COBOL–1 ORDER CODE

READ file-name-1.

READ file-name-1 **AT END** imperative- statement-1.

WRITE record-name-1.

ACCEPT data-name-1.

DISPLAY data-name-1.

MOVE data-name-1 **TO** data-name-2.

ADD data-name-1 **AND** data-name-2 **GIVING** data-name-3.

ADD data-name-1 **TO** data-name-2.

SUBTRACT data-name-1 **FROM** data- name-2 **GIVING** data-name-3.

SUBTRACT data-name-1 **FROM** data- name-2.

MULTIPLY data-name-1 **BY** data-name-2 **GIVING** data-name-3.

DIVIDE data-name-1 **INTO** data-name-2 **GIVING** data-name-3.

ON SIZE ERROR imperative-statement-1.   (option)

ROUNDED. (option)

GO TO procedure-name-1.

GO TO procedure-name-1, procedure- name-2, . . ., procedure-name-n **DE-PENDING ON** data-name-1.

IF conditional-expression-1 **THEN** imperative-statement-1 **OTHERWISE** statement-2.

PERFORM procedure-name-1.

PERFORM procedure-name-1 **UNTIL** conditional-expression-1.

PERFORM procedure-name-1 **VARYING** data-name-1 **FROM** data-name-2 **BY** data- name-3 **UNTIL** conditional-expression-1.

OPEN INPUT file-name-1, . . ., file-name- n, **OUTPUT** file-name-1, . . ., file-name-n.

CLOSE file-name-1, . . ., file-name-n.

STOP RUN.

Automatic Data-Processing Systems

Principles and Procedures

SECOND EDITION

Wadsworth Accounting and Data-Processing Series
Robert H. Gregory, Editor

FEDERAL INCOME TAX FUNDAMENTALS
William E. Dickerson and Leo D. Stone

AUTOMATIC DATA-PROCESSING SYSTEMS, Second Edition
Robert H. Gregory and Richard L. Van Horn

BUSINESS DATA PROCESSING AND PROGRAMMING
Robert H. Gregory and Richard L. Van Horn

IBM MACHINE OPERATION AND WIRING
Lawrence J. Salmon

PREPARING FOR THE CPA EXAMINATION, Volumes 1 and 2
Robert J. Smith

USING ACCOUNTING IN BUSINESS
Robert H. Van Voorhis, Clarence L. Dunn, and Fritz A. McCameron

Robert H. Gregory
Richard L. Van Horn

Automatic Data-Processing Systems

Principles and Procedures

SECOND EDITION

Wadsworth Publishing Company, Inc.

Belmont, California

Sixth printing: August 1966

L.C. Cat. Card No.: 63-15504
Printed in the United States of America

Preface

Automa: Data-Processing Systems: Principles and Procedures is an introduction to business data processing and does not require previous knowledge of electronic computing systems. Processor programming and systems analysis are covered in detail. New developments these areas and new tools and techniques for management information are discussed. The book attempts to blend a theoretical and a practical approach in order to explain the *why*, as well as the *what* and *how*, of data processing.

In the short time since the development of the first electronic computer in 1947, more than 12,000 electronic computers of various sizes have been built for business, engineering, and scientific purposes. However, despite the great advances in processor technology, electronic processors have not yet made business management a "pushbutton" process, nor are they likely to do so in the near future. In order to successfully apply automatic data-processing systems to business problems, it is necessary to have imaginative and analytical thinkers in systems analysis and design, programming, operation and management. For, since these systems are capable of producing such vast amounts of information, management may find lost in a morass of detail unless the systems are effectively controlled.

At the heart of this book is a distinction between information and data: the information that management wants must be distilled from data. Although the concept is simple, the problems of putting it to work are complex. Information must be defined and measured before system can be designed that will automatically produce more effective reports. And the value of such a system cannot be measured merely by its technical virtuosity; the costs of designing a better processing system must be compared to the value obtained having the improved information that is produced.

Systems analysis design in Chapters 6 and 7 include two new

v

features: information-flow analysis and decision tables. Unlike traditional systems-analysis work aimed at a single application, information flow analysis analyzes the flow of data about an *event* from its origin, through files, to output. This *event-chain* approach opens up the opportunity to use processors for analyzing the *actual flow* of data in an existing system and the *planned flow* in a proposed system. Thus it is both a systems-analysis and a systems-design technique at the data-flow level.

Decision tables are used to relate conditions and actions in a tabular form for the various rules that are applicable. Decision tables facilitate careful statement of conditions and actions, aid in developing correct and complete program logic, point up ambiguities and inconsistencies, and serve as a documentation device. Tables are a promising alternative to detailed flow-charting in both the design and programming-coding phases of systems development.

Programming is treated in this book in both problem-oriented and machine-oriented languages. COBOL-1, a simplified version of COBOL-61 (Common Business Oriented Language, 1961 edition), is covered first to bring out the fundamentals of processing business files. COBOL-1 is presented with the intricacies and options of COBOL-61 stripped away. It is more important, we think, to develop the concepts and drive home the fundamental points than it is to give encyclopedic but hasty sketches of numerous features of programming. The coverage of COBOL-1 in Chapters 8 and 9 introduces many features of problem-oriented languages. COBOL-1 is a real programming language compatible with COBOL-61. Instructions for compiling and running COBOL-1 programs on one processor serve as a guide to compiling and running programs on other processors. COBOL programs can be run on any processor for which the manufacturer has prepared a COBOL-61 compiler.

Programming in machine-oriented languages covered in Chapters 10 and 11, is discussed in terms of a fixed-length processor, WORDCOM, which is representative of a widely used class of machines. FIELDCOM, a "field" or variable word-length machine, is also covered to show the features of a class of machines. COBOL-1, WORDCOM, and FIELDCOM programming are covered at the introductory level to offer the reader some choice of where he wants to start. The sequence used here, and the one we recommend, is to study COBOL-1 in order to learn programming fundamentals with the fewest embellishments. Then the reader is ready, we think, to go to the machine-oriented languages of WORDCOM and FIELDCOM.

Although this book is written for those who are new to systems work, it is also intended for those experienced with electronic data processing and, therefore, it can be used in several ways. The reader may find the detailed summaries at the end of each chapter helpful in setting up his own reading program. Readers familiar with equipment and programming can profitably begin with Part V (Principles of Processing Systems). Management personnel might read Parts III (Systems Design), V, and VI (Equipment Acquisition and Utilization), since these sections discuss how to make informed decisions on systems design, proposed applications, and equipment selection. Systems analysts experienced in other processing methods may want to start with Part V; they may then find the earlier sections on equipment and processing more useful. Parts III and VI are especially appropriate for analysts because they deal with the effect of new processing techniques on systems analysis. At some point, and perhaps at the beginning, most readers will want to study Parts II (Automatic Equipment) and IV (Programming and Processing Procedures).

Automatic Data-Processing Systems is designed as a full semester or one-year text for a basic course. Appendix I contains numerous questions and problems (graduated in difficulty) designed to emphasize the important points in the chapter and to encourage methodical thinking about the problems of data-information systems. Appendix II is a glossary of terms common to the field of electronic data processing; it includes all terms given a new meaning in this book. Appendix III is a brief guide to literature useful in the field of business data-processing systems.

The idea for this text was suggested by members of the Office, Chief of Ordnance, U. S. Army Ordnance Corps, which supported the preparation of an earlier text for its own educational purposes; this version led to the first edition of *Automatic Data-Processing Systems*. We are indebted to Herbert Bryer for the basic tables in Chapter 5, to O. T. Gatto for the material on AUTOSATE in Chapter 6, and to Solomon Pollack for the material on DETAB-X in Chapter 7 and for many helpful suggestions. We owe much to our many friends and colleagues who have, in one way or another, contributed to this volume and especially to our readers and friendly critics in universities, government, and business: Arthur Carlson, Edward Chappelear, Richard W. Conway, James Gibbons, Howard C. Holland, Elmer F. Judge, and Robert Schlosser. We are also grateful to Mary Cole, who guided the book through typing and cheerfully did much of the work, and to our illustrator, Willard Harriss.

Robert H. Gregory
Richard L. Van Horn

Contents

PART I
ORIENTATION

1
The Why and How of Business Data Processing

Substantial changes in business activity during recent years have encouraged the creation of new data-processing systems. Conversely, changes in data-processing equipment and methods are suggesting new methods of doing business. Electronic data processing, operations research, and other new scientific and engineering developments are fast becoming a part of common business practice. And it is probable that data-processing and management-control methods will change more rapidly during the next decade than they have in recent years.

This progress will not make manual data processing and conventional control techniques completely obsolete, but it will make knowledge of automatic data processing invaluable for business managers, data-processing personnel, and systems and procedures analysts. All people who rely on facts for performing or managing business operations—people who need facts for answering questions and making reports—have a vital interest in the origination and processing of data.

WHY PROCESS DATA?

Data about business events are gathered, stored, processed, and reported for various reasons. Some of the more important reasons are to keep detailed *facts* about individual transactions; to produce routine *operating documents,* such as paychecks and purchase orders; to summarize masses of facts into useful, *informative reports,* such as reports on sales in given areas and on costs of production; and to make *analyses* of business problems, such as finding locations for factories and warehouses that will give minimum transportation costs.

Data Availability

Facts are the raw material of data processing. Initially, the collection of facts may be restricted to the minimum immediately required; but supplemental facts are often obtained at first in order to anticipate probable or possible demands for them in the future.

Often the solution of a problem has to be postponed until necessary facts are obtained. An efficient scheme for obtaining facts depends on balancing the *cost* of having them available—either too many or too few—against the *benefits* of having the necessary facts when they are wanted. The point is that it is usually impossible to obtain just the right set of facts about events "today." One must choose between trying to search out and reconstruct facts about yesterday, or waiting for tomorrow and gathering facts about events as they occur.

Document Production

The preparation of readable documents is an important phase of data processing. Documents are still a common means of communication among companies, and they are widely used within companies that have manual data-processing systems.

Where data collection is done by people and the output from processing goes to people, it is usually taken for granted that readable documents are required. This need is reduced, or even eliminated, when equipment is used for gathering and processing data. The output of machines at one stage—whether punched tape, cards, magnetic tape, or machine-readable printed characters—can be used as input at the next stage of processing, in either the same or a different company. The use of readable documents is sometimes restricted to small-volume operations where mechanization at the next stage is not feasible. Readable documents that are distributed to a wide audience—bills to customers and reports to managers—will continue to be used for many years.

Management Information

An important reason for developing elaborate data-processing schemes is to supply the management organization with the critical facts needed to control operations. The word *data* might be used to cover *all* the facts obtained; the term *information* is useful for denoting the *particular* facts management wants to know.

Although information derives from raw data, information has certain qualities that can serve as a guide in processing data. A manager in a company is interested in getting facts about operations he is responsible for. He wants these facts to be accurate, timely, and related to problems he can solve by his decisions. Furthermore, he is more interested in learning about unpredictable than about predictable developments. He has no need to be told repeatedly something he already knows. In short, the information given him should be accurate, have an element of newness or novelty about it, focus on a selected area, and deal with the unexpected.

Some examples will help distinguish *data* from *information*. Newspapers are bought for information. Someone who feels that a particular issue has little news to offer, either because so little is happening or because too many other editions are published, will not buy it. To stimulate their sluggish circulation, newspapers often try to create an air of bright novelty around the humdrum, or revive interest in old mysteries; the Loch Ness monster, for instance, is said to be a summertime phenomenon that obligingly reappears for the benefit of Scottish newspapers. Likewise, reports to management about unexpected or undesirable events, such as the costs of production jobs exceeding their standard, select and emphasize items to increase the reader's attention. The costs of jobs not exceeding standard may be included in reports for completeness or omitted for brevity, according to the reader's immediate interests or his needs for later reference to the whole picture.

The difference between a mass of facts and a few critical facts is illustrated by the plight of a businessman who furnished 1350 pounds of records to a tax collector. He was brought to court by the collector, who wanted five additional books, weighing only 10 or 20 pounds, that he considered critical. Every day businessmen are given pounds of reports when they want only a few critical facts. Managers do not really care about source reports, documents, and data, however useful they may be elsewhere in the organization.

The nature of information can be described, but it is difficult to measure information itself as a quantity. Whether a new system will produce better information than the old system did is difficult to determine, and will be even after the new system is introduced. Information production and the related areas of management control, including automatic decision-making, are challenging and profitable areas of study.

HOW DATA ARE PROCESSED

The basic functions of processing data are well established. Managers and operating personnel in business, government, and other enterprises have long been accustomed to processing data to obtain facts about operations and information for their control.

The basic operations in processing data are (1) to originate data, (2) to manipulate, according to some plan, the new data and files prepared in an earlier cycle, and (3) to report results.

Origination of Data

The origination of data in a form suitable for processing includes three necessary stages—collection, conversion, and verification.

Data Collection. Data collection captures facts when they are available; they may be processed later, when needed. For example, the time an employee starts or stops work on a particular job may be recorded in *writing* by a timekeeper, *stamped* in numerals by a time clock, or *punched* into a card. A storekeeper identifies and counts any material received in the stockroom in order to write a receiving report. Requisitions for material, on the other hand, specify desired quantities and serve as the original records of issuance. Employees of utility companies record customer meter readings by marking cards that are later run through equipment that "senses" the marks and punches them.

Data collection often starts with the *manual operation* of keyboards that punch cards or paper tape, or that record data on magnetic tape. Several devices recently developed for business use are capable of automatically collecting data in *machine-processable* form, though one class of these devices yields data in a machine-processable form that people cannot read. Examples of devices producing machine-readable media are point-of-sale recorders, transaction recorders, and time clocks that punch tape or cards. Another class of automatic data-collection devices produces numerals and letters on paper or cards in a form readable by both machines and people. Character-reading machines "read" the characters and convert them to a form suitable for automatic processing.

Other important techniques for data collection are pre-preparation of constant data, by-product preparation as a part of other operations, and duplication from card, plastic, or metal plates. A simple time clock records the basic facts for a transaction; a more complex clock might record all the facts—worker, time, job involved, and units produced—and thereby deserve the name "automatic transaction recorder."

New input data may be only a small part of the total data handled at each cycle. The inventory file, for example, is used repeatedly to introduce necessary changes for receipts, issues, and price changes, and to introduce and delete items. Data already in files are much easier to handle than new data, because master cards or tapes may be selectively duplicated for use as input data. The date, batch number or transaction serial number, and fixed data can be supplied automatically during the data-collection operation.

Data Conversion.   Data collected on the medium—paper, cards, or tape—that is most efficient at the first stage must often be converted to a different medium for further use. Some companies, for example, use audio tape recorders to record inventory counts. Until automatic voice-to-digital converters become practicable, conversion by people is required for further processing. People are able to work with oral, handwritten, or typed data, but equipment usually requires that data be recorded in a carefully prescribed form. Data from oral recordings or handwritten documents may be manually punched into cards or tape or written on magnetic tape for input to automatic processors. In many cases, punched cards or tape are prepared manually and the data are then converted automatically to magnetic tape for input.

Machines are used now to read typed, printed, and handprinted characters and to convert them to a form suitable for machine processing. Enough research has been done to indicate the feasibility of automatically converting the spoken word into a form suitable for further processing.

The form in which data are originally captured, and the manner in which data are converted, depend on several things: the volume of data involved, the number of points of origination, the permissible financial investment at each point of origination, transmission requirements, conversion costs, and the most efficient form for use in subsequent stages. Large volumes of data originating at a few points warrant big investments in elaborate collection and conversion facilities.

Data Verification.   Data are verified to obtain a desired degree of accuracy. The standard "a desired degree" does not imply perfection. Some inaccuracies—a slight misspelling of a name, for example—may be trivial, but other inaccuracies, such as crediting the wrong customer for a collection on account, can cause trouble unless they are corrected soon after they occur and before much processing is done. Verification includes checking data to determine whether they are in the approved format, convey the correct meaning to the reader, and will lead to the appropriate action.

The simplest type of *format* verification is to ensure that each data field contains the correct kinds of characters: numeric, alphabetic, or both. An alphabetic character in a numerical statement of amount—say, "$1,2A3.46" on a check—violates the rules of format, and it defies further processing because an alphabetic quantity cannot be handled arithmetically. Such an error in format must be corrected before processing.

A broader problem in format verification concerns the completeness of data input. Each business event requires these elements of data to describe it: (1) identification of parties to the transaction (one being the firm itself), (2) description by name and number of what is involved, (3) quantity involved, (4) the time of the transaction, and (5) the unit price or dollar amount, if money is involved. A receiving report, for example, must have the first four elements in order to be complete; it can be easily examined for correct format without referring to anything else.

More difficult problems of data verification arise from failures to originate documents for *all transactions* or to receive all of them for processing. Mechanical recorders, document numbering, and careful control over valuable items are used to assure complete reporting and correct handling.

The *meaning* of some data in terms of reasonableness serves to verify it. It is possible for an employee to work 80 hours in a week, but it is unreasonable to assume unquestioningly that he did, even with a two-shift operation. Detection of a possible error need not stop the checking process. After the questionable data are flagged or noted for verification before further processing, the checking activity may be continued.

Some data that pass the format and meaning tests may require some verification *action* before processing. For example, a check may be received, signed *John C. Smith*

—legible, but unaccompanied by any other identification. If there are several customers named John C. Smith, the only way to credit the check to the correct one is to take action to identify him. The clues are the signature itself (if a signature file is kept), account number and balance, amount of payment, and address. Without identification, it is not possible to credit the correct Smith—but he will take action when he receives his next statement.

To summarize, there are several ways to verify data before further processing, and the method chosen will depend on how easily the deficiency can be detected and corrected.

Processing of Data

The principal operations in processing data are rearranging input data and processing files.

Rearranging Input Data. Rearrangement involves classifying data by type and ordering them into sequence without changing their content by computation. There are many reasons why data are rearranged. Two or more kinds of transactions may originate together, but then require separate handling. Payroll, inventory, and sales data, for example, may be intermixed on arrival at the processing center. They are usually classified or sorted by type before processing, since procedures and files are designed to cope with only one class of transactions at a time. The task of sorting transactions into classes is made easier by arranging to have only one or a limited number of types of transactions originate together. This procedure also facilitates better control over who can originate certain kinds of transactions—that is, who can issue material, authorize payment of bills, or inquire into the contents of restricted files. This kind of arrangement for separate origination of each class of data is preferable to unscrambling mixtures of several classes.

A second way of rearranging data is to use each *type* of transaction to produce several outputs. Depending on the kind of output desired and the file arrangement, the transactions are arranged in different sequences for efficient processing. Consider the steps in processing customers' orders. Orders are the basis for sales analysis, customer accounting, inventory and production control, and salesmen's compensation. Data on sales might be summarized by geographic area or by product class, without sorting data into any sequence. If efficient magnetic-tape processing methods require that the customer or inventory file be kept in a certain order, transactions must be sorted into that sequence before updating a particular file. Still another sorting may be required before the transactions can be processed against a file organized in a different sequence. Two sets of sorted data already in the same sequence may be merged to obtain one over-all sequence. For example, inventory transactions for the first four days in a week can be sorted into sequence according to stock identification number, and transactions for the fifth day can be sorted separately. Merging the two sequences into one reduces the workload after the end of the week and permits processing against an ordered file.

In addition to the problem of arranging transactions in the same sequence as the file before processing them, there is the related problem of keeping the file itself in a specified sequence and eliminating inactive records. Maintaining a file of customers' accounts, for instance, may involve inserting records for new customers in alphabetic or customer-number sequence and deleting inactive records. Files kept on magnetic tape are often arranged in alphabetic or numerical sequence and are most efficiently processed in the same sequence.

Random-access equipment is designed to handle transactions without regard for file or transaction sequence. A file may contain records arranged in one sequence but the transactions may occur in a different, perhaps a *random sequence*. They may be processed together satisfactorily, if facilities are available for random-sequence processing. With these facilities, changes introduced into the file—and perhaps the file itself—need not be in any particular sequence; consequently, neither the file nor the transactions need be rearranged.

A third kind of rearrangement occurs when the elements of data in an item are in one sequence but are wanted in a different sequence. Data may be rearranged within an item during input conversion, processing, or output editing.

File Processing. "File processing" is restricted here to those operations not included in data origination, rearrangement, and output. It thus involves the following kinds of operations: updating files for inventory receipts and issues; computing gross and net pay; making decisions based on quantitative criteria, such as allowing a customer further credit if the amount and age of his balance are within credit limits; estimating sales based on predictions of market behavior, advertising expenditure, and economic forecasts; converting sales estimates into material requirements, labor estimates, and production schedules; summarizing numerous individual transactions into a few numbers; recognizing and dealing with exceptional cases; and looking up table values, such as prices or discounts applicable for various quantities.

In addition, the following processing operations are used to ensure accurate results: (1) verifying data by comparison with facts already in files, (2) controlling input data to guard against losing a valid transaction or introducing a spurious one, (3) checking arithmetical accuracy by repeating operations or by performing them in parallel through separate channels, as when two book-keepers in a bank post the same depositor's account on separate machines to reduce the risk of inaccurate results, and (4) determining that prescribed procedures are actually used. When such precautions are required to facilitate processing, they are incorporated in the main stream of processing. Other precautionary measures are used primarily to keep interested parties, such as managers and auditors, informed of the degree of accuracy. Such measures are used in addition to the main stream of processing rather than included in it.

Some operations are often considered nonproductive because they merely facilitate the performance of other operations directly related to the desired output. This classification corresponds to the indirect-direct labor classification in factory operations. Actually, all essential operations are productive because work done at one stage facilitates work at another. Consider, for instance, the damage that failure to verify input data could wreak at a later stage. An issue of materials charged against an incorrect number might later cause the creation of a new account with a negative balance, be sent to the wrong account, be set aside for investigation, or halt processing until the mistake is corrected. Verifying identification numbers against a master list at an early stage of processing may improve over-all efficiency. Keeping file maintenance—insertion and deletion of records in the file—separate from file processing—updating records in the file—may have some advantages for control purposes over trying to do both at once.

Output

Output preparation follows the origination and manipulation of data. Since processed results are seldom in precisely the form desired, it is often necessary to select what is wanted and present it in acceptable form. Job manufacturing costs are examples of *historical reports* about what has happened. A manufacturing schedule is a *forecast* of what is supposed to happen. A bill sent to a customer is an example of an *action document*. The content, frequency, and format of output are determined jointly by the people who use the output and those who prepare it.

Methods of output preparation depend on the way that demands occur—either scheduled or at random—the length of time available for meeting the demands, and the ability to forecast what will be demanded. Some examples will show how these factors bear on output preparation and, incidentally, will show that output requirements help determine the processing methods. There will be adequate time to prepare an *annual report* of fixed assets within one *month* after the end of the year if the assets are classified by number of years owned (less than one year, one to five years, and so forth). If the data about fixed assets are available and activity is low during the year, there will be ample opportunity to plan procedures, and the permissible one-month delay in reporting will allow fairly smooth scheduling of work.

Output preparation is more difficult, however, if the number of transactions is high and the reporting interval and permissible delay in processing are short. Buyers (merchandise managers) in a department store might want *weekly reports* of receipts, sales, and inventory for each item by the following Monday afternoon. This demand will put heavy loads on the system, but the work of output preparation will be several times greater if buyers want *daily reports* at 10 a.m. every day. Entirely different file-processing methods might be required, however, if buyers want *up-to-the-minute reports* on the sales activity or inventory of any one item. Furnishing quick answers to questions about current status involves continual updating of files and complex interrogation equipment.

Outputs not anticipated in advance may pose extremely difficult problems. Novel output requirements may require new methods of preparing output and new processing techniques to get the desired results. Still worse, *unexpected output* requirements may demand the use of data that are not readily available, if at all. Or the data available may be in a raw form that cannot be processed economically. In such a case, samples can be taken from the data and studied to determine whether they answer the questions, whether a complete analysis of the data is needed, or whether new data must be collected. An equally perplexing situation may arise when there is an immediate need for data which, although collected once, have since been discarded. In some cases, it may be possible to reconstruct data, but in others it is necessary to start afresh. For example, suppose an oil company were to ask, "Do service stations on the right-hand side of a street leading out from the center of town sell more gasoline than those on the left?" The answer may demand, for the first time, that data on station location be used in conjunction with sales data already available. Another question, "Do left-handed employees sell more than right-handed ones?" may not be answerable at all, either because data are not available or because the turnover of employees makes it impossible to reconstruct the data.

It is impossible to answer this disarmingly simple question until enough time elapses to permit the gathering of new data. Often, it is not possible to reconstruct even partially complete statistics, so unanticipated questions about the past cannot be answered. Reflection often shows, as in the case of the effect of left- and right-handed employees on gasoline sales, that the question is trivial and doesn't deserve an answer. The ability to distinguish between valid and worthless questions and take appropriate action is an important part of data processing.

The most *open-ended output* requirement, and the most difficult if not impossible requirement to deal with, springs from the question, "Look, we have these kinds of facts on file; what useful reports can we get out of them?" Exploiting unstructured facts is a task for researchers, rather than data-processing personnel. This situation, which is the bane of data processing, can be minimized by advance planning.

In summary, data processing involves (1) collecting data for new transactions; (2) manipulating new inputs and data already in files according to prescribed plans; and (3) producing output documents, reports, and instructions for various purposes.

PROCESSING FACILITIES

In order to reduce the *how* of processing data from general to concrete terms, we must consider the facilities that are used. These facilities must be able to receive input data, manipulate them according to some plan, and produce output. For processing, they must be able to control operations to follow the prescribed plan, hold data and processing instructions, and perform arithmetical and logical operations. Many kinds of facilities are used to process data; in the broadest sense, they range from people working without benefit of equipment to equipment operating with little aid from people.

People

The human being is the earliest form of data processor. A person receives input data chiefly by seeing or hearing them, and stores them in his brain, which also serves as an operating and control unit. His outputs are oral or written reports and various physical actions.

The human mind can *perform,* or at least *control* the performance of, many different operations: starting work, getting instructions and data; adding, subtracting, multiplying, and dividing; remembering results; performing the operations on a different set of data each round; comparing two items; modifying instructions to follow a path that depends on the outcome of a comparison; putting out results rearranged and edited as required; and, of course, stopping when the process is completed.

The ability to select the subsequent processing path dependent on the outcome at any stage is invaluable for modifying operations as they are performed. For example, suppose that a person calculating gross-to-net pay, is told to stop making voluntary deductions if net pay falls below a certain amount—say, $15.00. He would unconsciously apply this rule if gross pay appeared large enough to cover all possible deductions. He would exercise more care, and apply deductions one at a time, if net pay approached this criterion. He would skip any remaining deductions for that employee, but would, of course, return to the original procedure in calculating the next employee's net pay.

The human mind is an adaptable but often unreliable processor. It is slow in performing arithmetical operations and erratic in applying logical· rules. Where judgment is required, however, people are well-nigh indispensable because some operations of data processing and decision-making are inseparable. Even with elaborate data-processing systems people are needed to make decisions at some stages because of the extreme difficulty of planning to handle every eventuality. In short, a person unaided by other facilities is an efficient processor for small, relatively simple situations and is a vital element of every data-processing system.

Records

Records were the earliest aid developed to help process data. Consisting first of pictures and marks, writing now relies on "alphabets" of letters and numerals. Business alphabets consist of ten numerals, twenty-six letters, and other symbols, which allow the compact storage of huge quantities of facts. The alphabets are often represented as A through Z; 0 through 9; #, ., &, /, $; and, perhaps, a through z. Characters are also represented by punched holes in cards or paper tape and by positive and negative charges in magnetizable material. The familiar shape of A, B, C, and so on, is sacrificed in favor of other schemes that are more efficient for processing purposes, although often they are not readily usable by people.

Viewed in the broadest sense, records tremendously increase the size and reliability of data storage, which otherwise would be restricted to what people can remember. Schemes for representing characters in written form also provide a simple way to transmit data. People remain responsible for data input, control, and output, unless aided by other processing facilities.

Special-Purpose Office Equipment

Calculating machines perform simple arithmetical operations quickly and accurately and some print results on paper. Since people are slow and oftentimes inaccurate at arithmetical operations, the invention and improvement of calculating devices to add, subtract, multiply, and divide was an important step forward.

With the invention of the typewriter, writing speeds—about ten words a minute—were increased to sixty or more words a minute. More important, the typewriter improved legibility and enabled the preparation of multiple copies with carbon paper and duplicating devices.

The functions of the calculator and the typewriter were combined to create bookkeeping and accounting machines. These machines allow an operator to perform at the same time such multiple operations as preparing statements, ledgers, and journals. Electrically powered office machines for punching and reading paper tape are widely used to reduce data to a form that can be processed mechanically; they often do this as a by-product of other operations.

Punched Card Equipment

The basic operations of punched-card equipment are punching, sorting, calculating, and printing. Early punched-card machines required manual effort in punching data in cards, handling cards individually during the sorting operation, and counting the sorted cards. Since 1890 machines have become more nearly automatic, requiring less manual effort to originate data, sort cards, make calculations, and copy results from tabulators. People handle cards in bulk, and start, feed, tend, and stop machines. With people handling cards between stages, present-day punched-card machines and electronic calculators can receive punched input data, perform about a dozen different arithmetical and logical operations at the rate of 15,000 a minute, and produce printed reports or punched cards for further processing.

Electronic Data Processors

The most recent development in data-processing facilities is the electronic data processor. The unique feature of an electronic processor, also called an "internally stored program computer," is the fact that it stores operating instructions in the same way and in the same place as the data to be processed. Instructions read into storage direct the processor to perform specified operations in a desired sequence. Furthermore, like data, these instructions can be manipulated or changed. The capacity to *change instructions* while operations are in progress increases the applicability of instructions to a wider, although not unlimited, variety of situations that arise in processing.

Electronic digital processors execute a *variety of instructions,* both arithmetical and logical, ranging in number from about a dozen to two hundred. Speed of execution ranges from a few hundred to several hundred thousand or even millions of operations per second. High speed is an important feature of these computers. One company, for example, that spent 3 man-months calculating the critical shaft-speed for a steam generator found it could solve the same problem in 40 hours with punched-card machines, in 1 hour on an early-model electronic computer, in 15 minutes on a second version, in 15 seconds on a later version, and in about 3 seconds on a still newer model. With this last model, the ratio of computer to manual time needed to solve the problem was about 1:500,000.

Electronic Data-Processing Systems

An electronic data-processing system performs standard data-handling operations with a minimum of manual help. Thus, it greatly increases the ratio of equipment to labor used in processing data.

An electronic data-processing system consists of the following:

1. An electronic data processor (the central processing unit)
2. Associated peripheral equipment, such as data preparation, input, and output devices
3. Procedures that tell what data are needed and when, where they are obtained, and how they are used
4. Instruction routines for the processor to follow
5. Personnel to operate and maintain equipment, analyze and set up procedures, prepare instructions, provide input data, utilize reports, review results, and supervise the entire operation

The alphabet used in business for data, files, and reports is alphanumerical; that is, it includes both alphabetical and numeric characters. Large volumes of data about transactions are processed in conjunction with files to update the records in files and produce documents and reports. Records in files are analyzed to find relationships and searched to answer simple inquiries.

Business data processing involves repetitive cycles and tight time schedules for producing results that are intimately related to company operations. Scientific and engineering computation, on the other hand, generally deals with small volumes of data that may be drawn from the business file, from facts about current operations, or the engineering department. These data are processed intensively to answer specific questions, to prepare tables, or to control processes. However, the distinction between business and engineering computations is not radical, and today's electronic data-processing systems are often used for both purposes.

DATA–PROCESSING SYSTEMS

Brief descriptions of actual data-processing systems will give meaning to the why and how of processing data and the kinds of facilities used for processing. On-line and off-line processing systems, several arrangements for data origination-communication, and analysis and planning by means of simulation are described in this section.

On-Line Systems

An *on-line* system obtains data about operations while they are occurring, processes the data, and furnishes results quickly enough to be useful for controlling the outcome of a process. The chief feature of an on-line system is the fact that the data processing is done on a time scale comparable to the process being controlled. Operations, whether business or manufacturing, that are subject to rapid change, warrant the use of elaborate data-origination devices, communication networks, processing equipment, and control devices to shorten the time lag between the occurrence of events and the *feedback*—information sent to the control points—to carry out control instructions. If the system is fully automatic at all stages from data origination through processing back to the implementation of control, it is called a *closed-loop* system. Less elaborate systems, which utilize people for gathering data or carrying out the control instructions, are called *open-loop* systems. Most business data-processing systems are open-loop, although process control for oil refineries, rolling mills, and similar process operations are designed as closed-loop systems to take full advantage of high-speed data gathering and processing in order to control rapidly changing operations. Several examples of on-line systems are discussed here: airline reservations, savings banks, and process plant control.

Airline Reservations.   Airlines have important problems in controlling space availability, making reservations, and ticketing passengers. The "inventory" of items offered for sale—each flight between any two cities times the number of seats in each class, times the number of days into the future for which reservations are accepted—is huge, sales are made by a large number of widely scattered agents, and customers expect answers to most questions in a fraction of a minute. A number of electronic data-processing systems have been built and installed since the late 1940's to handle the availability of space on each flight, with customer reservations and ticketing controlled by paper or punched card records. More recently, comprehensive systems have been built to handle all three phases of airline reservations.

Newer airline reservation systems are built around an electronic data processor, a communication network, and input-output desk sets. The basic inquiry about space availability simply consists of a flight leg—flight number and origination-destination cities—class, date, and number of seats. An agent dealing with a customer merely selects the appropriate notched or punched plate from a set of plates and inserts it into a desk set to enter the flight leg, and depresses buttons for the date, number of seats wanted, and the kind of transaction: request, sell, or cancel. The data are sent directly to the electronic processor for it to determine whether the desired space is available for a request or to update the record of space available for a sale or cancellation. Information is sent from the data processor to the desk-set display in order for the agent to give information to the passenger and complete the transaction by preparing a ticket or doing whatever else is required. Customer reservations and ticketing are handled manually or with punched-card equipment in simpler reservation systems. In more elaborate systems that also control reservations and ticketing, the agent uses the typewriter on the desk set to enter name, telephone number, deadline for buying ticket, and other data wanted about the passenger to complete the ticket sale. This additional information for ticketing and passenger service, which involves much larger storage and intricate processing than space control *per se,* is placed in processor storage for use when needed to advise customers to obtain tickets, notify customers of changes in flight plans, and to prepare passenger lists.

This brief description of an airline reservations system merely gives a glimpse of operating systems, but it indicates the important aspects of an on-line system involving people for originating data and using the outputs to control operations. Other industries have essentially similar problems of on-line processing and control in serving numerous customers who may do business with any employee located at one of several offices. Some savings banks with branch offices, for example, have installed on-line data processing systems so that every teller can obtain from processor storage current information about any depositor's account. Each teller can offer service to any depositor and enter transactions, deposits, or withdrawals to update his record while he is at the window. Thus the electronic processor maintains current account status for all depositors and supplies it on demand to any teller.

Process Plant Control.   Process plants have several features that are different from the airlines reservation and savings bank applications described above. Process plant—oil refinery, steel rolling mill, etc.—operations occur at high speeds and require continuous monitoring of operations, calculations to determine what has happened and project what is going to happen, and rapid feedback to control operations. Data about operations are obtained by elaborate instrumentation located at strategic points throughout the plant for measuring temperature, pressure, rate of flow, volumes, and other key variables. The data processor is directly connected to each instrument for sampling it one or more times a minute to learn the conditions throughout the plant, and instrument readings may also be displayed on a control board so that people can monitor operations. The data processor uses an internally-stored program that is an elaborate mathematical representation of the important variables, reflecting what occurs in the process in order to calculate the results of operations after each set of readings is taken, determine the difference between the actual and desired results, and give corrective instructions to people to change the setting of control devices or issue instructions directly to automatic devices for controlling feed rates, fuel consumption, and other key factors. Whether the data processor issues instructions to human operators or directly to control devices depends on the reaction time of the process and the consequences of making corrections either quickly or slowly. Highly variable processes that may go completely out of control in a short period of time require frequent sampling of the monitoring instruments, elaborate calculations by means of a processor using a sophisticated program, and direct connection to control devices for quick feedback from the processor to take corrective action. Less dynamic processes may make important use of human operators for gathering data, introducing data to the data processor, and using the data processor's output for changing operation controls. In summary, the essential features of process control are: (1) frequent sampling of instruments for measuring numerous variables that indicate important features of the process, (2) quick transmission of the data about operations to a data processor for calculating what is happening and the kinds and amounts of corrections to make to return the process to its desired condition, (3) and feedback, either directly to control devices or via human operators, to make process control adjustments.

Off-Line Systems

Off-line systems might be thought of as on-line systems under relaxed conditions which reduce the need for direct connection between the operations and the data-processing unit. This relaxation in operating conditions doesn't mean that operations are uncontrolled; it merely reflects a difference in operating conditions—events are occurring less rapidly, operations are more stable, and the consequences of going out of control are less drastic—so that control can be achieved by less elaborate techniques operating at a slower pace. Two off-line data-processing systems are discussed here: utility billing and commercial banking.

Utility Billing. Preparation of public utility bills for the amount of service a customer consumes consists of the following steps: read each customer's meter; use the new reading and data in the customer's master record to calculate consumption, prepare his bill, and update the record; and post customer's payment to his account. There are, of course, some important preliminary operations—for example, connect service and set up the master record for each new customer—and ·many other repetitive operations—for example, follow through on overdue accounts and test meters for accurate operation.

The amount of money involved each hour or day is small for most customers, so that monthly or bi-monthly meter reading and billing is common practice. The master file for customers may be split into twenty (or forty) parts corresponding to meter reading districts, so that each business day a fraction of the meters can be read and bills calculated to keep the data-processing workload even.

Thus, each business day a part of the master file is updated for meter readings that were made a few days before and for collections received from customers during the past month. The three kinds of data—collections, present reading, and master record—are used to credit the customer's account for any collections, to calculate and print a new bill showing any uncollected balance; to update the master record for consumption history and other factors; to prepare follow-up notices for delinquent-bill collectors, instructions to meter testers, and customer records for account clerks; and to produce summaries for operating and management purposes. Utility billing is a typical example of *batch processing* because the master record file is updated only occasionally for all the transactions that occurred during the period of one or two months. File activity is so small—calculate one bill and post one collection—that more frequent updating of the master record file is not worthwhile. This means that the printed record of customers' accounts produced as part of the file batch-processing cycle for account clerks to use for answering inquiries are, on the average, two weeks old—one-twentieth of the records are one day old, one-twentieth two days old, etc., up to the whole batch-processing cycle of one month. Money collected from customers is, of course, processed for deposit in the bank each day and customer's identification and amount are prepared in a suitable data medium for input to master record processing on the batch-cycle basis. A supplementary daily record, or even a cumulative record since the master file was last updated, may be prepared for account clerks to use for answering customers' inquiries about payments, balances, and account status. The relaxed nature of off-line data processing for utility billing is reflected by the fact that each bill may carry the legend "Please subtract any recent payments" without even specifying the date of cut-off for collections included in the bill. Furthermore, an inquiry about account status may bring the reply, "Wait for next month's bill and see if it has been taken care of."

Commercial Banking.   Commercial banks handle checking accounts by off-line, batch-processing techniques that are, in many ways, similar to utility billing methods. Interestingly enough, to date commercial banks have found less need for on-line processing than savings banks, which superficially would appear to have less stringent data requirements.

For many purposes, the minimum unit of time in processing

checks is a business day—a depositor's account is considered satisfactory if it has a positive balance at the close of the banking day. Thus checks received through the clearing house, from correspondent banks, and in deposits are proved and sorted for processing against customers' accounts. After batches of checks are sorted to the accounts on which they are drawn, the checks are "paid" by posting to the accounts. Any checks that cause an overdraft—nonsufficient funds—are likely to be charged back to the source from which they are received—clearing house, correspondent bank, or depositor—and returned. For many purposes, check processing appears to be merely a paper-shuffling process, for almost any check will be accepted by a bank, subject to payment by the bank on which drawn. Much work has been done in recent years to increase the efficiency of processing paper checks. Before blank checks are issued to depositors, they are printed with bank clearing number and customer identification number in magnetic-ink characters that are readable by both people and machines. After a check is issued by a depositor and enters the banking system, the first bank may imprint the amount of the check in magnetic-ink characters so that proving and sorting work can be done by new types of character-reading, paper-sorting machines. Individual checks are, of course, easily handled, but the total volume of more than ten billion checks a year handled by the American banking industry poses a formidable problem.

The foregoing description of batch processing of checks seems leisurely, but there are situations—for example, the cashing of checks across the counter—in which banks want to know the current status of an account because it is not possible to recoup the amount of a cashed N.S.F. check merely by returning it to someone else. To guard against cashing such checks, banks may use on-line techniques to keep current balances of accounts readily available for reference by window tellers. But the introduction of on-line techniques for window tellers' reference may have an important impact on the design and operation of the whole system.

Data Origination-Communication

Data origination and communication are important aspects of data processing. Data need to be obtained at the point where they are first available and sent to the data-processing center for handling. Two examples of data origination and communication are discussed here: factory data collection and media prepared in advance for use on a turn-around basis. Several other methods for communication between firms which, to the receiver, serve the same purpose as data origination are also touched on.

Factory Data Collection.   Data collection in a job-shop factory consists of obtaining data about who performs what operations, the time required, and the number of units produced. Five kinds of data are basic: machine operator, machine used, job worked on, number of pieces produced, and start and finish time. Data originating at each work center throughout the factory can be collected quickly and economically by a device designed to accept the first four kinds of facts about the work done: a plate or card identifying the worker, a similar identification of the job, and settings of dials or buttons on a keyboard to indicate the operation performed and the number of pieces produced. When starting a job, a workman enters the first three kinds of data; and when finishing a job, he repeats them and enters the number of pieces produced. Each data-collection device is connected by cable or telephone lines to a central collection unit for accumulating the facts; the central unit also supplies the time from a built-in clock. The finish time minus the start time gives the elapsed time for the number of units completed on a production order by a particular workman. These facts can be used on a current basis to keep track of factory status and operations completed on jobs; the facts also show what did happen on an after-the-fact basis.

If an adequate data processor is available, the facts about each job may be fed directly into it for use in planning and controlling factory operations. Several facets of factory data collection are interesting: jobs may follow many different paths through the factory (a process plant, on the other hand, may have only one or a limited number of production flow paths); individual events—starting and stopping certain operations on each job—occur and need to be recorded; and workmen play an important role in performing individual operations, controlling the machine, and reporting what happened. All aspects of factory data collection are under the control of one company so that it is possible to design the kind of system wanted, place the devices where they are most convenient, and use the most efficient technique for each kind of input—plates or cards for identifying workers and jobs, manually-set dials for variables, and automatic clocks for indicating time. An important advantage of factory data collection over typical pencil and paper records is quicker and more accurate reporting which permits improvement of control over factory operations and can help reduce production costs.

Character Recognition.   When numerous people and data origination points are involved, data origination and communication problems become more difficult than those encountered in the factory. Simple and more economical techniques are necessary.

A commonly used technique for data origination is the gasoline credit card scheme of man-machine readable characters. A company issues each customer a plastic card embossed with his name, address, and identification number. A service station uses a customer's credit card to imprint a sales ticket (consisting of a blank punched card and paper copies) with carbon ink and writes in the item, quantity, and dollar amount of sale, or perhaps uses a special keyboard device to imprint the amount of sale in machine-readable characters. The service station sends the sales tickets to the oil company which puts them through a character-reading machine to decode the customer number and punch it into the same card that the customer signed at time of sale. The dollar amount of sale is keypunched into the card by people if it was manually written; but the amount is machine-read and punched if it was machine-imprinted. Two basic facts—customer number and dollar amount of sale—are enough for processing sales to customers either by using the original cards or by taking the data from them and using other media.

Machine-readable characters are also used in other situations where many people need to read the document and the volume for central processing is large enough to warrant machine processing. Examples are membership billing and accounting by large organizations and coupons distributed house-to-house by soap manufacturers for redemption through grocery stores and clearing houses.

Other techniques for efficient data origination on the part of an organization are the exchange between companies of punched cards for small volumes of data and magnetic tape for large volumes. Examples of interchanged data are purchase orders received from customers or progress reports from subcontractors. Many employers submit Federal Insurance Contribution Act tax reports for employees on magnetic tape instead of printing them on ordinary paper forms. The data on magnetic tape are ready for processing without any conversion.

Another interesting aspect of data communication is the development of elaborate communication networks for distribution of information retrieved from machine files. A simple example of an information retrieval-communication network is a stock market quotation service which replies to a keyboard inquiry about a particular stock by showing the most recent price (and perhaps other factors) on a display. Or it may give a voice reply after assembling the message from stock names and numerals previously recorded on a magnetic drum. More elaborate information retrieval systems are used to supply stock status to salesmen and others interested in the ability of a company to fill an order. Hospital insurance companies have direct wire communication service to hospitals to answer questions about the status of any member's account within minutes or seconds.

Simulation

The simulation of business systems on a data processor is an important application of data processors for analyzing and planning business operations. *Simulation* on a processor means to reproduce in a step-by-step fashion the important events that might occur in actual operations. For example, in a job shop orders for goods arrive at irregular rates, are scheduled into the shop, and proceed from one machine to the next until they are finished. Sometimes a large group of orders must wait for one "bottleneck" machine. Bottlenecks may be eliminated by different scheduling techniques or by using more machines; but it is difficult to predict in advance where bottlenecks will occur and the most efficient remedy—changing schedules, obtaining more machines, or whatever.

Several companies have approached the problem of analysis to predict results by simulating the operation of their job shop on an electronic data processor. Past history is analyzed to prepare a set of typical inputs: number of orders that arrive each hour or day, machines required for each job, and elapsed time to process each job on each machine. Of course, these numbers are different for each job and may vary for a particular kind of job so that a simple solution based on average values is not useful. The simulation concept accepts the various numbers and plays through day after day of operation to calculate what will happen: orders completed, bottlenecks, etc. In one hour, a large processor can simulate the handling of thousands of jobs or perhaps a year's operation of the shop. The analyst can try various scheduling policies and different numbers of machines until he finds a suitable, or perhaps even the best, combination. If any increase or decrease in workload is expected, the analyst can modify the input accordingly and obtain a projection of the changed plans.

The simulation approach to analysis can economically provide detailed measurement of long periods of "operation" on a before-the-fact basis without disturbing actual operations. Simulators are, of course, only models of reality and, like any projections of the future, may give misleading answers. When used correctly, however, simulators are valuable tools for analysis and projection and their use in business is increasing rapidly.

IMPLICATIONS FOR MANAGEMENT

The introduction of electronic data-processing systems into business has many implications for management. Reductions in manpower, space for processing and storage of data, and costs per unit of data processed may result. On the other hand, if the workload increases greatly, total costs may increase. The total workload often does increase when unit costs are reduced, because it is then practicable to collect and process data that were previously ignored.

Another advantage lies in the production of more *accurate and timely information*. Often the processing delay—the time between the occurrence of events and the availability of reports—can be greatly reduced. A shorter delay in processing may make more frequent reporting practicable. In some cases, the use of more equipment may actually increase the delay in getting certain results, even though the average delay is shortened for all output as a whole. An analogous situation occurs in manufacturing. The mass production of many units may take a longer time to set in motion than it would take to complete a few units or a special model by hand. Decreased manual handling of data increases accuracy by eliminating certain types of mistakes. Two major areas where mistakes occur—preparation of input data and interpretation of reports—require special attention for improvement.

Present and future developments in data processing will impinge on four fields of management: (1) decision-making, (2) human relations and supervision, (3) planning and operations, and (4) organization growth.

Decision-making will become more efficient because a manager will spend less time making routine decisions than he does now. Today, many problems go to top management because the simple facts that lead to specific answers are not available. In the future, decisions will follow a course based more on facts and less on intuition, although judgment will still be required. When sufficient facts are available and explicit decision rules are developed, more advanced systems will be programmed to make many decisions that managers now make. Of course, managers will continue to use their judgment and broad experience to make decisions when facts are missing or objectives are not explicit. Improvements in data processing will enable them to make better decisions by having more useful facts available, but managers will continue to deal with uncertainties that persist.

Human relations in business will change because equipment will do more of the work people now do. Improved processing methods will enable a manager to get more work from the same number of people because they are aided by more equipment. But an increased demand for more facts may require a larger over-all effort. Now, a manager frequently needs subordinates to collect and screen out control-information and to implement decisions. In the future, a data processor can do much of this work of data selection, thus allowing a manager to concentrate on the best plan of action. Improved information and control schemes will eliminate many routine problems that are now brought to a manager's attention. People will still have to direct, review, and maintain the operations of the most automatic systems now considered feasible. The main result of progress will be increased output per person. Thus, new ideas about the span of control and the training ground for future managers will become necessary.

Planning and operating a business will be different because an organization can respond faster to changed conditions. An entirely new program may be put into operation in a few minutes merely by giving the data processor a new set of objectives. Occasionally, a company connects the data system directly to the factory to control its operations, and it appears likely that this practice will spread. Management will take more preventive control action rather than having to rely upon after-the-fact corrective action.

Organization growth will be faster, if growth has been hindered by a lack of information for controlling operations and planning the future. Although larger equipment requires a higher investment in equipment and procedures, it can process more data at a lower cost per unit handled. A company may gain some competitive advantage by obtaining the largest-size equipment practicable for it.

To design a new data-processing system takes a long time and a huge amount of effort. Business management must learn to deal with developing data-processing and control systems that will become operational two or more years in the future. Whether an automatic system is desirable, and how it can be applied most advantageously, are questions that should be answered in advance by carefully planned and conducted studies. Systems studies involve selecting the objectives for the system, cataloguing all major data-processing areas, determining whether automatic techniques have merit, and investigating possible systems that appear to have merit. Following a systems study that leads to a positive recommendation, management will face problems of obtaining and installing equipment, training people, designing and testing the system required to go with the equipment selected, running old and new systems in parallel, cutting over from the old to a new system, and evaluating results from the new system to revise it as required.

A resourceful, carefully planned approach to a new system can yield large benefits—and a serious mistake, either from the wrong action or from inaction, can exact a severe cost. Electronic systems are not the answer to all data-processing problems, but they can prove highly effective when correctly designed and implemented.

SUMMARY

Important changes are occurring in the methods of business management and operation, and the widespread use of data-processing systems has accelerated the rate of change.

Data are gathered, stored, and processed in order to keep *facts* about transactions, produce operating *documents,* prepare informative *reports,* and make *analyses* of problem areas. The objective is to balance the quantity of data-processing work against the pay-off expected from the facts, documents, reports, and analyses produced.

Data and *information* have subtle but important differences. The term "data" represents collected raw facts. "Information" denotes the output after processing—sorting, organizing, file up-dating, and calculation. The information content of such output is measured in terms of accuracy, newness, degree of relevance to a selected area, and whether it deals with the unexpected. The distinction between data and information is important in systems-design, for there is a strong tendency to give too much attention to data collection and processing. It is in fact more important to concentrate on the information content of output to keep it at a high level.

This distinction is comparable to the difference of viewpoint between television station engineers and the people responsible for program content. Both station engineers and data-processing specialists concentrate on technical processes, with little concern for content, which they regard as someone else's responsibility. It is no wonder that business reports are often as barren a "wasteland" as television is accused of being.

The origination of data for processing involves collecting data as and when events occur and by whatever means will work efficiently. Origination in a form suitable for machine processing can simplify or eliminate subsequent conversion operations, but some conversion operations are usually necessary because different pieces of equipment with various operating speeds are used at each stage.

Data are verified to ensure that format is *correct,* that all the data elements appear to be *complete,* and that the meaning is *reasonable.* Initial origination and processing stages can include some verification steps. Complete verification often requires reference to files to obtain additional facts and answer questions that arise.

The processing of data includes the operations of rearranging input data and updating files for addition of new records and changes for records already in files. Initial data about transactions are classified by type and, if the files are kept in sequence, sorted into the same sequence for efficient processing. Transactions processed against several files may have to be re-sorted into the corresponding sequence before processing against each file.

The foregoing comments apply to files kept in a certain sequence, as magnetic-tape files usually are. Files maintained on random-access storage equipment, such as disks or large drums, need not be organized in any particular sequence. A stock item number, for example, or some variation of it, can serve as the "address" of a record, and any record in the file can be obtained about as quickly as any other. Therefore transactions need not be sorted into sequence before updating the file.

File processing consists of updating files for inventory transactions, calculating gross and net pay, making decisions based on numeric criteria, and calculating sales projections.

Output is taken from the facts on file and involves selecting, aggregating, editing, and rearranging in order to present results in a suitable form. Reports can be historical, forecast, or action documents. The frequency of report preparation—day, week, month, year, or when required—and the length of time available to prepare a report after the close of a period have important bearing on the design of the output subsystem if it is to operate as an efficient part of the whole data-processing system. Unexpected requests for reports pose great problems for a data system because of the need to try to anticipate them and have at least the basic facts available for preparing such reports. The problem is accentuated if the reports must be up-to-the-minute when released.

Broadly considered, processing facilities include people, records, special-purpose office equipment, punched-card equipment, and electronic data processors.

An electronic data-processing system consists of a central processing unit, associated peripheral equipment for input and output, a staff of operating personnel, procedures for them to follow, and instruction routines for the processor.

Many kinds of data processing systems have been installed and are in operation. On-line systems accept data about operations, process them, and supply results quickly enough to permit control of operations while they are going on. Open-loop control systems—for example, airline reservation systems—include people at some stage; whereas closed-loop systems—for example, oil refineries—are wholly automatic.

Off-line systems are useful for data processing and control when time requirements are not so pressing as for on-line control. Much business data processing—for example, payroll, accounts receivable, and similar applications—are handled by batch processing systems operating off-line.

Efficient techniques for data origination and communication play an important role in successful business data processing and will grow more important in the future. Simulation is a promising technique for analyzing and projecting the effect of business decisions.

For alert and progressive managers, electronic data-processing systems have important implications. Management will get more accurate and timely information. Decision-making will improve because managers will spend less time on fact-gathering and more time on using the available information. Human relations, business planning and operations, and business growth are likely to change greatly as data-processing systems gain wider acceptance.

2
Data for Machine Processing

The ability to obtain and store data for later use is invaluable to technical and cultural progress. The efficient storage and use of data depend on the combination of symbols, media, writer, and reader.

Symbols used to represent data are the numerals 0 through 9, the alphabet from A through Z, notes on a musical scale, and many others. Some alphabets are represented by symbols that, although useful for their intended purposes, are either difficult or impossible for people to read: dots and dashes for telegraphic transmission, holes in player piano rolls, punched cards and paper tape, and magnetized spots on a suitable surface.

Many *media* have been used for recording data: clay, stone, wax, sticks, papyrus, paper, cardboard, photographic plates, metal, and plastic. Two examples of plastic media are identification charge-plates with embossed characters, and magnetic tapes (plastic coated with iron oxide) for sound recorders and data processors.

The *writer* for recording data is an instrument and an operating or controlling element, although the two appear inseparable at first glance. Writing instruments have included the brush, pencil, knife, hammer and chisel, seal, movable type, typewriter, punch, and magnetic recorder. The operating or controlling element is commonly a person, either working alone or with the aid of electrical or mechanical power.

The *reader* for data can be a person, a punched-card or punched-tape reader, or a magnetic-tape reader. The reader may even be factory equipment; weaving machines, for example, read cards or tape with instructions for weaving a pattern in cloth or lace, and some milling machines are controlled by data stored on punched or magnetic tape.

MACHINE-PROCESSABLE DATA

Methods for recording business data in machine-processable form have been in use for about seventy years. Knowledge of the principles and methods involved in representing data in machine-processable form is vital to a study of automatic data processing. Some widely used methods of representing data are punched holes in cards and tape, marks in specified locations, specially shaped printed characters, and magnetic marks in a magnetizable material.

Punched Cards

Holes punched in cards are a basic way to store data for mechanized processing. Herman Hollerith invented the punched card and some rudimentary electric processing equipment while working at the U. S. Bureau of the Census in 1886. The punched cards he developed for census enumeration had space for punching 240 holes, each hole representing the presence or absence of a single fact in "yes-no" form.

This limit of 240 holes of course restricted the data content of a card. The content was increased by using smaller holes and punching more of them in a card, by adopting a numerical value (0 through 9) for the holes at each of ten positions in a column, and by using two or more columns together to represent larger numbers. In this way, three columns containing a total of 30 positions could provide for any number between 000 and 999, while 1000 positions would be required if each position were used to represent one fact.

Figure 2-1 shows numerals in 80- and 90-column cards. The standard 80-column card has *ten punching positions* (0 through 9) in each vertical column; only one hole is punched for each numeral to be represented. Each set of data punched in a card is assigned a group of columns called a *field*. Compare the punched with the printed numerals in the number "1734529." Although this number has seven digits, a field of twelve horizontally arranged spaces are allotted to it on the card. The first five spaces are punched with zeros so that the corresponding numbers on all cards are right-justified—that is, aligned on the right-hand digit. Filling out a field of spaces with leading zeros—zeros preceding the desired number—also helps in detecting skipped or double-punched columns, because each column is supposed to have only one punch for a numeral.

The data on a 90-column card are arranged in *two banks* of 45 columns each. The rows in each bank have a single or dual value:

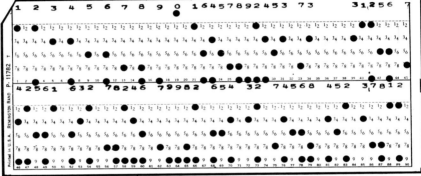

FIGURE 2-1. *Punched cards with numeric data.*

0, 1_2, 3_4, 5_6, 7_8, 9, although 0 and 9 are not marked. Zero and odd-value digits are punched by a single hole representing 0, 1, 3, 5, 7, or 9. Even-value digits are represented by punching both the appropriate dual value hole marked 2, 4, 6, or 8 (which are the same positions used for 1, 3, 5, or 7) and the 9 hole.

Another important development in punched-card data storage was the coding of letters and special symbols by two or three holes in the same column to increase the capacity for alphabetic data. Multiple punches consist of a *zone punch* to indicate the portion of the alphabet and a *numerical punch* to indicate a particular letter within that portion. Figure 2-2 shows cards with two kinds of codes for alphanumerical symbols.

Punched cards are important because data stored on them can be processed electro-mechanically. To do so, people must follow instructions for handling cards and insert suitable programs in the form of wired plugboards into the machine. A punched card is processed by being passed over a sensing device (electric brushes, feeler pins, or photoelectric cells) that reads the holes. Simple calculations

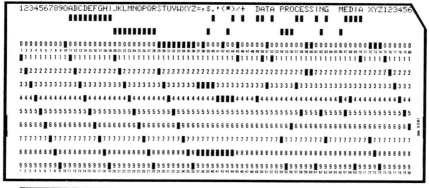

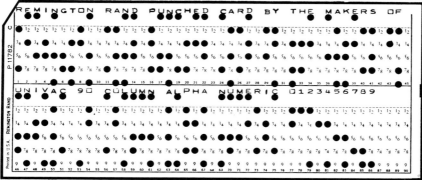

FIGURE 2-2. *Punched cards with alphanumerical codes.*

and *sorting* (arranging according to kind, class, or numerical sequence), *collating* or *merging* (combining two individually sorted decks of cards into one sequence) are done at speeds of 100 to 2000 cards per minute.

Punched cards are widely used for business data collection and processing. Examples of business uses are time cards, personnel records, inventory control records, and cost accounts. A punched card, perhaps of reduced size, can be attached to an item to identify it while in inventory. When the item is used or sold, the card can be detached and processed either directly or after conversion to a card better suited to machine handling. Punched cards are also used for documents that pass between companies and people, such as checks, bills, airplane and toll-road tickets, and purchase orders.

Punched Tape

A common type of punched paper tape has ten columns or frames per inch and can store an alphanumerical character in each frame.

Paper tape stores data more compactly than do punched cards, since it is narrower (about $^{11}/_{16}$ inches wide) and thinner. One basic format for paper tape allows holes for each character to be punched in only five positions or channels. Consequently, the schemes used to represent characters on punched cards will not work directly. If all possible combinations of holes and no holes in each of the five channels are used, a total of 32 different codes are possible ($2^5 = 32$). These 32 combinations, however, are inadequate to handle the required 10 numerals, 26 letters, and several punctuation symbols. To overcome this problem, two combinations are used for shifting between the figures and letters mode. These modes correspond to the upper and lower case key on a typewriter, which permits dual use of each position. In this way, 60 alphanumerical and special characters are practicable—the 64 possible characters, less the figure and letter mode shift characters that are the same in both modes: $64 - 2 \times 2 = 60$. (See Figure 2-3.) Actually, only

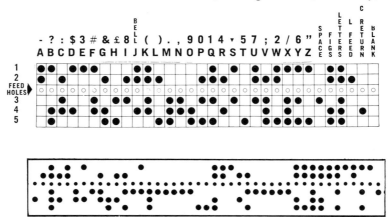

FIGURE 2-3. *Punched tape and five-channel code.*

52 characters are obtained because several more codes are used to control machine operations.

Wider tape will hold still more channels, of course, and thus further increases the number of possible characters. The characters possible with six-channel tape are basically the same as with five-channel, except that they include both upper and lower case letters. Seven-channel code is the same as a six-channel code with a checking channel to help detect mistakes in transmission.

Recent work on what is called *integrated data processing* has aimed at developing a system of completely mechanized handling from the original collection of data to the preparation of final documents and reports. An important facet of some integrated systems is the use of punched tape as a common language for communication among the many kinds of office equipment, ranging from cash registers to punched-card equipment, which punch or read the five-channel code. Five-channel code is not restricted to tape; it can be punched along the edges of ordinary or continuous-form cards used for filing, or even on standard-size cards that are punched in the usual fashion. Although commonly made of paper for single or infrequent use, tape may be laminated from paper and Mylar or paper and metal to withstand repeated runs.

Limitations of Punched-Hole Equipment

Although punched-card equipment is an important advance over manual methods, it has some serious drawbacks. The *mechanical problems* of punching, reading, and card-handling limit operating speeds. Since the plugboards in which wires are inserted to select and sequence operations hold only a small number of *fixed instructions*—for example, "multiply hours worked by wage rate to get gross pay"; or "subtract withholding and payroll taxes from gross pay to get net pay"—processing flexibility is limited for each pass of the cards. Simple arithmetical calculations can be readily handled, but extensive, complex calculations can be made only inefficiently if at all.

The *data density* of cards—the number of characters that can be recorded per square inch or other measure of area or volume—is low because of the hole size required, the alphanumerical codes used, the thickness of cards, and the fixed-field-length requirement. The fixed-field requirement means that the number of columns assigned to a field must cover the longest item that may occur—for example, if stock on hand may reach 10,000 units, then a field five positions long must be provided on every card even though, for most items, only a few hundred units are on hand. More data can be typed or printed on a card (up to 25 lines) than can be punched into the same card. Punched-tape strips are more compact than cards but are clumsy to handle and file. The difficulty of altering data punched in cards or tape is a desirable feature when they must be retained as evidence, but it restricts them to a one-time use. Paper or plastic file-cards, on the other hand, may be used repeatedly. Cards are bulky to send by mail, and transmission over a telegraph line is limited to a few cards a minute with one receiving-sending unit, although card transmission over telephone lines is much faster.

The *serial nature* of punched tape—one character follows another in a word although the holes for a character are in parallel across the tape as a *frame*—and its indefinite length speed up reading and perhaps calculating and tabulating, but it makes sorting more difficult because it is not feasible to cut a tape into short lengths and physically manipulate them to sort data into sequence. Despite these deficiencies, the widespread acceptance of punched-card and tape processing equipment has stimulated the development of more efficient means of storing data for machine processing.

Magnetic Recording

Magnetic recording of digital data corresponds to audio recording methods, except that signals are recorded separately instead of continuously. More care is also required, for the loss of even a few digits may be worse than losing part of a voice recording.

Magnetic spots, which represent data, are recorded in an iron oxide coating on a plastic, aluminum, or even cardboard backing. The iron-oxide-coated material is used in the form of drums, disks, cards, or reels of tape. Magnetic recording media are shown in Figure 2-4.

The operations in magnetic recording are (1) erasing of prior contents, (2) recording the desired data, and (3) reading whenever wanted. Two heads—one for erasing unwanted contents and another for recording and reading—are close to but usually not in contact with the iron-oxide surface. The magnetic spots can be erased and the material reused almost indefinitely.

Characters are often written on tape ½ or ¾ inches wide at densities ranging from 100 to 1500 characters per inch. The 80 alphanumerical characters that can be punched in a card can be recorded on 0.053 to 0.8 inches of tape. Recording density on drums is usually lower—not more than 100 characters an inch on each track around the drum, in eight or so tracks per inch along the drum in the direction parallel to the axis. Tapes are moved past the read-write heads at speeds ranging from 75 to 200 inches a second, and drums rotate at speeds between 1,000 and 20,000 revolutions a minute. The read-write process is controlled electrically and is extremely fast, being done while the tape or drum is in motion. Tape-reading or writing speeds range from 5,000 to more than 100,000 alphanumerical characters a second.

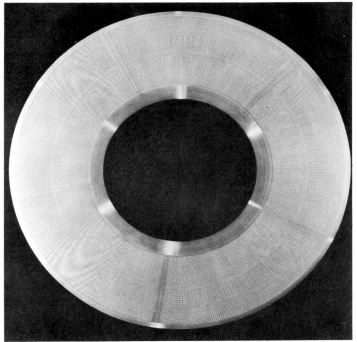

FIGURE 2-4. *Magnetic tape and disk (with data bits along tracks).*

Magnetic cores are small doughnuts of magnetizable material strung on stationary wires and are not moved. Electricity is sent through the wires to write or read the magnetic state of any desired core. Data can be written into or read out of magnetic cores in a few millionths of a second and, in newer equipment, in a fraction of a millionth.

Data Representation

At various stages in a data-processing system, many different methods can be used for representing data: handwriting; handprinting; punched holes; the positions of wheels, gears, and levers, as in a desk calculator; electric pulses; and magnetic states. The proper choice depends on whether people, machines, or both will use the data. Ordinarily, several methods are used and conversion is required among them, since, if a single method were used throughout, efficiency would drop.

Just as many different frequencies, shapes, and amplitudes of audio signals are used to record music on a magnetic tape, many different sizes and shapes of holes, spots, or electric pulses can represent alphanumerical data. Although few components would be needed to handle digital data represented in this way, they would be very complex. Thus, another approach is to have simpler components and use many of them. Automatic processing equipment is designed with many components that can exist in either one of two states. The two states may be represented in various ways: by a punched hole or no hole; by a magnetic spot with either north-south or south-north polarity; by a relay open or closed; by an electric pulse or no pulse; or by a dot or dash. The "yes-no," "on-off," or "0-1" scheme is popular because it is easier to design equipment that can be put in one of two states and make it stay there—equipment with two *stable* states—than it is to provide for many stable states. A light switch is a simple example of a two-state, "on-off" device. Combinations of the two symbols 0 and 1, called "binary digits" or "bits," are used in a variety of ingenious schemes to represent numerals, letters, and other symbols.

NUMBER SYSTEMS

The various number systems in use are treated here only in enough detail to show the relationship between schemes that people like to use and those preferred by computer designers.

People like the decimal number system because it seems "natural"; they learned to count on their fingers, and often still do. Many other number bases are widely used; however, we tend to think of them merely as counting schemes. Examples are 12 for a dozen, 16 for ounces in a pound, 3 for feet in a yard, and 5280 for feet in a mile. Nondecimal fractions are also used; for example, ⅛ for security prices and ¹⁄₁₆ for fractions of an inch. People even find the British monetary system of mixed radices comprehensible (4 farthings to a penny, 12 pennies to a shilling, 20 shillings to a pound, and decimal thereafter), although far more complex than a single-radix scheme.

The *base or radix* of a number system need only be greater than 1, and is usually but not always an integer. The radix in the decimal system is 10; in counting by the dozen it is 12, and for counting by pairs it is 2. The number of marks in a number system is equal to the radix used. The decimal system has ten marks or digits—0 through 9. The binary system has two digits, 0 and 1. The octal system has eight symbols, 0 through 7.

Decimal System

When counting goes beyond one position in the decimal system, the digit in the next position to the left is increased by 1 and counting is resumed at 0. Counting beyond 9 seems easy because of constant practice; it seems "natural" that 10 and 11 should follow 9, or that 1000 should follow 999. In brief, all large numbers make use of the same digits, 0 to 9.

By way of contrast, consider that in using roman numerals—I, V, X, L, C, D, M, $\overline{\text{X}}$, $\overline{\text{C}}$, and $\overline{\text{M}}$— the value of a number depends on the characters used and their sequence (if they are different), but not on their individual positions. For example, III is 3, IV is 4, VI is 6, both XC and LXXXX are 90, and $\overline{\text{MM}}$CLXVI is 1,001,166. In this system, representations of large numbers are difficult to create and to understand.

The concept of positional value is fundamental to simple, straightforward number systems. Whenever a digit is written, it has an individual value that is independent of the digits to its left or right. But—and this point is important in modern number systems—the over-all value of a digit is the product of its individual value and its *position value*—the number base raised to the power of the digit position occupied.

In a decimal number, digits have individual values of 0 through 9 and position values that are multiples of 10, the number base of the decimal system. The first digit to the left of the decimal point is multiplied by 10^0, which is equal to 1, so that the first digit is counted at face value. The second or tens digit is multiplied by 10^1, which is 10. The hundreds digit is multiplied by 10^2 or 100, and so on.

Digits to the right of the decimal point are divided by 10^1, 10^2, 10^3 (or multiplied by 10^{-1}, 10^{-2}, 10^{-3}), corresponding to each digit position to the right of the decimal point.

The complete number is *the sum of each digit multiplied by its positional value.* For example, the digits 4, 9, 7, 6, 5, written as the number 497.65, have positional values as follows:

Position Value	$\begin{cases} 10^2 \\ 100 \end{cases}$	$\begin{matrix} 10^1 \\ 10 \end{matrix}$	$\begin{matrix} 10^0 \\ 1 \end{matrix}$	.	$\begin{matrix} 10^{-1} \\ \frac{1}{10} \end{matrix}$	$\begin{matrix} 10^{-2} \\ \frac{1}{100} \end{matrix}$
Digits	4	9	7	.	6	5
Products	\multicolumn{6}{}{$(4 \times 100) + (9 \times 10) + (7 \times 1) + (6 \times \frac{1}{10}) + (5 \times \frac{1}{100})$}
Number	\multicolumn{6}{}{497.65}

Powers of 10 are used to find positional values because there are 10 symbols. The largest digit is 9, but it is possible to represent 10 by assigning a positional value to the smallest nonzero digit, 1, and attaching 0.

Long familiarity has led people to think that the decimal system is objectively "natural." It is easy for us to forget how difficult it once was to learn the sums and products of two decimal digits. The decimal addition and multiplication tables are difficult to learn because the table for single-digit numbers has a hundred entries.

Binary System

The fact that it is easiest to design and build equipment with two stable states, that might be thought of as "yes-no," "on-off," or "0-1," makes the binary system desirable. The 0 and 1 are the only two binary digits and are often referred to as "bits."

The bits in a *binary number* have position values of 2^0, 2^1, to 2^n, which are equal to 1, 2, 4, and so on. This is similar to the scheme of 10^0, 10^1, 10^2, etc., for decimal digit positions.

Position values in binary are as follows, to the left and right of the binary point:

$$\begin{matrix} 2^5 & 2^4 & 2^3 & 2^2 & 2^1 & 2^0 & . & 2^{-1} & 2^{-2} & 2^{-3} \\ 32 & 16 & 8 & 4 & 2 & 1 & . & \frac{1}{2} & \frac{1}{4} & \frac{1}{8} \end{matrix}$$

Counting in decimal and binary shows the positional values and the similarities in advancing to the next position each time:

Decimal	Binary
0	0
1	1
2	10
3	11
4	100
5	101
6	110
7	111
8	1000
9	1001
10	1010
11	1011
12	1100
50	110010
100	1100100
512	1000000000

To the right of the binary point, each bit is divided by 2, 4, 8, and so on. Examples of fractions in one number system also show how some numbers may be difficult to express in the other:

Decimal	Binary
0.5	0.1
0.25	0.01
0.125	0.001
0.375	0.011
0.33333 . . .	0.01010101 . . .

Codes Based on Binary

Users and designers of data-processing equipment have different viewpoints about the ideal number system to use. Business users generally prefer a decimal number system because input and output data are typically decimal. Computer designers, on the other hand, prefer a binary system because it is easier to design and build equipment with components expected to maintain two stable states rather than ten. There are two ways to compromise this conflict. One way is to retain decimal numbers for input and output, and design the machine to operate with pure binary numbers. However, this use of two number systems requires converting input from decimal to binary and output back to decimal. Because people find manual conversion so burdensome, the processor is designed to handle it. Converting a *decimal number* to a *binary number* may be done during a card-reading cycle, or after data are read in from magnetic tape. Since most modern machines handle the conversion, it is of little concern to the supplier of input which mode the machine is operating in.

Another way to reconcile the decimal-binary conflict is to represent each *decimal digit* in a code of four binary digits and avoid the task of converting the number as a whole into binary. The conversion of each *decimal numeral* into *binary-coded decimal* is simpler than that from decimal numbers to binary numbers, but this advantage is gained at the cost of longer numbers, since more digits are required. The decimal number 403, for example, might be written as 0100 0000 0011 in binary-coded decimal. Manipulating binary-coded decimal numbers also entails either more circuitry or slower processing.

Decimal	Binary	Binary-Coded decimal	
		8421	Excess 3
0	0	0000	0011
1	1	0001	0100
2	10	0010	0101
3	11	0011	0110
4	100	0100	0111
5	101	0101	1000
6	110	0110	1001
7	111	0111	1010
8	1000	1000	1011
9	1001	1001	1100

TABLE 2-1. *Numerical coding systems.*

Values for 0 to 9 are shown in Table 2-1 for several code schemes including two versions of binary-coded decimal. The 8421 version uses a straightforward binary representation with leading zeros to fill out a four-digit field. The "Excess 3" code scheme is similar to the binary, but the binary value of a decimal 3, which is 0011, is added to each numeral in binary to facilitate arithmetical operations—for example, the decimal complement of an Excess 3 digit can be obtained simply by changing each 0 to 1 and each 1 to 0.

Many other codes exist, some of which are used for processors. Business applications involve a higher ratio of input-output operations to computations than do engineering and mathematical applications; therefore, equipment intended for business applications may be designed with a machine code, such as binary-coded decimal, that is easily converted from (or to) a code that can be used by other machines and people.

ALPHANUMERICAL SYSTEM

Alphabetic characters are more difficult to represent than numerals since they are more varied—26 letters and a dozen or so special characters, instead of merely ten numerals. Furthermore, alphabetic characters are not convertible into binary numbers by the usual scheme of division. The name "John Jones" cannot be represented in binary in any easy way.

Six-Bit Code

The binary-coded decimal scheme in which four bits can represent 16 characters can be extended to six bits to represent 64 characters, since six bits yield 2^6 or 64 possible combinations. Using six bits for each character makes it possible to represent the alphabet A to Z in upper-case characters, the numerals 0 to 9, and 28 other characters in what might be called a *binary-coded alphanumerical* scheme.

Examples of special symbols, numerals (in Excess 3 code), and letters in binary-coded alphanumerical are as follows:

(	00 0010
)	00 0011
/	01 0010
0	01 0011
1	01 0100
7	01 1010
C	10 0010
D	10 0011
S	11 0010
T	11 0011

Notice that (, /, C, and S have the same four right-hand bits but differ in the two left-hand "zone" bits. In some ways this is comparable to the two top-row or zone punches—X and Y—that are used with punches for 0 to 9 to represent alphabetical characters in a standard 80-column punched card. The four right-hand bits, which yield 16 combinations, are used with two left-hand bits yielding four combinations for a total of 64. This range of characters serves for many purposes but does not provide for both lower-case (uncapitalized) and upper-case characters. An important and easily overlooked point is that the combination of bits "10 0010" does not mean "C" to a computer, but is merely assigned that value by people using the equipment. The bits 10 0010 can just as easily stand for any letter in any alphabet that does not use more than 64 characters. For readability by people, the desired letter is placed on keyboards used for preparing input and on printers for output.

Parity-Bit

An extra binary digit, called the *parity-bit,* is often attached to each character solely to detect whether the equipment is malfunctioning by dropping or gaining a bit. If the equipment designer chooses to use an *odd-parity-bit* rule, an odd number of bits is used to represent each character. The gain or loss of one bit results in an even number of bits and violates the odd-bit rule. In the illustration below, the character "B" is represented as 100001, with an odd parity-bit attached in the parity channel to give 1 100001. The loss of one bit leaves two bits or the gain of one bit gives four, and both of these violate the odd-parity-bit rule.

Channel		Character				
Name	Number	)	*	8	B	X
Parity-bit channel	7	0	0	1	1	0
Zone channels	6	0	0	0	1	1
	5	0	0	1	0	1
	4	0	1	1	0	0
Numerical channels	3	1	1	0	0	1
	2	0	0	1	0	1
	1	0	1	1	1	1
Number of bits		1	3	5	3	5

Some equipment is designed with the even-parity-bit rule—which is to add a bit, if required—to make the number of bits in a character even, giving essentially the same result as the odd-bit rule.

There are other ways of detecting the complete loss of a character, such as counting the number of characters each time they are handled, or using a parity-bit for each channel along a tape. The lengthwise, or *longitudinal parity-bit* scheme is useful for detecting the loss of a bit in a channel. In conjunction with the vertical parity-bit, the longitudinal bit can be used to detect and correct an equipment malfunction of one bit. The message "213786 42 390 JOHN

DOE" (with $<$ and $>$ for "start message" and "end message," respectively, and • for "item separator") might be recorded on tape with a parity-bit for each character in Channel 7 and for each channel in the position marked "p" as follows:

```
           < 2 1 3 7 8 6 • 4 2 • 3 9 0 • JOHN • DOE > p
Channel
   7       0 0 1 0 0 1 0 1 1 0 1 0 0 0 1 0 1 1 1 1 0 1 1 0 1
   6       1 0 0 0 0 0 0 1 0 0 1 0 0 0 1 1 1 1 1 1 1 1 1 1 0
   5       1 1 1 1 1 1 1 1 1 1 1 1 1 1 0 0 0 0 1 0 0 0 1 0
   4       1 0 0 0 1 1 1 1 0 0 1 0 1 0 1 1 1 0 1 1 0 1 0 1 1
   3       1 1 1 1 0 0 0 1 1 1 1 1 1 0 1 0 1 1 1 1 0 1 1 1 1←
   2       1 0 0 1 1 1 0 0 1 0 0 1 0 1 0 0 1 1 0 0 1 1 0 0 0
   1       0 1 0 0 0 1 1 0 1 1 0 0 0 1 0 1 0 1 1 0 1 0 0 1 0
                 ↑
```

If a bit were lost so that the first 3, for example, was recorded as 0010010 with only two bits, the odd-parity-bit rule would be violated in both the column and the row marked with arrows. With only one bit lost (or gained), correction could be made by complementing whatever exists at the intersection of lines drawn from the two arrows. The complementing of 0 to 1 or 1 to 0 would correct the malfunction of the recording equipment. More elaborate parity-bit schemes, especially longitudinal ones, are used to detect and correct more severe malfunctions. A six-bit code with parity-bit is commonly used to detect the loss of bits in alphanumerical codes on magnetic tape. When data are transferred into some processors, the parity-bit scheme is omitted because the risk of losing a bit during processing is far less than during tape-reading or writing.

Sorting Sequence

Figure 2-5 shows an example of a six-bit code with parity-bit at the left of the character. This code is arranged in the collating or *sorting sequence,* which means that data in this code could be arranged in numerical and alphabetic sequence. The five messages, < 4357 • DOE, JOHN $>$, < 2476 • ROE, RICHARD $>$, < 1289 • BAKER, CHARLEY $>$, < 2476 • ROE, JOHN $>$, and < 7365 • BAKER, ABLE $>$, could be sorted into two difference sequences by using either the whole message or only the second item (and following items, if desired) as a key to identify the message.

The sequence using the *whole message* as the sorting *key* would be correct numerically.

CHARACTER DESCRIPTION	SYMBOL	7 P* (2^5?)	6 (2^5)	5 (2^4)	4 (2^3)	3 (2^2)	2 (2^1)	1 (2^0)	OCTAL EQUIVALENT	CHARACTER DESCRIPTION	SYMBOL	7 P*	6 (2^5)	5 (2^4)	4 (2^3)	3 (2^2)	2 (2^1)	1 (2^0)	OCTAL EQUIVALENT
Blank	—	1	0	0	0	0	0	0	00	A	A	0	1	0	0	0	0	0	40
Space		0	0	0	0	0	0	1	01	B	B	1	1	0	0	0	0	1	41
Cross	‡	0	0	0	0	0	1	0	02	C	C	1	1	0	0	0	1	0	42
Open Parenthesis	(	1	0	0	0	0	1	1	03	D	D	0	1	0	0	0	1	1	43
Close Parenthesis	)	0	0	0	0	1	0	0	04	E	E	1	1	0	0	1	0	0	44
Quotes	"	1	0	0	0	1	0	1	05	F	F	0	1	0	0	1	0	1	45
Colon	:	1	0	0	0	1	1	0	06	G	G	0	1	0	0	1	1	0	46
Dollars	$	0	0	0	0	1	1	1	07	H	H	1	1	0	0	1	1	1	47
Percent	%	0	0	0	1	0	0	0	10	I	I	1	1	0	1	0	0	0	50
Semicolon	;	1	0	0	1	0	0	1	11	J	J	0	1	0	1	0	0	1	51
Ampersand	&	1	0	0	1	0	1	0	12	K	K	0	1	0	1	0	1	0	52
Apostrophe	'	0	0	0	1	0	1	1	13	L	L	1	1	0	1	0	1	1	53
Minus	⊖	1	0	0	1	1	0	0	14	M	M	0	1	0	1	1	0	0	54
Asterisk	*	0	0	0	1	1	0	1	15	N	N	1	1	0	1	1	0	1	55
Period	.	0	0	0	1	1	1	0	16	O	O	1	1	0	1	1	1	0	56
Carriage Shift (CS)		1	0	0	1	1	1	1	17	P	P	0	1	0	1	1	1	1	57
Page Change (PC)		0	0	1	0	0	0	0	20	Q	Q	1	1	1	0	0	0	0	60
Line Shift (LS)		1	0	1	0	0	0	1	21	R	R	0	1	1	0	0	0	1	61
Slant	/	1	0	1	0	0	1	0	22	S	S	0	1	1	0	0	1	0	62
Zero (Numeric)	0	0	0	1	0	0	1	1	23	T	T	1	1	1	0	0	1	1	63
One	1	1	0	1	0	1	0	0	24	U	U	0	1	1	0	1	0	0	64
Two	2	0	0	1	0	1	0	1	25	V	V	1	1	1	0	1	0	1	65
Three	3	0	0	1	0	1	1	0	26	W	W	1	1	1	0	1	1	0	66
Four	4	1	0	1	0	1	1	1	27	X	X	0	1	1	0	1	1	1	67
Five	5	1	0	1	1	0	0	0	30	Y	Y	0	1	1	1	0	0	0	70
Six	6	0	0	1	1	0	0	1	31	Z	Z	1	1	1	1	0	0	1	71
Seven	7	0	0	1	1	0	1	0	32	End File (EF)		1	1	1	1	0	1	0	72
Eight	8	1	0	1	1	0	1	1	33	End Data (ED)		0	1	1	1	0	1	1	73
Nine	9	0	0	1	1	1	0	0	34	Item Separator (ISS)	●	1	1	1	1	1	0	0	74
Comma	,	1	0	1	1	1	0	1	35	End Message (EM)	>	0	1	1	1	1	0	1	75
Number	#	1	0	1	1	1	1	0	36	Start Message (SM)	<	0	1	1	1	1	1	0	76
Carriage Normal		0	0	1	1	1	1	1	37			1	1	1	1	1	1	1	77†

* The parity bit (P) is shown as it appears on magnetic tape (odd parity); on paper tape, parity is even.

† 77 with odd parity (1111111) is a legitimate octal number on magnetic tape. On paper tape, 77 is a legitimate octal number only when there is no punch in the seventh (P) channel (even parity). The Paper Tape Reader ignores a row in which all seven channels are punched, interpreting this as a corrective measure.

FIGURE 2-5. *The RCA 501 code, with odd parity-bit.*

1289	BAKER, CHARLEY
2476	ROE, JOHN
2476	ROE, RICHARD
4357	DOE, JOHN
7365	BAKER, ABLE

The sequence using the *second item* as the sorting *key* would be correct alphabetically.

7365	BAKER, ABLE
1289	BAKER, CHARLEY
4357	DOE, JOHN
2476	ROE, JOHN
2476	ROE, RICHARD

Each of these sequences is in ascending order according to the key used and the values in the collation table. When keys contain both alphabetic and numerical characters, the resulting sorted sequence depends on whether numerals precede letters (as is true for the code shown above) or vice versa.

Multi-Mode Codes

A dilemma arises from the fact that four bits are enough for a numerical code whereas six are required for an alphanumeric code that has more than 32 characters but not more than 64. If a four-bit code is used for representing numerals, then one alphabetic character might be represented by a two-digit number—a *two-for-one* scheme. For example, "A" might first be assigned the decimal number 32 and then coded as 0011 0010 in binary-coded decimal. The two-for-one scheme is efficient for numerals—each one is represented by four bits. But it is inefficient for alphabetic characters because each one is represented by eight bits, whereas six bits are enough to represent 64 different characters. The two-for-one scheme is acceptable when the volume of alphabetic data is small and the equipment prints letters as letters and not as two decimal digits that people must convert into letters when they read output. In this case, as in all multi-mode codes, the bits can be used to represent a character in either one mode or another, but obviously the same bits cannot be used in two modes at the same time. The programmer must keep track of which mode is being used.

The *three-for-two* scheme is more compact for representing both alphabetic and numeric data than the two-for-one scheme. Three numerals require twelve bits which can, alternatively, be used to represent alphabetic characters. This condensation is possible because numeric characters do not need the fifth and sixth bits—called "zone" bits—that are required for representing alphabetic characters. Thus, three numerals or two alphabetic characters can be represented by the twelve bits ordinarily thought of as being adequate for two alphabetic characters. The four zone bits of two alphabetic characters can be used along with the eight other bits to represent three numerals. The scheme of representing either three numerals or two alphabetic characters with twelve bits is useful for compact storage on tape. Numerals can, if desired, be returned to the usual six-bit form for internal storage and processing. Alphabetic characters are represented by six bits on tape and also in internal storage for processing.

The multi-mode scheme is carried further in some equipment so that 24 bits treated as a word may be used as eight octal, six decimal, or four alphanumerical characters. These modes are alternatives to using the 24 bits as one binary number. Examples of these different uses are shown in the following illustration. One or more parity-bits may be used with the 24 data bits. Longer words of 36 and

48 bits, which also are multiples of 3, 4, and 6, are also used in similar fashion by some processors.

Twenty-four individual bits **Binary**	101001110100101101100100
Eight groups of three bits **Octal numbers**	5 1 6 4 5 5 4 4
Six groups of four bits **Binary-coded decimal** **(Excess 3)**	7 4 1 8 3 1
Four groups of six bits **Alphanumerical**	J U N E
One group of twenty-four bits **Decimal**	10963812

Multi-mode codes have important practical considerations. The fact that data can be packed more densely at some stages of processing permits higher tape capacity and reading speeds. But it becomes necessary for the programmer to keep track of the mode being used and deal with it appropriately.

The selection of an efficient data code depends on whether alphabetic or numerical data are involved and on the amount of processing to be done each time the data are handled. If numbers predominate in the data, a numerical code—either pure binary or binary-coded decimal—offers more compact storage than does an alphanumerical code, although at the cost of clumsy methods for handling letters.

Conversely, alphabetic data can be handled directly by alphanumerical codes, but they are not efficient for handling numerals because six bits are used for a numeral, whereas four would be enough in binary-coded decimal and about three and a third in pure binary. Processors handle binary numbers more efficiently, but a conversion is required to decimal or alphabetic form for people to use. Frequent conversion between alphanumerical and binary offsets some of the benefits derived from more efficient internal processing. Newer machines, however, are designed to handle data in binary, octal, decimal, or alphabetic modes. In order to process the data in the same code in which it was encoded—say, binary out of several possible codes—it is necessary to specify to the processor the mode selected.

ORGANIZATION OF DATA

Data-processing equipment senses, stores, and manipulates a wide variety of characters. Individual characters must be grouped together in a way that is practical for use by people and machines.

The organization of data can be illustrated by the Jameson Knitting Company's scheme for keeping track of customers' orders (see Figure 2-6). An order record is prepared on paper for each order received from a customer; it identifies the customer, lists the

Jameson Knitting Company

Jameson Knitting Company

Jameson Knitting Company
Order Record

Order No. __37259__   Date ____8/3/--____

Name __JOHN DOE CO.__   Ship to ___JOHN DOE CO.___

Address 10 WALNUT STREET   SAME

OSHKOSH, MINN.

Customer Code __23AM69__

Stock Number	Quantity Ordered	Quantity Shipped	Quantity Back Ordered
162	3	3	0
14982	20	16	4
432891	25	12	13

FIGURE 2-6. *Customer order record, paper.*

items ordered, and posts the quantity shipped or back-ordered. Each numeral, letter, punctuation mark, or symbol is a *character*. Characters are grouped into *data elements* to specify a particular order number, date, alphabetic name, street address, stock number, and quantity. Data elements are grouped into *records*.

Examples of records in this case are the customer's order and the shipping department's report of the quantity of each stock number shipped or back-ordered. These records comprise the back-order *file*. The organization of data on paper, from the smallest to the largest unit, is thus: character, data element, record, and file. The concept of organizing data into a structure running from element to file is an important one for business data processing.

Another aspect of data organization is the quantity of storage assigned to a character, data element, record, or file. Data elements and records are of primary interest here.

Selectable-Length Data Elements

A customer order file kept on paper records illustrates the use of selectable-length data elements. The maximum number of characters needed for any element is anticipated and provided for in printing the form. The length provided for each element can be fixed individually, so that a long space can be provided for customer name. Customer name is an example of externally-originated data—data whose format is selected by someone outside the organization that must process it. Customer name may take 30 or 40 characters, although it can be limited in size and excess characters merely cut off or dropped. Stock numbers, on the other hand, can be established as desired and restricted to a few digits, although 10 or 20 digits are often used for unique identifications in large inventory systems. Since space on paper records is inexpensive, field lengths can be set generously to handle the longest element likely to occur. And, of course, people are clever enough to modify the length of an item merely by writing in the margin.

Punched cards pose a more difficult problem for fixing item length. Since the total number of columns available in a card is usually 80 or 90, their use must be economized to prevent some records from carrying over to several cards. Once a field—the number of columns—is assigned to a data element, the maximum length is selected for punched-card processing. If the longest *stock number* is 20 characters, then a field of 20 columns is assigned for use with both long and short numbers. For example, the numbers 387-A4295725-9291 and B7070 are punched into a 20-column field as 000387-A4295725-9291 and 00000000000000B7070. The *quantities of items,* on the other hand, might range from 1 to 9999 and thus require only four columns. An entirely different number of columns might be used for customer *name and address* in the cards.

In short, the term "selectable" means that the number of characters allotted to a data element in a record is open or free until a certain number is assigned. Thereafter, the number of characters for that element is fixed, so that shorter elements are filled out and longer elements cannot be fitted into the space assigned.

Variable-Length Elements

If the facilities used for processing data can deal about equally well with long and short data elements—that is, elements of *variable length*—one need only identify the element and use the number of characters necessary. Blank paper, without any designation of length, is a simple example of a variable-length element record. On blank paper a record might contain explicit identification and elements in sequence without regard to format or spacing.

> Order No. 37259 Date 8/3/—Name John Doe Co. Ship to John Doe Co. Address 10 Walnut St. Same Oshkosh, Minn. Same Customer code 23AM69 Stock number Quantity ordered Quantity shipped Quantity back-ordered 162 3 3 0 14982 20 16 4 432891 25 12 13

The order record written in variable-length elements occupies less space on blank paper than does the selectable-length record on the printed form shown earlier. It takes more skill to associate headings—stock number, quantity ordered, shipped, and back-ordered—with the related elements in the line-by-line scheme shown here. The loss of one item, furthermore, might cause the others to be misinterpreted.

'The elements can be organized in more logical ways. Related data may be grouped together and then described as a particular element or set of elements that is repeated a specified number of times. A file of 10,000 customer orders, for example, is fully explained by a single description of the format to be used. The name of each element need not be listed explicitly but can be implied from the sequence in which it appears. The order for John Doe can be compressed if • is an element or item separator, < indicates start of record, and > indicates end of record.

< 37259 • 8/3/— • John Doe Co. • John Doe Co. • 10
Walnut St. • Same • Oshkosh, Minn. • Same • 23AM69
• 162 • 3 • 3 • 0 • 14982 • 20 • 16 • 4 • 432891
• 25 • 12 • 13 >

The item following the second item separator should be the
customer's name; hence if the date is omitted, two separators are
included for counting purposes: < 37259 • • John Doe Co. •
. . . .When records are organized in this manner, a repetitive pattern develops—stock number, quantity ordered, shipped, and back-
ordered—so that the tenth, fourteenth, or eighteenth item is always
the stock number. Computers designed to handle variable-length
items can store and process data recorded in this fashion on magnetic tape (see Figure 2-7). They are called "variable-length field"

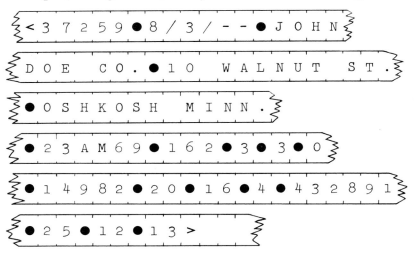

FIGURE 2-7. *Schematic for content of customer order record, magnetic tape,*
variable-length field.

or "character" machines since it is possible to use any number of
characters desired.

Fixed Word and Block

Word is often defined as a fixed number of characters or character locations that are treated as a unit. Word length is fixed by the
computer designer and incorporated in the circuitry. Common word
lengths are 10 or 12 alphanumerical characters and 24, 36, or 48
bits. Every computer word must contain the specified number of

characters or bits. Excess positions in *computer words,* occurring because the data elements are shorter, can be filled with zeros or spaces. Figure 2-8 shows the layout for a customer order on mag-

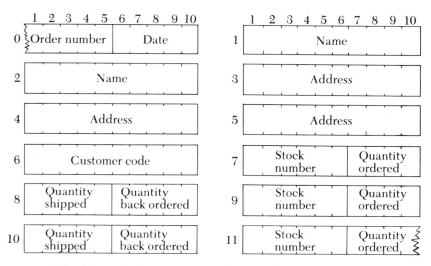

FIGURE 2-8. *Schematic for customer order record, magnetic tape, fixed word length, twelve words.*

netic tape with fixed word length. Longer items occurring in the data can be handled by using two or more computer words together to represent one item.

Fixed-word equipment uses extra storage space for shorter data elements because it fills out the word with spaces. If two or more short items of data are *packed* into one word, extra steps are required to separate or unpack them for individual processing. An opposite situation arises when an item is longer than a computer word so that two words are used to store an item. Both words must be treated together when making comparisons during sorting or when performing arithmetical operations.

Block means a fixed number of characters or words treated as a unit on magnetic tape and in computer storage. Data on magnetic tape can be read only while the tape is moving at speeds of about 100 inches a second. Inter-block gaps—blank spaces of about one-half inch on tape—are required for starting and stopping tape movement. If the tape-packing *density* is 200 characters an inch, ten characters in a word occupy one-twentieth of an inch of tape. Tapes written with individual words would have ten times as much start-stop space as data space. In order to conserve space on tape, data are handled as fixed-length blocks of characters; a block, for example, may contain 720 characters arranged in 60 words of 12 characters each. A computer designed to handle variable-length elements may handle blocks as short as several characters and without an upper limit for long records. In the conversion of data from punched cards to tape, the block length may be limited to the 80 characters in a card. Short blocks may be consolidated into longer blocks during the first processing run in order to reduce tape length and read-write time in subsequent passes. In such cases, the data are said to be "blocked" and the length of magnetic tape used for recording the data is reduced. Additional handling may be required to unblock the records and process them individually.

Because people and machines each work best with data in different formats, problems arise of placing two or more data words into one processor word and two or more data records into one block on tape, and subsequently separating them for processing.

SUMMARY

Many methods are used to represent, store, and process data. The efficient storage and use of data depend on the symbols, media, writer, and reader. Any particular combination selected from the available possibilities imposes restrictions on data-processing techniques, since all members must operate compatibly.

Punched cards and punched paper tape are widely used for storing business data. Both cards and tape involve the mechanical operations of punching holes in paper. The width, length, and thickness of cards and tape influence the code used, data density, and processing methods. As originally developed, the codes were mostly limited to numerals, but more recently they have been extended to include alphabetical characters.

Magnetic recording media are similar to cards and paper tape in some respects, but have two highly desirable features: they require fewer mechanical operations, and they can be reused for other data.

Number systems owe much to the historical context in which they originated and developed. Various number systems—decimal, duodecimal (base 12), hexadecimal (base 16), octal, and binary—are widely used today, although people seem to favor the decimal system. Computer designers prefer the binary system of data representation, because two-state devices are easier to build and operate than multi-state devices. As a result, conversion from one system to another often is required; this conversion is usually performed by the processor.

Four-bit codes, with sixteen possible combinations, are often used for numerals. Six-bit codes are used to represent numerals, letters, and special characters, but are, of course, limited to a total of 64 characters ($2^6 = 64$). Alphanumerical codes usually provide an additional parity-bit for detecting the gain or loss of a bit that would change a desired character to an illegal character. A total of seven bits—six bits for the character plus a parity-bit—will represent 128 characters ($2^7 = 128$); but only half the possible characters are considered legal. The adoption of an odd parity-bit scheme makes illegal all characters that have an even number of bits. The loss resulting from ruling out half the possible characters, when one bit is designated as a parity-bit, is considered a fair price to pay for the increased ability to detect errors. The general idea of parity-bits need not be limited to one bit for a character (*vertical parity*). Additional parity-bits may be used along the channel for several characters (*horizontal parity*). Both vertical and horizontal parity are sometimes used to increase the ability to detect and also correct errors in data recorded on tape.

Multi-mode schemes are used to represent different mixes of characters in a format that is basically binary. The eight bits designated for two numerals can be used for one letter—a two-for-one scheme—or the twelve bits designated for three numerals can be used for two letters—a three-for-two scheme. Some processors are designed to treat the bits of a word in any one of several ways at the programmer's option—binary, octal, decimal, or alphanumerical—to maximize the density of data storage for the particular kind of data involved.

Data are organized into four levels for processing:
1. *Character:* numeral, letter, punctuation, or other symbol.
2. *Data element:* characters grouped to specify a particular unit of information—order number, date, customer's name and address.
3. *Record:* one or more data elements related in some meaningful way—same transaction, same physical object, same customer, etc. Records can consist of several levels of data elements. For example, the data element "customer's address" can be further classified into "street," "city," and "state," as separate data elements.
4. *File:* a collection of related records.

There are several schemes for organizing data elements for processing, based on the fact that the length of the elements may vary greatly. Under the *selectable-length* scheme any length may be chosen for an element—say, the stock number—but, once chosen, all stock numbers must be given the same length at the expense of filling out short numbers with zeros. Selecting a long record to handle the longest stock number may entail additional processing for all records.

The *variable-length* scheme allows any item to be any length, without restraint. The end of each item is identified by an item indicator (which may be combined with its last character or the first character of the following item) or an item separator used between every two items. Under this scheme, an item is identified not by its location but by its sequential relationship to other items. To keep the item-count correct, this plan requires identification of any items omitted.

The *fixed-word-and-block* scheme specifies the number of characters that are treated as a word, and the number of words handled as a block. The word and block length are designed into the equipment by the manufacturer, and the user must adhere to his specifications.

PART II
AUTOMATIC EQUIPMENT

3

Processing Equipment—Basic Processor and Storage

A data-processing system consists of a number of individual components, each of which has its own tasks. Efficient processing requires units to prepare data in machine language, read the data into the processor, store the data, perform arithmetical or logical operations, accept data from the processor, present results in usable form, and control the entire operation.

MAJOR COMPONENTS

Figure 3-1 is a schematic diagram of the major components of a data-processing system. *Data preparation devices* include card punches, character readers, and by-product paper-tape punches. They convert data in written or verbal form into machine media—generally magnetic tape or punched cards. Special *communication devices* bring data to the processing system over telephone and telegraph lines from remote locations—different rooms, buildings, cities, or even countries. Sometimes data preparation or communication devices transmit data directly to high-speed storage, but generally they produce machine-processable media as an intermediate step. *On-line input units*—commonly magnetic-tape or punched-card readers—are directly connected to the processor in order to read data from the machine media into the processor.

The *basic processor* consists of a control unit, an arithmetic and logic unit, and a high-speed storage unit. The *control unit* is comparable to a telephone switchboard, for it sets switches to direct the flow of data through the system and to initiate the desired arithmetical or logical operations. The *arithmetic and logic unit* might be viewed as a combination of a desk calculator and a dependable, extremely fast clerk. This unit performs addition, subtraction, multipli-

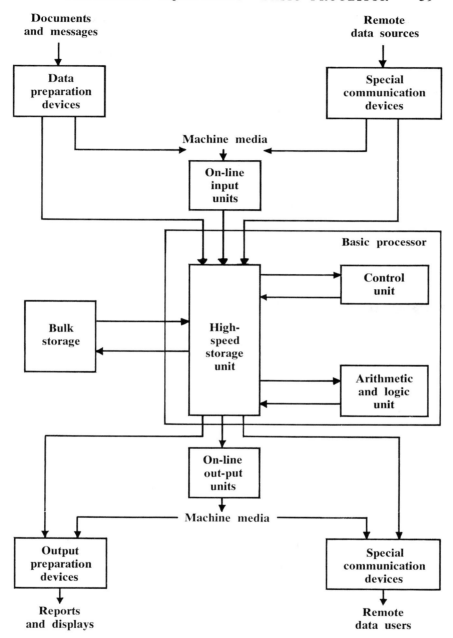

FIGURE 3-1. *Schematic of major components of a data-processing system.*

cation and division. By comparing data items, it decides whether Jones precedes or follows Brown in alphabetical sequence, or whether the quantity of a particular inventory item is above or below its reorder point. The *high-speed storage unit*—usually magnetic cores or a magnetic drum—receives data from input units, supplies data and instructions to the control and arithmetic units during processing, and furnishes results to the output unit. The high-speed storage unit contains thousands of individual locations that can store either data or instructions at any time.

Since high-speed storage is costly, and therefore limited in size, many processors have *on-line bulk storage* as an option to supplement the high-speed storage. All the contents of the bulk storage unit, which may contain both data and instructions, are available directly to the processor, but at a slower speed than data in high-speed storage. Bulk storage units—magnetic disk files and large drums—will hold millions of characters of data or instructions.

Processor *output functions* and equipment are similar to those used for input in many respects. Results of processing are often written out of high-speed storage onto magnetic tape, although the data may go directly to a printer, a card punch, or a communication device.

Modern data-processing systems are highly *modular*. Various input, output, and bulk storage devices can be attached to most basic processors and even to small-scale ones. The basic processor itself is generally available with two to four different sizes of high-speed storage plus many special options to increase processing speed and to simplify programming. The careful and informed user often can find, or assemble, a system closely tailored to his needs. If his workload grows or declines, he can modify, within limits, his processor to fit.

The remainder of this chapter discusses the equipment and operation of the basic processor and bulk storage. Input, communications, and output are covered in Chapter 4.

CONTROL AND OPERATIONS

The control and operation functions are at the heart of an electronic data processor; they are responsible for on-line data handling throughout the processing system. The *control function* includes the circuitry that selects each instruction in the proper sequence, interprets each instruction, and causes all other parts of the processor to carry out the actions specified in an instruction. The various operations—addition, subtraction, comparisons, rearrangement—are carried out by circuitry in the *arithmetic and logic function.* Briefly, the steps in over-all control and operations for read-in, process, and write-out are as follows. Under guidance of the control unit, the input units read data for transfer into specified locations of the high-speed storage unit. To process data, the control unit obtains an instruction from high-speed storage and interprets it. The control unit then sets up arithmetic and logic circuitry as specified by the instructions, gets data from high-speed storage, executes the specified operation on the data, and returns the result to high-speed storage. Later, the control unit interprets the output instructions to send results to an output unit.

Instruction Routines

The control unit causes other components to carry out the necessary operations. A list of coded instructions, called an *instruction routine* or *program routine,* tells the control unit what to do and what sequence to follow. The instructions might say "ADD X TO Y," "WRITE PAY-RECORD ON TAPE UNIT 3," or "STOP." Each instruction tells the control unit what operation to perform, which data to use, and where to place the results.

Instruction routines are supplied to data processors in several ways. The method used by *internally-stored program* processors is to read instructions into high-speed storage just as if they were data and then execute the instructions while they are in internal storage. Another method is to design the routine into the equipment to perform a special purpose. A third method is to set up the routine in a wiring board as an externally-stored program.

Internally-Stored Programs.   A processor with the capability for an internally-stored program reads instruction routines and data from input units and places them in high-speed storage (or perhaps bulk storage). The routines are then ready for execution by the control unit and can be used to operate on the data. Instructions and data look alike to the processor and can be placed anywhere desired in storage. The programmer must plan to have the processor *execute* instructions and *operate* on data. It is, furthermore, useful to operate on instructions to modify them; but it is not meaningful to try to execute data.

The important point here is that reading in another program enables the processor to do different things to a different kind of data.

The read-in operation takes seconds or only minutes depending on the length of the program and whether it is stored on magnetic tape, punched cards, or paper tape. Typical programs range from several hundred to many thousands of individual instructions.

The amount of work accomplished by each instruction in a program depends on the *instruction format* of the processor. Each instruction for a *single-address* processor consists of two parts: an *operation code*—ADD, SUBTRACT, READ, WRITE, or other verb—and the *address* of data in storage or the identification number of a device, such as a tape unit.

The instruction "ADD 200" has a *single address* and means, "Add the contents of high-speed storage location 200 to the contents of a special area where sums are formed." A *two-address* processor is designed for instructions that contain an operation code plus two addresses. "SUBTRACT 200, 300" might mean, "Subtract the contents of location 200 from the contents of location 300." Some processors are designed with a *three-address* format. "MULTIPLY 100, 200, 300" might mean, "Multiply the contents of location 100 by the contents of location 200 and store the product in location 300." Many variations of instruction format exist, but each consists of an operation code plus one or more addresses or special designators. Note the important point that the *references to storage* locations 100, 200, and 300 above are just that. Each reference *does not* say anything at all about what a storage location contains. The programmer must arrange, either by read-in or by prior processing, to have the desired *operand*—the data item to be worked on—in the correct storage location when an instruction involving the contents of that location is executed. This idea is basically a familiar one: desk calculators and adding machines will add whatever is set up in the keyboard when the add key is depressed. The add key is, in effect, an instruction to add the *contents* of the keyboard to the contents of the machine's accumulator. Of course, the number has to be set up in the keyboard, but that operation is a separate action.

Processors that use internally-stored programs have three highly desirable features. Most important is the ability to change programs easily and quickly merely by reading in another program from magnetic tape or punched cards. The second is the ability to select the next instruction on the basis of the results of processing up to that point. The instruction "IF ACCOUNT BALANCE IS NEGATIVE GO TO INSTRUCTION 37, OTHERWISE GO TO INSTRUCTION 85" allows the processor to select the appropriate next instruction—37 or 85—depending on whether "ACCOUNT BALANCE" is negative or positive when tested by this "IF" instruction. Finally, the control and operations functions can process or operate on instructions as well as on data. The processor can modify instructions to change the address part, operation part, or both, as required to cope with conditions encountered in the data during processing. Chapters 8 through 12 discuss the address format of instructions and these features.

Special-Purpose Equipment.   Special-purpose equipment with instruction routines designed into its circuits and wires can prove efficient for a single important application, such as inventory control or demand analysis. Special-purpose equipment is sometimes used for operations requiring many remote input-output stations. But special-purpose equipment has high research and development costs per unit since few systems are made from a particular design. The inherent inflexibility of special-purpose equipment exposes it to the risk of being discarded whenever the application changes for any reason; and most applications tend to change frequently.

Externally-Stored Programs.   Several models of small processors have instruction routines stored in a wiring board or plug board. Wires or pins are manually put into a board, which is later inserted in the machine. The wires or pins call up operations in their proper sequence. Each application requires the use of a separate, individually prepared control board for the processor. Wired instruction routines can make some decisions and choose different processing paths, but the wires or pins, being physically inserted by hand, are not alterable while the machine is running. Wired instruction-board equipment is more flexible than special-purpose equipment, but it is less readily adaptable to new applications than internally-stored program equipment. Instruction boards are powerful enough for most problems handled by small computers, but they are unwieldy for a lengthy routine because a different board is needed for each major phase of processing.

Arithmetic, Logic, and Control Unit

The arithmetic, logic, and control units for internally-stored program processors contain registers, decoders, and counters. A *register* is a special-purpose storage location that may be as large as a few hundred characters. It is designed as part of high-speed storage or as a separate device inside the basic processor. An *instruction regis-*

ter holds the program instruction that the processor is currently executing. An *address register* holds the address of the operand specified by the instruction. In simple terms, an *operand* is the content of a storage location that is to be operated on or that results from an operation. Examples of operands are inventory quantity and unit cost, which can be multiplied together to get inventory value. A *decoder* translates the operation code part of an instruction by setting up the appropriate arithmetic and logic circuits for its performance.

Instruction Counter. The instruction counter stores the address of the next instruction to be executed. If instructions in storage are being executed in sequence, the number in the counter is increased by one in each cycle. To change the sequence or go to a different part of the program, the counter is reset to zero or to any desired instruction by a "jump" instruction (also called "transfer," "branch," or "go to" instruction).

Accumulator. Circuits and devices in the arithmetic and logic function vary widely with equipment, but they are essentially similar from the user's viewpoint. An *accumulator* is a register to form sums and other arithmetic results for single-address equipment that handles one operand at a time.

The accumulator is as long as a processor word with provision for a plus or minus sign and an overflow bit to indicate the sum is too big to store.

For performing addition, the control unit instructs the equipment:
1. Copy the first number or operand from a storage location into the accumulator
2. Get the second number from a storage location and add to (or subtract a negative number from) the number in the accumulator
3. Continue to add (or subtract) other numbers or copy the accumulator content into a storage location

Note that the accumulator is necessary for single-address equipment. Since the processor handles only one number at a time, it needs a special location to "accumulate" the numbers it is working on.

A two-address or three-address processor brings up both operands simultaneously and adds them in an adder capable of forming the sum of two or more quantities instead of in an accumulator. Addition and subtraction of seven-digit operands (seven digits are used as a specific word size for discussion here and in Chapter 10) can be handled by an eight-digit accumulator. Seven digits are for the answer and the eighth digit is for *overflow* (a single bit would serve for overflow) to indicate when an answer outgrows the seven-digit space.

M-Q Register.   The M-Q register (short for multiplier-quotient register) is used in multiplication and division. Multiplication of two seven-digit numbers may give, a fourteen-digit product. The accumulator holds the first or high-order seven digits of the product, and the M-Q register (think of it as a right-hand extension of the accumulator) holds the right-hand seven digits.

All fourteen digits of the product in the accumulator and M-Q register are available and can be stored, if the degree of *precision*— the number of digits in the answer—warrants. Otherwise, the effect of rounding can be carried over from the discarded digits to the right-most digit in the accumulator and the seven significant digits saved. If any number of significant digits other than the seven in the accumulator or the M-Q register are to be saved, some shifting operations—movement to left or right of the digits in the product— will be required for positioning the desired digits in either the accumulator or the M-Q register before storing them. In division operations, the quotient ends up in the M-Q register and the remainder is in the accumulator.

Chapters 10 and 11 describe how arithmetic operations are carried on from the programmer's viewpoint. It is sufficient for our purposes to say that arithmetic operations are performed *quickly and accurately* at a rate from a few thousand to a million or more per second, with only one mistake in hundreds of thousands or millions of operations.

The foregoing comments about the location of the results of arithmetic operations refer to actual machine operations. When a programmer uses a higher-level language, say, COBOL (described in Chapters 8 and 9), he can use SUM, REMAINDER, PRODUCT, QUOTIENT, or some other convenient name to refer to the result of each of the arithmetic operations. A special program called a "compiler" is used to translate these names to the machine equivalent of accumulator and M-Q register before the program is executed. In this way, the programmer is not concerned with the precise arrangement and location of arithmetic results, although he may be able to improve processor performance if he understands the operating details.

Control Unit.   Somewhat simplified, the control unit of a typical processor operates in the following way to execute an instruction.

1. The control unit *reads* the instruction contained in the particular storage location indicated by the *instruction counter.*
2. The control unit *decodes* the pulses in the instruction received from storage. Each sequence of pulses causes the control unit to *carry out* a specific operation, such as compare, add, or store operands. Pulses also indicate the location of the operands involved in the operation.
3. The control unit reads either the next instruction in sequence or goes to one at another place, as directed by the instruction counter.

Instructions and data in processor storage are distinguished solely by the routing of pulses from internal storage. Pulses routed to the control unit are interpreted as instructions; those routed to the arithmetic unit are treated as data.

Operating Cycle

The operating cycle for a single-address processor is shown schematically in Figure 3-2. Assume that computations are in process and one operating cycle is observed just after an instruction is put into the instruction register. The instruction register contains an instruction, such as "ADD 268," copied from location 062. The instruction "ADD 268" means, "Add the contents of storage location 268 to the contents of the accumulator." The operating cycle, for present purposes, consists of seven steps repeated as many times as are required to execute a program. The numbers in the steps below correspond to those on Figure 3-2 showing data flow and control lines.

1. Transfer the operation part of the instruction, ADD, from the instruction register to the decoder.
2. Transfer the address part of the instruction, 268, from the instruction register to the address register.
3. Copy into the arithmetic unit the operand (which may be either data or an instruction) contained in storage location 268.
4. Execute the required operation, ADD, in the arithmetic unit, and notify the control unit that the operation is complete.
5. Increase the number 062 in the instruction counter by 1 to 063, to indicate the address of the next instruction.
6. Transfer the number 063 from the instruction counter to the address register.
7. Get the instruction located at address 063, "SUB 495," and put it into the instruction register.

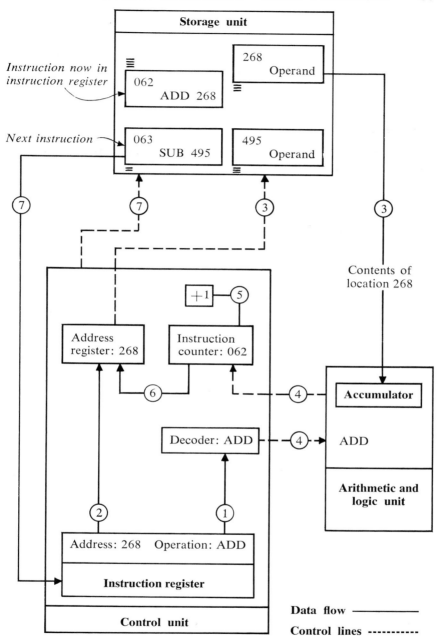

FIGURE 3-2. *Operation of control unit in a single-address processor.*

This simplified operating cycle is repeated in the sequence given unless the program instructs the processor to halt operations or some condition arises during program execution that forces it to halt. Examples of conditions forcing a halt are a nonexistent instruction or address encountered in the program and a sum that overflows accumulator or storage capacity.

Control Console

The operator and the machine communicate with each other through the machine console. Man-machine communication is necessary for several reasons. An operator places the first program instruction in the instruction register or sets its location in the instruction counter to start processing operations. The internally-stored program then takes over and controls operations.

The control console is used for detecting some program mistakes —a process often called "debugging." The console, along with test equipment, is useful for locating machine malfunctions. The console has neon lights or other means of displaying the contents of desired storage locations or registers. An operator can set switches to stop operations in order to read the content of a storage location, observe an instruction, or examine the arithmetic unit after each instruction. A console usually shows why a machine stops—defective input, a mistake in the program, an overflow condition, or the end of the program.

Debugging.   An operator or the programmer might trace a mistake by repeating the program step by step while he watches the console, but experienced users rule out *console debugging.* Console tracing of a routine is inefficient because machine speed is limited to the individual's reaction time. Special debugging programs— traces and post-mortems—are more efficient. While the program is running, a *trace* routine will obtain, for each instruction executed, the contents of the instruction counter, instruction register, accumulator, M-Q register, various cycle counters (to indicate the number of times a particular program segment has been executed), and other selected storage locations. This information on how the program operated while it was running can be printed for the programmer to study at a later time.

Post-Mortems.   A post-mortem routine causes the processor to record selected information about the contents of registers *after* a mistake causes the program to stop running. The programmer uses print-outs from the trace and post-mortem to locate mistakes without tying up the processor.

The console may be used to enter small quantities of data when the processor is stopped or to interrogate a file record stored on a drum or disk. The record desired is indicated on the console keyboard, the processor locates it in storage and sends it to the console typewriter for type-out.

The console may also be used in checking equipment operation to locate specific malfunctions when something is wrong. Some processors have a separate maintenance console since the problems and level of detail in checking equipment are different from those handled by the operator's console.

INSTRUCTION REPERTOIRE

Each data processor is designed to execute a repertoire of machine operations, instructions, or commands. The programmer uses combinations of these operations to process data in a desired fashion. Actually, a few basic operations—subtract, shift a number to left or right, store, read, write, and go to another point in the program if the result is negative—are sufficient to do extensive processing. This is true in much the same way that a pocketknife can be used to make anything out of wood—assuming that the whittler has enough wood and patience. However, several of these basic instructions would be needed for each step of a problem and their use would be slow and inefficient in both programming and machine operation. Therefore, manufacturers design a much larger repertoire of operations into each processor. Typically ranging from thirty to more than a hundred operations, it offers programming convenience and faster operating speeds. The instruction repertoire includes arithmetic, logic, and input-output control operations.

Arithmetic Operations

Commands to accomplish addition, subtraction, and multiplication of numbers are commonplace in most modern processors, but a command to perform division may be available only as a special option at extra cost. For economy of machine design the manufacturer may omit the divide command but provide a *subroutine*— a set of instructions—for division. A subroutine obtains the same result but uses more machine time than direct division. If the division operation is infrequently used in business data processing, then separate circuitry for it may be an unnecessary expense. This example typifies the design problem facing the equipment manu-facturer and user: "How to balance the convenience and speed of another machine command against the cost of providing it?" Arithmetic operations as a group are only a small fraction—say, one-fifth to one-third—of the processor operations performed in business data processing.

Program Modification. Arithmetic operations are performed equally well on data and on instructions. The programmer may wish to send an instruction to the arithmetic unit while the program is running in order to treat it as data and modify it. For example, the programmer's written instruction "ADD 485" could mean, "Add the *contents* of storage location *485* to the *contents* of the accumu-lator." This instruction is read into the processor as part of the in-struction routine, and converted by the processor into the number 010 485 for internal storage and execution. The "010" means ADD to the processor, although "ADD" is more easily understood by people. The instruction "010 485" can be altered by placing it in the accumulator and adding to it the contents of a storage location that contains "000 001" to get "010 486." When this modified in-struction is returned to storage and executed in a later cycle, it specifies the *contents* of location 486 for use in the next addition operation. The ability to operate on and change an instruction dur-ing processing is the most important feature of internally-stored program processors. Address modification, which in this example is done in a simple machine language, is handled more adroitly from the programmer's viewpoint by the programming languages de-scribed in Chapters 8 through 12.

Decisions. The arithmetic capability of processors is also used to make *simple decisions* or choices between alternatives. When *numbers* are involved, a decision is merely an extension of addition or subtraction operations. The arithmetic unit distinguishes be-tween positive and negative numbers. Depending on whether the remainder obtained by subtracting one number from another is positive or negative, the appropriate sequence of instructions is selected next. For example, a 5 per cent discount may be allowed on sales of $50.00 and over. To check for a discount, the $50.00 is first converted to 5000 pennies by eliminating the "$" and "." from the data before read-in. Processors will perform arithmetic operations on all-numeric operands, but not on operands that con-tain symbols such as "$" and ".". It is then possible to determine whether the amount of sale is 5000 pennies or more merely by subtracting 4999 pennies from the sales price and examining the remainder. If the remainder is positive, program control is sent to the subroutine for calculating discount. No discount is allowed, of course, if the remainder is zero or negative, so the program execution continues without going to the discount subroutine.

Logical Operations

Logical operations differ from arithmetic operations in several ways. First, logical operations can deal with any or all of the characters available to the processor—numerals, letters, punctuation, and special symbols. The business user does not want to do arithmetic on letters, punctuation, and frequently not on numbers. He wants to sequence, compare, or rearrange these data items. Second, logical operations treat data as a fixed set of symbols; there are no carries to or borrows from another position as is the case for arithmetic operations. Logical operations are important in business data processing.

Comparison.   The comparison operation is useful for examining the individual character positions of two fields. A data item containing letters usually cannot be subtracted from another item to find which is smaller or, more correctly, which comes first in the collating sequence. Most processors "hang up" when attempting to operate arithmetically on operands containing letters, for letter codes do not fit the rules for addition and subtraction operations.

Data items consisting of *letters, numerals,* or *both* can be compared in order to find which one is earlier or later in the *alphanumeric* sequence of the collation table. The binary value for B is higher than for A, that for C higher than for B, and Z has the highest binary value of the letters. Numerals may come before or after letters depending upon the particular processor. *Logical comparison* of the name entries "Jones, John" and "Brown, John" shows that "Jones, John" has a higher collation table value. In a sorting run using names, "Jones" will be placed after "Brown" to develop an alphabetic sequence. The essence of alphabetic sorting is comparison of keys so as to arrange records in the collation table sequence of letter values. One type of comparison instruction has three possible results—"less than," "equal to," and "greater than"—and the proper use is made of each outcome to branch—jump or send program control—to three places (or perhaps two if primary interest is in the greater case and the other two—say, less than and equal to—are treated alike) in the program to continue processing.

Numeric values—for example, stock numbers and invoice numbers—are also used as keys to sort items into numeric sequence. Comparison is preferable to subtraction for numbers (even though subtraction could be used) to find whether one item is smaller or larger than another. The comparison operation leaves the two numbers unchanged; subtraction, on the other hand, may change one number to a remainder.

Editing.   Editing by use of an extraction command is another logical operation provided by some processors. To "extract" means to remove from a set all the items that meet some criterion. Extraction is used to edit one or more selected characters either out of or into a word in the following way. An extractor consisting of 0's and 1's is placed in a storage register. The accumulator holds the data to be edited. Another storage location contains the editing symbols—such as decimal points, commas, and dollar signs—to be combined with desired characters in the accumulator to give the edited result. When the edit or extract command is executed, the extractor word guides the combining of the accumulator and the editing characters. Assume the following content in the processor:

Extractor	1000100
Accumulator	0684029
Storage location 379	$ - - - . - -

Execution of an *extract odd-character* order, written here for simplicity as EXO 379, will replace the characters in the accumulator with characters from location 379 that have *positions* corresponding to the odd-value characters in the extractor. The content of the accumulator after executing the EXO 379 order is as follows, with nothing else changed:

Accumulator	$684.29

The extract order or variations of it can be used for editing—inserting the dollar sign, commas, and decimal point and for replacing leading zeros with asterisks (* * *)—money amounts before printing checks to pay employees or vendors. Other schemes for output editing are discussed in Chapters 8 through 12.

Shifting. The *shift instruction* is another logical operation. Shifting involves moving a word to the right or left within the accumulator and M-Q register. That is, simultaneously all characters in a word are moved one or more positions to the right or left. An important use of shifting is to align data items containing letters before comparing them or to align data items containing numerals before adding them. Continued shifting in one direction causes characters to drop off at that end of a word; and zeros occupy spaces arising at the other end.

Many variations of the basic logical operations are possible. Each manufacturer supplies the set that he believes will be most useful to the user. The programmer then puts together combinations of these basic operations to do his particular jobs.

Input and Output Control

A user needs adequate capabilities for getting data in and results out of a processor; therefore, input and output operations are usually well represented in machine instruction repertoires. A processor with magnetic tape has commands to read data from tape into storage, write data from storage onto tape, back-space the tape, rewind it, and, perhaps, search the tape. It also has commands to read punched cards, or other form of data input from devices attached to the system. In addition to writing on tape, commands are available to write data out on printers and display data on console or remote typewriters and even on television tubes. Control features include the ability to specify format in printing: single or double space, skip any desired number of lines, and start new pages when desired.

Data Channels. A basic processor is designed to perform only one of three operations at any one time: read, process, or write. Performing only one operation at a time makes total processing time equal the sum of the individual times spent for reading, processing, and writing. By designing the system to handle three (or perhaps only two) of these operations at one time—called "concurrent" or "overlapped" operations—total processing time is reduced. It may be shortened to the longest one of the three operation times instead of being the sum of the three. There are several design schemes for getting overlapped operations between the central processor and input and output operations.

Large processors have *data channels* for input and output control. A data channel, which is almost a small processor by itself, compensates for the differences between processing speed and input and output speeds. When programming for a data-channel machine, the programmer merely writes an instruction—for example, "Read a punched card." When the processor encounters this instruction, it sets up the circuits to read the card and then continues other operations. While the card-reading unit is reading one card at the restricted speeds of card handling and reading, the processor can independently perform many thousands of other operations.

Trapping. After the card-reading operation is finished, the data channel *traps* or *interrupts* the main program, and transfers control to a special location simply by resetting the instruction counter. At this special location, the programmer has placed all the instructions he wants executed each time that a card-reading operation is finished.

With data-channel operation, an input or output unit that finishes its assigned task interrupts the main program and, in essence, asks for further instructions. By operating in this fashion a large processor can, at one time, be reading data from one unit, writing on another, and doing an arithmetic or logic operation. As might be expected, data channels are expensive. Small processors with slower internal speeds have less need for concurrent operations and generally are designed without channels.

HIGH-SPEED STORAGE

Fast and efficient processing of large volumes of data depends on the availability of adequate high-speed storage. In large processors, the arithmetic, logic, and control circuitry can perform a few hundred thousand or perhaps a million or more operations per second. Utilization of this capability requires that data and instructions be obtained and put away at corresponding speeds. Indeed, the development of more powerful processors is closely linked to the availability of larger and faster high-speed storage. Early processors had a few hundred to several thousand words of high-speed storage, with any word typically available for processing in several *milliseconds* (thousandths of a second). Today's large processors offer perhaps a hundred thousand words, and each word is available in a few *microseconds* (millionths of a second). Tomorrow's processors will probably have larger storage with access times measured in *nanoseconds* (billionths of a second).

Storage-Unit Characteristics

Proper evaluation and selection of high-speed storage is critical if one is to obtain balanced performance from a processor. However, selecting the most suitable storage unit on the basis of its characteristics and application requirements is a complex task. Even the informed user has difficulty in precisely stating his requirements. If one knows nothing of the jargon, diverse measures, and various attributes of storage, he might as well resort to flipping a coin. More rationally, data storage can be analyzed and evaluated by the way that data are represented, method used to get and put away data, time required to obtain data, capacity of the storage unit, and permanency of storage.

Data Representation.   Most units use some version of a *binary* scheme, as described in Chapter 2, to represent data in storage. Processors that handle numbers only may use four bits for one decimal digit. Many alphanumeric computers designed primarily for business applications use six bits for each letter, numeral, or other symbol. Some processors are designed to combine the eight bits that would be used for two numerals and store one letter—a "two-for-one" scheme. Others store two six-bit symbols for letters in the twelve bits that could represent three numerals—a "three-for-two" scheme. Some newer processors have dual or multiple modes: they represent numbers in pure binary, but use groups of six bits for alphabetic data. In this way, a binary word represents a number without wasting any bits, and represents alphabetical characters as efficiently as a machine with the six-bit, alphanumeric mode. Arithmetic and logic operations on binary data tend to be fast and efficient, but binary processors often must convert numbers from decimal to binary when they are first handled. After the numbers are converted, the binary form may be retained throughout all processing until the final stage, when a conversion from binary to alphanumeric mode and printing is necessary for people to read the output.

Addressing Schemes.   A storage unit may be designed so that numerals and letters can be stored at identifiable locations; this scheme is called *addressable storage*. When a data item is wanted, it is obtained from its known location. With *nonaddressable storage,* storage locations are not specified, and some type of scanning or searching through a file is required to locate a data-item.

An address is assigned to each location in addressable storage units. The programmer must organize data in storage to obtain data when wanted. A programmer can use as *absolute addresses* the numbers that identify locations in storage.

However, most manufacturers supply schemes that use the processor to assist the programmer in keeping track of the storage locations he assigns to data and program instructions. By these techniques, the programmer can use *data-names,* such as "CUSTOMER NAME" and "CUSTOMER ADDRESS," in his program to refer to the name and address data items in each record in the customer file. He also can use *procedure-names,* such as "CALCULATE NET-PAY" or "UPDATE INVENTORY," to refer to the sections in his program designed to perform these operations. The programmer must, of course, describe his identification scheme to the processor by means of a *data description* section in his program so that the processor can correctly associate the assigned names with storage locations. By following a specially written program, called an "assembler" or "compiler," depending on how it works, the processor can associate such names with specific addresses in storage. A programmer can refer to an item in storage by some identifying name when writing his program even though he does not know where it will be when the program is executed. He need not worry about the exact location of data or even program routines in storage so long as they actually will be there when wanted and he knows what name to call each one in his program.

The number of characters referred to by an address within a program is different for word and character machines. For a fixed-word machine, one address refers to a *word* of, say, 8, 10, or 12 characters as designed by the manufacturer. Processors designed to handle each character individually use an address to refer to one *character,* and any character can be addressed, if desired. Either the first or last character in a group being handled as a data-item or field is usually addressed, depending on the equipment design; and the other end of the field is indicated by a special field or item mark.

Mode of Operation. "Mode of operation" refers to the way that bits, characters, and words are moved. In the *serial* mode, the bits, characters, or words of data are moved one after another in time sequence. In the *parallel* mode, two or more bits are read simultaneously. Generally, some combination of the two modes is used. On magnetic tape the bits in a character are usually read in parallel, and characters that make up a word are read serially—parallel by bits and serial by character. If storage and arithmetic unit modes are different, data go through a buffer for modification as required. The problem of serial versus parallel operations, like most other problems, is resolved in terms of economics. The question is whether the increased speed achieved at a particular stage by using more equipment for parallel instead of serial operations is worth the cost.

Capacity.   The capacity of a storage device is expressed as the number of bits, decimal digits, alphanumeric characters, or words it can store at one time. Each of these units of measure is used under varying conditions, so that conversion from the various units to one standard is helpful for comparison. The cost of storage is closely related to the number of bits, so that bits are one possible standard. If most of the data handled are numeric, the capacity might be measured in numeric digits. If much of the data is alphanumeric, the capacity for alphanumeric symbols is relevant.

Effective capacity for storage organized as *fixed-length* words is often less than the stated capacity because short data items may waste some of the space allotted to each storage word. *Packing* two or more short data items into one word will save space; but packing and unpacking operations may increase processing time. Long data items may occupy more than one storage word. The loss of storage is small in a word machine if storage is used mainly to hold program instructions, most of which are designed just to fit in one word. But some processors are designed with a variable-length instruction format that uses fewer characters for short, simple instructions.

A *variable-field* processor, on the other hand, uses minimum space to store each data element, but it raises questions about how to keep track of where each element is. In addition, the special symbol that indicates the end of each field may occupy part of available storage. Similar comments apply to short data records because they may waste storage space on tape: either they are filled out to longer blocks or there are too many inter-record gaps, if stored individually in variable-length fields. *Blocking* data records together into longer blocks, depending on design and operation of the processor and tape units, can economize space, operating time, or both.

Access Time.   Another major characteristic of storage is its *access time*—the length of time between a call for data from storage and completion of the delivery. Some processors with magnetic core storage have access times of less than a microsecond, though most are in the range of 1 to 20 microseconds. These high speeds are obtained because data in core storage are electronically addressable and no mechanical movement, which is much slower than electronic switching, is involved.

In magnetic drum and disk storage units, another addressing method is used: the data move serially past read-write heads until the desired address or item is found. *Average access* time for data on drums ranges from 2 to 50 milliseconds. Average access for data in disk storage runs from 10 milliseconds to several seconds.

A third method for getting access to an item involves scanning the data because there is no specified address. The data on magnetic and paper tape, for example, are scanned until a desired item is found; however, this method is seldom used by high-speed storage devices.

Minimum access time is the length of the time required to get data from the storage location that is most readily available. *Maximum access* time applies to the least readily-available storage location. For magnetic core storage the minimum and maximum are the same. In most others—drums, disk, tapes—these times are substantially different. Both the average access time and the range from minimum to maximum have an important effect on over-all processing time. Transfer rates—the speed at which individual characters are handled after the first one is accessed—also bear on storage speed and its effect on processor control of storage and operating speeds.

Most magnetic and electronic storage devices are erasable and nonvolatile. *Erasable* means that previously stored data can be removed and replaced by new data. *Nonvolatile* means that stored data remain intact when electrical power is stopped; but the lack of this feature need not be critical. Either lost data can be reconstructed by reprocessing original data, or intermediate results can be stored as a precaution. Interestingly, some processors designed for military purposes are required to have volatile storage for security reasons. The contents of storage, and even the storage unit itself, can be destroyed whenever advisable.

High-Speed Storage Devices

Typically, high-speed storage facilities form an integral part of the basic processor circuitry, although the storage unit may be physically separated from the processor. The storage device holds the program that is being used and the data involved in processing. The data are read directly from storage to the arithmetic, logic, and control units for processing.

High-speed storage is organized into thousands of individual *locations*—at the level of character, word, or field—that can store data or instructions. Each location has a *unique address* so that it can be located by its number or by a simple description—as we would locate a house by its address: "1627 Ann Arbor Avenue." The access time for high-speed storage is short, but capacity is limited by economic considerations. Core storage to hold one bit may cost about half a dollar, whereas drums are less expensive though slower. Magnetic cores and magnetic drums are the most commonly used high-speed storage devices.

Magnetic Core. A magnetic core is a doughnut-shaped ring of iron the size of a match-head capable of retaining either one of two magnetic states. Magnetic cores are placed where *write* wires cross to form a grid. Electric current passed through selected "X" and "Y" wires goes through each core and changes the magnetic state of the core at the junction of the two wires. The state of other cores along each one of the two wires remains unchanged. A current passed in one direction through the wires magnetizes the core; a current sent in the opposite direction along the wires reverses the core's magnetic state. One state represents a 1, the other a 0.

Reading is done by writing a 0 in the core and watching what happens. In addition to write wires, *read* wires pass through every core and detect if its magnetic state changes when a 0 is written. If the core already contains a 0, nothing happens. If it is in the 1 state, a change occurs which is detected by the read wire. The magnetic state of the core is, in effect, "read" from the induced current caused by writing. For a core in the 1 state, this reading technique is destructive; its prior state must be regenerated by an appropriate write signal. Newer designs of magnetic cores have nondestructive readout, therefore no rewrite is required, and they can operate at higher speeds.

Each magnetic core holds one bit. Cores are arranged in planes (Figure 3-3) that may have, say, 32, 64, or some other number of cores in each direction for a total of 1024 or 4096. Many core planes—say, 37 or 48, depending on the number of bits for data and parity treated as a word by the designer—make up a storage unit. The bits that make up a word are often placed in the same X and Y position on each plane and read in parallel. Thus a word of 37

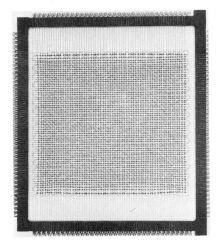

FIGURE 3-3. *Magnetic core storage plane and assembly.*

bits may be stored in the cores located in row 9 and column 53 of
every one of the 37 planes. The 37 cores may be used to store a
variety of data—a 36-bit binary number and sign, or 6 six-bit alphabetical characters, or 9 four-bit decimal numerals and sign.

The basic storage capacity of 1024, 4096, or 8192 words in a single set of core planes may be increased by using several storage units for one processor. Modular construction of storage units allows the user to order and "plug in" one or more units to meet his storage requirements.

Magnetic-core access time is in the range of a fraction of a microsecond to 200 microseconds and is the fastest and most common high-speed storage device in general use. It is both erasable and nonvolatile. Magnetic cores are individually inexpensive, but the associated electronic circuits make them much more expensive than a magnetic drum for each bit of storage capacity.

Magnetic Drum.   A drum is a metal cylinder coated with magnetic material. Read-write heads are mounted in the drum housing and the drum rotates past them. Circular recording tracks, or *bands* are thus formed around the drum by the heads, which are located close together so that there are several bands to the inch (Figure 3-4). Each band around the drum can be thought of as being divided into many small areas, each of which can store a bit. A magnetized area represents a 1; an area magnetized in the opposite direction, or perhaps left unmagnetized, represents a 0. A read-write head is usually located at one point for a band on the drum so that all data written on the band come into reading position once each revolution. A bit is written into or read from a particular unit area on a track as it rotates under the read-write head; and access time to data stored on a drum depends on rotational speed and the location of desired data. The maximum access time of a full revolution arises when data that are wanted have just passed the track reading head. The minimum access is for data just coming into reading position when wanted. The average access time is equal to one-half of a drum revolution, plus some time to set up the reading circuit.

There are several ways to reduce average access time. One is to space program instructions and data around the drum so that the content of each desired location becomes available just as it is needed.

Another is to place separate writing and reading heads at short intervals around one band. In such cases, a writing head records data on the drum, and a fraction of a revolution later, when the data move under the reading head, they are read and returned to the prior writing head. This combination of a writing head, a short space on the drum, and a reading head connected back to the writing head makes a *revolver loop*. All data in the loop are read

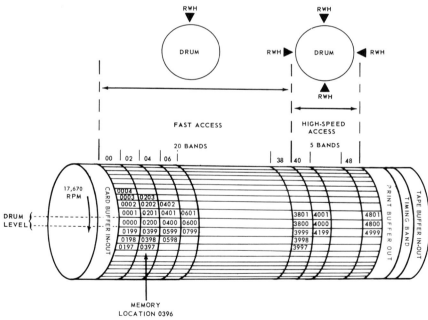

FIGURE 3-4. *Magnetic drum unit and schematic.*

continuously as the drum revolves and can be sent off for processing, if desired. Some drums have several revolver loops to shorten the access time for data on a few tracks to a small fraction of the maximum access time.

Magnetic drums in use today vary greatly in capacity and operating speeds. Drums used as high-speed storage range from 4 to 12 inches in diameter and rotate at speeds of 3,000 to 17,000 revolutions a minute to give average access times of 2 to 10 milliseconds. Capacities range from 10,000 to 60,000 numeric characters. It costs less to store a bit on a magnetic drum than on other devices used for internal storage; the data are erasable and nonvolatile.

Magnetic drums are sometimes utilized for high-speed storage in small or medium-sized processors, but slow access rules them out for primary storage in large processors. The use of slow-access drums to provide secondary storage—*bulk storage*—for processors will be discussed later.

Some large processors use a *combination* of devices for high-speed storage. For example, a machine with 4000 words of magnetic-drum storage may in addition have 100 words of magnetic-core storage. Data and instructions are moved from drum to core at the start of a series of operations. The cores are used to hold intermediate results and instructions during processing. When processing is complete, the results are returned to the drum.

A relatively small amount of *very fast storage* substantially increases processing speeds under other conditions. Machines with 4-microsecond-access magnetic cores as the main high-speed storage unit may have a hundred or so words of either ultra high-speed core or thin film storage with access times of a few hundred nanoseconds. *Thin film storage* consists of a glass or ceramic plate with small dots of magnetic material that operate in about the same way as magnetic core storage.

As mentioned earlier, the *registers*—accumulator, address registers, instruction counter, and others—in the arithmetic, logic, and control units are actually special types of storage devices. Sometimes these registers are reserved locations in the main high-speed storage unit; for example, word 1000 might be the accumulator, 1001 the M-Q register, and so forth. In other machines, special devices with fast access are used for registers. Registers in the main storage unit are generally cheaper, but slower than special devices.

BULK STORAGE

Two or more levels of storage are used in every data processor to achieve an efficient balance between access, cost, and capacity. Quick-access storage costs more per unit than slow-access storage. Most processors have limited amounts of fast-access storage and large amounts of slow-access bulk storage as an option. Bulk storage facilities are not an integral part of the basic processor, but they often are directly connected to the processor and controlled by it. The processor reads from bulk storage into high-speed storage before processing.

Some bulk storage is called *random access*. Carefully defined, random access means that access time to the next desired storage location is independent of the previously-accessed location. Among commonly-used storage devices, only magnetic core actually meets this criterion. But the name "random access" is widely used to mean large storage with relatively low access time. Some form of random access is imperative for on-line data flow. For this purpose, random access storage may be used to hold large master files while processing transactions that occur in random sequence.

Addressable Bulk Storage

Bulk storage units may be designed as addressable or nonaddressable. The most widely-used addressable bulk storage devices are magnetic disks and magnetic drums.

Magnetic Disk File. A magnetic disk file is a stack of metal disks with magnetic material on both sides which are mounted on a rotating shaft. An access arm with read-write heads, under program control, writes on or reads from a selected data track on either side of the disk. A typical disk file is shown in Figure 3-5.

One disk storage unit is designed to operate with 250 concentric tracks on a disk side, and each track holds a maximum of 2800 six-bit characters. A maximum of 40 disks (80 sides) in a unit holds 56 million characters. Five units can be attached to one processor to provide 280 million characters of storage. Each disk surface has its own read-write head and all the heads move in and out together like teeth on a comb to any one of the 250 track locations. At each head setting, one track on each side of the 40 disks can be read or written, so one revolution of the disks provides access to a maximum of 112,000 characters. If no head movement is required, average access time is 17 milliseconds (one-half of a disk revolution). Moving the heads between tracks requires from 50 to 180 milliseconds, depending on the distance moved.

Several other varieties of disk files are available. Some models have only one arm to hold the read-write heads at any particular setting, so that only two tracks on one disk or two adjacent disks are available. Access to other tracks and disks is obtained by moving the arm in or out and up or down. As one might expect, access time

FIGURE 3-5. *Magnetic disk file (with multiple arms).*

is large and averages 0.5 seconds. Another disk file has an arm containing six read-write heads for each disk surface. This arrangement permits operations with six tracks on both sides of all disks without any arm movement and yields short access times to a large block of data. A jukebox file arrangement moves the appropriate disk to the reading head, searches out the correct track and reads it. Although average access time is several seconds, this device provides a large amount of addressable storage at low cost. A slightly different type of file features removable disks. When the user is finished with one file, he can remove it and replace it with another in less than one minute.

Bulk Drums. Bulk storage drums also supplement the high-speed storage unit of many processors. One application uses file storage drums arranged in pairs that hold six million characters, and a total of ten pairs holding 60 million characters can be connected to the processor. Instead of the usual plan of one read-write head for each data track, one set of read-write heads is moved back or forth for use with all tracks on the drum. This scheme reduces the amount of equipment at the expense of mechanical movement and slower operating speeds.

Strips and Cards. In several devices, strips of magnetic material are used to provide addressable bulk storage. A *tape-bin* storage unit consists of strips of magnetic tape arranged so that a read-write device can move directly to a desired strip. The reading head then scans that strip to find a record. Access is faster than for an ordinary reel of tape but is slow compared to modern disk files. A *magnetic card file* contains a set of cards comparable to punched cards but with a magnetic coating. The desired card is selected from the "deck" by electro-mechanical indexing and passed under a set of read-write heads. Each unit of one version of this file contains 256 cards holding 21,700 alphanumeric characters each for a total of over 5.5 million; and 16 units will operate with one processor. The entire set of 256 cards may be manually removed and replaced with another set in less than a minute. This capability allows the user to process many files with only one read-write mechanism.

Several manufacturers have built or proposed addressable bulk storage files that use *photographic media* instead of magnetic. The storage density—number of characters stored per square inch—of photographic material is ten or more times greater than magnetic media but is nonerasable. To date, photographic storage units are used in special applications only.

Nonaddressable Bulk Storage

The majority of business data is held in nonaddressable bulk storage—either punched cards, punched paper tape, or magnetic tape. These media hold large amounts of data at low cost and in forms suitable for machine processing, but with high average access time. To select random data, the storage media is put into a suitable handling unit and each piece of data examined in sequence until the desired data are found. Nonaddressable bulk-storage, however, is seldom if ever used as a random access device.

The role of nonaddressable bulk storage is to hold data that are used either as one large block—say, a processor program—or a sequence of groups—a file containing a record for each customer arranged by customer number. In the large-block case, the object is quick transfer of the *entire block* from bulk storage to high-speed storage. In the sequence case, the object is quick transfer of the *next group* of data from bulk storage to high-speed storage. When used sequentially, the time required to find data in a particular storage location—access time—is not relevant. The important feature of nonaddressable bulk-storage is the *transfer rate* or read-write or read-punch speed.

Most medium- or large-scale processors and many small ones use *magnetic tape* as the main nonaddressable bulk storage. Magnetic tape is usually from ½ to 1½ inches wide and, ordinarily, a tape unit is designed to handle reels holding 1500 to 3600 feet of tape. Data are recorded in blocks ranging from one to a few thousand characters. Each block may consist of one or more data records for customers, employees, or stock items. Recording density commonly ranges from 100 to about 800 characters per inch, although some newer tape recording is at densities of 1500 characters per inch. A 2400-foot reel of half-inch tape can store about 3 to 16 million characters, but the effective storage capacity is less than the apparent maximum because of inter-block gaps. An *inter-block gap* of ¾ to about 2 inches of tape is left blank between successive blocks of data to permit the tape unit to start or stop and not lose any data by failure to read correctly. Also, the pause afforded this way enables the processor to handle the data—make calculations, update files, and write out results—that were read in from the previous block. Inter-block gaps may occupy a large fraction of the tape if short records are written on tape. For example, when data on cards are converted to tape as 80-character records, inter-block gaps exceed record lengths and occupy much more than half the tape. After read-in, several short records can be blocked to record them on tape as a larger block to improve tape utilization and increase effective read-write speeds. A 2400-foot tape with 200 characters per inch holds as many data as 25,000 eighty-column cards.

Maximum *data-transfer rates* depend on tape speed and data density; and rates of several thousand to several hundred thousand characters per second are common. Tape-movement speed is generally about 75 to 125 inches per second. Stop and start times between records reduce the effective transfer rates. Some tape-oriented processors will read or write a few hundred thousand characters per second from one tape and may simultaneously read or write on two or even more tapes. Reading a 2400-foot tape at maximum speed may take about four and one-half minutes, and rewinding ranges from one to three minutes. This time must be counted when calculating processing time, because rewinding and dismounting tapes (unless the manufacturer provides for dismounting unwound tapes and later rewinding them) takes another minute or more and may impede processing. Many tape-changes are done with little interruption of processing by using an alternate tape transport. The next tape is mounted before it is needed so that only a "tape-swap" is made under program control to the next reel of tape when the end of a reel is reached.

Effective reading speed is increased in some systems by reading tape while moving in either the *forward* or *backward* direction. For example, in sorting data stored on tape by means of the merging scheme to consolidate two or more sequences (as described in Chapter 13), output tapes from one pass can be read backwards on the next pass. In this way, the merging operation is continued without delay for tape rewinding, which is required for machines that read tape moving in one direction only. Many business data processors have about ten to twenty tape read-write units, and some can handle several dozen. Tapes are mounted for processing as required and returned to the tape library for storage after processing or for reuse after the data are no longer wanted.

Magnetic tape is durable under ordinary operating conditions, for tapes can be read satisfactorily several thousand times. Data on a worn tape can be transferred to a new tape but, of course, should be transferred while still readable. Maximum tape performance involves some precautions in handling: temperature and humidity variations cause magnetic oxide surfaces to crack, dust on tape may cause a reading head to miss a signal, and manual handling of tape leaves oil and moisture that catches dust and impairs reading. Extremely high-density tapes—1500 characters per inch—are packaged in "cartridges" to avoid exposure to handling and dust. Metal tape resists temperature variations and extreme heat better than plastic tape. Exposure to strong magnetic fields that can erase all the data on tape, although rare, requires precautions.

Tape unit operations are controlled by the processor program, which orders a read-in of data when more records are needed for processing. The processor may also provide for automatic backspacing and rereading of a tape for data that do not pass the parity test. If a malfunction is caused by dust or some other transient reason, then a second or third reading will probably be satisfactory. Repeated failure to read warrants engineering service for the processor or a new tape. While the rereading feature is designed as automatic for some processors, it must be programmed for others.

SELECTION OF STORAGE EQUIPMENT

The types and quantities of storage required for a business data processor depend on the nature of applications. Some applications require high-speed storage alone; others rely heavily on bulk storage. Some factors affecting storage requirements are outlined below.

The *type* of processing performed varies greatly. Problems involving extensive calculations can effectively utilize large high-speed storage. Lengthy instructions and many numbers are involved in calculations. If storage capacity is exceeded, instructions and data must be segmented for handling in several runs.

Business applications usually involve *limited* computations on *huge* files that are affected by numerous transactions, but the activity rate for master-file records may be low. Transaction and master-file data nearly always exceed high-speed storage capacity. One plan is to read in one or more transactions and master-file records, update these records, write them out, and repeat the cycle. Some applications often have long instruction programs that exceed the high-speed storage·capacity available at any reasonable price. In such cases, some scheme for *segmenting* instructions, transactions, and files is imperative for efficient processing.

The *time limit* between the occurrence of an event and the need for information about that event affects the selection of storage equipment. Reliance on nonaddressable bulk storage may be suitable, if the permissible elapsed time limits are not stringent. Transactions accumulated over a period of time can be sorted and processed in batches against a master file maintained on magnetic tape. External storage and batch-processing may be economical for huge master files. On the other hand, tight time schedules may require that files be available for frequent updating. The idealistic arrangement for tight processing and reporting schedules is to have all files available for processing at all times. If transactions must be handled immediately, the master file is usually kept in addressable bulk storage for *on-line processing*—data origination devices are directly connected to the processor for handling transactions as they occur. Core, disk, drum, magnetic cards, or tape strips are used for quick processing of transactions in random sequence.

Fast-access storage costs much more per unit than slow-access storage; hence, system design involving huge amounts of high-speed storage should be examined with care. Equipment and operating cost involved in meeting extremely short time limits may exceed the value of the information obtained.

Information requirements are reflected in the frequency and nature of reports prepared and references made to files. The nature of information required affects the selection of storage methods. A need for scheduled, formal reports may be met efficiently from files kept in external storage, if time limits permit. Scheduled processing at reasonable time intervals may be an efficient plan for updating huge files. Part of a file—one fifth or one twentieth—may be updated each day to complete the cycle over a period of a week or month. Current reports covering a part of the file can be prepared when that part is updated. If reports are needed immediately after events occur, quick-access storage is required. Examples of unscheduled reports are references to the file and *interrogations*—questions requiring quick answers. A need to know the quantity of stock on hand involves a file interrogation. Frequent interrogation of files demands storage devices suited to the need. Quick answers require quick-access storage. An event may trigger the need for information even though the event is part of the stream of regular transactions. A withdrawal below inventory reorder point is determined during inventory processing and, for example, triggers a replenishment order.

Interrogation of current files poses critical problems. Many solutions have been proposed, and special equipment has been designed to cope with file-inquiry problems. The point is often overlooked, but interrogation of relatively inactive files becomes more difficult as the volume of the files grows. External storage appears to be mandatory for historical files because of their huge volumes. Infrequent reference and loose time limits may make external storage useful for many purposes. In fact, the unit cost of high-speed storage precludes its use for mass storage. The reusability of storage has an interesting feature that makes it valuable for historical reference purposes. Some items in a record are useful for only a short period of time. Consider how the usefulness of data declines over a period of time. Data about individual receipts and issues of inventory may be vital for the current and past quarter. Monthly data pertaining to the third and fourth quarters in the past may be adequate. Quarterly summaries may suffice after one year and annual totals after three years, so that file volume can be reduced by condensing unwanted data. In summarizing data, some details will be lost unless they are available elsewhere. Condensing records on a reusable storage medium and discarding the parts no longer wanted corresponds to the transfer of paper or card records to inactive storage. But—and this is the important point—paper records must either be put into inactive storage as whole documents or destroyed, whereas records on magnetic tape can be *selectively condensed* in order to discard only those characters or words that are no longer wanted. Reusable storage that is released by condensing or discarding unwanted records can, of course, be used for other purposes.

Data *volume* is an important factor in selecting efficient storage methods. Huge volumes restrict system design to some method with low unit cost in order to keep total costs in bounds. Wider choices of methods exist for moderate volumes of data. Business applications involve large volumes of data and varied processing methods so that the use of two or more storage methods is likely to be more efficient than the use of a single method.

SUMMARY

Processor instruction routines are furnished by internal circuits or wires for some special-purpose equipment. External wiring or plugboards give other equipment limited flexibility. General-purpose equipment operates with programs that are read in like data and stored internally during execution. Quick read-in of programs makes the equipment highly versatile.

Internally-stored program equipment is designed with a particular instruction format. A *single-address* instruction specifies an operation and one operand. A *two-address* instruction specifies one operation and either two operands or one operand and the location of the next instruction. Each instruction format is best suited to certain applications.

The arithmetic unit has registers for storing words while they are being used. The *accumulator register* is long enough to hold a sum, overflow bit, and sign; it forms sums, remainders and other arithmetical results. The *M-Q register* holds the multiplier when the multiplication starts, but after multiplication, the left-hand digits of the product reside in the accumulator and the right-hand digits in the M-Q.

A control unit usually contains an instruction register, address register, and instruction counter. These elements hold the instruction being executed and the addresses of the operands and next instruction to execute. The control unit also sets up circuits for executing the instruction.

An operator communicates with the processor via the control console, which is used to start operations, monitor processing, read some data in and out of storage, detect certain kinds of mistakes, and keep a "log" of operations, including changes in instructions and insertion of data in a running program.

Instruction repertoires range from a few dozen to more than a hundred commands for various processors. A large repertoire affords the good programmer just the right instruction for many situations, but may prove overwhelming to the beginner.

The arithmetic unit performs the arithmetical operations of addition, subtraction, multiplication, and division. Variations of these operations give increased flexibility. The control unit executes instructions in the proper sequence by interpreting each instruction and applying proper signals to the arithmetic unit and other parts in keeping with an instruction.

Logical operations, which are a special kind of arithmetical operation, include comparison, extraction, and shifting.

Input facilities are used to bring in data; output facilities give results to users. High-speed input and output are obtained by fast magnetic-tape units and high-speed card transports. Data channels permit simultaneous operations of the processor and input-output units. Trapping mode operation enables the in-out device to interrupt the processor when the device is ready to give or accept data and simplifies the programmer's task of testing whether a device is ready to operate.

Important features of storage units are capacity, access time, and erasability. *Capacity* is the quantity of data that a storage unit holds. *Access time* is the length of time between a call for data from storage and completion of delivery. The *transfer rate* for delivery of successive characters (after the first is delivered) is another facet of storage speed. *Erasability* means that previously stored data can be replaced by new data.

Storage is classified here as high-speed storage and bulk storage that may be either addressable or nonaddressable. High-speed storage of magnetic cores is common (and some processors have a small quantity of ultra high-speed storage of magnetic cores, thin films, or other devices) for holding active data and program instructions. Addressable bulk storage "backs up" the high-speed storage with larger capacity but at slower access speeds. Examples are magnetic disk files, bulk drums, tape strips, and magnetic cards. Nonaddressable bulk storage on magnetic tapes or cards is not connected to the processor, but holds most of the business data that are kept in processable form.

Three levels of storage are used with most business processors to get an efficient balance between the volume of storage and unit cost of storage. But the equipment manufacturer decides what kinds of high-speed and addressable bulk storage units he will offer and thereby limits the user's choice.

Factors involved in selecting storage methods are the types of processing and their time limits, information requirements, interrogation demands, and volume of data. Time limits—the elapsed time between an event and required reports—are important. Short time limits and on-line interrogation demand quick-access storage units. If report preparation can be scheduled, files may be kept in nonaddressable bulk storage. References and interrogations that must be handled immediately after being triggered by events require file maintenance in addressable bulk storage to give quick replies.

4
Processing Equipment— Input and Output

Business data-processing systems handle a large volume of data that can originate in various forms and in widely separated locations. Although relatively simple, individual arithmetical operations are performed, the over-all processing may be complex, and the results of it put to a number of different uses. Input devices must originate data about events and move the data quickly to utilize the full capabilities of high-speed processing; expensive processors should not wait for data in the "pipeline." Output devices must handle results rapidly to keep up with the speed of the processor and furnish output in desired forms to meet the requirements of different users. Widely scattered operations rely heavily on communication networks for data input and output. Suitable input, output, and communications are costly but essential parts of an efficient system.

INPUT PREPARATION

Before considering the input devices available and how they are used, it is useful to look briefly at the activities involved in getting data into a form suitable for read-in to a processor.

Activities in Input Chain

The chain of activities leading up to the input of data to a processor is as follows:

1. Events occur and are detected or observed
2. The observed events are translated into symbols
3. Symbols are recorded as data
4. Data are converted into processable form
5. Processable data are transmitted to the processor

A simple example of this chain of events is illustrated by the steps in keeping track of the attendance time of workers—when they come and when they go. The arrival or departure of each worker from the plant is an *event*. A timekeeper *observes* each worker to identify him, decide whether he is coming or going, and note the time from a clock. He *translates* these observations into *symbols* that represent the worker's name or badge number, direction "in" or "out," and the clock time. The timekeeper *records* the symbols as *data* on a suitable form, which might be blank paper or a ruled form with appropriate spaces. Even in the simplest case, a form prepared in advance is likely to have some data already filled in, such as the employee's name and badge number. The data for each employee's daily attendance can be keypunched into cards as a suitably *processable form*. Messengers or ordinary mail can *transmit* the data to the point where the processor is located. The data about attendance time of workers are then ready for input to a processor. A card reader can read the cards directly into the processor for use with other records, say, job-time tickets, to reconcile the two reports of time from different sources and calculate costs and payroll.

This example merely illustrates the steps in the chain leading up to making data available for processing. There are more elaborate schemes for performing or combining operations in the chain. For example, a time clock that prints "time in" and "time out" for each employee and machine-stamps his time card, which is prepared before the start of the week, combines the occurrence and detection of an *event* with its translation into *symbols*. If the time clock is designed to punch the card instead of merely print it, then the event and symbols are originated in a *data form suitable for processing*. The data content of the cards can be transmitted by wire to a central location and repunched into cards. The cards may be used for input to the processor either directly or after conversion to some higher-speed media such as magnetic tape.

Input Preparation Devices

This section deals with the kinds of input equipment available and their use in each step of the input chain.

The usual procedure for getting input data ready for a processor is to convert the symbols concerning events into a suitable machine-processable medium—punched card, paper tape, or magnetic tape. Manual keyboard operators convert typed or written copy to a desired medium. Manual conversion is slow, and the error ratio is high enough that verification by duplicate operations, calculations, or editorial checking is used to detect mistakes and increase accuracy. The manual work in key-punching can be reduced and accuracy increased by pre-punching or otherwise mass-producing the elements that are common to many records. When possible, data output from one stage is retained in machine-processable form to simplify input operations at a later stage. Character-recognition devices optically or magnetically "read" typed or printed documents to prepare suitable media for processing. Data punched in cards are often converted to magnetic tape for faster read-in to a processor.

Input preparation devices are used for recording and converting data. The devices are called "off-line devices" because they are not connected to the processor when the data are first prepared. At a later stage, and after transmission, the data are introduced into the processor.

Paper-Tape Punches.   Simple devices of this kind merely punch paper tape; more elaborate ones also produce readable copy, duplicate other tapes, or control the content and format of the copy. Special electric typewriters, for example, will convert source data to punched paper tape. Manual keyboard operation thus produces paper tape and readable page "hard copy" at the same time. Some electric typewriters also type hard copy from punched paper tape or punch a second tape, or both, as desired.

Office machines are available that can punch paper tape as a by-product of preparing regular printed output. Many kinds of office equipment, including adding machines, calculators, and posting machines, produce five-channel paper tape and some produce six-, seven-, or eight-channel tape. Several of these devices are shown in Figure 4-1. Some office machines can also punch cards as a by-product of ordinary operations.

In preparing a sales order, for example, a suitable office machine also punches paper tape or cards containing either the same data or only a selected part of the data. The by-product tape or cards eliminate the duplicate work that would be involved in later punching the data. The sales order, which can be produced in multiple copies for ordinary purposes, is useful for checking accuracy since the hard copy and punched media must agree. The degree of accuracy achieved depends on the skill and care used in original preparation and verification plus the skill of subsequent users in

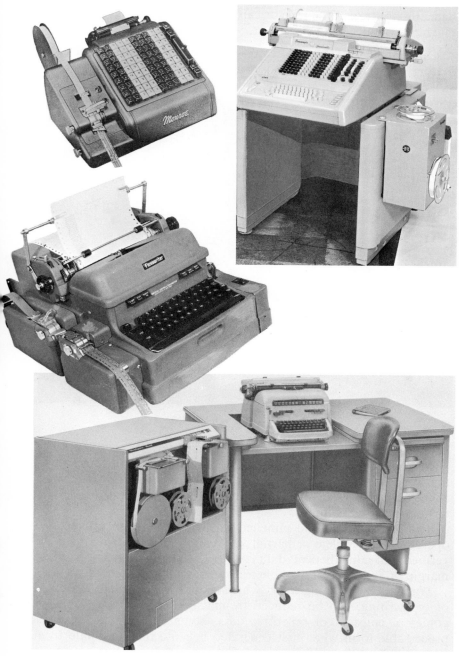

FIGURE 4-1. *Tape-punching office equipment.*

detecting mistakes. The tape or cards can be used for input to other machines or to a data processor.

Card Punches. Punched cards are a common medium for originating data in machine-processable form. When an operator strikes a key on a card punch (Figure 4-2), it punches a hole or

FIGURE 4-2. *Card keypunch.*

holes in a column to represent one character. A printing-punch prints each character along the top of a card above the corresponding punched column when a card is first prepared. Or a machine called an "interpreter" later reads the punches and prints the characters for selected columns.

The original data and punched cards may be given to a second operator for complete or partial verification. Numeric data may be verified but alphabetical data skipped, since sometimes a lower margin of accuracy is tolerable for letters than for numerals.

Manual keypunching work, which is done at about half the speed of typewriting, can be reduced by machine duplication of master copies of constant or repetitive data. Some data are in machine-processable form when first generated because they originate from card-punching time clocks or transaction recorders. Marking a card in specified locations with a special lead pencil enables a mark-sensing machine to punch the marked data. Several other schemes involving only a small amount of equipment are available for originating punched cards: portable hand punches, a stylus and punched platen for guiding the punching of characters in one or more of 40 columns in cards that are pre-perforated in all twelve positions, portable devices that punch a fixed set of repetitive data in certain columns and have a keyboard to set up and punch a small number of additional columns, and ink marks for optical reading and punching. After the cards are punched, ordinary card equipment can be used for processing.

Magnetic-Tape Writers. A manually operated keyboard machine will record data on magnetic tape directly from source data and produce a typed copy for record and checking purposes. The typed copy is an important aid to the operator because he cannot read magnetic tape as he can punched cards and paper tape.

The typical verification schemes of scanning hard copy or of preparing a second record on magnetic tape and comparing the two recordings can be used with magnetic-tape writing systems. A mistake can be erased from magnetic tape and the correct character substituted.

Prior Preparation

The input equipment and methods described above usually start with data on typed, handprinted, or handwritten documents that are not machine-processable. That is to say, the event that occurred was translated into symbols, and the symbols were recorded as data. The next step—manual character-by-character conversion of data on documents to a form suitable for processing—is expensive and fraught with mistakes.

The *prior preparation* of input data means that output from one stage is used directly as data input at the next stage of processing. This concept of data origination essentially eliminates two activities—translating events into symbols and recording symbols as data. Thus, the task of converting data into processable form is made much easier. It is necessary only to observe that the event occurred and the data are then ready for processing, although an automatic conversion step may be required.

The most interesting and challenging examples of prior preparation of data arise when numerous people originate data for processing. These people may be warehouse stockkeepers, customers, or agents. A common example of prior preparation of input data is the punched-card bill prepared and sent to a utility customer for him to return with his payment. When he does, a cashier gets the money and customer's bill card to identify the collection event. The collected bill card is then used as data input for crediting the customer's account, so that manual conversion of input data is eliminated. Bills printed with the correctly-shaped characters on paper are also being used in a similar way. Of course, a character reader, instead of a card reader, is used when the printed stub is received with the collection from a customer. Commercial checking-account numbers are printed in machine-processable characters on checks before they are issued to depositors. Pre-numbering facilitates sorting when checks reach the bank for payment. Preparation of data at one stage—say, bill issuance—can minimize manual conversion at the next stage—for example, account collection and posting.

Tag Readers.   Inventory control is facilitated by mass-producing punched cards or other machine media at the time inventory items are obtained. Special devices print and punch or otherwise prepare tags with the item name, size, manufacturer, and other desired facts. Tags may be designed for direct input to processors, otherwise machine conversion puts the data in the proper form.

A section of an inventory tag may be detached and placed in a transaction recorder at the point of transaction—sale to a customer, issuance to manufacturing department, or whatever. The recorder automatically reads the tag and produces a continuous punched tape or other specified media, which also includes the variable data that the operator manually enters on a keyboard. Whenever desired—hourly or daily—the data on tape can be converted to punched cards or fed directly into a processor for inventory, sales, and customer accounting. Direct wire-transfer of data from transaction recorders to a processor is useful for updating account balances fast enough to permit interrogating them about current inventory status.

Factory Data Collection.   The important data required to keep tabs on factory operations may be who operated the machine, which machine was used, and what was produced—the item and quantity. A data-collection device (Figure 4-3) located in each production center in a factory may collect data about factory operations in the following way. Machine-readable identification cards or tags are prepared once for each machine operator and each machine and as required for each new production order. When starting a

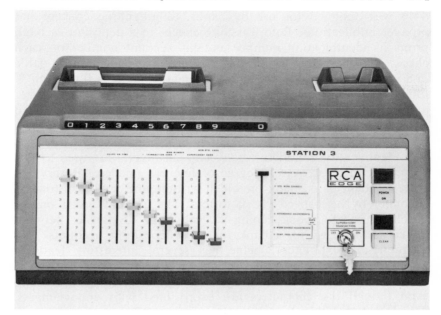

FIGURE 4-3. *Factory data collector.*

job, the operator inserts the three cards—man, machine, and job—
into the reading device in his production center. The data are read
and transmitted via wires or cable to a central unit that records the
data about the operator, machine, and job, and also the starting
time of the job, which is supplied by a wired-in clock. When an
operator finishes the job, he repeats the input cycle for the three
cards and then enters the quantity produced via a keyboard on the
reading device. After the central "compiler" receives these data
and also notes the stopping time, the essential data are available
for calculating and summarizing what items were produced, how
many units, on which machine, and who ran it. With little modification, records from a factory data-collection system may go
directly into the next stage of data processing.

Character Readers. Another data-input system reads characters
printed on ordinary paper documents. Character-recognition devices convert visually readable characters into machine-processable
form. There are several versions, but they can be classified into two
broad types: magnetic-ink and carbon-ink readers.

The most widely used *magnetic-ink character reader* (Figure

4-4) was designed for use by banks, although the concept has broader implications. Before issuing checks to a depositor, a bank prints its identification number and his account number on each check. The characters are printed with ink that contains iron-oxide in a visually readable type font consisting of the digits 0 through 9, four letters, and some special symbols to indicate data fields. After a customer writes a check, the first bank handling it is supposed to imprint the amount of the check in a similar way. Then the inks can be read magnetically by machines as well as visually by people. The identification numbers—bank and customer—are used to sort the check to the required degree of fineness (Federal Reserve or correspondent bank, bank on which written, and finally customer's account) by high-speed check sorters. The amount coded on the check is used for bookkeeping at each stage of transfer between banks and also within a bank for each depositor's accounts. The magnetic-ink character scheme has several interesting features. First, the character can be read by *both* people and machines. Second, readability and accuracy of machine handling remain high even though the characters are overprinted with endorsements. Third, and probably most important, it is the first significant application of machine-processable documents to gain acceptance throughout a large industry.

FIGURE 4-4. *Magnetic-ink character reader.*

Optical character readers work with documents printed or typed in ordinary carbon inks by typewriters, high-speed output printers, or special imprinters. Machines for reading characters imprinted from credit cards convert each customer's number from a man-machine readable form to punched cards or to magnetic tape for efficient machine processing. Accuracy of reading (or complete rejection) of each document is assured by a self-checking feature in the design of each character so that it differs from every other character in at least two of the horizontal and vertical bars that compose it.

When a retail gasoline station, for instance, makes a sale, the customer's name and account number are imprinted from his plastic plate to an unpunched card. The gasoline station is also identified by use of a similar plate. The product and quantity involved and dollar amount of sale can be recorded manually or the dollar amount can be imprinted from dial digits set by hand before imprinting. The station turns in the imprinted and written cards to the tank-wagon driver as payment for more gasoline. The driver delivers the cards to a central location where a reading unit reads the customer's number (and amount of sale, if printed in the machine-readable dial digits; otherwise a keypunch operator reads and punches the written amount) and punches the data into the same card. Optical equipment scans each numeral, and a logical network decodes the scan pattern into a character. These cards containing basic data— customer's number and amount of sale—are then used for billing customers and in any other ways desired.

Considered from the viewpoint of the utility cashier's department, character reading for utility bills is, as pointed out earlier, one step in advance preparation of data. The billing department need use only a suitable type font on its high-speed printer when printing bills to make them machine-readable when customers return the bills with payment in full. The bill stubs are put through a character reader to get the required data—customer number and dollar amount—for updating the customer's account in the files.

The concept of character recognition for near-ordinary type fonts printed with carbon inks has much wider application than the foregoing examples of prior preparation—tag readers, factory data collection, and magnetic-ink reading. It is useful for business documents of many types that can be standardized enough for machine handling and reading. Along these lines, it is interesting to note that the post office department has done experimental work with character readers for reading and coarse-sorting letter mail addressed in any reasonably standard type font—typewriter, high-speed printer, and duplicating plates.

Another use is the conversion of ordinary typed data to machine-readable form. For example, customer names and addresses for magazine subscription file-processing may be typed and then put through a character reader to convert to cards or magnetic tape for processor input. Typewriters are more economical—considering both equipment and labor for the output obtained—to operate and are more accurate than keypunch machines.

Input Converters

Automatic converters transfer data from one medium to another. The methods of recording (punched hole or magnetic spot) and of number-system representation (decimal, binary, binary-coded decimal, and five or more channel codes) are ordinarily changed during conversion. Efficient converters increase the compatibility and flexibility of different types of equipment, so that each unit of equipment can be selected on its own merits, with less regard for whether all use the same medium and data code. Current high-speed processors operate best from data on magnetic tape because of its high read-in rate; however, many accept data in other forms.

When electronic processors were first used for business applications, special converters were designed as separate units to convert data from one medium to another, such as from punched cards to magnetic tape, paper tape to magnetic tape, and magnetic tape to the others. On the output side, special control units were designed to work with a magnetic-tape unit and a high-speed printer or a card punch. Now small and medium scale processors are frequently used to handle the work formerly done by these special converters. The philosophy is that such a processor, acting as a satellite to a large processor, can handle all the conversion operations required throughout the system, perform extensive editing, and do some processing on its own if it still has idle capacity. Examples of processing considered suitable for a satellite processor are editing input data for completeness and format, maintaining disk files (updating, sorting, and answering inquiries), and editing and arranging the large processor's output for printing.

DATA TRANSMISSION

The transmission of data to the processor is the last stage of input prior to data read-in. In some cases—factory data collection, remote keyboard, or special set inquiry—transmission is an inherent part of the recording and conversion operations. However, communication arises as a separate facet when the transmission stage is not integrally related to data origination.

Communication Channels

Data are often transmitted from one location to another over some form of electrical or electronic circuit—wires, cable or microwave. The Bell System, Western Union, or other communication firms supply most of these communication circuits. With appropriate conversion equipment, the regular telephone and telegraph networks may be used as needed at standard prices. For example, the manager of a branch office might send data to a main office simply by dialing the telephone number of the main office and transmitting the data via an appropriate device after the main office answers the call.

Many different types of service are available. The occasional user may find it cheapest to use the dial telephone system and pay the price for a regular telephone call either local or long-distance. For transmitting a large volume of data, leasing a private telephone or telegraph circuit may be most economical. Charges depend upon the number of miles of leased circuits and the time of day and night that the circuits are used. The wide area service of the communication companies—for a fixed monthly fee a user has unlimited calling privileges in a prescribed area which may encompass the entire United States—is available for data as well as voice use.

Telegraph, Telephone, and Microwave Services. Circuits are classified mainly by their capacity—the rate at which they will transmit data. Teletype is low capacity, telephone is intermediate capacity, and microwave or a service called Telpak is high capacity. Actually, microwave, telephone, and telegraph circuits are closely related. A single high-capacity microwave circuit might be used as several Telpak channels, several hundred telephone channels, several thousand teletype channels or some combination.

Regular commercial *telegraph* service is used to transmit limited amounts of data sent to a telegraph office. If volume is sufficient, a telegraph grade circuit between offices or firms may be leased for exclusive use. Teletypewriter Exchange Service or TWX Service provides dialed connections between any two points on the TWX network. Manually and paper-tape operated typewriters and punched-card devices are often connected to teletype circuits. The maximum rate of data transmission over a telegraph grade circuit is ten characters a second.

Standard voice or *telephone* grade channels will transmit data at rates up to several hundred characters per second depending on the type of service. For example, circuits leased for exclusive use by one customer may have a maximum rate of 300 characters per second while circuits in the dial network may have a maximum rate of 250 characters per second for local service and 150 characters per second for long distance service. Telpak service is available on a leased circuit basis in several grades at data rates up to 60,000 characters per second. Transmission techniques for all circuits are improving and maximum rates are expected to increase.

Some companies have set up private *microwave* systems which are capable of extremely high-speed transmission rates of millions of bits per second. However, since relay stations must be within ten to twenty miles of each other, numerous stations make installation expensive enough to limit widespread private use of such systems.

Errors. Errors reduce the useful capacity of a circuit. If, for example, a circuit will handle 336 bits per second, then it can transmit six-bit characters with no error checking at a rate of 56 characters per second. Communication circuits, however, introduce "noise" similar to static on a radio, and this noise may change one character to another. If undetected changes are not acceptable, a seventh parity bit can be added to each character, but capacity is reduced to 48 characters per second. Furthermore, each time a parity check fails, the character must be retransmitted so that capacity is less than 48 valid characters per second. The valid characters, however, may well have more value to the receiver than a larger number of unchecked characters. Higher accuracy will result from two parity bits per character or special parity characters and words. Early teletype transmission provided no automatic error checking and was not satisfactory for some users. At present, leased lines are more error-free than the dial networks.

Modulation Equipment. Modulation units, often called Data-Phones, are required to translate data into an electrical form suitable for transmission. This equipment replaces the ordinary telephone with a device that connects to an input reader. When dial service is used, the modulator contains the dialing mechanism and may even contain a telephone for voice communication before or after the data are transmitted. Modulation equipment is available for use with punch-card, paper-tape, and magnetic-tape units, or for direct transmission between processors.

Transmitting Devices

Transmitting and receiving devices can handle all common machine-processable media. Since transmission circuits require data in a different form than most basic processors, each major data-processing equipment manufacturer has a special line of input and output equipment designed for use with standard modulators. However, some special modulators are built for direct hook-up to standard input-output equipment. In one way or another, compatibility between the input-output equipment and the circuit must be provided.

The data transmission rate is more often limited by the *grade of circuit* than by the characteristics of the transmitter. For this reason, maximum rates are often the same for various models of equipment produced by different manufacturers.

Paper Tape. Five-channel tape is standard for use with telegraph equipment. Tape data can be transmitted directly over telegraph wires. The Teletypewriter accepts and automatically transmits five-channel tape pre-punched for higher-speed read-in and produces a typed copy of data transmitted, if desired. The keyboard can be operated manually for direct, although slow, transmission. Receiving equipment prints messages or re-perforates them into paper tape at speeds of six to ten characters per second. Similar devices that operate over telephone grade circuits are capable of transmitting at rates up to 100 characters per second.

A device called Teledata transmits, receives, and checks data coded in five-, six-, or eight-channel punched-paper tape. As data in punched-paper tape are sent through the reader, they are simultaneously re-perforated and checked on the punch of the Teledata unit located at a distant point. For five-channel tape, parity checking is by words or groups of characters between space codes. Six- and eight-channel tape permit single and double parity checking. Transmission speeds are six to ten codes per second depending on the commercial telegraph channel grade used—60, 75, or 100 words per minute.

Punched Cards. Data on punched cards can be transmitted and received directly over telegraph or telephone circuits by many units. A widely used device called a Transceiver transmits three to five punched cards per minute over telegraph circuits and eleven cards per minute over telephone circuits. One telephone circuit can handle four units at the same time so that 44 fully punched cards can be transmitted per minute, and the card-rate output is increased if fewer columns are punched. Self-checking features assure the degree of accuracy in transmission necessary for accounting and computing.

The Kinecard Converter used in conjunction with a card read-punch unit transmits and reproduces data in standard punched cards at the rate of 100 cards per minute over a telephone circuit. Malfunctions in data assembly and transmission are detected by odd- and even-parity checks on each card; defective cards are isolated by offset stacking. Other card units read and transmit up to several hundred cards per minute.

Magnetic Tape. Several devices are available for transmitting data recorded on magnetic tape. They read data from magnetic tape, transmit the data over telephone wires, and record on magnetic tape at the destination. The transmission speed over commercial telephone channels is from 150 to 300 characters per second.

While tape-reading rates are only a few inches per second for transmission over wire circuits, forward and reverse tape speeds for editing and rewinding tape are very fast in some equipment. Automatic error checking and correcting features are obtained by character and channel parity-bits. Dual parity-bits (channel parity is introduced just before transmission if not already on tape) add enough redundancy to reproduce data at an undetected error rate as low as one error in 10,000 bits. A record containing a parity error, which usually is caused by interference on the voice circuits, is automatically retransmitted when a transmission error is detected. After three unsuccessful attempts, the machine halts to allow the operator to decide what to do.

Microwave and Telpak facilities transmit data from magnetic tape at much higher rates than those achieved over voice grade telephone lines. Effective transmission rate in an early microwave system was about 8000 characters per second. The magnetic-tape unit involved had a capability of 15,000 characters per second, but operating speed was reduced because of delays in moving data from a receiving buffer into the recording tape. Microwave and Telpak channels are capable of transmitting data from magnetic tape at rates over 60,000 characters per second.

Processor-to-Processor. High-speed transmission techniques and special control units permit direct communication between the internal storage of two processors. Since processors can make data

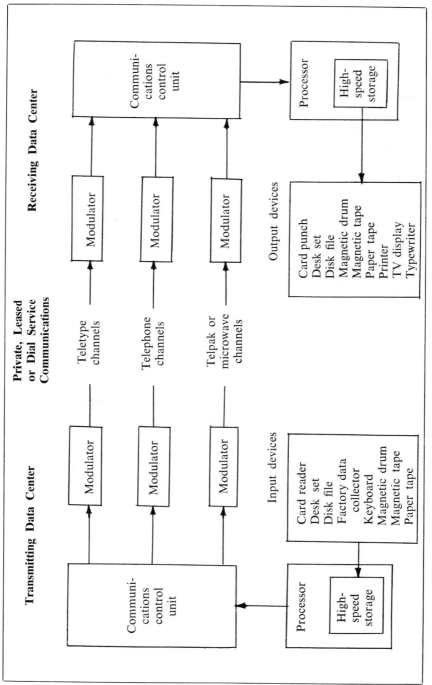

FIGURE 4-5. *Schematic of processor-to-processor communication.*

available at storage access speeds—many thousands to hundreds of thousands of characters per second—the limiting factor is the transmission circuit capacity that is economical to install and use. With processor-to-processor communication, any input device attached to the processor can be used indirectly as a transmitter and any output device as a receiver. Figure 4-5 shows a schematic diagram of a processor-to-processor hook-up.

INPUT READERS

Input readers are connected to a processor for direct read-in. Selection of a reader depends on data volumes, equipment speeds, and the permissible processing time. Magnetic-tape read-write units are used for large-volume data input, whereas punched-card or punched paper-tape readers are widely used for smaller volumes. Keyboard devices are used to read in limited amounts of data, program corrections, and file interrogations. The processor console switches may be used to read in some data or fragments of a program and especially the initial steps required to start program read-in.

Magnetic-Tape Units

Several features of magnetic tape for data storage were discussed in Chapter 3; others deserve discussion here. Magnetic-tape units, also called "tape handlers" and "tape transports," are used to read in huge volumes of data for processing.

A typical tape unit (Figure 4-6) moves tape past the read-write heads at speeds of 75 to 125 inches per second, depending on the tape unit specifications. A speed of 100 inches per second for tape written at a density of 400 characters per inch produces a data transfer rate of 40,000 characters per second, apart from interblock gaps. Actually, different magnetic tape units have transfer rates ranging from 5000 to 100,000 characters per second and more. Some tape units operate with tapes in both low- and medium-density modes. The tapes written on them can be used with higher-capacity tape units on larger processors that operate in medium- and high-density modes. Thus the medium-density mode is common between tape units operating with the two sizes of processors.

Steady high-speed movement of tape past the reading heads—there is one head for each data and parity channel on tape—generates a magnetic field for each bit recorded on the tape. Reading consists of sensing the magnetic field. Such high rates of data trans-

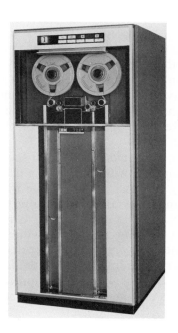

FIGURE 4-6. *Typical magnetic-tape units.*

fer would fill processor storage in a second or less; therefore, tape units operate intermittently to read in (or write out) data as required by processing.

Some tape units are designed to read or to write tape while moving in the forward direction only; other units can write in one direction and search tape moving in either direction. A few, however, have been designed to read and write in both directions. Two-direction capability speeds up some operations such as tape sorting, which requires many passes of the same tapes, as described in Chapter 13.

Many tape units have a high-speed rewind that takes a minute or so (compared with four to eight minutes to read or write during ordinary processing) to cut the time lost before the next tape reel can be mounted. Business data processors usually have enough tape units so that the next tape is merely mounted on another unit in order to continue processing while the used tape is being rewound. But some tapes are designed for demounting after reading or writing and later rewinding on a simple device. Many processors have two or more data channels for simultaneous operation of two or more tape units that are appropriately connected through the data channels.

Magnetic tapes are reusable because each tape unit is equipped with erase heads in addition to the read-write heads. The erase heads remove by electrical action any old data on the tape just before new data are recorded. Of course, precautions are required to avoid premature discard of data by erasing and writing over data that are still wanted.

Punched-Card and Tape Readers

On-line punched-card readers are used with many business processors. The processor can control the card reader and start and stop reading operations as required. Editing is done under program control to check for double punches, blank columns, and field consistency—no alphabetical characters in a numeric field and vice versa. Contents of columns can be omitted, altered, or rearranged for transfer into storage. Card readers usually verify operational accuracy by reading each card twice and comparing for identity, or by reading once and making a hole-count for each column for comparison with a second hole-count made at a read-check station. Conversion between the punched-card code and the code used in the processor is handled by read-in equipment, ordinarily with no loss in processor speed. Paper-tape readers are frequently used with small data processors and sometimes with large ones. Paper-tape readers may be useful for reading in data transmitted over wire circuits and punched into tape when received. Readers handle five-through eight-channel code under control of the processor.

Limited editing operations may be performed during read-in. Paper-tape readers can stop tape movement between any two adjacent characters, so that any one character can be read into the computer for examination and tape movement stopped, if required, before the next character comes into reading position. Thus, no special inter-block gap is required because the space between any two characters serves as a start-stop gap.

Keyboards and Multiplexed Input

A console keyboard may be used to enter data directly into processor storage. Keyboards are used for program testing, program alteration, and file interrogation. Console keyboards are seldom used for volume input because people type too slowly and are prone to error. It is desirable to perform the detailed steps of program testing and alteration away from the processor to save machine time and reduce mistakes.

Keyboard input, however, may be desirable even though limited by manual operating speeds. Simple interrogation can be made via a console or similar keyboard to all files under processor control that can be searched to give a rapid reply. This restricts such inquiry to files in magnetic-core storage, drums, disks, and, perhaps, magnetic-card records and short-tape files. Interrogation keyboards can be located on or near the processor console, or even in remote locations if suitable communication links are provided. For example, one medium-scale processor using disk files will accept inquiries transmitted via teletype, obtain an answer from the disk file, and send a reply to the inquirer without manual assistance.

Special-purpose input units called *desk sets* are designed for speed and accuracy in applications that require frequent access to large files, such as airline reservations or savings bank accounting. Each agent's desk set for airline reservations (Figure 4-7) accepts data from metal or plastic plates indicating flight number and times, and from a keyboard punched for date, class of service, and type of transaction—inquiry, reserve, sell, or cancel. Lights on the agent's set indicate the processor's reply to the agent's action and he can follow through as directed.

A large number of desk sets connected to the processor at one time—multiplexed input—effectively increases speed. Data from

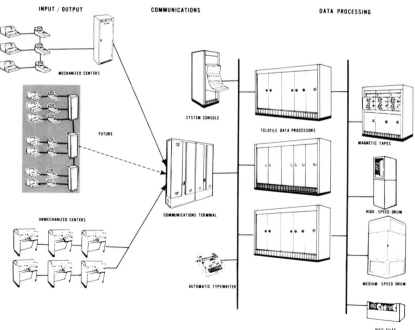

FIGURE 4-7. *Airline agent set and schematic of a reservations system.*

each keyboard are accepted in turn by multiplexing but priority may be given to some keyboards to accept their input ahead of others. A processor can handle a large number of keyboard inputs in this manner without excessive waiting time. A program-interrupt feature in some processors permits a read-in unit filled with data to take the initiative and interrupt the program just long enough to start the transfer of data to main storage. Processing of other data then continues during the read-in of new data to the buffer.

Buffer Storage

A processor can ordinarily accept and record data in storage faster than input units can supply data. *Buffer storage* is used to compensate for this difference in operating speeds. A buffer may be a small intermediate storage unit between and connected to the input unit and processor storage. In other cases, part of the main storage is used for buffering, alongside program and data storage.

Either the processor directs the input unit to read data into buffer storage, or the reader does so on its own initiative. The processor continues with other operations until the buffer loading operation is completed and then transfers data from buffer storage into main internal storage. This transfer can occur at high speed regardless of the speed at which the buffer was filled. Of course, buffering does not increase the speed of data read-in above the rated capacity of a card or tape unit, but it does minimize processor delay during data read-in and thereby speeds up processing.

Some processors continue processing throughout the whole read-in cycle. Concurrent operations of this type are called "read-while-process" or "processing overlap" and neither the processor nor the read-in unit is delayed by waiting for the other. Other processors can read in data from two or more devices at once. Concurrent operations of this type require the use of two or more data channels so that each active input device has access to the processor through a channel. There are various schemes for connecting input and output devices to data channels. Simple schemes divide devices into groups and connect each group to one line only. More elaborate schemes offer more flexibility by connecting all devices to all channels and switching to any device desired.

Although read-while-process increases the efficiency of data-processing operations, data input is still limited to the rated speed of read-in units. When data are wanted faster than they are read in, data-processing operations are said to be "read-in limited"; they are called "processor limited" when the processing cycle is longer than the read-in cycle. The processing and read-in cycles are rarely exactly the same length, but the two can be brought into closer balance by shifting part of the processing load from one run to another or by making other changes in operating routines. For example, data editing and checking might be done in the last pass of the sorting run instead of the first pass of the file-processing run to shift the balance of work, if file processing is processor-limited.

OUTPUT DEVICES

Processed results may go directly to an on-line output device, if output is needed quickly. Ordinarily, results are recorded in machine-processable form for off-line printing, since, if there is a great deal of output, slow on-line printers can hinder the processor.

On-Line Output

On-line devices convert processor output directly to magnetic tape, punched cards, paper tape, printed reports, or visual displays in television-like tubes. Magnetic tape is frequently used for large volume output, whereas typewriters and special desk sets are adequate for answers to a limited number of file interrogations.

A *magnetic-tape unit,* as described earlier for data read-in, is also used interchangeably for data write-out. A magnetic-tape unit is efficient for write-out because it accepts data much faster than a punched-card or tape device. Some processors do not buffer input or output to magnetic tape, so that processing stops during data read-in or write-out. Processors of higher capability provide for concurrent operations of read-in, process, and write-out, although some are designed for only two concurrent operations—read-process, read-write, or process-write. The comments made in this and the preceding chapter concerning magnetic tape—high density, rapid data-transfer, read-reverse, back-space, accuracy, and reusability—also apply here. In fact, reusability and the similarities of the reading and writing operations, which the same magnetic-tape unit performs, are the chief features that make magnetic tape suitable for both input and output.

Card punches are often connected to and controlled by the processor for on-line output. Buffering units take up the speed differences between processor output and card-punching rates. Results are first read from processor working storage to buffer storage; the processor then directs the card punch to take data from buffer storage, and it does so if the prior punching cycle is complete. During the punching cycle, other operations continue. Some processors are designed so that the card punch retains the initiative to interrupt the processor and call for output when ready. This processor-interrupt feature simplifies the program because it need not keep interrogating the card punch to determine whether it is ready to accept more output.

To verify the accuracy of punching, a processor may retain for one punch cycle either the data or a column-by-column hole count of what is supposed to be punched in a card. A punched card is moved to the punch-check station for check reading. Either the card's data content or the columnar hole-count is compared with the data retained by the processor. If a discrepancy is found, the faulty card can be rejected, the operator alerted, and operations halted.

Some processors have directly connected *paper-tape punches*. Once in operation, a punch produces one particular code, but most can be converted readily to punch any code ranging from five to eight channels. Some punches perform limited editing during read-out at punching speeds ranging from 20 to 500 or more characters per second.

Airline reservation-agents' sets and bank-tellers' machines, described earlier as input readers, are also *direct display* devices operating as on-line output. An agent's set will indicate to him by means of lights the seat availability on selected flights. The information a bank teller needs about account balances, restricted deposits, and other special conditions may be displayed or printed. Printing is useful to give the depositor a record of the transaction.

Large processors may have a cathode-ray output device similar to a television tube to receive and display data either directly from the processor or from magnetic tape. The desired data—alphanumerics, graphs, and line drawings—are displayed in suitable form for viewing, photographing, or perhaps printing. With a direct scope display, it is possible for the processor to show the solution while it is being calculated. On-line scopes might be useful for quick display of information wanted by managers.

Output Converters

Many processors have output facilities for only one or two media so that converters are used to transfer the data to other media. A wide choice of output methods from the processor may be available, although some of these are not necessarily efficient in practice. One efficient scheme is to use magnetic tape for fast write-out from the processor and then convert off-line from tape to other media while the processor continues operations. Conversion may be done by a limited-purpose converter or by a satellite processor which, as described earlier, can handle this and other kinds of conversions.

Some applications require both printing and punching on the same card. Elaborate processing schemes are sometimes used to print cards on continuous forms only, burst them apart, punch desired data in the cards, and finally (since punches are less reliable than printers) verify that the corresponding data are printed and punched on the same card. The traditional approach has been to punch the cards and then "interpret" them to print whatever is punched. A newer approach is to print first and then use a character reader to read the printed data on a card and activate a card punch. For data already punched and printed, a character reader and punched-card reader may be used jointly to verify identity of the two kinds of data. Or mistakes in punching or printing can be detected by reading the printed characters and comparing summaries of them with control totals prepared in the prior stage of processing. Some equipment has been designed solely for the purpose of printing and punching into each card the data—customer, name and address, account number, and amount of bill—required for utility billing. The printed-punched card returned by the customer with payment can be used for direct input to the accounting process—an example of prior preparation of data, as discussed earlier, but slightly different from the character-reader scheme.

Mechanical Printers

Page printers work from most forms of data media: magnetic tape, punched cards, and paper tape. Fast printers connected on-line to the processor save an intermediate step, but at the risk of delaying operations.

The traditional method of printing business documents, or any other, is well-known. It consists of holding the paper against a platen, placing an ink-bearing ribbon over the paper, and striking the ribbon with a metal type-slug embossed with the shape of the desired character. Variations of this plan are used to obtain high printing speeds, as described below.

Single-Character. A single-character device, such as an electric typewriter, types one character at a time and can produce five lines of 120 characters in a minute. Typing speeds of 600 characters per minute may be fast enough for a punched-card or punched paper-tape system with low-volume output. An electric typewriter is often used on-line with the processor for inquiries and replies, for typing out a log of machine operations, and for giving instructions to the machine operator. Some processors have a "locked-in" log and a program control routine that requires console type-outs before the operator alters internal data and their addresses by using the console.

Line-at-a-Time. A medium-speed line-printer uses either type bars or type wheels to print a whole line of characters at one time. Each printing position has a complete set of alphanumeric and special symbols on movable type bars. Each bar is raised until the desired symbol is in printing position and hammers strike the type-bars to print in all positions at one time. A type-bar printer produces up to 90 lines of 100 characters each in a minute.

A type-wheel printer has a wheel, instead of a type bar, at each printing position with numeric and alphabetical type faces arranged around the rim of each wheel. To print, each print wheel is rotated until its desired character turns into position. The print wheels move forward to strike the paper and produce a printed line at speeds of 150 lines of 120 characters each per minute.

One type of high-speed printer consists of a continuously rotating cylinder with raised characters arranged in bands around the rim of the cylinder. Every character to be used—and there are usually 50 to 60 in the "alphabet"—is located in each band to provide one printing position. A fast-acting hammer opposite each band of characters strikes the paper against the desired character at the correct time while the paper is momentarily stopped at each print line. Printing speeds of 1000 lines per minute of 160 alphabetical characters each, or 2000 lines of numerical characters, are obtained.

Another version of a high-speed printer uses five sets of characters attached to a chain that moves continuously in a horizontal path. A hammer at each of the printing positions across a line strikes the paper when the desired character reaches that position to print 600 lines of alphanumerical characters per minute. Much higher speeds for numerics only are obtained by substituting an all-numeric chain for the alphanumeric chain.

An interesting problem in trying to achieve high-speed printing is the fact that many business documents—checks and invoices are good examples—have more blank space than printed lines of data. A high-speed blank-paper skip feature that may operate at, say, 33 inches per second for skips up to eight lines and 75 inches per second for longer skips increases the effective handling rate for printing business documents. The combination of high-speed print and higher-speed blank-paper skip gives very high throughput rates for documents.

SELECTION OF INPUT-OUTPUT EQUIPMENT

Many characteristics of the business environment—the type of processing, time schedules, geographical location of operating units, report requirements, and the degree of accuracy required for output—influence the types and combinations of input-output equipment suitable for efficient operations. Some of the more important considerations in the development of an efficient input-output system deserve discussion here.

Business systems operate in *various environments* to cover many activities and functions. Data may originate in numerous forms at few or many points. Punched cards may be best suited for collecting data at one point, while paper tape is best for another. In a factory, transaction recorders are useful to capture original data, while special input-output sets are useful for airline agents and savings-bank tellers since they need to interrogate files and initiate transactions. Stock brokers use a simpler inquiry-reply device merely to obtain price quotations. Specialized equipment may be efficient for handling large volumes of repetitive data that originate on one medium and that can be brought to one point for mass-processing.

The *type of processing* required influences the selection of input-output equipment. Serial, periodic processing is efficient for files maintained on magnetic tape. Random-sequence processing is preferable when file-update cannot be scheduled, quick updating is wanted, and rapid reply to interrogations is needed.

Preliminary processing outside the processor is often justified, and design of the input system should exploit this possibility. Sorting a large number of records into sequence may be done more economically using punched cards than magnetic tape. The cards can be sorted and then read into the processor either directly or after conversion to magnetic tape. This is not to say that data already on tape should be converted to cards for sorting and then returned to the processor for further processing. Some factors other than economy of sorting are important. Sorting records with a data processor is often quicker than with punched-card equipment. The experience of some users has shown that processor sorting is both more accurate and less expensive than punched-card sorting and especially so for large numbers of records. The number of transactions to be processed and the need to sort them into sequence affects the point at which data are converted from card to tape.

Disk storage with multiple access arms, which permits use of the "cylinder" concept of high-speed reading and writing (the corresponding tracks on all disks are handled before the heads are re-positioned), offers new opportunities for fast sorting of large volumes of data.

Time schedules may be loose enough that off-line input and output are adequate. On the other hand, current information may be so critical for successful management decisions and for automatic control of operations that on-line input and output are imperative. Automatic control reaches its highest present form when the processor is tied directly to manufacturing control devices. Automatic input and output devices are imperative for processor control of physical processes. When the data-information system and plant operations are considered as an integrated whole, the timeliness of information can be evaluated in terms of improved operating efficiency.

The *geographical location* of company operations, decision-making, and data-processing activities affects the choice of communication facilities. Widespread operations and centralized data processing require a large communication network for the mass flow of data. Network installation and operating costs, in addition to technical factors, help determine how much geographic centralization is feasible. If time schedules permit, mail may work as well as an elaborate wire-transmission system. High rates of data transmission can be achieved by messenger, air mail, or surface mail.

Requirements for reports vary greatly: the volume needed ranges from small to large, the number of copies may be few or many, and the content and format may be strictly repetitive or wholly unpredictable. Although ordinary printed reports and documents are suitable for external and internal use in many cases, the careful planning of document preparation, based on the idea of prior preparation, may facilitate the next stage of data input. The volume, format, and method of preparing reports and documents determine what type of output devices are required and how much capacity they must have.

It is generally thought that business reports should achieve an extremely high *degree of accuracy* or even perfectly accurate output, with absolutely no discrepancy between the results actually obtained and the perfect results that might be obtained. It is true that the degree of accuracy can be increased by providing enough capacity within the system to handle both the message and the mistakes that arise—erroneous characters, dropped digits, lost messages, transpositions, and, most important, misunderstandings that occur about system logic and operating procedures. If a system has sufficient extra capacity designed into it and such capacity is efficiently used, it is possible to detect and even to correct substantially all mistakes in data origination, transmission, processing, and output. Increased capacity for accurate data processing can be obtained by using more sophisticated codes, more elaborate equipment, and better communication channels. In the final analysis, the question of what degree of accuracy is warranted must be answered by balancing the cost of achieving the higher degree of accuracy against the cost of using inaccurate results. Inaccurate results are seldom fatal in business: gross mistakes usually are soon caught and small ones rarely change important decisions; it is the intermediate-size mistakes in output that cause the most trouble in business management. These comments are not intended to condone mistakes, but simply to put them in correct perspective.

The problems involved in achieving a high degree of accuracy in communications deserve some elaboration here. Various methods are used to try to assure that the message received is identical to the one transmitted. The idea of some redundancy—character and channel parity-bits or check sums—may range as high as 50 per cent or more by duplicate transmission of messages containing parity-bits.

Two general points are worth considering. The first is that every scheme for improving the accuracy of data transmission increases costs, because more capacity—better equipment and lines, elaborate codes, and higher-skilled personnel—is required to accommodate the inherent "noise" while still transmitting the message. A second point is that there is never complete assurance that the message received is identical to the message as it originated. There are only varying degrees of probability that the input and output messages are identical. In other words, perfectly accurate transmission might, and probably would, cost an infinite amount of money. The optimum degree of accuracy to achieve in data transmission is reached at the point where the costs incurred in raising the level of accuracy increase faster than the benefits derived from having the higher degree of accuracy in reports; that is to say, the net benefit reaches a peak.

SUMMARY

The input and output subsystem consists of devices and media for getting data into and usable results out of a processor; it is a critical element of a successful data-processing system. The chain of activities leading up to processor input are (1) occurrence and detection of events, (2) translation of events into symbols, (3) recording symbols as data, (4) converting data into processable form, and (5) transmitting data to the processor for read-in. All of these activities exist for any particular situation, but some of them may be obscured because they are combined with others in the single operation of translate and record, or even translate, record, and convert.

Input preparation usually starts off-line from the processor because it is a relatively slow process. Devices used for converting data into processable form are paper-tape punches, by-product tape punches, keypunches, typewriters with connected card punches, and magnetic-tape writers. Various schemes of sight reading and duplicate operations with comparisons are used for verifying that the original record of symbols is correctly converted into processable form.

Prior preparation of data—the performance of work at one stage to facilitate input operations at a much later time and different place —can both improve operating results and reduce costs. Important examples of prior preparation are customer charge-plates with embossed characters for imprinting sales tickets for optical machine reading; commercial checks imprinted with magnetic-ink numbers for customer and bank before issuance; and factory data collection systems to capture data about man, machine, and job from cards or plates and the number of pieces produced from keyboards on recorders located throughout the factory.

Input-data conversion is commonly required to bridge the gap in format and speeds between the medium best suited for data origination and for processor read-in. Originally, special-purpose converters were used, but now small to medium scale data processors are used as satellites to large processors to handle data conversion and to perform editing and sorting operations.

A wide variety of data-transmission techniques is available: telephone and telegraph, TWX, Telemeter, private wire, and microwave. Common data media used for data transmission are punched tape and punched card. Magnetic-tape data transmission is used by some companies and there is promise that high-speed transmission and even direct processor-to-processor transmission may be used.

Input readers connected directly to the processor range from manual keyboards operating at a speed of a few characters per second to magnetic-tape units as fast as a few hundred thousand characters per second. Magnetic tape has the desirable features of high-density storage, rapid data transfer, read-reverse, back-space, reliability, and reusability.

A most interesting development in input readers is the use of desk sets designed for people to make file interrogations, read in transactions, and receive immediate replies from the processor. Special sets that accept previously-prepared plates or cards for fixed data and also have keyboards for introducing variable data are commonly used in some industries. These sets may be connected to the processor by special lines or operate over the switched teletype network on a per-call basis. Since file interrogation interrupts the processor's operations, a processor with overlapped operations—read, process, and write at the same time—is desirable for handling frequent interrogations and transactions from numerous desk sets. Processor features used to handle communications from desk sets on a demand basis, yet still maintain high speed for other processing operations, are buffer storage, multiplexed input-output, and processor-interrupt with priority.

The most common high-speed output medium is magnetic tape, since it has the same desirable features for writing that it does for reading. Card and tape punches may operate on-line but are likely to be run off-line from magnetic tape written by the processor. Direct display from a processor is used for desk sets via lights and printed listings. More elaborate direct displays of data—both digital and graphical—are made with cathode-ray tubes for viewing or photographing.

Processors are also connected directly to the factory to give instructions to operate automatic control devices. Processor output goes to operating control devices and people need not work in the control loop although they must prepare programs and monitor results. Automatic digital control was developed in the 1950's for metal-working equipment and for such process industries as oil refining and chemicals, but its use is quickly spreading to other industries.

High-speed printers that print 500 to 1000 full lines of alphanumeric characters per minute and two or three times as many numeric-only characters are now commonplace. High-speed blank-paper skip features give fantastic rates of business document throughput, since these documents usually contain more blank space than printed lines. Ingenious techniques are used to print and punch one document for a utility bill or a dividend check.

Important factors of the business environment affecting the selection of input-output equipment are the types of processing, time schedules, geographical locations of operating and data-processing departments, document and report requirements, and accuracy wanted in the output.

5
Processing Equipment— Systems

In this chapter, the individual components of basic processor, storage, and input-output equipment are treated as sets of equipment, often called "systems." These systems show, in general, what constitutes a small, medium, or large processor and, in particular, some of the computer systems that manufacturers offer for data-processing applications.

This chapter is a synopsis of the following characteristics of automatic processing systems: storage, speed, instruction repertoires, tape units, addressable bulk storage, and peripheral devices. In a sense, the chapter is a general model of comparative facts. However, the tables given throughout should *not* be used as a check list for accepting or rejecting a particular set of equipment, since they do not cover all the processors available and since, in addition, many factors that are not easily tabulated should be considered. Furthermore, a detailed list may be incorrect because equipment specifications are sometimes difficult to interpret in simple, equivalent terms. Tabulated details are, at best, useful as an initial guide to equipment, which must be further studied before a selection is made.

For business data processing, the data-processing systems discussed here are usually classified as large, medium, or small scale. The classification is somewhat arbitrary, however, because several factors are involved: storage capacity, operating speed, and input-output capabilities. In general, large systems have more internal storage and higher computing speeds than medium systems. Large processors usually handle both alphabetic and numeric data. Medium or small systems, on the other hand, are sometimes built as numeric machines and require special schemes to handle alphabetic data. Small machines have restricted internal storage, slower speed, or more limited capability to control input-output devices. However, some small processors designed to serve as satellites to large processors for handling input-output conversion and printing operations have excellent features for these specialized tasks. The list of equipment in the tables is *representative* of large, medium, and small processors; it is not meant to be exhaustive.

Two series of tables are included in this chapter. The first lists characteristics for typical processors in the small, medium, and large classes. "Typical" has its usual meaning here of exhibiting the common characteristics of a group. The numbers shown are developed in an approximate fashion; they are not averages, and do not necessarily reflect the whole range of values. More important, the values listed are indicative common values for the processors of each size class. The purpose of the first set of tables is to furnish an overview of three representative sizes of processing systems to serve as a guide to realistic systems and to give an introduction to the elaborate and detailed specifications about actual systems.

The second series of tables gives specific facts about a wide variety of equipment; these tables are placed at the end of the chapter for use later when details may be wanted about particular systems. Since different equipment has widely varying characteristics, it is difficult to set up a format by which their specifications may be compared. Equipment manufacturers should, of course, be consulted for additional details, for changes in specifications, and for the introduction of new and different equipment. The second series of tables is designed merely to serve as a guide to data-processing systems and is not complete either for all processors available or for all the facts worth knowing about the components in each system.

The two series of tables are related in the following way. Table 5-1, for example, shows the type of internal storage capacity and access times for typical small, medium, and large processors. Other tables covering typical processors are given in the body of this chapter and are numbered 5-2 to 5-9. At the end of this chapter, Tables 5-10 to 5-18 contain details about corresponding features for a large group of currently-used or available processors. For example, Table 5-10 corresponds to Table 5-1; 5-11 to 5-2, etc. The discussion throughout the chapter generally applies to both sets of tables.

FEATURES OF DATA-PROCESSING EQUIPMENT

The features of data-processing equipment discussed here are internal storage, operating speeds, instructions, magnetic tape units, addressable bulk storage, and peripheral devices. Some features useful for equipment appraisal and some of the problems in systems design are covered later.

Internal Storage

Table 5-1 deals with internal storage in terms of type, capacity, and access for typical processors; Table 5-10 at the end of the chapter gives more detail for a variety of processors. Magnetic-core internal storage is common to the whole range of processors; magnetic-drum storage is used in some small processors. Occasionally, both a

	Scale of Processor		
	Small	*Medium*	*Large*
Type of internal storage	Core or drum	Core	Core & thin film
Capacity			
Words	1000–4000	2000–16,000	8000–32,000
Alphanumeric characters	4000–32,000	8000–50,000	32,000–262,000
Decimal digits	4000–32,000	10,000–100,000	50,000–393,000
Instructions	1000–4000	4000–32,000	8000–64,000
Access time, microseconds per			
Word	32–500	6–32	1–8
Character	12–20	8	2

TABLE 5-1. *Internal storage type, capacity, and access for typical processors.*

small amount of core for speed and a large drum for volume are used in a small- or medium-size processor. Large processors may have a limited amount of ultra high-speed storage in the form of special cores, thin film, or other elements.

Basic storage is stated in words, alphanumeric characters, decimal digits, and instructions depending upon the methods available for representing data. Of course, some processors do not use all techniques, and some of the measures of capacity are not strictly applicable, although at first glance they may appear to have a simple equivalence. Character-addressable storage is organized as fields, frequently called "variable words," by the programmer to fit the requirements of each application. For the machines that do not have a fixed-length word, the use of a word of hypothetical length is assumed merely to describe character storage in terms of words. The number of decimal digits and alphanumeric characters that can be stored are the same except for machines that use a two-for-one or three-for-two scheme to represent alphanumeric characters in the bits ordinarily used for decimal digits.

Storage capacities for binary computers can be equated to decimal and alphanumeric capacities corresponding to magnetic tape codes, since six bits usually equal one character. However, if binary numeric representation is used, the capacity may be greater. For example, the largest number that 36 bits used as alphanumerics of six bits each can represent is 999,999. As four-bit decimals, 36 bits can represent a number as large as 999,999,999. The same 36 bits used as binary can represent a number as large as 68,719,476,735.

Access time is the length of time required to obtain either a word or a specified number of characters from storage and transfer them to a register ready for processing. Internal storage capacity and access time are two important features in which large processors are superior to medium and small processors. Since large processors have much more internal storage and access at least four times faster than medium and small processors, they are able to achieve a much higher data-handling capacity.

Table 5-2 shows parity checking used and the number of parity bits associated with each word in internal storage. Also of interest are the number of alphanumeric characters, decimal digits, and

	Scale of Processor		
	Small	*Medium*	*Large*
Parity check used	Yes	Yes	Yes
Parity bits for checking	1	1–2	—
Content, per word			
Alphanumeric characters	Variable	2–6; variable	6–8; variable
Decimal digits	Variable	3–12; variable	6–12; variable
Binary bits	—	20–36	36–48
Instructions	1	1–2	1–2

TABLE 5-2. *Storage parity and word content for typical processors.*

binary bits that can be stored in a word. The number of instructions per word, which is usually one or two, indicates the relationship between the capacity to store words and instructions.

Operating Speed

Operating speed, as shown in Table 5-3, is indicated by the storage cycle time, mode for performing arithmetic operations, and the addition and multiplication times. More details about these aspects are given in Table 5-12.

Storage cycle times range from a few to 500 μs—microseconds. Large processors have shorter storage cycle time than medium and small processors, especially in the upper range. The lower range is

	Scale of Processor		
	Small	*Medium*	*Large*
Storage cycle time, micro-seconds µs	4–500	8–32	1–6
Arithmetic mode	Decimal serial	Decimal serial or parallel	Decimal or binary parallel
3-address add time			
5 decimal digits µs	100–2000	10–50	5–20
10 decimal digits µs	200–3000	20–160	5–20
3-address multiply time			
4 digits × 5 digits µs	1000–8000	500–1000	20–80
4 digits × 10 digits µs	1500–10,000	500–1500	20–80

TABLE 5-3. *Operating speeds for typical processors.*

essentially the same for medium and small processors because several small processors have magnetic-core storage, although the cycle time is likely to apply to merely a character instead of a word. Some large processors have small quantities of thin film or special cores to furnish ultra high-speed storage in the range of a few hundred nanoseconds—billionths of a second. Storage cycle time is equal to the sum of a read and a write cycle for earlier types of core storage with destructive read-out that require rewriting the data just read if still wanted in storage. Some newer core storages have nondestructive read-out that obviates the need to rewrite, in a separate memory cycle, the data just read from storage.

Arithmetic modes are either parallel with all characters in a word handled at one time or serial on a character-by-character basis. Parallel operation is faster than serial, but involves more hardware. Addition time is stated in terms of synthetic three-address operations —add operands A and B and store in C—to achieve comparability even though the processor's instruction format is either one-address or two-address. The synthetic three-address addition time for typical processors runs from 5 to 2000 µs. The addition time for operands of ten-decimal digits is about twice as long as for five-decimal digits in several serial machines, as shown later in Table 5-12, although this tends to be concealed by the range of speeds given for typical processors in Table 5-3.

Similar comments apply to multiplication times, which are stated in terms of a synthetic three-address mode—multiply operand A by B and store in C. Times are shown for multiplying four digits by five digits and for multiplying four digits by ten digits. In some processors, a longer operand does not increase multiplication time; in others, a longer operand doubles or triples the time. In general, multiplication operations take from two to twenty times as long as addition.

Instructions

Instruction repertoires available in large processors range from several dozen to approximately two hundred distinct commands. Since all processors have comparable basic instructions, Table 5-4

	Scale of Processor		
	Small	*Medium*	*Large*
Characters per instruction	1 word	1 word	1 word
	1–12 char	5 char	24–48 bits
Addresses per instruction	2–3	1–2	1
Index registers	0–3	1–99	0–64
Modification time	12–48	6–90	0–3
Indirect addressing	No	Yes	Yes
Table look-up	Yes	No	No
Floating point	No	Yes	Yes
Character or bit addressing	Yes	Yes	Yes

TABLE 5-4. *Instructions characteristics for typical processors.*

lists only a few selected instructions and related features that may be of special interest in data-processing applications.

The number of characters in an instruction is measured in terms of words, characters or bits. Large processors use a word or a specified number of bits for an instruction, whereas medium and small processors often use a fixed or variable number of characters for an instruction, since they are likely to have character-addressable storage. Large processors typically have one address per instruction, medium processors one or two, and small processors two or perhaps three.

Although several processors have no index registers, some small ones may have three as optional equipment, and medium and large processors may have as many as a hundred. One machine features a substitute for index registers by addressing a group of special storage locations to increase or decrease the address contained in an instruction. The net effect is to develop an effective address, although neither the indexing word nor the instruction is altered by the process. Index modification times range from 0 through 90 μs, but large processors have much shorter modification times than medium and small processors.

Indirect addressing, which is available in medium and large processors, uses two stages of addressing to get an operand. The address in an indirect-address instruction refers to a location that contains the address where the operand itself is located, rather than the operand, as is true for direct addressing. The scheme is useful because the address within an indirect-address instruction in the program need not be modified. It simply refers to a storage location the content of which is modified as required to get the desired operand in another storage location. Some machines carry indirect addressing through two and even more stages.

Table look-up, which is available in several small processors, utilizes a table consisting of a series of reference facts—names or numbers—arranged in an ascending sequence. One or more values within the table are associated with each reference fact and are stored in the same word or a fixed number of words apart. The table is used by comparing a known name or number against the stored reference facts to find the address of the equal fact, or, if no equal is present the next higher one. The address of the "matching" fact is used to calculate the data address of the associated value, which can then be inserted into an instruction for processing. The table look-up instruction is useful for building and using simple tables—for example, the costs incurred by each department in a factory. The department numbers are the facts, which need only be in ascending sequence, and the costs for each department are the corresponding values. A department number in the input data is used for quickly finding its related value in the table.

Large and medium processors have floating-point arithmetic features that align and keep track of decimal points in arithmetic operations. Without these features, the programmer would have to keep track of decimal points, shift numbers to align their points before addition or subtraction, and calculate the location of the decimal point after completing multiplication or division. Operations research and engineering calculations make use of floating-point features, but ordinary business data processing seldom requires them. Subroutines are often available for performing floating-point arithmetic in machines lacking the built-in feature. Generally, processors with a built-in floating-point feature also perform arithmetic operations in fixed-point or ordinary arithmetic.

Character or bit addressing is available in typical processors of each size class. It enables the programmer to operate on one or more specific characters or bits within a word and gives a word machine some of the features of a character or binary machine for compact data representation and manipulation. A single bit is most efficient for representing one yes-no condition; a single character is less efficient since a six-bit character could represent six individual yes-no conditions. A word is entirely too inefficient to represent a single yes-no condition. It is necessary, of course, to isolate an individual bit or character—by means of bit or character addressing —in order to determine the status of the yes-no condition represented and to take appropriate processing action. Lacking this facility to address an individual character or bit, a programmer can isolate one or more of them by shift, extract, or mask instructions.

Several other instructions included in some processors, although they are not covered in the tables, deserve brief mention: add-to-storage, intra-storage transfer, repeat, and program interrupt. Instructions for sensing tape and for utilizing input-output status are covered later under selected input-output instructions and buffering.

An *add-to-storage instruction* performs the equivalent of adding the contents of the accumulator to the contents of a specified storage location and placing the sum in that location. This instruction, which is the basic addition operation in a two-address processor, is useful for accumulating various totals by summarizing a series of items.

An *intra-storage transfer instruction,* which is often called "memory-to-memory," is used for transferring words from one location to another in storage. It may be the only instruction that will transfer the content of an addressable register, other than the accumulator, directly to storage. Intra-storage transfers are useful for collecting associated fields of different records to produce the contents of reports. A modification of the intra-storage transfer order permits the transfer to take place between dispersed storage locations and a block of continuous locations. Such a transfer of data from dispersed locations may be performed independently or as part of an order to read from or write on tape, called "scatter read-write." The instruction refers to a stored table that specifies the addresses of the dispersed memory locations to be used.

A *repeat instruction* in a program causes the instruction following it to be repeated a specified number of times with the address part of the instruction modified as specified before each execution. This order is useful in the repeat-move combination to block-transfer an arbitrary number of words from one part of storage to another. It is also useful as a substitute for the table look-up operation.

A *program-interrupt feature* is often available in large processors. In one processor, this feature allows control to be transferred to a certain storage location, if bit position 40 of the word in the real-time input register contains a 1 supplied by the device that furnishes data. If it contains a 1, the regular program is interrupted and the address of the last instruction executed is stored for retrieval after the incoming data are stored and the regular program is to be resumed. The program-interrupt feature is indispensable for processors operating with many peripheral devices or as the nerve center of large communication networks to accept inputs from numerous devices and furnish immediate replies in order to control operations in real time.

Magnetic Tape

Magnetic tapes are widely used for file storage and for high-speed read-in of data and write-out of results. Features of magnetic tape that are of interest here are transfer rates, formats, and lengths; blocking and checking; and buffering and selected input-output instructions.

Transfer Rates, Formats, and Lengths. The maximum theoretical transfer rate, data density, data format, and tape length are shown in Table 5-5 for typical processors. The tape speed, ranging from

	Scale of Processor		
	Small	*Medium*	*Large*
Maximum theoretical transfer rate thousand characters per second	7–40	15–66	30–170
Density, alphanumeric or linear bits per inch	200–500	200–500	200–1500
Speed, inches per second	30–75	100–120	100–150
Tape width, inches	½ or ¾	½ or ¾	½ to 1
Tape length, feet	1200–3600	2400 or 3600	2400 or 3600

TABLE 5-5. *Magnetic tape: transfer rates, formats, and lengths for typical processors.*

30 to 150 inches a second, multiplied by the number of characters per inch, gives the maximum number of decimal digits that can be transferred per second, which ranges from 10,000 to about 200,000. In actual use, transfer rates must be reduced because of the time required to pass the inter-block gap even when running tape continuously. Some processors are designed to operate with

both low-density and high-density tape, although they may not be completely interchangeable.

The density of data along each channel ranges from 200 to 1500 frames—the group of bits across magnetic tape, usually consisting of one from each row that make up a character—per inch. The number of alphanumeric characters per inch is the same as the linear density of frames except when two or more character channels are recorded across tape. Some of the tape units described use two different densities. In general, selection of density is controlled by a hardware switch, although some systems control density by program instructions.

Tape widths are typically ½ or ¾ inches, and length is 2400 or 3600 feet, although some tape units handle shorter length tapes. Total tape length minus the space occupied by inter-block gaps times data density indicates the potential storage capacity of tapes. Large capacity tapes are useful for storing big files because they reduce the number of tapes and tape-handling time when running programs.

	Scale of Processor		
	Small	*Medium*	*Large*
Maximum block size	600 digits 100 words, or variable	1000 characters 100 words, or variable	Variable
Inter-block gap, inches	¾–1	¾–1	½–1
Start-stop time, milliseconds	4–20	4–18	3–8
Read-reverse	No	Yes	Yes
Rewind, inches per second	100–500	100–500	150–500
Checking Read after write	Yes	Yes	Yes
Horizontal parity or other	Yes	Yes	Yes

TABLE 5-6. *Magnetic tape: blocking, operations, and checking for typical processors.*

Blocking, Operations, and Checking. Table 5-6 shows selected features of magnetic-tape blocking, operations, and checking. Some of these factors help explain why the maximum data transfer rate is only theoretical. Block size represents the maximum number of words or characters that can be transferred by a read or a write command. Some magnetic tape units operate with fixed-size data blocks ranging from 100 words to 16,000 characters. But many units are able to handle variable-length fields of any length desired from one character up to complete capacity of processor storage.

The inter-block gap for accelerating and decelerating tape when reading or writing individual blocks ranges from about 0.5 inches to 1 inch. The inter-block starting or stopping time ranges from a few to about 20 milliseconds. In some cases the starting and stopping times between blocks are different, and they are also different for reading and writing. Since the reading head is placed after the writing head in terms of tape movement, the starting time for reading is longer. Accordingly, the tape times shown are average.

The read-reverse feature, which is available on large processors and some medium processors, permits reading a tape moving opposite to the direction it was written. Read-reverse is valuable for merge-sorting operations because an output tape from one pass can be used as an input tape on the next pass without rewinding. Of course, in those cases where read-reverse is not available, it may be possible to "overlap" some or most of tape rewinding time with other operations and cut preparatory time for the next pass. Rewinding speeds, which influence the amount of time required to change tapes that are in the forward position when processing is completed, vary from 100 to 500 inches a second, so that rewind time ranges from 1 to 5 minutes.

Most tape units provide for read-after-write checking for both the alphanumeric character and its parity bit that make up a frame of data across tape. A longitudinal parity feature is also included in many processors to give two-way parity protection and to reduce further the possibility of undetected errors in reading. Some other features to improve accuracy of data on tape, as listed in Table 5-15 at the end of the chapter, are dual recording of each character, diagonal parity, fixed-block character or word count, and self-correction of errors. A few processors have a dual-head rereading feature that automatically reads and checks all data that are written, and in some cases uses a dual-level signal-sensing capability.

Selected Input-Output Instructions and Buffering. Table 5-7 shows some selected input-output instructions for magnetic tape and the number of tapes that can be connected to the processor or to one or more input-output buffers.

Large processors may have a scatter-read-write instruction. The scatter-read instruction enables the processor to read a block of data from tape, break it up into processable elements, and place them wherever desired in storage under program control. Desired

	Scale of Processor		
	Small	*Medium*	*Large*
Scatter-read-write	No	No	Yes
Program-interrupt	No	Yes	Yes
Test peripheral device for availability	No	Yes	Yes
Number of control buffers per system	0–3	1–8	2–16
Maximum number of tapes per control buffer	6	12	16
Maximum number of tapes per system	6–12	10–64	14–180
Multiple read-write	None or partial	1 Read and write	Read-process-write or combinations

TABLE 5-7. *Magnetic tape: selected input-output instructions and buffering for typical processors.*

elements are isolated ready for processing without further movement. Similarly, when writing records on tape, the scatter-write instruction assembles data elements as one continuous block from separated locations in storage. The scatter-read-write instruction eliminates the need to use internal storage and separate operations to break up or to assemble a block of data when the arrangement wanted for most efficient processing is different from the sequence on tape.

The program-interrupt feature on medium and large processors enables a tape unit that is ready for the read or write operation to take the initiative and interrupt a program just long enough to start the transfer of data and allow other processing to resume while the transfer continues.

The instruction to sense the availability of a tape unit provides for a transfer of program control based on the status of an individual tape transport, a tape coordinator, or a tape controller, depending on the design and construction of the system. This order is useful in avoiding delays in the main program caused by execution of a tape command involving a busy transport or controller.

The status of an input-output unit can be indicated by an indicator that is turned on when the unit reaches an end-of-file or end-of-tape condition and remains on until turned off by the program or by a manual operation. When the end-of-file indicator is turned on, a transfer can be made to an instruction location specified by the transfer-on-signal instruction. The end-of-file subroutine may provide for the console typewriter to notify the operator to change tape or to alternate automatically between tapes already mounted and to continue operations. Magnetic-tape interrupt conditions may be end-of-file, end-of-tape, or other designated control characters.

A test for the availability of peripheral devices operates in a similar fashion and takes over the programmer's chore of intermittently testing for availability of a tape unit in order to transfer data.

The efficiency of tape operations is also affected by the number controllable by a processor directly or through buffers at one time and the ability to perform simultaneous operations. Large and medium processors generally have buffers for controlling data transfers to and from magnetic-tape units while processing operations continue. The control buffer for a large processor can, for example, control up to 16 tapes, although medium and small processors usually have limited capacity. The maximum number of tapes that a processor can have connected to it is determined by the buffers it can control and the number of tape units that each buffer can control. Small processors can efficiently control only a limited number of tape units—say, 6 to 12; whereas large processors can control as many as 180 tape units by means of buffers.

Parallel-transfer capability indicates the number of tape units that a processor can read from or write on at one time. Ordinarily, each control buffer (or in some processors, channel, subsystems, or in-out processor) can operate one tape unit, although small processors may have such low data transfer rates that they can operate only one tape unit at a time despite buffering arrangements.

The capacity to perform simultaneously various combinations of reading, processing, and writing ranges from nil in some processors to all three in others. In some processors, concurrent operation may be restricted to reading and writing. A processor may have a tape-search feature that can operate simultaneously with internal processing. Some large processors are designed to execute several programs concurrently by interlacing them, while performing read-write simultaneously. With a sufficient number of tape controllers, the maximum data-transfer rate may be several million decimal digits per second, which is determined by the number of tape controllers times tape units per controller times data transfer rate per tape unit. However, processing speeds may be slowed when several operations are done simultaneously.

Addressable Bulk Storage

As shown in Table 5-8, there are two kinds of addressable bulk storage typically available: magnetic disk for small processors, and disk or drum for medium and large processors. Some processing systems use entirely different types of bulk storage, namely, magnetic cards or short lengths of tape, which involve the physical movement of either the card or a tape read-write head.

Type of storage	Scale of processor		
	Small	*Medium*	*Large*
	Disk	Disk or drum	Disk or drum
Disks per unit	25–50	25–50	25
Capacity, alphanumeric million characters	3–20	3–50	3–50
Maximum number of units	2–5	2–5	5
Access arms per disk unit	1–3	3–16	24
Read-write heads per arm	1–6	6–64	48
Access time, milliseconds Minimum	100	10	10
Maximum	800	350	180
Addressed in records of	200 char	64–1000 or variable, cylinder	Variable, cylinder
Theoretical transfer rate, thousand characters per second	2–22	90–150	90–500

TABLE 5-8. *Addressable bulk storage for typical processors.*

The number of disks per unit ranges from 25 to 50 with a tendency for smaller processors to handle the larger number. Storage capacity per disk or drum unit ranges from about 3 to 28 million characters and the maximum number of disk or drum units connectable to a processor is typically two to five, although it is more in some cases.

Disk access times are determined by the number of access arms, which range from 1 to 24, and the number of read-write arms per head, which range from 1 to 64. A large number of arms and heads gives access to more data with less need for mechanical movement and reduces access time. Access times range from 100 to 800 milliseconds for disks, but are much shorter for limited data in some units. In some systems, addressing is by records a few hundred characters long; others address a variable-length record ranging up to a whole disk track. When one or more read-write heads is used for each disk face, the corresponding tracks under each read-write head can be read or written without moving the heads and gives rise to the "cylinder" concept of data handling. Actual transfer rates for the cylinder scheme for disks are very high, ranging from 90,000 to 500,000 characters a second.

Peripheral Devices

Table 5-9 lists characteristics of some peripheral devices: punched cards, paper tape, and line printers. The important features of card and tape devices are their operating speeds and the number of them that can be connected to a processor.

	Scale of processor		
	Small	*Medium*	*Large*
Punched card, cards per minute			
Read	200–800	200–1500	250–2000
Punch	100–250	100–250	100–300
Paper tape			
Number of channels	5–8	5–8	5–7
Speed, characters per second			
Read	20–500	200–1800	200–1000
Punch	60–300	60–300	60–300
Line printer, lines per minute	600–1000	600–1000	600–1000
Remote-inquiry typewriter	Yes	Yes	Yes
Magnetic-ink document reader	Yes	Yes	No
Satellite processor available	No	No	Yes

TABLE 5-9. *Peripheral devices for typical processors.*

Card-reading speeds range from 200 to 2000 cards per minute. Punching speeds are typically 100 cards per minute, although some equipment punches 250 or 300 cards per minute. The number of card devices that can be connected to a processor ranges from one reader only to a total of 63 devices. Format control of the data being read from the card reader into the processor may be by means of a plugboard inserted in the reader, but is frequently handled internally by the processor after read-in.

Punched paper-tape reading speeds range from 200 to 1800 characters per second, whereas punching speeds are commonly 60 to 300 characters per second. From 1 to 63 paper-tape devices can be connected to some processors, although many make no provision whatever for paper-tape input and output. Processors that do handle punched paper tape usually work with five, six, seven, or eight channels.

Printer speeds range from 150 to 1000 or more lines per minute. Many use program control of copy format; others have plugboard format control. The number of character positions per line is typ-

FIGURE 5-1. *Small scale processors: Univac Solid State II (top) and IBM 1440 (bottom).*

ically 120, although some printers have 80, 132, 144, or 160 positions per line, and can produce a reasonable number of carbons. Some printers are restricted in the sense that they operate solely as either on-line or off-line devices.

Remote inquiry stations are available for processors in all size ranges. Such stations enable an inquirer to interrogate the processor and receive an answer without manual intervention. This feature is useful if the processor has a large amount of data readily available in addressable bulk storage and the inquirer can quickly use the output for either decision-making or operating purposes.

FIGURE 5-2. *Medium scale processors: General Electric 225 (top) and RCA 501 (bottom).*

Small and medium processors are designed to control magnetic-ink document readers, as described in the chapter on input-output devices. Document readers handle 1000 to 2000 documents per minute, which is considered high for paper documents of different sizes in various physical conditions. But a small or medium processor is adequate to accept the data read from the documents.

Satellites are small processors designed for use in conjunction with large ones. A satellite may be connected directly to a large processor to share the processing load. More often, a satellite is used separately for preparing data—for example, for card-to-tape conversion, for direct input to the main processor, and for handling magnetic tapes to print or punch output data. These uses require that the main and satellite processors have compatible tape units in order to work with the same tapes.

Pictures of small, medium, and large scale processors are shown in Figures 5-1, 5-2, and 5-3, respectively.

FIGURE 5-3. *Large scale processors: Philco 212 (top) and Honeywell 800 (bottom).*

Communication Devices

A wide variety of data-communication devices is available for either off-line operation—to produce data in punched cards, paper tape and magnetic tape—or on-line operation—direct to a central processor with immediate reply to the input unit originating the message. Many kinds of data-communication devices are not directly related to the capacity of equipment and operate with small, medium, or large processors. Table 5-19 at the end of this chapter describes specific data-communication devices available.

Off-Line Devices. Off-line data-communication devices can handle all standard machine media. Paper-tape readers and punches operating at transmission speeds of ten to 100 characters per second are available for five-, six-, seven-, and eight-channel tape. Punched-card equipment operates at speeds of several hundred cards per minute. Magnetic-tape data transmission speeds, limited primarily by circuit channel capacity, range from several hundred to many thousand characters per second.

Punched-card, paper-tape, and magnetic-tape devices transmit and receive over standard telephone circuits and, at lower speeds, over telegraph-grade circuits. Most devices, except for five-channel paper tape, have one or more error-checking schemes—for example, horizontal and vertical parity checks.

The off-line communication devices are similar to, but may not be interchangeable with, those used for processor input and output operations. Some specialized off-line devices are used for communication only. For transmission over standard dial-telephone circuits, a low-cost card reader reads a punched card that is manually inserted and removed. Figure 5-4 shows a device, complete with Data-Phone modulation unit, for receiving and transmitting data from punched-paper tape. Factory data-collection devices transmit data from manually inserted punched cards and from dials or buttons set by a machine operator. The data are transmitted over wires or cables for collection, without processing, by a low-capacity recording device, such as a paper-tape punch; however, more elaborate data-collection systems operate on-line to process the data received.

The devices described above require manual data handling at origin and destination. An operator places the machine media containing data in the transmitter and a second operator removes the data media from the receiver for further processing.

FIGURE 5-4. *Receiver, transmitter, and modulators for data communication with paper-tape media.*

On-Line Devices. On-line communication devices are directly connected to the data-processing unit. Many processors have remote interrogation devices consisting of a keyboard and an electric typewriter. The user makes an inquiry by keying in an address in high-speed or bulk storage, and the processor replies by printing the requested data on the typewriter. Alternatively, the keyed input may call on a program to perform some processing and provide the desired answer. Low-cost interrogation devices operate with minimum control and adapter units. Small processors generally lack buffers and interrogations interrupt processing. Furthermore, the cables connecting inquiry-reply devices to the processor are limited to lengths of a few thousand feet.

Special purpose on-line interrogation devices may be provided for numerous employees—for example, airline ticket agents. Three kinds of input are used in some airline reservation systems to introduce data: (1) buttons for action—request, sell, or cancel space,

(2) a special card for fixed information—the desired flight, fares, services, etc., and (3) a keyboard for variable information—the customer's name and address. A message consisting of the three parts is communicated to the processor which replies to the agent by lights indicating space availability and a printer produces a reservation card for filing. Standard telephone or telegraph circuits have adequate capacity for transmitting data and replies between agents' sets and the central processor.

A special-purpose processor supervises the flow of messages between agents' sets and the main processor. A large special-purpose communications control unit supervises message-flow for a thousand or so agent's sets. A general-purpose communications control unit supervises inputs from several hundred assorted units: factory data collectors, two-way communication via teletype units, and direct transfer between the high-speed storage units of two processors. A small general-purpose communication control unit serves a limited number of devices operating at lower speeds. It accepts telephone-line input from paper tape, punched cards, or keyboard, and sends output to paper tape punches and to printers.

EQUIPMENT APPRAISAL AND SELECTION

The prospective user of equipment within a business data-information system needs to evaluate the equipment as an integral part of the total system. Equipment appraisal and selection, and even the initial decision to introduce more equipment, requires examination of both the hardware itself and the applications environment in which the equipment will operate. This section looks at some of the implications for the business organization as a whole and examines the features of equipment that are important to appraisal and selection for business data-processing applications.

Equipment and the Business Organization

The equipment being considered for one or more particular applications is likely to be in fairly widespread use or at least be fully designed so that its operating specifications—read-write speeds, storage cycle time, arithmetic operating speed, capability for parallel operations, reliability, programming, software package, and date of availability—are either well-known or easily determinable. Some of the equipment being studied—and usually a substantial percentage of the total configuration—will be carried over from prior models with, perhaps, some important improvements in certain features, such as card-reading speeds, tape read-write reliability and speeds, and printer speeds. Newly-designed features—and some of the most important hardware improvements during recent years have been in the processor operating speed and tape transfer rates—can be studied, along with the equipment carried over from the prior model, to predict how the new set of equipment is likely to operate in practice. That is to say, any new model of data-processing equipment consists of a large percentage of previously-existing units so that there are valid bases for estimating performance. Furthermore, a positive interaction exists between units of equipment so that improvement in one individual unit may permit other units to operate more efficiently.

The point that improvement in one unit of equipment has a positive effect on other units is important, for a similar relationship may not hold true for those parts of a system involving people. A change in one part of such a system—by introducing equipment or modifying the nature of the work done by people—may either improve or degrade the performance of other people and, therefore, the total system.

A proposed data-processing system may be essentially like the existing system with merely newer models of equipment, more equipment, or perhaps improved communication channels. Such changes reflect the mechanization approach to data systems design described in Chapter 6. However, important changes in equipment are likely to be associated with or to cause some important changes in the data-processing system and perhaps the business organization itself. Important changes in equipment and operating practices represent the data systems redesign or information systems design approach to developing a new system, which are also described in Chapter 6. The important point is that both the data system and the business organization into which more or different equipment is being introduced are likely to change so that the broad implications of equipment introduction need to be appraised. The introduction of equipment, being the causal factor, deserves credit for improvements in the operating environment—better outputs, improved use of outputs, and reduced costs. Conversely, the introduction of equipment should be charged with any worsening of the operating environment as reflected by increased costs to operate the data system or to run the business because of changes required in operating practices.

Results Produced by a System

Any new or modified data system—the equipment and the related operating procedures and practices—is expected to produce outputs that are at least equal to those produced by the prior system. Furthermore, many people expect the new system to do so for an amount equal to or less than the existing expense.

On the other hand, a system is frequently expected to produce improved results in terms of the quantity, quality—accuracy, timeliness—and usefulness of information for operating and management purposes, as described in Chapters 14 and 15. Any improvement in information is reflected in improved operations—smaller inventory, better fill rate, and in other ways. Since it is difficult to estimate the amount of improvement attributable to a better data-processing system, as described in Chapter 15, it seems customary in practice to ignore the value aspects when deciding whether to make an important systems change.

Careful and complete appraisal of equipment requires knowledge about how it actually performs in an operating environment. But it is difficult to obtain this information because a data system is not a suitable testing environment; adequate testing is precluded by the time, expense, and disruptive influence caused by introducing new equipment and a related system throughout an organization. Therefore, when appraising equipment performance, emphasis is placed on how it operates in an abstract environment that has some resemblance to the real applications to be handled.

In general terms, business-data processing systems requirements can be appraised in terms of the *nature of processing* and kinds of outputs wanted. One classification of outputs and operating requirements is useful because it emphasizes the demands made on the equipment and communication network:

1. Periodic accumulation of data for processing and periodic reporting—for example, insurance premium, utility billing, and accounts receivable accounting.
2. File maintenance and processing to answer interrogations whenever made—for example, inventory position or the current status of jobs throughout a job shop.
3. Real-time processing with outputs to control operations by taking direct action or issuing instructions to people to take specified action—for example, control a manufacturing process by direct connection to the factory or communicate with people via display boards and desk sets.

Another approach to the appraisal of equipment in an operating environment is to determine how well it operates with a *test problem* representative of the applications to be handled by the equipment.

The test problem may be a segment of a planned application—for example, processing inventory transactions, preparing shipping and order documents, etc. Such processing involves accepting inputs, processing files—making calculations, logical choices, and other program steps—and producing outputs. The test problem, which may be treated as either a benchmark or typical problem, can be programmed for running on each set of equipment under study. The use of a common language like COBOL, as described in Chapters 8 and 9, may simplify the programming task by allowing the user to write one program for the test problem and give it to all manufacturers. Each manufacturer can compile the test problem prepared by the user in COBOL and produce a machine-language program for his equipment, as described in Chapter 12, ready to run with data. The efficiency of program execution may be increased (or decreased) appreciably by the way that, say, a COBOL file structure is laid out and the way that the program is written, since each machine has various features that can be fully utilized (or perhaps neglected) by a particular COBOL program.

However, a manufacturer may prefer to program the test problem in one of the languages—assembly or compiler—designed specifically for his machine in order to exploit the machine's unique capabilities. A tailor-made program also reflects the capabilities of the men who program the test problem. They may be more skilled in machine programming but less familiar with the user's operating problems than the user's personnel. A manufacturer that has skilled analysts and programmers to prepare programs is, of course, likely to show better performance on its equipment than manufacturers with less capable personnel. A user needs to appraise the two elements—equipment and skills of manufacturer's personnel—contributing to test problem performance and determine whether his personnel are likely to be able to duplicate the skills that the manufacturer's personnel applied to the test problem.

The test problem itself may be developed with simulated data or actual data from the past that have been screened to remove the mistakes and inconsistencies not planned for in the test problem program. The use of simulated or purified real data has the advantage of removing the effect of inaccuracies and inconsistencies caused by people from the files and transactions being used. It is then possible to study how the equipment will probably function in a system where people do not make mistakes. The existence of several mistakes in the data can easily vitiate the test of equipment operation and, instead, indicate the difficulties of dealing with the real data that people originate and supply to the system. Problems of coping with erroneous data are basically separate from testing machine performance and should be studied individually.

The test problem approach to equipment evaluation is advantageous, for it permits a prospective user to observe how a set of equipment functions under realistic test conditions and is, therefore, likely to perform under actual operating conditions. However, since test problems are difficult to prepare, they may be restricted in size and scope, thus being neither realistic nor allowing a high-speed machine to give a good workout and to demonstrate its full potential. Program preparation may be more expensive than formulation of the test problem, and manufacturers are generally unwilling to run them unless either the user prepares a program in, say, COBOL, or the pay-off from success is high—that is, there is a potential sale of several sets of equipment for similar installations.

Somewhat simpler than the test-problem approach is the use of the timed-application approach for evaluating equipment in a realistic environment. The prospective user may, with the help of one or more equipment manufacturers, analyze an application and describe it by record designs and flow charts or decision tables, as discussed in Chapter 7. The application description is submitted to manufacturers to analyze and plan programs for estimating the equipment configuration required and calculating the running time for the central processor and the input and output devices.

The timed-application approach has some of the advantages of the test-problem approach, for it tries to relate the equipment to a particular application. Estimates of running times for applications have the advantage in that they cost less to make and are quicker than programming and running a test problem. Timed-application estimates suffer, however, from being based on educated guesses of an approach to handling an application, the machine procedures to use, and the program instructions required to handle the data. The educated guesses about approaches, procedures, and programs are subject to error because the manufacturer's analysts and programmers may misunderstand the logic of the application or overlook some of its finer points. Furthermore, since a manufacturer has a strong interest in making his equipment appear as favorable as possible in order to make a sale, he may resolve doubtful points in his favor. In many ways, equipment can be made to appear more capable than it really is, when the study is limited to a paper analysis of a hypothetical application. Merely restricting the scope and depth of analysis for an application will make it seem simpler and easier than it actually is to program and run. Many complexities and subtleties of an application are discovered only by thorough and careful examination.

The most rudimentary approach to estimating how equipment will function in an operating environment is to develop an index or profile of machine capabilities. Indexes of machine speed alone have been used for a long time as a simple indicator of machine capability for performing engineering and scientific computations. Such an index may be built from the total time for some combination of addition, multiplication, and storage instructions representative of all the computation operations performed. Because of their importance in mathematical calculations, emphasis is correctly placed on central processor computation operations, rather than input and output operations.

For appraising the capability of equipment for business data processing, a broad profile of performance is more useful than a narrow index of internal speeds. A profile should encompass various processing functions—for example, data conversion, file read-in, calculation and logical operations, file read-out, and printing— that can be reduced to detailed machine operations. Alternatively, the functions may be stated in terms of classes of operations that machines are used for: file maintenance and processing, sorting, and matrix calculations. Facts for the detailed machine operations related to functions or to classes of operations can be combined with other aspects of the equipment to develop an over-all profile.

Similarly, a profile can be developed for an actual or hypothetical application and matched against a profile developed for the equipment. The equipment with the profile most closely matching the application profile, after penalties are charged for deficiencies and small bonuses allowed for extra features likely to be used, ranks highest on the profile-rating scheme.

The profile approach to equipment evaluation, while based on calculations rather than on realistic test runs, has the advantage of being economical and of eliminating the hidden biases that may influence the timed applications approach and even the test problem approach. Indexes and profiles, in effect, deal with extremely simple problems or applications—the time required to perform a specified number of operations. These measures of equipment operation are useful for selection purposes because they indicate the capability of equipment to handle a broad variety of problems or applications that, on average, make similar demands on the equipment.

Equipment Extras

Any set of data-processing equipment usually has some features that are valuable from the user's viewpoint but not easily appraised in terms of producing results or of reducing operating costs. Nevertheless, the long-run value of these extra features is worth estimating even though the short-run value may be nebulous.

One equipment extra is the point in time that equipment will be available. If equipment is already available, the design has shaken down and most of the production and operating difficulties eliminated. Equipment delivery dates are a matter of production scheduling rather than of design and testing. If it is important to implement an application as soon as it can be analyzed and programmed, readily available equipment is advantageous for several reasons. Equipment ready to operate will be available when promised and will enable the user to gain benefits at an earlier point in time. Equipment will be available at the manufacturer's plant or elsewhere for program testing and debugging and avoid the need to test on different kinds of equipment by means of simulators or other schemes. Manufacturers' and users' personnel can gain real experience in programming and operations at an earlier point in time and a large body of knowledge will exist concerning the features of the equipment and how to exploit them. Back-up equipment will be available at other users' locations, which permits trading time to guard against excessive down-time.

Many of the aspects of ready availability are reflected by some aspects of off-the-shelf equipment versus special-design equipment. Special-design equipment is likely to require several years for analysis and design before the equipment is built and ready for use. While special-design equipment may have superior features for its specific intended use, the time delay and the limited availability of such equipment poses important problems from the user's viewpoint in terms of the advantages described above for readily-available equipment.

The feature of ready availability of equipment has another side. A manufacturer may be about ready to replace with improved or new models the equipment that has been offered for several years even though it has been in use for only a short time—equipment either in use or available for several years is likely to be a good candidate for supercession. The user should consider the equipment he is about to obtain as the first in a long series of equipment to be used, so that the first decision should be considered as merely a link in a chain. Before obtaining the first set of equipment, a user is reasonably free to acquire an available set or to continue with present manual-mechanical methods for a year or so and obtain a successor model of equipment. A user's freedom to choose is greatly curtailed after he makes his first decision. In order for newer equipment to be worth installing to replace some equipment already in use, it must be enough superior so that its total costs—both conversion and operating—are smaller than the out-of-pocket costs of the existing equipment. Since this hurdle is a difficult one for new equipment, and especially so if the existing equipment was purchased instead of rented, the user needs to examine carefully the prospective rate of improvement in equipment design and manufacture when making a commitment to any particular model. The rent-purchase question is discussed more fully later in this chapter.

Equipment maintenance and reliability affect the user's productivity or operating costs. If maintenance and reliability are good, the user can write programs and plan operations aimed more at productive operations and less at coping with the machines' foibles. For example, fewer check points and rerun procedures need be included in programs for restarting processing in case of machine malfunction; and a higher fraction of machine time will be available for scheduling processing operations. Well-maintained and reliable equipment may enable the user to reduce his costs by doing productive work in less time and by requiring fewer man-hours for machine operations, even though the equipment manufacturer gives full credit for all running time lost because of machine malfunction and reruns required. The mere occurrence of malfunctions leads to reruns and unscheduled maintenance both of which increase the total elapsed time to get good production, even though machine down-time is not paid for.

Manufacturer support for systems planning, programming, and operations can have an important effect on the user's costs and production. One of the most important items of support is the software package. A comprehensive software package to support the hardware, as described in Chapter 12, includes the following: a compiler-level language and compiler (in addition to the machine-level language) to aid the user in writing tailor-made programs for business and scientific applications; generators—canned routines—for the user to fill in and prepare routines to fit his requirements for sorts and merges and for reports; executive routines to take over much of the operator's functions during test runs and even during production runs to handle one program immediately after another and to reduce the machine time lost between programs or between short runs; monitor routines for controlling operations during program debugging and for preparing traces of program execution and snapshots of programs that fail to run to completion; and industry application packages that handle certain important problems.

An adequate software package cuts the user's expense and elapsed time for preparing programs tested and ready to run. The user's analysts and programmers can work at the level of compiler, generator, executive, and monitor routine and avoid the near-fruitless task of repeating essentially the same work done at a hundred and one other installations. Early availability of a comprehensive software package is important because many components are needed before programming starts in order to plan the most efficient approach toward programming: whether to use a compiler language or machine language, what generators are suitable, etc.

The responsiveness of equipment to a user's needs are measured in terms of whether the equipment will meet his needs in both the short and long run. Short-run requirements pose many difficulties in trying to translate them into machine loads because it is easy to misunderstand requirements or make estimates that prove erroneous. Longer-run estimates are fraught with more hazards because of the changes that are almost certain to occur over time. Some examples of these changes are the increase in the skills of analysts, programmers, and operators, which leads to more efficient operations and to more sophisticated applications, and the growth of the business organization itself in terms of both volume and complexity, which leads to higher demands on the data-processing system.

The user's solution to the problem of long-run responsiveness of equipment to his needs depends on whether the equipment is modular in capacity and how much the equipment loads are likely to grow. If equipment is modular, then additional or higher capacity units may be added to or substituted for existing units so that total capacity keeps up with the demand. If equipment is nonmodular, then increased workloads may be handled by introducing satellite equipment and shifting some of the load from the main processor to the satellite. Alternatively, another main processor may be acquired to handle the loads. Presumably, of course, second- and third-shift operation possibilities are fully exploited before additional equipment is acquired. However, the practical productive operating time for equipment is usually less than 18 hours or so per day. After a sufficient growth in loads and machine utilization, newer equipment with higher capacity may be obtained to replace several sets of lower-capacity equipment.

Costs

Available data-processing equipment has a wide variety of costs with broad ranges of amounts for each. Such costs may be viewed in terms of their object (personnel, equipment, or overhead), when they are incurred (preparation, transition, or operation), or their function (analysis, design, programming, or operations). Costs are examined here in terms of when they are incurred.

One of the most important preparatory costs for introduction of a new system is for manpower to analyze the old system and to design a new system. It is estimated to be three-quarters, more or less, of the total costs for preparation, including systems analysis, design, and programming. These costs are incurred by the user and it is his responsibility to keep them under control and obtain efficient results. Since a large percentage of the early preparatory costs are independent of equipment, the supplier may provide little help with them. In fact the manufacturer's assistance may prove a hindrance because his training programs have, understandably, a strong bias toward the introduction and use of his equipment. Such emphasis is reflected in the concentration upon programming rather than on systems analysis and design, which should, at least in the early stages, be essentially independent of particular equipment.

The user needs to know the contents of the equipment manufacturer's software package during the planning stage when selecting programming methods and must have the whole package during the programming-coding phases. A good software package cuts the user's costs of program preparation, checkout, and operation by reducing the amount of manpower and elapsed time to develop and debug an operating program, unless the user's programmers are above average in skill and experience.

Transition costs from the existing to the proposed system include the physical facilities for equipment and people, conversion of data from old to new media, and duplicate operations during the conversion phase until cut-over is completed.

Minimum costs for physical facilities are determined by the equipment itself—amount of space, floor construction, power and air conditioning—and the work requirements of people. Additional costs are determined by the show-room effect wanted for the installation to produce an attractive and pleasing layout. Additional space and other facilities are usually required for the initial installation of equipment. Subsequent installations of second and third generation equipment are likely to be small enough in size and power requirements that they occupy only a fraction of the space and use only a fraction of the power and air conditioning required by first generation processors.

Data conversion costs may be huge when paper records or cards are first converted to magnetic tape or disks. The problem, which reflects the degree of completeness and accuracy of existing records, as well as the change from one medium to another, is essentially independent of the particular equipment to be used. In order to reduce the peak workload caused by data conversion, outside clerical help is sometimes called in or the task may be subcontracted to an outside service organization. Huge peaks in workload are likely to result from converting all the records to a new media in parallel with equipment installation and system implementation.

Duplicate or parallel operations arise when both the old and new systems are operated jointly. A complete duplication of operations is difficult to maintain over an extended period. Too much manpower is required and duplication seems wasteful because of the confusion from the work involved in straightening out discrepancies. Duplicate operations may be continued only long enough to prove the validity of the new system. Parallel operations may disclose numerous deficiencies in a manual-mechanical system and entail huge efforts if they are corrected. Therefore, the previous system is likely to be discontinued at the earliest possible stage to cut the costs of system transition.

The amount of system operating costs is a second important factor. Operating costs will continue for the life of the system. Some costs are directly related to the equipment in use: equipment and maintenance, machine operators and supporting personnel, power, air conditioning, tapes (to add to the library and replace those worn or damaged), and supplies. Other costs are more closely related to the particular data-processing system in use: the methods used for data origination and communication, systems analysis, systems design, programming, reprogramming to correct errors discovered and to cope with changed conditions, and analysis and design to extend existing applications and to add new ones. To these should be added the costs for personnel only indirectly related to the system but whose activities are affected by it—for example, production and marketing personnel who originate data inputs for the system or who use the outputs produced by it. Introduction of new equipment and a data system may materially change these indirect costs of systems operation.

How to Choose Equipment

Much of the preceding discussion dealt with the question of whether to use a certain class of equipment. The next question, assuming a positive decision to acquire equipment, is to select specific equipment.

The selection of one set of equipment from several is easy if they are effectively identical in that they produce the same results in terms of filling the user's needs; it is simply a matter of choosing the equipment with lowest cost. Similarly, if several sets of equipment have the same cost, the choice should be the one that best fills the user's needs. However, neither the costs of two sets of equipment nor the results they produce are likely to be identical; hence, some analysis of costs, results, and their relationship is useful.

In the selection of equipment, a point-scoring scheme may be used to measure the strength of each machine in terms of ten, twenty, or more features common to all equipment. The equipment with the highest total score is deemed superior on an absolute scale. But if the criterion for machine superiority is performance per dollar, the point score is divided by dollar cost to find the equipment that is superior on a relative scale. Point-scoring schemes need a broad base to cover all aspects of a machine's performance in an actual operating environment—speeds, reliability, maintenance, software package, and availability. Otherwise, the scoring scheme is likely to overemphasize characteristics of the machine without regard for the supporting features, which may count for as much as the machine itself. The number and kinds of points included in the scoring scheme have an interesting feature that is easily overlooked. A long and detailed list of points tends to bury individual features: no one feature stands out because it is merely one among many. Furthermore, one feature may be reflected several times within the various points that are included. Many factors—for example, storage access time, addition and multiplication times, tape read-write speeds, and the speed of index registers—reflect the speed of the main processor, though they reflect other aspects as well. If the point-scoring scheme also includes the processing time—actual program, test-problem, calculated time for an application, or merely the time to perform certain operations—then the machine speed is counted several times even though the intention was to count it only once.

The user is interested in what a proposed system and set of equipment will accomplish for him in a real, operating environment. Much of the success of a system depends on the user's management and operating personnel, since their abilities, attitudes, and initiative determine, in large part, whether a system succeeds or fails. Success may depend on such intangible factors as what equipment the management and operating personnel wanted to obtain (and they may have had different choices), their prior experience with equipment of the class and brand to be used, and their general attitudes about the merits of the data systems design and its prospects of success. Large organizations have gained enough experience to show that one group can design and implement a system, whereas a less experienced group cannot copy it and make it work; or, alternatively, one group can succeed·with a certain brand of equipment, whereas another group using similar equipment for the same application fails because it wants to prove that its choice for a different brand was correct. The attitudes of people toward system success are extremely difficult to measure and use as a factor in system design and equipment selection.

In short, there are many factors to consider in equipment selection but many of them are interrelated, some are nebulous, and some are more closely related to the operating environment than to equipment. It is incorrect to focus on equipment, prepare elaborate scoring schemes, and select equipment primarily in terms of point scores with any strong prospect of system success; much more is involved.

Equipment selection has some aspects of being penny-wise and pound-foolish, since people are likely to examine data-processing equipment in terms of an application or problem that is only roughly related to reality and may actually be unreal in some aspects. Regardless of the degree of reality and care used in formulating an application or problem for evaluating equipment, the equipment is only a part of the total system. The whole system encompasses the environment: ability of management and operating personnel to estimate future activities and the workload generated and the skills and initiative of people for analysis, design, programming, and implementation work. When important systems changes are planned, there is no easy formula for evaluating these factors.

Rent or Buy

Assuming that a decision is made to obtain equipment and a specific set of equipment selected, there remains the question as to whether it should be rented or bought. The basic rule for a decision to rent or buy is well known: purchase equipment if (1) the present worth of the future rent for the period the equipment is likely to be used, when discounted at the rate of return the organization can earn on its best available investment opportunity, exceeds (2) the purchase price of equipment.

The rent-or-buy question is actually an extremely narrow one and hinges on the following: (1) the rate of return on investment opportunities used in discounting the future rents for (2) the period that the equipment is likely to be used measured in terms of technical obsolescence of equipment, system changes that make it obsolete, or perhaps purely economic terms, and (3) the present worth of the salvage value of the equipment when it is likely to be replaced by newer equipment.

Rental rates for data-processing equipment have a fixed and variable element. For many years the data-processing equipment industry used a prime-shift charge covering eight hours of basic operation with no additional charge for the lunch hour and unscheduled overtime. Second- and third-shift use rental were each about half of prime-shift rental, although it is not ordinarily practicable to plan production operations for more than eighteen to twenty hours a day. Scheduled maintenance, down-time, and unscheduled maintenance generally take several hours a day.

The standard eight-hour day and 22-day month were combined into a standard work month of 176 hours for the prime shift. The eight-hour day and shift-plan for billing machine users was dropped and only the standard work-month of 176 hours per month was retained. A user now can use equipment at any time during the month within the limit of 176 hours for the basic rental rate without regard to the number of hours per day, prime shift, and other schemes that have artificial aspects which may conflict with the user's varying workloads throughout the week, month, or year. Nevertheless, the user must examine his operations and try to select the most economical operating plan—for example, whether it is most advantageous to work more hours per month on one set of equipment, upgrade the equipment by obtaining either more or faster components, rent time at a service bureau or from other users, obtain a second set of identical equipment, or turn in the equipment on hand for entirely new and faster equipment.

Manufacturers furnish engineers for scheduled maintenance of rented equipment and now usually perform it outside the time charged to the user; also, the user may be given credit for production time lost because of equipment malfunctions. Engineers are on hand during prime shift hours and may be on call during other hours.

Each manufacturer offers equipment for sale at a price which is equivalent to a certain number of months' rent that ranges from about 33 to 50. Maintenance contracts are offered separately at a fixed monthly charge so that it is necessary to combine the one-time purchase price and recurring monthly charge when calculating whether to rent or buy. Some equipment with important mechanical and electromechanical elements may have such expensive maintenance contracts when purchased that the user may find it cheaper to continue renting these units and restrict his purchase to the units that are primarily electronic.

The length of time that equipment can be used before it should be replaced by newer equipment has a crucial impact on a purchase decision. A forecast of a long economic life favors a decision to buy, whereas a forecast of short economic life favors continued rental. The economic life of equipment is limited to the point in time when the total average cost per period of using replacement equipment is less than the out-of-pocket cost of using the existing equipment plus the amount that the salvage value will decline. Economic life of installed equipment may terminate when (1) it deteriorates enough that its operating costs grow large, (2) its effective production dwindles because of malfunctions and down-time, or (3) new equipment is superior enough in terms of capability and reliability to have lower average costs than existing equipment. Since equipment owned and in operation should be charged with only the out-of-pocket operating costs and decline in salvage value (despite any allocation scheme for charging each period with depreciation expense), new equipment is likely to have difficulty overcoming this hurdle with the result that owned equipment may be used longer than it would if it was merely rented. Or viewed differently, it is advantageous for the user to rent equipment when the technical rate of improvement is high; and it is advantageous to own equipment when the rate of change is low. However, customers pay for technical changes, to the extent that the manufacturer is successful in including them in the price structure, through either equipment rental or sales.

A decision to purchase equipment may be further complicated by the terms of the purchase option that the manufacturer offers. Some manufacturers credit a user with a large fraction of rentals paid during the first year or two, if purchased during that period at the initial list price. A decision to purchase made after this period may be at a negotiated price. In some cases, a manufacturer restricts the freedom of equipment users to buy equipment after installation to those users that bought and paid a nontrivial amount—say, one percent of equipment sales price—for an option to purchase equipment when the original rental contract became effective. If the option to purchase was not bought initially, then the user has no rights to purchase the equipment later. Of course, any rental-purchase agreement is subject to bargaining and revision if the parties want to change it.

These comments about the acquisition of equipment, its rent or purchase, and sale or trade-in do not consider the tax aspects of such decisions. In an actual situation, taxes, and especially income taxes, may have an important bearing on equipment decisions. Tax regulations should, of course, be consulted, and their effect determined before making final arrangements for equipment.

SUMMARY

In this chapter, individual components of equipment are treated as data-processing systems. Specific details about a large number of processors are included in Tables 5-10 to 5-18. They are organized in the same fashion as the typical processor Tables 5-1 to 5-9 and the discussion throughout the chapter also applies to these tables: Table 5-10 corresponds to Table 5-1, etc. Table 5-19 lists communication devices and their operating features. Again a word of caution and guidance: the tables should *not* be used as a check-list for accepting or rejecting a particular set of equipment. The reasons are, first, the tables do not cover all business data processors available for use, and, second, many factors not readily tabulated should be considered before making a decision. At most, the tabulated details may be useful as background or initial guidance for studying the features of equipment preparatory to a broader survey and much more intensive study.

Internal storage usually consists of magnetic cores or perhaps a drum. Storage capacity ranges from a few thousand to a couple of hundred thousand characters. Word length may be as large as ten or twelve digits, but is much shorter in some equipment. Character-addressable storage enables the programmer to treat each item of data, whether long or short, as an individual field in storage. Each approach to organizing internal storage, either as fixed words or as fields to fit the data, has certain implications for equipment cost, data storage capacity, and programming.

Input and output devices may operate either on-line or off-line. Large processors use magnetic tape and small ones use punched cards or paper tape for on-line input and output. Off-line printing of data from tape and cards is used to produce readable copy. Consoles and direct-connected keyboard inquiry stations are used for small-volume on-line input and for inquiries. Printers, either of low or high speed, may be used for on-line output, but are generally used off-line.

Equipment appraisal and selection covers the range of problems from the broad one of the initial decision to introduce equipment to the narrow one of the decision to acquire a specific type of equipment. The nature of the operating environment and the constraints imposed by it are important to successful operation of equipment. But since the environmental conditions are difficult to assess, they are often taken for granted, and sometimes incorrectly so, when appraising equipment for selection.

The performance of equipment may be evaluated by various means, depending on the amount that the prospective user and manufacturer are willing to spend. The user and manufacturer may jointly program an application for running on a processor with live or test data to get a realistic representation of the actual situation. A less ambitious scheme is for the user to develop a test problem and have each manufacturer program and run it on his equipment. The user may prepare the initial program in a suitable compiler-level language, such as COBOL, to give to each manufacturer to compile and run.

A commonly-used plan for analyzing machine performance, although it is open to mistakes and biases, is for each manufacturer to plan the program and calculate running time for an application or problem that is merely described by the user. The simplest scheme for estimating equipment performance is to calculate the length of time to execute a specified set of instructions—read records, make certain calculations, and write records, etc.

Costs are incurred for personnel, equipment, and overhead support. Analysis, design, and programming costs may run as much as the equipment, and, like the equipment costs, continue for an indefinite period. A manufacturer's software package is valuable in the programming-coding phase, but doesn't help much in the analysis and design phase where most of the costs of system development are incurred. ·

A decision to rent or buy equipment hinges on questions of how long the equipment will be useful or will be displaced by technical obsolescence or economic factors, the rate of return obtained by the company on available investments, the ratio of rental to sales price set by the manufacturer, and the maintenance costs for purchased equipment. Many rental rate schemes and purchase plans have been offered by manufacturers over a period of time and the user may have difficulty choosing a wise course of action.

Company Model No.	Type	Words Minimum Maximum	A/N Char. Minimum Maximum	Dec. Digits Minimum Maximum	Instructions Minimum Maximum	Access Time Microsec. per Word or Char.
Burroughs 5000	Core	4,096 32,768	32,768 262,144	49,152 393,216	16,384 131,072	3w
Control Data 1604A	Core	8,192 32,768	65,536 262,144	114,688 458,752	16,384 65,536	2.2w
GE 210–215	Core	4,096 8,192	12,228 24,576	20,480 40,960	4,096 8,192	32w (210) 36w (215)
GE 225–235	Core	4,096 16,384	12,288 49,152	20,480 81,920	4,096 16,384	18w (225) 6w (235)
Honeywell 400	Core	1,024 4,096	8,192 32,768	11,264 45,056	1,024 4,096	20w
Honeywell 800	Core	4,096 16,384	32,768 262,144	45,056 360,448	4,096 32,768	6w
Honeywell 1800	Core	8,192 32,768	65,536 262,133	98,304 393,216	8,192 32,768	2w
IBM 650	Drum	1,000 4,000	5,000 20,000	10,000 40,000	1,000 4,000	480w
	Core	60	300	600	60	96w
IBM 1401	Core	—	1,400 16,000	1,400 16,000	175 2,000	11.5c
IBM 1440–1460	Core	—	4,000 16,000	4,000 16,000	730 2,900	11.1c (1440) 6c (1460)
IBM 1410–7010	Core	—	10,000 100,000	10,000 100,000	1,250 12,500	4.5c (1410) 2.4/2c (7010)
IBM 1620	Core	—	20,000 60,000	20,000 60,000	1,666 5,000	10–20c
IBM 7070–7074	Core	5,000 10,000	25,000 50,000	50,000 100,000	5,000 10,000	6w (7070) 4w (7074)
IBM 7080	Core	—	40,000 160,000	40,000 160,000	8,000 32,000	2/5c
IBM 7040–7044	Core	4,096 32,768	24,576 196,608	24,576 196,608	4,096 32,768	8w (7040) 2.5w (7044)
IBM 7090–7094I&II	Core	32,768	196,608	196,608	32,768	2.4w (7090) 2–1.4w (7094)
NCR 304	Core	2,400 4,800	24,000 48,000	24,000 48,000	2,400 4,800	60w
NCR 315	Core	2,000 40,000	4,000 80,000	6,000 120,000	1,000 20,000	6w
Philco 210–211–212	Core	4,096 65,536	32,768 524,288	61,440 983,040	8,192 131,072	4w (210–211) .9w/(212)
RCA 301	Core	—	10,000 40,000	10,000 40,000	1,000 4,000	7c
RCA 501	Core	—	16,384 262,144	16,384 262,144	2,048 32,768	12/4c
RCA 601	Core	8,192 32,768	65,536 262,144	98,304 393,216	4,096 32,768	1.5w
Univac III	Core	8,192 32,768	32,768 131,072	49,152 196,608	8,192 32,768	4w
Univac 490	Core	16,384 32,768	81,920 163,840	81,920 163,840	16,384 32,768	6w
Univac Solid State-II	Core	1,280	9,387	14,080		17w
	Drum	2,600 8,800	17,334 58,667	26,000 88,000	2,600 8,800	425w or 1700w
Univac 1105	Core	8,192 12,288	49,152 73,728	49,152 12,288	8,192	8w
Univac 1107	Core	16,384 65,536	98,304 392,216	98,304 392,216	16,384 65,536	4w
	Film	128	768	768	—	0.6w

TABLE 5-10. *Internal storage type, capacity and access.*

163

Company Model No.	Parity Check	Bits	Word Content Alphanumeric Characters	Decimal Digits	Binary Bits	Instructions
Burroughs 5000	Yes	1	8	12 equiv.	48	4 syllables
Control Data 1604A	No	None	8	14 equiv.	48	2
GE 210	No	None	3	6	28	1
GE 215	Yes	1	3	Sign + 3	20	1
GE 225–235	Yes	1	3	Sign + 3	20	1
Honeywell 400	Yes	4	8	Sign + 11	48	1
Honeywell 800	Yes	6	8	Sign + 11	48	1
Honeywell 1800	Yes	6	8	Sign + 11	48	1
IBM 650	2 of 5	None	5	Sign + 10	—	—
IBM 1401	Yes	1/c	1	1	—	—
IBM 1440–1460	Yes	1/c	1	1	—	—
IBM 1410–7010	Yes	1/c	1	1	—	—
IBM 1620	Yes	1	1	1	—	—
IBM 7070–7074	2 of 5	None	5	Sign + 10	—	1
IBM 7080	Yes	1/c	1	1	—	—
IBM 7040–7044	Yes	1	6	6	36	1
IBM 7090–7094	No	No	6	6	36	1
NCR 304	Yes	1/c	10	10	—	1
NCR 315	Yes	1	2	3	—	1
Philco 210–211–212	Yes	1	8	12	48	2
RCA 301	Yes	1/c	1	1	—	—
RCA 501	Yes	1/c	1	1	—	—
RCA 601	Yes	2	8	12	48	Variable
Univac III	Yes	2	4	6	24	1
Univac 490	No	None	5	5	30	1
Univac Solid State-II	Yes	1/c	22/3w	Sign + 10	44	1
Univac 1105	No	None	6	6	36	1
Univac 1107	No	None	6	6	36	1

TABLE 5-11. *Storage parity and word content.*

Company Model No.	Storage Cycle Time	Arithmetic Mode	3-Address Add Time 5 Decimal Digits	10 Decimal Digits	3-Address Multiply Time 4 Digits × 5 Digits	4 Digits × 10 Digits
Burroughs 5000	6	Octal parallel	9	9	37	37
Control Data 1604A	2.2	Binary parallel	21.6	21.6	58.8	58.8
GE 210	32	Decimal concurrent	192	288	678	1900
GE 215	36	Binary or decimal	216	324	342	342
GE 225	18	Binary or decimal	108	162	288	288
GE 235	6	Binary or decimal	36	54	84	84
Honeywell 400	10	Binary or decimal parallel	120	120	2000	2000
Honeywell 800	6	Binary or decimal parallel	24	24	162	162
Honeywell 1800	2	Binary or decimal parallel	8	8	54	54
IBM 650						
Drum avg.	480	Decimal serial	15,648	15,648	23,166	23,166
Core	96		1,440	1,440	3,072	3,072
IBM 1401	11.5	Decimal serial	540	885	16,000	18,000
IBM 1440	11.1	Decimal serial	535	875	15,500	17,500
IBM 1460	6	Decimal serial	270	440	8,000	9,000
IBM 1410	4.5	Decimal serial	115	171	4032	6016
IBM 7010	2.4	Decimal serial	60	85	2000	3000
IBM 1620	20	Decimal serial	480	960	15,500	17,700
IBM 7070– 7074	6	Decimal serial parallel	180	180	624	624
	4	parallel	24	24	60	60
IBM 7080	2.18	Decimal	15.3	26.2	135	165
IBM 7040– 7044	8		48	48	72	72
	2.5	Binary parallel	15	15	38	38
IBM 7090– 7094	2.18		14.4	14.4	47.6	47.6
	2	Binary parallel	12	12	18	18
NCR 304	60	Decimal serial	600	600	2,760	2,760
NCR 315	6	Decimal serial	72	144	900 avg.	900 avg.
Philco 210– 211	10	Binary parallel	25	25	60	60
Philco 212	1.5	Binary parallel	4	4	5.4	5.4
RCA 301	7	Decimal serial	189	330	Subroutine handles 10 × 10	8100
RCA 501	12	Decimal serial	288	468	4584	7464
RCA 601	1.5	Binary or decimal serial & parallel	15.2	15.4	80	100
Univac III	4	Decimal or binary serial	24	36	100 avg.	100 avg.
Univac 490	6	Binary parallel	28.3	36	75 avg.	75 avg.
Univac Solid State-II	17 (core) 425+ (drum)	Decimal serial	136 1470	136 1470	688 1990	1088 2730
Univac 1105	8	Binary parallel	48	48	192	192
Univac 1107						
Film	.6	Binary parallel	12	12	20	20
Core	4					

TABLE 5-12. *Operating speeds, microseconds.*

Company Model No.	Instruction Size	Addresses per Instruction	Index Registers	Modification Time, Microseconds	Indirect Addressing	Table Look-up	Floating Point	Character or Bit Addressing
Burroughs 5000	12 bits per syllable	Polish Notation				No	Yes	Yes
Control Data 1604A	8 char.	1	6	0	Yes	No	Yes	No
GE 210	6 char.	1	1	32	No	Yes	No	Yes
GE 215	20 bits	1	4 or 128	36	No	No	Yes	No
GE 225	20 bits	1	4 or 128	6	No	No	Yes	No
Honeywell 400	48 bits	3	3	12	No	No	No	Yes
Honeywell 800	48 bits	3	64	6	No	No	Yes	Yes
Honeywell 1800	48 bits	3	64	2	Yes	No	Yes	Yes
IBM 650	1 word	1	3	0	No	Yes	Yes	No
IBM 1401	1–8 char.	2	3	.34.5	No	No	No	Yes
IBM 1440	1–8 char.	2	3	33.3	No	No	No	Yes
IBM 1460	1–8 char.	2	3	18	No	No	No	Yes
IBM 1410	1–12 char.	2	15	24	No	Yes	No	Yes
IBM 7010	1–12 char.	2	15	9.6	No	Yes	No	Yes
IBM 1620	12 char.	2	0	—	Yes	No	Yes	Yes
IBM 7070–7074	1 word	1	99	6	Yes	No	No	Yes
IBM 7080	5 char.	1	0	—	Yes	No	No	Yes
IBM 7040–7044	1 word	1	3	—	Yes	No	Yes	Yes
IBM 7090	1 word	1	3	0	Yes	No	Yes	Yes
IBM 7094	1 word	1	7	0	Yes	No	Yes	Yes
NCR 304	1 word	3	10	60	No	Yes	No	Yes
NCR 315	2 words	1	32	—	No	Yes	No	No
Philco 210–211	24 bits	1	8	0	No	No	Yes	No
Philco 212	24 bits	1	8	0	Yes	No	Yes	No
RCA 301	10 char.	2	3	21	Yes	Yes	Yes	Yes
RCA 501	8 char.	2	7	90	No	No	No	Yes
RCA 601	4–20 char.	0 to 3	8	4.5	Yes	No	No	Yes
Univac III	1 word	1	9–15	0	Yes	No	No	Yes
Univac Solid State-II	1 word	1	9	17	No	No	No	No
Univac 490	1 word	1	7	0	No	No	No	Yes
Univac 1105	1 word	2	0	—	No	No	Yes	No
Univac 1107	1 word	1	15	0	Yes	No	Yes	Yes

TABLE 5-13. *Instruction characteristics.*

Tape Unit Model No.	Systems Using	Maximum Transfer Rate Thousand Char. per Second	Density per inch A/N Char.	Density per inch Linear Bits	Speed, Inches per Second	Lateral Format Parity	Lateral Format Data Bits	Tape Width
B422	Burroughs	24	200	200				
	5000	66.7	556	556	120	1	6	½
CDC 606	CDC 1604A	30	200	200				
		83.5	556	556	150	1	6	½
GE 210	GE 210	30	500	250	60	1	8	¾
GE 215	GE 215	15	200	200	75	1	6	½
Honeywell Economy	H-400	32	533	400	60	1	8	¾
Honeywell Standard	H-400, H-800	64	533	400	120	1	8	¾
Honeywell Hi-Density	H-400, 800 H-1800	89	1100	555	120	1	8	¾
Honeywell Super-Density	H-800 H-1800	124	1500	777	120	1	8	¾
IBM 727	IBM 650, 704, 705	15	200	200	75	1	6	⅓
IBM 7330	7010, 7040, 7072, 14—	7.2	200	200				
		20	556	556	31	1	6	½
IBM 729 II	IBM 1401, 1410 1460, 7010	15	200	200				
		41.6	556	556	75	1	6	½
IBM 729 IV	7040, 7044 7070, 7074 7080, 7090	22.5	200	200				
		62.5	556	556	112.5	1	6	½
IBM 729 VI	7094	22.5	200	200				
		62.5	556	556	112.5	1	6	½
		90	800	800				
IBM 7340 Hyper Tape-I	7080, 7074 7090, 7094	170	1511	1511	112.5	2	8	1
Hyper Tape-II	1400 Series	34	1511	1511	22.5	2	8	1
NCR 304	NCR 304	30	200	200	150	1	6	½
NCR 315	NCR 315	24	200	200				
		40	333	333	120	1	6	½
		60	500	500				
Philco 234	Philco 210, 211, 212	90	750	375	150	2	12	1
Philco 334	Philco 212	240	1200	600	133	2	12	1
RCA 381	RCA 301	10	333	333	30	1	6	½
RCA 382	RCA 301	20	333	333	60	1	6	½
RCA 581	RCA 301, 501, 601	33	333	333	100	2	12	¾
RCA 582	RCA 301, 501, 601	67	666	666	100	2	12	¾
Uniservo II-A	Univac III, SS-I, 490	12.5	125	125				
	1106, 1107	25	250	250	100	1	6	½
Uniservo III-A	Univac III 490, 1107	133	1333	1000	100	⅔	9	½
		120	1200			1	6	
Uniservo III-C	Univac III, 490, 1107	22.5	200	200				
		62.5	556	556	112.5	1	6	½

TABLE 5-14. *Magnetic tape units: tape transfer rates, formats, and lengths.*

Tape Unit Model No.	Maximum Block Size	Inter-block Gap, Inches	Start-Stop Time, Millisec.	Read Reverse	Rewind Inches per Sec. or Total Mins.	Max. Tape Length (Feet)	Read After Write	Horizontal Parity	Other
B422	Variable	.75	5	Yes	340	2400	Yes	Yes	—
CDC 606	Variable	.75	8	Yes	—	2400	Yes	Yes	—
GE 210	100 words	1	4.5	No	160 min.	3600	Yes	No	—
GE 215	Variable	.75	12	Yes	150	2400	Yes	Yes	—
GE 225	Variable	.75	.12	Yes	150	2400	Yes	Yes	—
Honeywell Economy	Variable	.67	—	—	—	—	Yes	No	Orthotronic
Honeywell Standard	Variable	.67	4	Yes	360	2500	Yes	No	Orthotronic
Honeywell Hi-Density	Variable	.67	3.5	Yes	—	2400	Yes	No	Orthotronic
Honeywell Super-Density	Variable	.67	—	Yes	—	2400	Yes	No	Orthotronic
IBM 727	Variable	.75	10.8	No	500	2400	No	Yes	—
IBM 7330	Variable	.75	20.8	No	22 min.	2400	Yes	Yes	—
IBM 729 II	Variable	.75	10.8	No	500	2400	Yes	Yes	—
IBM 729 IV	Variable	.75	7.3	No	500	2400	Yes	Yes	—
IBM 729 VI	Variable	.75	7.3	No	500	2400	Yes	Yes	—
IBM 7340 Hyper Tape	Variable	.45	3.0	Yes	1.5 or 3.8 min.	1800	Yes	—	Self-correcting
NCR 304	100 words	None, reposition head, 11.5 ms. avg.	5 plus repositioning time	No	225	3600	Yes	Yes	Diagonal parity
NCR 315	16000 char.	.75	4.8 accel.	No	—	3600	Yes	Yes	—
Philco 234	1024 char.	.9	5	Yes	225	3600	Yes	Yes	Fixed block count
Philco 334	Variable	.65	2.5	Yes	180	3600	Yes	Yes	—
RCA 381	Variable	.4	7	Yes	90	1200	No	No	—
RCA 382	Variable	.54	5.7	Yes	120	1200	Yes	No	Echo check
RCA 581	Variable	.4	3.5	Yes	100	2400	No	No	Dual recording each character
RCA 582	Variable	.6	3.5	Yes	150	2400	Yes		
RCA 681	Variable	.9	6	Yes	225	2400	Yes	No	Self-correcting
Uniservo IIA	120,720 or 1000	1 or 2.4	17.8 11.0	Yes	100	1500 2400	No	No	Block character count, fixed
Uniservo IIIA	Variable	.75	4–13	Yes	150	3500	Yes	No	—
Uniservo IIIC	Variable	.75	4–14	No	330	2400	Yes	Yes	—

TABLE 5-15. *Magnetic tape units: blocking, operations, and checking.*

Company Model No.	Scatter Read-Write	Program Interrupt (Trap)	Test Peripheral Device for Availability	Max. No. of Control Buffers Per System	Max. No. of Tapes Buffer	Max. No. of Tapes System	Parallel Transfer Capability
Burroughs 5000	No	Yes	Yes	4	16	16	1 per channel
Control Data 1604A	No	Yes	Yes	6	4	24	1 per subsystem
GE 210	No	No	Yes	13	8	8	1 read and 1 write
GE 215	No	Yes	Yes	1	8	8	1 per controller
GE 225	No	Yes	Yes	8	8	64	1 per controller
GE 235	No	Yes	Yes	7	8	56	1 per controller
Honeywell 400	No	No	Yes	1	8	8	1 per channel
Honeywell 800	No	Yes	Yes	8	8	64	1 per channel
Honeywell 1800	No	Yes	Yes	8	8	64	1 per channel
IBM 650	No	No	No	1	6	6	1 per system
IBM 1440	—	—	—	—	—	None	—
IBM 1401	No	No	No	0	—	6	1 per system
IBM 1460	No	No	No	0	—	6	1 per system
IBM 1410	No	Yes	No	2	10	20	1 per channel
IBM 7010	No	Yes	No	2	10	20	1 per channel
IBM 1620	—	—	—	—	—	None	—
IBM 7070–7074	Yes	Yes	Yes	4	10	20	1 per channel
IBM 7080	Yes	Yes	Yes	4	10	40	1 per channel
IBM 7040–7044	Yes	Yes	Yes	4	10	40	1 per system
IBM 7090–7094	Yes	Yes	Yes	8	10	80	1 per channel
NCR 304	No	No	Yes	8	8	64	1 copy or search per controller
NCR 315	No	Yes	Yes	0	—	8	1 per system
Philco 210, 211, 212	No	Yes	Yes	4	31	64	4 transfers per I/O processor
RCA 301	No	No	Yes	2	12	14	1 per control
RCA 501	Yes	Yes	Yes	8	8	63	1 read and 1 write per channel
RCA 601	Yes	Yes	Yes	4	24	48	1 read and 1 write per channel
Univac III	Yes	Yes	Yes	13	2	32	1 read and 1 write per channel
Univac Solid State-II	No	No	Yes	2	10	20	1 per channel
Univac 490	No	Yes	Yes	12	12	144	1 per channel
Univac 1105	No	Yes	Yes	2	10	20	1 per channel
Univac 1107	No	Yes	Yes	15	12	180	1 per channel

TABLE 5-16. *Magnetic tape: selected input-output instructions and buffering.*

Company Model No.	Type	Alphanumeric Characters per Unit (Millions)	Maximum Number of Units	Access Arms per Unit	Access Time millisec. Min.	Access Time millisec. Max.	Addressed in Records of	Max. Transfer Rate, 1000 Char. per Sec.
Burroughs 5000	Drum	32,768 words	2 (1 req)	—	8.5	17	480 char.	120
	B472 Disk	9.6	100	None	20	40	480 char.	100
Control Data 1604A	—	—	—	—	—	—	—	—
GE 210	—	—	—	—	—	—	—	—
GE 215, 226, 235	Disk	18.8	4	16	199	305	64 words	62.5
Honeywell 400	H-460	37.5	4	—	—	—	—	—
Honeywell 800–1800	H-860 Disk	67.5/135	8	—	100 avg.		64 words	—
IBM 650	355 Disk	6	4	3	175	850	—	22.5
IBM 1440	1311 Disk	3	5	5	—	400	100 char.	77
IBM 1401	1405 Disk	10/20	2	1–2	100	800	200 char.	22.5
	1311 Disk	3	5	5	—	400	100 char.	77
IBM 1460	1311 Disk	3	5	5	—	400	100 char.	77
IBM 1410	1405 Disk	10/20	5	1–2	100	800	200 char.	22.5
	1301 Disk	3	5	5	—	400	100 char.	77
IBM 7010	1311 Disk	3	5	5	—	400	100 char.	77
IBM 1620	1311 Disk	3	4	5	—	400	100 char.	77
IBM 7070–7074	1405 Disk	3/6	4	3	100	800	300 char. 600 digits	—
IBM 7080	1301 Disk	28/56	5	24	—	180	Variable, cylinder	90
IBM 7040–7044	1301 Disk	28/56	5	24	—	180	Variable, cylinder	90
IBM 7090–7094	1301 Disk	28/56	5	24	—	180	Variable, cylinder	90
NCR 304	—	—	—	—	—	—	—	—
NCR 315	Cram Magnetic Cards	5.5	16	1	14 re-access	170 per card		150
Philco 210, 211, 212	Disk	41.9	4	—	—	117	—	—
RCA 301	Record Disk	4.6	5	1	2000	—	900 char.	2.5
	Data Disk	22	8	12	—	150	160	32
RCA 501	None	—	—	—	—	—	—	—
RCA 601	None	—	—	—	—	—	—	—
Univac III	—	—	—	—	—	—	—	—
Univac Solid State-II	Randex Drum	24	10	—	5	540	48 char.	4.8
Univac 490	FH-880 Drum	4	96	—	17 avg.		Variable	150
	Fastram Drum	64.8	96	—	5	156	Variable	50
Univac 1105	—	—	—	—	—	—	—	—
Univac 1107	FH-880 Drum	4.7	96	—	17 avg.		Variable	360
	Fastram Drum	66	96	—	5	156	Variable	150

TABLE 5-17. *Addressable bulk storage.*

Company Model No.	Punched Card Read Speed	Punch Speed	Channels	Paper tape Read Speed Char. per Sec.	Punch Speed Char. per Sec.	Line Printer Speed Lines per Min.	Remote Inquiry Typewriter	Document Reader Docs. per Minute	Satellite Processor
Burroughs 5000	800	300	5–8	1000	100	700	Yes	No	No
Control Data 1604A	250	100	———None———			150	Yes	No	CDC 160
GE 210	400 1500	100	7	200 or 500	60	1000	No	1200 Magnetic	No
GE 215, 225, 235	400 1500	100 300	5–8	250 or 1000	110	900	Yes	1200 Magnetic	No
Honeywell 400	240 650	100 250	5–8	200 1000	60	900	Yes	312 Optical	No
Honeywell 800	240 650	100 250	5–8	200 1000	60	150 900	Yes	312 Optical	H400
Honeywell 1800	240 650	100 250	5–8	200 1000	110	150 900	Yes	312 Optical	H400
IBM 650	250	100	5–8	20	None	150	Yes	No	No
IBM 1440	400	91	5–8	500	150	240	Yes	950 Magnetic	No
IBM 1401	800	250	5–8	500	150	600	Yes	Magnetic	No
IBM 1460	800	250	5–8	500	150	600/3300	Yes	400 Optical	No
IBM 1410–7010	800	250	5–8	500	150	600/1100	Yes	Optical	No
IBM 1620	250	125	8	150	15	240	No	No	No
IBM 7070–7074	500	250	———None———			150	Yes	No	IBM 1401, 1460
IBM 7080	————Off-line————						Yes	No	IBM 1401, 1460
IBM 7040–7044	250	125	———None———			600/3300	Yes	No	IBM 1401, 1460
IBM 7090–7094	250	100	———None———			150	Yes	No	IBM 1401, 1410, 1460
NCR 304	Off-line		5–8	1800	60	680	Yes	No	No
NCR 315	400 2000	250	5–8	400 1000	110	680	Yes	1620 Optical	No
Philco 210, 211, 212	2000	100	5–8	1000	60	900	Yes	No	Philco 1000
RCA 301	800	250	5–8	1000 100	300 100	1000	Yes	Yes	No
RCA 501	600	200	7	1000	300 100	600	No	No	No
RCA 601	Off-Line		7	300	10	1000	No	Off-line	RCA 301
Univac III	700	300	5–8	500	110	700	No	No	Univac SS-II
Univac Solid State-II	150 600	150	5–8	500	110	600	No	No	No
Univac 490	600	150	5–8	500	110	600	Yes	No	Univac SS-II
Univac 1105	120	120	7	200	60	Off-line	No	No	No
Univac 1107	700	150 or 300	5–8	400	110	700	Yes	No	Univac SS-II

TABLE 5-18. *Peripheral devices.*

171

Company Model No.	Type Unit	Grade of Channel	Speed Char/Sec.	Input Media	Output Media	Error checking
Collins 8000	Comm. Control	Telephone	300	C, PC, MT	C, P, PC, MT	Char. & block parity
Dashew 702	Off-line	Telephone	20	PT	PT	Vert. parity
Dashew 1000	Off-line	Telephone	20	PC, KB	PC	1 hole/col.
Dashew 1500	Off-line	Telephone	105	PT	PT	Vert. parity
Digitronics 506	Off-line	Telephone	100	PT, PC, MT	PT, PC, MT	H & v parity
Digitronics 520	Off-line	Telephone Telpak	300 62,500	MT	MT	H & v parity
Frieden TD	Off-line	Telegraph	14	PT	PT	Parity
Frieden 30	Factory Input	Cable	30	PC, Badge	None	Parity
IBM 357	Factory Input	Cable	18	PC, KB, Badge	None	Column check
Honeywell 880	Comm. Control	Telephone	150	C	C	Parity, validity
IBM 1001	Low volume Off-line	Telephone	12	PC, KB	PC	Parity, field length
IBM Transceiver	Off-line	Telephone	14	PC	PC	4 of 8 code
IBM 1009	Proc. to Proc.	Telephone	300	C	C	Parity, validity
IBM 7710	Proc. to Proc.	Telpak	5100	C	C	Parity, validity
IBM 1013	Off-line	Telephone	80	PC	PC	Parity, validity
IBM 1050	Off-Line or Proc. Remote	Telegraph Telephone	15	PC, PT, P, KB	C, PC, P, PT	Char. & block parity
IBM 1060	Agent set	Telegraph or telephone	15	KB	P	Char. & block parity
IBM 7702	Off-line	Telephone	300	MT	MT	H & v parity
IBM 1945	Tape Control	Telpak	62,500	MT	MT	Parity, validity
IBM 7750	Comm. Control	Telephone	300	C, MT, PC	C, MT, PC	H & v parity, validity
RCA 5901	Off-line	Telegraph	7	PT	PT	Parity
RCA 5903	Off-line	Telephone	100	PT	PT	Parity
RCA 5907	Off-line	Telephone Telpak	300 66,000	MT	MT	Parity
RCA EDGE	Factory Input	Wire	15	PC, KB, Badge	None	Parity
Soroban DTD	Off-line	Telephone	150	PT	PT	H & v parity
Standard Register	Off-line	Telephone	—	PC, KB	PC	2 of 8 code
Stromberg	Factory Input	Cable	15	KB, PC, Badge	None	Parity
Systematics	Off-line	Telegraph	10	PT, PC, KB	PT, PC, P	Check character
Tally Register Mark 3	Off-line	Telephone	75	PT	PT	H & v parity Block check
Teleregister LRT 401	Agent set	Telegraph	8	KB	P	None
Teleregister LRT 580	Agent set	Telephone	133	KB	P	Vert. parity
Teletype 28	Off-line	Telegraph	10	KB, PT	P, PT	None
Teletype, Mod 2	Off-line	Telephone	105	PT	PT	None
Univac 8110	Agent set	Telephone	127	KB	P	H & v parity
West. Union Telex	Off-line	Telegraph	7	KB, PT	P, PT	None

Abbreviations: C—core MT—magnetic tape PC—punched cards
KB—keyboard P—printer PT—punched paper tape

TABLE 5-19. *Data communication devices.*

PART III
SYSTEMS DESIGN

6

Systems Analysis, Evaluation, and Approaches to Design

This chapter and the next one deal with systems primarily from the viewpoint of the objectives set for them and the environment in which they operate. Most of the discussion is independent of equipment, although equipment must be considered during the implementation phase. This chapter covers *systems analysis*—fact finding and critical examination of the facts—and *approaches to systems design*—deciding what general plan will be followed in design. Together they are the search and initial creative phases: what the present system does, what the proposed system should do, and what schemes can be devised to achieve the desired objectives. Creativity is the first phase of systems synthesis.

Systems design is the development of a plan or scheme for processing data based on the facts learned in the analysis stage and within the framework developed in the approaches-to-design phase. In addition to building on the analytical phases, systems design requires all the designer's ingenuity in devising new and improved systems. The designer must synthesize or put together the parts to devise an operating system. This is an entirely different job from that of the analyst, who analyzes—literally takes apart—the process he is investigating in order to understand it.

The *implementation* stage builds on the analysis and design phases by devising procedures, selecting and installing equipment, obtaining and training people to support a system, and putting the equipment and system into operation.

Although systems analysis, selection of design approaches, design, and implementation are discussed one at a time for simplicity, they are closely related and each one affects the others. When a new system or revision of an existing one is begun, each phase may be handled in sequence. But a question about one phase—say, systems design—often requires more systems analysis, or rethinking of the design approach, so that all three are soon carried on together. In later stages, the process becomes iterative and it may be necessary to cycle through the four phases of analysis, design approaches, design, and implementation several times in order to build an efficient system that is based on a thorough analysis of requirements and is well designed to use the most suitable equipment and techniques.

SYSTEMS ANALYSIS

Systems analysis involves collecting, organizing, and evaluating facts about a system and the environment in which it operates. This requires determining the demands for outputs—the data and information requirements of an organization for both operating and management purposes—the sources of data, and the processing methods and files that serve as a link between input and output.

Environmental features of interest in systems analysis are the business activity and the management pattern, since these bear on the kinds and volumes of information wanted for operating and control purposes. The nature and organization of the business also affect the types and quantities of data that are needed to produce the desired information. The number and variety of origination, processing, and use points determines the communication pattern, organization and location of files, processing procedures, and the techniques and equipment used at each stage.

Objectives of Systems Analysis

As used here, the word *analysis* is restricted to fact-finding and to examining systems to learn how they work; such analysis is applicable to existing or proposed systems. The act of synthesizing a system by devising, copying, or inventing is a design function, and is covered later. But, and this is the important point here, as soon as a proposed system is designed, it can be analyzed to estimate how well it is likely to work if put into practice. More elaborate testing in the form of simulation of a proposed system is possible, and may be extremely valuable.

The objective of systems analysis, then, is to learn enough about a system—equipment, personnel, operating conditions, and demands on it—to establish the foundation for designing and implementing a better system, if it is feasible to do so. A data-information system is *better,* if it increases the net over-all output of the organization after considering the cost of systems design as part of the total costs.

Closely related to the objectives of systems analysis are the questions "Why analyze?" and "How much analysis is worthwhile?" Analysis is usually the first step in either partial or complete redesign and implementation of a new system. Analysis may be triggered by dissatisfaction with those operating results of the business which can be attributed to the output of the present system. Important causes of dissatisfaction are late, insufficient, or inaccurate information; an excessive burden on operating personnel to collect data; or excessive system operating costs. Such dissatisfaction may occur following poor design or inadequate installation of the existing system. Or, because of new products, different management organization, additional manufacturing plants or marketing outlets, and increased competition, operating conditions may change, thus requiring revision of the data-processing system in order to regain its original or hoped-for level of adequacy.

Analysis may be worthwhile because of potential improvements arising from technical developments in equipment, advances in the state of the systems art, or increased capabilities of people. Analysis following improvements in one or more of these factors can lead to the design of either a superior system at the same cost or a system equal to, but more economical than, the one in use.

Some analysis of a system is warranted in any situation except the steady-state case. In the steady-state or static case, the system is considered to be performing satisfactorily, operating conditions within the business are not changing, and technical changes in data-processing equipment are at a standstill. This combination of circumstances, as one might expect, seldom occurs.

How much analysis is worthwhile? More analytical work is worth doing, if it is likely to lead to design and implementation of a new system with a total value exceeding all the costs involved. The expected value of an improvement depends on the combined probability of making the improvement and the amount of such improvement. Small improvements are almost certainly achieved from any analysis and design work, although substantial improvements are made infrequently. This pattern is typical, for important gains are uncommon in any field.

On the other hand, the costs of systems analysis are likely to continue at a steady pace and somewhat independently of the expected value of improvements. There is a continuing risk that the expected value of systems improvement will drop below the best estimate of costs still to be incurred to implement the improvement. If so, the project should be abandoned, since, according to best available estimates, continuing will lead to a net loss. Note that the criterion for continuing or stopping analysis and design work is not how much has been spent to date, but how much will be spent to completion. Past costs are "sunk," and only future outlays count in making the decision to continue or to stop.

The feeling is widespread that initial estimates of system improvements are optimistic and that estimates of costs of analysis, design, and implementation are conservative. If so, only those projects that have a large pay-off when initial estimates are made should be pursued seriously.

Analysis of Processing Procedures

Processing procedures are the common thread running between input data, facts in files, and output reports. Raw data originate on documents or other suitable media as events occur—business transactions with outsiders, transfers between departments, and operations within a department. Event data are processed against files to update existing records and to introduce new records into files. System output ranges from brief answers in reply to specific questions, through listings of raw data with little or no processing, to highly condensed summaries and periodic analyses of files.

Since data-information systems are large and complex, a systems analyst can remember only a small part of the details at one time. But an analyst must do more than obtain and remember facts about the existing system. In order to understand and appraise the system in broad terms, he must organize the facts, or get them organized with the aid of others and, perhaps, data-processing equipment. An understanding and appraisal of the existing system, coupled with some clear thinking, are necessary for selecting a design approach and designing a new data-flow system.

Steps in Analysis. There are five steps the systems analyst must perform in analyzing a typical data-information-processing system that is operated by people and uses readable documents.

First, *obtain facts* by interviewing people and observing activities about the events—their type, volume, and timing—that lead to the origination of documents, maintenance of files, issuance of reports, processing steps done at each work station, and flow of documents between stations. Both physical action and clerical events lead to the creation of more documents or initiation of more action.

Second, *collect sample copies* of filled-in documents, file papers, and reports with facts on activity—smallest, average, and largest number—during each period and the number of lines and characters of data per line to indicate the volume of activity.

Third, *study processing operations* to learn the how and why of every document that each person receives or issues, what processing steps he performs, the nature of files he keeps or uses, and the contents of any reports he prepares.

Fourth, *organize the facts* obtained into flow charts, flow lists or other suitable form to trace the path of data from origin, through each stage of communication and processing, into files, and out of files to reports. Systematic methods for organizing facts make them easier to deal with and help disclose gaps and mistakes in the analyst's data gathering and comprehension.

Fifth, *interview each user* of documents and reports to learn what information he uses in his work and what he thinks he needs. The systems analyst should determine what criteria management originally set up for the present system and is likely to establish for a proposed or merely prospective system. Management and operating-personnel demands for outputs influence the systems analysis work in determining how well the present system does or can meet such demands. These demands also influence selection of an approach to systems design and the design work, as described later.

With this catalogue of facts organized in a systematic fashion, it is possible to discover system weak points. These include failure to report data origination, duplicate origination, breaks in the flow because documents issued by the originator are either not received or not properly handled by the recipient, redundancy in file content, and delays in handling and transmitting data or taking the action called for by the output.

Documentation.   Documentation is the first step in analyzing a data-processing system. It consists of detailed fact-finding about information flows: data inputs, processing actions, outputs, control points, quantities, file identification, frequencies of transfer, and special time requirements. Analysts interview people, gather specimen forms, and analyze activities. A standardized form, such as the Message Specification Sheet in Figure 6-1, can be used to collect uniform and complete facts about each form prepared in the organization.

In one approach to the fact-gathering stage, attention is focused on the *event* that creates the document and the *station*—a person, group of persons, or area where similar data originate. Tracing the series of events related to one document results in an *event chain,*

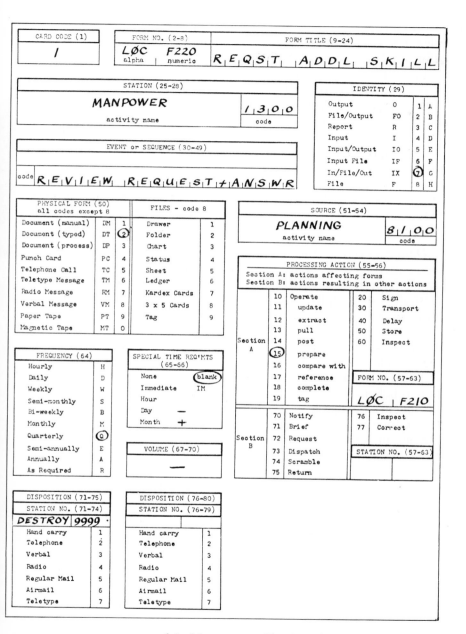

FIGURE 6-1. *Message specification sheet.*

as described below. Neither the data system as a whole nor individual applications are considered at this stage because it is difficult to assign each operation to an application. Boundaries between applications are ambiguous because events are interrelated and people often don't know how the papers they create fit into the broader picture—for example, one copy of a form prepared by production clerks goes to payroll and another copy goes to inventory control. Although many other approaches to analysis are used, the event and station one, which has several unusual features, will be pursued here.

The analyst interviews people and identifies them by the station to which they are assigned—say, the maintenance department, order-processing department, or a shop in the factory. The division by station seems arbitrary, but it has an advantage in that it follows the organization pattern and identifies the nodes—the points at which data-handling events occur—in the data-flow network.

Data Collection Sheet. Special data collection forms—document, message, file, and report specification sheet—are filled out during interviews at each station. The analyst also obtains copies or facsimilies of completed documents and reports, and descriptions of files during each interview. Data-flow in and out, as well as data retained at the station, are noted on the data collection sheet. Local documents and verbal messages are also covered in order to study the complete information-communication network.

The analyst assigned to a station—and several analysts can work in parallel at different stations—obtains the following facts for each document: official forms control number, name of form, station where interviewing is done, identity—its role at the station (input, file-output, or similar combinations), event that causes the form to be prepared, sequences within files, physical form, originating stations for documents being processed at a station, processing action, frequency of preparation, special processing-time requirements, volume, and disposition.

Completion of the data collection sheet yields enough information about data-flows to perform the systems analysis steps described below and closes the fact-finding phase.

Editing. An analyst or editor reviews the data collection sheets for completeness and correctness to facilitate coding and also key-punching, if machine processing is used to supplement manual analysis, and flow charting, as described later. He obtains codes for station source and disposition from a master listing, which he must prepare if unavailable. He assigns numbers to unnumbered local forms and files, and reviews and abbreviates descriptions. Editing and completing the data collection sheets is an important task for the editor when reviewing the work of all analysts. Many analysts can work in parallel to gather data quickly since the subsequent editing stage helps make their individual work uniform.

Conclusions from Analysis

The most important conclusion obtainable from the analytical scheme described here is a comprehensive, quantified understanding of data-flows throughout an organizational area. This involves examining the characteristics of different stations, their relationships with each other, and location of major files in the network.

Station Characteristics and Relationships. Station characteristics include a description of files and the type, frequency, volume, and special requirements of data processed at the station. These facts indicate whether a station is an origination, control, storage, or satellite point in the system. This knowledge is useful for deciding where to place input, terminal, processor, display, and storage equipment. Volumes for each station compared to total volume determine the relative importance of different stations.

Station relationships point out potential areas for integration or centralized processing. Local systems are preferable for stations that send or receive few documents from other stations. However, stations having large volumes of communications with each other might be efficiently integrated into a comprehensive system.

Major *file analysis* shows the need for different storage media— magnetic tape, random access, automatic display—and the redundancies in files. Redundancies arise when similar or identical data appear in two or more files. Analyses are made of document activity, document flow, and files to serve as a foundation for designing system improvements.

Network Load Analysis. The data obtained on the original message specification sheets are used to prepare a load analysis of the data-flow network. The data are sorted by station, identity, form number, and card code to develop volumes of documents for each station by identity codes, frequency of processing, and special time requirements. Calculating the workload percentages by data type is useful, along with total volumes, for comparing the activity of stations.

The *station* load analysis in Figure 6-2 lists all documents, forms, and reports processed at a work station grouped by identity code, frequency of processing, and special requirements. The volume of documents is listed by frequency of processing and converted to a monthly basis to facilitate comparison among work stations. Percentages can be calculated for each frequency. The immediate processing case deserves special consideration because it imposes extra loads on the system.

From an analysis of the volume associated with each identity code—output, file-output, report, input, input-file, etc.—the analyst can determine whether a station is primarily a terminal area, a control point, or a storage area. These conclusions can also be translated into needs for input-output, display, storage, or main-frame processing capability. Quantities and percentages about frequency and special time requirements suggest the need for random access, remote inquiry, or other processing capability.

The *network load summary* report (illustrated in Figure 6-3) shows activity volumes by identity and frequency for the total data-flow network and each station. Percentages are useful to indicate the importance of each category at a station, each station in relation to the total functional area workload, and each station in relation to the whole organization's workload.

Document Activity Analysis.   An analyst uses the document activity report to see the document flow between different data processing systems, functional areas, and stations at various locations.

The document activity analysis is based on the same data used for the network data load analysis. Documents are identified by stations and compared by sources and dispositions to determine functional activity. The document activity report identifies documents processed at a particular station and a separate listing can be prepared for documents created and used by the same station.

The analyst obtains clues about the degree of potential integration within and between functional activities from the document activity report. (See Figure 6-4.) Independent stations are highlighted because they have little or no transfer of documents to or from other stations. Furthermore, the importance of various functions and their relationship with geographically separate segments of the company are indicated. These facts guide the analyst toward a sound decision about centralized or decentralized processing. Closely

NETWORK DATA LOAD DETAIL REPORT

STATION CODE 4000 STATION NAME COST ACCTG

ID	FREQ	SPEC TIME REQ	NO.	TITLE	PRESCRIBING DIRECTIVE	FREQ	MONTHLY H	ID VOL	H	D	W	SM	BW	M	Q	SA	A	AR	SPEC TIME IM
2	M		LOC 108	DM OP COST REPT		01	1. 1												
2	M		LOCF012	OCR DM LBR HOURS		01	1. 1												
2	M		LOCF014	OCR DPEH ANALYS		01	1. 1												
2	M		LOCF130	OCR BUD VAR SCHD		01	1. 1												
2	M		LOCF140	OCR DM GEN EXP		01	1. 1												
2	M		LOCF150	OP COST REPT/BR		05	5. 1												
2	M		LOCF160	OCR DM SUMM		01	1. 1												
2	M		LOCF170	OCR SHOPS DIV		01	1. 1												
2	M		LOCF175	OP COST REPT/WC		34	34. 1												
2	M		LOCF232	OCR SHOP GEN EXP		01	1. 1												
2	M		LOCF234	OCR MATL VAR		01	1. 1												
				TOTAL			48.	1.86											
6	B		LOC 130	ACT PAYRCLL LIST		34	74. 1												
6	M		LOC 107	EARNED HR ANAL		01	1. 1												
6	D		LOC 131	ACT EXPENDTR LST		01	1. 1												
6	E		LOCA240	WORK REQUEST		25	525. 1												
6	M		LOCE100	END ITEM COST RP		10M	1667. 1												
6	E		LOCE190	MTCE COST SUM/MO		-0	0. 1												
6	M		LOCE191	MTCE COST SUM/SA		-0	0. 1												
6	M		LOCE250	MATL IN MTCE		29	29. 2												
6	M		LOCE300	MATL VAR ANALY		34	147. 2												
6	M		LOCE440	STD + ACT LABOR		34	34. 1												
6	C		LOCF012	OCR DM LBR HOURS		01	1. 1												
6	M		LOCF014	OCR DPEH ANALYS		01	1. 1												
6	M		LOCF075	MO DIST/APRV BUD		12	3. 1												
6	M		LOCF130	OCR BUD VAR SCHD		01	1. 1												
6	M		LOCF140	OCR DM GEN EXP		01	1. 1												
6	M		LOCF150	OP COST REPT/BR		05	5. 1												
6	M		LOCF160	OCR DM SUMM		01	1. 1												
6	M		LOCF170	OCR SHOPS DIV		01	1. 1												
6	M		LOCF175	OP COST REPT/WC		34	34. 1												
6	M		LOCF232	OCR SHOP GEN EXP		01	1. 1												
6	M		LOCF234	OCR MATL VAR		01	1. 1												
				TOTAL			2528.	98.14											
F	Q		LOCE260	MATL STD COST LS		-0	0. 2												
				TOTAL			0.	0.											

GENERAL FREQUENCY

TOTALS FOR THIS STATION   2576.   0.   20.4 5.7 0. 2.9 5.2 0.1 64.7 0. 0. 0.

FIGURE 6-2. *Network data load detail report.*

183

NETWORK DATA LOAD SUMMARY REPORT

STATION CODE	STATION NAME
8100	PLANNING

IDENTIFIER — FREQUENCY

	O	FO	R	I	IO	IF	IX	F	SA	A	AR	GEN
PCT	7.48	0.01	0.	0.67	0.20	3.97	87.66	0.	0.	0.	0.	0.
VCL	22260.	30.	0.	2000.	600.	11819.	260754.	0.	0.	0.	0.	0.

	H	D	M	SM	BW	M	Q	SA	A	AR	GEN
PCT	0.	98.27	0.05	0.	0.	0.	1.68	0.	0.	0.	0.
VCL	0.	292320.	147.	0.	0.	0.	4995.	0.	0.	0.	0.

TOTAL STATION VOLUME 297462.
PERCENT STATION TO FUNCTIONAL AREA 96.60
PERCENT FUNCTIONAL AREA TO BASE 1.67

STATION CODE	STATION NAME
8110	CLERICAL

IDENTIFIER — FREQUENCY

	O	FO	R	I	IO	IF	IX	F	SA	A	AR	GEN
PCT	0.	16.27	0.	0.	0.	67.47	16.27	0.	0.	0.	0.	0.
VCL	0.	1701.	0.	0.	0.	7056.	1701.	0.	0.	0.	0.	0.

	H	D	M	SM	BW	M	Q	SA	A	AR	GEN
PCT	0.	100.00	0.	0.	0.	0.	0.	0.	0.	0.	0.
VCL	0.	10458.	0.	0.	0.	0.	0.	0.	0.	0.	0.

TOTAL STATION VOLUME 10458.
PERCENT STATION TO FUNCTIONAL AREA 3.40
PERCENT FUNCTIONAL AREA TO BASE 1.67

STATION CODE	STATION NAME
8200	SCHEDULING

IDENTIFIER — FREQUENCY

	O	FO	R	I	IO	IF	IX	F	SA	A	AR	GEN
PCT	0.	0.32	0.	6.79	0.	92.82	0.06	0.	0.	0.	0.	0.
VCL	0.	1000.	0.	21000.	0.	287001.	188.	0.	0.	0.	0.	0.

	H	D	M	SM	BW	M	Q	SA	A	AR	GEN
PCT	0.	97.99	0.08	0.	0.	0.01	1.27	0.	0.	0.65	0.
VCL	0.	302967.	255.	0.	0.	29.	3938.	0.	0.	2000.	0.

TOTAL STATION VOLUME 309189.
PERCENT STATION TO FUNCTIONAL AREA 62.74
PERCENT FUNCTIONAL AREA TO BASE 2.67

FIGURE 6-3. *Network data load summary report.*

DOCUMENT ACTIVITY REPORT

STATION	NO	FORM TITLE	F VOL	TYPE 1 STATIONS – INTERACTIONS FROM	TYPE 1 STATIONS – INTERACTIONS TO	TYPE 2 STATIONS – INTERACTIONS FROM	TYPE 2 STATIONS – INTERACTIONS TO	TYPE 3 OFF BASE
2000 DATA SERV			D 1000		0	0	0 9999	0 0
			D 026M	2000 2000	0 2000	0 8400	0	0 0
	LOCC050	REQUISITION	R	2000 2000 2000	1 2000 2000 2000	1 8200 8200 8500	2	0 0
			D	2000 2000	0	0 8400	0 9300	0 0
			M		0	0	0 8200	0 0
			Q 108M		0	0	0 8300	0 0
	LOCC060	ROUTED ITM CARD	D 1000	2000 2000	0 2000 2000 2000	1 8220 8210	0 8220	0 0
			M		0	0	0 8210	0 0
			Q 015M		0	0	0 8210	0 0
	LOCC070	SCH SKILL DEGRSE	D		0	0 5000	0 5000	0 0
	LOCC090	UNASSGN CONT CD	D 0031		0 2000	0 8110	0	0 0
	LOCC080	STD ADJUSTMT CD	Q 7000	2000	0 2000	0 7000	0	0 0
			Q 011M	2000 2000 2000	2	0	0 9999	0 0
			Q 018M X	2000	0	0	0 8100 7000	0 0
	LOCC090	UNASSGN CONT CD	D 0081		0	0 8110	0 8110	0 0
	LOCD010	CONTROL NO CD	D 0081		0	0	0 8110	0 0
			M		0	0	0 8110	0 0
	LOCD020	CONT NO CROSS RF	D 0081		0	0	0 8110	0 0
			M		0	0	0 8200 8100 5000	1 0
	LOCD050	STK LIST CHG REF	M 0125		0	0	0 5000 8200	0 0
	LOCE010	ACTUAL LABR UTIL	D 0034		0	0	0 5000 8200	0 0
	LOCE020	MATL COST TRANS	D 0100		0	0	0 4020	0 0
	LOCE030	SKILL ANALYSIS	Q 0029		0	0	0 5000 8500	0 0

FIGURE 6-4. Document activity report.

185

interrelated data-processing activities at numerous stations suggest a strong case for centralized processing, and vice versa.

Flow-Listing Analysis. The event-oriented approach to flow-list analysis emphasizes the fact that an *event* creates a document or action at a particular station and focuses analysis on the chain of related events. Event chains are studied rather than the flow of documents for individual applications, which is the customary approach. Flow lists showing all links in each event chain are easier to prepare, analyze, and modify than charts, and can be prepared by a data processor, as will be described later. Flow lists can, of course, be used to prepare flow charts, if a more graphic display seems useful.

It is important to have a complete chain of documents corresponding to the whole series of events from initiation to completion of some action. As an example, the chain of events related to the major failure of a machine in the factory might run as follows. The operator tells his supervisor of the failure; the supervisor diagnoses the trouble and calls the head of the machine repair section. He dispatches specialists to repair the machine and they may call back for parts and other workers. Upon completion of repairs, the repair specialists advise their heads and the departmental supervisor and return the machine to its production status. In the interests of speed, most of these communications are by voice or telephone; the documents for work orders, labor, time, and material used by the repair crew follow later. The interviewing analyst prepares a message specification sheet for each event, whether verbal or written, in the chain of data flow. An attempt to prepare a flow chart or a flow list will disclose any breaks that may exist in an event chain.

The event-type flow list in Figure 6-5 shows a particular event and its sequence in the chain of events listed by station and document identified with it. Message specification sheets are also identified with each event. The processing actions taken as a result of receiving a document at a particular station are identified on the flow list as affecting the document alone or as also initiating some physical operations.

Producing a flow list consists primarily of tracing the flow of documents throughout an organization and linking them to the events and documents that created them. Any incomplete event chains require further investigation to cure the fault: event chains may be incomplete because the functional area is still to be investigated, the interviewer's analysis was not complete and accurate, or

Figure 6-5. Event-type flow list.

SEQ NUMBER	EVENT	STATION	DOCUMENT NUMBER	ID	FM	F	SPEC TIME	VOL	PROCESSING	ACTION VERB	DOC/STAT	DISPOSITION HOW	DISPOSITION STATION	SEQ NUMBER
4 0.	RECORD CURRENT WKLDS	DATA SERV	FILT080	IO	MT	E		0183	X	PREPAR	FIL 60		DATA SERV	4 1000000.
4 100000.	APLY NEW FAC TO WKLD	DATA SERV	FIL 60	IF	MT	E			X	COMPUT	FIL 61		DATA SERV	4 200000.
4 200000.	DET SPAC REQ BY WKLD	DATA SERV	FIL 60	IF	MT	E			X	COMPAR	FIL 61		DATA SERV	4 300000.
4 300000.	AFTER APPLY FACTORS	DATA SERV	FILT180	IX	MT	E			X	PREPAR	FILT180		DATA SERV	4 400000.
4 310000.	SUMMARIZ TO DCSN COD	DATA SERV	FILT180	IF	MT	E			X	COMPAR	FILT150		DATA SERV	4 320000.
4 320000.	SEMI-ANNUAL PROCESSG	DATA SERV	FILT180	IF	PC	E								4 330000.
4 330000.	AFTER SUMMARIZATION	DATA SERV	FILT180	IF	MT	E			X	UPDATE	FILT180		DATA SERV	4 340000.
4 340000.	PREPARE REPORT	DATA SERV	LOCE110	IF	MT	E			X	PREPAR	LOCE110		AFLC HQS	4 340000.
4 341000.	DISTRIBUTION	DATA SERV	LOCE110	O	DP	E						HNDCY	INDUST ENG	4 350000.
4 342000.	DETERMIN NEW WKLDS	INDUST ENG	LOCE110	IF	DP	E						TRANS	INDUST ENG	4 343000.
4 344000.	DETERMIN CHANGE RQD	INDUST ENG	LOCE110	IF	DP	E			X	COMPAR	LOCE180		INDUST ENG	4 344000.
4 345000.	AFTER E180/55 COMPAR	INDUST ENG	LOCE110	IX	DM	E			X	COMPAR	FIL 55		INDUST ENG	4 345000.
4 345100.	FORWARD FOR PROCESSG	INDUST ENG	LOCA020	O	DM	E			X	PREPAR	LOCA020		INDUST ENG	4 346000.
4 345200.	KEY PUNCH	INDUST ENG	LOCA020	IO	PC	E						HNDCY	DATA SERV	4 345200.
4 345210.	RECORD BUILD MEASURE	DATA SERV	LOCB020	IO	DM	E			X	PREPAR	LOCB020		DATA SERV	4 345300.
4 345211.	NEW SPACE/MAN RATES	DATA SERV	FIL 61	IF	MT	E			X	PREPAR	FIL 61		DATA SERV	4 345210.
4 345212.	MATCH SPACE/WKLD REQ	DATA SERV	FIL 61	IF	MT	E			X	COMPUT	FIL 60		DATA SERV	4 345212.
4 345213.	AFTER COMP SP/MN RAT	DATA SERV	FIL 61	IX	MT	E			X	COMPAR	FIL 61		DATA SERV	4 345213.
4 345214.	SEMI-ANNUAL PROCESSG	DATA SERV	FIL 61	IF	PC	E				UPDATE	FIL 61		DATA SERV	4 345214.
4 346000.	AFTER E180/55 COMPAR	INDUST ENG	LOCE110	IX	DP	E			X				DATA SERV	4 345215.
4 346100.	FORWARD FOR PROCESSG	INDUST ENG	LOCA030	O	DM	E				PREPAR	LOCA030		INDUST ENG	4 347000.
4 346200.	KEY PUNCH	DATA SERV	LOCA030	IF	DM	E			X			HNDCY	DATA SERV	4 346200.
4 346210.	RECORD BLD/WKLD IDTY	DATA SERV	LOCB030	IF	PC	E			X	PREPAR	LOCB030		DESTROY	4 346300.
4 347000.	AFTER E180/55 COMPAR	INDUST ENG	LOCE110	IX	DP	E			X	UPDATE	FIL 60		DATA SERV	4 346220.
4 347100.	FORWARD FOR PROCESSG	INDUST ENG	LOCA050	O	DM	E			X	PREPAR	LOCA050		INDUST ENG	4 348000.
4 347200.	KEY PUNCH	DATA SERV	LOCA050	IF	PC	E			X			HNDCY	DATA SERV	4 347200.
4 347210.	RECORD CURRENT UTILZ	DATA SERV	LOCB050	IO	DM	E			X	PREPAR	LOCB050		DESTROY	4 347220.
4 348000.	AFTER E180/55 COMPAR	INDUST ENG	FIL 61	IF	PC	E			X	UPDATE	FIL 61		DATA SERV	4 349000.
4 348100.	FORWARD FOR PROCESSG	INDUST ENG	LOCA060	IX	DP	E				PREPAR	LOCA060		INDUST ENG	4 348000.
4 348200.	KEY PUNCH	DATA SERV	LOCA060	O	DM	E						HNDCY	DATA SERV	4 348300.
4 348210.	RECORD FUTURE UTIL/N	DATA SERV	LOCB060	IF	PC	E			X	PREPAR	LOCB060		DESTROY	4 348220.
4 349000.	AFTER E180/55 COMPAR	INDUST ENG	LOCE110	IF	DP	E			X	UPDATE	FIL 61		DATA SERV	4 350000.
4 349100.	FORWARD FOR PROCESSG	INDUST ENG	LOCA170	IX	DP	E				PREPAR	LOCA170		INDUST ENG	4 349200.
4 349200.	KEY PUNCH	DATA SERV	LOCA170	O	DM	E						HNDCY	DATA SERV	4 349300.
4 349210.	RECORD SPACE ALLOC	DATA SERV	LOCA170	IF	DM	E			X	PREPAR	LOCB170		DESTROY	4 349220.
4 343000.	REFERENCE + ANALYSIS	AFLC HQS	LOCE110	IF	DP	E			X	UPDATE	FIL 61		DATA SERV	4 351000.
4 350000.	PREPAR BLDG DRAWINGS	INDUST ENG	LOCE110	IF	DP	E			X	STORE	FIL 65		AFLC HQS	4 352000.
4 352000.	AFTER LOC55 COMPARE	INDUST ENG	LOCE110	IX	DP	E			X	COMPAR	LOC 55		INDUST ENG	4 353000.
4 352100.	DISTRIBUTION	AFLC HQS	LOC 56	O	DM	E				PREPAR	LOC 56	AMAIL	AFLC HQS	4 352200.
4 352200.	REFERENCE + ANALYSIS	AFLC HQS	FILT180	IF	MT	E			X			AMAIL	AFLC HQS	4 352300.
4 350000.	SEMI-ANNUAL PROCESSG	AFLC HQS	FIL 63	IF	MT	E				STORE	FIL 64		AFLC HQS	4 360000.
4 351000.	SEMI-ANNUAL PROCESSG	AFLC HQS	FIL 63	IF	PC	E				PREPAR	FIL 63		AFLC HQS	4 352000.
4 400000.	SLMI ANNUAL PROCESSG	DATA SERV	FIL 60	F	PC	E			X				DATA SERV	4 500000.

END OF THIS CHAIN

187

there are actually gaps and inconsistencies in the data system being studied by reason of documents having been prepared but not issued, or received but not utilized.

From the flow list of event chains, the analyst obtains an over-all view of how the organization contributes and reacts to events. The document activity and relationships within each event chain are clearly depicted as an aid in redesigning data flow. Producing flow lists from data collection sheets and tracing them through to their logical conclusions force complete documentation and point up deficient areas resulting from incomplete interviewing and the possibility that either stations do not realize what documents they receive, or they fail to use them properly. Event chains that remain incomplete after further study point up a need to improve the present system either by discontinuing delivery of the document to that station or by advising the station of the existence of such information at no cost.

File Analysis.   Facts collected for each file include details about data elements, activity volume by frequency of processing and activity type, and other characteristics. File analysis determines file characteristics, locates file redundancies or similarities, and compiles a list of documents and data elements in the files.

The data about inputs and files are analyzed to identify file redundancies in two ways. First, the forms that affect a file are identified with it; this is a *forms-to-file* approach. Second, files are examined to determine which ones are based on data taken from the same documents; this is a *file-from-forms* approach.

If one form is used in the preparation of two or more files, there is some duplication in file content. However, close examination of format, arrangement of items, time periods covered, and degree of detail is required to determine the actual degree of redundancy in the files and whether it should be eliminated.

A broad-gauge approach isolates obvious redundancies in files, so that people can study the most promising cases. First, a list is made of all the forms and documents used with each file. The lists are then arranged in the numerical sequence of the identification numbers for all documents going into that particular file; for example, file A: forms 180, 213, 550, and 672.

Out of a given number of files, three selected files, A, C, and F, each based on certain forms and documents, may be listed as follows:

File	Forms and document numbers going into each file
File A	180, 213, 550, 672
File C	109, 267, 435, 863
File F	109, 213, 267

Next, the form and document source numbers can be compared for two files at a time to determine the degree of repetition or uniqueness of file content. The comparison can be made visually for a small number of files. For a large number of files, a data processor can be used to compare the document numbers and make the redundancy search. Comparing the contents of files A and C indicates no documents in common. Comparing the contents of files A and F indicates one common document—213. Comparison of C and F indicates that two documents—numbers 109 and 267—are common to both.

By analyzing all files and their source documents, it is possible to determine redundant files that may be merged with little or no loss of information. In the example above, file F could be dropped if one more document—213—were used in keeping file C, for it would be based on documents 109, 213, 267, 435, and 863. File A, on the other hand, is based on only one form—213; which is in either file C or F. Viewed differently, files A and C together contain the same documents as file F. If files A and C are suitably arranged so that the file F content—degree of detail, format, time period, and user convenience—is available in them, file F can be dropped with no loss of information.

Redundancy in files can occur in another way. Assume that several files contain mostly dissimilar data from many different types of documents, but that they also contain a small amount of the same data from a limited number of other documents. Each time data in the common part of each file changes, all the users must update their files. In such a case, it may be worthwhile to design a new file for this common element alone in order to increase user convenience. The actual problem of redundancy in files is much bigger and more intricate than these simple illustrations indicate. They merely give an inkling of the nature of the problem. An equally big redundancy problem exists for reports.

A file analysis report can be prepared to identify all the data elements throughout the whole organization and prepare an alphabetic list by name. It also identifies files by the station location and the particular data elements contained. The analyst can learn several things about data storage from file analysis as described here. Calculation of activity in and out of a file provides a check on the correctness of statistics gathered during interviews. Developing file-activity volume by frequency period for processing gives the analyst some idea of the static or dynamic nature of the files and therefore the type of storage media best suited for the files—magnetic tape, random access, punched cards, or microfilm.

File analysis for data elements, similarities, and redundancies serves as a guide to file reorganization. No hard conclusion is possible about each factor because other features of the operating organization—say, the need to have files nearby for ready reference in the sales department—may warrant keeping a file that is nearly a duplicate of one kept by inventory control. But it may be possible, through technical changes, to offer the several users a superior storage and reference technique even though files are centralized.

Automated Analysis.   The analysis of processing procedures described above is similar in many ways to what people commonly do with paper and pencil alone in traditional office systems and analysis work. But it also has the interesting feature that data processors can do much of the routine work after systems analysts obtain the initial facts. One approach to using data processors for organizing the facts obtained about the flow of documents was developed at The RAND Corporation and has been named AUTOSATE (Automated Data Systems Analysis Technique). The introduction of an electronic processor for completely organizing and analyzing the facts collected about the flow of data in a system has three important features. First, input collection is simplified and standardized so that nonanalysts can be trained to collect facts. Second, most of the routine work that analysts do to organize and understand—checking, tracing, reconciling, verifying and flow-charting—can be turned over to the processor. Freeing people from these chores enables them to do more rigorous and thorough analysis. Third, analysts can devote their attention to higher-level analysis and creative design work. Schemes, whether manual or automatic, for analyzing data flows are applicable to proposed as well as existing systems. They can, therefore, be used during the design stage to test the feasibility of a system and discover weak points before the system is introduced. Such searching analysis during the design stage can lead to better systems design.

SYSTEMS EVALUATION

A major aspect of systems analysis and design is the evaluation of any proposed system both as a comprehensive system and in terms of its component subsystems. System evaluation has three phases: (1) formulate reasonable alternatives to the proposed system, (2) appraise the costs and benefits associated with each alternative, and (3) explicitly describe both the alternatives and the results of appraising them.

System development projects are often large and the people responsible may prefer to dispense with the formulation and appraisal of alternative systems as a way of selecting the most promising one from among several possibilities. The work involved in analyzing and designing one large system is a major task that can easily occupy all available personnel so that it may seem as though no one is available to evaluate the proposed system. Evaluation and constructive criticism may be more difficult than the original creative design work. Furthermore, electronic data-processing systems are new and exciting enough that some people consider them to be both inherently good and inevitable. There appears, so the argument commonly runs, to be little or no need for critical evaluation of a proposed system.

The results of unquestioning acceptance of a system design may be catastrophic. Design and implementation schedules set up in terms of months may stretch out to years. New system performance may be little or no better than with the prior system, but costs may be much higher. When a system is viewed in its entirety without regard for its segments, the two or three most profitable applications may be lost among a dozen marginal ones. Thus, even though few people are capable of evaluating major system proposals, careful evaluation is vital. The potential payoff from improved design and reduced mistakes is worth the cost of temporary diversion of personnel from basic design work.

Reasonable Alternatives

The first step in systems evaluation is to develop a good set of reasonable alternatives in order to select the best system from the set. When developing alternative systems, it is necessary to examine problems that are more fundamental than merely selecting different kinds and arrangements of hardware: the job itself deserves re-examination. Requirements for data processing may seem, at first, to be fixed, but closer examination of surrounding circumstances often reveals that the application requirements have some flexibility. For example, initial plans may call for daily updating of the entire inventory master file consisting of 800 character records, which, upon re-examination, functions nearly as well with a short record and weekly updating. For a third possibility, an elaborate system of on-line updating of longer records may increase ability to fill customers' orders and offset any increase in data system costs. The important point is that, for stated requirements, it is possible to design a number of different systems with varying features, costs, and benefits. Many systems may have to be designed and all of them analyzed in order to find one that is near optimum. It is not feasible to ensure that the optimum system be included in the group for analysis because it is often possible to design a system superior to any already designed. The real objective is to get a near optimum system, although not necessarily the best conceivable.

The notion of a reasonable alternative system deserves emphasis. Each possible alternative system evaluated should be as efficient as possible. A company might, for example, have an expensive manual data system. In preparation for automation, the analyst may identify many superfluous functions and inefficient operations. To develop a fair basis for choosing between alternatives, a modified manual system should be designed containing the same functions and improved flows as the proposed automated system. If the existing manual system is treated as an alternative to a newly-designed automatic system, two errors can occur. First, all credit for potential improvements in the old system go to the new system, and, second, the new system may be less efficient than it should be because the competition is not keen.

Appraise Alternatives

The keystone of systems evaluation is to appraise the costs and benefits associated with alternative systems. At first, electronic data-processing equipment was applied to system areas that were well defined and efficiently operating, such as payroll or billing. Often the equipment was devoted to one or a few applications, and the output was essentially the same as before: paychecks or bills. Since the system outputs were the same as before, the benefits remained constant, and the criterion for selecting the best system was simply economy of operation.

Currently, data-processing systems are expected to furnish improved outputs: produce information useful to management, facilitate business operations, or provide better service to customers. The analyst needs to evaluate both the costs of operating the system and the benefits it will produce because both may change. In practice, the appraisal of benefits is likely to be quite difficult. An analyst can hypothesize that more frequent reports on inventory position—weekly instead of monthly—will permit reduction of inventory without unduly increasing the risk of running out of stock. But the actual amount of benefit from more frequent inventory reports can be learned with certainty only after the system is built and operating. Obviously, a company cannot afford the luxury of building alternative data-processing systems for the sole purpose of learning which one is best.

The problem of systems appraisal is further complicated by the advent of large data processors that are versatile enough to handle many applications. The processes of systems analysis, design, development, implementation, and operation for all applications are closely related, and many costs are common to several applications —joint costs—so that calculation of costs for individual applications is difficult, if not impossible. As a result, new systems evaluation is likely to be made in terms of total cost versus total benefits for all applications. Marginal and unprofitable applications may survive to dilute the highly profitable ones because individual appraisal is difficult. These difficulties of estimating costs and benefits require that adequate manpower and calendar time be allotted to systems evaluation. Tentative results of evaluation should be available early enough to guide selection of a particular design before commitments are firmed up and large-scale development starts.

Two approaches to evaluation of alternatives are (1) the simple procedure of identifying and listing the relevant costs and benefits, and (2) the use of simulation techniques to estimate the outcome of certain courses of action if they are adopted.

Costs and Benefits. The simple approach to appraising alternative systems is to make a list of costs and benefits, such as that shown in Table 6-1, for each system studied.

The costs of the hardware selected for each proposed data processing system can be obtained from the equipment manufacturer. The operating expenses contain several elements of costs that are often ignored in system planning. Programming expenses may remain high throughout the life of a large system. Few large systems work properly initially so that they need continuous modification and improvement for several years. For companies that face constantly changing conditions, as is true for most, the amount of reprogramming effort may be high throughout the life of a data-processing system.

Proposed System Costs

  Hardware

    Basic processor
    Storage and input-output
    Communications
    Facilities
    Equipment maintenance

  Operating Expenses

    Programmers to maintain the system
    Equipment operators
    Keypunchers and media preparers
    Data collectors
    Data control and correction
    Electricity, heating, and air conditioning
    Cards, paper, and tapes

  Development Costs

    Hiring and training programmers and analysts
    Salaries of programmers and analysts
    Salaries of additional study team or developmental personnel
    Disruption of normal operations
    Retraining of displaced personnel
    Establishment of new files

Proposed System Benefits

  Decreased Operating Costs

    Fewer people
    Less inventory
    Fewer penalties for late delivery or payment
    Reduced spoilage of goods
    Lower transportation or purchasing costs for material
    Fewer shortages to interrupt production
    Better scheduling of production

  Increased Revenues

    Ability to handle more customers with existing facilities
    More customers by faster or more dependable service
    Higher price or more customers from better quality of product

TABLE 6-1. *Proposed system costs and benefits.*

The operating costs for collecting data and correcting mistakes are likely to be large, but are frequently underestimated. Clerical or production workers are expected to collect large amounts of data. While each data collection event may appear trivial, the total during a day can easily run an hour or so per person. Electronic data-processing systems have immense capabilities to process data, but their rigid requirements for input format and completeness increase the cost of data collection over that for an existing manual system.

Most new systems contain extensive provisions for checking input data and rejecting incorrect data since errors degrade the accuracy of records. Much systems design work presumes that a person will correct and resubmit each rejected transaction. Large costs are likely to be incurred in controlling erroneous data during the correction process to make sure they are returned for processing. Data control costs are high, especially for a new system, but continue throughout the life of a system.

New system development is an expensive process. Unless a firm has adequate personnel, it must incur large hiring and training costs. Tens or hundreds of man years are commonly spent on development, implying outlays of many thousand to several million dollars. The costs for developing alternative systems may vary as much as the hardware costs. For example, simple modifications to an existing manual system may require little development, whereas a large automated system has high costs for both hardware and development.

New or improved data systems offer two major types of benefits: decreased operating costs, or increased revenues, or both. The precise nature of benefits depends on the company so that only a few general guides are possible here. A typical benefit associated with a new system in paper handling firms—for example, banking and insurance—is a reduction in clerical personnel. Many industrial companies implement inventory control systems to reduce the total investment in inventory and the costs of maintaining it. Improved scheduling and production control are becoming common applications to cut production costs. These decreases in operating costs are listed as benefits here, although many people prefer to treat them as negative costs.

Increases in revenues may be obtained in several ways: through better utilization of equipment, faster service, or a higher price for a better quality product. Airlines reservation systems help bring in more revenue by increasing the number of passengers carried per flight. Mail order companies attract more business by a prompt, dependable, order-filling system. An electronics equipment manufacturer can obtain a higher price for a more nearly uniform product by means of a superior quality-control system. Each of these firms can pay more for a new data system if it receives a correspondingly greater increase in revenues. Assignment of dollar values to system benefits is difficult, but it is an important aspect of appraising alternative systems. Many decisions must still be made on the basis of judgment, but a careful listing of cost and benefits is a powerful aid to judgment.

Simulation.   The key to the desirability of a new data-processing system is the benefits that it will produce; but the benefits are difficult to measure until the system is actually implemented and operating. The search for better ways to estimate the overall performance of a proposed system, as reflected in either reduced costs or increased revenues, has led to the development of simulation as one analytical tool with much promise.

The simulation technique follows through, step-by-step on paper, in a data processor or in other symbolic fashion, the events that are likely to occur in the proposed system. The simulation analyst uses past experience plus forecasts for the future to estimate the type, timing, and quantity of events that result in data input. For example, the events under study may be the arrival of customer orders. In designing the proposed system, the analyst describes how each order is handled. He can play the input event against the proposed system and keep track of what happens as each order arrives: how long the order waits until someone handles it, what happens to an order containing an error, how often goods are unavailable to fill the order, etc. By keeping track of what happens in processing numerous orders in simulated operations, the analyst can estimate performance of the proposed system. Manual simulation with pencil and paper is slow; however, in a few minutes a large data processor can follow through thousands of events and months or years of operations to yield, at low cost, a large amount of simulated experience.

An example of simulation to evaluate a system for a mail order firm with one wholesale warehouse and several retail centers will clarify operation of the process. Customers phone or mail orders to the retail centers, which fill the orders, if possible, from available stock. When a particular item runs low, the center sends a request to the warehouse for more stock.

Under the existing system, each retail center returns about twenty percent of customers' orders with a suggestion that they reorder in fifteen days because the center is out of stock. Sales department analysis shows that fifty percent of the orders returned are not placed later. Furthermore, twenty-five percent of the customers whose orders are refused do not order again. On the basis of this data, the sales department estimates that each one percent reduction in the rate of orders refused will increase the merchandising margin by $5,000 per month because of increased sales to existing customers and reduced turnover of customers.

Information about the consequences of a certain action is vital to evaluating the impact of changes in system performance on revenue. Investigation indicates a number of causes for the high rate of refusals. The current data system uses batch processing to update one-fifth of the stock item balances each day, check balances against reorder points, and place requests with the warehouse for more stock. Since each item is updated and checked only once a week, a big increase in sales of an item may go unnoticed until it is too late to prevent a stockout.

The data systems design group proposes three schemes to decrease the order refusal rate. The first scheme is to install a random-access data-processing system to update stock balances as each sale is processed so that a request is sent to the warehouse as soon as an item reaches its reorder point.

A second scheme is to retain batch processing but install a larger data-processing system to update balances for one-half of the items every night so that each item is checked every two days instead of once a week. A third scheme is to retain the present data system but increase the quantity of stock on hand at each center. Rather than pay for more information, the company will maintain more inventory and incur larger costs for warehousing and stock control.

The costs of these three schemes can be estimated readily, but selection of the best scheme depends on both its costs and benefits. Irregular arrival of customers' orders makes it difficult to analyze benefits. Few orders arrive on some days and huge numbers on other days. Furthermore, the mix of items ordered by customers varies from day-to-day so that average sales figures are not useful for evaluating the proposed schemes.

The simulation procedure for dealing with the irregularity of customer order volume and product mix is to prepare a list of customers' orders showing the arrival time, item, and quantity for each order based on, say, last year's orders as an estimate of next year's orders or on mathematical methods for generating typical order patterns. The inventory used when starting the simulation of the first two schemes can be the quantity actually on hand at a selected date or perhaps an ideal inventory with the same total cost. For the third scheme, a larger investment in inventory is planned, so that the larger inventory is set up and used in starting the simulation.

Simulated operations start by advancing time in constant intervals of, say, one hour or from one major event to the next. In each interval, the simulated orders arrive for filling. Each stock item is updated for the balance remaining on hand and resupply is requested from the warehouse if the quantity on hand goes below the reorder point.

When simulating the first scheme, each customer's order is processed immediately. If stock is available, the order is recorded as filled and the quantity-on-hand of each item requested is reduced by the amount ordered. If stock is not available, the order is recorded as refused either in total or for individual lines. If a stock item is below its reorder point, a resupply request is sent to the warehouse and after a delay of several simulated days, the new stock arrives and the balance on hand is increased. No stock is really involved, of course, for the entire process is simulated by appropriate changes in the numbers representing balances on hand.

The same process is followed when simulating the other schemes. However, for the second scheme, the balances for half the stock items are updated on alternate days instead of immediately. For the third scheme, the balances are updated once each week, but the inventory used to start the simulation is larger and the reorder points are set higher than in the first two simulations in order to maintain larger inventories.

Each major event is recorded throughout a simulation period of suitable length, and the analyst obtains detailed facts about system performance: number of orders, pattern of orders, items ordered, percent of orders refused, number of resupply actions, and inventory balances.

After all three schemes are simulated, the analyst can evaluate proposed system costs and benefits as shown in Table 6-2 which uses the existing batch data-processing system as a benchmark. The cost shown for each scheme is merely the change in cost from the present system. Similarly, the benefits are the change in revenue from the present system.

The results shown in Table 6-2 might be interpreted as follows. The random access system appears to produce the largest net benefit, but it entails a substantial increase in cost. A conservative company may prefer to improve the batch system since it produces large net benefits at a small increase in cost. System costs become largely fixed after a company installs a new data system, but benefits may not actually arise. The third scheme appears clearly undesirable for it incurs large costs and produces only a small net benefit.

Alternative	Percent of Orders Rejected	Increase in Margin	Increase in Cost	Net Benefit
Current system	20	......	......	......
Random-access system	5	$75,000	$31,000	$44,000
Improved batch system	11	$45,000	$10,000	$35,000
More stock	10	$50,000	$41,000	$ 9,000

TABLE 6-2. *Results of simulating three proposed schemes for improving order filling by a mail-order company.*

The simulated results may, of course, be erroneous; however, they are probably superior to mere estimates of system performance, and especially so for complex situations.

Explicit Description

A written description of a system evaluation study is most important. There is an obligation to state clearly and explicitly what the analyst does regardless of the study technique—mere listing of costs and benefits, simulation, or some other. Managers reviewing the study need to know much more than simply which scheme the analyst concludes is best. Managers may have information unavailable to the analyst—for example, plans for company expansion or introduction of a new product—that will influence system selection. Furthermore, results are seldom clear-cut. Managers need to examine the preparation of cost and benefit estimates to appraise their validity and merits. For these reasons, detailed discussion of the assumptions and reasoning serving as the foundation for a study is more important than description of conclusions.

Numbers are invaluable for explicit description. For example, the phrase "a large reduction in order refusal rate" is ambiguous; whereas, "a reduction in refusal rate from twenty percent to ten percent" is meaningful. But, quite often numbers are only estimates and should be described as such. An attempt to assign a number to system benefits or refusal rate helps to sharpen the problems involved and clarify the assumptions—which might otherwise remain implicit—that are required for their solution.

From beginning to end, systems evaluation is difficult. However, systems evaluation is a valuable aspect of systems analysis if reasonable alternatives are selected, costs and benefits are analyzed, and the study results are described in clear, explicit fashion.

APPROACHES TO SYSTEMS DESIGN

Systems design is the creative act of devising or inventing a partially or completely new scheme for processing data. Design work, which follows systems analysis, should attempt to cope with more than just the problems discovered during the analysis phase. Systems designers should pay special attention to demands by management and operating personnel for information outputs from the system. These demands are important and even controlling objectives of systems design.

It might seem that both analysis and design work could be done by analysts because they have the best insight into problems and are best armed to solve them. Although this may be so, analysis and design have an important difference. One involves fact-finding, whereas the other depends on creativity, imagination, and an awareness of what might be done. The important point here is that systems analysis is only a base, and not the sole foundation for creative systems-design work.

The degree of freedom offered systems designers in any particular situation ranges from nearly none to almost carte blanche to design whatever seems useful for the organization. The approaches to systems design that are of interest here range from merely simplifying the present system, through mechanization, to developing either a new data system or a completely new management-information system. Each of these approaches to systems design and the conditions for which it is suitable will be considered.

Simplification

The systems designer may merely simplify the existing system. The techniques long used by systems and procedures analysts are suitable for this job, which may include designing forms that are easier to prepare and use, eliminating useless data, planning for more efficient flows of data, consolidating files, and devising improvements in the existing processing techniques. Simplification might be considered the *economy approach* to systems design. It requires a relatively small amount of manpower, time, capital, and technical skill.

The simplification approach is often appropriate, but its implications should be recognized. Its adoption implies that analysis shows the system is basically satisfactory in that it produces or, with minor changes, will produce the kinds of operating and management information wanted throughout the business. This approach may be adequate when inefficiencies exist that can be eliminated by simplifying or eliminating operations, documents, files, and reports that have only limited value. When, however, an important opportunity for technical improvement exists, then a broader approach is desirable.

Mechanization

The mechanization approach to systems design has an important feature in common with the simplification approach: the inputs, data flows, files, and outputs are considered essentially fixed. New equipment and processing procedures are then introduced to get a more efficient combination of hardware and people. This might be considered the *efficiency approach*. The existing structure of the data-processing system is, to the extent possible, merely retained while new equipment is introduced. Systems redesign is minimized, although some changes are required merely to utilize equipment or to take advantage of its best features.

The introduction of more equipment may be warranted merely because such equipment becomes available or because the nature of the business changes enough to deserve more elaborate techniques. Since some important technical changes are involved in the mechanization approach, advance planning is necessary to develop an efficient combination of equipment, people, and procedures. Advance planning extends to the preparation of detail specifications for the system designed around new equipment; the appraisal of system data loads, information requirements, and equipment capability in order to match them; and planning and debugging to make the equipment operate efficiently. Of course, mechanization requires installation of new equipment and displacement of some existing methods.

Example of Mechanization. An interesting example of an increase in the degree of mechanization with other system changes limited is that provided by one version of an integrated data-processing approach. This version of integrated data-processing started in the early 1950's by joint action of several industrial companies and many office machine and processing equipment manufacturers.

The concept of integrated data-processing discussed here was developed to cope with the inefficiencies of fragmentary processing. In fragmentary processing, the over-all task is divided into small parts for people and limited-purpose equipment to handle. The high degree of specialization needed to handle large, complex applications leads to excessive duplication for individual operations at each work station. Duplication reflected in merely recopying constant or repetitive data—for example, names, addresses and item descriptions—is an important cause of inefficiency resulting in high clerical costs and errors.

Each department in an organization wants documents and reports that may vary only slightly in content, but these small differences often require preparation of entirely new copies. Mechanization for repeating constant or common data at each stage of document processing is an important element of integrated data processing. Integrated data processing uses basically standard office machines— typewriters, calculators, cash registers, adding machines, and book-keeping machines—that are modified to produce and to operate from some low-speed media such as punched paper tape or edge-punched cards. Repetitive data are punched in tape or cards when first originated or as soon thereafter as feasible. Tapes are stored and run through the machines to repeat the repetitive data when preparing new documents. New data are introduced at each stage through the machine keyboards. Selected portions of the old and new data are repunched into tape by the read-punch office machines in any department handling the transaction. Tapes are filed and later used when required.

Data in punched paper tape are transmittable over wire circuits. But some organizations mail punched tape overnight to save money yet suffer little delay in processing. Others convert punched cards to tape for mailing to avoid the cost of mailing cards or of wire-sending either the card or tape data. Rapid communication by one means or another is important for efficient processing in a geographically-scattered organization.

The fundamental point is that mechanization reduces the manual element in duplicating repetitive data. Operations are similar, in many respects, to those in a manual system except that five-channel tape or a similar media ties them together and increases the degree of mechanization. Of course, planning and personnel training are required to set up an integrated system, but the amount of preparatory work is limited, since procedures continue basically unchanged even though mechanized.

Data System Redesign

If the systems designer has fairly broad freedom to select an approach to design, he may devise a new data system. Management procedures, as reflected in the data-processing outputs, may be firmly established, but the processing procedures and data inputs may be modifiable. If so, the most that a systems designer can hope to do is develop a new data system consisting of new input and processing techniques that will improve operations yet produce essentially the same outputs as before. The designer can simplify inputs—for example, adopt a scheme of single point origination of data—consolidate files, and change processing. This greater freedom compared to the simplification and mechanization approaches may lead to designing a system to supply more data faster and cheaper than before.

After a new data system is designed, and to some extent during the design phase, it is useful to apply the analysis techniques described earlier to study the origination and flow of data, file redundancies, and preparation of outputs. Analysis helps ensure that the system will supply the outputs that management and operating personnel demand as necessary. In developing a new data system with the degree of freedom considered here, changes are not contemplated in the outputs wanted by management or in the way that management makes decisions. Such changes require a broader degree of freedom, which will be covered later.

Example of Data System Redesign. File processing is a typical area for data system redesign. Fragmentary processing implies multiple runs of the master files. Transactions are classified by type in a logical order for processing and then sorted into sequence corresponding to the file, if records are maintained in an orderly sequence. Logical ordering by transaction type—receipts ahead of issues—is required for correctly processing files regardless of storage technique. But sequencing within each type of transaction is not required for files in random-access storage.

In the more extreme case, all files for a business might be kept in one consolidated master file. Such consolidation minimizes duplication of file contents that ordinarily occurs throughout an organization. Any transaction, assuming an appropriate instruction program and capable processing facilities, can be processed against the files whenever desired. If access to files is quick enough, transactions can be handled on-line without any delay.

For a more realistic approach, the *functionally integrated* or *consolidated* approach means that the segments in a fragmentary system are combined into larger but not completely comprehensive units. Some degree of consolidation is warranted if various parts of the operating organization are closely related and if input, processing, files, and output have some usage in common. Consolidated processing requires larger-scale facilities than fragmentary processing, but eliminates the duplicate parts of files so that total file requirements are reduced. Any type of transaction can be handled in any logical sequence, since all files are available for processing. A master program calls up the appropriate operating program for completely processing each transaction encountered. Both kinds of instruction routines—the master and operating—are likely to be large and complex, and exceptional situations usually involve elaborate programming.

Functional integration goes much further than mechanized duplication because it cuts across departmental boundaries for the purpose of consolidating data processing as such. Inventory files containing quantity and dollar values illustrate the features of separate and consolidated files. Two groups of clerks—accounting and stock control—keep and maintain separate files in a manual system. Each group wants sole control over records for convenience and to fulfill its responsibility. However, electronic processors can handle equally well the dollar value and quantity transactions against both files. The two kinds of transactions and files are so closely related that one consolidated file for joint processing may be most efficient.

Functional integration may require fundamental changes in the organizational structure to achieve the most efficient combination of new equipment, procedures, and people. This *may* result in merging departments and making far-reaching procedural changes. Developing and installing a system to integrate functions is likely to involve large-scale equipment, personnel orientation and training, and intensive planning. Consolidated files permit more efficient processing because transactions can be entered in one or a few runs of the central file, whereas separate files require individual processing.

Management System Design

When the system designer has essentially complete freedom, the optimal approach may be to overhaul the present management information system or develop a new one. This means that the decision rules used by management and the information required to implement them are open for examination and possible change, but the power to make changes in the decision rules remains with management.

This broad-gauge approach to designing a management-decision system places the data-processing system in proper perspective as one of the factors of production for the whole organization. Each factor of production—factory worker, equipment, and material—has certain costs associated with it and makes some contribution to the organization's operations. Information about operations and the decision rules used to control operations also have their costs and benefits. Costs arise, first, in developing and testing a data-information and decision-making system, and second, in operating it to produce information and make decisions.

Measurement of the cost of information involves uncertainties because some data-processing operations are obligatory—for example, data gathering, processing and reporting for tax purposes. Some data are necessary for operating purposes almost independently of management considerations. Only a few circumstances require data gathering and manipulation solely for management and these may be primarily for operations-research type studies to answer such questions as, "What will happen if we make certain changes to operate this way instead of that?" Sometimes the study of available data will answer these questions, but in many cases new data must be gathered. Gathering new data is likely to increase costs for systems planning and design, for the operating department involved, and also for the data-processing department. Sometimes answers to specific questions are derived by intensive analysis of existing data.

The benefits that accrue from information and decisions are reduced costs or increased revenues throughout an organization. Some aspects of information output that are valuable for operating purposes are the degree of detail and arrangement of reports, frequency of reporting, time period covered, time limits permitted for issuing routine reports and answering special questions, completeness, the degree of focus on important problems, ease of use by management, accuracy, and precision. The benefits obtainable from having more information depend on the improvement achieved in operating results. Measurement, therefore, involves the same difficulties as measuring the results obtained for many of the support services in an organization or the overhead factors of production. The net value of having more or better information is equal to the increase in benefits minus the increased costs of supplying it.

Example of Management System Design.   The steps taken by a large organization to overhaul its inventory control and resupply policies illustrate the design of a substantially new data-information system. Before redesign, each sales-office warehouse kept books for stock on hand, managed its own stock position, and placed orders for its optimal resupply quantity when the balance reached the reorder point. Customer orders were cleared centrally for credit since many customers were located throughout wide regions and ordered from several sales offices. The warehouse nearest the customer filled the order, but the home office issued invoices and collected accounts receivable.

There were many possibilities for system redesign in this organization, but the one of most interest here is inventory control and resupply action. Problems were presented by the fact that each warehouse tried to manage its own inventory and guard against running out of stock. These precautions resulted in increased costs from carrying excessive inventories. Safety levels were higher than necessary and resupply action was earlier, more frequent, or for larger amounts than was required to maintain the company-wide optimum inventory. Economic order quantities and reorder points were recomputed for each warehouse each six months on a scheduled basis without regard for the stock level at that time and when reorders were placed. Such a system might be characterized as a *pull* system, for each warehouse kept its records, managed its inventory, and took its own resupply action to get its inventory.

Management was not satisfied with the scheme in use because customers' orders were not filled promptly, as reflected in the back-order and cancellation rate; inventory policies were sub-optimized at the warehouse level instead of optimized company-wide, and data-processing output seemed unsatisfactory and costs excessive. Furthermore, the prospects for improving the system seemed small, unless a radically new approach for data processing and management control was adopted.

One approach proposed for dealing with the problems described here is to centralize inventory management and switch from a pull to a push scheme for resupply action. *Push* means that action will be initiated centrally to send stock to each warehouse—literally to push it out of the factories to the warehouses. Adoption of the push approach to warehouse stockage implies important changes in the data-processing and management system. This plan involves centralizing inventory recordkeeping and discontinuing local records. Since orders are checked centrally for credit approval, information on customer demand is available when orders are first handled. Data for actual issues can be obtained as a by-product of invoicing. Factory shipments to warehouses will serve, with appropriate adjustments for time-delay, nonreceipts, and mistakes, as warehouse receipts. Thus adequate data are available centrally to keep stock records and manage inventory. Centralized calculation of reorder points and quantities permits optimum planning on a company-wide basis instead of sub-optimizing at the local level. Each time the balance at any warehouse drops to the reorder point, the position for all warehouses and the factory can be reappraised to determine the desired total stock throughout the company and the best allocation between warehouses and factories, including transfer between warehouses, if appropriate.

The important implications of the push system of inventory control are centralized recordkeeping and company-wide stock management. Recordkeeping and inventory control at sales offices can be virtually eliminated, thus allowing concentration on selling, warehousing, and order-filling. Local management may believe their authority reduced, since they are likely to consider inventory management inseparable from recordkeeping. However, the ability of local management to forecast and plan sales can and should be used as an input to central planning of stock levels and resupply action. The company gains in several ways from centralized control. Better information about customers' demands are available for inventory management, since original order data can be analyzed at the earliest point. Company management is not forced to rely on warehouse resupply action, which is, at best, a delayed and erratic indicator of customer demand. Inventory optimization is easier to achieve because the whole company's position—all warehouses and factories—are considered together instead of as individual units; and the company-wide position can be reappraised whenever inventory action is indicated for any warehouse.

The inventory control and analysis problems described in this example are not unique; many companies have similar problems of processing data for and managing nation-wide inventories. As an outstanding example, airlines have developed the most elaborate solutions to the control of seat sales, since the stakes—the value of unsold or oversold seats—are high.

Selection of an Approach

Many factors enter into the selection of a suitable approach to systems design. Some of the important factors are (1) the skill of the designers in developing, devising, and inventing new methods, (2) the degree of satisfaction throughout the organization with the present information output and management decision policies, (3) the availability of important technical improvements in equipment, (4) increases in capabilities of people, (5) the possibility of inventing new design schemes, (6) time schedules, (7) financial considerations, (8) how recently an important change has been made and whether it is fully "digested," and (9) the receptivity of operating and management personnel to important changes.

Factors that contribute to substantial redesign of data systems and even the creation of entirely new concepts are management dissatisfaction with existing information and decision-making structures, important improvements in the capabilities of equipment and people, adequate financial budgets, and suitable lead times before a system must be operational. But, regrettably, there is no ready formula for relating these factors to the design approach selected in a particular situation.

SUMMARY

There are four phases or stages in introducing a new system: analysis of the existing system, selection of a design approach, design of the new system, and implementation of the new system to displace the existing one. Initially, the plans may be to handle each phase in turn since they have a logical order, although they are closely interrelated. For example, the optimum amount of analysis depends on the possibility of implementing any system likely to be designed. Thus, each phase requires some consideration of the implications of other phases. After the first pass through all phases, it may be useful to recycle through one or more phases. At some point in introducing a new system, all four phases may be active.

The systems-analysis phase involves fact-finding and critical examination of the facts about a system. This requires determining the demands for data and information for operating and managing an organization, the sources of data, and the processing methods and files serving as a link between input and output. The organizational environment has important bearing on the kinds and volumes of information wanted for operating and control purposes. The objective of analysis is to learn enough about a system and the demands on it to serve as the foundation for designing and implementing a better system. Analysis is worthwhile if there is dissatisfaction with the outputs because they are late, insufficient, or inaccurate. Processing activities may be troublesome because of excessive costs or burdens placed on other departments to collect data. The timing and amount of analysis is geared to the prospective improvement in over-all operations after counting all costs of analysis, design, and implementation of any changes that are made. Some analysis is warranted whenever conditions either inside or outside the business change enough to offer some opportunity for potential improvements.

Systems analysis consists of five steps: (1) obtaining facts about the types, volumes, and timing of events that lead to the preparation of documents, maintenance of files, and other processing steps; (2) collecting sample copies of filled-in documents, file papers, and reports with facts to indicate activity volumes; (3) studying the how and why of every document each person receives or issues, the processing steps performed, the nature of files he keeps or uses, and the contents of reports; (4) organizing the facts about the flow of data arising from any event into lists or charts to disclose breaks in the event chain between origination and destination; and (5) interviewing document and report users in order to learn what information they use and what they think they need.

There are several ways to obtain and organize facts about the flow of data throughout an organization. AUTOSATE uses formal methods to gather facts about each event chain as it is reflected in messages, inputs, files, outputs, and reports. Formal methods have several desirable features: systems analysts and others with less training can prepare specification sheets about data flow for events, editors can scan the data for completeness and uniformity, and processors can manipulate the data to prepare the event chain reflecting the flow through the organization of the data related to an event.

Event-oriented analysis enables the analyst to develop numerical measures about the characteristics and relationships of stations— the points where similar data originate—and to determine what kinds and amounts of processing capability each station needs, and whether a station should be handled separately or integrated into a comprehensive system. File analysis indicates the nature of files and the need for different storage media and the nature and importance of redundancy. Redundancy is more than a simple matter of two or more files containing the data from one or more identical types of documents. File redundancy can be studied from the viewpoint of one document going into several files—the *forms-to-files* approach; or from the viewpoint of the documents that make up a file—the *files-from-forms* approach. Some redundancy may be planned to provide users with the desired combination and arrangement of data for quick reference. Network load analyses indicate the nature of processing work done at each station and its importance in relation to other work at that station and throughout the organization. People or processors can prepare flow lists showing the source and destination of each document throughout the whole event chain growing out of an initial event. Flow lists are desirable in that they quickly disclose gaps and inconsistencies in the event chain. Also, they are useful during design-planning stages to determine the consequences of various proposed changes. Flow charts can be prepared from the flow lists, if the graphics seem worthwhile.

Systems evaluation, which is important to efficient systems design, has three phases: (1) formulate reasonable alternatives to the proposed system, (2) appraise the costs and benefits of each alternative, and (3) explicitly describe the alternatives and results of appraisal. Systems evaluation is laborious because it requires formulating various systems using different design concepts as well as equipment in order to select the best from the whole range of possibilities including the present system. Remember that two or more choices are needed in order for a decision maker to have any choice.

Cost and benefit estimates are required for each proposed design structure and method of implementation to find the one with the best payoff—the largest excess of benefits over costs. Costs can be easily calculated if the equipment, personnel, space, and supplies required can be estimated correctly. Estimation of benefits is more difficult because systems seldom operate exactly as planned to produce the kinds of information needed to bring about the anticipated management and operating improvements.

Simulation is a useful technique for estimating the benefits that a proposed system is likely to produce by playing through various versions of the system. Furthermore, simulation is useful for design purposes because it furnishes some guidance toward further improvements by testing, under realistic conditions, numerous variations on original plans.

Explicit descriptions of the alternative systems designs considered and of the results obtained in appraising them are useful aids for managers making decisions. Careful, detailed descriptions are also useful for building a systems history so that the organization can develop a "memory" to serve as a foundation for future progress.

Selecting a design approach is often considered part of either the analysis phase or the design phase. The design-approach phase is considered separately here in order to show that some important decisions should be made between the completion of the analysis and the start of the design phase. Knowing all about a system through careful analysis is only a foundation for systems design. An explicit statement of system objectives and selection of a design approach are equally critical to successful design and implementation.

The design approaches discussed here are simplification, mechanization, data system redesign, and information system design. Simplification is a suitable approach when the system produces the desired output and is basically satisfactory except that it is cumbersome or inefficient in certain limited respects. Simplification involves redesigning forms for easier preparation and use, elimination of unwanted data and files, and improvements in existing processing techniques. On the surface, little is changed, although big improvements may be made within the limits imposed.

The mechanization approach to design aims at introducing new equipment and processing procedures to develop a more efficient system while leaving data inputs and report outputs essentially unchanged. Emphasis is placed on mechanizing a system that requires only such moderate advance planning as run diagrams and flow charts for applications to be handled by new equipment, appraisal of system loads and information requirements to match against equipment capability, and planning and debugging to make the equipment operate efficiently. For example, integrated data processing, is built on the concept that data should be captured in machine-processable form when first originated and mechanically reproduced for later use, whenever possible. Integrated data processing uses ordinary types of office machines redesigned to punch and read either punched tape or edge-punched cards. Introduction of this version of integration increases the degree of mechanization but leaves unchanged the basic procedures of the office.

The data system redesign approach presumes a freedom to change both the inputs and processing methods yet still produce the same outputs. This freedom permits the designer to introduce entirely new equipment, develop novel data-origination schemes, and make almost any changes in processing that seem worthwhile. One example of data system redesign is the consolidation of files maintained throughout an organization to achieve functional integration. Other changes may be made in data origination—say, single-point origination of data about an event for dissemination of data to all users. Functional integration cuts across departmental boundaries and may result in merging some functions. Developing and installing a new data system involves large-scale equipment, personnel orientation and training, and intensive planning.

The management-information-system design approach implies essentially complete freedom to develop and produce entirely new kinds of information for management use in running the business. Such freedom may lead to complete overhaul of the present information system or to the design of a new one. The costs and benefits of any proposed system, considering all ramifications throughout the organization, should be estimated to appraise its merits. An example of a new management information system is the shift from warehouse data processing and resupply action to centralized processing and inventory management. The switch from the "pull" to the "push" control approach has important implications for company-wide inventory control and also for management; for example, how the skills and experience—the decision-making know-how—of local managers are utilized, since they are likely to feel left out when recordkeeping and most decision-making are done centrally. Ingenuity is required to make the best use of local management in the inventory-control area.

7
Systems Design

The steps following the systems-analysis work and selection of an approach to systems design are the design and installation of the proposed system. In order to design a proposed system, there must be agreement on the kinds of changes to be made—the outputs wanted, inputs needed, and the organization and content of files required to serve as connecting links between inputs and outputs. It is at the start of the design process that inventiveness and ingenuity offer the biggest pay-off in the development of new and different systems design.

SYSTEMS DESIGN AND LAYOUT

Systems design brings a proposed system much closer to reality by describing the nature of inputs, files, and outputs, and showing the processing procedures by which they are connected. The initial design of processing procedures can be *machine-independent*—they need not be related to particular equipment or even classes of equipment. But as design progresses further, classes and even particular types of equipment must be selected, subject to later revision, of course.

Run diagrams and flow charts are useful for representing the flow of data throughout a business, the processing done at each stage, and the relationships between inputs, files, and outputs. Later, the diagrams and charts are used to prepare detailed routines for equipment and people to follow in implementing the system and making it operational.

The design of inputs, outputs, and files are discussed first; run diagrams, flow charts, and implementation are covered later in the chapter.

Input, Output, and Files

For the purposes of this book, *input* means the facts gathered about events that flow into the data-processing system. *Output* covers the reports, summaries, lists, documents, and answers to questions that the system furnishes to management, operating personnel, and outsiders. *Files* are the accumulated inputs still available to the system for use in preparing output. The data in files may be in their raw state or processed through one or more stages of condensation and summarization and organized in various ways.

Specifications. The development of suitable specifications for content and arrangement of inputs, outputs, and files is an important part of systems design. Output design is the most critical because outputs are the link between the data-processing system and information users—operating and management personnel and outsiders. Consumers do not really care about machines and procedures; they simply want results. The system outputs therefore should be designed to meet the users' requirements. The users may set criteria for content, degree of detail, format, timeliness, and accuracy. These factors affect file and systems design, since anything wanted as output must be planned for in designing files and data inputs and in setting up processing procedures that link inputs to outputs through files. Unless planned for, outputs are likely not to be available when and in the fashion they are wanted.

Summary reports—for example, total company sales for a year—may be readily prepared and these are adequate for evaluation of the organization as a whole. But a higher *degree of detail* is required for management purposes: sales by months or weeks, by products, by salesmen, to customers, by territories, etc. Each additional level or kind of detail requires finer classifications or rearrangement within files that may be most efficiently handled by setting up more files. Some higher-level requirements can be met by summarizing detailed-level files; for instance, territory sales are the total for all salesmen assigned to that territory. But the need for cross-classifications and intricate analyses can lead to files that contain the same data yet are not duplicative because they are organized differently. For example, sales may be classified once by salesman and once by customers, especially where the same customers operate in several sales territories, and a unique relationship does not exist between salesmen and customers.

Timeliness of reporting affects file and systems design in two ways. First, frequent reports at short intervals require the separation of events into successive *reporting periods* by setting up new records or by distinguishing between the several time periods within each record. To keep files from growing indefinitely in content, facts about earlier reporting periods may be purged from the record or the whole record transferred to less active storage. The second aspect of output timeliness is the *reporting delay*—the length of time between the close of a period and distribution of reports. Reporting delay needs special consideration when the reporting system is *event-triggered,* as when the event that a stock item reaches its reorder point triggers some action. Interrogations to learn file content require short-delay reporting because people want quick answers to their questions. Since the system must be designed with adequate capacity to process files and produce outputs within the permissible time, demands for extremely quick reporting lead to high peak loads for equipment, difficult scheduling problems, and elaborate equipment with large costs.

The *degree of accuracy* wanted in system outputs raises problems in designing an adequate data-origination scheme to obtain a high degree of completeness and correctness. Safeguards are also required throughout communication networks to preserve the fidelity of messages and during processing to achieve logical and arithmetical accuracy.

Careful planning for system outputs may permit the complete specification of all files to be maintained and the inputs entering such files. That is, anything wanted as an output must be planned for and obtained as an input; both files and inputs are limiting factors for output. Any output wanted must either be in the files or be derivable from the files, otherwise it is necessary to try to resurrect such facts from outside the system or wait until it is possible to gather the required data. Although it may seem a truism, many people overlook the limitation that a system cannot supply desired outputs unless it contains the necessary inputs. And to supply outputs quickly the inputs must already be in essentially the desired arrangement for output: content, degree of detail, classification, and time periods covered. Only minimal processing is permissible, if output is wanted quickly.

File Content. Of course, files and inputs may contain more, much more, data than reach the output stage. Efficient design depends on keeping excessive data at a minimum consistent with the ability to meet output demands planned in advance and a good probability of meeting demands that arise unexpectedly.

File content depends on input data and the methods of aggregation used in classifying, combining, and summarizing for products, different parts of the organization, and different periods of time. The structure and organization of files depend on the nature of demands for outputs. If output requirements are fully specified in advance, the files can be carefully structured, data inputs used to prepare the specified files, and the inputs discarded. In fact, there is only a limited need for files themselves, if output requirements are so carefully pre-specified that they can be filled and no further demand made for additional information. In such a case, it may be most efficient merely to produce the specified outputs and discard both inputs and the intermediate stages of summarization ordinarily saved as files. This extreme case—prepare reports and discard all else—is unusual. But for most operating situations, some of the utilize-data-and-discard feature is worth considering because it is costly to try to reanalyze raw data and relate them to the whole situation on a retrospective basis. So many pieces have to be fitted back together and people have so much trouble remembering all the circumstances for interpretive purposes that reanalysis may not be worthwhile.

If output requirements are only partly pre-specified and, therefore, depend partly upon new questions that may later arise, files cannot be quite so carefully structured and highly condensed. Files must contain more data than are immediately required in order to meet a high fraction of later demands for information. In fact, some input data may be retained in its raw form for processing on an *ad hoc* basis to meet output requirements when they arise. The most difficult case of file organization occurs when output requirements are so inadequately specified that it is impossible to design organized files to meet requirements. To cope with this uncertainty, much of the input data may be retained in their original form with little organization or condensation to await processing for output requirements when someone decides what he wants.

The practical approach to file design is likely to maintain more voluminous files than are needed for short-run requirements. This extra content assures that many unanticipated requests for output can be filled. In addition, raw input data may be retained for further analysis to prepare reports and answer questions not formulated initially but likely to arise later. Since usually it seems to cost little to obtain and store input data in raw form, the practical approach to gathering and retaining all potentially useful data has some merit. The difficulty lies in the high costs of retrieving and processing data to classify, summarize, and analyze to determine significant relationships. Masses of input data retained in their raw form are difficult to cope with and may result in excessive processing costs, both in money and elapsed time, when trying to prepare useful reports.

Example of File Content. In the work-a-day world, a routine record in a file for an inventory item is likely to contain several dozen data elements and several hundred characters. Cursory examination of the simpler inventory record in Figure 7-1 indicates it is useful for keeping a substantial, even though limited, quantity of data about each inventory item. It can be used for preparing catalogue lists, quantities on hand and on order, items with balances

Stock Number	1 4 3 0 7 5 3 1 3 9	*Ten-digit number*

Stock name	GASKET	*Twenty alphanumeric*

Quantity on hand	0 1 2 0 0	*Five-digit number*

Quantity on order	0 0 2 8 8	*Five-digit number*

Reorder point	0 1 3 9 0	*Five-digit number*

Warehouse location

Building number	3 7	*Two digits*
Aisle number	A 5 2	*One letter and two digits*
Bin number	3 5	*Three digits*

Unit cost	0 0 1 5 0	*Five digits, including cents*

Stock value		*Seven digits, including cents*

FIGURE 7-1. *Inventory file master record (schematic).*

below the reorder point, contents of warehouses, stock values, and financial commitments on purchase orders. However, some data about inventory items may be available only in the original documents or handbooks; other desired facts may not be available anywhere in the company.

Run Diagram

A run diagram is a general or broad-brush picture of how files, transactions, and data are handled together. A simple example of a run diagram is one that shows how to update the inventory file and handle the reorder procedure on a periodic basis. File processing uses the master file from the prior run and new input transactions to produce several outputs: an updated version of the master file, lists of transactions applied, errors or discrepancies arising during processing, summaries or lists for use in subsequent processing runs, and documents for operating and management use. In this example of the mechanization approach to systems design, an electronic processor is being considered for handling inventory processing—file updating with the inputs, outputs, and files essentially fixed. The degree of freedom open to the systems designer is simply to mechanize by introducing more equipment than is presently used. Inventory-control schemes, of course, may offer incentive for designing a superior system rather than merely mechanizing the existing system.

A simplified and condensed version of a weekly run diagram to update the inventory master file and prepare a reorder list is in Figure 7-2. Each rectangular box represents a run—the processing of one set of inputs. The arrows show whether a file or document is an input to or output from a run and the numbers tell the volume of input or output records. In Run 1, the data in the inventory transaction file—receipts, issues, and orders—are first sorted into sequence by stock number to correspond with the master-file sequence. The transactions are also sorted into a logical sequence for processing by transaction type. Each type of transaction must be processed in a certain order; for example, receipts are processed ahead of issues because processing an issue before a receipt for the same item may lead to an incorrect entry on the reorder list. Numbering the receipts, issues, and orders as transaction types 1, 2, and 3, respectively, makes it easy to sort transactions into the desired sequence in one operation. The combination of stock number and transaction type is used as the sorting key.

In Run 2, both the sorted inventory transaction file and the in-

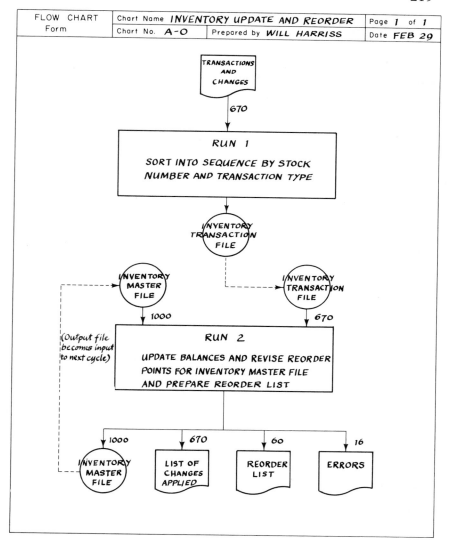

FIGURE 7-2. *Run diagram for inventory updating and reorder procedure.*

ventory master file are inputs to processing. The outputs from processing are the updated master file for use in the next cycle, lists of changes applied, a reorder list, and errors. Errors in this case consist of transaction records that lack corresponding master-file records, records out of sequence, negative balances, and other anomalous situations.

A point to observe is that even this extremely simple case contains two runs. First, the transactions are sorted into stock-number sequence corresponding to the master-file sequence and arranged in a logically correct order by transaction type for processing. Second, the sorted transactions and the master file are processed together to produce the desired outputs. If the inventory master file is stored on a media not requiring sequential processing, then sorting into stock number sequence can be omitted. But arrangement of transactions in a logical processing order by type is still required.

A master file is usually much longer than the transaction file. Each master record for an inventory item contains many data elements: stock number, name, quantity on hand, reorder point, location, unit cost, value, etc. But a transaction record for the same item need contain only a few data elements: stock number, transaction type, quantity, and, perhaps, the dollar amount. Also, a master file contains a record for every item in inventory, but transaction records arise for only the items that are active between processing cycles. The processor reads the master file and transactions to update each record that is affected. Unchanged master-file records are merely carried over to the new master file along with updated records to give a current and complete master file.

In designing a file run for magnetic-tape input and output, the work load can be estimated in terms of the length of the master-record file that the processor must read and write. The amount of processing time required to handle each transaction to update the master file should be estimated in terms of processor instruction steps. Since the program for updating each record is simple, a processor with concurrent read-process-write often can perform the whole operation within tape-reading time for the master file.

For another example, files for depositors' accounts can have appreciably different operating requirements than inventory files, although they are basically quite similar. The master file for depositors' checking accounts may be maintained in a bulk storage device with faster access than magnetic tapes to handle a high rate of change and permit immediate reporting. Possibilities for storage are disk, bulk drums, short tapes, or magnetic cards. Changes are processed to update the file soon after they occur; there is no need to wait for the weekly processing cycle. Reports can be prepared with any frequency wanted, whether weekly, daily, or after each change, and interrogations can be readily answered. However, reports and interrogations need careful appraisal since their preparation may interfere with routine processing.

FLOW CHARTS

Flow charts show the documents, conditions, actions, and outputs that make up a particular data-processing system. They contain various levels of detail below run diagrams. Unique symbols for each major class of items are connected by lines to represent the flow of documents, data, information, and action.

Structure Flow Charts

Structural flow charts are used in the general design of a system. They deal with the types, times, and quantities of input, processing, files, and output. They do not, however, indicate how jobs are performed. A flow chart of the system structure might show that inventory balances are required, for example, but not specify whether they are to appear on a typed list, punched cards, or magnetic tape. The structural flow chart represents, in basic terms, the information and data needs of an organization.

Only a few basic symbols are needed for flow charting; as illustrated in Figure 7-3, these are input-output document, operation, file, decision, connector, and line of flow. Card and magnetic-tape symbols are shown, in addition to a general symbol for files. The three-choice decision symbol is useful because three different possibilities often arise from making comparisons—for example, "less than," "greater than," or "equal to." The three-choice symbol, of course, can also be used for the two-choice—"yes" or "no"—decisions.

A sample flow chart at the system structure level is shown in Figure 7-4. It illustrates a scheme for updating the inventory master file and for writing a list of items that have balances below their reorder points. The *identification* names (or numbers) are given to major blocks, documents, and files. The same name or number should be used on all flow charts and sheets to identify the same item. Since keypunches and other machine-media devices produce only upper-case letters, it often is convenient to use all upper-case letters on flow charts. The INVENTORY MASTER FILE contains the complete record for each item in inventory: stock number, quantity on hand, reorder point, and other data elements shown earlier in Figure 7-1. The INVENTORY TRANSACTION FILE contains all the transactions received for processing since the INVENTORY MASTER FILE was updated in the prior processing cycle.

The *main flow* path of action is represented by lines and arrows

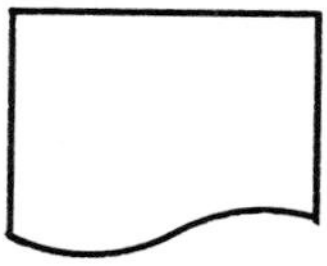

Input or output document symbol — shows data or information coming in or going out

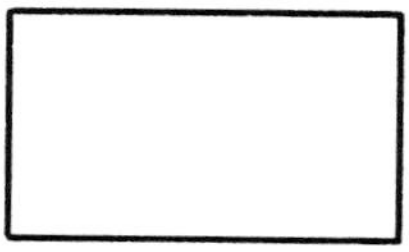

Procedures symbol — indicates action such as sorting, calculation, or output

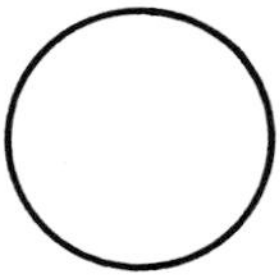

File symbol — represents data stored in organized fashion

Card symbol — represents data stored in punched cards

Magnetic tape symbol — represents data stored on magnetic tape

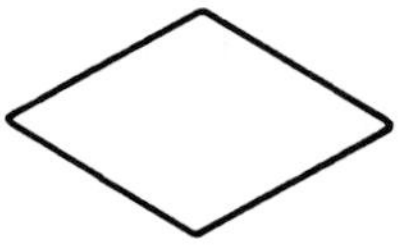

Decision symbol — shows a choice must be made between two or three paths on the basis of a comparison

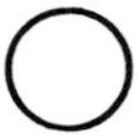

Connector symbol — identifies location that an item or action comes from or goes to

Line and arrow — indicates flow of action or data

FIGURE 7-3. *Symbols for flow charting.*

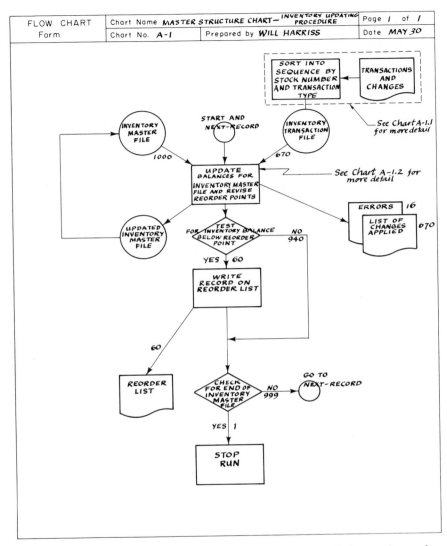

FIGURE 7-4. *Flow chart of structure for inventory updating and reorder procedure.*

entering at the top of a symbol and leaving at the bottom. Action lines may leave the points of the diamond-shaped decision symbol to indicate that the line of action branches into several choices, as shown here. Use of these conventions in flow charting makes the main action paths easier to follow.

Flow charts can show the volume of activity—the number of records or the times that each path is followed. The number 1000, which appears beside the line from the INVENTORY MASTER FILE, means that the inventory contains 1000 items. There are 670 inventory transactions, as indicated. The number 60 on the YES branch from the TEST FOR INVENTORY BALANCE procedure indicates that, according to systems analysis, an average of 60 items are below the reorder point and are written on the REORDER LIST. Volume figures are valuable for calculating work load and processing times.

At the TEST FOR INVENTORY BALANCE diamond, branching occurs when action lines split in two directions depending on whether an item is below the reorder point. The TEST procedure has only two branches, because the "equal to" and "greater than" cases are lumped together as NO. The "less than" case, YES, leads to the WRITE RECORD box. Branching at the CHECK FOR END procedure depends on whether more items are to be processed or the last item in the file has been handled. The CHECK procedure has only two branches because it is merely testing for the end-of-file condition after all records are processed. A line of action may branch into three lines, however, if all three possibilities of "less than," "greater than," or "equal to" are wanted from comparing one item with another.

Merging, the opposite of branching, occurs if the two lines of action that branched at some prior block come back together. Each branch may pass through one or more operations and then merge: In Figure 7-4, both the YES and NO branches of the TEST diamond come back together above the CHECK FOR END diamond. Other merging branches are shown in some of the illustrations that follow.

A loop may be indicated by an arrow to or from a small circle called a *connector.* The connector on the NO branch of the CHECK FOR END diamond contains the note GO TO NEXT RECORD and the NEXT-RECORD connector is located above the UPDATE BALANCE box. Therefore, each time processing is complete on one record, the path of action returns to the UPDATE BALANCE box and processing of the next record begins. The same action can be indicated by drawing a line from the NO branch of the CHECK FOR END diamond to the UPDATE BALANCE box; however, on complex charts the lines become too involved and hard to follow.

Flow charts disclose *common elements* that might be overlooked.

The first chart drawn for the inventory reorder procedure might, for example, have an end-of-inventory test in two different paths. A flow chart should disclose that tests for the end-of-file condition are common elements in two lines of action, so that the designer can merge the two lines of action in his next draft of the chart and merely test once. Flow charts are tools for discovering and developing improvements. Thus a chart is only tentative when first drawn, and each new draft may reveal simplifications and improvements.

The precise method used to perform a job is not important at this stage. The INVENTORY MASTER FILE may be in a book, on punched cards, on magnetic tape, or in a random-access storage unit of a data processor. A clerk, punched-card equipment, or an electronic processor can update the file and prepare a reorder list. Because of the high degree of generality, a structural flow chart is useful to sketch the general design of a system.

Technique Flow Charts

Technique flow charts show data and information requirements and the particular methods proposed for filling them. These flow charts specify the media used for input and output and indicate the nature of files and types of processing equipment. A separate set of flow charts is required for each set of equipment considered. Selection of a particular technique may require modification of the structure already developed. Although a wide variety of symbols are sometimes used for technique flow charts of a proposed system, a limited set of symbols and brief explanations are often adequate.

Flow charts can be prepared with different *levels of detail*. A general outline, which concentrates on the major divisions of the operation and contains little detail, may be prepared first for designing the system and to help plan and control further design work. However, more details are required in flow charts as systems design progresses. Very detailed charts are useful when the systems designer wants to offer the programmer-coder more guidance in complex situations. One set of flow charts with only one level of detail may serve for small-scale operations, but many levels of detail are required for flow-charting large-scale operations.

The transaction-sequencing part of the structure flow chart for the inventory update and reorder procedure in Figure 7-4 is developed for one particular technique in Figure 7-5. Since the processor selected here takes only magnetic-tape input, the data on documents are first punched in cards and then converted to tape. The data on tape are then sequenced to produce the INVENTORY TRANS-

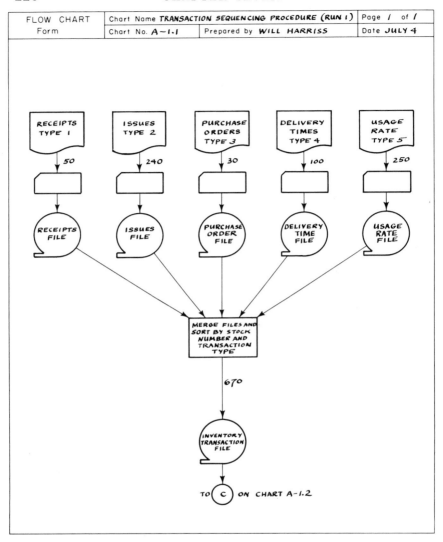

FIGURE 7-5. *Transaction sequencing procedure.*

ACTION FILE. Several other techniques might be used to handle these procedures, but each decision made restricts the freedom to make other choices. The programmer-coder responsible for preparing instruction routines will use the technique flow charts as a guide in his work.

Figure 7-6 is a technique flow chart for that part of Figure 7-4

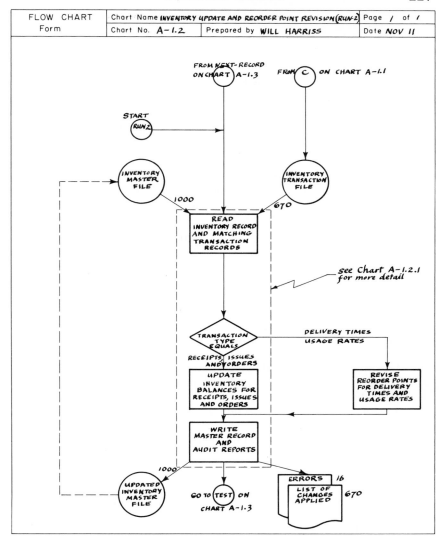

| FLOW CHART | Chart Name **INVENTORY UPDATE AND REORDER POINT REVISION (RUN-2)** | Page *1* of *1* |
| Form | Chart No. **A-1.2** | Prepared by **WILL HARRISS** | Date **NOV 11** |

FROM NEXT-RECORD ON CHART A-1.3

FROM **C** ON CHART A-1.1

START (RUN 2)

INVENTORY MASTER FILE

INVENTORY TRANSACTION FILE

1000

670

READ INVENTORY RECORD AND MATCHING TRANSACTION RECORDS

see Chart A-1.2.1 for more detail

TRANSACTION TYPE EQUALS RECEIPTS, ISSUES AND ORDERS

DELIVERY TIMES USAGE RATES

UPDATE INVENTORY BALANCES FOR RECEIPTS, ISSUES AND ORDERS

REVISE REORDER POINTS FOR DELIVERY TIMES AND USAGE RATES

WRITE MASTER RECORD AND AUDIT REPORTS

1000

UPDATED INVENTORY MASTER FILE

GO TO **TEST** ON CHART A-1.3

ERRORS 16

LIST OF CHANGES APPLIED 670

FIGURE 7-6. *Inventory update and reorder point revision.*

covering master file processing—updating the inventory balances and revising the reorder points. Only four major procedures— READ, UPDATE, REVISE, and WRITE—and the associated files, input, and output are shown. But each procedure can be expanded to a detailed flow chart, since more details are required as systems-design work progresses. The connector above the IN-

VENTORY TRANSACTION FILE shows that its preparation is explained on Flow Chart A-1.1 (Figure 7-5).

Figure 7-7 shows more detail for the READ and UPDATE operations. Essentially, it shows the sequence of operations involved in reading a record from the INVENTORY MASTER FILE and the INVENTORY TRANSACTION FILE, comparing them to determine whether they match, and updating the master record with data from the transaction record. Both a transaction record and master record are needed to start the process, so the first two boxes on the START path contain read instructions for both files. Several steps of this type, called "set up" operations, are required to prepare for a repetitive process. The START path is followed only *once*; thereafter a new record is needed from *either* the INVENTORY MASTER FILE or the INVENTORY TRANSACTION FILE.

After reading, the next step is to compare the stock numbers of the transaction and master records (TRANSACTION RECORD NUMBER : MASTER RECORD NUMBER). The three outcomes and their meanings are as follows:

1. *Greater Than* ($>$). The transaction has a larger stock number than the master record; therefore it should match a master record later in the file. The desired action is to write the existing master records and read new ones until a master record matches the transaction record. The action path goes to the TEST procedure on Chart A-1.3.1 (not illustrated) and returns to this chart at the NEXT-RECORD connector.
2. *Less Than* ($<$). A transaction with a smaller stock number than the master record indicates an error in sequence.
3. *Equal To* ($=$). When both numbers are equal, the transaction will be used to update the master.

If the transaction is type 4 or 5, it is a change in delivery time or usage rate, respectively. The action path branches to the RE-VISE operation on Chart A-1.2.2 and returns to this chart at the END-OF-REVISE connector. Transactions of types 1, 2, and 3 are processed as shown in Figure 7-7. If no transaction record remains (the YES branch of the LAST TRANSACTION diamond), no further processing is required and the action path goes to Chart A-1.2.3, which contains a special process to write the remaining INVENTORY MASTER FILE RECORDS on the output file. Otherwise, the next transaction record is read and the process repeated.

Many charts with the degree of detail shown in Figure 7-7 may

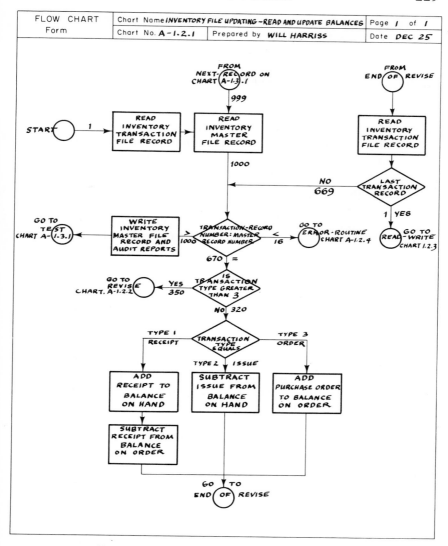

FIGURE 7-7. *Procedure for file reading and balance updating.*

be needed to cover the whole inventory updating and reorder procedure. The programmer may prepare charts with even more detail for his guidance.

Accuracy, simplicity, and understandability are prime considerations when preparing flow charts for systems analysis and design. *Simplicity* means that all relevant facts are presented as clearly as possible. Frequent explanatory comments, even brief ones, are helpful in developing and understanding a flow chart. Files, input, output, and operations should be labeled for flow-charting business problems. The flow-chart symbols used in this chapter are merely illustrative, and system designers can select the set or sets of symbols best suited to their needs and the problem at hand. However, a standard set for use by all programmers in an organization will help communications and reduce confusion.

Identification of all the inputs, outputs, operations, flow charts, and documents is useful in systems analysis and design. Documents and files should be named, numbered or given some other non-ambiguous identification for referring to them. Actions, files, or other items dealt with on two or more flow charts should be cross-referenced, and charts at various levels of detail for the same operation should be cross-referenced to each other. Extreme care is necessary to keep all the relations and details straight.

DECISION TABLES

An examination of detailed flow charts for processes such as inventory file updating reveals some severe deficiencies. First, flow charts are difficult and laborious to draw because of the symbols and spacing. Clarity presents a second and more serious problem. Conditions and actions of the type, IF Condition 1, THEN Action 1, are individually simple, but a series of condition-action phrases may become difficult to follow. There may not be a clear and obvious path from beginning to end through a flow chart, since action for any particular condition depends on all *prior* condition-action phrases. For example, the user might wish to determine from the flow chart in Figure 7-7 whether any master record is written before all the transactions affecting that particular record are handled. The answers to questions of this type are not obvious from a study of the flow chart, and it is easy to get lost while tracing an action path through several branches. If the designer must determine whether all conditions are covered or whether there exist alternative methods that may be superior, then flow charts offer little help. It is little wonder that people are willing to accept incomplete statements of a problem, quit trying to formulate the logic of an application, and stop searching for better methods. Instead, they simply skip to programming for the machine.

Decision tables are a design tool used to overcome some of the deficiencies of the flow-chart approach to systems design. These tables are similar in use and construction to flow charts, but they show conditions and operations in a more clear and orderly fashion, thus facilitating careful and complete development of the problem logic during both the problem analysis and programming stages.

Example of a Decision Table

Table 7-1 is a typical decision table. It parallels the flow chart in Figure 7-7 to facilitate comparison and understanding. The mechanics for constructing a decision table are simple. The table, as illustrated in Table 7-1, is divided vertically into two parts— the stub and the body. All the *conditions* that are relevant to the problem are listed in the upper part of the stub in any order that is convenient. These conditions are the same as the contents of the diamond or branch symbols on a conventional flow chart. *Actions*— the contents of the rectangular symbols on a flow chart—are listed in the lower part of the stub in the sequence desired for execution.

The possible *outcomes* for each condition—such as the YES, NO, EQUAL, TYPE 1, and others used in conventional flow charts to identify the outgoing branches of a decision diamond—are listed in the upper part of the body. To conserve space, "Y" is used for YES and "N" for NO. A "–" indicates that the outcome is irrelevant and should be ignored. Each column in the body makes up a *rule*. When *all* the condition outcomes in the top half of a rule are satisfied, then the actions with an "X" opposite them in the bottom half of that particular rule are executed. A rule corresponds, therefore, to *one* of the several or many possible paths through a flow chart.

Rule 1 handles the first cycle or set-up operations. For the first cycle, the START condition outcome is YES, and other conditions are immaterial. The action wanted for Rule 1 is to read a transaction record, read a master-file record, and return to the beginning of this table. Rules 2 through 8 handle the main body of processing. The NO's for these rules mean that this is *not* the start cycle. The last transaction record has *not* been used yet. In Rule 2, the transaction number exceeds the inventory master-file record number; therefore, either all transactions for this master record have been processed or there were none. The transaction type in this case is irrelevant. The resulting action is to write out the inventory master-file record, perform whatever action is specified in the test table, read in another

DECISION TABLE	Table Name	INVENTORY FILE UPDATE		Page 1 of 1
Form	Chart No. T-1.2.1	Prepared by WILL HARRISS		Date FEB 29

Stub	Body														
	Rule Number														
Conditions	1	2	3	4	5	6	7	8	9	10	11	12	13	14	15
START	Y	N	N	N	N	N	N	N	N						
LAST TRANSACTION RECORD	–	N	N	N	N	N	N	N	Y						
TRANSACTION NO : MASTER RECORD NO	–	>	=	=	=	=	=	<	–						
TRANSACTION TYPE EQUALS	–	–	1	2	3	4	5	–	–						
Actions															
ADD RECEIPT TO BALANCE ON HAND			X												
SUBTRACT RECEIPT FROM BALANCE ON ORDER			X												
SUBTRACT ISSUE FROM BALANCE ON HAND				X											
ADD PURCHASE ORDER TO BALANCE ON ORDER					X										
GO TO ERROR-ROUTINE TABLE								X							
PERFORM REVISE TABLE						X	X								
READ INVENTORY TRANSACTION FILE RECORD	X		X	X	X	X	X								
WRITE INVENTORY MASTER FILE RECORD		X													
PERFORM TEST TABLE		X													
READ INVENTORY MASTER FILE RECORD	X	X													
GO TO INVENTORY FILE UPDATE TABLE	X	X	X	X	X	X	X								
GO TO READ-WRITE TABLE								X							

TABLE 7-1. *Decision table for inventory file updating.*

inventory master-file record, and go to the beginning of this table. The action, GO TO INVENTORY FILE UPDATE TABLE, directs the processor to return to the *beginning* of this particular table and test the conditions again for the new master record.

The PERFORM TEST TABLE procedure in Rule 2 has some special features. This statement causes the action path to go to a subtable—the TEST TABLE—to find the appropriate rule, execute it, and return to the next action in the rule being executed in the main table—the INVENTORY FILE UPDATE TABLE. Therefore, after the appropriate actions in the TEST TABLE are executed, the path of action returns to the INVENTORY FILE UPDATE table and the last two actions of Rule 2—READ and GO TO—are then executed. The PERFORM statement, in effect, allows one table to contain other tables within it. Note that this PERFORM TEST TABLE process corresponds to the action path of Figure 7-7, which leaves at TEST and returns at NEXT-RECORD.

Rules 3, 4, 5, 6, and 7 apply to a transaction record and master-file record with matching numbers. Therefore, the transaction type —1, 2, 3, 4, or 5—determines the kind of action—ADD RECEIPT TO BALANCE ON HAND, etc.,—for updating the master-file record. Rules 6 and 7 contain PERFORM statements for the REVISE TABLE, which contains the processing logic for type 4 and 5 transactions. The next step is to read another transaction record and go to the beginning of the table to handle the new transaction. Rule 8 covers the out-of-sequence transaction because its stock number is less than the master-file stock number. The action, GO TO ERROR-ROUTINE TABLE, might result in punching a card for immediate study or writing the out-of-sequence transaction on a tape for printing. Action for a short error-routine might be included in the present decision table. Rule 9 deals with the condition in which *all* transactions have been handled, but more master-file records must be read and written on the output tape.

General Form for Decision Tables

Two important features of decision tables are described above. One is that conditions and actions are kept separate. Another is that all conditions are tested to find an applicable rule before any action is executed. Other features of interest in this method of problem analysis are (1) the uniqueness of rules, (2) the sequence of execution, (3) limited and extended entries, (4) the else-rule, and (5) the relationship of decision tables to programming.

Unique Rules. The set of conditions specified by each rule must be unique to avoid ambiguity. Equivalent sets of conditions leading to different actions are erroneous. The converse—different conditions leading to the same action—is permissible and may be desirable. Often, however, careful examination of two or more rules leading to the same action will disclose that a redundancy exists and that either the problem logic is incorrect or one rule is contained in another. Several rules might be simplified to a smaller number of rules by, perhaps, using an "it doesn't matter" for one condition to cover YES in one rule and NO in another, or by broadening the limits of outcomes so that one outcome will cover another when no distinction was actually intended.

Sequence of Execution. All conditions within a rule are tested at once to find if the rule applies to a particular situation in the data—in effect, parallel testing. The rules are sequence-numbered for convenience, as shown in Table 7-1; however, this does not imply that the rules must be executed in this sequence. If each rule is unique and does not have to rely on other rules or the sequence in which they are written, then that sequence which is most desirable— easiest to program, fastest running, or takes least high-speed storage —can be selected at the time of programming. The programmer can, for example, indicate the frequency of occurrence of each rule for processor guidance during the compiling pass to develop a faster-running program. But under these circumstances the programmer cannot be sure that rules will be executed in exactly the hoped-for sequence.

Each action desired for a rule is marked "X"; an action not wanted for a rule is simply marked "–" or left blank. Actions marked "X" for a rule are executed in their *row-sequence.* Any desired sequence can be obtained by an appropriate listing; thus, the actions A and B can be executed in both the A-B and B-A sequences by listing A, B, and A, and then selecting A and B for one rule and B and A for another.

Limited and Extended Entries. The decision table in Table 7-1 has "limited entries" for all actions and for the START and LAST TRANSACTION conditions. Limited-entry rules are restricted to the notation "Y," "N," for condition outcomes, and "X" and "blank" for actions.

The two conditions involving transaction number and transaction type have "extended entries." Part of the record-number condition— the operators ">," "=," and "<"—extends into the rules column. For transaction types, the numbers "1," "2," and "3" are placed in the rule column as the second operand. The extended entry form is compact; one extended entry may have the capability of several limited entries. For example, the extended entry conditions of $>$, $=$, $<$, MASTER RECORD NO. requires the following limited entries (in the context of Table 7-1):

CONDITIONS	RULES
	1 2 3 4 5 6 7 8 9
TRANSACTION NO > MASTER RECORD NO	– Y N N N N N N –
TRANSACTION NO = MASTER RECORD NO	– N Y Y Y Y Y N –
TRANSACTION NO < MASTER RECORD NO	– N N N N N N Y –

Similarly, actions can be written as extended entries to place either an operand or both an operator and an operand in the rules area. For example, acceptance of a customer's order on account may be conditioned on both credit bureau ratings and the amount of his account overdue. For the AMOUNT OF ORDER TO ACCEPT, the "$<$" is an operator and the amounts of $7000, $5000, and $2000 are operands.

Limited and extended entries can be used in the same decision table, but each row must be in one form only. Obviously, condition rules of YES and NO are incompatible with EXCELLENT, $<30,000$, and $>20,000$. Nor can X and blank for actions be mixed with ANY, <7000, and NONE.

STUB	BODY				
CONDITIONS	RULE NUMBER				
	1	2	3	4	5
CREDIT RATING	EXCELLENT	EXCELLENT	GOOD	GOOD	POOR
AMOUNT OVERDUE	$<30,000$	$>30,000$	$<20,000$	$>20,000$	–
ACTIONS					
AMOUNT OF ORDER TO ACCEPT	ANY	<7000	<5000	<2000	NONE

Else-Rule. The number of rules required to handle all possible conditions grows rapidly with the number of conditions. For the simplest case, in which each condition is filled by either YES or NO, as the number of conditions increases $1, 2, 3, 4, \ldots n$, the possible number of rules grows $1, 4, 8, 16, \ldots 2^n$. The complete set of rules soon becomes burdensome to write, and many are likely to have the same actions. The irrelevant, seldom-used, or logically-impossible rules may be omitted and an ELSE-rule with all conditions blank introduced to handle the situation when none of the other rules apply. The action associated with the ELSE-rule may be to halt processing, note the unanticipated case, or take some corrective action and return to this table, as appropriate. The ELSE-rule is executed when *none* of the other rules apply.

Relationship to Programming. Decision tables are described here as a method for organizing the logic for problem solution. However, they can also be used as a programming language. The brief coverage of decision tables here is consistent with the DETAB-X (Decision Table, Experimental) Programming Language, which is a combination of decision tables and COBOL, the Common Business Oriented Language discussed in Chapters 8 and 9. In the DETAB-X Language the contents of a decision table are treated as a single *procedure* and can be executed whenever desired in a COBOL program. The main processing program uses a PERFORM or GO TO statement to send program control to any desired decision table. When a PERFORM statement is used, the main program regains program control after all the data involved are handled by that table. One table can, of course, send program control to another table before returning to the main program. Viewed in this way, a program may consist of an executive control routine with a high fraction of the processing operations organized as decision tables.

SUMMARY

In the development of a new system, systems design and implementation follow the analysis and selection of the design approach. Designing a system involves making decisions about the kinds of changes proposed, the outputs wanted, the inputs and files needed, and the processing procedures that will be adopted to link input and output. Ingenuity and inventiveness, coupled with clear, sound thinking, have the biggest pay-off in the early stages of systems design.

The initial design is performed almost independently of the type of equipment that may be introduced. Attention is centered on the nature and content of inputs, files, and outputs, and on the kinds of processing required. Design decisions about outputs are critically important because they are the products delivered to system customers—management and operating personnel. System outputs can be appraised in terms of their content, organization, degree of detail, format, accuracy, and timeliness—the frequency of reporting and the delay in issuing reports. Careful planning may make it possible to specify in advance all the output requirements and thereby simplify the design of files and procedures. However, conditions are seldom so predictable that all required outputs can be pre-specified. Generally, many new demands for output arise that may be handled fairly well by gathering and storing additional data in files for possible later use. One measure of the efficiency of file design is the percentage of unusual requests for information that can be filled without having to cram the files full of data on the mere prospect of use. However, the cost of keeping excessive data in files is small compared to the cost of not having data when wanted. Therefore, the practical approach to file design of retaining large quantities of data is, within limits, a wise one.

Run diagrams are a broad-brush presentation of files, transactions, and data that are handled together. The treatment of data entering a run depends on the organization of files and the nature of processing. Sequenced master files require a similar arrangement of transactions for processing. Each kind of transaction must be handled in a logically correct sequence; for example, receipts of stock should be handled ahead of issues to avoid having transactions rejected during processing by illogical intermediate results.

The inputs to a processor run are the prior-run master file, new transactions, and a program. The outputs are an updated master file, list of transactions applied, errors, summaries or listings for use in subsequent runs, and reports for operating and management personnel. Even simple processing operations are likely to involve several runs for editing and sorting transactions, for updating the master file, and for preparing printing outputs. For a processor with concurrent read-process-write capability, processing times can be estimated as the longer of master-file read-write time or transaction processing time.

Structure flow charts are used in systems design to cover the types, times, and quantities of inputs, processing, files, and outputs. Structural flow charts are drawn without showing the equipment to be used or how jobs are performed. A small number of symbols, with explanations where needed, are adequate for drawing structural charts. There are many conventions to flow-charting that make preparing and understanding them easier: direction of flow lines, identification of files and procedures, volumes through each path, repetitive loops, branching into two or more paths, merging of several paths into one, and connections between different charts. Each version of a chart should be considered tentative and simplified, if possible, by combining common elements and eliminating unnecessary steps until an efficient final version is prepared.

Technique flow charts show data and information requirements and the methods for filling them. They specify data media and equipment for input, output, and operations. The level of detail in flow charts should be attuned to their use, and charts for guiding programmers and coders are the most detailed. Accuracy, simplicity, and understandability are prime considerations when preparing flow charts for systems analysis and design.

Decision tables are an alternative to flow charts for the description of problem logic. They show conditions and actions in a clearer and more orderly fashion than flow charts and thus facilitate careful and complete development during the problem specification and programming stages. DETAB-X is a programming language based on a combination of decision tables and COBOL.

PART IV
PROGRAMMING AND PROCESSING PROCEDURES

8
Programming—Cobol-1

A *program* consists of a set of instructions on how to perform a particular task. The nature and detail of instructions depends on many factors. These include the complexity of the immediate task, knowledge about performing this or similar tasks, the tools available, and the language the instructor or programmer thinks best for communicating on this particular occasion. Instructing a person to do a certain task has many facets, though most of them are taken for granted because of long practice in giving and using instructions, the wealth of languages available for communication between people, and the built-in experience of people in performing tasks.

Careful and explicit instructions are required when machines are used to perform tasks. At the present stage of development, machines have little capability to fill in missing parts of their instruction routines; in other words, they have limited learning power. But enough research work has been done to bring processors up to about the "cave-man" stage of development, and further advances in the ability of machines to adapt to their environment and solve problems will come.

PROGRAMMING

In more concrete terms, programming does and, for the foreseeable future, will consist of the following steps:

1. Analyze a problem area to determine what the problem is and to learn as precisely as possible the boundary conditions—what *outputs* are wanted, the *inputs* needed to produce the required outputs, and the *files* that relate input to output.
2. Formulate a plan or *program*—invent, improvise, or copy a solution—to produce the outputs from the inputs by appropriate processing techniques that will develop and maintain any files necessary. First develop the solution in broad terms and then in more detail as the occasion warrants.

3. Learn what *capabilities* are available—processing and communications equipment, people, and the organizational environment—how they operate, and how to communicate with them in a suitable language.

The important point from this broad-brush description of programming is the requirement to know the whole background situation in order to develop the instructions aimed solely at the machine. From this background it is possible to develop a solution that is detailed enough to put into operation. Implementation involves selecting equipment, people, and procedures, and preparing detailed descriptions of outputs and inputs and the processing steps for people and equipment to follow.

The Essence of Programming

In addition to the narrow, specific task of preparing machine instructions, the following background information must be developed: (1) precise descriptions of the information *outputs,* data *inputs,* and *files* used for organizing partially processed data; (2) *instruction lists to guide people and equipment* to carry out the required procedures; and (3) specifications of the available *equipment*—the central processor, high-speed and bulk storage, and input-output facilities— to run the program. In briefest terms, these points about programming might be called data description, procedure description, and equipment environment.

Example of a Program

Suppose you are going to see a friend; the set of directions for finding the friend's house is a program for the occasion of a visit. The objective—to reach his house—is explicit and both of you understand it, although he may need to identify the house for you by its appearance or street number and name. If you are resourceful, the address—street number and name, city, and state—is adequate to guide you to his house. You can, if you interpret his address into geographical location, plan a route from your starting point to his house, obtain a suitable means of conveyance, and execute your plan.

If your friend wants to help you by planning your route, several facts must be made explicit. You must agree where you will start from—*the input*—and what conveyance you will use, whether auto, bus, or on foot—*the equipment environment.* In order to describe an efficient route—*the procedure*—it is necessary to take into consideration simple and intricate routes, fast and slow roads, traffic conditions at that time of day, and miscellaneous factors such as road-construction obstacles.

Having answers to questions about the input point, equipment environment, and operating conditions, your friend probably visualizes he is driving from your house to his and says, "Go out Route 138, turn right at the second barn after the third house, and, at the end of the road, turn left and go to 2321 Sylvan."

Features of a Program

This brief program of instructions about how to reach a friend's house has features in common with processor programming that are worth noting.

1. The inputs, outputs and equipment environment are agreed upon before the procedures are prepared, but they are related to each other—any change in one may require some change in another.
2. An agreed-upon language is used—in this case, a subset of English suitable for giving instructions to people driving cars on highways. If two languages are involved—say your friend is a Frenchman—translation is required at some stage to convert French to English.
3. Instructions are at a macro or aggregate level—"go out," "turn right," and "go to"—for they say nothing about the details, such as how to make turns—slow down, signal, check traffic, get into the proper lane, check traffic, turn the wheel, check traffic, etc. Each instruction becomes many lower-level or detailed instructions upon execution. The instruction "second barn after the third house" requires the ability to count in the same way as intended by your programmer. Situations such as "end of road" and "Sylvan" must be recognized. A count-down or count-up to 2321 is required, depending on whether you approach the house from the high- or low-number side.
4. The sequence must be followed as stated—go out, turn right, turn left, etc.—since a left turn before a right will spoil execution of the whole program and will spoil it completely unless you are able to detect you are off the route, stop, and call for further directions or return to a point you can identify as correct.
5. Execution of the program is up to you since your programmer will not be in the car with you. You can "interpret" each instruction as you go and take your chances. But in this particular case you have instructions in advance and can "compile" more detailed instructions by studying maps and by questioning your instructor. Does the "second barn after the third house" mean that the two barns are in succession with no intervening houses? Does "at the

second barn" mean "before," "after," or "what?" Some of these ambiguities are resolved merely by reading the instructions and applying logical tests that you have developed by trying to follow similar instructions at other times. The most thorough test is to execute the program in advance so that after each mistake you can return to the last point you are sure about and repeat the erroneous parts until you *debug* the program or conclude it is unworkable and call for help or give up.

6. No provision is made for contingencies—engine failure, lack of gas, flat tire, or bridge out of use. Engine failure, like any central processor failure, may be near-fatal to the program. Others which may cause only minor annoyance on the road also have their equivalents in processor operations: out of cards, a magnetic-tape unit that doesn't work, or failure of a data channel to carry data.

PROGRAMMING LANGUAGES

Programming specialists have developed a rich variety of languages for writing instructions to data-processing machines. The earliest languages were *machine-oriented;* it was considered enough to operate processors without worrying about the niceties of the language itself. Subsequent programming research has focused on *problem-oriented* languages to ease the user's task of writing programs. Further schemes have been developed to make the processor handle many of the bookkeeping and clerical tasks required for program operation. Thus, the program writer is free to concentrate on the essential features of his problem and do so in a language that he is familiar with.

Machine-Oriented Language

Actual processor instructions are expressed in numbers that indicate to the machine what operations to perform and what data to use. For example, the instruction to add regular pay to overtime pay giving total pay might look as follows in machine language:

$$10 \quad 100 \quad 101 \quad 200$$

The 10 indicates an ADD instruction. The 100 and 101 are *addresses* of storage locations that contain the numbers for regular and overtime pay; 200 is the storage location for the sum, total pay. The programmer must arrange to have the desired operands in the specified locations before the processor executes this instruction. It will add whatever is in location 100 to whatever is in location 101 and put the result in location 200 (displacing whatever is there). He must also plan to line up the decimal points and guard against overflow—numbers becoming too large to fit into storage locations. In short, machine-language programming places a large burden on the person writing the program to keep track of the details involved.

Problem-Oriented Language

Problem-oriented languages are designed around a language ordinarily used to solve the relevant type of problem. Engineers or scientists use mathematics and formulas to solve technical problems and hence have algebraic programming languages—for example, FORTRAN or *For*mula *Tra*nslating System.

The use of English is natural when coping with business problems. Business applications often are described in English and detailed instructions are prepared in English for clerks. Similarly, English-language instructions are useful for people to communicate with business processors. The instruction to calculate gross pay, instead of using the numbers shown above—10 100 101 200—might be written as

ADD REGULAR-PAY TO OVERTIME-PAY GIVING GROSS-PAY

An instruction written in English is perfectly clear to any reader, whether programmer, programmer supervisor, payroll-department head, controller, or even the president. The burden of translating the instruction to machine form in order to execute it is placed on the processor in contrast to machine-oriented languages that place the burden on people. Programming specialists have developed schemes —compilers—that enable the processor to convert English-language instructions to machine-language instructions. Other programmers are then able to concentrate on solving problems with English-language instructions that a processor will compile into machine language.

The COBOL Language

The problem-oriented language of major concern to business users is COBOL, the Common Business-Oriented Language. COBOL is near-English in form, represents a long chain of development from early languages, and is still developing as more refinements are added. COBOL-1961 (the 1961 version) was developed by a committee composed of government users, computer manufacturers, and other organizations. The language was first described in a report of the Conference on Data-Systems Languages (CODASYL), issued by the United States Government Printing Office in April, 1960. Each equipment manufacturer publishes detailed descriptions covering each processor for which he has implemented COBOL.

Since the processor shares in the programming job when COBOL is used, it must be given a considerable amount of data about each problem. The programmer must provide data about three facets of the program, just as are required for a trip to a friend's house: data division, procedure division, and environment division.

Data Division. The Data Division is a description of each item of data used in input, output, or temporary storage during processing. For each element of data, the Data Division includes a *data-name* such as EMPLOYEE-NAME, AMOUNT-ON-HAND, PAY-RATE, or TODAYS-DATE, and a description of its type—numeric or alphanumeric—and its length expressed in number of characters. The Data Division is a dictionary in which the programmer tells the processor that a particular set of characters, for example PAY-RATE, is used with a certain meaning in a problem. COBOL allows capital letters only, and has certain punctuation rules with special meanings. The programmer must conform to these rules even though their use upsets the rules for grammar and appearance of ordinary English text; COBOL is a programmer's English, not a grammarian's.

Procedure Division. The Procedure Division is the programmer's opportunity to specify what he wants done with the *data-names* described in the Data Division. The COBOL procedure statement, MULTIPLY PAY-RATE BY HOURS-WORKED GIVING GROSS-PAY, means just what it says. The data-name PAY-RATE—meaning "data identified by the name PAY-RATE"—is multiplied by the data-name HOURS-WORKED and the answer has the data-name GROSS-PAY. If the next instruction says, WRITE GROSS-PAY, the processor will write on magnetic tape the product resulting from the multiplication. PAY-RATE, HOURS-WORKED, and GROSS-PAY are data-names of items of data that the programmer wants to use in his program. A hyphen is used between words in a data-name since blanks are not permitted within a COBOL name. The programmer does *not* specify which storage locations should be used. The task of assigning a specific storage location to a data-name is handled by the processor in a *compiling* run; the compiled program can then be executed or carried out in a later *execution* run.

Environment Division. The Environment Division describes certain characteristics of the equipment that affect the way a program runs. For example the Inventory File may be a deck of punched cards in the card reader or a magnetic tape mounted on any one of twenty or so tape units. The Environment Division may specify the type and location of each file and other machine-related items. The precise form and content of the Environment Division depends on the equipment used at each of the two stages—compiling and executing—for a COBOL program. The equipment configurations may be different and more equipment capacity, especially storage, may be required for compiling than for executing a program.

COBOL-1

The remainder of this chapter describes COBOL-1, a programming language based on COBOL-61. COBOL-1 is a simplified version to facilitate learning the fundamentals of programming. It preserves the essential structure of a powerful business programming-language, but minimizes the number of rules and variety of options in the initial stage. The discussion of COBOL-1 is designed to communicate the fundamentals of programming without becoming enmeshed in details or esoteric features—enough of them will arise later.

COBOL-1 is a completely compatible subset of COBOL-61 in much the same way that the 800 or so words of basic English are a subset of the King's English of thousands of words. Programs written in COBOL-1 are real and operational, not just hypothetical. They will compile and run on any machine that has a COBOL-61 translator, *if* the additional instructions given at the end of this chapter are followed. COBOL-1 is, therefore, a realistic language, and experience with it is a valid introduction to writing in the full COBOL-61 language. There is much more to learn but nothing to unlearn.

THE DATA DIVISION

An important aspect of programming, briefly reviewed here, is the systematic organization of data for processing. First this section will consider files from the viewpoint of records on cards for manual processing, since most people are familiar with them. Then the organization of data will be discussed from the viewpoint of COBOL-1, which requires more careful organization for efficient processing.

Levels of Organization

As described in Chapter 2, data are organized into three levels, starting with a character—numeral, letter, punctuation mark, or symbol, as follows:

1. *Data element:* A group of characters to specify an item at or near the basic level—date, alphabetic name, address, order number, stock number, and quantity on hand. An item may be used as an elementary item or several may be grouped—a group item—for some purposes. For example, the group item "customer's address" contains the elementary items of the customer's name, street address, city and state.

2. *Record:* One or more data elements that are usefully associated with a person, thing, or place. A record for an inventory item includes a stock number, stock name, amount on hand, warehouse location (and, perhaps, building number, aisle, and bin number), unit price, cost, and as many other elements as seem useful.

3. *File:* One or more records concerning people, things, or places that are closely related in an operational sense—all records for inventory items can be grouped together as a stock-record file.

The following description of the stock-record file for the ABC Company is organized in outline form with an indication of the content of each data element:

Inventory File: A group of Stock Records; one for each of the several thousand parts stocked by the ABC Company. (Other files are kept for employees, customers, etc.)
  Stock Record: One record for each stock item containing the following data-names.
  Stock Number: A ten-digit number from the official catalogue.
  Stock Name: Not more than twenty letters or numerals.
  Quantity on Hand: Not more than five digits.
  Quantity on Order: Not more than five digits.
  Warehouse location:
   Building Number: Two digits.
   Aisle Number: One letter and two digits.
   Bin Number: Three digits.
  Unit Cost: Two digits for cents and not more than three for dollars.

Card Records

The stock-record file of the ABC Company is kept on cards, as shown in Figure 8-1. The maximum number of spaces permitted

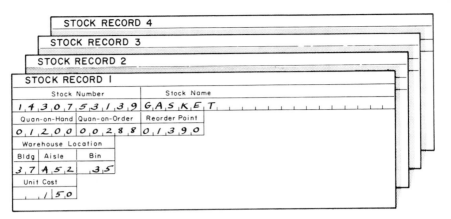

FIGURE 8-1. *Card layout for stock records in inventory file.*

for writing each data item is indicated and will guide the keypunch operator if the data are punched into other cards. The meaning of space allocations will become clearer when COBOL Data Descriptions are discussed.

This card record focuses on stock status, for it shows only the current quantity on hand, quantity on order, and unit cost. It does not show a prior balance or the transactions that resulted in the present balance. If these are wanted, the inventory card needs to be redesigned to show date, quantity, and type of each transaction. As presently designed, either a new stock record needs to be written after each receipt or issue in order to show current balances, or the recordkeeper must erase and write new amounts in place of old. In this respect—erase and rewrite—the card record corresponds to magnetic-tape or disk records.

The programmer, when designing a new or modified data-processing system, may rearrange or modify the contents of the existing records. Some of the items of data may not be relevant to his program; others, perhaps, can be fitted into less space or arranged for more efficient machine processing. For example, in analyzing the stock record shown earlier, the programmer may conclude that the reorder point is not needed and that bin numbers do not exceed two digits. He may also rearrange the items on the record to put them into a more efficient sequence for processing. The objective is to develop an efficient arrangement for the data actually used throughout the system.

COBOL Data Description

The stock record illustrated in Figure 8-1 is described in the proper form for COBOL-1 in Figure 8-2. The COBOL-1 rules for writing data descriptions must be carefully adhered to.

Data-Name. Data-names shown in Figure 8-2 are used to identify each piece of data during processing by a COBOL-1 program. When the program, for example, refers to STOCK-NUMBER, the data called STOCK-NUMBER is obtained and processed. The programmer's first problem, therefore, is what to call each kind of data that he wishes to process. The data-names used in COBOL-1 are arbitrarily selected by the programmer to suit his needs. It is often easier to use COBOL-1 data-names that are similar to normal business names, but any name that fits the rules is acceptable. After adoption, a name must be used consistently.

Names are formed in the following way. A name may use only the capital letters A through Z and the numerals 0 through 9. The length of a name is limited to 30 or fewer characters, as indicated by the space provided on the form: columns 12 to 41 for *data-name*. At least one of the characters must be a letter. Dashes may be used to separate the words or phrases in a name for easier reading, for example, STOCK-RECORD; but blanks are not permitted. Finally each data-name must be unique in that it differs from all other names used in the same program by one or more characters.

Level. The two digits in the column headed "Level" indicate the structure of the data. The description of each file used in a COBOL-1 program must begin with the level entry FD followed by the *file-name*—in this case, INVENTORY-FILE.

The *record-name* within a file has a level number of 01; therefore STOCK-RECORD is level 01. Each data-name contained within a record is given a larger number to indicate a lower level—02, 03, etc. The data elements, STOCK-NUMBER, STOCK-NAME, QUAN-ON-HAND, and QUAN-ON-ORDER are all part of the STOCK-RECORD and have, therefore, a level of 02. Figure 8-2 shows that a *group item*—WAREHOUSE-LOCATION—within the STOCK-RECORD also has a level number of 02. The *elementary items*—BUILD-NO, AISLE-NO, and BIN-NO that make up WAREHOUSE-LOCATION—have level numbers of 03. Level numbers are the COBOL equivalent of the indenting shown earlier in the description of the ABC Company inventory file. Note that

COBOL-1 Program Form

Program Name STOCK-VALUE CALCULATION
Program Number SVC-1
Prepared by WILL HARRISS
Date NOV 23
Page 1 of 1

Line No.	Level No.	Data-Name	Picture
010		DATA DIVISION.	
020	FD	INVENTORY-FILE	DATA RECORD IS STOCK-RECORD.
030	01	STOCK-RECORD.	
040	02	STOCK-NUMBER	PICTURE 9(10).
050	02	STOCK-NAME	PICTURE X(20).
060	02	QUAN-ON-HAND	PICTURE 99999.
070	02	QUAN-ON-ORDER	PICTURE 99999.
080	02	WAREHOUSE-LOCATION.	
090	03	BUILD-NO	PICTURE 999.
100	03	AISLE-NO	PICTURE XXX.
110	03	BIN-NO	PICTURE 999.
120	02	UNIT-COST	PICTURE 999V99.

FIGURE 8-2. COBOL-1 data division for stock-record in inventory file.

250

UNIT-COST returns to the 02 level since it is not a subelement under WAREHOUSE-LOCATION. The general rules for assigning level numbers are as follows:

1. Level numbers consist of
   FD for a File
   01 for a Record
   Two digits—from 02 through 49—for data elements and subelements in a Record.
2. An item contains within it all items directly below it that have larger numbers for level.

Picture. A symbolic picture of each data element goes in the right-hand column of the COBOL-1 Form. The item with dataname QUAN-ON-HAND consists of five numeric characters and, therefore, has the description PICTURE 99999, which can be read "Picture is 99999." The character "9" in a PICTURE indicates the location of a single numeric digit. Any data element that consists only of numerals—numeric data—has an appropriate number of 9's in its picture to show its maximum size. If an item contains one or more letters or punctuation marks—alphanumeric data—its size is shown by "X's" in PICTURE. AISLE-NO consists of one letter and two digits in no specified sequence; therefore, PICTURE XXX properly covers it.

The STOCK-NUMBER was originally described in Figure 8-1 as a ten-digit number, so its description is 9999999999, or in shorthand form, 9(10). The number before the parenthesis tells the type of character—numeric or alphanumeric; the number within the parentheses specifies the number of these characters in the data element. Thus, 9(10) means that provision is made for ten numeric digits. This notation can also be used with the X symbol for letters.

All data used for computation must be numeric only. Alphanumeric data such as AISLE-NO consisting of three alphanumeric digits can be read into the processor, sorted into sequence, compared, or read out of storage, but such data cannot be used in an addition, subtraction, or other arithmetic operation.

The symbol "V" in a PICTURE indicates the location of the decimal point. PICTURE 999V99 for UNIT-COST means it has three numeric digits for dollars on the left of the decimal and two numeric digits for cents on the right of the decimal. The decimal point itself *cannot* appear in a number stored inside the processor for use in arithmetic operation. It is not a numeric character and, therefore, is not allowed in a numeric item used in arithmetic operations. If UNIT-COST is $127.13, the input data should contain merely the numerals 12713.

The PICTURE 999V99 for UNIT-COST instructs COBOL to assume that the decimal point is located two positions from the right and to treat 12713 as 127.13. COBOL will correctly align the decimal points of data elements indicated by a V before performing any arithmetic operations. The programmer need not worry about decimal-point location after the data description is written. However, he must assure that all input data has the appropriate number of digit positions. If UNIT-COST is to be $127.00 and PICTURE 999V99, the input then must be 12700 for correct handling. An input of 127 might be treated by the processor as though it were $1.27.

Pictures are used only with elementary items—items that do not contain any other items. The item with data-name WAREHOUSE-LOCATION is a group item (not a single element) of data and therefore does not have a PICTURE. STOCK-RECORD is a record-name containing several data elements and must rely on their description. Files need a special entry in place of a picture that identifies the records within the file. This entry has the general form of DATA RECORD IS *record-name,* and in Figure 8-2 is DATA RECORD IS STOCK-RECORD.

The rules for describing data in COBOL-1 are as follows:

1. The PICTURE shows the number and type of characters comprising each data element by means of the symbol 9 for each numeric character, and X for each alphanumeric character. A number in parentheses indicates repetition of the preceding character.
2. A PICTURE is required only for elementary items (the lowest level); it is not permitted for group items, records, or files.
3. Data elements used for computation must be entirely numeric.
4. A V inserted at the appropriate place in a PICTURE indicates the location of an *assumed* decimal point. Input data for arithmetic operations must not contain an actual decimal point.

All data-names should be described in the Data Division *before* actually writing COBOL-1 procedures, but, of course, the data-names and procedures are closely interrelated and must be developed together.

PROBLEM EXAMPLE

The following problem example will be developed throughout much of the remainder of this chapter. Suppose that, in processing a file, the first requirement is to calculate the dollar value of one inventory item. Dollar value is equal to quantity on hand multiplied by unit cost. The input will be one STOCK-RECORD (Figure 8-2) and the output will be a VALUE-RECORD, as described below.

The Data Division for this example is shown in Figure 8-3. The upper part shows the INVENTORY-FILE, which is identical to the file described earlier. It contains the input data that are of special interest here: STOCK-NUMBER, STOCK-NAME, AND UNIT-COST. The bottom part of Figure 8-3, starting on line 140, is a second file identified as STOCK-VALUE-FILE. It is designed to receive the output data of stock number and stock value.

Since each data-name in COBOL-1 must be unique, the part number of an item is named STOCK-NUMBER in the INVEN-TORY-FILE and STOCK-NUMBER-O ("O" might be thought of as Output) in the STOCK-VALUE-FILE, as shown on line 160. The data element STOCK-VALUE, line 170, is unique to the VALUE-RECORD, for it was not used in the STOCK-RECORD.

The STOCK-VALUE-FILE, lines 140 through 170, contains only two items: STOCK-NUMBER-O and STOCK-VALUE. If other information about a stock item is desired, it can be carried over from the STOCK-RECORD—for example, STOCK-NAME, QUAN-ON-HAND and WAREHOUSE-LOCATION. In each case the data-name in the VALUE-RECORD must be different by one or more characters from the corresponding data-name in the STOCK-RECORD.

THE PROCEDURE DIVISION

In the Procedure Division, the programmer specifies what he wants to do with the data described in the Data Division. As initially stated, the problem here is to calculate the value of inventory on hand for one item in the inventory file. The operation proceeds as follows. Read in a stock record, multiply the balance on hand for an item by its cost, and write out the value record.

The data required for both the input and output files was described in the Data Division in Figure 8-3. In actuality, the procedures and data descriptions are developed jointly since they are closely interrelated. Some procedures planning is often required to firm up the content of files.

Flow Chart

Figure 8-4 illustrates the value-calculation process in flow-chart form. The flow chart to handle one item is as simple as it looks.

COBOL-1 Program Form

Program Name	STOCK-VALUE CALCULATION	Page 1 of 1
Program Number	SVC-1	
Prepared by WILL HARRISS	Date AUG 17	

Line No.	Procedure-Name / Level No.	Data-Name	Picture / Procedures
010	DATA	DIVISION.	
020	FD	INVENTORY-FILE	
030	01	STOCK-RECORD.	DATA RECORD IS STOCK-RECORD.
040	02	STOCK-NUMBER	PICTURE 9(10).
050	02	STOCK-NAME	PICTURE X(20).
060	02	QUAN-ON-HAND	PICTURE 99999.
070	02	QUAN-ON-ORDER	PICTURE 99999.
080	02	WAREHOUSE-LOCATION.	
090	03	BUILD-NO	PICTURE 99.
100	03	AISLE-NO	PICTURE XXX.
110	03	BIN-NO	PICTURE 99.
120	02	UNIT-COST	PICTURE 999V99.
140	FD	STOCK-VALUE-FILE	DATA RECORD IS VALUE-RECORD.
150	01	VALUE-RECORD.	
160	02	STOCK-NUMBER-0	PICTURE 9(10).
170	02	STOCK-VALUE	PICTURE 9(6)V99.

FIGURE 8-3. COBOL-1 data division for stock-record and value-record.

254

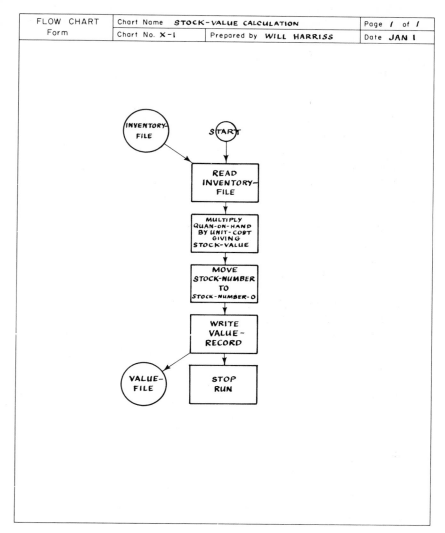

| FLOW CHART | Chart Name **STOCK-VALUE CALCULATION** | Page *1* of *1* |
| Form | Chart No. **X-1** | Prepared by **WILL HARRISS** | Date **JAN 1** |

FIGURE 8-4. *Flow chart for calculating the stock-value of one inventory item.*

START identifies the beginning point for the program. Five steps are involved in processing and calculating the value of one inventory item. The first step, READ in a stock record, brings in one record. The second step, MULTIPLY quantity by unit cost, is the heart of the process, for it fulfills the original requirement for calculating stock value.

The MOVE operation simply copies the stock number that was read in from tape into another location, so that it is available for use with stock-value as part of the output records. The final two operations are WRITE out the desired record, and then STOP the operations.

The names used in preparing the flow chart can be any descriptive name that the programmer wishes. However, as shown here in Figure 8-4, it is highly desirable to use Data-Division names and COBOL-operation names when preparing the flow chart in order to reduce the risk of discrepancies when procedures are written. One good way to prepare a COBOL-1 program is as follows. A very general flow chart is drawn showing all known inputs and outputs and a brief description of each processing activity. This chart is essentially the run chart described in Chapter 7. The Data Division entries for inputs and outputs are next written up for each processing activity. Then a detailed COBOL flow chart is prepared using the data-names from the Data Division and COBOL operation names: READ, MULTIPLY, MOVE, WRITE, and STOP. When writing on the procedures form, the programmer must use the exact data-names from the COBOL-1 Data Description, as shown in Figures 8-2 and 8-3 and also in Figure 8-5. Although a programmer is free at the beginning to choose any file-names, record-names, and data-names that he wants, he must adhere to them after he selects them. No deviation in spelling, abbreviation, or punctuation is permitted.

At the conclusion of flow-charting, the programmer should have a complete and integrated description of both logic and data. Writing COBOL procedures is then a relatively straightforward step.

Procedures Form

The spaces across the COBOL-1 form for use as a procedures form are headed Procedure-Name and Procedures. They are arranged in the following manner to guide the programmer when preparing the program for processor input:

> *Line number:* A line number identifies each line on the page. The programmer may number lines 010, 020, etc., to permit insertion of additional lines of program where desired by writing on a free line and assigning the desired intermediate number.
>
> *Procedure-Name:* A procedure-name is assigned to individual portions of a program so that one procedure statement can refer to another. The programmer selects and assigns a procedure-name to each paragraph and section of a program that he wishes to refer

FIGURE 8-5. *COBOL-1 procedures division for stock-value calculation program.*

COBOL-1 Program Form

Program Name	STOCK-VALUE CALCULATION	Page 1 of 1
Program Number	SVC-1	
	Prepared by WILL HARRISS	Date FEB 14

```
Page    Line    Level
1-3     No.     No.     Data-Name / Procedures                                    Picture / Procedures

001     010             DATA DIVISION.
        020     FD      INVENTORY-FILE
        030     01      STOCK-RECORD.                    DATA RECORD IS STOCK-RECORD.
        040     02      STOCK-NUMBER                     PICTURE 9(10).
        050     02      STOCK-NAME                       PICTURE X(20).
        060     02      QUAN-ON-HAND                     PICTURE 99999.
        070     02      QUAN-ON-ORDER                    PICTURE 99999.
        080     02      WAREHOUSE-LOCATION.
        090     03      BUILD-NO                         PICTURE 999.
        100     03      AISLE-NO                         PICTURE XXX.
        110     03      BIN-NO                           PICTURE 99.
        120     02      UNIT-COST                        PICTURE 999V99.
        140     FD      STOCK-VALUE-FILE                 DATA RECORD IS VALUE-RECORD.
        150     01      VALUE-RECORD.
        160     02      STOCK-NUMBER-O                   PICTURE 9(10).
        170     02      STOCK-VALUE                      PICTURE 9(6)V99.
        180             PROCEDURE DIVISION.
        190             START.
        200             READ INVENTORY-FILE.
        210             MULTIPLY QUAN-ON-HAND BY UNIT-COST GIVING STOCK-VALUE.
        220             MOVE STOCK-NUMBER TO STOCK-NUMBER-O.
        230             WRITE VALUE-RECORD.
        240             STOP RUN.
```

257

to so that he can use it in a different sequence. The broken line at Column 12 indicates that the procedure-name can run into the space for Procedures, if desired. Each procedure-name is followed by a period. The procedure-name START must always appear in each program before the first procedure to be executed.

Procedures: Procedures specify action—program verbs—to be carried out by the program on the data when the program is executed, although a few verbs merely direct the processor. Notice that each statement is followed by a period.

Program Verbs

The way that the program verbs are used in this program, and also their general form, deserve discussion.

READ Instruction. The READ instruction on line 200 of Figure 8-5 causes the processor to read in the contents of the first STOCK-RECORD in the INVENTORY-FILE. The FD entry in the Data Description for INVENTORY-FILE, which says DATA-RECORD is STOCK-RECORD, indicates this is the record for the processor to work with.

The general form of the READ instruction is

READ *file-name.*

The processor executes this instruction by bringing in the next record from the file-name specified. The words in italics, *file-name,* indicate the number and kinds of data-names that a programmer can use with an instruction. The READ instruction can be used with any file-name that is correctly described in the Data Division of the program. A period is placed at the end of each COBOL sentence to indicate it is complete.

MULTIPLY Instruction. The instruction on line 210 is the multiplication instruction. The general form is

MULTIPLY *data-name-1* BY *data-name-2* GIVING *data-name-3.*

This instruction causes the data element described by *data-name-1* to be multiplied by *data-name-2;* it places the product at *data-name-3.* The data referred to by each *data-name* must be all numeric. Decimal point location is handled automatically, if the assumed decimal point is properly located in each PICTURE.

MOVE Instruction. An instruction to move data, such as that on line 220, copies the data into a receiving area. It does not destroy the original data. The general form of the MOVE instruction is

MOVE *data-name-1* to *data-name-2*.

Processor execution of the MOVE instruction causes the contents of the item, which may be an elementary item or group item, identified by *data-name-1* to become the contents of the *data-name-2* item also. In Figure 8-5 MOVE merely copies the contents of STOCK-NUMBER into STOCK-NUMBER-O. This transfer is needed to put the elementary item STOCK-NUMBER into VALUE-RECORD in order to identify STOCK-VALUE when it is written out.

WRITE Instruction. The WRITE instruction shown on line 230 is similar to the READ instruction, for it writes out one record from processor storage onto magnetic tape. The general form is

WRITE *record-name*.

The COBOL-1 compiler, as described later, is instructed by means of the Data Division for this program that the VALUE-RECORD goes in the STOCK-VALUE-FILE.

STOP Instruction. The STOP instruction on line 240 consists simply of two words, so its form is

STOP RUN.

DATA FLOW

Execution of the program for the problem example is illustrated by a series of figures that show the essential features at each step. Schematic diagrams are used here only for discussion purposes, for this is not the way things really work. More careful descriptions are given later.

Assume that the procedure division (Figure 8-5) is read into high-speed storage as shown in Figure 8-6(a). The data descriptions for the Stock-Record and Value-Record (Figure 8-3) are used by the processor to assign storage locations for these two records, as is also shown in Figure 8-6(a). The amount of storage set aside here for each data-name is that specified by the PICTURE of the data element. The input file is ready for read-in at this point. Note that the data elements are stored exactly as wanted on tape and, for readability here, heavy rulings separate the items. The output file is merely a blank tape at this point.

When the READ instruction is executed the processor reads into the pre-assigned storage area the data contained in the first STOCK-RECORD, as shown in Figure 8-6(b). Observe the effect of this instruction by looking at the active parts, which are emphasized for

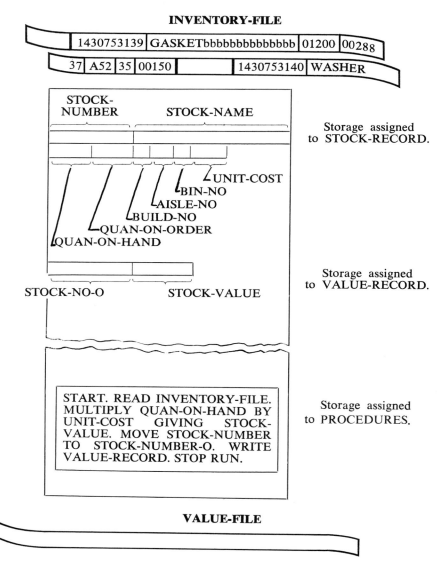

FIGURE 8-6(a). *Files and processor storage after program read-in and storage assignment (schematic).*

readability. The data items exactly fit the storage space assigned according to the data description. Alphabetical items are left-justified in the input stage to facilitate sorting, if required, and the remaining spaces are filled with blanks. The Stock-Name appears as "GASKETbbbbbbbbbbbbbb" in storage, because it was described as 20 alphanumeric characters long by the PICTURE X(20). Each "b" indicates a blank character position. The numeric

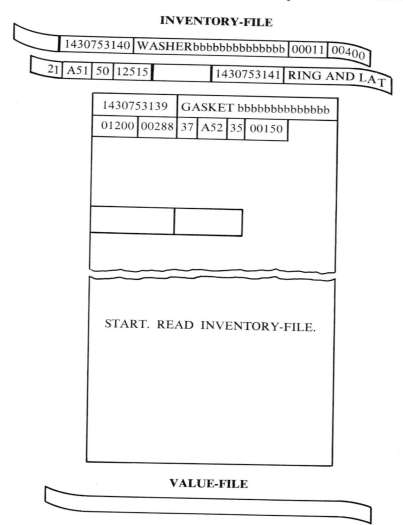

FIGURE 8-6(b). *Files and storage content after reading inventory-file.*

data items QUAN-ON-HAND, QUAN-ON-ORDER, and UNIT-COST are right-justified to align their units positions and decimal points, if any, to perform arithmetic correctly. The inputs 01200, 00288, and 00150 correctly fit their PICTURES, as shown in Figure 8-6(b).

After the MULTIPLY instruction is completed, Figure 8-6(c), the product from multiplying QUAN-ON-HAND BY UNIT-COST is stored as the STOCK-VALUE. Note that use of these two operands in the MULTIPLY operation does not change their

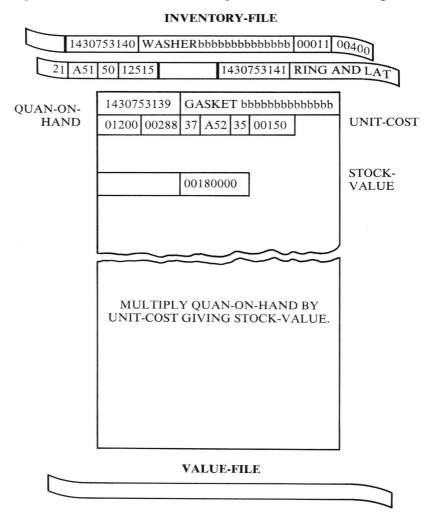

FIGURE 8-6(c). *Files and storage content after multiply order executed.*

existence in the STOCK-RECORD; they remain just as before. Any number in the location identified by STOCK-VALUE is replaced by the new product STOCK-VALUE. In general, data used as input to an operation also remain unchanged at their original location, and the results of an operation, when placed in storage, replace any data already in that location.

The MOVE instruction, as indicated in Figure 8-6(d) transfers the data called STOCK-NUMBER to the location called STOCK-NUMBER-O. Since the data-name STOCK-NUMBER is merely

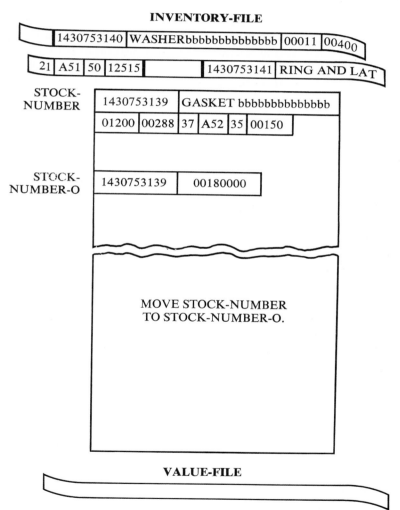

FIGURE 8-6(d). *Files and storage content after move order executed.*

the operand copied into another location, it continues to appear unchanged as an item in the STOCK-RECORD. The result: STOCK-NUMBER, which is 1430753139, now appears in two locations in storage.

In the last stage, the WRITE instruction causes the processor to write out (by copying) the VALUE-RECORD. Operations STOP as indicated by Figure 8-6(e), and the program is finished. Both records—STOCK-RECORD and VALUE-RECORD—remain in high-speed storage. The VALUE-RECORD is written in the output file just as it appears in storage without any editing. It might be useful to edit the STOCK-VALUE of 00180000, which has the PICTURE 9(6)V99, as shown in Figure 8-5 to make it readable as $1,800.00. Such editing would require suppression of leading zeros, and insertion of dollar sign, comma, and decimal point. Editing is described later in this chapter.

File Processing

The example described above shows how to calculate the value of a single inventory record. But most business data processing deals with many or all the records in a file; not merely a single record.

Cycling. The brute-force approach to handling more than one record is for the programmer to repeat the set of instructions for each additional record. Such repetition may be efficient for a few records, but is intolerable for a large file. Since an identical set of instructions is used to process each record, one set of instructions should handle a whole file of records by performing the set one time for each record in the file. The idea of repeatedly using a single set of instructions to process numerous records in a file is called *cycling.* The program cycles through the data one time for each record and thereby greatly increases the usefulness of a program. Cycling is an essential and widespread programming practice.

Figure 8-7 is a flow chart of the cycling procedure to calculate the value for each stock-record in inventory. It must, of course, stop when the end of file is reached. In the first cycle, the processor reads the first stock-record in the inventory-file, obtains a NO answer to the end-of-file question, and exits vertically. It multiplies quantity by cost to get value, and writes an output record containing the stock number and value of the first inventory item. Instead of STOP RUN, the next step is GO TO START. This GO TO transfer returns program control to the first operation, READ INVENTORY-FILE and the calculation process is repeated. From

INVENTORY-FILE

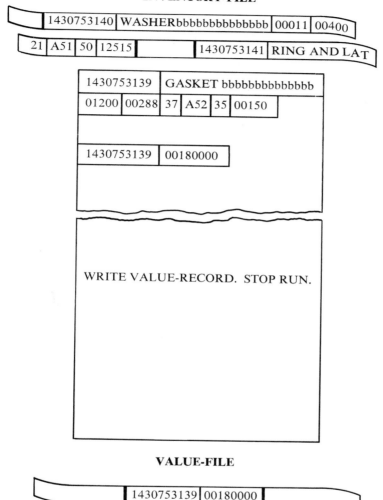

FIGURE 8-6(e). *Files and storage content after write order executed and stop.*

the flow chart in Figure 8-7, an instruction routine can be developed easily, as shown in Figure 8-8. It is similar to the routine for a single record in Figure 8-5 except that line 240 is GO TO START instead of STOP RUN and the READ instruction is conditional, as discussed below.

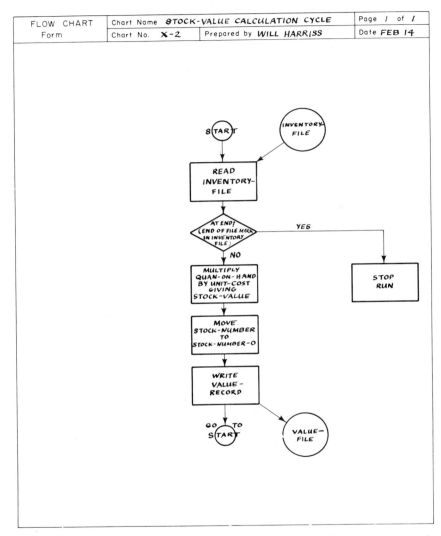

FIGURE 8-7. *Flow chart of cycle to calculate stock-value for each stock-record.*

COBOL instructions are executed in the same sequence as they are written, unless otherwise specified. The program sequence in Figure 8-8 is READ, MULTIPLY, MOVE and WRITE, with a new type of instruction: GO TO *procedure-name*.

COBOL-1 Program Form

Program Name **STOCK-VALUE CALCULATION**
Program Number **SVC-2**
Prepared by **WILL HARRISS**

```
Page 001

Line
No.

010   DATA DIVISION.
020   FD INVENTORY-FILE         DATA RECORD IS STOCK-RECORD.
030   01 STOCK-RECORD.
040   02 STOCK-NUMBER           PICTURE 9(10).
050   02 STOCK-NAME             PICTURE X(20).
060   02 QUAN-ON-HAND           PICTURE 99999.
070   02 QUAN-ON-ORDER          PICTURE 99999.
080   02 WAREHOUSE-LOCATION.
090   03 BUILD-NO               PICTURE 199.
100   03 AISLE-NO               PICTURE XXX.
110   03 BIN-NO                 PICTURE 199.
120   02 UNIT-COST              PICTURE 9999V99.
140   FD STOCK-VALUE-FILE       DATA RECORD IS VALUE-RECORD.
150   01 VALUE-RECORD.
160   02 STOCK-NUMBER-0         PICTURE 9(10).
170   02 STOCK-VALUE            PICTURE 19(6)V99.
180   PROCEDURE DIVISION.
190   START.
200   READ INVENTORY-FILE AT END STOP RUN.
210   MULTIPLY QUAN-ON-HAND BY UNIT-COST GIVING STOCK-VALUE.
220   MOVE STOCK-NUMBER TO STOCK-NUMBER-0.
230   WRITE VALUE-RECORD.
240   GO TO START.
250
```

FIGURE 8-8. *Procedure for cycling through stock-value calculation for the inventory file.*

267

GO TO Instruction. The GO TO instruction changes the normal sequence of executing instructions and causes the program to continue from the specified location. The general form of the GO TO instruction is

GO TO *procedure-name-1.*

The *procedure-name-1* is any valid COBOL name for a procedure section or paragraph as listed in the Procedure Division. The processor executes the GO TO instruction by finding the place in the program where *procedure-name-1* appears in the procedure-name column. It then executes the instructions starting at *procedure-name-1* and continues in normal sequence until it encounters another GO TO order to change sequence or encounters a STOP. In Figure 8-8, the GO TO START instruction on line 240 causes the processor to go back to START on line 190 to repeat the cycle of READ, MULTIPLY, etc. The program as written will cause the processor to continue processing records until it handles every record in the inventory file. It will then stop because of the conditional read instruction.

Conditional READ Instruction. The simplest plan for stopping the cycles—the repetitive execution of the program, described above—is to use a conditional READ instruction of the general form

READ *file-name-1* AT END *imperative-statement-1.*

The processor tries to read a record each time it reaches the conditional READ instruction in the program, which is basically similar to the READ instruction first described. But the conditional READ instruction differs in the following way. If one or more records remain in the file, the processor reads a record and continues with the following instruction. But, if no record remains in this file, the processor senses an end-of-file mark, previously placed on the tape. Since this mark indicates it is AT END of the file, the processor does whatever is directed by *imperative-statement-1*.

The READ-conditional instruction with an imperative-statement of STOP RUN will terminate the processing cycle when the end-of-file mark is encountered during execution of a READ instruction.

The programmer may want to perform some other operations—say, write out totals or perhaps go to another routine after processing all records in the file. For this purpose, the conditional READ instruction with an imperative GO TO statement is useful. The *procedure-name* TOTAL might identify the routine for writing out totals accumulated while processing the files. If so, the instruction READ STOCK-RECORD AT END GO TO TOTAL will cause the processor to execute the write-out routine that starts at TOTAL.

The conditional READ instruction enables the programmer to plan the processing of all records in a file without the bother of programming for the exact number in the file. The processor performs one cycle to handle each record in turn until the whole file is processed. A careful programmer is interested in how many records a file contains in order to control the accuracy of file processing, even though it is desirable to have instructions that save him the chore of testing after every READ operation to determine whether the last record was read. It is easier merely to count and check the number of records that are handled than it is to program for executing a cycle a specified number of times.

ADDITIONAL FEATURES

The COBOL programming language has many other features. Some of the basic features included in COBOL-1 are the standard arithmetic operations, special features for rounding and error control, branching or decision-making operations, and various data-editing operations to handle decimal points, commas, dollar signs, and zero suppression.

Arithmetic Instructions

The multiplication instruction was described above. COBOL-1 also has instructions for the other standard arithmetic operations—addition, subtraction, and division. Examples in Figure 8-9 illustrate the operation of each of the arithmetic instructions, and a brief description is given below. Each operand may be viewed as consisting of dollars and cents, although the "$" and "." are omitted because only numeric symbols can be present in data operated on arithmetically.

ADD GIVING Instruction. The addition instruction, ADD GIVING, provides for adding two numbers together and storing the total in another location. The general form of this instruction is

ADD *data-name-1* AND *data-name-2* GIVING *data-name-3*.

When the ADD GIVING instruction is executed, the processor adds the contents of *data-name-1* to the contents of *data-name-2* and stores the result at *data-name-3*. More simply, ADD A AND B

Instruction	Data-Name	Storage Contents	
		Before Execution	After Execution
ADD SELLING-PRICE AND TAX GIVING TOTAL-PRICE	SELLING-PRICE	5100	5100
	TAX	204	204
	TOTAL-PRICE	—	5304
ADD EACH-PURCHASE TO TOTAL-PURCHASES	EACH-PURCHASE	13200	13200
	TOTAL-PURCHASES	62100	75300
SUBTRACT DISCOUNT FROM GROSS-PRICE GIVING NET-PRICE	DISCOUNT	7300	7300
	GROSS-PRICE	73000	73000
	NET-PRICE	—	65700
SUBTRACT AMT-OF-CHECK FROM BANK-BALANCE	AMOUNT OF CHECK	4521	4521
	BANK-BALANCE	2001	–2520
DIVIDE NO-OF-ITEMS INTO TOTAL-COST GIVING AVERAGE-COST	NO-OF-ITEMS	12	12
	TOTAL-COST	4836	4836
	AVERAGE-COST	—	403

FIGURE 8-9. *Results of arithmetic operations.*

GIVING C. By using more data-names, a series of items can be added—for example, ADD A AND B AND C AND D AND . . . AND Y GIVING Z. An example of this instruction is: ADD SELLING-PRICE AND TAX GIVING TOTAL-PRICE.

ADD TO Instruction. A second addition instruction, ADD TO, corresponds more closely to the desk-calculator or adding-machine scheme for adding each number to the prior total to get a new total. Remember that a desk calculator forms a subtotal after each addition operation and has only one total for a whole series of additions. More simply ADD A TO B. The general form of this addition instruction is

ADD *data-name-1* TO *data-name-2*.

This instruction is useful to accumulate individual items into a total—for example, ADD EACH-PURCHASE TO TOTAL-PUR-CHASES.

SUBTRACT FROM GIVING Instruction. There are two forms of subtraction operations, corresponding to the two instructions for addition operations. The SUBTRACT FROM GIVING instruction means: subtract *data-name-1* from *data-name-2* giving *data-name-3*. This operation retains the operands and the remainder resulting from a subtraction operation: SUBTRACT A FROM B GIVING C. The general form of this instruction is

SUBTRACT *data-name-1* FROM *data-name-2* GIVING *data-name-3*.

The two operands *data-name-1* and *data-name-2* are unchanged by this operation. The remainder is stored as *data-name-3*. An example of this instruction is SUBTRACT DISCOUNT FROM GROSS-PRICE GIVING NET-PRICE, which makes the three items available for printing as three lines on an invoice.

SUBTRACT FROM Instruction. The SUBTRACT FROM instruction places the remainder in the location of *data-name-2*. It corresponds to subtraction performed on a desk calculator that calculates a new remainder after each operation, but doesn't retain the prior amount. The general form is

SUBTRACT *data-name-1* FROM *data-name-2*.

It causes the processor to subtract the contents of *data-name-1* from *data-name-2* and store the result at *data-name-2*. An example is SUBTRACT AMT-OF-CHECK FROM BANK-BALANCE, or simply, SUBTRACT A FROM B.

DIVIDE INTO GIVING Instruction. The divide instruction simply causes the processor to divide A into B giving C. The general form of the instruction is

DIVIDE *data-name-1* INTO *data-name-2* GIVING *data-name-3*.

The processor divides the contents of *data-name-1* into the contents of *data-name-2* and stores the quotient as *data-name-3*. All three items are available after execution of the DIVIDE INTO GIVING operation since three storage locations are used. However, the remainder from the division operation is not available, though it can be calculated if wanted. An illustration of the divide instruction is DIVIDE NO-OF-ITEMS INTO TOTAL-COST GIVING AVERAGE-COST.

Decimal-Point Alignment

COBOL-1 handles decimal-point alignment automatically on the basis of information in the data description for each program. For example, the data description includes data-names and pictures as shown. At time of execution of an addition operation, the contents are as indicated:

Data-Name	PICTURE	Contents
QUANTITY-X	99V9	327
QUANTITY-Y	99V99	9165
QUANTITY-Z	9999V999	

The addition operation ADD QUANTITY-X, QUANTITY-Y GIVING QUANTITY-Z causes addition in the following manner. (Remember that the hyphen is used to avoid a blank space yet keep the name readable; it does not mean minus or negative when used with data-names such as X, Y, or Z, even though the value itself may be negative.) The data content identified by QUANTITY-X and QUANTITY-Y are aligned according to the assumed decimal point in their pictures, as indicated by the V's, and any unused space at either the left or right in the result is filled in with zeros. The result of addition from the machine and the programmer's viewpoint can be compared as follows:

Data-name	PICTURE	Processor Operation	Programmer's Viewpoint
QUANTITY-X	99V9	327	32.7
QUANTITY-Y	99V99	9165	91.65
QUANTITY-Z	9999V999	0124350	0124.350

The processor stores the sum as 0124350 without a decimal point to conform to the PICTURE for QUANTITY-Z of 9999V999. The processor uses the picture 9999V999 to keep track of alignment during subsequent calculations and for inserting the decimal point by proper output editing to get 0124.350 for reports. The zeros will appear at both the left and right ends unless they are suppressed during editing to get 124.35 without unwanted zeros. A "$" sign can be inserted in any position wanted during the editing operation. Editing will be discussed in more detail later.

Size Error

The processor will keep track of decimal points according to the PICTURE described for each item. But the risk arises that a PICTURE is not of appropriate length for the data it is supposed to store. A data-name described by a PICTURE that is too short to hold the results assigned to that data-name will discard some digits.

If the PICTURE for QUANTITY-Z were 99V9, the result from the addition operation would be stored as 243 instead of 0124350, as above. The PICTURE 99V9 is too short to hold the sum of 12435 so that one or more significant digits—the leading 1 in this case—are lost. There are two remedies for the leading digit(s) size error. The obvious one is to make the PICTURE for any result large enough to store the result. As a further precaution, each instruction that may result in a size error should be written with an option for size error to transfer processor control to another program point. The programmer may choose to stop processing or to take remedial action such as shifting the operands to the right (as described in Chapter 10) and repeating the arithmetical operation. The general form of the SIZE ERROR option in an instruction can be illustrated by the ADD GIVING instruction:

ADD *data-name-1* AND *data-name-2* GIVING *data-name-3*
   ON SIZE ERROR *any imperative statement.*

The *imperative statement* corresponds to the *imperative statement* in the conditional READ instruction described earlier. It can be a STOP or a GO TO another point in the program to take remedial action. The size-error option can be used with any of the arithmetic instructions, and can also be used with the rounding option, as described below.

Rounding

Digits on the right-hand end of a result that exceed the picture field can be dropped with little or no harm. In fact, results should be shortened by dropping right-hand digits to get a suitable answer. Invoices, for example, are rounded to the nearest penny after adding taxes, deducting discounts, etc. Rounding is initiated by inserting the word ROUNDED in the instruction after the last data-name. The form of the multiplication instruction with the rounding and size error option is

MULTIPLY *data-name-1* BY *data-name-2* GIVING *data-name-3*
   ROUNDED ON SIZE ERROR *imperative statement.*

The rounding option—increasing the right-hand retained digit by 1, if the left-hand discarded digit is 5 or more—can be used also for the addition and subtraction operations. The options for rounding and size error can be used independently, or together, if desired.

Decision-Making

Three basic types of operating instructions were discussed above:

1. *Input-output:* READ and WRITE
2. *Arithmetic:* MULTIPLY, ADD, SUBTRACT, and DIVIDE
3. *Rearrangement:* MOVE

The fourth type of operation of interest here is *decision-making.* The programmer uses it when he wishes to choose one out of two or more possibilities.

Two-Choice Situations. The READ AT END instruction discussed earlier can be rephrased into a two-choice situation for decision-making. The question can be stated as, "Is this record the end-of-file mark?" If the answer is no, then, as shown in Figure 8-7, the program should continue in normal sequence to process this record and read the next record.

If the answer is yes, then the whole file will have been read, as indicated by the fact that this record is the end-of-file mark following the last ordinary record. The imperative statement after READ AT END may be either STOP or GO TO another part of the program for additional processing—summaries, write out, or whatever.

An inventory reorder routine also illustrates a situation involving two choices within a program. The quantity on hand for each inventory item can be compared with the reorder point for that item. If BAL-ON-HAND is less than REORDER-POINT, a purchase order can be prepared. If the balance equals or exceeds the point, the order routine is skipped and the processing cycle continued. The segment of a COBOL-1 program dealing with this decision-making aspect is shown in Figure 8-10.

IF Instruction. The instruction that starts IF BAL-ON-HAND in the inventory-ordering routine in Figure 8-10 is one version of the IF instruction. It is useful for situations that have two possible outcomes—action A or action B. Its general form is

IF *conditional-expression-1* THEN *statement-1* OTHERWISE *statement-2*.

Conditional expression-1 is first set up and tested. If *conditional expression-1* is true—that is to say, the condition set up is filled— *statement-1* is executed and *statement-2* is ignored. But if *conditional*

COBOL-1 Program Form | Page 001

Program Name INVENTORY-REORDER PROCEDURE | Page 1 of 1

Program Number IRP-3 | Prepared by WILL HARRISS | Date JUL 14

Procedures

```
Line No. | Procedure-Name / Level No. | Data-Name | Picture
010 START.
020     READ INVENTORY-FILE AT END STOP RUN. IF BAL-ON-HAND IS LESS
030     THAN REORDER-POINT THEN GO TO ORDER OTHERWISE GO TO START.

040 ORDER.
        NOTE THE ROUTINE TO GENERATE A PURCHASE ORDER STARTS HERE.
```

FIGURE 8-10. *Procedure to make a decision.*

expression-1 is false—not filled by the condition when the test is made—*statement-1* is ignored and *statement-2* is executed. That is, the option executed should correspond to the true condition. These rules can be expressed in decision table form, as follows:

	Conditional Expression-1	Statement-1	Statement-2
Rule 1	True	Execute	Ignore
Rule 2	False	Ignore	Execute

In the IF BAL-ON-HAND instruction of Figure 8-10, *conditional-expression-1* is BAL-ON-HAND IS LESS THAN REORDER-POINT, *statement-1* is GO TO ORDER, and *statement-2* is GO TO START.

Besides the conditional expression of the type *data-name-1* IS LESS THAN *data-name-2* discussed above, two others are available—the equal and greater conditions. The range of conditional expressions for the IF—THEN—OTHERWISE instructions is as follows:

IF *data-name-1* IS GREATER THAN *data-name-2* THEN *statement-1* OTHERWISE *statement-2*

IF *data-name-1* IS LESS THAN *data-name-2* THEN *statement-1* OTHERWISE *statement-2*

IF *data-name-1* IS EQUAL TO *data-name-2* THEN *statement-1* OTHERWISE *statement-2*

Any one of these can be used, but some care is needed to make sure that the "equals" case is handled correctly. A test on greater condition, for instance, lumps the equal and less conditions together. In general, a test for one condition lumps the other two conditions into the OTHERWISE *statement-2*.

Comparison to Zero. A simple type of conditional expression is formed by testing the relationship of *data-name-1* to zero. The condition is stated in terms of whether *data-name-2* is positive, negative, or zero—in effect "sign" condition. These correspond to the conditional expressions IF *data-name-1* GREATER THAN *data-name-2*, etc., with *data-name-2* now equal to zero. The range of expressions to examine sign condition of a single data element A is as follows:

> IF *data-name-1* IS POSITIVE THEN *statement-1* OTHER-WISE *statement-2*
>
> IF *data-name-1* IS NEGATIVE THEN *statement-1* OTHER-WISE *statement-2;*
>
> IF *data-name-1* IS ZERO THEN *statement-1* OTHERWISE *statement-2*

As an example, the IF—NEGATIVE instruction can be used in processing checks against depositors' accounts to determine whether to reject them for nonsufficient funds. After subtracting the amount of a check from account balance the over-draft charge and rejection instruction are IF ACCOUNT-BALANCE IS NEGATIVE GO TO SERVICE-CHARGE OTHERWISE GO TO NEXT-CHECK.

Inclusion of Action Statements.   The action statements associated with an IF instruction are commonly GO TO instructions, but any valid COBOL-1 imperative statement is allowed. That is to say, an operation can be incorporated with the IF instruction. For example, an instruction might be written as IF BALANCE IS GREATER THAN CHECK-AMT THEN SUBTRACT CHECK-AMT FROM BALANCE OTHERWISE WRITE BAD-CHECK-RECORD. In this expression, *statement-1* is a SUBTRACT command and *statement-2* is a WRITE command. Since each of the statements to be executed is an imperative command, both can be included in an IF statement. After the appropriate one of these commands is executed, the statement following the IF statement is executed next, since the processor is not sent to another procedure-name.

It is also proper to have a second IF instruction within an IF—THEN statement as the OTHERWISE clause. For an example, IF BALANCE IS GREATER THAN CHECK-AMT THEN SUBTRACT CHECK-AMT FROM BALANCE OTHERWISE IF CUSTOMERS-CREDIT-RATING EQUALS GOOD THEN WRITE POLITE-BAD-CHECK-RECORD OTHERWISE WRITE BAD-CHECK-RECORD.

Output Editing

The purpose of output editing is to present results in a format useful to the reader. Output editing for alphanumeric elements causes little trouble for they often can be used just as they were read in. If changes are needed to select and emphasize certain items or to improve readability, the output data descriptions can be used to select and edit desired items.

Numeric output, on the other hand, poses a different problem. First, the size of each item that is wanted in the output depends on the calculations involved and cannot be determined in advance. Second, the data description for each item must be long enough to handle the biggest result likely to arise in order to minimize the loss of digits at either end; however, this results in zeros filling in excess spaces in numeric PICTURES. Third, arithmetic operations will accept only all-numeric data. Special symbols—dollar signs, commas, and decimal points—must be excluded from COBOL-1 input, for they cannot be present in data-names during computation.

The user, however, still insists on results in an attractive, readable format. The current value of inventory is more comprehensible when stated as $1,268,453 than as 0000126845302. It is unrewarding for the processor to automatically keep track of the decimal point during a lengthy series of computations, unless it tells the user where the decimal point belongs in the final result and gives him the right number of digits.

Fortunately, COBOL provides the user with good facilities for editing output data. The editing process consists of two parts. First, when the Data Description is prepared for a program, certain data-names are set up to serve as editing areas. The PICTURE of these data-names will contain special editing symbols. The second part of the editing process is included in the Procedures Division of a program. The programmer writes program instructions to move data to the desired data-name that serves as an edit-area. The MOVE operation results in inserting editing symbols—decimal point, dollar sign, and comma—in the data-name, shortening it to the desired length, and suppressing any unwanted characters.

Decimal Point. Insertion of the decimal point is a common operation in editing. The *data-name* COST, for example, may have a PICTURE of 9999V99. The value of COST in one record in the input file might be 13726. This would mean $137.26 when used with the PICTURE 9999V99, although the "$" and "." are implicit from the digit positions in a card field and are omitted from the data when prepared for input. COST will appear as 013726 during processor computation in keeping with the PICTURE, and the V in the PICTURE tells the processor how to keep track of the decimal point. Thus the *data-name* COST may have the content 013726 from either data read-in or from processor calculations.

To insert the decimal point in the output data, an edit-area is set up by means of the Data Description, with a PICTURE containing a decimal point in the desired location. For example, COST-EDIT with the PICTURE 9999.99 may be set up as an edit-area for COST which was originally defined with the PICTURE 9999V99. Execution of the instruction MOVE COST TO COST-EDIT will make COST-EDIT contain 0137.26. The number now has the decimal point where it is wanted, but the "$" is missing, and there is an extra "0". These problems will be discussed shortly.

The important point about the editing operation, of which decimal-point insertion is a simple example, is that it involves two or more control stages as data move from input through processing to output. The input-file PICTURE controls input data. The PICTURE for each *data-name* that receives the results of calculations also controls the format of such results. The PICTURE for each edit-area controls the format and content of results before they go to output.

The symbol 9 in an edit-area PICTURE represents only a location for a numeric digit, which corresponds to the scheme for an input PICTURE—the actual content of the specified edit-area can be any numeric digit. The decimal point in the edit-area PICTURE is a *literal,* for it appears as the actual contents of a location and also indicates its position relative to others. When data are moved to the COST-EDIT area, with the PICTURE 9999.99, the characters fill the locations represented by the 9's and a decimal will occupy the third character-position from the right.

The processor will align the V-position of the source data (from read-in or from calculation) with the decimal point of the edit area, assuming that it exists in both cases. Figure 8-11 illustrates some of the possibilities that result from editing. Case 1 is the example described above in which the edit-area PICTURE and source PICTURE correspond to the input data so that the edited result has the same decimal point and digits. In Case 2, the edit-area contains only one digit to the right of the decimal point, so the right-hand digit is dropped and rounding does *not* occur.

In Case 3, the source PICTURE indicates that the decimal point is located four digits from the right, which corresponds to 1.3726 as input. Since the edit-area provides for only two places to the right, the edited result is 1.37 and the 2 and 6 are dropped. Editing

	COST		COST-EDIT	
	Input or Source		Edit-Area	
Case	*PICTURE*	*Contents*	*PICTURE*	*Contents*
1	9999V99	013726	9999.99	0137.26
2	9999V99	013726	9999.9	0137.2
3	99V9999	013726	9999.99	0001.37
4	9999V99	013726	99.99	37.26
5	999999	013726	99999.9	13726.0

FIGURE 8-11. *Result of moving data from the location described by input picture to the location described by edit-area picture.*

places zeros to the left of the decimal point to fill out the edit-area PICTURE.

Case 4 shows how leading digits can be lost by use of a short edit-area. The edit-area PICTURE has only two digits to the left of the decimal point, so that the leading 1 is dropped and the processor prints out a message on the console to indicate loss of a leading digit.

In Case 5, the input picture does not have a V, and the processor assumes that the source number is an integer—it consists of digits to the left of the decimal point only and none to the right. The edit operation correspondingly places the source data-item to the left of the decimal point, since the input PICTURE accepted all of it, and places a 0 to the right.

Dollar Sign and Comma. The other editing symbols, the dollar sign and the comma, are inserted in essentially the same way as the decimal point. First, the edit-area PICTURE is described in the Data Description with the dollar sign and comma in the character positions where they are wanted in the final output. The dollar sign, comma, and decimal point are three literals that also specify locations; each symbol both represents and is the location's content. The 9's in the PICTURE merely represent positions for numeric digits. The second step is to MOVE the data-name to be edited to the edit-area to associate the editing symbols with the data. Figure 8-12 illustrates some results from using these editing symbols.

In summary, dollar signs, commas, and decimal points are inserted into numeric data by developing an appropriate set of sym-

Case	COST Source Area PICTURE	COST Source Area Contents	COST-EDIT Edit-Area PICTURE	COST-EDIT Edit-Area Contents
1	9(5)	18710	$99,999.99	$18,710.00
2	9(7)	5371321	99,999,999	05,371,321
3	9999	0321	$9999	$0321
4	9999V99	132167	$9,999.99	$1,321.67

FIGURE 8-12. *Result of editing for dollar sign, comma, and decimal point.*

bols in an edit-area PICTURE, and moving the numeric data into the edit-area.

Zero Suppression. In Figure 8-12, both Cases 2 and 3 result in leading zeros that are undesirable; they interfere with quick comprehension and are unsightly. COBOL-1 has a zero-suppression editing symbol—Z—for replacing leading zeros with blanks. The Z, used in place of the 9 symbol in an edit-area PICTURE, has the following effect. When an item is moved into the edit-area, the digits fill in the Z locations just as they fill in the locations indicated by 9's. Leading zeros, however, become blanks. Examples of the use of zero suppression are shown in Figure 8-13.

Case	COST Source Area PICTURE	COST Source Area Contents	COST-EDIT Edit-Area PICTURE	COST-EDIT Edit-Area Contents
1	9(5)	17591	ZZZZZ	17591
2	9(5)	00018	ZZZZZ	18
3	9(5)	03040	ZZZZZ	3040
4	9(5)	03040	$ZZ,ZZZ	$ 3,040
5	9999V99	001734	$$,$$$.ZZ	$17.34
6	9999V99	000000	$Z,ZZ9.99	$ 0.00

FIGURE 8-13. *Result of editing for zero suppression (with dollar sign, comma, and decimal point).*

The other editing symbols—dollar sign, comma, and decimal point—are usable with zero suppression in the same manner as described above for 9's. The comma, however, has an additional feature, for it disappears if suppression eliminates all digits to its left. But the dollar sign and decimal point used in an edit-area PICTURE remain after zero suppression with the dollar sign "floated" into the desired position (between the left and right $'s) if the edit-area PICTURE contains two or more $'s in the positions to the left of the digits that are wanted in the output.

The use of Z's alone in an edit-area PICTURE will result in all blanks for an item containing all zeros. If the programmer wishes to retain one or more leading zeros, he may use 9's to the right of the Z's. But 9's must not be written to the left of the Z's.

The rules for editing data items for zero suppression, and insertion of dollar sign, comma, and decimal point can be summarized as follows:

1. [Z] Numeric data moved into an edit-area PICTURE fill in the spaces represented by the Z's. Zeros to the left of the first nonzero character become blanks and the decimal point does not stop zero suppression.
2. [9] Numeric data moved into an edit-area PICTURE occupy the spaces represented by 9's. Any 9's positions not filled by the source data become zeros.
3. [.] The V in the source data from input or calculations (or the right-most character if no V is present) is aligned with the decimal point in the edit-area PICTURE. The decimal point always carries through to the position shown by the picture of the edit-area.
4. [$] The dollar sign appears in the position shown by the edit-area PICTURE. Two or more $'s in the edit-area PICTURE "float" one $ to the position occupied by the right-most leading zero in the data that is indicated by a $.
5. [,] A comma in the edit-area PICTURE will appear in the edited result, *unless* zero suppression eliminates all digits to its left and it is then dropped.

TRANSLATING AND RUNNING A COBOL-1 PROGRAM

Programs written in COBOL-1 can, with minor modifications, be run on a data processor. Two phases are involved in using a COBOL program. First, a program written in COBOL, commonly called a *source program,* is translated into a program in machine language, called an *object program,* under the control of a special program called a *COBOL translator.* Second, the object program is run to process data. The idea that two processor runs and three programs are involved in writing, translating, and running a COBOL program is shown in Figure 8-14. Any processor that has a COBOL-61 translator can translate and run COBOL-1 programs. This section outlines the procedures required to prepare COBOL-1

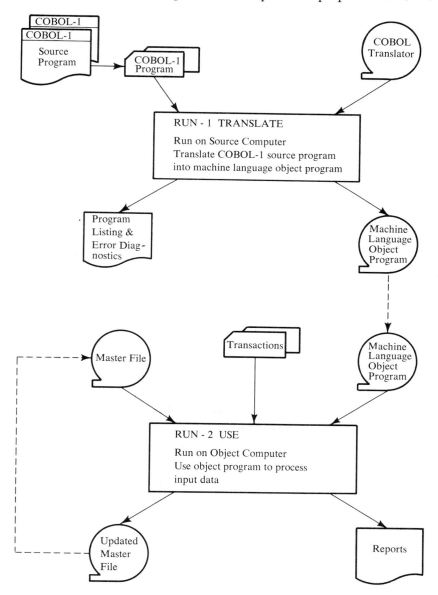

FIGURE 8-14. *Run diagram for translating and using a COBOL program.*

programs in a form suitable for translating on a particular processor. The exact method for preparing source programs varies, of course, from one model processor to another and even between different configurations of one model.

COBOL Running Requirements

In order to translate and run a source program written in COBOL, a programmer must adhere to the COBOL rules for writing programs. Furthermore, he needs access to a computer that has a COBOL translator available *and* the particular machine he is working with must meet the manufacturer's minimum specifications for translating COBOL programs. In general, each equipment manufacturer provides a COBOL translator for his large and medium scale business processors. Table 8-1, at the end of this chapter, shows a list of manufacturers and their processors with COBOL translators, which are often called *compilers.*

Reserved Words. One of the rules a programmer must follow in selecting COBOL names is *not* to use any of the words reserved for all versions of COBOL-61 or any of the additional words reserved for the machine he plans to use for translating his program. Certain words have a special meaning in COBOL and may not be used as data-names, file-names, or procedure-names. COBOL defines a word as a group of letters written together without spaces, although the parts of a COBOL word may be separated by hyphens for readability. For example, INVENTORY-FILE is treated as one word in COBOL and is a legal name; FILE by itself is a reserved word; and INVENTORY FILE is illegal for it violates the rules by containing a blank. The words reserved for all versions of COBOL-61 are listed in Table 8-2 at the end of this chapter. The additional reserved words for the IBM-1401, which is used here to illustrate a COBOL-1 program, are as follows:

ADVANCING	NO-PRINT-STORAGE
BEFORE	1402-R
LINES	1402-P
VALUES	1403-P
ID	1403-CT
RETENTION-CYCLE	1403-P-CB
TAPE	1403-P-C9
TAPES	1403-P-CV
NO-RELEASE	1401-SS
NO-OVERLAP	

Source Computer.   A manufacturer specifies the minimum configuration of a computer, commonly called a *source computer,* for efficiently translating or compiling a source program written in COBOL into an object program in machine language. The minimum specifications for a source computer usually state the number of magnetic tapes needed, the size of high-speed storage, and the availability of index registers and other logic features. A data processor, commonly called an *object computer,* used to run the resulting object program is subject to few restrictions for minimum size. The fact that the source computer may have to be fairly large to operate efficiently reflects the fact that compiling a program is likely to be more difficult than running it. Big configurations of medium and most versions of large scale processors will compile COBOL source programs. For example, to use the IBM 1401 as a source computer requires that it have at least the following:

12,000 positions of magnetic-core storage
Four magnetic-tape units
A 1403 'Printer, Model II
A card-reader punch
Advanced programming features (index registers)
A high-low-equal compare instruction
Sense switches
A multiply-divide instruction.

Object Computer.   After the source program is compiled, the resulting object program will run on any IBM 1401 that has at least 4000 positions of magnetic-core storage. Even card systems—that is, systems without magnetic-tape units—can run COBOL object programs.

Sample Program

The sample program shown in Figure 8-15 brings together many subjects discussed in this chapter. The basic problem used here is the simple one for calculating stock value described earlier, but several new points are added to make the problem and program more realistic and interesting. Since the new points are simple, they can be discussed along with the program. Of course, a complete statement of the problem and flow charts in one place would be useful, but they are easily prepared. The program shown in Figure 8-15 is complete and, when keypunched, can be compiled and run on any IBM 1401 that meets the COBOL configuration require-

COBOL – 1 Program Form	Program Name STOCK-VALUE CALCULATION	Page 1 of 3
	Program Number SVC-3	
	Prepared by WILL HARRISS	Date FEB 22

Page 1 / 001	Line No.	Procedure-Name / Level No. 12	Data-Name	Procedures 41	Picture
		COBOL RUN			
	001	IDENTIFICATION DIVISION.			
	002	PROGRAM-ID. STOCK VALUE.			
	003	AUTHOR. WILL HARRISS.			
	010	ENVIRONMENT DIVISION.			
	020	CONFIGURATION SECTION.			
	030	SOURCE-COMPUTER. IBM-1401			
	040	MEMORY SIZE 12000 CHARACTERS			
	050	NO-RELEASE NO-PRINT-STORAGE.			
	060	OBJECT-COMPUTER. IBM-1401			
	070	MEMORY SIZE 12000 CHARACTERS			
	080	NO-OVERLAP NO-RELEASE NO-PRINT-STORAGE.			
	090	INPUT-OUTPUT SECTION.			
	100	FILE-CONTROL.			
	11C	SELECT INVENTORY-FILE ASSIGN TO 1402-R.			
	120	SELECT STOCK-VALUE-FILE ASSIGN TO 1403-P.			

FIGURE 8-15. Sample COBOL-1 program.

COBOL-1 Program Form

Program Name: STOCK-VALUE CALCULATION
Program Number: SVC-3
Prepared by WILL HARRISS
Page 2 of 3
Date FEB 22

Page 1-3: 002

Procedures

Line No.	Procedure Name / Level No.	Data-Name	Picture
200		DATA DIVISION.	
210		FILE SECTION.	
220	FD	INVENTORY-FILE LABEL RECORDS ARE OMITTED DATA RECORD	
230	01	STOCK-RECORD.	
240	02	STOCK-NUMBER	PICTURE 9(10).
250	02	STOCK-NAME	PICTURE X(20).
260	02	QUAN-ON-HAND	PICTURE 99999.
270	02	QUAN-ON-ORDER	PICTURE 99999.
280	02	WAREHOUSE-LOCATION.	
290	03	BUILD-NO	PICTURE 99.
300	03	AISLE-NO	PICTURE XXX.
310	03	BIN-NO	PICTURE 99.
320	02	UNIT-COST	PICTURE 999V99.
330	02	FILLER	SIZE IS 28.
340	FD	STOCK-VALUE FILE LABEL RECORDS ARE OMITTED DATA RECORD	
341	01	IS VALUE-RECORD.	
350	01	IS VALUE-RECORD.	
360	02	STOCK-NUMBER-O	PICTURE 9(10).
370	02	FILLER	SIZE IS 5.
380	02	STOCK-NAME-O	PICTURE X(20).
390	02	FILLER	SIZE IS 5.
400	02	STOCK-VALUE	PICTURE 9(6)V99.
410	02	FILLER	SIZE IS 5.
420	02	STOCK-VALUE-E	PICTURE $222,229.99.
430	02	FILLER	SIZE IS 68.

FIGURE 8-15. Sample COBOL-1 program (cont'd).

287

COBOL-1 Program Form — Program Name: STOCK-VALUE CALCULATION — Program Number: SVC-3 — Prepared by WILL HARRISS — Page 3 of 3 — Date FEB 22

Page 003

```
500  PROCEDURE DIVISION.
510  START.
520  OPEN INPUT INVENTORY-FILE OUTPUT STOCK-VALUE-FILE.
530  NEXT-RECORD.
540  READ INVENTORY-FILE AT END GO TO FINISH.
550  MULTIPLY QUAN-ON-HAND BY UNIT-COST GIVING STOCK-VALUE.
560  MOVE STOCK-NUMBER TO STOCK-NUMBER-O.
570  MOVE STOCK-NAME TO STOCK-NAME-O.
580  MOVE STOCK-VALUE TO STOCK-VALUE-E.
590  WRITE VALUE-RECORD.
600  GO TO NEXT-RECORD.
605  FINISH.
610  CLOSE INVENTORY-FILE STOCK-VALUE-FILE.
620  STOP RUN.
```

FIGURE 8-15. Sample COBOL-1 program (cont'd).

ments. It can be used to demonstrate the operation of COBOL-1 and to gain actual introductory experience to COBOL-61.

A complete COBOL-1 program must have four divisions in the following sequence: Identification Division, Environment Division, Data Division, and Procedure Division.

Identification Division. The Identification Division is simple and has only three entries:

> IDENTIFICATION DIVISION
> PROGRAM-ID. *The program name.*
> AUTHOR. *The author's name.*

Each entry starts in the left-hand column under Procedure Name, as shown by the sample Identification Division in Figure 8-15 (lines 001 through 003).

Environment Division. The Environment Division describes the specific hardware to be used to compile and later to run this COBOL-1 program along with the assignment of files during the run phase. The Configuration Section specifies both the source computer and the object computer. It also includes an Input-Output Section to identify the particular piece of hardware—card punch, card reader, tape unit or printer—used for each input and output file; and it may also specify other equipment features. The exact content of this division depends upon the particular processor involved and is independent of the program except for the file names.

The Environment Division for the IBM 1401 processor to be used for the sample program is shown in the second part of Figure 8-15 (lines 010 through 120). The first two entries are the standard division and section titles. The *source computer paragraph* starts at line 030 to state the source computer is an IBM 1401. Line 040 specifies that it has 12,000 positions of core storage, which is the minimum permissible for use as a source computer. When a machine with 16,000 positions of core is used, the entry should be 16000 instead of 12000 in order to get more efficient compilation. The entries on line 050—NO-RELEASE, NO-PRINT-STORAGE— state that two special options available from the manufacturer— read-punch release and print-storage—are *not* included on this machine. If either of these features is available, the corresponding NO entry on line 050 is omitted. Note that a period follows the last entry in the paragraph for source computer.

The *object computer paragraph,* comparable to the source computer paragraph, specifies on line 060 that an IBM 1401 is the object computer to run the program. Line 070 indicates the object computer has 12,000 characters of core storage. The range of storage capacity for an IBM 1401 that can run COBOL programs is from 4,000 to 16,000 characters and the number actually available should be entered. Each NO entry on line 080 is omitted for each special feature that is available.

In the *Input-Output Section,* the programmer assigns each input and output file to a specific input-output unit. The section title appears on line 090 and the paragraph title FILE-CONTROL appears on line 100. The general form for each line assigning a file to a piece of equipment is:

SELECT *file-name* ASSIGN to *device-name.*

The entry on line 110 assigns INVENTORY-FILE, the input file described earlier in this chapter, to 1402-R, which is the code name for the card reader in the 1401 system. The next line assigns STOCK-VALUE-FILE, the output file, to 1403-P, which is the code name for the printer.

As mentioned earlier, the exact contents of the Environment Division vary widely among different processors. The description given here is typical, but it is appropriate only to one configuration of the IBM 1401. A manufacturer's manual for the particular processor used should be consulted for a detailed description.

Data Division.   The Data Division in Figure 8-15 corresponds to the Data Division for the stock value calculation problem given earlier in Figures 8-2 and 8-3. Some modifications are necessary to write it in correct form ready for compilation.

First, the title FILE SECTION must appear on the next line after DATA DIVISION (line 210). Second, after each FD and *file-name* entry the statement LABEL RECORDS ARE OMITTED must be inserted before the statement naming the data record (lines 220 and 340). Label records are special messages placed at the beginning and end of files that may contain an identification of the file, the date last processed, a record count, and other similar items. Label records are not used with punched-card files and are optional with magnetic-tape files. Two new data elements in the output record are STOCK-NAME-O (line 380), which is moved from the input record, and STOCK-VALUE-E (line 420), which will produce an edited version of stock value complete with a dollar sign, decimal point, comma, and zero suppression. For comparative purposes in this example, the program will print both the edited and unedited version of stock value in the output.

COBOL for the IBM 1401 imposes a special restriction on files that pass through the card reader or printer. These files must have a record length equal to the normal record length for the device that is used, which is 80 characters for the card reader or punch and 132 characters for the printer. The total number of data characters in STOCK-RECORD is 52. Since it must have a total of 80 characters, a pseudo-data element of 28 characters called FILLER is added to the STOCK-RECORD at line 330. Since FILLER is not a real data element, size is its only characteristic and is specified by a statement SIZE IS *number-of-characters*. The FILLER entry is used only for spacing and any number of elements with the same name, FILLER, can appear in the Data Division, but it must not be mentioned in any procedure statement.

The COBOL language implicitly assumes that output is in the form of magnetic-tape files, which can be printed later, if readable reports are wanted. As a result, general COBOL-61 makes little reference to printing, although specific processors may have COBOL instructions for line spacing, starting new pages, and so forth. When printed output is produced by a COBOL program, FILLER entries can be used to separate data elements. The entries on lines 370, 390, and 410 will each result in a blank space that is five characters wide during printing and make the report easier to read. The FILLER entry on line 430 is used to make the total characters in the Output record a full line of 132 print positions as required by the printer.

Procedure Division. The Procedure Division in Figure 8-15 corresponds to Figure 8-8, but several modifications are necessary to open the files only once for all records, to move three items (instead of one) to the output area, and to close the files after finishing processing.

The Procedure Division prepares files for use prior to executing a file READ instruction and for removal of file at the end of processing. The initial preparation is caused by inserting the following statement on line 520 as the first instruction:

OPEN INPUT *file-names* OUTPUT *file-names*.

The input *file-names* are written after INPUT and the output *file-*

names after OUTPUT. Before the STOP-RUN instruction, a file closing statement is written in the form:

CLOSE *file-names.*

All files are listed together regardless of type in the CLOSE instruction as shown on line 610.

The program reads many stock records, but it should OPEN the files only once. The *procedure-name* START, therefore, refers to the OPEN statement (line 520), and the record-processing part of the program (lines 540 through 600) is given the *procedure-name* —NEXT-RECORD (line 530). Finally, two new MOVE instructions are inserted (lines 570, 580) to transfer stock names from the input to the output record and to edit stock value.

At the last step of preparation for compiling, the COBOL-1 program is converted into punched cards or paper tape, depending on what media the source computer reads. The COBOL-1 programming form was designed to facilitate keypunching as well as to simplify writing the program. The data from each line filled in is punched as an entry on card or tape, but blank lines are ignored. For each entry, the page number of the COBOL-1 form is punched in the first three columns of a card (or characters on tape) and the rest of the entry copied intact from its line on the COBOL-1 form. Consequently, Line No. is punched in columns 4 through 6, Procedure-Name in columns 8 through 11; Data-Name in columns 12 through 41; and Picture in columns 43 through 49.

The maximum length of an entry depends upon the processor. For the IBM 1401, an entry is not permitted to exceed 72 columns because only the first 72 columns of an 80-column punched card are read by the IBM 1401 COBOL translator. Processors that accept punched paper tape can, of course, read entries of any length, although a limit is often imposed. When a COBOL-1 statement will not fit in one line on the COBOL-1 form, it is continued at the beginning of the *data-name* column on the next line. Therefore, one sentence may become two or more machine-media entries, but successive inputs are treated by the processor as a single statement until it encounters a period.

Most processors require some type of job or run card as the first card in the COBOL program. For the IBM 1401, this card is punched with COBOL in columns 6 through 10 and RUN in columns 16 through 18. The entry COBOL RUN is shown on the first line of Figure 8-15.

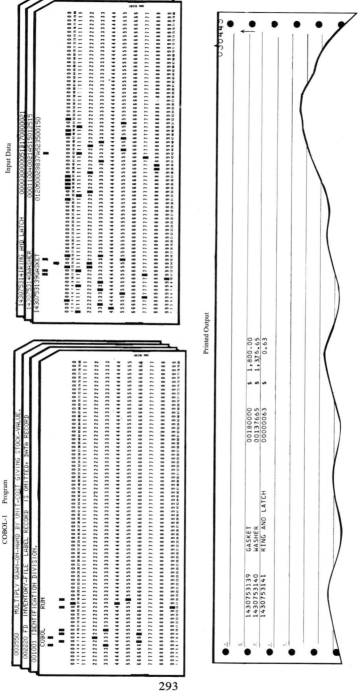

FIGURE 8-16. *Machine media: COBOL-1 program, input data, and output.*

293

Figure 8-16 shows part of this COBOL-1 program punched into cards and ready for read-in to a processor.

This simple program has many of the features of a typical file-processing application for it explains and illustrates each of the four COBOL divisions of a program. It shows how specific equipment is described and the data and procedures required. Although real COBOL programs are much longer, most of this length is due to more detail, not new features.

SUMMARY

When stated in ordinary terms, programming is a familiar subject to everyone. It consists simply of planning a solution and giving instructions for a way to do a particular task. The art of giving instructions to machines has much in common with that of giving instructions to people. However, more careful and explicit instructions in a special language are required for machines than is the case for people.

Programming consists of the following steps. First, define the *requirements*—inputs, outputs, files, and boundaries of the problem. Second, formulate a general *solution*. Third, identify available *capabilities*—people, organization, and hardware. Finally, match the general solution to the capabilities and arrive at a specific solution—a detailed set of *instructions* written in a particular language.

There are many types and varieties of programming languages. Machine-oriented languages reflect the engineering structure of a specific processor. Problem-oriented languages are designed with the symbols and format commonly used to solve a particular type of problem. Since English is commonly used in business, a language designed for solving business problems is built around English words and phrases.

The problem-oriented language described in this chapter is COBOL-1, a compatible subset of COBOL-61, the Common Business Oriented Language, which is planned for widespread use with different processors. COBOL-1 provides both an effective means of learning about programming and a practical tool for subsequent use, since COBOL-1 programs may be test-run on any of the many processors supplied with COBOL translators.

COBOL specifications require data descriptions in terms of *characters*—letters, numerals, and punctuation or special marks; *elements*—a set of related characters such as part name or stock number; *records*—a set of related elements, such as stock record; and *files*—a set of related records such as an inventory file. COBOL is designed primarily for *file processing*—reading a record, processing it, and writing it out, then repeating this cycle.

A COBOL-1 program contains four parts in the following sequence. First, the Identification Division simply identifies the program and the author. Second, the Environment Division describes the source computer for translating the COBOL program into machine language, and the object computer for running the translated program to process data. This division also specifies the particular media and device used for each file—cards, magnetic or paper tapes, or printer. Third, the *Data Division* describes each element, record, and file used in input, output or processing. Each entry in the Data Division consists of a *level number*—FD for files, 01 for records, and 02 to 49 for elements within records; a *file-, record-,* or *data-name*—a unique combination of 30 or fewer numerals and letters; and a *picture* that shows the type and maximum number of characters in each elementary item. Fourth, the *Procedure Division* specifies what operations the programmer wants to perform on the elements, records, and files described in the Data Division.

Instructions are available to read data in, move data inside the processor, and write out results. Arithmetic instructions provide for the operations of add, subtract, multiply, and divide. A third group of instructions are used to change the program sequence either unconditionally or depending on the outcome of a comparison. The order code for COBOL-1 is summarized in Table 8-3, at the end of this chapter.

After a programmer analyzes a problem and defines a solution, the process of writing a COBOL-1 program involves the following steps. First, a flow chart of the logic is drawn using COBOL data-names and instruction-names. Second, as each new data-name appears on the flow chart, its description is written in the Data Division. Third, the flow chart is translated into COBOL procedures using the exact data-names defined earlier. Both the description of data and the procedure statements are written on the COBOL-1 Programming Form. This form is designed for both writing programs and converting them to machine media.

COBOL is particularly well adapted to file-processing applications, which involve treating each record in a file in a similar manner—read the record in, perform some arithmetic or logic operations on it, and write out the results. Since this pattern of actions exists, one set of instructions can often be used repeatedly to process all the records in a file. This approach to repetitive

Company	Model of Equipment
Bendix Computer Division	G–20
Burroughs Corporation	B–5000
Control Data Corporation	CDC–1604 CDC–924
General Electric Company	GE–225 GE–304B
International Business Machines Corporation	705–II 705–III/7080 709/7090 7070/7074 1410 1401
Minneapolis-Honeywell Regulator Company	MH–400 MH–800
National Cash Register Co. (Joint implementation effort with General Electric Co.)	NCR–315–Tapes NCR–315–CRAM NCR–304A NCR–304B
Philco Corporation	200 series computers (210, 211, & 212 main frames)
Radio Corporation of America	RCA–301 RCA–601 RCA–501
Remington Rand UNIVAC	UNIVAC II UNIVAC Solid State UNIVAC III UNIVAC 1107 UNIVAC 490
Sylvania Electronics Systems Data Systems Operations	9400 MOBIDIC

TABLE 8-1. *Equipment manufacturers and processors with COBOL-61 compilers.*

use of programs is called cycling and is fundamental to programming.

The output-editing feature is of special interest in COBOL. Data used in computation must be numeric and not contain blanks, a decimal point, or other non-numeric symbols. Report users, however, want data in a readable and understandable format. COBOL editing features allow a programmer to suppress leading zeros and to insert dollar signs, commas, and decimal points.

Using a COBOL-1 program involves two steps. First, the COBOL-1 source program is translated into a machine language. Second, the resulting object program is run with data. With minor additions, a COBOL-1 program will compile and run on any machine that has a COBOL-61 translator and that meets the minimum configuration required for COBOL-61. The actual translation and execution of COBOL-1 programs should clarify its features and serve as an introduction to the operation of a typical business programming language.

ABOUT	CHARACTERS	END-OF-FILE
ACCEPT	CHECK	END-OF-TAPE
ADD	CLASS	ENTER
ADDRESS	CLOCK-UNITS	ENVIRONMENT
ADVANCING	CLOSE	EQUAL
AFTER	COBOL	EQUALS
ALL	COMPUTATIONAL	ERROR
ALPHABETIC	COMPUTE	EVERY
ALPHANUMERIC	CONFIGURATION	EXAMINE
ALTER	CONSTANT	EXCEEDS
ALTERNATE	CONTAINS	EXIT
AN	CONTROL	EXPONENTIATED
AND	COPY	FD
APPLY	CORRESPONDING	FOR
ARE	DATA	FILE
AREA	DATE-WRITTEN	FILE-CONTROL
AREAS	DECLARATIVES	FILLER
AS	DEFINE	FILLING
ASSIGN	DEPENDING	FIRST
AT	DIGIT	FLOAT
BEFORE	DIGITS	FORMAT
BEGINNING	DISPLAY	FROM
BEGINNING-FILE-LABEL	DIVIDE	GIVING
BEGINNING-TAPE-LABEL	DIVIDED	GO
BIT	DIVISION	GREATER
BITS	DOLLAR	HASHED
BLANK	ELSE	HIGH-VALUE
BLOCK	END	HIGH-VALUES
BLOCK-COUNT	ENDING	I-O-CONTROL
BY	ENDING-FILE-LABEL	IF
CHARACTER	ENDING-TAPE-LABEL	IN

TABLE 8-2. *Reserved words for all versions of COBOL-61.*

INCLUDE	OPEN	SEQUENCED
INPUT	OPTIONAL	SIGN
INPUT-OUTPUT	OR	SIGNED
INTO	OTHERWISE	SIZE
IS	OUTPUT	SOURCE-COMPUTER
JUSTIFIED	PERFORM	SPACE
LABEL	PICTURE	SPACES
LEADING	PLACES	SPECIAL-NAMES
LEAVING	PLUS	STANDARD
LEFT	POINT	STATUS
LESS	POSITION	STOP
LIBRARY	POSITIVE	SUBTRACT
LINES	PREPARED	SUPERVISOR
LOCATION	PRIORITY	SUPPRESS
LOCK	PROCEDURE	SYNCHRONIZED
LOW-VALUE	PROCEED	TALLY
LOW-VALUES	PROTECT	TALLYING
LOWER-BOUND	PROTECTION	TAPE
LOWER-BOUNDS	PURGE-DATE	TEST-PATTERN
MEMORY	QUOTE	THAN
MEMORY-DUMP	RANGE	THEN
MEMORY-DUMP-KEY	READ	THROUGH⎱ *Equivalent*
MINUS	RECORD	THRU ⎰
MODE	RECORD-COUNT	TIMES
MODULES	RECORDING	TO
MOVE	RECORDS	TYPE
MULTIPLE	REDEFINES	UNEQUAL
MULTIPLIED	REEL	UPPER-BOUND
MULTIPLY	REEL-NUMBER	UPPER-BOUNDS
NEGATIVE	RENAMING	UNTIL
NEXT	REPLACING	UPON
NO	RERUN	USAGE
NO-MEMORY-DUMP	RESERVE	USE
NOT	REVERSED	VALUE
NOTE	REWIND	VARYING
NUMERIC	RIGHT	WHEN
OBJECT-COMPUTER	ROUNDED	WITH
OBJECT-PROGRAM	RUN	WORDS
OCCURS	SAME	WORKING-STORAGE
OF	SECTION	WRITE
OFF	SELECT	ZERO
OMITTED	SENTENCE	ZEROES
ON	SENTINEL	ZEROS

TABLE 8-2. *Reserved words for all versions of COBOL-61 (cont'd).*

READ *file-name-1*. Read into the processor the record from the input file identified by *file-name-1*.

READ *file-name-1* AT END *imperative-statement-1*. If a record remains in the input file identified by *file-name-1*, then read it. If none remains, execute the instruction contained in *imperative-statement-1*.

WRITE *record-name-1*. Write the data identified by *record-name-1* in the output file set up to receive them.

MOVE *data-name-1* TO *data-name-2*. Move the data identified by *data-name-1* to the location called *data-name-2*.

ADD *data-name-1* AND *data-name-2* GIVING *data-name-3*. Add the data identified by *data-name-1* to the data identified as *data-name-2* and call the result *data-name-3*. Any number of *data-names* may be added together by placing them in the instruction between the ADD and the GIVING.

ADD *data-name-1* TO *data-name-2*. Add the data identified by *data-name-1* to the data identified by *data-name-2* and call the result *data-name-2*. Any number of *data-names* may be added to *data-name-2* by placing them in the instruction between the ADD and the TO.

SUBTRACT *data-name-1* FROM *data-name-2* GIVING *data-name-3*. Subtract the data identified by *data-name-1* from the data identified by *data-name-2* and call the result *data-name-3*. Any number of *data-names* may be subtracted from *data-name-2* by placing them in the instruction between the SUBTRACT and the FROM.

SUBTRACT *data-name-1* FROM *data-name-2*. Subtract the data identified by *data-name-1* from the data identified by *data-name-2* and call the result *data-name-2*. Any number of *data-names* may be subtracted from *data-name-2* by placing them in the instruction between the SUBTRACT and the FROM.

MULTIPLY *data-name-1* BY *data-name-2* GIVING *data-name-3*. Multiply the data identified by *data-name-1* by the data identified by *data-name-2* and call the product *data-name-3*.

DIVIDE *data-name-1* INTO *data-name-2* GIVING *data-name-3*. Divide the data identified by *data-name-1* into the data identified by *data-name-2* and call the quotient *data-name-3*.

ON SIZE ERROR *imperative-statement-1*. If an arithmetic instruction with this phrase attached results in the loss of leading digits, follow the instruction in *imperative-statement-1*. Otherwise ignore *imperative-statement-1*.

TABLE 8-3. *COBOL-1 instructions.*

ROUNDED. (option) When an arithmetic instruction with this phrase attached results in the loss of trailing digits, the right-most retained digit is increased by 1 if the discarded digit is a 5 or greater.

GO TO *procedure-name-1*. When this instruction is encountered, the program continues with the first instruction that follows *procedure-name-1*.

IF *conditional-expression-1* THEN *statement-1* OTHERWISE *statement-2*. If *conditional-expression-1* is a true statement, then execute *statement-1;* otherwise execute *statement-2*.

STOP RUN. This instruction marks the end of a COBOL-1 program and will cause the processor to halt.

TABLE 8-3 *COBOL-1 instructions (cont'd)*.

Chapter 9
Programming—COBOL-1 (Continued)

The essential techniques of COBOL discussed in the preceding chapter—how to read and write records, perform arithmetic, make simple decisions, and edit output—can be used to handle simple business applications, as illustrated by the inventory problem. However, actual business applications are far more complex, and COBOL or similar compiler languages are designed with features to make them more adaptable.

The inventory problem, slightly modified, will again be used in order to illustrate the additional instructions and features of COBOL. The purpose of each instruction is discussed in conjunction with a typical application; in the last section, many of the applications are combined into a program for inventory updating. The complete instruction set for COBOL-1 is given in Table 9-2 at the end of the chapter.

INVENTORY-UPDATING LOGIC

The selected inventory-updating operations shown in the flow chart in Figure 9-1 are based on the transaction-processing portion of the inventory-updating example discussed in Chapter 7. Chart B-1 (Figure 9-1) shows the major flows, decisions, and actions. The upper half of the flow chart contains a scheme for checking whether the transaction being handled has a valid date and for counting the number of transactions handled. Date-validity checks and transaction counts are representative of a wide variety of control checks that can be performed on input data. The lower half of the flow chart shows how transaction numbers and master-record numbers are matched with the appropriate processing action.

Date-Validity Check and Transaction Count

The process of checking the validity of transaction dates starts when a date limit and the present date are brought into storage. The

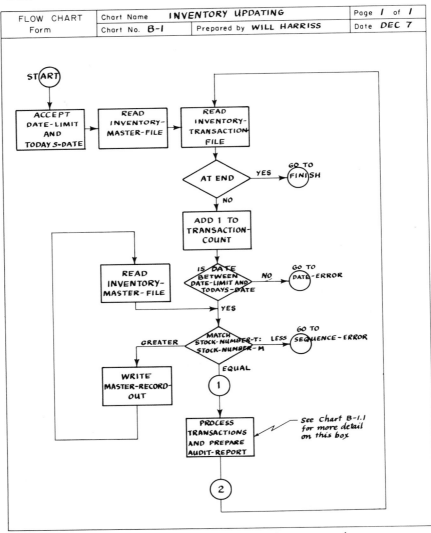

FIGURE 9-1. *Selected inventory updating operations.*

date limit is the date of the oldest valid transaction. If the present date (specified by day of the year) is 261 and transactions more than seven days old are not acceptable, then the date limit is 254. Any transaction with a date between the limit and the present date is considered valid for processing; a transaction with a date outside these limits is rejected for investigation. The set-up operations to accept these checkdates and read the first master record are performed only once.

The first operation in the repetitive part of the program is an instruction to read a record from the inventory-transaction file. The second operation tests for the end of the inventory-transaction file. If a transaction is available, meaning that it is not the end of the inventory-transaction file, the transaction count is increased by one, and the validity of the transaction date is checked. If the date is valid, the stock numbers of the transaction record and master record are compared. If the stock number of the transaction is greater, the matching master record has not been reached; the current master record is then written out and another one read.

The cycle of match-write-read for master records is repeated until a master record is reached with a stock number that matches the number of the existing transaction. When a hit occurs, the transaction type is determined in order to process the transaction and prepare the audit report. The action path then returns to read the next transaction. After all the transactions are processed, the end-of-file test directs the action path to the finish operation. The finish operation contains instructions to transfer any remaining records in the inventory master file to the output file, so that the updated inventory master file will contain both active and inactive inventory records. Any desired summaries of results for the entire run also are prepared at this time. All processing is then complete and operations stop.

Transaction Processing

The detailed procedures for the transaction-processing section of Chart B-1 are applied to issues in Chart B-1.1 in Figure 9-2; the processing of receipts and orders is merely suggested. The quantity of a stock item issued is subtracted from the quantity on hand, and three operations are performed for inventory financial accounting. The department withdrawing the material and the project using the material are charged with its cost for departmental cost control and for job cost accounting. The audit count of the number of issue transactions processed is increased by one. An issue is then completely processed and a test is made for a negative balance of quantity on hand. This sequence—process and then test—is selected because a negative balance merely indicates that something is amiss. The current transaction may be entirely correct.

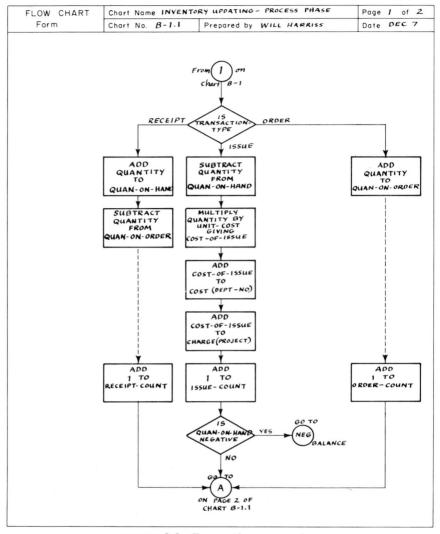

FIGURE 9-2. *Transaction processing.*

More detailed accounting is often required for receipts and orders. For simplicity, however, only the updating and record counts appear on the chart and in the subsequent program.

The second page of Chart B-1.1 in Figure 9-3 shows the steps in auditing during the processing phase. In order to control data-preparation operations, batches of exactly 50 transactions are prepared

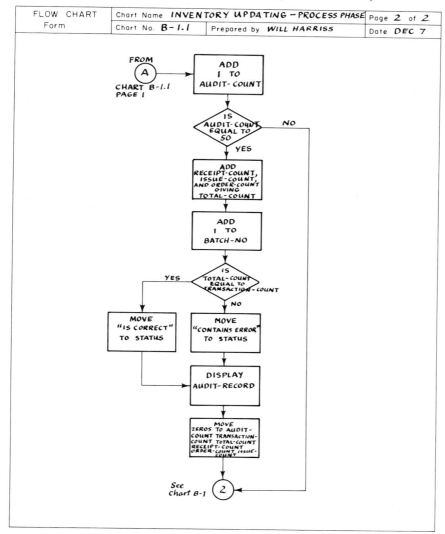

FLOW CHART Form	Chart Name INVENTORY UPDATING – PROCESS PHASE		Page 2 of 2
	Chart No. B-1.1	Prepared by WILL HARRISS	Date DEC 7

FIGURE 9-3. *Auditing during the processing phase.*

and submitted to the inventory-update run. For each batch of 50 transactions, an audit report is printed showing batch number, status, and counts for the number of transactions, receipts, issues, and orders. The status for a batch is either "Is correct" or "Contains error," depending upon whether the transaction count equals the sum of the other counts.

This audit routine should detect the loss of a transaction from input after batches are prepared or reveal that processing of a transaction has been duplicated because of a program or machine error. A batch that contains an error will be carefully checked and the error corrected during the next processing cycle. The audit count must be reset to zero—move zeros to audit count, etc.—each time the audit report is prepared in order to prepare an individual audit report for each batch of 50 transactions. If it is not reset, only one audit report is produced by the program instead of one for each batch of transactions. Each of the totals also must be reset to zero in preparation for the next batch. The heavy emphasis placed on error checks in this program is indicative of their importance. Errors are a serious problem and, especially in new programs, can result in confusion and high processing costs. After the program has run for several months and has shaken down, the programmer may remove some of the error checks, but enough should be retained to continually check input validity and operation of the program to maintain control over processing.

The flow charts in Figures 9-1, 9-2, and 9-3 are used as the basis of illustrations throughout this chapter. The entire program for this example of inventory updating, including sample Identification and Environment Divisions, is given in Figures 9-6, 9-7, and 9-8 near the end of the chapter. Although this example is more complex than earlier ones and more nearly approximates typical business applications, it deals with only a small part of a realistic inventory-processing scheme; for example, the reorder process and reorder point revision discussed in Chapter 7 are not included.

The line numbers used in the illustrations throughout the chapter correspond to the same line numbers in the complete program given in the last three figures of the chapter. Since the lines illustrated are only segments selected for explanations of COBOL features—in some cases they are neither whole lines nor contiguous lines—it is useful to trace the numbered lines to the complete sample program to see how they fit into the other segments. A second series of line numbers, consisting of four digits, is also used throughout the chapter; these line numbers identify points that are discussed but not included in the sample program. This numbering scheme is used, even though it is outside COBOL rules to keep the discussion of alternative approaches to programming from becoming confused with the updating program itself. In a few cases, both explanatory lines and actual program lines are used together in the text illustrations.

DATA HANDLING

COBOL-1 has advanced features to describe and manipulate individual items of data—for example, literals, low-volume input and output, working storage, constants, and condition-names. These features are interrelated—each makes use of another. These features will first be described separately, then combined in the sample program in order to illustrate their format and usage.

Literals

As described in Chapter 8, one procedure for getting data to use in processing is to read it in from an input file. In order for the programmer to use an instruction such as ADD ONE TO TRANS-ACTION-COUNT to maintain the transaction count, he must describe ONE as a data-name in the Data Division and read in the content "1" for it from an input file. Similarly, in order to have an alphanumeric error-message such as CONTAINS ERROR available as output, he must define the message and read it into storage from an input file.

A more convenient way to procure certain numbers and words for use in a program is for the programmer to write *literals*—actual numerals or letters—in *procedure* statements. A literal, therefore, is a pseudo data-name in which the name itself is the content.

An example of procedure statements using the numeric literal 1, alphanumeric literal INVALID TYPE, and figurative literal ZEROS is as follows:

Line No.	Proce-dure Name	Procedures
545		A D D 1 TO TRANSACTION-COUNT.
790		MOVE 'INVALID TYPE' TO REASON.
750		MOVE ZEROS TO AUDIT-COUNT

A *numeric literal* consists of one to 18 numeric characters. A numeric literal can be used for counting records by executing the ADD statement (line 545, above) each time a record is processed. One decimal point may appear within a numeric literal, but it must not be in the rightmost position, since the COBOL processor treats any decimal point followed by a space as though it were a period. A numeric literal contains numerals only and is thereby distinguished from data-names, which must contain at least one alphabetic character.

An *alphanumeric literal* may contain from one to 120 characters: numerals, letters, blanks, or punctuation marks; but not single quotation marks. In COBOL-1, alphanumeric literals are enclosed in single quotation marks (') to distinguish them from data-names. The double quotation mark (") serves its ordinary function of setting off words for emphasis in the text, since the double quotation mark is not a valid character in COBOL.

The MOVE statement (line 790, above) will place INVALID TYPE in the storage location called REASON. Like other alphanumeric data, an alphanumeric literal may not be used in an arithmetic statement. When moved within storage, numeric and alphanumeric literals are, of course, subject to the receiving area PICTURE description for length and kinds of characters. If REASON has a PICTURE X(10), its content after executing the instruction on line 790, above, will be INVALID TY. Any picture that contains less than 12 characters will discard some of the data at the right. Furthermore, alphanumeric literals must not be used with data-names that are described as all numeric.

A *figurative constant* is the name of a character used as a literal. For example, the MOVE statement (line 750) will fill AUDIT-COUNT with zeros. Figurative constants exactly fill a specified location, whatever its length and description. If the receiving location has a picture 99, then its contents become 00 when zeros are moved into it. The figurative constant SPACES is used in similar fashion to generate blanks.

Low-Volume Input-Output

In order to use COBOL instructions for reading and writing records from files, appropriate descriptions for files and records are required in the Data Division.

Writing file and record descriptions is warranted if numerous records will be read or written, but it represents unnecessary work in programming and may be inefficient during compiling and running if only one or a few records are wanted. To handle low volumes of data, COBOL-1 has the ACCEPT statement for input and DISPLAY statement for output, which are used as follows:

Line No.	Proce- dure Name	Procedures
520		ACCEPT TODAYS-DATE.
745		DISPLAY AUDIT-RECORD.
835		DISPLAY
836		'TRANSACTION WITH STOCK-NUMBER ' STOCK-NUMBER-T
837		' WAS LISTED BECAUSE OF ' REASON.

ACCEPT Instruction. The accept instruction in a program brings in data from an input device. The particular device, which is generally the punched-card reader, is specified in the Environment Division. For example, in order to check the validity of a transaction date against the present date during a file-processing run, it is necessary to have the correct date available. A convenient way to supply the date is to punch it in a card and read it in by an ACCEPT statement (line 520) at the beginning of the program. A series of accept statements will bring in any kind and quantity of data placed in the low-volume input device.

DISPLAY Instruction. The display instruction writes a limited amount of data on a device, usually a printer or a typewriter, specified in the Environment Division. The DISPLAY statement (line 745) will print the contents of the AUDIT-RECORD, which consists of one or more elementary or group items. For a transaction with an invalid date, the program branches to and executes the statement on lines 835 to 837, in which the characters within quotes are alphanumeric literals, and STOCK-NUMBER-T and REASON are data-names not enclosed in quotation marks. The data-name REASON (line 837) contains a message passed down from a prior point in the program, which, for the INVALID DATE, is line 765 in Figure 9-8. If the stock number of the record with an invalid date is "1430702901" the display statement on lines 835 to 837 will print the message

TRANSACTION WITH STOCK NUMBER 1430702901 WAS LISTED BECAUSE OF INVALID DATE

The DISPLAY instruction can be used to print any desired combination of data-names and valid literals. Each blank wanted in a display statement to keep items from running together must be planned. Blanks (b) wanted within alphanumeric literals—for example, TRANSACTIONbWITHbSTOCKbNUMBER—are simply written in the program statements. In order to have a blank before and after a data-name or a message passed down from a prior point in the program, a blank is enclosed within the quotation marks—for example, ...STOCKbNUMBERb'...'bWASbLISTEDbBE-CAUSEbOFb'..., as shown on lines 835 to 837.

Working Storage

The file section of the Data Division of a program contains descriptions of files and records. Often, however, the programmer will want to use data-names for dates, counts, or work areas that are not part of an input or output file. He can do this by describing these data-names in the Working Storage Section of the Data Division.

The Working Storage Section is a work area for the programmer to use as he wishes. Within Working Storage, he might define data-names called TODAYS-DATE and TRANSACTION-COUNT in order to have the present data available or to keep a count of the number of transactions processed. A data-description must be set up in working storage before any item not in a file can be brought in by an ACCEPT instruction, printed by a DISPLAY instruction, or manipulated by any other instruction.

Data-names in working storage are described in the same fashion as data-names in the file section. Each entry consists of a level number, the data-name, and a picture. For example, the descriptions of date limit, today's date, and audit count might have the following entries:

Line No.	Level No.	Data-Name	Picture
350	77	DATE-LIMIT	PICTURE 9(3).
355	77	TODAYS-DATE	PICTURE 9(3).
365	77	AUDIT-COUNT	PICTURE 99.

The level number of 77 indicates that TODAYS-DATE is an *independent work area;* it is not subdivided and is not a part of another item. Each of the other two is also a single item and has a level number of 77. All level 77 items are written at the beginning of the working storage section in a program.

Working storage also provides for *group* work areas to describe records or items that contain other items and uses the ordinary COBOL scheme of level numbers 01 to 49 for data-elements. The sample problem requires the display of an AUDIT-RECORD for each batch of 50 transactions. A group work area can be used to hold this record, which consists of several items—batch number, status, transaction count, and total count—and which is described as follows:

Line No.	Level No.	Data-Name	Picture
385	01	AUDIT-RECORD	
390	02	BATCH-NO	PICTURE 9(4).
395	02	STATUS	PICTURE X(14).
400	02	TRANSACTION-COUNT	PICTURE 9(2).
405	02	TOTAL-COUNT	PICTURE 9(2).

Transfer of data to and from working storage results from MOVE, ACCEPT, DISPLAY, or arithmetic instructions, since items in working storage can, for example, be added to items in the file section, or vice versa. The READ and WRITE instructions are not relevant, however, because items in working storage do not belong to an input or ouput file.

Items in independent and group work areas can be given *initial values*—the value or content of a data-name when program execution starts. An initial value is established by adding a VALUE IS *any-literal* clause to the data description for an item. For example, a program might read one record in a set-up operation before starting the regular file-processing cycle. In order to make the record count equal one to reflect this operation before starting regular processing, the programmer writes the following:

Line No.	Level No.	Data-Name	Picture
1000	77	RECORD-COUNT	PICTURE 9(4) VALUE IS 1.

The record count starts with a value of 1 and, by other instructions, can be increased by 1 for each record read during processing. The programmer may also set the value of an item to an alphanumeric literal or to a figurative constant by using ZEROS for a numeric item and either ZEROS or SPACES for an alphanumeric item.

A working storage item established by an initial value clause has the specified value at the beginning of the program, but subsequent operations usually change the initial value.

Constant Section

The Constant Section of the Data Division describes items that have the same value throughout a program. The *constant* value for an item is specified by the standard VALUE IS *any-literal* clause. For example, a special record with a stock number of 9999999999 might be put after the final item record to indicate the end of the master file. If the programmer defines LAST as shown below, he can determine when the end of the file is reached by comparing the stock number of each new master record to LAST.

Line No.	Level No.	Data-Name	Picture
455	77	LAST	PICTURE 9(10) VALUE
456		IS 9 9 9 9 9 9 9 9 9 9.	
1010	77	SALES-TAX	PICTURE 9V99 VALUE IS 0.04.

Named constants are standard terms such as SALES-TAX, discount percentages, and tax rates which are set up in the Constant Section and given appropriate values. Constants may be either independent items with a level number of 77 or group items with level numbers from 01 to 49. As before, the data class—numeric or alphanumeric—of the value-literal should correspond with the class of data described by the picture.

Condition-Names

A *condition-name* is a name associated with each outcome or value of a data-name that may occur during the course of a program. Transaction type, for example, may have a value of 1 for receipts, 2 for issues, and 3 for orders. The data description consists of a level number of 88 (which is reserved exclusively for condition-names), a condition-name, and a value clause, as follows:

Line No.	Level No.	Data-Name	Picture
1020	02	TRANSACTION-TYPE	PICTURE 9.
1030	88	RECEIPT	VALUE IS 1.
1040	88	ISSUE	VALUE IS 2.
1050	88	ORDER	VALUE IS 3.

The definition of a data-name with a level number 02 to 49 controls the condition-names, so that they do not need individual pictures. After a condition-name is defined, it can be used in place of a conditional phrase that equates the data-name to the value of the condition-name. For example, the phrase VALUE IS 1 means that the single condition-name RECEIPT is equivalent to (serves the same purpose as) the conditional phrase TRANSACTION-TYPE IS EQUAL TO 1. To test whether a transaction is a receipt, the programmer might write either one of two procedures (as shown on lines 1060 to 1065 or lines 1070 to 1075):

Line No.	Procedure Name	Procedure
1060		IF TRANSACTION-TYPE IS EQUAL TO 1,
1063		THEN GO TO PROCESS-RECEIPT, OTHERWISE
1065		NEXT-SENTENCE.
1070		IF RECEIPT, THEN GO TO PROCESS-RECEIPT,
1075		OTHERWISE NEXT-SENTENCE.

Either of these sentences produces the same result, but the use of a condition-name in the second scheme makes it easier to write and check the program. The condition-name RECEIPT and pro-cedure-name PROCESS-RECEIPT are obviously compatible, which helps reduce the possibility of writing ORDER or ISSUE in a sentence that contains an instruction to PROCESS-RECEIPT. On the other hand, the 1 in line 1060 has no mnemonic relation to PROCESS-RECEIPT, and a programmer might easily write a 2 instead of 1 for transaction type.

The phrase NEXT-SENTENCE in line 1065 or 1075 above serves as the imperative-statement for the IF instruction and is a legal imperative-statement after either THEN or OTHERWISE. NEXT-SENTENCE sends program control to the first COBOL sentence following the IF instruction.

Redefinition

One location in storage may be used to store different kinds of data; for example, transactions can be read one after another into the same storage locations even though there are several types of transactions. Some items are the same in each type of transaction record—for example, stock number, transaction type, date, and quantity. But other items of data—for example, project number or vendor name—are used for only one type of transaction. If each transaction is read into the same storage location, the programmer must be able, by using different data-names, to call for selected parts of this location in order to get the item he wants.

Figure 9-4 shows the record formats for an issue and an order. It also shows how the same character positions are used for dif-ferent data items in the two transaction records. The first 19 char-acters are the same for both types of transactions, but the last 12 are used differently. When working with an issue of stock, the pro-grammer wants the last nine characters—670321101 for AU-THORIZATION-CODE. However, when processing an order for stock, he wants the first eight characters of the unique data—41167032 for PURCHASE-ORDER-NO. Similarly, it is useful to get PROJECT or DEPT-NO when working with an issue trans-action and to get VENDOR-NO when working with an order. In other words, the data contents of a transaction record are divided differently depending on its type. The issue format and order format are called *masks* for the data.

The REDEFINES Clause.   The REDEFINES clause enables the programmer to provide two or more masks for one data-storage

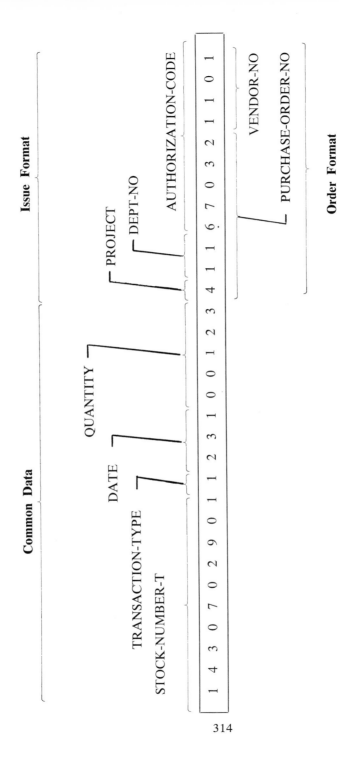

FIGURE 9-4. *Issue and order formats for the same data storage area.*

area. A data description for the transaction file illustrated in Figure 9-4 is as follows:

Line No.	Level No.	Data-Name	Picture
210	FD	INVENTORY-TRANSACTION-FILE	
212			DATA RECORD
213		IS TRANSACTION.	
215	01	TRANSACTION.	
220	02	STOCK-NUMBER-T	PICTURE 9(10).
225	02	TRANSACTION-TYPE	PICTURE 9.
230	02	DATE	PICTURE 999.
235	02	QUANTITY	PICTURE 9(5).
240	02	ISSUE-DATA.	
245	03	PROJECT	PICTURE 9.
250	03	DEPT-NO	PICTURE 99.
255	03	AUTHORIZATION-CODE	PICTURE 9(9).
260	02	ORDER-DATA	REDEFINES ISSUE-DATA.
265	03	PURCHASE-ORDER-NO	PICTURE 9(8).
270	03	VENDOR-NO	PICTURE 9(4).

The level 02 items—STOCK-NUMBER-T through QUAN-TITY—are common data for characters 1 through 19, inclusive, in both kinds of transactions; hence, only one set of descriptions is required. Both ISSUE-DATA and ORDER-DATA describe the unique 12 characters of the transaction record; this is possible because ORDER-DATA redefines the data described by ISSUE-DATA. The elementary items within the order and issue descriptions are freely available just as though the descriptions were entirely independent. The data-name used in a processing procedure should correspond to the kind of transaction available for processing, that is, the one most recently read in. The point is that, even though there are two descriptions, there is only one set of data available at one time, and only one description is relevant because a transaction is either an issue or an order.

A data-name that redefines another data-name must have the same level number as the original data-name and must contain the same number of characters. The data-name used for redefinition must also follow immediately after the group that it redefines. Any group item (below the record level) in the file section or in working storage may be redefined.

Multi-Record Files.   Records in the file section are redefined in a different manner from other group items. For a file containing various types of records with various data-name arrangements, the programmer may set up an entirely different mask for each record. If so, he lists each record-name in the data records clause of the FD entry. He then writes the first record name and a normal description of its contents followed by the next record and its contents. For a transaction file containing issue records and order records (with the order record arranged entirely differently), the file description as a multi-record file is as follows:

Line No.	Level No.	Data-Name	Picture
1100	FD	INVENTORY-TRANSACTION-FILE	DATA RECORDS ARE
1105		ISSUE-RECORD, ORDER-RECORD.	
1110	01	ISSUE-RECORD.	
1120	02	ISSUE-TRANSACTION-TYPE	PICTURE 9.
1130	02	ISSUE-STOCK-NUMBER	PICTURE 9(10).
1140	02	ISSUE-DATE	PICTURE 9(3).
1150	02	ISSUE-QUANTITY	PICTURE 9(5).
1160	02	PROJECT	PICTURE 9.
1170	02	DEPT-NO	PICTURE 99.
1180	02	AUTHORIZATION-CODE	PICTURE 9(9).
1190	01	ORDER-RECORD.	
1200	02	ORDER-TRANSACTION-TYPE	PICTURE 9.
1210	02	ORDER-QUANTITY	PICTURE 9(5).
1220	02	VENDOR-NO	PICTURE 9(4).
1230	02	ORDER-STOCK-NUMBER	PICTURE 9(10).
1240	02	ORDER-DATE	PICTURE 9(3).
1250	02	PURCHASE-ORDER-NO	PICTURE 9(8).

The organization of the two records is entirely different; only one item—the transaction type—has the same location for both order and issue transaction records. The ISSUE-RECORD and ORDER-RECORD are merely different masks for a single set of data, and execution of the READ INVENTORY-TRANSAC-TION-FILE instruction brings in the next record in the file and stores it in the single input area reserved for read-in of this file. The programmer determines which record is available by checking the transaction type and uses the appropriate data-names when processing it.

There are other ways to solve the problem of redefinition for multi-record files. The programmer can minimize the description of an input record by merely defining the transaction type and lumping the rest of the record together—for example, TRANSAC-TION-TYPE with PICTURE 9 and OTHER-DATA with PIC-TURE 9(30). He also defines an ISSUE-RECORD and ORDER-RECORD in working storage. After reading in a transaction, the kind of transaction is determined by means of the TRANSAC-TION-TYPE, and the data are moved to the appropriately defined work area. The important point is that, in one way or another, the programmer must provide a mask for each arrangement of data that may occupy the same storage location.

SUBROUTINES

Programs are often viewed as a main program and a series of subroutines. The main program has the control function of directing the action path to the appropriate subroutine. A *subroutine* is a group of related instructions and may be used repeatedly in a cycling fashion to handle a particular part of an over-all job. Subroutines are of interest because repetitive processing—performing a set of operations for each of the thousands of records in a file—is an important aspect of business data processing. Even the simple problem example described in this chapter involves numerous subroutines and helps illustrate how COBOL-1 offers several different approaches to the use of subroutines within programs.

GO TO Subroutines

The GO TO instruction is used in programs to maintain control and execution of subroutines. Part of a program to handle the processing in the inventory-update example might be written as subroutines for (1) determining the type of transactions record just read in from the file and now ready for processing, (2) processing receipts, (3) processing issues, (4) processing orders, and (5) auditing the transaction-batch count following each of the processing subroutines.

Line No.	Proce-dure Name	Procedures
1260		IF RECEIPT THEN GO TO PROCESS-RECEIPT OTHERWISE NEXT-SENTENCE.
1270		IF ISSUE THEN GO TO PROCESS-ISSUE OTHERWISE NEXT-SENTENCE.
1280		IF ORDER THEN GO TO PROCESS-ORDER OTHERWISE GO TO TYPE-ERROR.
		.
		.
		.
635	PROCESS-RECEIPT.	
		.
		.
		.
655		GO TO AUDIT.
660	PROCESS-ISSUE.	
		.
		.
		.
695		GO TO AUDIT.
700	PROCESS-ORDER.	
705		ADD QUANTITY TO QUAN-ON-ORDER.
710		ADD 1 TO ORDER-COUNT.
715	AUDIT.	

The procedure on lines 1260 to 1280 will transfer control to one of several subroutines, depending on transaction type. For a receipt, the GO TO PROCESS-RECEIPT action is executed and transfers program control to the subroutine for processing a receipt. After the arithmetic statements following line 635 are executed in the subroutine to process a receipt, the GO TO statement (line 655) directs the action path to the audit procedure to resume the remainder of the program. In one pass through the program only one of the process subroutines for receipt, issue, or order is used, and, of course, the others are ignored.

The approach to subroutines shown above is built around the use of GO TO statements in two different ways. The first statement is written in the main program and directs the action path to the subroutine. The statement at the end of each subroutine directs the action path to the appropriate point in the main program or to another subroutine.

Subroutines offer a number of advantages over straight-line coding. First, the use of subroutines allows the total programming job to be divided among several programmers. After the basic design for processing is developed in flow charts or decision tables, one programmer can write the main control program while other programmers work on individual subroutines. When designing the records, each programmer must, of course, be careful to use the standard data-names developed. Subroutines also simplify program revision because a change in the procedures for handling a receipt may involve only the subroutine for handling a receipt transaction and not affect the main program.

Control of Subroutines

The main program needs a mechanism for getting to and from the appropriate subroutine. If a subroutine is to be executed on every pass through a main program, a simple GO TO statement alone will direct the action path to the subroutine. In the example above, a series of three IF statements with GO TO clauses are used to select one of the three process subroutines or an error subroutine. Other selection mechanisms are available for specific situations.

The *selective GO TO* is a simple and powerful way to select subroutines or alternate action paths. The three IF statements in the previous example can be replaced by a single statement with a selection feature—the DEPENDING ON clause, which is written as follows:

GO TO PROCESS-RECEIPT, PROCESS-ISSUE, PROCESS-ORDER
DEPENDING ON TRANSACTION TYPE.

This instruction causes the action path to branch to the procedure-name at the position that corresponds to the value of the
data-name following the DEPENDING ON clause. If the transaction type in the input data is *1,* indicating a receipt, then the
action path branches to the *first* procedure-name in the list of three,
PROCESS-RECEIPT. Similarly a value of 2 for transaction-type
sends program control to the second procedure-name, and a value
of 3 sends control to the third procedure-name.

The selective GO TO statement requires certain conditions in
order to work correctly. The DEPENDING ON clause data-
name—TRANSACTION-TYPE—must have positive integer
values and must not exceed the number of procedure-names listed
after the GO TO. In this example, the data-name must have a value
of 1, 2, or 3, since there are only three procedure-names. Any other
value occurring in the data for transaction type—0, 4, 5, 2.3, or
−1—will cause the action path to skip to the next sentence after
the selective GO TO statement. For this reason, a GO TO *error-
routine* statement is often placed immediately after each selective
GO TO. If an illegal value occurs for the data-name, the action
path goes to the error routine.

The use of GO TO statements at several points in the main
program to transfer control to one subroutine presents some difficulties in returning program control to the correct point in the
main program. It is not sufficient to put a GO TO statement at the
end of a subroutine to direct the action path back to the main
program. Since the transfer to the subroutine may come from any
of several exit points in the main program, it is necessary to return
to the next instruction following the particular exit point that was
used. A substantial amount of "bookkeeping" is required to keep
track of the exit point from the main routine to the subroutine
in order to return to the next instruction after the exit point.

The Simple PERFORM

A perform statement copes with the problem of sending program
control to a subroutine and automatically returning program control to the next instruction in the main routine. Thus a subroutine
can be entered from any number of points in the main routine with
no need for bookkeeping by the programmer about the return point.
A statement to perform a procedure will direct the action path to

the procedure named, execute that procedure, and return control to the main program. Executing a PERFORM *procedure-name-1* statement in a program causes the action path to branch to procedure-name-1 and execute the statements that follow until another procedure-name is encountered. At that point, the action path automatically returns to the statement immediately following the PERFORM statement. The PERFORM statement, therefore, handles program control so that the subroutine needs no instructions to direct return of the action path to the main program.

The PERFORM is used in the inventory-update program as follows:

Line No.	Proce-dure Name	Procedures
570		GO TO PROCESS-RECEIPT, PROCESS-ISSUE, PROCESS-ORDER
575		DEPENDING ON TRANSACTION-TYPE.
580		GO TO TYPE-ERROR.
		.
		.
		.
785	TYPE-ERROR.	
790		MOVE 'INVALID TYPE' TO REASON.
795		SUBTRACT 1 FROM TRANSACTION-COUNT.
800		PERFORM ERROR-ROUTINE.
805		GO TO NEXT-TRANSACTION.
		.
		.
		.
830	ERROR-ROUTINE.	
835		DISPLAY
836		'TRANSACTION WITH STOCK NUMBER ' STOCK-NUMBER-T
837		' WAS LISTED BECAUSE OF ' REASON.
840		MOVE TRANSACTION TO REGULAR-TRANSACTION-DATA.
845		WRITE CHECK-RECORD.
900	SEQUENCE-ERROR.	
		.
		.
		.

As described earlier, an incorrect value for transaction type in the DEPENDING ON clause (line 575) will cause the action path to skip to the next statement (line 580) and execute it to go to the subroutine for type-error. That subroutine will move the alphanumeric literal 'INVALID TYPE' to an independent work area called REASON. After reducing the transaction count, the following statement, PERFORM ERROR-ROUTINE (line 800) directs the action path to the subroutine called ERROR-ROUTINE. If the record with the invalid transaction type has a stock number of 1830921604, the DISPLAY statement on lines 835 to 837 prints the following message.

TRANSACTION WITH STOCK NUMBER 1830921604 WAS LISTED BECAUSE OF INVALID TYPE

The error subroutine (line 840) then moves the entire transaction to an output area and writes it, along with a description of the error (line 845) in a file for later checking. At this point, the program encounters the next *procedure-name* (line 900), so the action path automatically returns to the main program at the statement (line 805) that follows the PERFORM.

Because of the automatic return feature of the PERFORM statement, a subroutine can be called upon by several PERFORM statements placed throughout the program. After execution, the action path will automatically return to the point in the main routine where it came from. The ERROR-ROUTINE described is used for several different types of errors detected at different places in the main program. For example, the sample problem uses the same error routine to process errors for both invalid date and negative balances.

Line No.	Proce-dure Name	Procedures
		.
		.
		.
760	DATE-ERROR.	
765		MOVE 'INVALID DATE' TO REASON.
775		PERFORM ERROR-ROUTINE.
780		GO TO NEXT-TRANSACTION.
		.
		.
		.
810	NEG-BALANCE.	
815		MOVE 'NEGATIVE BALANCE' TO REASON.
820		PERFORM ERROR-ROUTINE.
825		GO TO AUDIT.
830	ERROR-ROUTINE.	
		.
		.
		.
900	SEQUENCE-ERROR.	
		.
		.
		.

When a negative balance or date error is detected, the appropriate subroutine moves the proper description to REASON (lines 765 and 815), and then causes the error-routine to be performed (lines 775 and 820). The error-routine prints the error-description and writes out the record for later research. The action path returns to the line following the PERFORM statement that caused execution of the ERROR-ROUTINE in this particular case. After a date error, the return is to line 780, which causes the program to GO TO NEXT-TRANSACTION, and, after a negative-balance error, the return is GO TO AUDIT (line 825). The processor, not the programmer, keeps track of the proper return location following execution of a subroutine after a perform statement.

The statements included in a subroutine are determined by the arrangement of procedure-names in both the PERFORM statement and the subroutine area. A PERFORM followed by a procedure-name starts executing statements under the specified procedure-name and continues until the next procedure-name is encountered. If a PERFORM is followed by a section name—any valid *procedure-name* followed by a space and the word SECTION—the subroutine executed will consist of all statements following the specified section name until another section name is encountered. Any intervening procedure-names, being of a lower rank, are simply ignored.

At a still higher level, the PERFORM statement may also specify a *range* of procedure-names or section names. The statement PERFORM ORDER-ROUTINE THRU PURCHASE-ROUTINE results in execution of the subroutine starting at ORDER-ROUTINE and continuing through all of the statements following PURCHASE-ROUTINE until the next procedure-name is encountered. Any procedure-names between ORDER-ROUTINE and PURCHASE-ROUTINE are ignored. Figure 9-5 shows the way in which subroutine statements called upon by different PERFORM statements are executed.

PERFORM with Conditional Exit

The programmer may wish to perform a subroutine repeatedly until some condition is satisfied. For example, after the program handles all inventory transactions, it is necessary to read the remaining records in the master file to write them on the output tape. The end of the inventory master file can be indicated by a special record that follows the last valid record and that contains a special stock number of 9999999999, which indicates the end of the file. Each master-file record read in is checked to determine whether

COBOL-1 PERFORM STATEMENTS

Statement No.	Type	Statement
1.	Single paragraph	PERFORM DATE-ERROR.
2.	Group of paragraphs	PERFORM TYPE-ERROR THRU ERROR-ROUTINE.
3.	Single Section	PERFORM TEST SECTION.
4.	Group of Sections	PERFORM TEST SECTION THRU PROCESS SECTION.

RANGE OF EACH STATEMENT

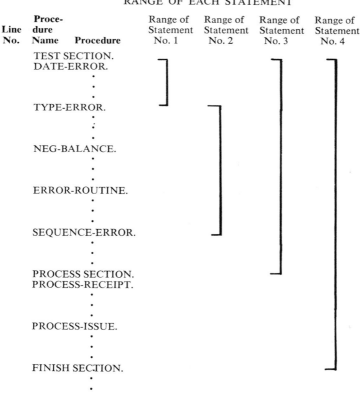

Line No.	Proce-dure Name	Procedure	Range of Statement No. 1	Range of Statement No. 2	Range of Statement No. 3	Range of Statement No. 4

TEST SECTION.
DATE-ERROR.

TYPE-ERROR.

NEG-BALANCE.

ERROR-ROUTINE.

SEQUENCE-ERROR.

PROCESS SECTION.
PROCESS-RECEIPT.

PROCESS-ISSUE.

FINISH SECTION.

FIGURE 9-5. *Range of the perform statement.*

it is the end-of-file record because its stock number is equal to LAST, which was given a value of 9999999999 in the constant section (line 455 to 456). If the record just read is not the end-of-file record, it is written on the output tape. But when the end-of-file record is encountered, the update process is complete and operations can be wound up. The PERFORM statement with a conditional exit will handle the read and write operations for the remainder of the master file, as follows:

Line No.	Proce-dure Name	Procedure
925		PERFORM NEXT-MASTER UNTIL STOCK-NUMBER-M IS EQUAL TO LAST.
		.
		.
		.
605	NEXT-MASTER.	
610		MOVE MASTER-RECORD-IN TO MASTER-RECORD-OUT.
615		WRITE MASTER-RECORD-OUT.
620		READ INVENTORY-MASTER-FILE.

In this case, the PERFORM statement causes NEXT-MASTER to be executed repeatedly until the stock number read in from the master file is equal to LAST, which has a value of 9999999999, indicating it is the end-of-file record. The phrase following UNTIL can be any desired conditional expression. For example, a routine can be repeated until a counter equals some value, a balance becomes negative, or one quantity is greater than another.

TABLE PROCESSING

The processing procedures discussed have centered on master-record files and transaction-record files containing many records. Each transaction record, for example, represents one transaction and consists of a stock number, transaction type, quantity, price, and other data-elements. A single description of the elements in a transaction record applies to the entire transaction file. The data description for a record is, therefore, a shorthand way of describing the repetitive contents of a file.

Other forms of repetition occur in business data. A *table* consists of one data-element repeated within a record. Table 9-1 (page 328) shows a Department Cost Summary for inventory issued to each department during the week ending on day 291. The data-element, cost, is a table arranged by department number. The format of each cost entry is identical—six characters for dollars, a decimal point, and two characters for cents. The entries differ because they are the costs of issues for different departments.

Table Description

The Data Division must describe all data processed by a COBOL program. A table, as shown in Table 9-1, is part of a record and can be described in the usual fashion. Since this record will appear in working storage, a description of a file is not needed:

Line No.	Level No.	Data-Name	Picture
425	01	DEPT-COST-RECORD.	
1300	02	COST-1	PICTURE 9(6)V99.
1305	02	COST-2	PICTURE 9(6)V99.
		.	
		.	
		.	
1350	02	COST-11	PICTURE 9(6)V99.
1355	02	COST-12	PICTURE 9(6)V99.

The preceding description is correct, but it is inefficient to write the identical description for each of the 12 cost entries and it is especially inefficient for several hundred departments. A simple and more efficient scheme, the OCCURS clause, requires only one entry to describe all the items in a table. The description of the department cost record by means of the OCCURS clause is as follows:

Line No.	Level No.	Data-Name	Picture
425	01	DEPT-COST-RECORD.	
430	02	COST	PICTURE 9(6)V99 OCCURS 12
431		TIMES.	

The record description written with the OCCURS clause is a shorthand version of the one with 12 explicit names and pictures. The OCCURS clause states that the eight numeric characters of the COST data-element are repeated in the record 12 times. The complete COST record, therefore, contains 96 numeric characters—8 × 12, and serves as a data-name for 12 items.

Subscripts

The programmer needs a way to identify individual items that he wants to use from a table. Tables are described by their size or the number of times the data-element OCCURS and an item in a table is identified by its position. For example, in the table containing 12 items, the third item in the table is the cost for Department No. 3 and, for the week ending on day 291, is $ 7,831.07. Any item in this table can be identified by one number, so the table has one *dimension,* which in this case is department number.

A *subscript* is a numeric literal or data-name placed in parentheses after the data-name for the table to identify a particular item. A subscripted data-name refers to the one item with a corresponding position in the table. When used in a procedure statement, the subscripted data-name COST (3)—written with a space between data-name and subscript—refers to the third item in the list—the cost for Department No. 3 of $ 7,831.07. By placing the appropriate numeric literal in parentheses, the programmer can select any desired item from a table.

A data-name such as DEPT-NO can also serve as a subscript—for example, COST (DEPT-NO). The item referred to depends on the current value of the subscripting data-name. If DEPT-NO has a value of 2, then COST (DEPT-NO) refers to the second item in the cost list. The subscripting data-name must have its own data description entry. The data description to develop a table for accumulating cost of issues by department number is as follows:

Line No.	Level No.	Data-Name	Picture
200	DATA	DIVISION.	
205	FILE	SECTION.	
		.	
		.	
		.	
215	01	TRANSACTION.	
220	02	STOCK-NUMBER-T	PICTURE 9(10).
235	02	QUANTITY	PICTURE 9(5).
250	03	DEPT-NO	PICTURE 99.
280	01	MASTER-RECORD-IN.	
285	02	STOCK-NUMBER-M	PICTURE 9(10).
310	02	UNIT-COST	PICTURE 999V99.
345	WORKING-STORAGE SECTION.		
		.	
		.	
		.	
370	77	COST-OF-ISSUE	PICTURE 9(6)V99.
375	77	DEPT-COST	PICTURE $ZZZ,ZZ9.99.
425	01	DEPT-COST-RECORD.	
430	02	COST	PICTURE 9(6)V99 OCCURS 12
431		TIMES.	

The procedure for calculating the costs of stock issues and posting to the cost department record is as follows:

Line No.	Procedure Name	Procedures
660	PROCESS-ISSUE.	
670		MULTIPLY QUANTITY BY UNIT-COST GIVING COST-OF-ISSUE.
675		ADD COST-OF-ISSUE TO COST (DEPT-NO).

This routine assumes that an issue is in the process of being posted against the correct master record. The input record for the issue (lines 215 to 250) contains the quantity issued and identifies the department that receives the stock. The inventory master record (lines 280 to 310) contains the stock number and unit cost. The total cost of an issue is calculated on line 670 as a QUANTITY multiplied by UNIT-COST. This instruction uses data-elements from two different records.

The data-element DEPT-NO for the department receiving the stock is part of the transaction record and is used for subscripting COST (DEPT-NO). By subscripting, the appropriate COST in the table is used when the COST-OF-ISSUE (line 675) is added. If DEPT-NO is 04 for a transaction, the computed value of COST-OF-ISSUE will be added to COST (04)—the fourth entry in the table, which is the cost for Department No. 4. As each stock issue is processed by this routine, the cost of the issue is calculated and added to the cost for the appropriate department using the stock.

A table with an OCCURS clause and subscripts can be used for any item with a level of 02 or greater; however, records are at the 01 level and may not be subscripted. Both literals and data-names used as subscripts must have positive integer values between 1 and the number of items in the table. After an item is described as a table by the use of an OCCURS clause, that item must be subscripted every time it is used in a procedure statement. Conversely, subscripting is incompatible for an item not defined as a table.

Table Manipulation

Data in the form of tables are handled somewhat differently from records in files. Whereas each record in a file is processed in turn by a common set of instructions, some of the instructions to process data in a table are *modified* for each new cycle. There are several ways to modify the instructions to prepare the departmental cost summary for the illustrative problem. The simplest way is to use the data-name DEPT-NO as a counter. It is, of course, part of the input area reserved for transactions, but the programmer may use it in other ways, as follows:

Line No.	Proce-dure Name	Procedures
1360	OUTPUT-ROUTINE.	
1370		MOVE 1 TO DEPT-NO.
1380		PERFORM DEPT-SUMMARY UNTIL DEPT-NO
1390		IS GREATER THAN 12.
1400		GO TO ELSEWHERE.
1410	DEPT-SUMMARY.	
1420		MOVE COST (DEPT-NO) TO DEPT-COST.
1430		DISPLAY 'COST FOR DEPT. ' DEPT-NO ' IS ' DEPT-COST.
1440		ADD 1 TO DEPT-NO.

Line 1370 is a set-up operation. Any value remaining from the prior transaction is removed and DEPT-NO, which has a two-digit picture contains 01. The PERFORM statement on lines 1380 to 1390 causes the instruction on lines 1420 to 1440 to be repeated until costs for all 12 departments are listed.

If the data description for DEPT-COST is $ZZZ,ZZ9.99, the statement on line 1420 produces an edited version of COST (DEPT-NO) by inserting dollar sign, comma, and decimal point, and by suppressing leading zeros. The DISPLAY statement on line 1430 prints a line such as COST FOR DEPT. 03 IS $ 7,831.07.

When the subroutine DEPT-SUMMARY is performed the first time, the DISPLAY uses the 01 for the department number that was transferred by the MOVE operation on line 1420. Execution of line 1440 increases the department number by 1, so that the department number is 02 when the subroutine is repeated. The subroutine DEPT-SUMMARY is repeated until it produces the output for Department No. 12 and DEPT-NO is increased to 13. The PERFORM statement (lines 1380 to 1390) has a conditional UNTIL phrase that stops the PERFORM, and the action path continues to the statement on line 1400.

The subroutines for OUTPUT-ROUTINE and DEPT-SUMMARY will produce the body of the report shown in Table 9-1,

```
COST FOR DEPT. 01 IS $   5,124.60
COST FOR DEPT. 02 IS $   5,973.51
COST FOR DEPT. 03 IS $   7,831.07
COST FOR DEPT. 04 IS $       0.00
COST FOR DEPT. 05 IS $     499.83
COST FOR DEPT. 06 IS $   1,367.25
COST FOR DEPT. 07 IS $   6,777.71
COST FOR DEPT. 08 IS $  20,651.04
COST FOR DEPT. 09 IS $  11,212.73
COST FOR DEPT. 10 IS $   1,800.55
COST FOR DEPT. 11 IS $   3,183.40
COST FOR DEPT. 12 IS $   1,561.23
```

TABLE 9-1. *Record format for a department cost summary.*

although a simpler scheme using the PERFORM VARYING instruction below is included in the illustrative program. If report title, date line, and other headings are desired, they can be produced by additional DISPLAY statements located ahead of the first execution of the statement printing department costs.

Perform Varying

The PERFORM statement shown above relies on an arithmetic operation, ADD 1 to DEPT-NO, to advance the department number and to serve as a criterion for completion of table printing. Table processing is simpler when the PERFORM VARYING statement is used, which handles all three operations in table manipulations; it causes the subroutine to be performed, advances the department number, and counts whether the correct number of cycles has been performed. The procedures given above can be simplified by using a PERFORM VARYING procedure, as follows:

Line No.	Proce-dure Name	Procedures
920	FINISH.	
930		PERFORM DEPT-SUMMARY VARYING DEPT-NO
931		FROM 1 BY 1 UNTIL DEPT-NO IS GREATER THAN 12.
950	DEPT-SUMMARY.	
955		MOVE COST (DEPT-NO) TO DEPT-COST.
960		DISPLAY 'COST FOR DEPT. ' DEPT-NO ' IS ' DEPT-COST.

The PERFORM statement (lines 930 to 931) contains the clause, VARYING DEPT-NO FROM 1 BY 1. The phrase FROM 1 sets DEPT-NO to 01, and thus serves the same purpose as the instruction shown earlier, MOVE 1 TO DEPT-NO. In essence, the result is that a counter with an initial value of 1 is set up before the cycle is performed the first time. The phrase BY 1 adds 1 to DEPT-NO after the subroutine is performed each time. This statement has the same effect as the prior procedure, ADD 1 TO DEPT-NO.

The FROM and BY phrases may contain any number that does not exceed the picture limitations of the data-name that follows VARYING. The programmer can write FROM 7 to set the data-name equal to 7, and write BY 5 to increase it by 5 in each cycle, which would be consistent with subscript values of 7, 12, 17, etc. Of course, the UNTIL criterion would need to be the appropriate value that would handle the number of entries in the table.

The makeup of the UNTIL clause is important, for the clause is tested in each cycle before the PERFORM is executed. As soon as the conditional phrase is true, the action path branches to the statement that follows the PERFORM. Use of the clause UNTIL DEPT-NO IS EQUAL TO 12 will stop the cycle before the cost for Department No. 12 is printed. The desired value for the conditional phrase in a test depends on the location of the test. Since the test for completion of cycles is made before the action, the correct condition to use is GREATER THAN the desired number of cycles (line 931). However, for some other kinds of cycle testing, the test is made after the action, and the appropriate condition to use is equal to the desired number of cycles. The programmer must understand the conditional expression, otherwise the subroutine may be performed one more or less times than was intended.

INVENTORY-UPDATING PROGRAM

The segments of the program given throughout this chapter forming part of the inventory-updating program—those with three digit line numbers—are combined here and additional segments are introduced to produce a complete COBOL-1 program. The program, which corresponds to the flow charts in Figures 9-1, 9-2, and 9-3, is given in Figures 9-6, 9-7, and 9-8, corresponding to description in the text. The complete program consists of four main divisions similar to the divisions in the sample program in Chapter 8: Identification, Environment, Data, and Procedure, in that order. The form of the program illustrated here is only one of many possibilities. Other formats can be prepared using COBOL-1, and the COBOL language for any specific processor will offer other possibilities for writing a simpler or more efficient program. Good programming demands continuing analysis, innovation, and testing.

Identification and Environment Division

The Identification and Environment Divisions for inventory updating are shown in Figure 9-6. Although the Identification Division is simple, it is important, since the COBOL translator will not accept a program lacking an Identification Division.

The Configuration Section of the Environment Division (lines 120 to 131) describes the source and object computers, and the Input-Output Section (lines 135 to 160) specifies the input-output units assigned to each file used by the program.

The Configuration Section lists two hypothetical computers— WORDCOM-2000 and WORDCOM-1000. Lines 125 and 126 state that a WORDCOM-2000 with 30,000 words of high-speed storage will translate the COBOL-1 source program into machine

COBOL-1 Program Form	Program Name INVENTORY UPDATE		Page 1 of 8
Page 001	Program Number INV-381	Prepared by WILL HARRISS	Date MAY 10

```
Line  Procedure-Name /
No.   Level No.         Data-Name                                   Picture
100   IDENTIFICATION DIVISION.
105   PROGRAM-ID.  INV-UPDATE.
110   AUTHOR.   WILL HARRISS.

115   ENVIRONMENT DIVISION.
120   CONFIGURATION SECTION.
125   SOURCE-COMPUTER.  WORDCOM-2000
126          MEMORY SIZE 30000 WORDS.
130   OBJECT-COMPUTER   WORDCOM-1000
131          MEMORY SIZE  4000  WORDS.
135   INPUT-OUTPUT SECTION.
140   FILE-CONTROL.
145          SELECT INVENTORY-TRANSACTION-FILE  ASSIGN TO 1 TAPE-UNIT
146          FOR MULTIPLE REEL.
150          SELECT INVENTORY-MASTER-FILE  ASSIGN TO 2 TAPE-UNITS FOR
151          MULTIPLE REEL.
155          SELECT UPDATED-MASTER-FILE  ASSIGN TO 2 TAPE-UNITS FOR
156          MULTIPLE REEL.
160          SELECT TRANSACTION-CHECK-FILE  ASSIGN TO CARD-PUNCH.
```

FIGURE 9-6. *Identification and environment divisions for inventory updating.*

language. Since WORDCOM-2000 is a large scale machine with microsecond addition time and up to 20 tape units, it can efficiently translate the COBOL-1 program into machine language under control of the Environment Division to produce a machine language program for the object computer, which is WORDCOM-1000.

The WORDCOM-1000, listed as the object computer on lines 130 and 131, is a medium scale processor with 4000 words of high-speed storage, a smaller instruction repertoire, and slower operating speeds than WORDCOM-2000. WORDCOM-1000 is efficient for large file processing applications, but it is slow and inefficient for translating COBOL source programs into machine language. The use of different source and object computers may be more efficient than using either one for both purposes. A special translator routine is required, of course, to enable one processor to produce programs for another. Most translators require that one computer be used as both source and object computer, although a few manufacturers are writing translators that allow one computer to prepare programs for another.

The Input-Output Section starts with the standard File Control paragraph on line 140. The two input files are read from magnetic tape, one output file is written on tape, and the other output file is punched in cards. The file containing inventory transactions (line 145) normally occupies only part of one reel and is assigned to 1 TAPE UNIT. The transaction file occasionally consists of more than one reel, so the phrase FOR MULTIPLE REEL, must appear as part of the file entry. When processing a multi-reel file assigned to one tape unit, the processor stops at the end of each reel and waits for an operator to mount another reel and push a restart button.

The master file described on lines 150 and 151 currently occupies three tape reels. Two tape units are assigned to the file, and, each time a mark indicating end of reel is reached, the processor automatically switches from one tape unit to the other. While the processor is reading data from one tape unit, the machine rewinds the other tape and the operator has several minutes to mount a new tape on that unit before it is required. By means of tape-swaps, any number of reels can be processed using only two tape units and with no delay for changing tapes. The new master file is also assigned two tape units, as shown on lines 155 and 156.

The desired number of tape units is assigned but individual units are not identified because an executive or operating system routine is used to control program execution and handle the assignment of specific tape units. For example, tape units 4 and 5 may be the two tape units assigned by the executive program to the UPDATED-MASTER-FILE. The programmer merely specifies the type and quantity of input-output units needed in order for the executive routine to assign them.

Data Division

The Data Division was prepared in conjunction with the flow charts. When a new file or data name was entered on the charts, it was immediately recorded, described, and expanded as necessary in the Data Division. After the flow charts were finished and checked, the corresponding procedure statements were then prepared for the program.

The Data Division for inventory updating in Figure 9-7 consists of three sections: File, Working Storage, and Constant. The File Section (lines 205 to 340) describes all the files—Inventory Transaction, Inventory Master, Updated Master, and Transaction Check —used for regular input and output operations. The Working Storage Section (lines 345 to 441) describes work areas for counters, totals. and for low-volume input and output items. The Constant Section (lines 450 to 456) defines any data-names that will have one fixed value throughout the program.

File Description. The magnetic-tape files used here for transactions and master records offer two possibilities for condensation and identification not available with card files or printed output. First, since the records are short and each will occupy only a fraction of an inch of tape, the programmer may wish to combine several records and write them as one block on tape. Second, magnetic labels can be written on the tape itself to identify the tape contents. If record blocking and label descriptions are used, they are described following the FD entry for each file.

Record *blocking* is indicated in COBOL by inserting the phrase BLOCK CONTAINS *numeric-literal* RECORDS in the file description. For the inventory-transaction file description (lines 210 to 213), each block contains 50 records of 31 characters each (lines 220 to 255), which results in a block of 1550 characters. Tape units for the WORDCOM-1000 record data at the rate of 500 characters per inch with half-inch gaps between blocks. Consequently each block occupies 3.1 inches of tape and blocks are separated by a half-inch gap. One thousand transactions require 62 inches of tape for data and 10 inches for gaps, or a total of 72

	COBOL-1 Program Form	Program Name INVENTORY UPDATE	Program Number INV-381	Prepared by WILL HARRISS

Line No.	Level No. (Procedure Name)	Data-Name	Procedures 41	Picture
200		DATA DIVISION.		
205		FILE SECTION.		
210	FD	INVENTORY-TRANSACTION-FILE		
211		LABEL RECORDS ARE STANDARD		BLOCK CONTAINS 50 RECORDS
212		'INV TRANS' VALUE OF REEL-SEQUENCE-NUMBER IS 1		VALUE OF FILE-IDENTIFICATION IS
213		IS TRANSACTION.		DATA RECORD
215	01	TRANSACTION.		
220	02	STOCK-NUMBER-T		PICTURE 9(10).
225	02	TRANSACTION-TYPE		PICTURE 9.
230	02	DATE		PICTURE 999.
235	02	QUANTITY		PICTURE 9(5).
240	02	ISSUE-DATA.		
245	03	PROJECT		PICTURE 9.
250	03	DEPT-NO		PICTURE 99.
255	03	AUTHORIZATION-CODE		PICTURE 9(9).
260	02	ORDER-DATA		REDEFINES ISSUE-DATA.
265	03	PURCHASE-ORDER-NO		PICTURE 9(8).
270	03	VENDOR-NO		PICTURE 9(4).
275	FD	INVENTORY-MASTER-FILE		
276		LABEL RECORDS ARE STANDARD		BLOCK CONTAINS 25 RECORDS
277		'INV MASTER' VALUE OF REEL-SEQUENCE-NUMBER IS 1		VALUE OF FILE-IDENTIFICATION IS
278		IS MASTER-RECORD-IN.		DATA RECORD
280	01	MASTER-RECORD-IN.		
285	02	STOCK-NUMBER-M		PICTURE 9(10).
290	02	STOCK-NAME		PICTURE X(20).
300	02	QUAN-ON-HAND		PICTURE 9(5).
305	02	QUAN-ON-ORDER		PICTURE 9(5).
310	02	UNIT-COST		PICTURE 999V99.

FIGURE 9-7. Data division for inventory updating.

334

Page 003	COBOL-1 Program Form	Program Name	INVENTORY UPDATE
		Program Number	INV-381
		Prepared by WILL HARRISS	Date MAY 11

Page No. 6-7	Line No. 4	Procedure Name / Level No. 7	Data-Name	Picture / Procedures 41
	315	FD	UPDATED-MASTER-FILE	BLOCK CONTAINS 25 RECORDS
	316		'LABEL RECORDS ARE STANDARD	VALUE OF FILE-IDENTIFICATION IS
	317		'INV-MASTER' RETENTION-PERIOD IS 10	
	318		DATA RECORD IS MASTER-RECORD-OUT.	
	320	01	MASTER-RECORD-OUT.	
	321	02	MASTER-DATA	PICTURE X(45).
	325	FD	TRANSACTION-CHECK-FILE	
	326		LABEL RECORDS ARE OMITTED	DATA RECORD IS CHECK-RECORD.
	330	01	CHECK-RECORD.	
	335	02	REGULAR-TRANSACTION-DATA	PICTURE 9(31).
	340	02	REASON	PICTURE X(16).
	345		WORKING-STORAGE SECTION.	
	350	77	DATE-LIMIT	PICTURE 9(3).
	355	77	TODAYS-DATE	PICTURE 9(3).
	360	77	ERROR-DISPLAY-CODE	PICTURE 9.
	365	77	AUDIT-COUNT	PICTURE 99.
	370	77	COST-OF-ISSUE	PICTURE 9(6)V99.
	375	77	DEPT-COST	PICTURE ZZZ,ZZ9.99.
	380	77	PROJECT-CHARGE	PICTURE $ZZZ,ZZ9.99.
	385	01	AUDIT-RECORD.	
	390	02	BATCH-NO	PICTURE 9(4).
	392	02	FILLER	SIZE IS 2.
	395	02	STATUS	PICTURE X(14).
	397	02	FILLER	SIZE IS 2.
	400	02	TRANSACTION-COUNT	PICTURE 9(2).
	402	02	FILLER	SIZE IS 2.
	405	02	TOTAL-COUNT	PICTURE 9(2).
	407	02	FILLER	SIZE IS 2.
	410	02	RECEIPT-COUNT	PICTURE 9(2).
	412	02	FILLER	SIZE IS 2.
	415	02	ISSUE-COUNT	PICTURE 9(2).
	417	02	FILLER	SIZE IS 2.
	420	02	ORDER-COUNT	PICTURE 9(2).

FIGURE 9-7. Data division for inventory updating (cont'd).

335

COBOL – 1 Program Form

| Program Name | INVENTORY UPDATE |
| Program Number | INV-381 |

Prepared by **WILL HARRIS**

Page **4** of **8**

Date **MAY 11**

Line No.	Procedure Name / Level No.	Data-Name	Procedures / Picture
425	01	DEPT-COST-RECORD.	
430	02	COST	PICTURE 9(6)V99 OCCURS 12
431		TIMES.	
435	01	PROJECT-CHARGE-RECORD.	
440	02	CHARGE	PICTURE 9(6)V99 OCCURS 5
441		TIMES.	
450		CONSTANT SECTION.	
455	77	LAST	PICTURE 9(10) VALUE
456		IS 99999999.	

FIGURE 9-7. *Data division for inventory updating (cont'd).*

336

inches of tape, whereas unblocked records would take the same 62 inches for data and 500 inches for gaps, or a total of 562 inches.

Each time a READ instruction is encountered, the COBOL translator automatically sets up instructions to get the next record from a block and brings in a new block after the current one is handled. However, adequate high-speed storage must be available to hold an entire block of 1550 characters read in at one time.

Label records are recorded as the first and last record—called *header* and *trailer* labels—on each tape reel. COBOL-1 provides a standard header-label record which contains the following information:

1. File identification: one to ten alphanumeric characters to identify the file
2. Creation date: the date on which the file was written
3. Retention period: one to four numerals to describe the number of days the file is to be retained
4. Reel-sequence number: one to four numerals to identify the sequence of reels in a multi-reel file

The trailer label at the end of each reel is simpler and contains (1) a type code to indicate end of reel or end of file, and (2) a count of the number of blocks on the reel.

The programmer specifies the use of labels by inserting the phrase LABEL RECORDS ARE STANDARD in the FD entry for each file, lines 211, 276, and 316. When this statement appears for an input file, the labels are automatically checked by the executive routine. The programmer also writes desired values in the FD entry—for example, lines 211 to 213 for the inventory-transaction file, and VALUE OF FILE-IDENTIFICATION IS 'INV-TRANS' and the REEL-SEQUENCE-NUMBER IS 1 for the first reel.

The executive routine checks the header label on the first reel processed of a file against the values supplied in the program and any discrepancy causes the processor to stop and print an error message. As each succeeding reel of a multi-reel file is used, the reel-sequence-number stated in the FD entry is automatically increased by one and checked against the corresponding entry in the header label. The block count accumulated during the processing of a reel is checked against the trailer-label block count and any discrepancy noted, often on the console printer.

When the statement for a standard label appears in an output file description, labels are automatically written. The programmer merely specifies the value of FILE-IDENTIFICATION and RE-

TENTION-PERIOD to put in the label (lines 316 and 317). The executive routine prepares a header label consisting of the specified data plus the date the tape was written, and numbers each reel in sequence starting with the first. At the completion of processing for each reel, the executive routine writes the block count in the trailer label.

Before beginning a new output tape by writing a new label on it, the executive routine checks the existing label to make sure the retention period for the tape has expired. If the present date is day number 291, the executive routine will not allow a tape to be used as an output tape if it has, for example, a creation date of 285 and the retention period is 007. The executive program check for expiration of tape files prevents the files from being used before the planned date.

Files. The input files for transactions and master records are the same as shown in the chapter except for the blocking and labeling schemes described above. The INVENTORY-TRANSACTION-FILE (lines 210 to 270) contains two masks for the last twelve characters—called ISSUE-DATA (lines 240 to 255) and ORDER-DATA (lines 260 to 270). The INVENTORY-MASTER-FILE is similar to that used in Chapter 8 except that warehouse location data are omitted.

The main output file, UPDATED-MASTER-FILE, consists of only an FD entry (lines 315 to 318), a record entry (line 320), and one entry to hold all the contents of the record (line 321). The input record is processed and moved as a whole to the output record for writing. Consequently, individual data-elements in the output record need not be identified.

The TRANSACTION-CHECK-FILE (lines 325 to 340) receives those transactions that need investigation—negative balances, invalid dates, etc. Since it is a punched-card file, it does not use blocking or label records. Each record in this file is made up of the input data for the transaction (line 335), plus a verbal description of why it appears in the check file (line 340).

Working Storage. Working storage is divided into group work areas and independent work areas, the latter, 77 level items, all being written first. Lines 350 to 360 are items to be read in as low-volume input; line 365 is a counter; line 370 is an intermediate result of an arithmetic operation; and lines 375 to 380 are edit pictures for low-volume output data.

Group work areas are set up on lines 385 to 441 for the AUDIT-

RECORD and for two tables of department costs and project charges. The filler entries provide spacing when the AUDIT-REC-ORD is printed. Costs are accumulated for twelve departments and five projects treated as two tables, as shown by the OCCURS clauses on lines 430 and 440. A constant with a value of 9999999999 (lines 455 and 456) is given the name LAST and is used to test for the end of the master file. The exact use of each item in the Data Division will be discussed in the Procedure Division.

Procedure Division

The Procedure Division in Figure 9-8 contains instructions for the program for inventory updating. The major parts of the program are the set-up to start processing and the main program to read in transactions, check their validity, read in master-file records, and find a match for processing. For each matching transaction number, the main program calls on one of the three processing subroutines for a receipt, issue, or order. When necessary, the main program also calls on the error routines to handle erroneous conditions. After all transactions are processed, the main program calls on the FINISH subroutine to initiate close-out operations and stop the program run.

Set-up Operations. The set-up operation, OPEN (lines 510 and 511), prepares the input and output files for use, checks header labels on input files, and writes header labels on output files. The three ACCEPT statements (lines 515 to 525) bring in several pieces of data for later use in the program. The READ statement (line 530) brings in a master record for comparison with a transaction record (line 565) in the first cycle. In subsequent cycles, a new master record is brought in by a routine read operation (line 620).

Main Program. The main program, with paragraph-name NEXT-TRANSACTION, begins (line 535) and reads in a transaction (line 540). The transaction count is increased to keep track of the number of transactions (line 545). The next two statements (lines 550 to 555) check date validity. A transaction failing either of the date-limit tests is not processed but causes the action path to go to DATE-ERROR (lines 760 to 780). If the date of the transaction is between DATE-LIMIT and TODAYS-DATE—neither of the conditional phrases is true—the action path continues to the MATCH paragraph. The first sentence of the MATCH paragraph (lines 565 to 568) is an IF instruction with an OTHERWISE

Page 3 005	COBOL-1 Program Form	Program Name INVENTORY UPDATE	Program Number INV-381	Prepared by WILL HARRIS	Page 5 of 8 Date MAY 11

Line No.	Procedure Name Level No 12	Data-Name	Picture	Procedures 4|
500	PROCEDURE DIVISION.			
505	START.			
510	OPEN INPUT INVENTORY-TRANSACTION-FILE INVENTORY-MASTER-FILE			
511	OUTPUT UPDATED-MASTER-FILE TRANSACTION-CHECK-FILE.			
515	ACCEPT DATE-LIMIT.			
520	ACCEPT TODAYS-DATE.			
525	ACCEPT ERROR-DISPLAY-CODE.			
530	READ INVENTORY-MASTER-FILE.			
535	NEXT-TRANSACTION.			
540	READ INVENTORY-TRANSACTION-FILE AT END GO TO FINISH.			
545	ADD 1 TO TRANSACTION-COUNT.			
550	IF DATE IS LESS THAN DATE-LIMIT GO TO DATE-ERROR.			
555	IF DATE IS GREATER THAN TODAYS-DATE GO TO DATE-ERROR.			
560	MATCH.			
565	IF STOCK-NUMBER-T IS GREATER THAN STOCK-NUMBER-M THEN GO TO			
566	NEXT-MASTER OTHERWISE IF STOCK-NUMBER-T IS EQUAL TO			
567	STOCK-NUMBER-M THEN NEXT-SENTENCE OTHERWISE			
568	GO TO SEQUENCE-ERROR.			
570	GO TO PROCESS-RECEIPT, PROCESS-ISSUE, PROCESS-ORDER			
575	DEPENDING ON TRANSACTION-TYPE.			
580	GO TO TYPE-ERROR.			
600	SUBROUTINES.			
601	NOTE THE FOLLOWING PROCEDURES ARE SUBROUTINES CALLED UPON BY			
602	THE MAIN PROGRAM.			
605	NEXT-MASTER.			
610	MOVE MASTER-RECORD-IN TO MASTER-RECORD-OUT.			
615	WRITE MASTER-RECORD-OUT.			
620	READ INVENTORY-MASTER-FILE.			
625	RETURN.			
630	GO TO MATCH.			

FIGURE 9-8. *Procedure division for inventory updating.*

COBOL – 1
Program Form

Program Name **INVENTORY UPDATE**
Program Number **INV-381**

Prepared by **WILL HARRISS**

Page **6** of **8**   Date **MAY 11**

Page 3 — 0016

Line No.	Procedure-Name / Level No.	Data-Name · Picture · Procedures
635		PROCESS-RECEIPT.
640		ADD QUANTITY TO QUAN-ON-HAND.
645		SUBTRACT QUANTITY FROM QUAN-ON-ORDER.
650		ADD 1 TO RECEIPT-COUNT.
655		GO TO AUDIT.
660		PROCESS-ISSUE.
665		SUBTRACT QUANTITY FROM QUAN-ON-HAND.
670		MULTIPLY QUANTITY BY UNIT-COST GIVING COST-OF-ISSUE.
675		ADD COST-OF-ISSUE TO COST (DEPT-NO).
680		ADD COST-OF-ISSUE TO CHARGE (PROJECT).
685		ADD 1 TO ISSUE-COUNT.
690		IF QUAN-ON-HAND IS NEGATIVE THEN GO TO NEG-BALANCE OTHERWISE
695		GO TO AUDIT.
700		PROCESS-ORDER.
705		ADD QUANTITY TO QUAN-ON-ORDER.
710		ADD 1 TO ORDER-COUNT.
715		AUDIT.
720		ADD 1 TO AUDIT-COUNT.
725		IF AUDIT-COUNT IS EQUAL TO 50 THEN NEXT-SENTENCE
726		OTHERWISE GO TO NEXT-TRANSACTION.
730		ADD RECEIPT-COUNT ISSUE-COUNT AND ORDER-COUNT GIVING
731		TOTAL-COUNT.
735		ADD 1 TO BATCH-NO.
740		IF TOTAL-COUNT IS EQUAL TO TRANSACTION-COUNT THEN MOVE
741		'IS CORRECT' TO STATUS OTHERWISE MOVE 'CONTAINS ERROR'
742		TO STATUS.
745		DISPLAY AUDIT-RECORD.
750		MOVE ZEROS TO AUDIT-COUNT TRANSACTION-COUNT TOTAL-COUNT
751		RECEIPT-COUNT ISSUE-COUNT ORDER-COUNT.
755		GO TO NEXT-TRANSACTION.

FIGURE 9-8. *Procedure division for inventory updating (cont'd).*

341

COBOL - 1 Program Form

| Program Name | INVENTORY UPDATE |
| Program Number | INV-381 |

Prepared by **WILL HARRISS**

Page 007	Line No.	Procedure Name / Level No.	12 ... Data-Name ... Procedures 41 ... Picture
	760	DATE-ERROR.	
	765		MOVE 'INVALID DATE' TO REASON.
	770		SUBTRACT 1 FROM TRANSACTION-COUNT.
	775		PERFORM ERROR-ROUTINE.
	780		GO TO NEXT-TRANSACTION.
	785	TYPE-ERROR.	
	790		MOVE 'INVALID TYPE' TO REASON.
	795		SUBTRACT 1 FROM TRANSACTION-COUNT.
	800		PERFORM ERROR-ROUTINE.
	805		GO TO NEXT-TRANSACTION.
	810	NEG-1BALANCE.	
	815		MOVE 'NEGATIVE BALANCE' TO REASON.
	820		PERFORM ERROR-ROUTINE.
	825		GO TO AUDIT.
	830	ERROR-ROUTINE.	
	835		IF ERROR-DISPLAY-CODE IS EQUAL TO 1 THEN DISPLAY
	836		'TRANSACTION WITH STOCK-NUMBER ' STOCK-NUMBER-T
	837		' WAS LISTED BECAUSE OF ' REASON.
	840		MOVE TRANSACTION TO REGULAR-TRANSACTION-DATA.
	845		WRITE CHECK-RECORD.
	900	SEQUENCE-ERROR.	
	905		DISPLAY 'SEQUENCE ERROR WITH TRANSACTION ' STOCK-NUMBER-T
	906		' MASTER RECORD STOCK-NUMBER-M ' BATCH ' BATCH-NO.
	910		STOP RUN.

FIGURE 9-8. Procedure division for inventory updating (cont'd).

COBOL-1 Program Form	Program Name INVENTORY UPDATE		Page 8 of 8
	Program Number INV-381	Prepared by WILL HARRISS	Date MAY 11

Line No. 4 6 7	Procedure-Name	Level No. 12	Procedures Data-Name	41 Picture
920	FINISH.			
925	PERFORM NEXT-MASTER UNTIL STOCK-NUMBER-M IS EQUAL TO LAST.			
930	PERFORM DEPT-SUMMARY VARYING DEPT-NO FROM 1 BY 1 UNTIL			
931	DEPT-NO IS GREATER THAN 12.			
935	PERFORM PROJECT-SUMMARY VARYING PROJECT FROM 1 BY 1 UNTIL			
936	PROJECT IS GREATER THAN 5.			
940	CLOSE INVENTORY-MASTER-FILE INVENTORY-TRANSACTION-FILE			
941	UPDATED-MASTER-FILE TRANSACTION-CHECK-FILE.			
945	STOP RUN.			
950	DEPT-SUMMARY.			
955	MOVE COST (DEPT-NO) TO DEPT-COST.			
960	DISPLAY 'COST FOR DEPT.' DEPT-NO ' IS ' DEPT-COST.			
965	PROJECT-SUMMARY.			
970	MOVE CHARGE (PROJECT) TO PROJECT-CHARGE.			
975	DISPLAY 'CHARGE FOR PROJECT' PROJECT ' IS ' PROJECT-CHARGE.			

FIGURE 9-8. Procedure division for inventory updating (cont'd).

343

phrase that is a second IF instruction. The instruction has three possible exits to subroutines:

Condition	Action
1. STOCK-NUMBER-T > STOCK-NUMBER-M	GO TO NEXT-MASTER
2. STOCK-NUMBER-T = STOCK-NUMBER-M	(GO TO) NEXT-SENTENCE
3. STOCK-NUMBER-T < STOCK-NUMBER-M	GO TO SEQUENCE-ERROR

The first condition—stock number for the condition is greater than for master file record—indicates a record farther along in the master inventory file is wanted and directs the action path to the NEXT-MASTER (lines 605 to 620) in order to write the current master record and read another one. Following NEXT-MASTER, the program automatically continues to RETURN on line 625 where GO TO MATCH (line 630) returns program control to check transaction number against master record number.

The second condition—matching stock-numbers for transaction and master file—directs the action to the selective GO TO statement (lines 570 to 575) to select the appropriate processing subroutine. After a valid transaction is processed by a subroutine (discussed below), the action path returns to NEXT-TRANSACTION to read a new transaction. If a transaction is not a receipt, an issue, or an order, the action path drops to line 580 and is sent to the TYPE-ERROR paragraph on lines 785 to 805.

The third condition—stock number for the transaction is less than for the master-file record—indicates that the transaction is out of sequence for its matching master-file record (if any) has been passed. The erroneous-sequence condition, which is indicated by a failure to execute the greater than or equal to condition, executes the GO TO SEQUENCE-ERROR, which is a subroutine (lines 900 to 910).

Every cycle through the main program on lines 530 to 580 causes the action path to branch to one of the following subroutines: (1) to write a master record and read a new one, (2) to process a transaction, or (3) to display an error. The point of return from each subroutine to the main program is important for program execution and can be summarized as follows:

From Subroutine	Line No.	Return to Main Program	Explanation
DATE-ERROR	780	NEXT-TRANSACTION	The current transaction was rejected, so a new one is needed.
TYPE-ERROR	805		

From Subroutine	Line No.	Return to Main Program	Explanation
PROCESS-RECEIPT PROCESS-ISSUE PROCESS-ORDER	655 695 710	NEXT-TRANSACTION (by way of AUDIT)	The current transaction was processed, so a new one is needed.
NEXT-MASTER	630	MATCH	The current master record was written out and a new one read. A new transaction is not needed, so the action path enters the main program in the middle.
SEQUENCE-ERROR	910	No return; stops run	The action path does not return. A sequence error stops the run.

Next-Master Subroutine. Subroutines constitute the program from line 600 onward. The NEXT-MASTER (lines 610 to 620) applies to a master record ready for writing in order to read in another one for processing. This subroutine moves the current master from the input area to the output area, writes it on an output tape, and reads in a new master record. The program path continues from line 620 to line 630 so that the GO TO statement on line 630 is effectively part of this subroutine, and sends the program to MATCH. However, the GO TO statement on line 630 has a separate procedure-name because a subsequent PERFORM statement (line 925) uses only lines 605 to 620 for a different purpose and does not use lines 625 to 630. The dual use of part or all of a subroutine will be discussed later with the FINISH routine.

Processing Subroutines. The three transaction-processing subroutines on lines 635 to 710 correspond to the flow chart shown in Figure 9-2. The process-issue subroutine calculates the cost of inventory issue (line 670) and posts it to both the appropriate department (line 675) and the project (line 680). The three instructions on lines 670 to 680 use data from many places in storage: QUANTITY is part of the input record for transactions, UNIT-COST is part of the input for master records, and COST-OF-ISSUE is an independent work area. COST and CHARGE are entries in tables in the group work area. The subscripts DEPT-NO and PROJECT are obtained from the input area for transactions by using the ISSUE-DATA mask, lines 240 to 255.

The first two transaction-processing subroutines—receipts and issues—end with GO TO statements directing the action path to

AUDIT. The order-processing routine is followed by AUDIT and the action path merely continues to AUDIT after an order is processed.

Audit Subroutine. The AUDIT routine corresponding to Figure 9-3, consists of two parts. The first (lines 720 to 726) checks whether the current transaction is the last of a batch of 50. If the transaction is not the last of a batch, the action path immediately returns to the main program to read the next transactions. If the current transaction is the last of a batch, the second part of the routine (lines 730 to 755) is executed.

The individual counts for each type of transaction are summed (lines 730 and 731), and the batch count is updated (line 735). The correct verbal message is put in STATUS (lines 740 to 742), and the audit record described in lines 385 to 420 of the Data Division is displayed (line 745). A typical display, with names added for clarity here, is as follows:

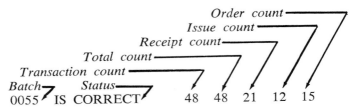

The DISPLAY statement prints out a single line with no heading. The spaces between data-elements are produced by the FILLER entries in the data description (lines 392, 397, . . . 417). The total count of 48, instead of the batch count of 50, indicates two erroneous transactions were rejected. All counters except the batch counter are reset to zero (lines 750 and 751) to prepare for handling the next batch of transactions. Any number of data-names can be listed in the MOVE TO statement. The action path returns (line 755) to the main program to read the next transaction.

Error Subroutines. An error subroutine is executed if an error is detected during processing. The three error subroutines for invalid date, transaction type, and negative balances use a common ERROR-ROUTINE (lines 830 to 845). For example, the DATE-ERROR (lines 760 to 780) moves the alphanumeric literal INVALID DATE to REASON. Since a transaction with a date error is rejected from processing, the transaction count, which was increased (line 545) when the transaction was read, is adjusted to reflect the rejection (line 770). The action path transfers to perform the ERROR-ROUTINE.

The ERROR-ROUTINE can display by printing (lines 835 to 837) the reason for the erroneous transaction. The contents for REASON (line 837) were passed down to the ERROR-ROUTINE by the DATE-ERROR routine (line 765). Often one routine will pass down values for data-names before it calls on that routine to use the data-names.

The display-print instruction (lines 835 to 837) is conditional. If the operator wants the error message printed, he reads in the value 1 for ERROR-DISPLAY-CODE (line 525) at the beginning of the program. If any other digit is read in, the display print is suppressed. Processor console switches can be used for the same purpose. The phrase IF KEY-1 IS ON, THEN DISPLAY . . . will print a message if switch number 1 on the console is down. In either of these ways, the operator can control the printing of error messages. With a new program or new inventory procedures, the operator may wish to examine every error, but, after the program is running smoothly, these details are not needed and can be suppressed.

The remainder of the ERROR routine (lines 840 to 845) sets up a record consisting of the transaction input data and the verbal error description and writes the record. Since line 900 starts a new paragraph, the action being performed terminates and action automatically returns to the statement following the PERFORM in the program that caused execution of the ERROR-ROUTINE, which in this case is line 780.

The TYPE-ERROR routine (lines 785 to 805) works in the same fashion as DATE-ERROR except that it passes down different data to REASON. The NEG-BALANCE routine (lines 810 to 825) uses the ERROR-ROUTINE the same way as the two routines above, but does not subtract 1 from the transaction count. Issue-transactions are already processed before they result in negative balances, and cannot be backed out merely by subtracting 1 from the transaction count. Furthermore, since the issue transaction is processed, the action path (line 825) goes to AUDIT rather than returning directly to read a new transaction.

The SEQUENCE-ERROR subroutine (lines 900 to 910) operates differently from the other subroutines. The transactions and master file are supposed to be in sequence when processing starts; an incorrect sequence is likely to make processing impossible. The error subroutine therefore prints out a message and stops the run. An actual program may have a routine to attempt to straighten out a minor mix-up in sequence, but the logic for such a routine is outside the scope of this illustration.

Close-out Operations. The FINISH routine (starting on line 920) is executed after all transactions are processed. This subroutine is reached by executing the READ...AT END GO TO FINISH statement (line 540) when the end of the transaction file is reached. The PERFORM statement on line 925 transfers each remaining master record from the input file to the updated master file by performing the NEXT-MASTER statement (lines 610 to 620) used earlier by the main program for moving, writing, and reading the next record in the master file. However, only those statements in the NEXT-MASTER paragraph are executed. The paragraph-name RETURN (line 625) terminates the execution of the PERFORM NEXT-MASTER; therefore, the GO TO MATCH statement (line 630) is not executed. The move-write-read cycle will continue until the last master record with a pseudo-stock number of 9999999999, defined in the Constant Section as the value of LAST (lines 455 and 456) is read in and action goes to line 930 to summarize department costs.

The PERFORM (lines 930 and 931) uses the DEPT-SUMMARY (lines 950 to 960) to print the table for department costs using the routine described earlier in the chapter. Lines 935 and 936 together with lines 965 to 975 print the table for project charges.

The CLOSE statement (lines 940 and 941) writes an end-of-file label for UPDATED-MASTER-FILE and rewinds the three tape files. No further processing of files is possible, for the STOP RUN statement (line 945) terminates all processing activity. The program has started, run, and stopped.

SUMMARY

The unique features of COBOL-1, which make it readily adaptable for file processing, have been described by a typical inventory-updating problem. The inventory example processes receipts, issues, and order transactions against a master file to produce an updated master file, audit reports, error messages, a summary report for financial inventory accounting, and a file of erroneous transactions. Special attention is paid to error checks, since new programs need extensive error checking and all business data-processing applications require precautions to ensure valid inputs and program operation.

Input and Output

READ *file-name-1*. Read into the processor the record from the input file identified by *file-name-1*.

READ *file-name-1* AT END *imperative-statement-1*. If a record remains in the input file identified by *file-name-1*, then read it. If none remains, execute the instruction contained in *imperative-statement-1*.

WRITE *record-name-1*. Write the data identified by *record-name-1* in the output file set up to receive it.

ACCEPT *data-name-1*. Data are read in from the standard low-volume input device and stored in the location called *data-name-1*.

DISPLAY *data-name-1*. Data from the location called *data-name-1* are read out to the standard low-volume output device. Any literal may be used in place of *data-name-1*.

Data Transfer

MOVE *data-name-1* TO *data-name-2*. Move the data identified by *data-name-1* to the location called *data-name-2*. A literal may be used in place of *data-name-1*. Any number of data-names may be listed after *data-name-2*.

Arithmetic

ADD *data-name-1* AND *data-name-2* GIVING *data-name-3*. Add the data identified by *data-name-1* to the data identified as *data-name-2* and call the result *data-name-3*. Any number of *data-names* may be added together by placing them in the instruction between the ADD and the GIVING. A numeric literal may be used in place of *data-name-1* or *data-name-2*.

ADD *data-name-1* TO *data-name-2*. Add the data identified by *data-name-1* to the data identified by *data-name-2* and call the result *data-name-2*. Any number of *data-names* may be added to *data-name-2* by placing them in the instruction between the ADD and the TO. A numeric literal may be used in place of *data-name-1*.

SUBTRACT *data-name-1* FROM *data-name-2* GIVING *data-name-3*. Subtract the data identified by *data-name-1* from the data identified by *data-name-2* and call the result *data-name-3*. Any number of *data-names* may be subtracted from *data-name-2* by placing them

TABLE 9-2. *COBOL-1 instructions (complete).*

in the instruction between the SUBTRACT and the FROM. A numeric literal may be used in place of *data-name-1* or *data-name-2*.

SUBTRACT *data-name-1* FROM *data-name-2*. Subtract the data identified by *data-name-1* from the data identified by *data-name-2* and call the result *data-name-2*. Any number of *data-names* may be subtracted from *data-name-2* by placing them in the instruction between the SUBTRACT and the FROM. A numeric literal may be used in place of *data-name-1*.

MULTIPLY *data-name-1* BY *data-name-2* GIVING *data-name-3*. Multiply the data identified by *data-name-1* by the data identified by *data-name-2* and call the product *data-name-3*. A numeric literal may be used in place of *data-name-1* or *data-name-2*.

DIVIDE *data-name-1* INTO *data-name-2* GIVING *data-name-3*. Divide the data identified by *data-name-1* into the data identified by *data-name-2* and call the quotient *data-name-3*. A numeric literal may be used in place of *data-name-1* or *data-name-2*.

ON SIZE ERROR *imperative-statement-1*. If an arithmetic instruction with this phrase attached results in the loss of leading digits, follow the instruction in *imperative-statement-1*. Otherwise ignore *imperative-statement-1*.

ROUNDED (option). When an arithmetic instruction with the phrase attached results in the loss of trailing digits, the right-most retained digit is increased by 1 if the discarded digit is 5 or greater.

Sequence Control

GO TO *procedure-name-1*. When this instruction is encountered, the program continues with the first instruction that follows *procedure-name-1*.

GO TO *procedure-name-1, procedure-name-2, . . . , procedure-name-n* DEPENDING ON *data-name-1*. Control is transferred to the procedure-name with a position in the list that corresponds to the current value of *data-name-1*.

IF *conditional-expression-1* THEN *imperative-statement-1* OTHERWISE *statement-2*. If *conditional-expression-1* is a true statement, then execute *statement-1;* otherwise execute *statement-2*.

PERFORM *procedure-name-1*. Control is transferred to *procedure-name-1* and all following statements are executed until another procedure-name of equal rank is encountered. At that point, control returns automatically to the statement following the PERFORM. In this and all other versions of PERFORM statements,

TABLE 9-2. *COBOL-1 instructions (complete) (cont'd).*

the phrase *procedure-name-1* THRU *procedure-name-2* may be used in place of *procedure-name-1*.

PERFORM *procedure-name-1* UNTIL *conditional-expression-1*. If *conditional-expression-1* is false, the statements referenced by *procedure-name-1* are executed. The process is repeated until *conditional-expression-1* is true. At this point, control returns to the statement that follows the PERFORM statement.

PERFORM *procedure-name-1* VARYING *data-name-1* FROM *data-name-2* BY *data-name-3* UNTIL *conditional-expression-1*. First, *data-name-1* is set equal to *data-name-2*. If *conditional-expression-1* is false, the statements referenced by *procedure-name-1* are executed. Then *data-name-1* and *data-name-3* are added together. If *conditional-expression-1* is still false, the statements are again executed. The process continues until *conditional-expression-1* is true at which point control returns to the statement that follows the PERFORM statement. Both *data-name-2* and *data-name-3* may be replaced by numeric literals with positive integer values.

Processor Control

OPEN INPUT *file-name-1, . . . , file-name-n*, OUTPUT *file-name-1, . . . , file-name-n*. Prepare the input and output files for use.

CLOSE *file-name-1, . . . , file-name-n*. Prepare the files for removal from the processor.

STOP RUN. This instruction marks the end of a COBOL-1 program and will cause the processor to halt.

TABLE 9-2. *COBOL-1 instructions (complete) (cont'd)*.

COBOL-1 has advanced features to describe and manipulate individual pieces of data. A *literal* has contents identical to the data-name itself. A numeric literal consists of one to 18 numerals and a decimal point. Alphanumeric literals consist of one to 120 alphanumeric characters enclosed in quotation marks and may not be used in arithmetic statements. All literals are subject to picture limitations of the receiving area. The figurative constants, ZEROS and SPACES, are used as literals for the characters that they name.

Two statements are available in COBOL-1 to handle low-volume input and output. The ACCEPT statement reads in data from a standard low-volume device, and the DISPLAY statement writes data by printing on the console typewriter or punching a card. *Data-names* used in low-volume input-output statements must be defined in the Data Division, but a File Description is not required for the data.

The Working Storage Section of the Data Division defines data-names and records that are not part of an input or output file. A data-name with level number 77 is an *independent* work area without subdivision and is unrelated to any other item. Records or items containing other items are described in *group* work areas. An item in either an independent or group work area may be given an initial value by a VALUE IS *any-literal* clause. The Constant Section describes data-names with values that remain unchanged during the program.

A condition-name is associated with each value of a data-name and has an entry consisting of level number 88, the condition-name and value clause that must immediately follow the data-name involved. A condition-name for *data-name-1* with a value of *n* is equivalent to the phrase *"data-name-1* IS EQUAL TO *n."* An area in storage for any item below the record level 01 can be redefined according to different masks by using one data-name to REDEFINE another. The redefining data-name must follow immediately after the entries for the redefined data-name. Multiple masks for a record are obtained by listing the several record-names in the DATA RECORDS ARE clause of the file description and defining each record in the normal manner.

Programs are often viewed as a main program to direct the action path to appropriate subroutines as required. A subroutine is a group of related instructions that are often used repeatedly. A GO TO statement in the main program sends the action path to a subroutine, and a GO TO in the subroutine returns the action path to a specified point in the main program. The selective GO TO statement directs the action path to one of *n* subroutines, depending on the value of data-name-1, which must have a positive integer value between 1 and *n*. A statement directing the action path to an error routine is often placed after one or more selective GO TO statements in case none of them was executed.

The simple PERFORM statement directs the action path to a subroutine and automatically returns to the statement following the PERFORM. When a single subroutine is called by any one of several different PERFORM statements, the action path each time automatically returns to the correct location—the next statement after the PERFORM that directed the transfer. The PERFORM statement may refer to a paragraph or section or a range of either.

A PERFORM statement with an UNTIL *condition-1* tests condition-1 each time before execution and repeats the subroutine until condition-1 is true. The programmer must carefully construct the condition, else the program will execute one cycle more or less than was intended.

A table is a set of repetitive data elements repeated n times within one record. The OCCURS n TIMES clause is added to the data-element description to describe the table. A subscript—a numeric literal with a value between 1 and n or a data-name—is enclosed in parentheses after the data name for the table to identify a particular item in the table. A data-name used as a subscript must have a data-description of its own.

The subscripted data-name for table items is used in regular COBOL instructions. The subscript can be set up as a counter and varied by standard arithmetic operations. More simply, the PER-FORM...VARYING...FROM...BY...UNTIL... statement sets the subscripts to any desired initial value, executes a subroutine using the subscript value, increases the subscript value by any desired constant, repeats the execution, and increases the subscript until the specified condition is true.

The program for inventory updating contains all four COBOL-1 divisions in correct sequence: Identification, Environment, Data, and Procedure. Different computers, WORDCOM-2000 and 1000, are specified as the source and object computers. Inventory master-file input and output tapes are assigned to multiple tape units so that tape-reel mounting and dismounting can be done by means of tape swaps while processing continues. The transaction input file is on tape, and the file for erroneous transactions is punched into cards.

The Data Division consists of a File Section, Working-Storage Section, and Constant Section. All input and output files are described in the File Section. Records on the three magnetic-tape files are blocked to increase tape capacity and reduce read-write time. The tape files contain standard labels, which the executive routine checks automatically and rejects any tape with the wrong identifier or reel number. The use of a tape for output is restricted until expiration of the retention period specified in its label.

The Procedure Division contains set-up operations, the main program, a series of subroutines, and close-out operations. The set-up operations open files, bring in some low-volume input, and read the first master record. The main program reads a transaction, checks it for valid date, and attempts to match it with the corresponding master record. Master records are written and read by a subroutine until a match with a transaction is found. A matching transaction is processed against its master record by one of three subroutines, and the action path returns to the main program.

An audit subroutine checks the total number of each type of transaction processed against the count for transactions read in and prints results of the comparison. Subroutines handle errors in transaction date or type, negative balances in the master record, and file sequence. The close-out operations transfer to the output file any master records remaining after all transactions are processed, close the files, print cost summaries, and stop the run.

COBOL-1 illustrates a business programming language with substantial capabilities. Equally important, the inventory-updating example programmed on COBOL-1 reflects many of the problems and practices of business data processing.

10
Programming—Machine-Oriented
Languages—WORDCOM

This chapter deals with machine-oriented languages for programming data processors. In many ways machine-oriented language programming corresponds to COBOL. The problem-solving process is basically the same whether a machine-oriented or other programming language is used. Many of the principles of input, output, and cycling remain the same for any language, but the programmer works with them at a different level of detail in each language.

The machine-oriented languages discussed in this chapter are still one or more stages removed from basic machine languages. They use mnemonic operation codes—for example, ADD, PNC, and WT for "add a number," "punch data in a card," "and write a data record on tape," respectively. These codes are easier to remember and use than the numbers, such as 11, 32, and 24, to represent operations in near-machine language. The mnemonic instruction codes are converted to numbers on a one-for-one basis by means of the processor using an assembly program: ADD to 11, and PNC to 32. The assembled program consisting of numbers for operations and addresses is converted by the processor to binary for execution.

Absolute addresses are used for instructions in most of this chapter. Each instruction address refers to a certain location in the machine—for example, ADD 267—to deal with the *contents* of storage location 267. Results are developed in certain registers—the accumulator and M-Q—and can be returned to storage. Since instruction addresses are absolute, they refer to specific locations in storage and are ready to execute as written in a program without conversion, except for decimal to binary. The programmer deals with words and characters for machine-oriented languages instead of data elements as he does with COBOL.

355

A machine language is designed for a particular processor and exploits its unique capabilities better than COBOL does. COBOL, it will be recalled, is designed as an English-like language for data processing with a wide variety of processors. Thus a judicious mixture of languages may be most efficient: COBOL for most of a program and the particular machine-language for situations best handled by unique features of the processor. COBOL provides for transition between languages by use of the ENTER verb and the name of the desired language—the particular machine language or COBOL. This transition from one language to another makes programming bilingual, in a sense.

This chapter discusses machine-oriented language programming for a *fixed*-word-length processor. WORDCOM, which works with data represented at the character level, is covered throughout most of the chapter. WORDCOM II, which is a bit machine, is treated briefly.

WORDCOM

WORDCOM (for fixed-*word*-length *com*puter) is a medium scale, internally-stored program processor. It is designed as a simplified machine to present machine-language programming for this important class of processors. It has arithmetic, control, and storage units as described in Chapter 3, and input-output units as described in Chapter 4. The features of WORDCOM of interest here are, briefly, as follows:

1. *Storage:* One thousand words of sign and seven alphanumeric characters each in high-speed storage. Addresses are 000 through 999 (999 is followed by 000).
2. *Arithmetic unit:* Accumulator and M-Q registers of sign and seven characters each.
3. *Control unit:* Instruction counter and three index registers.
4. *Input-Output:* One card read-punch machine and up to ten magnetic-tape units.
5. *Instruction repertoire:* Twenty-four different single-address instructions can be executed.

WORDCOM INSTRUCTIONS AND PROGRAMMING

As described earlier, a single-address instruction is a set of characters that specifies an operation and indicates a storage address or register that contains an operand. The address can also indicate where to put the results of an operation. The address part is used for special purposes in some instructions.

Instruction Repertoire

The list of instructions that WORDCOM executes can be described as follows. The instructions are defined in this chapter and a summary list is given in Table 10-1 near the end of the chapter.

1. *Input and Output*
   a. Read a card and place data contents in storage.
   b. Punch a card with data from storage.
   c. Read from tape a block of data and place in storage.
   d. Write on tape a block of data from storage.
   e. Rewind a tape.
2. *Cycling to repeat an instruction routine a desired number of times*
   a. Set an index register to prepare for counting the number of cycles.
   b. Increase an index register to count each time the cycle is executed.
   c. Compare an index register to a criterion to test whether the desired number of cycles is executed.
3. *Tests*
   a. Compare two items and, depending on whether the results are "less than," "greater than," or "equal to," jump to one of three locations.
   b. Jump, if accumulator is negative.
   c. Jump, if content becomes so large it overflows accumulator.
4. *Load and store accumulator and M-Q registers*
   a. Clear accumulator and add a number to it.
   b. Clear accumulator and M-Q register and add a number to M-Q.
   c. Store contents of accumulator.
   d. Store contents of M-Q register.
5. *Arithmetic*
   a. Add a number to contents of accumulator.
   b. Subtract a number from accumulator.
   c. Multiply a number in storage by a number in the M-Q register.
   d. Divide a number in the accumulator by a number in storage.
6. *Miscellaneous*
   a. Halt processor operations.
   b. Shift contents of the accumulator and M-Q to the left.
   c. Shift contents of the accumulator and M-Q to the right.
   d. Edit by combining contents of the accumulator and an edit word under control of an extractor.
   e. Unconditional jump in the program by transferring control to a specified instruction location.

Instruction Format

Each single-address instruction for WORDCOM consists of the following elements:

1. An instruction operation code of three characters which causes the processor to read, write, compare, add, subtract, and so forth, for a total of 24 different instructions.
2. A single-letter designation of index registers, which are special units of the machine.
3. Three characters for identifying (a) the address in storage of data to be operated on, (b) the location to store a result, or (c) the storage location of an instruction. These three characters may also be a special number—a literal that is used as such.

The format of an instruction written on programming sheets or punched in cards, for read-in to internal storage is as follows:

Sign	1	2	3	4	5	6	7
+	R	E	C		0	2	3

Positive   *Operation* *Refers to* *Address or*
sign for   *code*   *an index*   *special*
instructions   *register*   *constant*

Input-Output Instructions

WORDCOM has one card read-punch unit and can have up to ten magnetic-tape units. Data are first punched in cards and either read in directly or converted to tape for high-speed read-in. Output is punched in cards or written on tape. Any readable copy desired is printed later by an off-line printer operating from cards or tape. Programming in machine-oriented language for WORDCOM requires complete format details for input and output.

Punched Cards. A card read-punch unit is connected to WORDCOM for on-line operation. Reading and punching are independent and operate on separate decks of cards. The REC xxx instruction activates the card reader to read 80 character positions of a card. The read operation stores the data in ten or fewer words of eight characters each (sign and seven alphanumeric) in consecutive storage locations starting with the address specified in the instruction. Read-in replaces anything previously in the storage locations used. The PNC xxx instruction activates the card punch to accept ten words of data in processor storage, starting with word location xxx, and punch them in a card without changing the contents of storage; read-out is nondestructive. The ten words will fill 80 characters in a card, with no option for the programmer, although blanks in storage are merely blanks in a card. The format and explanation of the instructions for WORDCOM to read or to punch a card are as follows:

Code	Explanation
REC xxx	*Re*ad the next card in card reader. Store the data in ten consecutive word locations starting with word xxx, where xxx is a three-digit number 000 through 999.
PNC xxx	*Pu*nch the next card in the card-punch unit with ten words from ten consecutive word locations starting with word xxx. Contents of storage unchanged.

A simple routine can be developed from these two instructions for reading into storage the data from one or more cards and punching the data into other cards. The program given below will read data from one card, punch the same data in another card, and repeat the read and punch operations. The program itself can be read in from punched cards and placed anywhere in storage by a read-in program described later in this chapter. For simplicity, it is assumed that this program will be read into storage locations 100 to 103. Execution of the read instruction will read data from each card into storage locations 150 through 159 and the data from the last card (the second in this case) will remain there after punching is completed.

Loc.	Content	Explanation
100	REC 150	Read ten words from the first card in the reader and place them in storage locations 150 through 159. The prior contents of these locations are replaced.
101	PNC 150	Punch ten words in storage locations 150 through 159 in the next card in the punch unit. Read-out does not change the contents of storage.
102	REC 150	Read ten words from the next card in reader into locations 150 through 159. The prior contents of these locations are replaced.
103	PNC 150	Punch ten words in the next card in the card-punch unit. Storage content is unchanged.

The repetition in duplicating cards becomes burdensome if many cards are involved. To avoid this, various program schemes are used to handle the cycle of read-punch, read-punch, as described later under cycling.

Magnetic Tapes. WORDCOM can have up to ten magnetic-tape units. Data can be read from or written on any tape mounted on a tape unit by addressing that tape unit, numbered 0 through 9. The reel of tape mounted on tape unit number 3, for instance, is available when tape unit 3 is addressed in an instruction. A file label can also be recorded as the first record on tape for identifying its contents.

Data on tape are handled in "record blocks" to facilitate movement between high-speed storage and input-output units. WORD-COM reads or writes magnetic tape in blocks of 60 words, which is much longer than the ten words handled for cards. The tape read, write, and rewind instructions are as follows:

Code	Explanation
RTt xxx	*R*ead the next block of data on *t*ape unit *t* and place the data in 60 consecutive words in storage starting with location xxx. Prior contents of these locations are destroyed.
WTt xxx	*W*rite on the tape in *t*ape unit *t* the block of data in 60 consecutive words in storage starting with location xxx. Storage contents unchanged.
RWt	*R*e*w*ind the tape on tape unit *t* and position for removal.

A simple program, similar to that for reading and punching cards, shows how card data can be read into storage and written on tape.

Loc.	Content	Explanation
010	REC 100	Read ten words from the first card in the card-
011	REC 110	read unit and place in storage locations 100
012	REC 120	through 109. Repeat for next five cards placing
013	REC 130	in succeeding locations ten words later: 110–119,
014	REC 140	120–129, 130–139, 140–149, 150–159.
015	REC 150	
016	WT4 100	Write on the tape in tape unit 4 the 60 words in storage locations 100 through 159.

The two input-output routines given here illustrate card duplication and conversion of cards to tape—read cards and write blocks of 60 words on magnetic tape. Data conversion and writing operations are used with other instructions for processing data.

Cycles

The simplified input-output routines given above appear inefficient because they contain almost identical instructions. Repetitive instructions for handling large volumes of input and output occupy too much storage. For example, to read 3000 cards and write them on tape would require 3500 instructions—six card-read and one tape-write instructions for each six cards—but WORDCOM has only 1000 words. More efficiently, this short seven-instruction routine can be repeated 500 times to handle 3000 cards. Both program steps and storage can often be saved by devising a cycle that the processor repeats the desired number of times. The steps a programmer might take to make the processor perform an operating cycle a certain number of times are as follows:

1. Before cycling starts, *set up* or initialize a cycle counter and a criterion for counting cycles and for testing when to leave the cycle.
2. *Perform* the desired cycle of read, write, or other operations.
3. Increase the *count* in the cycle counter.
4. *Compare* the contents of the cycle counter with the criterion to determine whether to repeat the cycle *or* to leave the cycle because the desired number of cycles has been completed.
5. *Jump* to the appropriate instruction in the program to repeat the cycle *or* go to another part of the program, depending on the results of the comparison.

Index Registers. WORDCOM uses index registers identified as A, B, and C to count cycles. An index register is a counter that can be set to any desired number from storage, increased by a certain number, and tested to find whether the new number is equal to a criterion in storage that was set up before cycling started. Each index register can hold a three-digit number from 000 to 999 that can be set, increased, and tested whenever desired in a program by means of the following *indexing instructions:*

Code	**Explanation**
SISyxxx	*Set in*dex register y (y designates index A, B, or C) with the three right-hand digits contained in *s*torage location xxx. Storage location xxx contents unchanged.
INCynnn	*Inc*rease the number in register y by the number nnn (nnn is the *number* itself and not an address).

Code	Explanation
CISyxxx	Compare the number in *i*ndex register y to the criterion (right-hand three digits) in *s*torage location xxx. If index and criterion are unequal, take the next instruction in sequence, which should be a jump. If equal, skip one instruction and take the second instruction. Contents of index register and location xxx remain unchanged by the comparison operation.

The format of an instruction involving an index register is shown below. Character 4 identifies the register—A, B, or C. Positions 5 through 7 indicate a storage location whose contents are used to set a register initially in a SISyxxx instruction, or the location of a criterion for comparisons in a CISyxxx instruction. For an INCynnn instruction, positions 5 through 7 contain *the number* used for increasing index contents.

Sign	1	2	3	4	5	6	7
+	S	1	S	y	3	2	0

Positive sign for instructions   *Operation code*   *Identifies register A, B, C*   *Address or special constant*

Sequence Changes. One more instruction is required to complete the cycling scheme. A jump instruction is placed after the comparison instruction to return program control to the beginning of the cycle, if it is supposed to be repeated. If the cycle is not completed enough times when the CISyxxx is executed—as indicated by the contents of index register y and storage location xxx *not* being equal—the next instruction should be executed in sequence, a jump. If the cycle is complete—contents of the index register and location x are equal—the jump instruction should be skipped and the main program path continued. The jump instruction (also called *branch* or *transfer*) merely changes the sequence of program execution.

Code	Explanation
JMPyxxx	Change the content of the instruction counter to xxx. The result is to *jump* unconditionally and take the next instruction from storage location xxx, indexable.

The instruction required to halt operations at a desired point, and always at the end of a program, is defined as follows:

Code	Explanation
HLT xxx	*Halt* unconditional. Processor halts after this instruction with instruction counter set to address specified by xxx. Leave unchanged at next sequential instruction location if xxx is blank.

Indexed Read-In. The instructions for setting, counting, and comparing index registers can be illustrated for the simple read-write program given earlier. Assume that a cycle is run for reading cards containing ten words each and writing the 60 words in one block on tape. To read 3000 cards, this cycle will be repeated 500 times. The flow-chart for this operation is in Figure 10-1.

Before the cycle starts, the programmer provides for initializing the index register used for cycle counting and placing a criterion of 500 in storage. During each cycle the program should increase the index register count by 1 and test the index-register number against the criterion of 500 to find whether the cycle has been performed 500 times. If the cycle has not been performed 500 times—the index-register number *is not equal* to the criterion—the program repeats the cycle. If performed 500 times—the index register number *is equal* to the criterion—the processor exits from the cycle and continues with the main program. The instructions to repeat the card reading cycle 500 times, rewind tape, and halt the processor are as follows:

Loc.	Content	Explanation
011	+0000500	Criterion for counting 500 tape blocks (500 blocks × six cards per block = 3000 cards).
012	+0000000	Zero used to set index register.
013	SISA012	Set index register A to 000 from contents of location 012 and use for counting 500 tape blocks.
014	REC 100	Read next card in reader and store in ten consecutive word locations: 100–109, 110–119, etc., to 150–159.
015	REC 110	
016	REC 120	
017	REC 130	
018	REC 140	
019	REC 150	

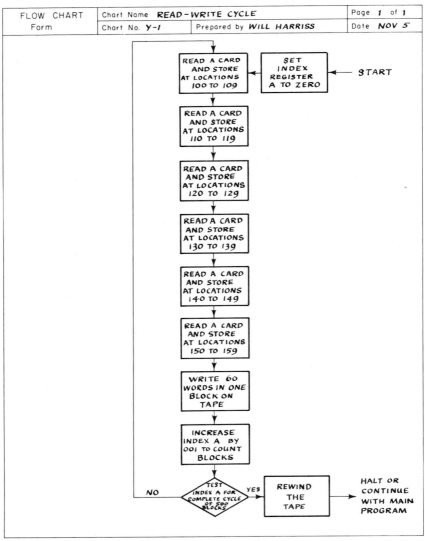

| FLOW CHART | Chart Name **READ-WRITE CYCLE** | | Page **1** of **1** |
| Form | Chart No. **Y-1** | Prepared by **WILL HARRISS** | Date **NOV 5** |

FIGURE 10-1. *Flow chart of read-write cycle using indexes.*

Loc.	Content	Explanation
020	WT9 100	Write on the tape mounted on tape unit 9 the block of 60 words in locations 100–159.
021	INCA001	Increase the number in index A by 001 from 000 to 001 on first cycle, 001 to 002 on second, and so forth, to 500.

Loc.	Content	Explanation
022	CISA011	Compare number in index register A and criterion in storage location 011. If contents unequal, take next instruction in sequence; if equal, skip one instruction and take second instruction.
023	JMP 014	Arriving here means cycle for writing 500 blocks on magnetic tape not complete; go to location 014 to read six more cards.
024	RW9	Arriving here means 500 blocks written on tape; rewind tape on tape unit 9.
025	HLT xxx	Halt processor with instruction counter set to any desired program location xxx to start other operations (or omit the HLT xxx and continue the main program).

The program to read 3000 cards and write their content in 500 blocks on tape deserves brief examination from the viewpoint of length and use. Three instructions are used for initializing, increasing, and comparing index A with the criterion. One jump returns to the beginning of the cycle. Only seven instructions—six read-card and one write-block-on-tape—are used directly to perform the card-to-tape conversion operations. Two instructions close up by rewinding tape and halting. While the seven *operating* instructions seem outnumbered by the eight *housekeeping* instructions and constants, the routine is efficient, for it repeats each instruction in locations 014 through 023 to perform the read-write cycle 500 times, although 023 is not executed in the last cycle. Instructions in locations 013, 024, and 025 are executed only once each. Thus thirteen instructions in locations 013 through 025 result in executing 5002 instructions. Written as straight-line coding without the use of a cycle, 3500 instructions would be required for this card-to-tape conversion. Cycling means less work for the programmer and less space in storage, but more operations for the machine to do the same work.

Effective Addressing. The card-to-tape conversion can also illustrate the idea of effective addressing with index registers, because the card-read instruction is used six times with merely different addresses: 100, 110, . . ., 150. A second or inner cycle can be set up to handle this repetitive operation by using one indexable read instruction: RECy100. In order to gain this dual use of the read instruction, the programmer associates index register B with the read-card instruction and writes the instruction as RECB100. Instructions, such as this one, that can have their addresses, as written, modified by the number contained in index register to get an effective address during program execution are called *indexable* instructions. The programmer writes the program so that index B contains 000 in the first cycle, 010 in the second cycle, etc., up to 050 in the fifth cycle in order to get the desired number for effective addressing. The effective address, when the RECB100 instruction is executed, is the sum of the number in register B and the 100 in the read instruction. The effective address is thus $000 + 100 = 100$ in the first cycle, $010 + 100 = 110$ in the second, etc., and $050 + 100 = 150$ in the sixth cycle. The jump following the comparison test is made five times to execute the inner cycle a total of six times. Note that it is executed once before the operations for increase and compare index B are first executed. *After* the sixth card-read cycle, index register B is increased to 060, and comparison of index B and the criterion of 060 sends program control to the second following instruction to write the block on tape.

The tape-write operation is followed by counting and testing index A, as in the prior example, to determine whether 500 blocks have been written. If not, program control is returned to the beginning of the read cycle to *reset* index B to zero and repeat the inner cycle to read six more cards. Executing the outer loop the 500th time causes program control to skip one instruction and continue operations. The program using a second index register for counting card-reading cycles and for effective addressing to store card data, is given below. Only new instructions introduced into the prior example are explained.

Loc.	Content	Explanation
011	+0000060	Criterion for counting 60 words read from six cards containing ten words each.
012	+0000500	
013	+0000000	
014	SISA013	
015	SISB013	Set index register B to 000 and use for *counting* 60 words read from cards *and* for *effective addressing* to put card data in desired storage locations.

Loc.	Content	Explanation
016	RECB100	Read next card and put data in storage at *effective address* equal to number in index B plus the 100 in this instruction. This is an *indexable* instruction because the address of 100 as written is modified by the contents of an index register to get an effective address each time the instruction is executed. The other instructions involving index registers in this example are *indexing* instructions because they initialize, increase, or test an index register and do not involve another instruction.
017	INCB010	Increase the number in index B by 010 in each cycle: from 000 to 010, 010 to 020, . . ., to 060. (But B is reset to 000 after the sixth cycle, when the instruction in 015 is repeated.)
018	CISB011	Compare number in index register B and criterion of 060 in location 011.
019	JMP 016	Arriving here from the comparison instruction means that the card-reading cycle has not been completed six times to get 60 words. Return to the read instruction.
020	WT9 100	Arriving here from the comparison instruction indicates six cards have been read to get 60 words; write a tape block.
021	INCA001	
022	CISA012	
023	JMP 015	Less than 500 blocks have been written on tape; go to 015 to reset index B to 000 and repeat the card-reading cycle.
024	RW9	
025	HLT	

A program using two index registers for the card-to-tape conversion routine happens to occupy the same storage space but results in *more* instruction executions than the first conversion scheme using only one index. That is to say, six instructions are not a long enough loop to deserve using the inner cycle. A longer and more varied instruction loop warrants use of cycles and indexes to save programming work and processor storage space, as a later example will show. An index register can be used with as many instructions as desired to get a different effective address for each one. It is important to understand that effective addressing *per se* changes neither the instruction nor the index register. The use of indexes for effective addressing is similar to chemical catalysts: they make operations possible but are not themselves affected.

Arithmetical Instructions

The WORDCOM instructions discussed above were limited to input-output and cycling instructions. These types of operations make up a large part of many business data-processing programs. Along with them, the arithmetical operations of add, subtract, multiply, and divide are used to calculate bills, inventories, sales forecasts, and production schedules. Arithmetical operations are explained briefly and their use in programs illustrated.

Addition and Subtraction.   Addition and subtraction operations are performed in the processor's arithmetic unit and the results are located in the accumulator. The sequence of instructions is as follows: The accumulator is cleared to remove any prior result, the first number is added from storage, each desired number is added or subtracted, and the result placed in storage for further use or for read-out. The instructions to clear the accumulator, add, subtract, and return the results to storage are as follows:

Code	Explanation
CAAyxxx	Clear the *a*ccumulator and *a*dd contents of location xxx, indexable; contents of location xxx unchanged. (This starts the addition operation *and* adds the first number.)
ADDyxxx	*Add* contents of storage location xxx, indexable, to contents of accumulator, which will contain the sum.
SUByxxx	*Sub*tract contents of storage location xxx, indexable, from contents of accumulator, which will contain the remainder.
STAyxxx	*Sto*re *a*ccumulator contents in storage location xxx, indexable. Accumulator contents remain unchanged, but prior contents of location xxx are destroyed.

Addition and subtraction operations may be started by a clear-accumulator-and-add instruction, which corresponds to clearing a desk calculator *and* adding the first number from location xxx. Each number is added to the number in accumulator by an ADDyxxx instruction, or subtracted by a SUByxxx. These instructions might be used for posting receipts and issues to inventory-control accounts, for summarizing inventory on hand, or for myriad other purposes.

WORDCOM operates on a whole word from storage when performing arithmetical operations. The programmer is responsible for aligning operands for decimal points and coping with overflow of accumulator capacity. Alignment can be handled by punching each number in the appropriate positions on a card when preparing input, so that the *assumed* decimal point will occupy the desired position within a word in storage. A WORDCOM storage word consists of a sign and seven characters that occupy eight positions on a card. Ten words punched in a card can be read directly into ten words in storage. For example, a money amount with three positions for dollars and two for cents can be punched in a card, as +0036742 with two zeros for filler. The decimal point is assumed (as was true for COBOL) and is not punched in a card or represented in storage for amounts used in arithmetical operations. If a plus sign and seven-digit money amounts are punched in a card starting in columns 1, 9, 17, etc., to 73, each one will occupy a whole word when read into storage. Other numbers to be added or subtracted from these must be similarly positioned. Of course, the card-reader plug board can be wired to arrange the words and characters in the card in various ways—spread them out, compress, or resequence them—during read-in to WORDCOM storage. The program can also shift a word in the accumulator and M-Q to the left or right to discard unwanted parts and to align decimal-point positions. Such operations are covered later in this chapter under packing and shifting.

Overflow. Continued addition or subtraction of numbers may give an answer that is too large for the accumulator to hold. For example, adding +6000000 to +7000000 gives an eight-digit total of +13000000. The eighth digit results in an *overflow* condition, when addition is tried in WORDCOM. To indicate overflow in a yes-no fashion, an extra bit is available in the accumulator. Whenever overflow is likely to occur in a routine, the programmer should test immediately, and if the overflow bit is on, go to a correction routine. One correction scheme is to shift the operands one position to the right before repeating the operations that caused overflow, continue with the main program, and later make adjustment for the shifting. Another scheme is to split each word into two parts in separate storage locations, operate separately on the two parts—double-precision arithmetic—and later join them together. A third scheme useful in some cases, such as adding a series of numbers, is to save the subtotal just prior to overflow, start afresh, and later combine all the subtotals. If an overflow occurs and a test is not made in the next instruction, the processor halts and indicates the condition on the console. The jump-on-overflow instruction to test occurrence of overflow and go to a correction routine, if required, is defined as follows:

Code	Explanation
JOV xxx	Jump on *overflow*, if one occurs, to take the next instruction from storage location xxx. If no overflow, continue regular sequence of operations. The processor halts if an instruction causing overflow is not followed by a JOV xxx instruction.

Multiplication. The multiplication of two seven-digit words gives a fourteen-digit product, although many of the left-hand digits may be zeros. The accumulator and M-Q registers are used together for multiplication in the following way:

1. The accumulator and M-Q registers are cleared to zero and the multiplier placed in the M-Q by the CAMyxxx instruction.
2. The multiplicand is obtained from location xxx, indexable, and the multiplication operation performed by the MLTyxxx instruction.
3. The product is stored from the M-Q register alone, if seven digits or less, by means of the STMyxxx instruction. If more than seven digits, the product extends into the accumulator and that part can be stored by a STAyxxx instruction.

The M-Q clear and add, multiplication, and M-Q storing orders are defined as follows:

Code	Explanation
CAMyxxx	*Clear* accumulator and M-Q and *add* to *M-Q* register the contents of location xxx, indexable; contents of location xxx unchanged.
MLTyxxx	*Multiply* contents of location xxx, indexable, by contents of M-Q. Low-order digits of the product will be in M-Q, and high-order in accumulator, although many may be zero. Storage-location contents are unchanged.
STMyxxx	*Store* contents of *M-Q* register in location xxx, indexable. (Use STAyxxx to store accumulator contents.)

The programmer is responsible for keeping track of the decimal point in the operands and the product. For example, multiplying the unit cost of $1.50 each by 1200 items on hand can be summarized as follows:

Multiplicand	+00001V50	Location x, indexable
Multiplier	+0001200	M-Q register
Product	+000000001800V00	Accumulator and M-Q

The desired answer of +01800V00 can be placed in storage by a STMyxxx instruction and, in this case, the accumulator content of +0000000 ignored.

Example of Inventory Calculation.   From the earlier example of converting inventory records from 3000 cards to 500 blocks of data on tape, an example of arithmetic operations can be developed. Suppose that the problem is to read in a block of data on tape containing six stock records, calculate stock value for each item (quantity on hand times unit cost) to complete each record, write out each completed record, and summarize stock value to find total stock value. For the six records in each of the 500 blocks on tape, the calculations must be repeated six times.

Since individual words in each record are handled here, the record format must be considered. The inventory-record layout used is similar to that for the COBOL-1 example in Chapter 8, but some changes are made to facilitate WORDCOM processing. A WORDCOM word consists of a sign and seven characters; therefore, ten words fill a card, as shown in Figure 10-2. Positions 1, 9, 17, etc., are reserved for signs, although they are needed only with numbers used for arithmetic operations. The record layout is designed so that the three words used here—quantity on hand, unit cost, and stock value—occupy whole words 6, 9, and 10, respectively, on each card, thus making these words directly available for use. Packing and shifting operations to handle elements not precisely fitting WORDCOM words are covered later in this chapter. The cards in Figure 10-2 also illustrate the stock records.

Each tape block of six records read into storage occupies 60 words starting at, say, word 201 with the three desired words of the first record occupying locations 206, 209, 210, of the second record locations 216, 219, 220, etc., and of the sixth record locations 256, 259, and 260. The program is given below for reading in a block from tape, calculating the stock value for each of six records in storage, subtotaling stock value, testing for overflow,

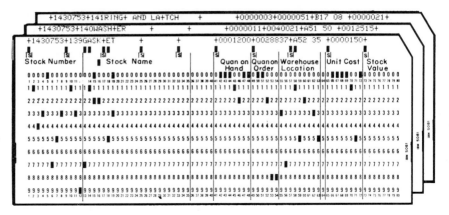

FIGURE 10-2. *Sample stock record for WORDCOM processing.*

writing the block, repeating the cycle 500 times and punching the total value:

Loc.	Content	Explanation
010	+0000000	Constant for setting and resetting index registers.
011	+0000000	Zero at first; use to hold stock-value subtotal.
012	+0000060	Criterion for testing completion of tape-block-processing cycle.
013	+0000500	Criterion for testing completion of file-processing cycle.
014	SISB010	Set to zero and use to count tape blocks read—the outer loop.
015	SISA010	Set to zero and use to count record-handling cycles and for effective addressing of records—the inner loop.
016	RT3 201	Read a tape block from tape unit 3 into locations 201–260 inclusive.
017	CAMA206	Clear accumulator and M-Q and add quantity on hand to M-Q from location 206, indexed by register A: 206 first cycle, 216 second cycle, etc., to 256 in the sixth.
018	MLTA209	Multiply unit cost in 209, 219, etc., to 259 in following cycles by quantity on hand to get stock value.

Loc.	Content	Explanation
019	STMA210	Store stock value in 210, 220, etc., to 260 in following cycles. (Assuming that only seven digits are wanted in product.)
020	CAA 011	Clear accumulator and add contents of location 011, which contains zero on first cycle and thereafter the subtotal of stock value.
021	ADDA210	Add stock value from 210, 220, etc., to 260 in following cycles to get new subtotal.
022	JOV 035	If addition causes overflow, jump to location 035 to punch the previous subtotal and restart operations for the record causing overflow. Overflow total not stored.
023	STA 011	Store stock-value subtotal in 011 after each addition.
024	INCA010	Increase index A by the number 010 for the spacing of data in records in storage since each record is ten words long.
025	CISA012	Compare index A to criterion 060 in location 012 to test completion of arithmetic operation cycle six times. (Criterion of 60 instead of 6 because index A is also used for effective addressing for *words* as well as for *record* counting.)
026	JMP 017	Return to repeat arithmetic cycle, if not completed six times.
027	WT9 201	Write block on tape, if six records handled.
028	INCB001	Increase index B by the number 001 to count tape blocks handled.
029	CISB013	Compare index B to criterion 500 in location 013 to test completion of block read-write cycle.
030	JMP 015	Return to read next block, if not all blocks handled.
031	PNC 011	Punch total stock value in a card (or subtotal if prior overflow occurred) after all records handled.
032	RW9	Rewind output tape.
033	RW3	Rewind input tape.

Loc.	Content	Explanation
034	HLT 001	Halt with instruction counter set at 1 to indicate program completion.
035	PNC 011	Punch stock-value subtotal for all records handled prior to overflow.
036	CAA 010	Clear accumulator to zero.
037	STA 011	Reload location 011 with zero, use to hold stock-value subtotal.
038	JMP 017	Return to repeat calculation for stock record that caused overflow and continue main program.

Division. WORDCOM also does division. Division is performed, from the programmer's viewpoint, in the following way. The accumulator is cleared by a CAAyxxx instruction and the dividend added. The divisor in storage location xxx is divided into the dividend in the accumulator by use of the DIVyxxx instruction. The quotient can be stored by a STMyxxx instruction and the remainder, if wanted, by STAyxxx.

In essence, the division operation subtracts the divisor from the dividend as many times as possible, places the count in the right-hand position of the M-Q and shifts the contents of both the accumulator and M-Q one position to the left. The subtract, count, and shift operations are repeated seven times to form the quotient in the M-Q and leave the remainder in accumulator. Division has a special rule: the divisor "as stored" must be larger than the dividend to avoid stopping the machine in a "divide-halt" condition. The programmer is responsible for anticipating relative sizes of the dividend and divisor and making adjustments to avoid a divide-halt condition. The division instruction is defined as follows:

Code	Explanation
DIVyxxx	*Div*ide the dividend in the accumulator by the divisor in location xxx, indexable. Quotient is formed in M-Q register and remainder is left in the accumulator.

Comparisons

The program illustrated earlier in this chapter for card-to-tape conversion accepted the sequence of records as given and simply wrote them on tape. Two choices exist, if data must be in sequence for efficient processing. The first is to leave the cards unsorted, convert them to tape, and use a processor program to sort the records into sequence by one of the schemes to be described in Chapter 13. The second is to sort the cards into sequence on a card sorter and merely check their sequence by comparing the numbers on each two successive cards during the conversion for subsequent processing. If the cards are in the correct sequence, the read-in should be continued; if out of sequence, the read-in operation halted. For cards almost in sequence, the sequence should be rechecked with a card collator and any cards out of sequence manually refiled. Cards in badly-mixed sequence should be rerun through the card sorter. After correction by either method, the cards will be ready for processor read-in and a second sequence check.

Comparison and Three-Way Exit. The comparison instruction with a three-way exit is useful for card-sequence checking and many other purposes. The comparison operation determines whether one number is less than, greater than, or equal to another. For names, the outcome is expressed in alphabetic-sequence terms: earlier, later, or same. To perform the comparison operation, the key word from one record is first placed in the accumulator and compared to the key word of another record in a specified storage location. The flow-chart block for the comparison operation, with the colon indicating the comparison operation, is as follows:

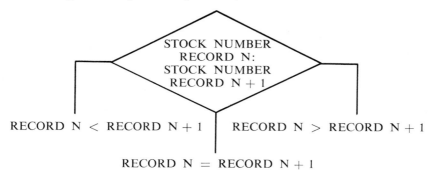

WORDCOM is designed to go to the first instruction following the comparison instruction for the *less-than* condition. In that location the programmer should place a jump instruction to send program control to the desired point in the program to handle that condition. The less-than condition can indicate that the card-read instruction just executed should be repeated, because the card examined is in sequence.

The second jump after the comparison is reserved for the *greater-than* condition. This outcome indicates a card is out of sequence and a jump instruction in that location can send program control to an error routine, which will either halt the processor, merely duplicate the out-of-sequence card and return to the main program to read the next card, or take other action.

The third location after the comparison instruction is reserved for the *equal* condition. If this condition indicates the main processing path should continue, the programmer can place the first instruction in the subroutine here.

The comparison instruction is defined as follows:

Code	Explanation
CMPyxxx	*Compare* content of accumulator with content of storage location xxx, indexable.
	Go to *next* instruction, if content of accumulator < content location xxx.
	Go to *second* instruction, if accumulator > content location xxx.
	Go to *third* instruction, if accumulator = content location xxx.
	Content of accumulator unchanged. For alphabetic comparisons, <, >, and = mean "earlier than," "later than," and "same," respectively.

File Sequence Checking. The use of comparison operations for sequence checking can be illustrated for the stock record card-to-tape conversion described earlier. Assume that the cards were sorted on the first seven digits that are the sequence part of the stock number. As a further check on card sequence before processing, the first word of one card may be put in the accumulator and compared with the first word on the next card. For the purposes of this example, each in-sequence card may be written on tape, each out-of-sequence card punched into another card for examination, and duplicate cards in the input deck ignored. The accumulator is first filled with blanks to act as a "prior card" before making the first comparison, so that the first card is correctly treated as in-sequence.

The simplified routine to read cards, check for numerical sequence, write in-sequence stock records in blocks on tape, punch out-of-sequence cards, and ignore duplicates is given in Figure 10-3

Location	S	1	2	3	4	5	6	7	Explanation

WORDCOM Program Form — Program Name: FILE SEQUENCE CHECKING — Page 1 of 1 — Program No. WC-1 — Prepared by WILL HARRISS — Date MAY 5

Instruction — Sign / Op Code / Index / Address

Location	S	1	2	3	4	5	6	7	Explanation
050	+	O	O	O	O	O	O	O	Constants.
051	+	O	O	O	O	O	6	O	
052	+	O	O	O	O	5	O	O	
053	+	C	A	A		O	5	O	Set accumulator to zero initially so that the first comparison will treat the first record as in-sequence.
054	+	S	I	S	B	O	5	O	
055	+	S	I	S	A	O	5	O	
056	+	R	E	C	A	1	O	O	Read card and store in locations 100-109, indexed, to build an in-sequence block of 60 words from six cards.
057	+	C	M	P	A	1	O	O	Compare stock number in accumulator (zero in the first comparison) with stock number in location 100, indexed.
058	+	J	M	P		O	6	1	Arriving here indicates card in sequence; go to load accumulator with stock number for next comparison.
059	+	J	M	P		O	7	1	Indicates out-of-sequence; go to punch card.
060	+	J	M	P		O	5	6	Indicates duplicate; ignore by reading next card (without changing index) into same storage locations over the duplicate cards.
061	+	C	A	A	A	1	O	O	Put current stock number in accumulator for next comparison.
062	+	I	N	C	A	O	1	O	
063	+	C	I	S	A	O	5	1	
064	+	J	M	P		O	5	6	
065	+	W	T	9		1	O	O	
066	+	I	N	C	B	O	O	1	
067	+	C	I	S	B	O	5	2	
068	+	J	M	P		O	5	5	
069	+	R	W	9					
070	+	H	L	T					
071	+	P	N	C	A	1	O	O	Arrival here means out-of-sequence card in location 100, indexed; punch a card for later examination.
072	+	J	M	P		O	5	6	Return to read the next card without increasing index A, which makes the new card read into storage over the prior card.

FIGURE 10-3. *Sample WORDCOM program for file sequence checking.*

on a programming form. This routine is similar to the routine for card-to-tape conversion given earlier, so only new instructions are explained here.

Test Negative and Two-Way Exit. The comparison instruction described above involves contents of the accumulator and a specified storage location. The jump-if-negative instruction is simpler. It tests the accumulator *sign* alone and branches in one of two ways for the negative or nonnegative condition. The jump-if-negative is useful for determining whether one number is smaller or larger than another. For example, quantity on hand minus reorder point quantity, if negative, indicates an order should be placed, but, if positive, no action should be taken. The jump-if-negative instruction is executed *only* if the sign of the accumulator is negative. It is defined as follows:

Code	Explanation
JINyxxx	*J*ump *i*f content of accumulator is *n*egative, to location xxx, indexed, for next instruction; otherwise continue regular sequence of instructions. Accumulator content unchanged.

Packing and Shifting

The input-output, cycle, arithmetic, and comparison instructions operate with whole words. Shifting instructions, however, operate on individual characters within a word. To save input preparation and read-in time, it is sometimes useful to pack two or more *data items* into seven characters when preparing input. The seven characters can then be stored as one WORDCOM *storage word* to save internal storage. *Shifting* operations can be used to *unpack* the storage word to separate the individual data items for processing. Processed results that occupy less than a whole word can be packed together for storage or read-out and punching in a card or writing on tape.

Shifting is the simplest method for unpacking and packing data. It uses the accumulator and M-Q registers together as a "shifting register" but ignores their sign positions. For shifting data, the M-Q register can be considered as simply an extension of the right-hand end of the accumulator, as follows:

Shifting Register

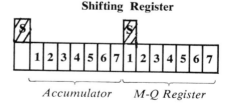

Character positions involved in shifting

S							S						
1	2	3	4	5	6	7	1	2	3	4	5	6	7

Accumulator   *M-Q Register*

An example of utility billing shows use of the shifting register. A utility punches a card with the following word, which consists of three different facts about a customer's meter reading:

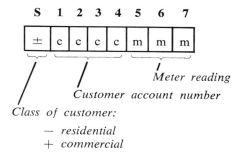

One word of new input, along with the master-file record is enough (with an appropriate program, of course) to compute a customer's bill. The master file is kept in customer account-number sequence in two blocks: residential ahead of commercial accounts, since minus numbers are smaller than plus numbers. For the four-digit numbers, the sequence is -9999, -9998, ..., -0001, $+0001$, ..., $+9999$. The cards punched with customer class, account number, and meter reading are sorted into sequence on sign and digits 1 to 4 before processor read-in. After read-in, the program checks sequence by using the whole word consisting of sign and seven characters to avoid the trouble of extracting the account number. The processor compares whole words, but meter reading in the low-order positions is minor to account number (which is major) and does not affect the sorting sequence. For shifting to unpack, as shown schematically in Figure 10-4, first clear both the accumulator and M-Q registers, and add the meter-reading word to accumulator.

To Unpack	**Explanation**
Customer account number	Shift right the shifting-register contents three character positions, so that customer account number is in accumulator positions 4 to 7. Store for later use as a separate word.
Meter reading	Next, shift left seven positions to discard customer account number. Meter reading is then in accumulator positions 1 to 3, unpacked. Store meter reading for later use or shift right four positions to 5 to 7 of accumulator for calculating consumption.

Shifting Register

	Accumulator								M-Q Register							
Character positions	S	1	2	3	4	5	6	7	S	1	2	3	4	5	6	7
Contents after clearing	+	0	0	0	0	0	0	0	+ 0	0	0	0	0	0	0	
Add meter-reading card (*c* for customer account; *m* for meter-reading digits)	+	c	c	c	c	m	m	m	+ 0	0	0	0	0	0	0	
Shift right three positions	+	0	0	0	c	c	c	c	+ m	m	m	0	0	0	0	
Shift left seven positions	+	m	m	m	0	0	0	0	+ 0	0	0	0	0	0	0	
Shift right four positions	+	0	0	0	0	m	m	m	+ 0	0	0	0	0	0	0	

FIGURE 10-4. *Shifting register to unpack customer meter reading.*

Instructions used in shifting the contents of the shifting register are defined as follows:

Code	Explanation
SHL nn	*Sh*ift *l*eft the contents of shifting register nn places, where nn is 01 through 13, inclusive. Sign positions of accumulator and M-Q unchanged. Discard any characters shifted out of left end of accumulator; fill with zeros the spaces vacated on right.
SHR nn	*Sh*ift *r*ight the contents of shifting register nn places. Discard any characters shifted out of right end of M-Q; fill with zeros the spaces vacated on left.

Data Read-In

To simplify the earlier discussion of programming, any program written was assumed to be available in the processor whenever wanted. Actually, the programmer must arrange to load his program into storage for processor use. The first step is to get enough instructions into the processor by manual means to make the processor bring in other instructions. Thus, a few instructions are used to "bootstrap" in more instructions.

General Scheme. The essential features of the four stages in loading WORDCOM with a program already punched in cards, and illustrated later are as follows:

1. Use the console and card reader switches to read the first card in the program load-routine into a desired location in high-speed storage.
2. The first card bootstraps the second into storage.
3. The load routine on the first two cards will read in an indefinite number of program cards.
4. The last program card makes a transfer to the start of the program, which includes data read-in and execution of the program itself.

The bootstrap load-routine cards, the program cards, and transfer-card to start execution of the card sequence-check program described above are shown in Figure 10-5. The program cards are

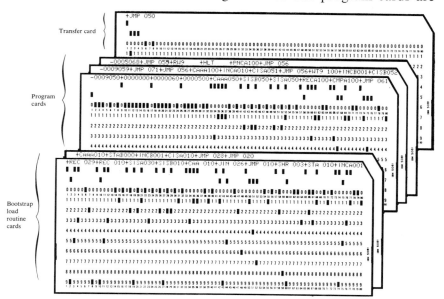

FIGURE 10-5. *Bootstrap load routine, card sequence-checking routine, and transfer card.*

discussed first here because their format affects the design and operation of the bootstrap load routine. Each program card will have from two to ten words on it. The first word on each card, called *word-*

count and location, is used solely for guiding the processor in storing the other words and has the following format:

S	1	2	3	4	5	6	7
—	0	0	0	w	x	x	x

The word-count character "w" indicates that one to nine words are to be read in from that card, corresponding to the number of instruction words in the card. The location part xxx, indicates where the second word on a card (the first program word on that card) will be put in storage. Other words on that card are stored in sequential locations.

The last card to be loaded, called a *transfer card,* contains +JMP xxx. The plus sign, instead of a minus, distinguishes the transfer card from the program cards to execute the +JMP xxx instruction. Execution of the +JMP xxx instruction transfers control to location xxx where the main program starts. Its format is:

S	1	2	3	4	5	6	7
+	J	M	P		x	x	x

Bootstrap Load Routine. The load routine starts from manually-set console switches to read one card into the locations specified in the program for the first card—say, 019 through 028, in this case. The processor is directed to execute the instruction in location 019. The instruction in location 019 causes the processor to read one more card, which contains the rest of the bootstrap load routine. The load routine of 16 instructions punched into the first two cards illustrated in Figure 10-5 is listed under Card Content below, with the location in storage and explanation added for clarity. The plus or minus sign that should be used with each word in WORDCOM has been omitted from instructions illustrated earlier, but is included here. The sign is used to indicate whether a card contains more program steps or all the program has been read in and program execution should start.

Loc.	Card Content	Explanation
		Use console switches to read first card into storage locations 019 to 028 and then transfer control to the first instruction in 019 for the processor program to take over the load routine.
019	+REC 029	Read second load-routine card into locations 029 through 038.
020	+REC 010	Read a card from main program into locations 010 through 019 for temporary storage while examining the first word to determine what to do with the other words. (The instruction in location 019, +REC 029, is not needed again and is destroyed when the first main program card is read into locations 010 through 019.)
021	+S I S A030	Set index register A with the three right-hand digits of location 030 which are 000. The 000 is taken from another instruction word, which contains 000, to economize storage.
022	+S I S B 010	Set index B with the right-hand three digits of the first word of a card in location 010—the word-location digits.
023	+CAA 010	Clear accumulator and add the first word from a card in order to get its sign.
024	+J I N 026	If sign of accumulator is negative, the accumulator contains a word-count and location for the other words on the card.
025	+J M P 010	If sign of accumulator is positive, then the word in location 010 is the transfer word to the first program instruction for execution. Make two jumps—one to location 010 and a second to execute the jump instruction there.
026	+SHR 003	The word-count and location word wxxx loaded into accumulator by the CAA 010 operation above is shifted right three places to put the "w" in the right-hand position. The location digits were set in index B by the SISB010 operation above and need not be retained here.
027	+S TA 010	The word-count in the right-hand position of the accumulator is stored in the right-hand position

	Card	
Loc.	**Content**	**Explanation**
		of the word-count, as follows: —000000w. Prior contents destroyed.
028	+INCA001	Increase index register A by 1 to count the number of words stored from the current program card.
029	+CAAA010	Clear accumulator and add the word in effective address location 010, indexed: 011 in first cycle, 012 in second, etc., to 019 in ninth cycle, if there are nine words to be stored from the card.
030	+S T AB000	Store accumulator content in effective address of 000 plus the content of index register B set in operation 022 with the desired location for the first word to be stored.
031	+I N CB001	Increase index register B by 1 to load program words into consecutive storage locations when repeating the cycle.
032	+C I S A010	Compare the count of words stored as contained in index register A with the number of words to be stored, which was placed in location 010 by instruction 027 to determine completion of word-storing cycle.
033	+J M P 028	Contents of index register A and location 010 are not equal; therefore, go to location 028 to repeat loop for storing a word.
034	+J M P 020	Contents of index register A and location 010 are equal; therefore, go to location 020 to read the next card.

A load routine of sixteen words punched in two cards, as illustrated here, can read in an indefinite number of other program cards and start execution of the program. Loading a program and starting its execution is similar to a chain reaction. If everything is ready, a small event triggers the whole operation for loading and executing the main program. Use of the load routine illustrated above precludes storing any part of the main program in locations 010 through 034, except for temporary storage of the data from each card in locations 010 through 019 to examine them before transfer to desired locations. Anything else stored in locations 010 through 034 will either destroy the load routine or be destroyed upon reading the next card. A similar load routine can be stored elsewhere, if these locations are required for the main program. After the main program is read in, the load routine area can be used for other purposes. The point is that storage must be allocated among load routine, main program, data, and working storage so that they do not interfere with each other.

Locations 000 to 009 are not used in the load routine shown above. They may be reserved for jump instructions after a halt occurs in order to start the program running again. Certain halt instructions (HLT xxx) in the program may specify a storage location from 000 to 009 for setting the instruction counter when the processor halts. A JMP xxx instruction stored in one of these locations can transfer control to an error-correction routine, when the processor is restarted. Used in this way, the jump instruction serves to connect the program halt and the error-correction routine with a temporary stop. The fact that the program arrives at location 003, for instance, indicates that HLT 003 was encountered in the program and may give some indication of the nature of the halt.

Editing

Programming WORDCOM for output of alphanumeric data items is simple. An alphanumeric data item occupying a whole word in storage, including blanks used to fill out the item, is ready for printing on the high-speed printer after writing on tape or punching in cards. If two or more items of data are stored in one seven-character word, each can be isolated by unpacking. Unpacking involves placing a word in the shifting register—accumulator and M-Q registers—and shifting left, right, or both to isolate the desired data item and discard others. During shifting operations, the desired item should be right- or left-justified as wanted for printing.

Editing numbers ready for printing with suitable symbols is more involved. It requires the use of an edit word containing editing symbols and an *extractor* to control editing these symbols into the data word. Two operations are involved for a data word that is already unpacked. First, zeros are placed in the data item to provide spaces for inserting the desired edit symbols of "$," "," and "." or perhaps others. Second, the data item is placed in the ac-

Instruction	**Explanation**
Op.	
Code Address	

Input and Output

R E Cyxxx	*R*ead a *c*ard and store contents in location xxx and following, indexable.
P N Cyxxx	*P*unch a *c*ard with ten words from storage at location xxx and following, indexable.
R T t yxxx	*R*ead a block of 60 words from *t*ape on *t*ape unit *t* and place in storage location xxx and following, indexable.
WT t yxxx	*W*rite on *t*ape *t* a block of 60 words from location xxx and following, indexable.
RW t ——	*R*ewind tape on *t*ape unit *t*.

Indexing

S I S yxxx	*S*et *i*ndex y from contents of *s*torage location xxx (not indexable).
I NCynnn	*I*n*c*rease contents of index y by the number nnn (not indexable).
C I S yxxx	*C*ompare *i*ndex y to contents of *s*torage location xxx (not indexable). Next two instructions in sequence are used for "not equal" and "equal" exits.

Tests

CMP yxxx	*C*om*p*are contents of accumulator and contents of location xxx, indexable. Next three instructions in sequence are used for exits for accumulator $<$, $>$, and $=$ location xxx.
J I N yxxx	*J*ump, *i*f accumulator *n*egative, to xxx, indexable.
J OV xxx	*J*ump, on *ov*erflow condition in accumulator, to location xxx.

TABLE 10-1. *Order code for WORDCOM.*

cumulator and the edit word is extracted into it under control of the extractor. The result of the operation is to give the edited data item in the accumulator ready for use. To *extract* means to remove from a word all the characters that meet some criterion and replace them with other characters.

Instruction	**Explanation**

Op.
Code   Address

Load and Store Accumulator and M-Q

CAAyxxx	*Cl*ear *a*ccumulator and *a*dd contents of location xxx, indexable.
S T Ayxxx	*St*ore contents of *a*ccumulator in location xxx, indexable.
CAMyxxx	*Cl*ear *a*ccumulator and *M*-Q registers and add contents of location xxx into M-Q, indexable.
S TMyxxx	*St*ore contents of *M*-Q register in location xxx, indexable.

Arithmetic

ADDyxxx	*Add* contents of location xxx to accumulator, indexable.
S UByxxx	*Sub*tract contents of location xxx from accumulator, indexable.
MLTyxxx	*Mul*tiply contents of location xxx, indexable, by content of M-Q register.
D I Vyxxx	*Div*ide the dividend in accumulator by divisor in location xxx, indexable.

Miscellaneous

HLT xxx	Unconditional *halt*, with instruction counter set to xxx. (Leave unchanged at next sequential instruction, if xxx is blank.)
S HL nn	*Sh*ift combined contents of accumulator and M-Q registers nn places to the *l*eft.
S HR nn	*Sh*ift combined contents of accumulator and M-Q registers nn places to the *r*ight.
EXOyxxx	*Ex*tract *o*dd replaces characters in the accumulator with characters from storage location xxx that have *positions* corresponding to odd-value characters in extractor, indexable; nothing else changed.
J MPyxxx	Unconditional *jump* to location xxx, indexable.

TABLE 10-1. *Order code for WORDCOM (cont'd).*

A data item in storage to be edited, 0068429, which should read $684.29 for printing, is opened up and zeros inserted by shifting and addition operations to give 0684029. Editing by extracting works in the following way. An extractor, say 1000100, consisting of 0's and 1's or any "even" and "odd" characters is read into processor storage. An edit word consisting of $——— . — is read into, say, storage location 379. The conditions just before extraction are as follows:

Edit word in location 379	$——— . —
Data item in accumulator	0684029
Extractor	1000100

The extract *odd*-character order, EXO 379, will replace the characters in the accumulator with characters from location 379 that have *positions* corresponding to the odd-value characters—the 1's—in the extractor, without changing anything else. The result of an extract odd order is to give $684.29 in the accumulator but not change the edit word or extractor. The extract *odd*-character order is defined as follows:

Code   **Explanation**

EXOyxxx   *Ex*tract *o*dd replaces characters in the accumulator with characters from storage location xxx that have *positions* corresponding to the odd-value characters in extractor, indexable; nothing else changed.

This scheme for editing is closely akin to the manual process, but it is less adroit than the COBOL-1 editing operation in which the EDIT order causes the processor to assemble the instructions to do the work.

The orders that WORDCOM executes (see Table 10-1) serve as a brief, simplified guide to the operation of internally-stored program processors with word-organized storage.

WORDCOM II

The first WORDCOM was designed with a fixed word of seven characters. This fixed length controls the organization of storage into words of seven characters, the capacity of the accumulator and M-Q registers, and the format of instructions. Since WORDCOM has a single address instruction, each instruction need identify only the following: one operation code out of 24, one index register out of three, and one operand address from 000 to 999. A word easily holds the five characters required for operation, index, and address. In fact, the seven characters of a word are used lavishly with three characters for a mnemonic operation code such as ADD and PNC.

It is more useful to consider how the instruction format of WORDCOM might be made more efficient by redesigning it as WORDCOM II. Some other interesting features of fixed-word processors are also considered.

Partial-Word Logic

WORDCOM II also has a fixed word consisting of sign and seven characters. It is designed with the same repertoire of 24 instructions that WORDCOM has. One character is enough to identify each of the 24 operations—A, M, S, C, and J for add, multiply, subtract, compare, and jump. Some of the mnemonic value is lost when only a single letter is used, since some letters have no apparent relationship to an operation name. Actually, one character can identify each of 64 operations if any alphanumeric or special symbols, such as /, !, ., ?, are considered suitable for an operation code. The machine can be designed to work satisfactorily with any symbol representing any operation. The question is whether programmers are willing to work with such operation codes.

Shortening the operation code to one character opens up two positions in a WORDCOM II instruction word. Engineers might redesign for *partial-word* logic—that is, so that characters in these two positions can be used to identify a selected part of a word wanted in an operation. The digit in position 2 of an instruction can indicate the high-order character and position 3 the low-order character of an operand. Two digits together indicate the high- and low-order characters of a partial word; if they are the same, the partial word is merely one character. When blank, the whole operand is used. An example of the format for WORDCOM II partial-word logic instructions is as follows:

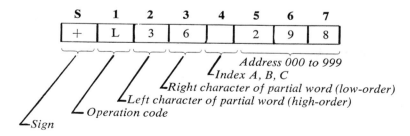

The instruction L36b298 means load—clear accumulator and add character positions 3 to 6, inclusive, of the contents of storage location 298—and ignore other character positions—1, 2, and 7 of location 298. The load instruction has right justification, so that the four characters in positions 3 to 6 from location 298 will occupy positions 4 to 7 in the accumulator and other positions will contain zeros. For example, executing the instruction L36b298 has the following effect:

	Positions **1234567**
Contents of location 298	$+8635492$
Contents of accumulator after execution of L36b298	$+0003549$

This load instruction is equivalent to clear and add location 298, shift left two places to discard the 86, and shift right three places to move the 9 into character position 7 of the accumulator. Operations to store accumulator contents also have partial-word logic and right justification. Partial-word logic has interesting features for unpacking a data item from a packed storage word and opening up a data item to insert edit symbols. Division by 10, 100, etc., can be done merely by dropping one or more digits when loading a partial word into the accumulator. Various instructions of WORDCOM II— including the arithmetic operations, load accumulator or M-Q register, store accumulator or M-Q, and the comparison instruction—can make good use of the partial-word feature.

Compact Addressing

WORDCOM uses three characters to identify 1000 storage locations numbered 000 to 999. Although three characters for addressing storage and 1000 addressable locations in storage are compatible, 1000 words of storage is small for a high-speed processor. The question arises whether it is possible to have a larger internal storage and still address it with three characters in each instruction. Of course, a longer word would provide more characters in the instruction for addressing storage, but here we are interested in the possibility of using the three characters more efficiently for addressing storage or index registers since the question of efficient use of each character arises regardless of word length.

More Storage Addresses.   Each character position has six bits in storage and can represent 64 alphanumeric characters ($2^6 = 64$). Only four bits are actually used to represent the digits 0 through 9 in each position, and they are not really efficiently used because six possibilities are idle, since $2^4 = 16$. Two bits in each character are spare and might be used for other purposes. The two spare bits could be combined with the four numeric bits to represent a total of 64 alphanumeric characters, since $2^6 = 64$. The "alphabet" of 64 alphanumeric characters includes the digits 0 through 9, letters A through Z, and special symbols, such as $, /, ., &, %, and +. If programmers are willing to use an alphanumeric as the first character along with two numerics in the operand address, then three characters have a range from 0000 to 6399: 0 to 63 in the first position and 0 to 9 in the second and third positions. An example is given below of the WORDCOM II condensed-addressing scheme for the instruction "Load the accumulator with character positions 3 to 6 inclusive of storage location 5498, indexed by contents of index register B":

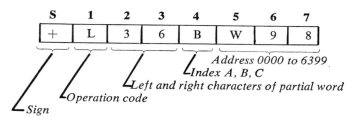

The programmer writes W to represent 54, its value in the collation table. During program execution, the processor decodes W to mean 54, and addresses location 5498.

Indexing. In a similar fashion, the two spare zone bits over position 7 in an instruction might be used to identify an index register. Two bits will identify four registers ($2^2 = 4$), which is adequate for WORDCOM II with only three index registers. Position 7 is numeric in instructions that are not indexed, since only 0 through 9 is needed. But in indexed instructions, the combination of numeric and zone bits in position 7 results in an alphanumeric symbol. The preceding instruction using the digits position of the address to mean both index register B and the digit 8 can be written +L36bW9H, since a zone bit to identify index B and the bits for 8 can be represented by the letter H. Position 4 is blank, for it no longer need be used to identify an index register. The address W9H to represent storage address 5498, indexed B, is compact, but it is hard for the programmer to work with. A compiler program, as will be described in Chapter 12, permits a programmer to write in ordinary format—

5498B—and make the processor compile instructions into compact form for internal storage and processing. A programmer should be familiar with the compact format, since program traces and snapshots will ordinarily be in this format. A programmer can write in one language but must be bilingual to debug his program.

Two-Address Instructions. Incorporating the identification of index registers A, B, and C with position 7 frees position 4 in the instruction format. Partial-word addressing, which uses positions 2 and 3, may not be considered important and therefore dropped from the design. If so, the three positions 2, 3, and 4 can be used in each instruction for addressing another operand in much the same way as the first address. The instruction format and an example of Add contents of location 5137, indexed B, to location 5246, is as follows:

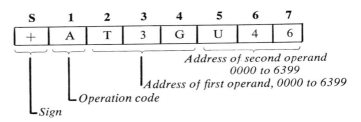

The switch from a single- to double-address machine requires design changes in equipment. The accumulator and M-Q registers might be eliminated and add-to-storage logic introduced. The instruction +AT3GU46 will add the contents of location 5137, indexed B, to location 5246 for T = 51, U = 52; G represents 7 and B together. The sum is formed in storage location 5246 and replaces the prior contents. Other two-address instructions, designed by engineers to operate as follows, give some idea of the order code:

Subtract contents of first address from second address and give remainder in second address

Multiply contents of first address by second address and give product in second address

Compare contents of first address with second address and take "less than" and "greater than" exits from the first and second addresses, respectively, in the next sequential instruction; the "equal" exit is the second sequential instruction. Or the processor might be designed with "switches" that the comparison operation sets for program testing to take the appropriate jump, whenever desired.

Two-address instructions are more compact and versatile than single-address instructions, but may result in slower operating speeds and extra steps to save the operands used in arithmetic operation.

It is useful to summarize at this point how WORDCOM II uses the 43 bits—seven characters of six bits each and sign—in each word.

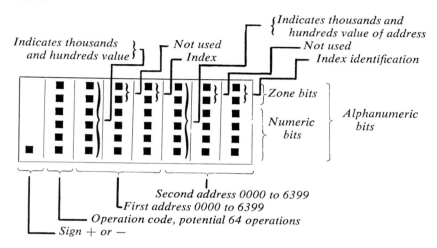

As mentioned earlier and as described in Chapter 3, the exact format of an instruction is not likely to be of concern to programmers until after they gain experience. At first, anyway, programmers prefer to write in a noncompact format, using mnemonics, symbolic names, or complete absolute addresses, and separate identification for index registers. The instruction ADD BILL TO AMT-DUE has a mnemonic operation code and symbolic addresses. After the compiling and assignment of absolute addresses, it may be represented ready for execution as A M36 Q94.

Binary Operations

WORDCOM II makes reasonably efficient use of the bits in a word by representing operations, addresses, and indexes with the near-minimum number of characters required. If the 42 bits in a seven-character word could be organized without regard for characters, it would be possible to represent an instruction with 35 bits as follows: operation code of five bits to represent any of 32 instructions, operand address of thirteen bits for up to 8192 addresses, and two bits to identify up to four index registers. The remaining seven bits might be used for addressing more locations if processor storage is increased to 16,384, 32,768, etc., words; each additional bit in an address doubles the number of locations that can be addressed. Or the spare bits could be used to indicate modifications of present instructions or to develop a larger order code.

All the bits in a word may represent one number 42 bits long. Chapter 2 showed how binary numbers are more compact than alphanumeric numbers. A 42-bit binary number can represent a number as large as 4,398,046,511,103, which is $2^{42} - 1$. It will be recalled that the largest number that seven alphanumeric characters can represent is 9,999,999.

Some processors can handle data and perform arithmetic operations in various modes—alphanumeric, decimal, binary, and octal. A programmer indicates the desired processing mode for an instruction, and some bits in the instruction keep track of the mode specified. Thus it is possible to perform a decimal add or a binary add depending on the data mode when the instruction is executed, although, of course, the data and the instruction must be compatible. WORDCOM II can represent and operate with data in the following modes:

Alphanumeric: 7 alphanumeric characters of 6 bits each
Decimal: 10 decimal digits of 4 bits each (2 parity or spare)
Octal: 14 octal digits of 3 bits each
Binary: 42 binary digits of 1 bit each

WORDCOM II has been discussed in some detail as a modified WORDCOM in order to show some of the variations possible within the framework of a fixed-length word. It is hoped that the discussion will also give the reader some idea of how the demand for compact instruction and data representation for efficient storage makes equipment more versatile, although this demand is somewhat in conflict with the programmer's desire for readable and recognizable instructions.

SUMMARY

The precise instruction format devised by engineers must be adhered to by programmers. The format specifies the use of each character position for operation code, index register, and address or special constant.

The example of a program given in the chapter to read the data from one deck of cards or a tape, and punch another deck of cards or write on tape is trivially simple, but the program shows address modification for cycling through instruction loops to cut the number of program steps to be written and stored. Index registers are special counters that can be set and increased or decreased by specified numbers—in WORDCOM, an increase by 995 is equivalent to a decrease of 005, since storage location 999 is followed by 000. A register is tested to determine its contents during each loop in a cycle. An indexable instruction adds the contents of an index register to the specified address in the instruction to form and use an "effective address" at the time of instruction execution. The indexing scheme is invaluable for performing repetitive operations on data stored in an organized fashion or brought in one record after another.

Comparison orders are at the heart of the decision-making process. Various comparisons can determine, for example, whether an inventory balance is larger or smaller than the reorder point, whether one item belongs ahead of another in a sequence, and whether a cycle has been performed the desired number of times. Jump instructions are used after comparisons to transfer processor control to the desired routine in the program to perform the required operations—for example, prepare shipping papers for a customer's order if his credit is satisfactory.

Instructions for addition, subtraction, multiplication, and division perform arithmetical operations, but arithmetical instructions are only a small fraction of the operations involved in business processing. The programmer has many responsibilities for arithmetical operations. He must keep track of the decimal point, avoid the possibility that results will overflow the accumulator, make correction for overflow, and edit results for dollar signs, commas, and decimal points. Shifting operations are used to line up characters before comparison or addition operations and to isolate desired characters—unpack and pack—during processing.

WORDCOM II illustrates some of the possibilities for making more efficient use of the characters in an instruction and giving greater versatility. Two of the possibilities are the use of one character to represent an instruction, and partial-word logic for selecting certain characters from a word, which is similar to shifting in WORDCOM for unpacking. The use of all six bits in a single character permits addressing 0 through 63 positions in storage with one character instead of merely 0 through 9 with a single digit. Similarly, a zone bit and the digits 0 through 9 can be combined as a letter or special symbol for addressing both storage and an index. Thus, three positions in an instruction can refer to 6400 words in storage and to four index registers. Double-address instructions are possible within seven-character words. As an example, AT3GU46 can mean "add contents of location 5137, indexed B, to location 5246" for $T = 51$, $U = 52$, and G, which represents 7 and B together. Binary operations make more efficient use of storage than do digital operations. The 42 bits in a seven-character word can be used in the following ways: seven alphanumeric, ten decimal (with 2 for parity or spare), fourteen octal, or 42 binary. The programmer can execute certain instructions in any mode by using the same mode for an instruction and the data.

11
Programming—Machine-Oriented Languages—FIELDCOM

FIELDCOM (for *field com*puter) is a medium-scale, internally-stored program processor that is in many ways similar to WORD-COM. But, since FIELDCOM storage is organized into "fields" instead of "words," its order code and programming therefore are different. FIELDCOM storage is 8000 individual *characters* as compared to WORDCOM's 1000 *words* each with seven characters and a sign. It is left to each programmer to plan the efficient use of FIELDCOM's 8000 characters for data items and instructions, though naturally this planning must be consistent with FIELD-COM's engineering design features.

One way to cope with storage assignment for each data item in FIELDCOM is to *select fields* of characters long enough to handle the longest example of each particular item likely to occur in all the records. Another storage assignment scheme is called *variable field,* which provides the exact number of characters required for every data item, whether short or long. However, in either scheme of storage assignment, each instruction may be the minimum number of characters required to indicate the operation code, the operands involved, or such features as field shifting and condition switches, to be discussed later. While a programmer is responsible for assigning storage to instructions and data, an assembly or compiling program handles most of the details, as will be described in Chapter 12.

Before delving into FIELDCOM, it is useful to review briefly some of the features of WORDCOM discussed in Chapter 10 and show their relationship to FIELDCOM design and operation. WORDCOM has a fixed-length word that makes it representative of a large class of data processors. This fixed-length word was designed by engineers to be long enough to contain either an instruction or a useful amount of data. In addition to containing an operation code and the address of a word in storage, an instruction may identify an input-output device and an index register. The discussion of WORDCOM II showed how the bits in a word may be used more efficiently for storing instructions or data. It also showed that a close relationship exists between the minimum number of characters required in an instruction word and the length of a word designed into the equipment. An important point in the discussion of word length was the emphasis on the composition and minimum length of an instruction; the argument was not primarily whether a long or short word would be most efficient for data storage and handling. Fixed-length-word design simplifies some aspects of programming, but freezes other aspects of data and program organization for the programmer. Any instruction or operand can be placed anywhere and easily interchanged, since word length is constant. The control unit obtains a whole word—instruction or operand—from storage and processes it at one time; such parallel processing makes possible higher operating speeds. However, difficulties arise because shorter items require packing into a word for efficient storage and unpacking for processing. Longer data items occupy two or more words and may entail elaborate handling operations.

An alternative to fixed-length-word storage design is for the equipment designer not to organize individual characters into words, as is the case for FIELDCOM. Instead, he can offer each programmer the freedom to organize the characters in storage into fields suited to the lengths of the data items processed. Of course, then other changes in equipment design and programming are required; for example, the processor must operate on a character-by-character basis instead of a whole field. Therefore, each character must be addressable in such a way as to indicate the end of a field or the separation between two fields. A *fieldmark*—a bit associated with, say, the left-hand character in a field—is one way to indicate the end of a field. An operation addresses the right-hand character in a field, and the processing unit handles one character at a time until it reaches the fieldmark. Another way of indicating field length is to place a unique symbol called a *field separator* between data items to indicate their end.

Two versions of FIELDCOM—FIELDCOM-S and FIELD-COM-V—are considered here to show the nature of data organization and processing for selectable- and variable-length fields for data.

FIELDCOM-S

FIELDCOM-S is a character-addressable processor designed in such a way that a programmer can *select* the length of each field for a data element. The ability to select corresponds to the assignment of fields to data when planning for the use of punched cards. It will be recalled that any number of card columns can be assigned to each item of data in a record. But after a particular length is selected to cover the longest instance likely to occur for that particular item, it must be used for that item in all records making up a file. Chapter 2 discussed the selectable-length organization of data items into records.

Machine Characteristics

FIELDCOM-S has a simplified design with a shortened order code planned to illustrate the essence of programming for character-addressable processors. Many features are similar to a widely used medium-scale processor in order to convey an understanding of the nature of programming. But some short cuts and simplifications have been made to permit focusing on essential aspects. The features of FIELDCOM-S of interest here briefly are as follows:

1. Storage: 8000 addressable positions in high-speed storage, each capable of holding one alphanumeric character. Three areas are assigned to input and output, although they can be used for other purposes at some risk of interference: character positions 0001 through 0080 for card read-in, 0101 through 0180 for card punch, and 0201 through 0320 for printing one line of 120 characters.
2. Operating logic: executes operations one character at a time and places results in storage—add-to-storage logic.
3. Control unit: instruction counter addresses an instruction by its left-hand character and advances one character at a time from *left to right*. It addresses an operand by its right-hand character and handles one character at a time from *right to left*.
4. Input-output: can have one card read-punch unit and up to ten magnetic-tape units.
5. *Instruction repertoire:* Executes 25 different two-address instructions.

Storage and Data Organization. Each of the 8000 addressable positions of FIELDCOM-S high-speed storage can hold one alphanumeric character. Six bits per character make it possible to represent 64 different symbols, covering the alphabet, numerals, and 28 special symbols, although some are reserved for processor control.

A seventh bit in each position is used for parity and an eighth solely to indicate a fieldmark for that character. A fieldmark indicates the left character of each operand and instruction in FIELDCOM-S.

A programmer can fieldmark any desired character position in storage—indicated "xxxx"—by means of the FMxxxx instruction, and can use it to set up fields of appropriate length. A fieldmark occupies the eighth bit and is independent of the character in that position; fieldmarking a position does not disturb the character and its parity in bits 1 through 7. Similarly, reading a character and parity into bits 1 through 7 in a position and manipulating it does not ordinarily disturb the fieldmark. The chief purpose of fieldmarks is to control field length for data movement and manipulation. The right-hand character of a field serves as its address and the first fieldmark to the left indicates the left-hand character. Thus a field can be as short as one character—the position addressed contains a fieldmark—or as long as several hundred characters, although there is a limit of twenty numerals for fields used in arithmetic operations.

A programmer organizes storage for data as selected-length fields to suit the requirements of each application. He might select a field of ten characters for stock number, twenty for stock name, five for quantity on hand, etc. The characters in storage between the character addressed and the fieldmark, inclusive, make up a field—an item of data for processing. For example, Figure 11-1 shows a simple stock record—the same one used to illustrate programming

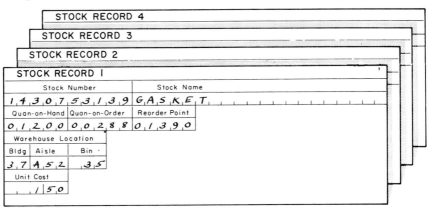

FIGURE 11-1. *Layout of stock-record card for FIELDCOM-S processing.*

in earlier chapters. Figure 11-2 shows storage content after the processor *reads* the contents of one card into storage positions 0001 through 0080 assigned for read-in and *copies* the contents into

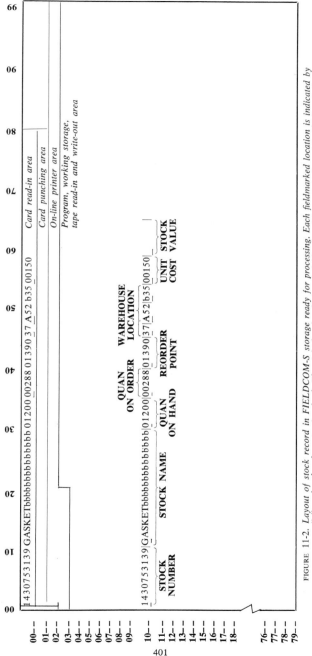

FIGURE 11-2. *Layout of stock record in FIELDCOM-S storage ready for processing. Each field—marked location is indicated by "⌐" under the character involved. The right-hand end of each field—the address—is indicated by "⌐" for clarity.*

locations 1001 through 1080 for processing. To consider a particular item, quantity on hand of 1200 units can be stored in a five-digit field to provide for numbers up to 99999. The address of quantity on hand is 1035 in this particular case, and the fieldmark, previously placed at location 1031, indicates the left end of the field. Quantity on hand also remains in the read-in area with address 0035 (position 0031 not fieldmarked) after the copy operation and until the program reads the next card into locations 0001 through 0080. A card-read operation reads in a whole card. But card contents can be copied into the punching, printing, or working-storage areas with some items omitted, and, if desired, with some expansion or shortening. On the other hand, some processing operations may require longer fields than in the input data and therefore require expansion of the input fields. Printed reports require expansion of fields for editing with "$" and "." and for spacing between fields to make them readable. Fields are shortened to discard some digits or even a whole item no longer wanted.

Data ready for read-in must have vacant spaces in numbers filled with zeros and in alphanumerics with blanks, "b." Every character position must contain a symbol, zero, or blank.

Figure 11-2 also shows that input-output operations are restricted to areas in storage. Character positions 0001 through 0080 are assigned to receive data when reading cards or paper tape. After read-in, the program can copy data into other locations in storage for processing. Any characters in these positions will be destroyed when the next card is read, but any fieldmarks previously set remain unchanged.

Positions 0101 through 0180 are assigned to hold data awaiting punching into cards or paper tape. They can be used for merely recopying from other storage locations or they can also be used for composing the contents of a card or even for calculation. When making calculations in these positions, the programmer must be sure to clear the area to remove any unwanted characters before punching in the next cycle. Similarly positions 0201 through 0320 are used to compose one line of 120 characters, including blanks, for printing on the high-speed printer.

Logic. FIELDCOM-S has add-to-storage logic. This permits direct addition of one field—say, units received—to the quantity-on-hand field. The sum will be stored in the quantity-on-hand field. The addition instruction format is ADxxxx xxxx, which means add the contents of the A address, the first xxxx, to contents of the B address, giving a total at the B address, with prior contents destroyed. This corresponds to the ADD TO operation in COBOL, which performs an addition operation with one instruction and places the results in storage at the second address. If contents of the B address are wanted afterwards, they must be placed in another field before the addition is performed, or separate working storage must be used to calculate the total.

Each instruction is designed to work with whole fields, although there are exceptions. For example, the addition operation is terminated upon reaching the first fieldmark. The addition operation is usually completed satisfactorily if field A is shorter than B, since A is added to B. But if field B is shorter, termination of addition at the B fieldmark leaves part of field A unadded. To guard against overflow, field B should be made longer than A. Continued addition of numbers to a particular field may give a sum longer than the field can store. The result is a field mistake corresponding to an overflow in WORDCOM. A field mistake sets a "switch," which is a device to indicate the occurrence of overflow. The switch can be tested whenever desired for the occurrence of a field mistake in the program and a jump made to a correction routine or to a program halt. The point here is that even in FIELDCOM-S, with selectable-length fields, a programmer must consider probable lengths of operands and allocate enough storage to handle most conditions.

FIELDCOM-S handles operands on a character-by-character basis from right to left under control of an address register and terminates execution *after* the fieldmarked character is handled. The address register then contains the address of the *right-hand* character of the next lower-address operand in storage. If that operand is wanted in the next instruction, it is already available and its address need not be specified. Implicit addressing in this way is called *chaining,* and permits the programmer to write instructions omitting the B address or both the A and B addresses.

Instruction Format. The FIELDCOM-S instruction format is variable in length, and each instruction can be as long as required to perform a complete function. Most instructions contain one or two addresses, although some—for example, card-read, card-punch, and chained instructions—have implicit addresses and are not written. The instruction format showing the instruction, Add field A, address 2376, to field B, address 4895, is as follows:

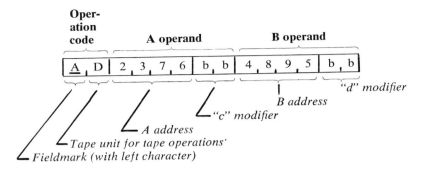

There are several important points to note about the FIELD-COM-S instruction format. The operation code consists of two characters with a fieldmark associated with the left character. An instruction is addressed by its *left-hand* character position. Instruction execution on a character-by-character basis is stopped when the next fieldmark is encountered. That is, an instruction is terminated one character before the next fieldmark. The second character indicates the tape unit used in a read or write operation. The A and B operand addresses each have six characters consisting of four for operand address and two for modifier. The "c" modifier can identify the switch to be tested for jump instructions. Either modifier can indicate "field shifting" positions, which resembles the shifting in WORDCOM when the field wanted in an operation is the field as stored but shifted left or right from one to nine positions.

The instruction format *represents* the way an instruction is stored in the processor ready for execution. Actually, it would be condensed by using a compact addressing scheme similar to one of those described for WORDCOM II. Since it is the instruction format that is of primary interest, rather than the exact plan for representation, the possibility of more compact operation codes and addresses will not be considered here.

Instructions and Programming

FIELDCOM-S is a two-address processor with add-to-storage logic. The addresses indicate where to obtain or to store operands in storage. Some modification of field addresses is possible by means of the "c" and "d" modifiers associated with the A and B field addresses, respectively. The word "position" is used here to indicate a single-character location in storage.

Instruction Repertoire. The FIELDCOM-S order code is given in Table 11-1 near the end of this chapter. Some of the orders correspond to WORDCOM instructions, but there are some important differences because of the features of selectable-field length and two-address instructions. Their use in simple programs is illustrated throughout this chapter, but a brief listing is useful at this point to serve as an overview of the instruction repertoire:

1. *Input and Output*
   a. Read a card or punched tape and place contents in locations 0001 to 0080.
   b. Punch a card or paper tape with contents of locations 0101 to 0180.
   c. Read a block of data from a tape and store in specified address, downward to blockmark.
   d. Write a block of data on a tape from specified address downward through first blockmark.
   e. Mark tape with file mark to indicate end of file on reel.
   f. Rewind a tape ready for removal.
   g. Print a line of 120 characters on the high-speed printer from storage locations 0201 to 0320.
   h. Read a specified sector from a disk and store at specified address in high-speed storage.
   i. Write a specified sector in disk storage from high-speed storage address.
   j. Seek a disk sector preparatory to reading or writing.

2. *Load and Store*
   a. Clear storage of both fieldmarks and characters between two specified positions and fieldmark the low-order character position.
   b. Fieldmark one character position in storage without disturbing contents.
   c. Copy contents of field at first address into field at second address, leaving contents of first unchanged.
   d. Copy and edit whole content of one field into a second field.
   e. Set the contents of a field to zero.
   f. Blockmark a position in storage to indicate end of block for tape-writing.

3. *Arithmetic*
   a. Add contents of one field to a second.
   b. Subtract contents of one field from a second.
   c. Multiply contents of one field by a second.

4. *Tests*
   a. Compare contents of one field with another and set a switch indicating result of comparison.
   b. Test the setting of a switch and make the appropriate jump, depending on condition of the switch.

5. *Miscellaneous*
   a. Halt processor operations with appropriate setting of instruction register.
   b. No operation—a "dummy" operation placed in a program for forming an operation later; otherwise skipped.
   c. Assign a literal value to a field with the absolute or relative address specified and fieldmark it.
   d. Assign an absolute or relative address to the symbolic address listed.

Card Input-Output. FIELDCOM-S controls either one card read-punch unit or a paper-tape read-punch. New data are usually punched in cards or tape and then read in for processing. Output may be punched in cards or tape for later use. Also, FIELDCOM-S often serves as a satellite to a larger processor by converting data from cards to tape for high-speed read-in and by printing output written on magnetic tape by the large processor.

A read-punch unit is connected directly to FIELDCOM-S for on-line operations. Reading and punching are independent and operate on separate decks of cards or reels of tape. For brevity, "card" means punched card or paper tape for input and output for FIELDCOM-S. The read-card instruction—simply RC with an implicit address of 0080, for none is stated—activates the card reader to read 80 characters from a card. The processor stores the 80 characters in locations 0001 to 0080, replacing any alphanumeric characters already there, but without disturbing any fieldmarks. In a simple case —say, punching a new deck of cards to replace worn cards, or converting cards to tape—all 80 characters can be copied as one field to the appropriate location for output to card or tape. Locations 0101 through 0180 are reserved for card output. A punch-card instruction—simply PC, without an address—activates the card punch to punch 80 characters from locations 0101 through 0180 into the next card in the card-punch hopper. Contents of the punch area in storage remain unchanged after the punch operation.

Since different areas are reserved for reading and punching data from cards, a copy instruction—CP 0080 0180, with A and B addresses for the read and punch areas of 0080 and 0180, respectively—will duplicate the contents of the read area into the punch area. Contents are then ready for punching into a card. These three instructions—RC, CP 0080 0180, and PC—can be used as often as desired to read the data from a card, copy them into the punch area, and punch them into another card.

One preliminary instruction is necessary to clear storage positions 0001 to 0180, inclusive, and to set a fieldmark at 0001 to indicate the left-hand end of the 80-character field for the copy operation after each card is read in.

Inst. Addr.	Op.	Addresses A	c	B	d	Explanation
STRT	C S	0001		0180		Clear storage positions 0180–0001, inclusive, and fieldmark position 0001.
	RC					Read a card into the read area, positions 0080–0001.
	C P	0080		0180		Copy the field at address 0080 (positions 0080–0001, which is fieldmarked) into address 0180 occupying positions 0180–0101.
	P C					Punch a card with data from punch area, positions 0180–0101.
	RC					Same as before to read, copy, and punch more cards.
	C P	0080		0180		
	P C					
	A A	0321		STRT		Assign the absolute address 0321 to the symbolic address STRT in this source program during the compiling run. The instruction CS 0001 0180 will have address 0321—left-hand character addressing for instructions—when the object program is loaded to run.
	b					b, blank with fieldmark to indicate end of preceding instruction.

Several points about this card read-punch routine are worth noting. The first instruction has the symbolic address STRT—any combination of four characters with the first one alphabetic serves as a *symbolic* address. A programmer writes a *source* program with symbolic addresses for instructions, mnemonic codes for operations, and operand addresses in symbolic, absolute, or relative form. The processor makes a preliminary run of the source program, under control of an assembler or compiler program, to prepare an *object* program ready for the processor to execute. The object program will then have instructions and addresses in a compact form best suited for machine execution. In the source program shown here, the instruction AA 0321 STRT will assign absolute address 0321, or any other free address that the programmer chooses, to the symbolic address STRT during the compiling run. The compiled object program, when read into the processor for execution, will be stored at absolute addresses 0321 and following. Compilers and assemblers are discussed in Chapter 12, but since it is more important that the reader learn the fundamental ideas, this chapter will forego discussing absolute addresses, which are difficult to determine for character-addressable storage, and instead will concentrate on symbolic source programs.

An instruction is addressed by its left character, which is field-marked, and the last instruction must be followed by a fieldmarked blank "b" to terminate the preceding instruction. Instructions occupy only the minimum number of storage positions—two for RC, ten for CP 0080 0180, etc. A field is addressed by its right position—0080 or 0180 for the card read and punch areas—and the fieldmark in 0001 terminates the copy operation. In this particular case no other fieldmark is required because this duplication routine is supposed to operate with all 80 characters from a card. However, if many cards are involved, the repetition of three instructions per card is burdensome; hence, various schemes for repeating the cycle are used, as will be described later under cycling.

Card Input, Tape Output. FIELDCOM-S can control up to ten magnetic-tape units. A program reads data from, or writes data on, the tape mounted on a particular tape unit by addressing the unit, which can be numbered 0 through 9 by manually set switches. FIELDCOM-S can write any desired length block on tape, although a block at least several hundred characters long is desirable to keep a suitable ratio of block length to inter-block gap. With tape density of 400 characters per inch and .75 inch inter-block gaps, tape blocks must average 300 characters to get 50 per cent utilization of tape capacity. A write-tape order, Wt xxxx, specifies the tape unit "t" and the address of the data block, which is its right-hand character position. A blockmark previously placed to the left of the last character in the block to be written terminates the tape-write instruction.

A simple program similar to that for reading and punching cards illustrates reading a card, assembling its contents into a block in storage locations 1001 through 1480 for a total of six cards, and writing the block on tape. Assume that there are 3000 cards to read and write on tape in six-card blocks of 480 characters each for a total of 500 blocks. The program is given in symbolic form with explanations for instructions in Figure 11-3 on a FIELDCOM-S programming form.

This card-to-tape conversion routine will read six cards, one at a time, while copying their contents into a tape-write area to compose a block of 480 characters of data. It also writes each block and a blockmark on tape. The jump-switch instruction, JS xxxx C, is a conditional jump that depends on the condition of the switch to be tested, as indicated by the explanation of the "c" address in Table 11-1. But the "U" in the JS READ U instruction in the program means the jump is an unconditional one to the symbolic address READ. Lacking any plan to test for end of data, this program will run until the card hopper is empty, whether it contains 3000 cards, as stated, or more or less. The tape-write instruction executes after reading each block of six cards. If the cards placed in the reader are not an exact multiple of 6, then some cards will remain in storage without being written on tape when operations stop. Along with the data from the cards not written on tape, locations 1001 through 1480 will contain data from cards in the prior block not written over by new cards. This aspect of remnants from a prior cycle can readily be tested by tracing through the treatment of merely seven cards, which in many ways corresponds to handling 3001 cards. The next section, cycle counting, discusses how to remedy the problem of counting the number of cards handled, properly handle all cards, and how to wind up operations involving tapes.

The two input-output routines illustrate card duplication and conversion of cards to tape. Data conversion and writing operations are seldom an end in themselves, but they are used with other instructions for processing data; in fact, elementary data handling is an important aspect of business data processing.

Cycle Counting. The card-to-tape conversion routine has a repetitive cycle, so that it continues to read six cards and write blocks on tape until the card hopper empties. However, it is not really satisfactory merely to handle all the cards that simply happen

FIELDCOM-S Program Form	Program Name READING CARDS AND WRITING ON TAPE		Page 1 of 1
	Program No. RW-100	Prepared by WILL HARRISS	Date MAY 17

Location	Opera- tion	A	c	B	d	Explanation
STRT	CS	0001		0080		Clear storage of fieldmarks and characters from
	CS	1001		1480		positions 0080-0001 for input and 1480-1001
						for output; fieldmark locations 0001 and 1001.
	BM	1000				Blockmark location 1000 to terminate block
						when writing a block on tape.
READ	RC					Read first card to read-in area.
	CP	0080		1080		Copy card contents from read-in area to
						1080-1001 in tape-write area.
	RC					Read second card to read-in area.
	CP	0080		1160		Copy card contents from read-in area to
						1160-1081 in tape-write area.
	.					Repeat the card read and copy operations for
	.					cards 3, 4, and 5 in each block using CP
	.					instructions with B addresses of 1240, 1320,
	.					and 1400.
	RC					Read card 6 to read-in area.
	CP	0080		1480		Copy contents of card 6 to address 1480.
	W3	1480				Write on tape unit 3 the block of data at
						address 1480 which terminates with the
						blockmark at location 1000.
	JS	READ	u			Jump on switch unconditional — "U" in c
						modifier — to address READ to read the
						first card in the next block of 6 cards.
	AA	0401		STRT		Assign absolute address 0401 to symbolic
						address STRT during assembly pass.
	b					Fieldmark merely to indicate end of
						preceding instruction.

FIGURE 11-3. *FIELDCOM-S program for reading cards and writing blocks on tape.*

to be ready. Good operating practices call for a *control count* at the earliest point in processing for checking the accuracy of the next operation. Several control counts can be used at one stage—for example, a file-record count and transaction count to control both the number of records and of transactions handled. Also, *control values*—quantities and dollar amounts—are useful for controlling the accuracy of processing. In this particular case, it seems useful to find the *actual count* of cards converted by revising the program to count each card as it is read for conversion to tape. Then the actual count is compared with the control count made when the cards were first prepared to determine whether the correct number of cards has been converted. Two choices are available: (1) process all cards and then check the actual count against the control count to determine whether the correct number of cards, more, or fewer has been converted; (2) stop when the actual count reaches the control count for the number of cards supposed to be converted.

Actual Count Control.   The first scheme of actual-count control is illustrated in the program below; the second scheme is discussed briefly afterwards. As described for WORDCOM, index registers are useful for counting cycles. But FIELDCOM-S has index registers only as extra equipment, so it is desirable to devise another technique to count the number of cards handled. One technique is to assign a four-character field for the actual count—to go to a limit of 9999 cards—set it at 0000 initially, and add 1 to it at some point in each card-handling cycle. At any point, the actual count will indicate the number of cards already handled. Three thousand cards are supposed to be converted to tape in this example, and a header card in the deck contains the control count in columns 7 through 10. After converting all cards to tape, the program is supposed to punch a card with CONTROLbCOUNTbXXXX in columns 1 through 18, ACTUALbCOUNTbYYYY in columns 21 through 37, and DIFFERENCEb±ZZZZ in columns 40 through 55. The card layout, with "b" for blank, and column assignment can be summarized as follows:

```
CONTROLbCOUNTbXXXXbbACTUALbCOUNTbYYYYbbDIFFERENCEb±ZZZZ
1              13 15 18 21          32 34 37 40       49 51  55
```

The program to convert all cards to tape and punch a card with the desired message is as follows:

Inst. Addr.	Op.	Addresses A	c	B	d	Explanation
STRT	CS	0001		0080		Clear card read and punch areas
	C S	0101		0180		of fieldmarks and characters and fieldmark 0001 and 0101.
	FM	0115				Fieldmark fields within the punch area for control count,

Inst. Addr.	Op.	Addresses A	c	B	d	Explanation
	FM	0 1 3 4				actual count,
	F̄M	0 1 5 1				and difference.
	B̄M	1 0 0 0				Blockmark location 1000 for tape writing.
	R̄C					Read control count card.
	C̄P	0 0 1 0		0 1 1 8		Copy control count into control-count field in punch area.
CLRS	C̄S	1 0 0 1		1 4 8 0		Clear tape-write area at the start of each cycle before copying card contents into it.
	R̄C					Read data card.
	J̄	S PRTB		C		Jump if last card, switch "C" is on, to PRTB to write partial block of less than six cards; the rest are blanks.
	C̄P	0 0 8 0		1 0 8 0		
	ĀD	O N E		ACNT		Add 1 to ACNT—actual count of cards.
	· · · · · ·					Repeat the four prior instructions —RC, JS, CP, AD—five times with higher B addresses for the copy—1160, 1240, 1320, 1400, and 1480—to store each card in successively higher locations. (Total of twenty instructions required.)
	W̄3	1 4 8 0				Arriving here from the sixth card-handling cycle means full block to write on tape *and* that last card not yet read. Write the full block on tape unit 3.
	J̄	S CLRS		U		Jump unconditional to CLRS— clear storage for assembling next block of data to write on tape.
PRTB	W̄3	1 4 8 0				Arriving here from the JS PRTB C instruction in the card-handling cycle means that last card has been read; last block will contain zero to six cards, the rest blanks.

Inst. Addr.	Op.	A	Addresses c	B	d	Explanation
WNDP	M 3					Mark tape with filemark to indicate end of file on reel.
	T 3					Rewind tape on tape unit 3.
	C P	0 1 3 7		0 1 5 5		Copy actual count into difference field.
	S B	0 1 1 8		0 1 5 5		Subtract control count from actual count.
	P C					Punch card with card-count message.
HALT	H L	HALT				Halt with instruction counter set to address HALT.
	A L	O N E	+1			Assign value of "+1" to symbolic address ONE.
	A L	0 1 1 3	CONTROLbCOUNT			Assign each literal to the absolute
	A L	0 1 3 2	ACTUALbCOUNT			address specified to form the
	A L	0 1 4 9	DIFFERENCE			card-count message.
	A A	0 1 3 7	ACNT			Assign absolute address of 0137 to ACNT for actual count of data cards handled.
	A A	*	01	O N E		Assign the next single free position as indicated by * and 01 the symbolic address ONE for storing the literal +1, assigned above.
	A A	0 4 0 1		STRT		Assign absolute address 0401 to STRT.
	b					Fieldmark to indicate end of preceding instruction.

This card-to-tape conversion routine for handling and counting all cards has several interesting features. After reading the header card for the deck, the program copies the control count from address 0010 into the field with address 0118 in the punch area; the fieldmark at 0115 terminates the copy operation, since the source field at address 0010 in the card-read area is not marked. The program assigns three literals—CONTROLbCOUNT, ACTUALbCOUNT, and DIFFERENCE—to specific addresses in the punch area. The symbolic address ACNT is used to maintain the running total of the actual count and could be located anywhere in storage, although it is assigned address 0137 in the punch area where it is later wanted. The absolute address 0137 could be used here instead of the symbolic address ACNT, since it is assigned an absolute address by the program; however, symbolic addresses are easier to use and it is desirable to get initial experience with symbolic addresses in simple situations. The difference (actual count minus control count) is both calculated and stored in the output area. Before starting to read the next block of cards, the program clears storage locations 1001 through 1480 for the block-assembly area to hold six cards in each cycle. This ensures that the last block written on tape, even though it contains fewer than six cards, will consist of only these remaining cards and not contain any data left over from cards read in the prior cycle. After each card-read instruction, the program tests for last-card condition, and, if the last card was read, transfers control to PRTB—the partial-block write instruction and wind-up. At PRTB, the program writes on tape the last block, which consists of data from six or fewer cards. This block is filled out with blanks and a tape mark, and the tape is then rewound for removal. Next, the program calculates the difference between actual count and control count, punches a card, and halts. The actual count of cards converted to tape and other control or identifying information could, if desired, also be written as a separate *trailer block* on tape following the data but before the tape mark and rewind instructions. The machine operator should be given instructions about how to proceed when the control and actual counts are different—rerun the operation, examine the card deck, or call the supervisor.

Planned Count Control.   A second scheme suggested earlier for controlling the number of cards converted to tape is to stop reading when the actual count equals the control count. Since the program reads one card at a time, it is possible to stop when actual count exactly matches the control count. However, when controlling on dollar amounts or quantities on hand, received, or issued, the actual sum may skip over the control total so that an equality match is not suitable; then, both "equal" and "greater than" tests are required.

The scheme for stopping card conversion when the control count is reached can be handled by the preceding program with minor modifications. After reading a card and increasing the actual count of cards by 1, the new actual count simply is compared with the control count, both of which are in the area reserved for card punching.

The comparison operation sets a switch that can be tested by an instruction—"jump on switch equal." While the actual count is less than the control count, which is true during all card-read operations except the matching one, the "jump on equal" is *not* executed; instead, the next sequential instruction is executed. When the actual count of cards read reaches the control count, the "jump on equal" instruction is executed and program control goes to the wind-up operations. The wind-up writes the last block on tape, writes a tape mark, and rewinds the tape. It also punches, if still wanted, a card showing card control count, actual count, and difference. The corresponding message may merely be printed on the processor console.

The card-to-tape conversion stops when the control count is reached, according to the planned count control, and any extra cards remain in the card-read hopper. If the actual number of cards is less than the control count, the "jump on last card" is executed to transfer control to the wind-up. The card-read cycle shown in the prior program, modified to stop when actual count reaches the card control count, is given below along with explanations for the two new instructions. As before, this cycle of card-read, copy, and related instructions must be written six times with successively higher addresses for the B address of the copy instruction.

Inst. Addr.	Op.	A	Addresses c	B	d	Explanation
	R C					
	J S	PRTB		C		
	C P	0 0 8 0		1 0 8 0		
	AD	O N E		ACNT		
	CM	0 1 1 8		ACNT		Compare field at address 0118 with field at relative address ACNT (which is assigned absolute address 0137 during the compiling pass) and set switch for equal, low, or high condition.
	J S	PRTB		E		Jump, if switch indicating equal is on, to write partial block, and wind up. (These six instructions must be written a total of six times with higher-B addresses for the CP instruction to handle six cards per block.)

Address Modification.   The second version of the control scheme for card-to-tape conversion has six instructions to read and handle each card, or a total of 36 for the six cards in a block. A programmer must write and check each of these 36 instructions and they will occupy 36 fields in storage when the program is run. Since only the copy instruction is slightly different each time—its B address increases by 0080 for each card—it should be possible to write the cycle once and perform it six times after modifying it as required.

The copy instruction should be CP 0080 1080 when executed for the first card, CP 0080 1160 for the second, and so forth to CP 0080 1480 for the sixth card in each block. To return to the first card in the next block, the copy instruction needs to be returned to its original status of CP 0080 1080. It will be recalled from the original discussion of internally-stored programs that addresses of operands are merely numbers and can be modified by addition or subtraction. This feature can be used in the following way. After each card-handling cycle, the number 0080 is added to the B address of the copy instruction CP 0080 1080 to increase the B address to 1160, 1240, etc. to 1480. A simple way to determine when the sixth card in each block has been handled is to compare the copy instruction used in each cycle—CP 0080 1080, CP 0080 1160, etc., up to CP 0080 1480—with a *criterion* consisting of the instruction supposed to be used in the sixth cycle— CP 0080 1480. If the copy instruction just executed is lower than the criterion, jump to repeat the cycle for the block. If it is equal, meaning that the sixth copy operation was executed, the copy instruction should be reset to its initial value to start the cycle afresh, a block written on tape, and the card-reading cycle then restarted. A segment of the card-to-tape conversion program, using instruction modification with an instruction as a criterion, is as follows:

Inst. Addr.	Op.	Addresses A c	B	d	Explanation
READ	R C				
	J S	PRTB	C		
COPY	C P	0 0 8 0	1 0 8 0		
	A D	O N E	ACNT		
	C M	0 1 1 8	ACNT		
	J S	PRTB	E		

Inst. Addr.	Op.	A	Addresses c	B	d	Explanation
	AD	ATEY		COPY+9		Add +0080 to B address of instruction with symbolic address COPY. Requires field shift of nine positions to right of the instruction address, which is the C in CP.
	CM	COPY		CRIT		Compare contents of symbolic address COPY with contents of symbolic address CRIT, which is CP 0080 1480, and set switch for low, equal, high.
	J S	READ	L			Jump if switch is low to symbolic address READ to repeat the card-handling cycle; if not low (but equal or high), continue in sequence.
	C P	BEGN		COPY		Copy the contents of symbolic address BEGN into symbolic address COPY to reset it for starting the next cycle.
CRIT	C P	0080		1480		Criterion for comparison test.
BEGN	C P	0080		1080		Instruction for resetting the instruction at COPY back to its initial value.
	AA	*		5 ATEY		Assign next five free positions the symbolic address ATEY.
	A L	ATEY	+0080			Assign the literal value +0080 to symbolic address ATEY.

In this particular case, four instructions are required to modify the address of the copy instruction, test for completion of reading six cards, and take the appropriate steps of either continuing the card-handling cycle or resetting the copy instruction to start afresh. Each card-reading cycle involves six basic instructions—RC, JS, CP, AD, CM, and JS—and three instructions to handle address modification—AD, CM, and JS.

Only one additional instruction, CP BEGN COPY, is required to reset the copy instruction, with symbolic address COPY, to its original value. Two fields are required to hold the CP 0080 1480 to serve as a criterion and CP 0080 1080 to reset the copy instruction in the program back to its initial value. Thus a total of four instructions and two constants can serve the same purpose as writing the card-handling cycle of five instructions five more times for a total of 25 instructions. By using cycles, a programmer writes fewer instructions and the program occupies less storage, but the processor achieves the same net result at the cost of executing more house-keeping instructions.

Magnetic-Tape File Processing.   A basically simple example of magnetic-tape file updating will illustrate some features of this important method of keeping business data files. The utility bill calculation and customer file update are highly simplified in order to concentrate on the basic points and avoid the confusion resulting from numerous details. Inputs for a processor run to update customer files are the master file from the prior run and mark-sensed cards that meter readers prepare showing customer number and meter-reading quantity. The outputs wanted here are an updated master file and a printed bill. Also, for each meter-reading card that does not match the master-file customer number, a duplicate card should be punched for an account clerk's investigation. Assume that the meter-reading cards are punched and in sequence without any duplicate cards, although some customers' cards are not available because readers missed meters on their routes.

Input and output formats of interest here are as follows:

1. Meter-reading card, columns:
   - 1–10   customer number
   - 11–15   current meter-reading quantity.
2. Master-file record on tape, same record format for old and new files, one record per tape block, characters:
   - 1–10   customer number
   - 11–15   most recent meter-reading quantity
   - 16–17   customer rate class (1 of 24 classes applying to all customers)
   - 18–22   most recent period's consumption
   - 23–30   most recent bill in dollars and cents, unedited
   - 31–299   name, address, consumption history, collection record, etc., handled as one field here for simplicity.
3. Bill, skeleton form only, print positions with blanks between items:
   - 1–10   customer number
   - 13–17   current meter-reading quantity
   - 20–24   current period's consumption
   - 27–28   customer rate class
   - 31–40   current bill in dollars and cents with format $$$,$$9.99; leading zeros are suppressed down to units position and the dollar sign is floated into position of rightmost sup-

pressed zero.
4. Investigator's card for meter-reading card number not matching file, card columns:
  1–10 customer number (not matching)
  13–17 current meter-reading quantity.

The flow chart in Figure 11-4 deserves some comment to clarify new points and describe the calculation scheme before plunging into

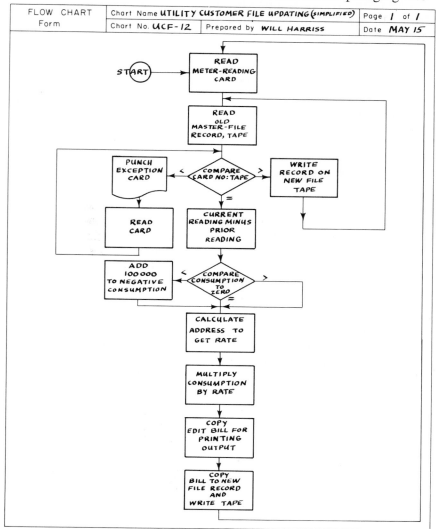

FLOW CHART Form	Chart Name **UTILITY CUSTOMER FILE UPDATING (SIMPLIFIED)**		Page **1** of **1**
	Chart No. **UCF-12**	Prepared by **WILL HARRISS**	Date **MAY 15**

FIGURE 11-4. *Flow chart for utility customer-file updating (simplified).*

the program itself. The flow chart shows that processing starts by reading a transaction *card* and an old master-file *record* from tape. Next, customer numbers from card and tape should be compared to search for matching numbers. The two nonmatching situations—customer number on a card is less than or greater than the master-file record—can be disposed of quickly since they require little processing. If the customer number on the card is *high,* the matching master record is further along in the file; therefore, the master record from storage should be written to the new master-file tape and another record read from the old master file. If the card number is *low,* the number does not match any master-file number, since the cards are in sequence and the potential file match for this card has been passed. Therefore, a duplicate card should be punched so that account clerks can investigate why a meter reader turned in a card with a nonmatching number. More information is required, of course, to track down the problem, but it is not of concern here.

A match—card customer number *equals* master-record number—starts the calculation process. Consumption equals current meter reading minus prior reading. A positive remainder is satisfactory, but a negative result indicates the meter dials passed from 99999 to 00000; therefore, 100000 must be added to the negative result to make it positive and to get the correct consumption. The programmer should start forming the records for printing the bill and writing the new master-file record. The obvious plan is to calculate the amount of bill by multiplying the kwh consumed by that particular rate out of 24 which applies to the customer involved. Each customer class has a four-digit rate expressed in pennies and decimals—$.XXXX. Since each rate is four digits long, the 24 rates can be stored consecutively as a simple "table" with addresses of, say, 6904, 6908, . . . , 6996, so that a particular rate can easily be associated with a customer's rate-class code. The customer's rate class can be used to calculate the address for his corresponding rate in the table. The obvious scheme is simply to multiply the customer's rate class number by 4, corresponding to the length of each table entry, and add 6900, which is the starting point of the table, to give results of 6904, 6908, . . . , 6996 to calculate the rate-address. Then the calculated rate-address can be inserted into a second multiplication instruction as the A address with the kwh consumed as the B address (multiplier) to compute the billing amount.

The multiplication operation in FIELDCOM-S with add-to-storage logic is a bit tricky, since it does not have an accumulator and M-Q register, as such. Any field in storage can be used as a "multiply field" for performing multiplication, but it must be as long as the two factors involved plus one extra position. The sequence of operations is as follows: the programmer must clear the multiply field, copy the multiplier into the *left* end of this field, and then execute the multiplication instruction—ML xxxx xxxx. Of course, the multiplier may already be in the left-hand end of the multiply field, and thus only the right-hand end need be cleared before executing the multiplication order. The multiplication instruction A address is for the multiplicand field located anywhere in storage, and the B address is the right-hand position of the multiply field containing the multiplier in its left end. Upon completion, the product is in the right-hand end of the multiply field. All of the product can be used or some right-hand digits may be cut off by addressing the rightmost digit wanted or, as will be described, by field shifting when storing the product in another field. In this particular case, a multiply field ten positions long is used for calculating the bill: five at the left to hold kwh and five at the right (four for rate $.XXXX and one for a space) to hold the product as it starts forming. The remainder of the output messages can then be formed for printing and for writing on tape.

Selected parts of the program for calculating utility bills are described here; assuming that another programmer supplies more careful testing procedures for last card and other conditions, housekeeping, and winding up. The general layout of storage in Figure 11-5 shows areas with fieldmarks for card read and punch, print, and billing-rate table. Areas for master-file tape read-in and tape write-out have both fieldmarks and a blockmark. Note that positions 0400 through 5999 are assigned to instruction storage and 6000 through 6899 to working storage, but that few fieldmarks are indicated. The program given below is written with symbolic instructions and addresses. The programmer provides for assigning address 0401 to the first instruction, since instructions are fieldmarked *and* addressed at the left-hand end. He also provides for assigning an appropriate address to the first item in working storage so that its fieldmark occupies position 6001 and the item itself occupies positions 6001 upwards. The compiler program actually makes the assignments during a compiling pass, as will be described more fully in Chapter 12, but, for some purposes, it will be assumed that the program has been compiled at least for assignment of addresses.

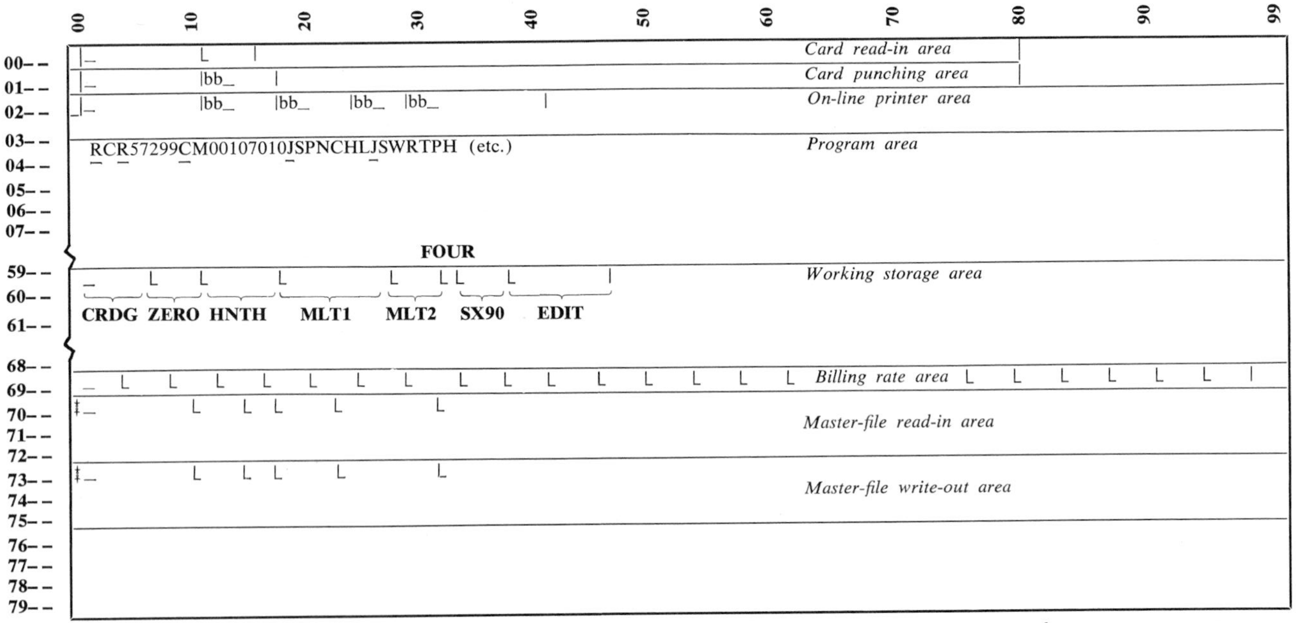
00
10
20
30
40
50
60
70
80
90
99
00--
01--
02--
03--
04--
05--
06--
07--
59--
60--
61--
68--
69--
70--
71--
72--
73--
74--
75--
76--
77--
78--
79--
Card read-in area
Card punching area
On-line printer area
Program area
RCR57299CM00107010JSPNCHLJSWRTPH (etc.)
FOUR
Working storage area
CRDG ZERO HNTH MLT1 MLT2 SX90 EDIT
Billing rate area
Master-file read-in area
Master-file write-out area

FIGURE 11-5. *Layout of storage for utility bill processing with fieldmarks and symbolic addresses for working storage.*

Inst. Addr.	Op.	A	Addresses c	B	d	Explanation
RDCD	RC					Read a meter-reading card.
RDTP	R5	7299				Read a master-file record from tape unit 5 into positions 7299–7001
CMPR	CM	0010		7010		Compare customer number on card to master-file number.
	JS	PNCH	L			If card customer number low (L), incorrect number; jump to PNCH to punch investigator's card.
	JS	WRTP	H			If card customer number high (H), no match; jump to write tape for inactive master-file record.
	CP	0015		CRDG		Arriving at this point indicates a match, start processing by copying current meter-reading quantity to CRDG—current reading—in working storage.
	SB	7015		CRDG		Subtract prior meter-reading in master file from current reading in CRDG to calculate consumption.
	CM	CRDG		ZERO		Compare calculated consumption with zero (has the symbolic address ZERO) to determine if negative—meter passed 99999.
	JS	CALC	H			Calculated consumption higher than zero, go to start calculation.
	JS	WRTP	E			Calculated consumption equals zero. Desired processing not specified, treat as inactive and go to write out master record; perhaps should punch a card for investigation to determine why consumption zero—broken meter, etc.
	AD	HNTH		CRDG		Calculated consumption is negative, add 100000 (symbolic address HNTH for 100000) to correct meter passing from 99999 to 00000 and start calculation.

Inst. Addr.	Op.	A	Addresses c	B	d	Explanation
CALC	ZR	MLT1				Zero the field MLT1 to eliminate remnants of prior multiplication.
	C P	CRDG		M L T 1	−5	Copy calculated consumption (CRDG) into multiply field number 1 (MLT1) with field shift of five positions to left to provide space at the right for multiplication by rate of four positions.
	ZR	MLT2				Zero the second multiplier field MLT2.
	C P	7 0 1 7		M L T 2	−2	Copy customer rate class from master-file area to multiply field number 2 (MLT2) with field shift of two positions to left to provide space for multiplication by 4 to develop the address of the rate.
	ML	FOUR		M L T 2		Multiply 4 (FOUR) by customer rate class to develop the spacing in rate table of four positions in the multiply field MLT2.
	AD	MLT2		S X 9 0		Add rate spacing in table to 6900 (SX90) to get rate-table address; should contain one of the following: 6904, 6908, . . ., 6996.
	C P	S X 9 0		R A T E	+5	Copy rate-table address from SX90 into instruction with symbolic address RATE, field shifted five positions to right to form the A address of the instruction. (Remember that RATE is the symbolic address of an instruction that is addressed by its left character.)
RATE	ML	0 0 0 0		M L T 1		Multiply rate from table (the A address is supplied by preceding instruction) by consumption previously placed in MLT1 by the instruction CP CRDG, MLT1 −5. Ten-digit product has six positions for dollars and four for cents: XXXXXXVXXXX.

Inst. Addr.	Op.	Addresses A	c	B	d	Explanation
	C P EDIT		0 2 4 0			Copy the editing field $$$,$$9.99 (EDIT) into the amount field of the printing area.
	C E MLT1	−2 0 2 4 0				Copy-edit amount of bill from MLT1 to 0240. Field shift of −2 for A address cuts off two right-hand characters from product in MLT1. Result is one to six positions for dollars, two for pennies with floated dollar sign, comma (if required), and decimal point.
	C P 7 0 1 7		0 2 2 8			Copy customer rate class from old master file to bill print area.
	C P CRDG		0 2 2 4			Copy current consumption calculated above to bill print area.
	C P 0 0 1 5		0 2 1 7			Copy current meter reading from 0015 in card-read area to 0217 in print area.
	C P 0 0 1 0		0 2 1 0			Copy customer number from 0010 in card-read area to 0210 in print area.
	P T					Print on high-speed printer the bill (skeleton form only) from positions 0201–0320.
	C P 7 2 9 9		7 5 9 9			Copy old master-file record positions 7299–7031 to new master-file positions 7599–7331.
	C P MLT1	−2				Copy, without editing, the amount of bill with format XXXXXXVXX into new master tape area at address 7330 by deleting two positions at right. B address chained since already at 7330 from prior copy.
	C P CRDG					Copy current consumption into master-file write-out area.
	C P 7 0 1 7					Copy customer rate class from old to new master-file areas.
	C P 0 0 1 5					Copy current meter reading.
	C P					Copy customer number.

Inst. Addr.	Op.	A	c	B	d	Explanation
	W 3	7 5 9 9				Write tape block of one up-dated master-file record, positions 7599–7301 with block-mark at 7300.
	J P	RDCD	U			Jump unconditional to read next card and repeat the processing cycle.
PNCH	C P	0 0 1 5		0 1 1 7		For a nonmatching card, copy content from read to punch area. Punch a copy of nonmatching card for account clerk.
	C P	0 0 1 0		0 1 1 0		
	P C					
	R C					Read next meter-reading card.
	J S	CMPR	U			Unconditional jump (U) to compare new card to prior record number.
WRTP	C P	7 2 9 9		7 5 9 9		Copy inactive master record from file-read to file-write area; record consists of six fields. "Chaining" both the A and B addresses is useful here since all fields in each inactive record are merely copied from file-read to file-write area. The read-in area might be used for write-out, apart from the usual objection to such dual use of a storage area because of risk of losing a record.
	C P					
	C P					
	C P					
	C P					
	C P					
	W 3	7 5 9 9				Write inactive record on new master tape keeping whole file in sequence.
	J S	RDTP	U			Jump, unconditional, to read next record in master file and repeat cycle.
HALT	H L	HALT				
	A A	6 0 0 5	5	C R D G		Assign the address 6005 to a five-position field 6001–6005 and give it the symbolic name CRDG, for current reading.

Inst. Addr.	Op.	A	Addresses c	B	d	Explanation
AA	*		5	ZERO		Assign the five next free positions in storage—6006–6010—and name it ZERO. The "*" means relative address and the compiler assigns the next five free positions; here follows 6005 from the preceding assignment.
AA	*		6	HNTH		Assign next six positions the symbolic name HNTH for 100000.
AA	*		10	MLT1		Assign next ten positions the symbolic name MLT1 for multiplier 1 field.
AA	*		4	MLT2		Assign next four positions the symbolic name MLT2 for multiplier 2 field.
AA	*		1	FOUR		Assign next one position the symbolic name FOUR.
AA	*		4	SX90		Assign next four positions the symbolic name SX90 for 6900.
AA	*		10	EDIT		Assign next ten positions the symbolic name EDIT.
AL	ZERO	00000				Assign the literal 00000 to symbolic address ZERO.
AL	HNTH	100000				Assign the literal 100000 to symbolic address HNTH.
AL	FOUR	4				Assign the literal 4 to symbolic address FOUR.
AL	SX90	6900				Assign the literal 6900 to symbolic address SX90.
AL	EDIT	$$$,$$9.99				Assign the literal $$$,$$9.99 symbolic address EDIT.
AA	0401			RDCD		Assign first instruction in program to location 0401.
ND	RDCD					ND indicates END of program; program to start at RDCD.
b						

The preceding discussion of FIELDCOM-S instructions and programming concentrated on punched cards and magnetic tapes. Card and tape records are arranged in files in an orderly sequence on a key such as customer number or inventory stock number, and transactions affecting files are customarily handled in the following way. First, a "batch" of transactions is accumulated, and, if not already classified, is organized according to the file the transactions affect—inventory, customers, employees, etc. Second, each classified batch of transactions is sorted into sequence on the key used for the file and also the logical sequence for transactions—receipts ahead of issues, etc. Third, the appropriate program is used with the transactions and file to process the file and prepare desired outputs, which consist of reports and an updated file. If a transaction also affects another file, all the steps must be repeated with that file and appropriate program. Batch handling takes time at each stage—accumulate, classify, sort, and process—and delays the production of desired output so that results may not be available as quickly as wanted.

Addressable Bulk Storage Processing. Addressable bulk storage, as described briefly in Chapter 3, speeds up transaction processing by providing a large bulk storage directly connected to and under processor control. This bulk storage, which may be magnetic disks, large drums, magnetic cards, or strips of magnetic tape, holds one or more files and the programs used for processing them. From the standpoint of programming and processing, the important points about addressable bulk storage are the methods of data organization, techniques for addressing, and the speed of operation. FIELD-COM-S disk storage is organized in the following fashion, but the concept is basically the same for other devices:

Units: 1 to 10 at the user's option numbered 0–9 and identified "u" in addressing
Disks: 100 disk faces numbered 00–99 per unit—dd
Tracks: 100 tracks numbered 00–99 per disk face—tt
Sectors: 10 sectors numbered 0–9 per track, each containing 100 characters—s.

Data capacity of a disk unit is, therefore, 10 million characters: 100 disk faces × 100 tracks per disk face × 10 sectors per track × 100 characters per sector. A "sector" is a unit of 100 characters of data in disk storage and is the lowest level of data addressable on disks. In view of the length and organization of data records, a sector of 100 characters may or may not be a convenient quantity of data, but the disks were designed to store exactly 100 characters of data and a programmer has to plan the processing and storage of records with this feature in mind. Of course, some addressable bulk storage, including disks, is designed to store variable-length records, which simplifies the task of organizing records for storage. The variable-length feature raises other problems of rewriting records in storage to make way for a longer record at the address where a short record was previously stored, but since it is the basic ideas that are of interest, only fixed-length sectors will be considered.

By appropriate programming, any 100 characters in high-speed storage, including blanks for padding a shorter record, can be written as a sector on a disk and any sector can be read from disk storage and written anywhere in high-speed storage. A unique address makes it possible to write in or read from any sector. A sector address is six characters long—uddtts, with the letters standing for *u*nit, *d*isk, *t*rack, and *s*ector, respectively. Each character position has a possible value of 0 through 9, as described above. The address of each sector in disk storage is permanently recorded at the start of that sector to identify it so that the processor can check the position of the read-write head before reading or writing. Sector addresses in high-speed storage have a dual purpose. The six characters, uddtts, address the disk sector involved in a disk instruction. They also identify the high-speed storage area involved in a disk instruction by the simple expedient of using the 100 storage positions to the left of the location of the address to contain the data serving as the operand for the particular instruction. Thus, a unit of data in high-speed storage for writing on a disk consists of 107 positions from right to left—six for the sector address, 100 for data, and one for the blockmark to indicate the end of the data to be written as a sector. A similar storage arrangement is used for reading a sector from disk into high-speed storage.

The layout of data in high-speed storage for reading or writing a disk sector using, for example, address 6806 to hold the sector address, is as follows:

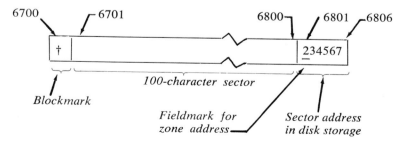

Two addresses are involved here; 6806 is the high-speed storage address holding the sector address. The sector address itself is 234567, meaning unit 2, disk 34, track 56, sector 7. The next lower hundred positions—6800 through 6701, in this particular case—are automatically associated with the disk address at address 6806 and should be followed by a blockmark at position 6700. After the processor executes a write-disk instruction, the disk sector with the corresponding address, 234567 will contain the same 100 characters of data and the blockmark. Each disk sector has its address permanently recorded just ahead of its 100-character space for data storage, as described above; therefore, the identical 107 characters are in both high-speed and disk storage after a write-disk instruction. Conversely, a read-disk instruction will read the disk sector addressed and store its contents of 100 characters in the 100 positions adjoining the sector address in high-speed storage.

The nature of the disk read and write orders should be almost obvious from the discussion of data organization. A read disk instruction, RD xxxx, simply specifies the address in high-speed storage which contains the six-character address—uddtts—of the disk sector to read. This is a simple example of *indirect* addressing: the address included in an instruction refers to a second address that contains an operand, or as in this case, the address of the disk sector to be used in executing the instruction. While indirect addressing may seem foreign, it is merely an extension of ordinary *direct* addressing in which the address in an instruction refers to an operand or another instruction. Indirect addressing is useful because the same sector address is used at least three times—to seek, read, and write, as explained below—in updating a disk file. It is easier to put the sector address at one place in storage and refer to it three times than to put it in each of the three individual instructions. Indirect addressing saves storage, first, by using an address of four characters instead of six in each instruction and, second, by implicitly locating the 100 characters in high-speed storage used for the instruction. Furthermore, housekeeping is simpler, since only one address need be modified to work with a different disk sector. Individual addresses in the seek, read, and write instructions can remain unchanged.

The instruction WD xxxx writes in the disk sector address stored in the field at the A address of the instruction. The instruction writes the 100 preceding characters from high-speed storage and is automatically followed by a read-check operation. If the data just written on disks do not correspond to the data supposedly copied from high-speed storage, the processor halts. The seek disk instruction, SD xxxx, uses indirect addressing similar to the disk read and write instructions. A seek-disk instruction is, if possible, placed far enough ahead of a disk read or write instruction in the program so that the disk mechanism will find the desired sector by the time the read or write order is executed. The processor continues program execution while the disk unit seeks the sector to read or write. After a seek and read, the disk sector is readily available for the write instruction; a second seek is not required.

For a simple example, suppose it is necessary to update the data with sector address 234567—calculate new balance or whatever—and rewrite the updated data in the same sector. Assume that the locations in high-speed storage described above are used—sector address at 6806, which fixes the location of 100 characters of data as 6800 through 6701—and that the instruction BM 6700 has been used to blockmark position 6700.

Inst. Addr.	Op.	Addresses A c B d	Explanation
	S D	6806	Seek the sector specified at address 6806—sector 234567.
	· · ·		Other instructions to permit processing to continue while the disk arm is seeking the sector specified.
	R D	6806	Read the sector specified at address 6806—sector 234567 into the 100 positions in storage preceding the sector address, 6800–6701.
	· · ·		Read additional sector(s), if the data record is more than 100 characters long.
	· · ·		Processing, as required, to update by calculating the new balance, etc., in high-speed storage.
	WD	6806	Write the 100 positions in storage preceding the sector address 6806— 6800–6701 into the sector specified, 234567; check-read data on disk against data in storage and, if not identical, halt. Write additional sectors if the data record is longer than 100 characters.
	· · ·		Continue processing to repeat disk update.

This brief discussion of processing data in addressable bulk storage merely gives a hint of some of the possibilities involved. Bulk storage can contain files for, say, customers, inventories, salesmen's commissions, and others. Bulk storage also should contain programs for processing transactions against these files. Any transaction involving these files can be processed as soon as it occurs. A master program in the processor examines each transaction for type—sales, receipt, issue, cancellation, etc.—and calls in the appropriate program from bulk storage to handle that transaction. The particular program takes over to read each record sector that the transaction affects, updates each record, and returns it to bulk storage. The processor can handle each transaction as it arrives for processing without regard for type or sequence.

There are certain technical problems in compactly assigning records to bulk storage even though the key—stock number, salesmen's number, or whatever—may have many skips. Some schemes for assigning records to bulk storage perform arithmetic on the identification numbers to compact them at the risk of developing identical addresses for two or more different stock numbers. If the calculation leads to an identical address, the second record is placed in an overflow area. Addressable bulk storage is more expensive than serial storage on magnetic tape or punched cards. The value derived from random-sequence processing of bulk storage should be weighed against the costs; if more timely information is valuable, random processing warrants the costs. In many cases, sequential file processing meets the time constraints for operating control and management.

Op. Code	Instruction Addresses			
	A	c	B	d

Input and output

R C		*R*ead a *c*ard or punched tape and store contents in storage locations 0001–0080.
P C		*P*unch a *c*ard or paper tape with contents of storage locations 0101–0180.
R t xxxx		*R*ead a block of data from tape *t* and store in A address in high-speed storage downward to blockmark.

TABLE 11-1. *Order code for FIELDCOM-S.*

Op. Code	**Instruction** **Addresses**			
	A	c	B	d

Input and output

W t xxxx — Write a block of data on tape *t* from A address downward through first blockmark in high-speed storage.

M t — Mark tape *t* with filemark to indicate end-of-file on reel.

T t — Rewind *T*ape *t* ready for removal.

P T — *Print* a line of 120 characters from high-speed storage locations 0201–0320.

RD xxxx — Read the *d*isk sector specified by the six-character address—uddtts—for unit, disk track, and sector, in high-speed storage at the A address indicated by this instruction and place the contents in the 100 positions of storage preceding the sector address.

WD xxxx — Write the *d*isk sector specified by the uddtts address in high-speed storage at A address in this instruction, using the contents of the 100 preceding positions of high-speed storage.

S D xxxx — Seek *d*isk sector specified by uddtts at the A address in this instruction.

Load and Store

C S xxxx xxxx — Clear *s*torage of fieldmarks and characters from B position through A position and fieldmark A position.

FM xxxx — *Field*mark one position at A; contents undisturbed.

C P xxxx ±n xxxx ±n — *Copy* contents of field at A address to B address; stop with first fieldmark, can shorten but not edit a field; —n shifts the field address n positions to the left; +n to the right.

C E xxxx ±n xxxx ±n — Copy and *e*dit whole content of A address into B address, erasing any fieldmarks in B address. B address may contain, for ex-

TABLE 11-1. *Order code for FIELDCOM-S (cont'd).*

Op. Code	**Instruction Addresses**			
	A	c	B	d

Load and Store

ample, $$$b,bb9.99. Leading zero(s) and comma(s) suppressed from left to right down to first 9; float $ within its left and right limits as indicated by the series, "$$$." The four characters "$" "," "9" and "." each count in the edited field as a character position.

Z R   xxxx   Set contents of field at A address to *zero*.

BM   xxxx   *B*lock*m*ark one position at A for indicating low-order end of block for writing on tape or of a sector (100 characters standard) for writing on disk.

Arithmetic

A D   xxxx ±n   xxxx ±n   *Ad*d contents of A address to B address, stopping at first fieldmark; if length of B exceeded, field mistake occurs; field shiftable.

S B   xxxx ±n   xxxx ±n   *Sub*tract contents of A address from B address, stopping at first fieldmark; if length of B exceeded, field mistake occurs; field shiftable.

ML   xxxx ±n   xxxx ±n   *Mul*tiply contents of A address by B address, giving product in B address—the "multiply field," which must be as long as multiplicand (A) and multiplier (B) field +1. Multiplication starts with multiplier in *left* part of B and zeros to the right; product obtained in right end of multiply field; field shiftable.

Tests

CM   xxxx   xxxx   *Com*pare contents of A address with B to first fieldmark and set a switch to indicate conditions tested by jump switch instruction, described below.

TABLE 11-1. *Order code for FIELDCOM-S (cont'd).*

Op. Code	A	Instruction Addresses c	B	d	

Tests

J S xxxx   C   Jump if *s*witch is on, indicating condition resulting from comparison: C, last card condition—preceding read operation not executed because hopper empty;

E   E, equal;

F   F, fieldmistake;

H   H, high (A > B);

L   L, low (A < B);

N   N, negative sign from the first preceding arithmetic operation;

R   R, last record read from tape in preceding read operation;

U   U, unconditional.

Miscellaneous

H L xxxx   *H*alt, with instruction register set to A address; can be the start of program if it is to be repeated; or address of the halt instruction itself to ensure halt, if processor restarted.

N P xxxx   xxxx   *N*o operation; ignore this operation even though it contains addresses; use as "dummy" to form an instruction later.

A L xxxx   11111...1   *A*ssign *l*iteral "ll...l" written in "c" columns and following to the address A, relative, absolute, or symbolic; the literal can be alpha, numeric, alphanumeric, or blank ("b" indicates a blank) up to thirty characters; fieldmark the left character.

A A xxxx nn   ssss   *A*ssign A *a*ddress, relative or absolute, to symbolic address "s" shown in the B address nn characters long.

TABLE 11-1. *Order code for FIELDCOM-S (cont'd).*

FIELDCOM-V

FIELDCOM-V is a variable-field processor with storage organized at the character-level similar to FIELDCOM-S. But FIELD-COM-V was designed to handle completely variable-length data fields. A variable field is just the length required for each item of data. A special character, called a field separator, precedes each item to separate it from the preceding one. There is no need to fill out short items with zeros or blanks as is required for the fixed word of WORDCOM or the selected-length fields of FIELDCOM-S.

A record in FIELDCOM-V consists of data fields arranged in sequence corresponding to the items in the record design. The sequence of fields in a stock record might be the same as illustrated earlier in Figure 11-1. With ◀, •, and ▶ used for start record, field separator, and end record, respectively, the stock record in FIELDCOM-V format is:

◀ • 1430753139 • GASKET • 1200 • 288 • 1390 • 37 • A52 • 35 • 150 • • ▶

The control unit locates an item by its sequence in a record. Stock number, 1430753139, is field 1; quantity on hand, 1200, is field 3; unit cost, 150, is field 9, and stock value is blank—between • • —until calculated and placed in field 10. To keep the sequence count for fields correct, a field separator is included to indicate a field even though its value in a particular record is zero or blank.

Addressing an operand in FIELDCOM-V storage can be explained simply as starting from the first location occupied by the record plus a field-sequence count. If the ◀ symbol is placed in location 0801, then quantity on hand is 0801,3; unit cost is 0801,9; and stock value is 0801,10—now blank, but to be filled in when calculated. Addressing an operand is thus a combination of a fixed address followed by a field-sequence count. The record design is used to control the assignment of storage for fields created after data read-in. In this case, the record design might assign seven characters to field 10 at time of read-in to hold stock value when calculated. Or field 10 might be opened up by moving the record within storage when the program is ready to insert the stock value.

Input data can be originated on punched-paper tape or other media suitable for a continuous string of variable-length fields. Each field separator is punched explicitly in the input data and occupies a character position during read-in and processor storage. Compared to WORDCOM and FIELDCOM-S, this may, but does not necessarily, mean additional characters for punching and storing. Their storage schemes require filling out short items with blanks or zeros to make fixed words or selected-length fields.

FIELDCOM-V has single-address instructions similar to those used for WORDCOM. Each instruction is treated by the control unit as being the same length and is addressed by its left character position; separators are not required between instructions. The arithmetic unit of FIELDCOM-V is twenty characters long and is adequate to handle most results encountered in business data processing; overflow is still possible, but the probability of its occurring is small. FIELDCOM-V can handle fields up to 120 characters long —a full line for the printer—if arithmetic operations are not performed on them. Editing for output printing inserts punctuation— dollar signs, commas, and periods—and deletes leading zeros and all field separators.

SUMMARY

The FIELDCOM-S order code in Table 11-1 serves as a quick guide to many of its features for programming. FIELDCOM-S storage consists of 8000 positions, each of which can store any one of 64 characters—alphabetic, numeric, and 28 special symbols. Storage is organized at the character level and a programmer is responsible for organizing storage into fields suitable for operands and instructions. The manufacturer supplies assemblers and compilers to handle most of the details of assigning storage for symbolic addresses and translating mnemonic instructions to machine-language instructions. The programmer needs to use the symbolic-mnemonic language and prescribed format for writing instructions. Generally, he must be able to debug in some other language such as machine language and absolute addresses.

FIELDCOM-S has double-address instructions with add-to-storage logic, which permits addressing two operands in one instruction. The addition instruction, for example, places the sum of the fields at the A and B addresses in the B address. An instruction addresses a field by its right-hand character; processing goes character-by-character leftward and terminates with the fieldmarked character. The shorter field usually stops processing when two fields are involved, as in the copy and arithmetic instructions. Thus, a field may range from one to hundreds of characters, although the limit is twenty for arithmetical operations.

Address modifiers permit modification of the A and B addresses to indicate field shifting or which switch should be tested for a conditional jump instruction. A negative field shift moves the effective address of an operand to the left and a positive shift to the right. The result is to shorten or lengthen a field much like the shifting in WORDCOM. FIELDCOM-S has a variety of switches that the processor sets automatically—for example, by reading the last card or reading the last tape block. The programmer can set certain switches—equal, high, low, and negative—by using the comparison instruction. A switch can be tested by a jump-switch instruction at subsequent points in the program, until the particular switch is reset by another operation, such as a comparison. The no-operation instruction, NP xxxx xxxx, has an interesting feature; it is written with addresses for use with an instruction code to be inserted in place of the NP when a certain condition is reached in the program. The processor passes over the NP instruction in each cycle until the program inserts the desired instruction; thereafter, the program executes it. The NP instruction might, for example, be used to insert an unconditional jump ahead of card-reading and processing operations to go directly from tape-read to tape-write to copy the remaining master-file records after the last transaction card is read.

FIELDCOM-S has addressable bulk storage with data organized into sectors of 100 characters. Program instructions seek a sector, read it into high-speed storage for processing, and write it back (with read-check) to a disk sector. Disk input-output instructions use indirect addressing—the address in an instruction refers to a storage address where the desired disk-sector address is located. The disk-sector address is located in high-speed storage just to the right of the 100 characters of data to use in the read or write instruction.

Selectable-length field storage has peculiar features the programmer must cope with. A fieldmark is required to define the left character of each operand and instruction. An instruction address is its left-hand position and decoding goes to the right. An operand address is its right-hand position and execution goes to the left, so that the instruction register ends up at the address of the next operand to the left. If that operand is wanted in the next instruction, "chaining" permits omitting the B address (or both the A and B addresses) in the next instruction.

Chapter 12
Programming—Advanced Techniques

In the fifteen years since automatic processors were invented, the art of programming has gone through several important stages of development. This chapter surveys these developments and examines some of them in detail.

With some early electronic processors, programmers set up instructions by setting switches or dials, or in other mechanical ways. For several processors, they wrote orders and addresses in binary code, which could be used directly by the machine. Very early, octal or decimal numbers, shortened to make them more readable, were used for order codes and addresses to facilitate programming. Later, mnemonic or memory-aiding codes were devised to simplify the neophyte's task of learning and writing order codes. The invention of symbolic addresses made it easier for the programmer to keep track of addresses and to modify them by inserting program changes. More importantly, with symbolic addresses a programmer could write a *source* program without regard to particular storage locations and, by means of a special program, direct the processor to organize the source program into an *object* program and assign specific locations. In a subsequent machine run (or, in some schemes, the same run), the object program and data are used to produce desired results.

Only the first type of program—orders and addresses written in binary—is ready to run as originally written. In the others, the written code must be converted to machine code. The simpler methods for writing orders and addresses and the conversion required before they are executed are as follows; the same numerical example is used for each:

Order	Address	Conversion Required
Binary	Binary	No conversion; input to run.
11011	1001110101	

Order	Address	Conversion Required
Octal 33	Octal 1165	Order and address converted to binary.
Decimal 27	Decimal 629	Converted to binary-coded decimal for a decimal machine, otherwise to binary.
Mnemonic code A	Decimal 629	Order converted to binary-coded alphanumeric, or both order and address converted to binary-coded decimal or to binary.
Mnemonic code ADD	Symbolic WKSALE	Both converted to binary-coded decimal or to binary. Conversion of the symbolic address requires use of a symbol table in order to assign absolute addresses.

Although these conversions can be handled manually, it is much cheaper to have the processor do them with special routines. The conversion of octal orders and addresses to decimal or binary is merely an arithmetical operation, though a tedious one. For mnemonic codes, simple translation tables are required to make the one-for-one conversion from the prescribed alphabetic code to the numeric order code designed into the machine. Similarly, a symbol table is required to convert symbolic addresses to absolute addresses; however, this conversion is likely to be more elaborate, since a programmer may have a wide variety of alphanumeric addresses available which must be converted to the numeric addresses used by the machine during program execution. For the simpler schemes described above, manufacturers have developed program routines called *assemblers* to handle the clerical tasks of converting from nonmachine to machine codes and addresses.

Repetitive use of the same routines for certain purposes led to the idea of *subroutines* written in general terms for use whenever needed in new source programs. The concept basically was simple: before transferring program control to a specified subroutine and executing it, the programmer wrote in his program a *calling* sequence containing the information needed by the subroutine and providing for return to the main program. After the instructions in the subroutine were executed, program control returned to the main program at the designated point to continue processing. If a large number of subroutines was used, the main program served primarily to link them together and supply new and unique parts of the program.

If only a few subroutines were used at a particular data-processing installation, it was possible to write them so that they would not overlap in storage. It was also possible to use any subroutine desired in a program, although there was often some loss of programming effort and storage in fitting subroutines into a program. But if numerous subroutines were used—especially if they were prepared by people at different installations—then conflicts in use of storage were certain to develop. To eliminate these conflicts, subroutines were designed that could be relocated in storage and called upon whenever desired for use in a program. As the number of subroutines written for various purposes increased, subroutine *libraries* developed. When the combined length of the subroutines exceeded storage capacity, it became necessary to keep them on tape, drum, or disk; programmers then had to be furnished with adequate descriptions—information required, running time, error conditions, etc.—so that they could determine which subroutine to use for a particular situation and how to use it. When processed, the handwritten source program obtained the specified subroutines from the library and *assembled* them as *open* subroutines into a program at each and every point they were wanted ready for execution. Alternatively, each subroutine could be called into play as a *closed* subroutine and merely interpreted each time it was needed in a program.

A *macro* instruction is one that does the work of many typical instructions. An example is the macro instruction READ in COBOL, which, in machine language, is expanded into a number of instructions each of which performs an individual step.

In addition to schemes to aid in *writing* programs, manufacturers offer numerous programs that can be used with little effort. A programmer has only to select an appropriate program, supply specific facts about requirements of the application, and the processor will *generate* a program suited to the requirements. Examples of generator routines, which convert a skeleton program into a program ready to run, are *file-sequence checking* generators for determining whether records in a file are in sequence, *sort* generators for sorting records into sequence, and *print* generators for printing output reports. For simpler situations, *utility* and *test* routines can be used merely by supplying facts about the desired operations of converting data, loading disks, or tracing the progress of a program during testing to debug it.

Manufacturers also supply *application packages* designed to fill the specific programming requirements of such major business applications as savings and loan accounting or brokerage accounting. The objective is to supply the user with programs that fill his requirements by reducing the analysis and programming work entailed in utilizing electronic equipment.

With *executive routines,* execution of programs is directed by the processor (not the programmer), which can do it more efficiently than can the machine operator. Executive routines perform such basic functions as setting up initial conditions and supervising the execution of a single program or a series of programs one after another. They can even multi-program several programs at the same time, a task clearly beyond an operator's capabilities.

The foregoing comments are a brief sketch of the development of programming techniques from the most basic machine language to advanced schemes for compiling programs and supervising their execution.

CODING AND ADDRESSING SCHEMES

Programming techniques were discussed in terms of mnemonic instructions and numeric addresses in Chapter 10 for WORDCOM, and in mnemonic instructions and symbolic addresses in Chapter 11 for FIELDCOM. It is desirable to describe the relationship between the various coding and addressing schemes and indicate how they are converted to machine code and absolute addresses ready for execution.

Machine and Mnemonic Codes

The name *mnemonic code* is used for a code designed to aid a programmer in writing programs. Each mnemonic code instruction must be translated into machine code before a program can be run in a processor.

The instruction codes described for WORDCOM in Chapter 10 consisted of two or three letters for each instruction. Some examples are ADD (add), SHL (shift left), STA (store accumulator), and RC (read a card). To make the instructions easy to remember, the code letters were selected from the description of the operation; STA, for example, is the abbreviation for *sto*re *a*ccumulator. The three instructions of "add," "shift left," and "store accumulator" might be abbreviated A, L, and S, and still retain some of their mnemonic value. If the number of instructions designed into the processor exceeds 26, some odd codes arise if each code is restricted to one of the 64 characters that can be represented by 6 bits—for example, $, %, /, and (.

Equipment designers prefer to use numbers for instruction codes. Two-digit decimal numbers permit representation of 100 instructions—00 through 99. Numerals can be manipulated more readily than letters if a programmer wishes to modify an instruction by, say, addition operations performed on the order code part itself. The programmer's interest in a mnemonic code for writing programs must be balanced against the assembly operations required to convert to numeric code for use inside the machine. As often happens, a difference of interest is compromised by giving each group at least part of what it wants—mnemonic codes for the programmer and numeric codes for the equipment designer. For example, both types of codes are used with one processor as follows:

Operation	Mnemonic	Numeric
Add (to upper accumulator)	AU	10
Shift left	SLT	35
Store (upper) accumulator	STU	21

A programmer can write in a mnemonic code by using easily recognizable abbreviations for operation codes instead of numbers, and then convert the abbreviations to the numeric code by writing the corresponding numeric instruction code before the program is read in for execution. Since the one-for-one conversion of an instruction written in letters to an instruction represented by numerals is basically a clerical task, it can be done by the processor. A special program called a *symbolic assembly program* performs the conversion. But assembly programs usually do much more than merely convert instruction codes from alphabetic to numeric equivalents.

Absolute and Symbolic Addresses

Programs written with absolute addressing—the actual locations in storage of particular units of data—appear to be simple and efficient for short programs. The processor assigns the same address as the programmer, which facilitates comparing the contents of storage with the original program at any time. Consider, for example, a three-instruction *loop* in locations 067 to 069 for modifying the *address part* of the instruction CAA xxx in location 070 and restoring the modified instruction to that location.

Loc.	Content	Explanation
067	CAA 070	Clear *accumulator* and *add* contents of location 070—the instruction to be modified.
068	ADD 010	*Add* the contents of location 010, which contains the constant 006.
069	STA 070	*Store* contents of *accumulator*, which is the modified instruction, in location 070.
070	CAA( )	Initial value 200 to be increased by 006 each loop.

The simplicity of absolute addresses has its price. If a mistake is found and correction requires inserting another instruction at some earlier point in the program, the instructions in locations 067 to 070 may simply be shifted up by one, giving the following program:

Loc.	Content	Explanation
068	CAA 070	
069	ADD 010	
070	STA 070	This instruction will be modified by the revised routine.
071	CAA( )	This instruction is not changed.

The changed program has entirely different results than was originally intended. The STA 070 instruction in location 070 will be modified by instructions 068 and 069. Modification of the instruction in location 070 is diabolical because it will store *itself* in location 076 when the loop is executed the first time, in 082 in the second loop, and so forth and may spoil the whole program. Chaos may result if the programmer fails to change the address parts of some instructions when the instructions to which they refer are relocated in storage. But since address changes tend to mushroom after they start, some erroneous addresses are almost certain to slip through any important program modification.

Absolute addressing also hinders the use of a subroutine in more than one main program because the addresses must be changed to fit each particular program. Furthermore, absolute addressing makes it difficult for two or more programmers to work on one program since each programmer will be unsure which location the other is using for certain data and it is difficult to combine the segments of a program.

One remedy for some of the deficiencies resulting from the use of absolute addresses is to use *symbolic addresses*. A symbolic address is a unique combination of characters—letters, numerals, or both—that refers to an item of data in a routine, and that is independent of the sequential location of that item within a routine. To be useful as a symbolic address, the same set of unique characters must be used to identify the location of *one* operand—number, alphabetic word, instruction, etc.—although it can, of course, be used many times as addresses in instructions that refer to the operand. However, only the operands that are referred to by instructions in the program need be identified by labels. The labeled operands may be restricted to the first words in blocks of data and to specific instructions that are referred to in jump or other instructions. Operands that follow the labeled operand are merely stored in sequence. Labels and, of course, symbolic addresses, must be converted to absolute addresses for running the program, but this conversion can be done by an assembly program on the processor, as will be explained shortly.

The fragment of a program given above for address modification can be rewritten as follows to illustrate the use of symbolic addresses.

Label	Mnemonic Order	Symbolic Address	Explanation
CHANGE	CAA	MODIFY	The label CHANGE identifies the first location. The symbolic address MODIFY refers to the location identified by MODIFY.
	ADD	PLUS SIX	PLUS SIX refers to the location identified by PLUS SIX which contains +006.
	STA	MODIFY	
MODIFY	CAA	FILE1	The label MODIFY identifies the location of the instruction to be modified. The symbolic address FILE1 refers to the location identified by FILE1.

Only the fourth instruction is referred to by the instructions shown here, and need be assigned a label. The label CHANGE is not needed except, perhaps, to enter this part of the program. These four instructions can be placed anywhere desired in storage, or one or more instructions can be inserted at any point without there being any changes in the addresses, since MODIFY is a suitable label wherever the instruction CAA FILE1 is located in the program. The symbolic addresses CHANGE, MODIFY, PLUS SIX, and FILE1 can be used repeatedly as addresses in instructions, but *must* be defined in one and only one way—given one absolute address—to avoid ambiguities when absolute addresses are assigned for labels and symbolic addresses.

Relative Addresses

Relative addressing is an extension of the concept of symbolic addressing. A relative address is a label used to identify an operand in relation to other operands. The fragment of a program given above can be written with relative addresses as follows:

Loc. Label	Content	Explanation
CHANGE CAA CHANGE +3		This location is identified by CHANGE; CHANGE +3 identifies the third location after this one.
	ADD PLUS SIX	
	STA CHANGE +3	
	CAA FILE1	

Inserting another instruction within this routine requires changing the relative address CHANGE +3 to CHANGE +4. This job is similar to, but far simpler than, the task of changing the absolute addresses to permit insertions, as in the example for absolute addressing given above. Relative addresses have an important advantage for preparing subroutines. After a subroutine written with relative addresses is checked out, it can be used wherever desired in the main program. The four instructions listed above can be used following the instruction identified by CHANGE whether it is given an absolute address of 321, 400, 512, or any other location. To a certain extent, the programmer can control the processor's assignment of absolute addresses to labels and, therefore, to symbolic addresses by specifying an origin point for the program or an origin point for each segment of it; but it is necessary, of course, to avoid interfering with absolute addresses previously assigned.

Symbolic and relative addresses can be converted to absolute addresses either by manual methods or by using the processor and an assembly program. For assigning absolute addresses for two selected labels, the programmer may use a symbol table, such as the following:

Label	Absolute Address Assigned	Explanation
CHANGE	321	The program will be stored in locations 321 and following.
FILE 1	600	The first file will be stored in locations 600 and following.

Storage locations will be assigned in turn to each succeeding instruction with a label that is not assigned an absolute address. If only the first label is assigned an absolute address, then each succeeding instruction will be assigned to storage with no intervening locations. If no address assignment is made, an assembly program provides for assigning a standard origin location to the first label and simply assigns sequential storage locations thereafter.

By convention, the symbolic addresses used to identify storage locations during programming are restricted to at least one letter and one or more numerals; the letters I and O may be prohibited in symbolic addresses to avoid confusion with the numerals 1 and 0.

Macrocodes

Although the preceding coding and addressing schemes are a variation of machine language, they are closely related to it, since they have a one-to-one correspondence: each instruction in a source program becomes one instruction in the object program ready to run for processing data, as will be explained later under assemblers and compilers.

Macrocodes are a higher-level language than machine language, and one instruction does the work ordinarily requiring many instructions. For example, the READ instruction in COBOL is expanded into a large number of instructions in machine language to handle the following operations: bring a record into storage; recognize end-of-reel conditions to perform ending-label procedures; make tape swaps (or stop and wait for the operator to mount a new reel if only one tape unit was assigned); perform beginning label procedures and make the next record available; and recognize the end-of-file condition to perform ending-label procedures and execute the at-end procedures.

A macro instruction in a source program serves to call in a miniature generator, tailor it to fit the requirements, and incorporate it into the object program. Macros may be supplied by the manufacturer to call in library routines for performing multiplication or division in machines that do not have this feature built into the circuitry. With library routines, it is possible to perform multiplication and division operations fairly efficiently by means of addition, subtraction, and other instructions built into the machine. Another example of a macro for a processor with disk storage is a procedure for checking the accuracy of a write-disk operation.

For each routine in the library that he wishes to use in his program, the programmer writes a macro at the appropriate point, assigns a label to the first statement in the generated symbolic routine, and specifies the various parameters required in the sequence for use by the model statement required for the particular object routine.

The macro generator extracts the appropriate routine from the library and selects the model statements specified by the parameters in the macro instructions and by the macros in the library routine. It also substitutes parameters where indicated in the model statements to produce the symbolic routine.

MACHINE-ORIENTED AND PROBLEM-ORIENTED LANGUAGES

The coding and addressing schemes described above have features designed to make the programmer's task easier and, therefore, might be called *programmer's language*. If they are designed for a particular set of problems, then they deserve the name *problem-oriented language*.

Both languages are some distance removed from the basic language of the machine. In order to execute a program written in a problem-oriented language and process data, it is necessary to convert the instructions—mnemonics or macros—to the basic order code of the machine and to convert symbolic and relative addresses to absolute addresses.

There are three methods for converting from a nonmachine language to a machine language: assembler, interpreter, and compiler.

Assembler

Assembly from programmer's language to machine language is simple and straightforward. The assignment of machine order code and absolute addresses to the instructions in a program, called *assembly,* can be done by people after writing a program or can be done by a processor using an assembly program written for that express purpose. Assignment of absolute addresses to symbolic addresses includes the following operations: (1) the construction of a symbol table to find where labels used as locations for instructions and operands will be placed in storage, starting from some specified origin, and (2) assignment of these absolute addresses to the symbolic addresses within instructions.

The conversion of symbolic address to absolute address ranges from extremely simple to fairly involved. The simplest scheme is for the programmer to assign an absolute address origin for the first instruction or operand in the program and have the assembly program assign an address to each succeeding instruction or operand in the source program. The process of assigning addresses also determines an absolute address for each label to use for symbolic addresses referring to that label.

To retain control over the assignment of absolute addresses to labels, the programmer can, if he wishes, assign an origin point to each segment of a program, but he must be careful to avoid overlapping various segments or wasting storage between segments spaced too far apart. Of course, each label used to identify the location of an instruction or element of data should also be used as a symbolic address within an instruction in order to make use of the instruction or data element with the corresponding label. A symbolic address without a corresponding label is undefined; if the samel label is used two or more times for different instructions, it is multiply defined. Either case can be detected by the processor during the assembly stage and called to the programmer's attention for correction.

The backbone of an assembly system consists of its imperative mnemonic code and symbolic-addressing scheme. The use of symbolic addresses instead of absolute addresses increases a programmer's freedom to use whatever areas he wants for data, constants, and work areas. Symbolic addressing also facilitates the joint work of several programmers on various phases of one program.

Statements defining work areas and statements to store constants are likely to be incorporated in an assembler. The definition of an area in storage may work in essentially the following way. The programmer writes a line in the source program containing an instruction to define an area, gives the area a symbolic label, and then lists the constant to be stored in the area. The assembler allocates a field in processor storage for use at object time when the object program is loaded for execution. The assembler also inserts the equivalent address of the label in place of the symbol wherever it appears as an operand in another symbolic program entry. The result is to place the constant in storage when the object program is loaded for execution and assign it the symbolic name indicated in the source program.

It is necessary to have a list of the order codes used by the programmer and its equivalent code in machine language. The order code written by the programmer is located in the list and its machine equivalent substituted for it on a one-for-one basis.

The assembled program, consisting of machine-language instructions and absolute addresses, is ready for execution in another machine run to process data. Since the processor operates under the guidance of an assembler to produce the assembled program, it is available for reuse. Important changes in the program require complete reassembly, although small changes might be patched into the assembled program.

In summary, in order to use mnemonic instructions with symbolic addresses, the programmer writes the mnemonic operation code for the instruction, and, if the instruction is to be referenced elsewhere in the program, gives the instruction a symbolic label. During the assembly pass, the processor substitutes the actual machine-language operation code for the mnemonic operation, substitutes the absolute address for the symbolic label, assigns the actual machine-language instruction an area in storage for use when the object program is loaded and executed, and prepares a program ready for execution whenever it is wanted.

Interpreter

With an interpreter, a programmer can write only a few lines of coding, but the processor will execute many instructions by calling upon any one of a number of subroutines prepared by expert programmers and maintained in a subroutine library. According to the interpretive concept, one pass through the hand-written program is interpreted into subroutines from the library and executed with data. A *subroutine* is a set of instructions that directs the processor to·carry out a sub-unit of a routine. After a subroutine is written and checked, it can be used in any program that requires the operations it will perform. An example of a simple subroutine is the program load routine described for WORDCOM in Chapter 10, which is useful for loading any program written for that processor. COBOL-1 programming in Chapter 9 utilized several subroutines for error checking in the inventory-calculation program.

The interpretive approach to programming makes use of a library of closed subroutines in high-speed storage, or in bulk storage—

drums, disk, or tape—if they exceed high-speed storage. The closed subroutines are basically independent of the main program and are stored outside the main program sequence.

A calling routine in the source program calls in a subroutine each time it is needed in the main program, supplies certain facts needed by the subroutine, and prepares for the return to the main program. The main program goes to a subroutine when it is wanted, and, after executing the subroutine, returns to continue executing the main program. Entering and leaving the subroutine involves keeping track of where the subroutine is stored, arranging to have the desired operands in correct locations to be handled by the subroutine, and returning to the correct point in the main program. Furthermore, the contents of some registers and indexes may have to be saved so that they will be available on the return to the main program. Depending on the program language, these steps may be elaborate, with much red tape, or quite simple. For example, as described in Chapter 9 for COBOL, the programmer can cause execution of one of the small subroutines in the inventory-updating program by means of a GO TO instruction for the subroutine and a second GO TO for returning program control to the main routine. Or, instead of doing this in two steps, he can do it in one with a PERFORM statement, which provides for both executing the subroutine and for automatic return to the main program.

The concept of interpretive coding to execute any one of a number of closed subroutines at various points in the main program and return to the main program can be illustrated as follows, using a line to indicate one or more lines of coding. The arrows show jumps to a subroutine and returns to the main program. Solid lines indicate unconditional jumps and broken lines conditional jumps.

Several points are worth noting about the illustration. The subroutines can be stored in any sequence desired and need not be in contiguous locations. After a subroutine is executed, program control may return to one of several points in the main program—subroutine 2 has alternate returns—depending upon conditions that arise during execution of the program. A subroutine may be used several times—subroutine 3 in this case—with a return to a different point in the main program each time. Pushed to the extreme, the main program is reduced to little more than a *calling sequence,* which is a series of jump instructions that guide the program from one subroutine to another.

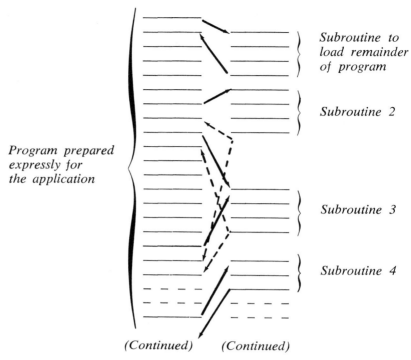

Program prepared
expressly for
the application

Subroutine to
load remainder
of program

Subroutine 2

Subroutine 3

Subroutine 4

(Continued)   (Continued)

Processor execution time is likely to be shorter for a program built of subroutines than for a program especially prepared for the problem, except when prepared by expert programmers. Subroutines also have the advantages of saving programming costs and elapsed time for preparation and testing, especially when each program is used only a few times.

There are three important differences between interpretive programming and assembly systems, as described above. (1) Some instructions are interpreted into many instructions in a subroutine, instead of being restricted to a one-for-one instruction conversion. (2) The program is interpreted and executed to process data in one pass, rather than being assembled in one pass and executed in a later pass, as is true for the assembly scheme. (3) An interpretive program must be interpreted afresh each time it is used to process data because the interpretation approach does not produce a complete program, as such, ready for execution.

Compiler

A compiler is a method used for converting a source program consisting of (1) *macrocodes* for conversion into machine code, and (2) *pseudocodes*—entries that look like coding but do not result in machine instructions—for bringing in subroutines in order to produce an object program. The object program can be executed in a later pass to process data. In the first pass, a *source program* is compiled on a source processor under the control of a compiler program, producing an *object* program punched in cards or written on tape ready to run on an object processor. Thus, a program in some form of nonmachine language is converted to a program in machine language. A compiler expands each macrocode into several—perhaps a dozen or more—machine instructions and, therefore, has an important leverage factor in expanding the program as written by a programmer. Each pseudocode brings in a subroutine and permits further expansion of the source program.

The programmer must provide several kinds of information in his source program for the compiler to prepare the object program, including area definitions, processor controls, and perhaps a description of the source and object processor to be used. For a source program, the compiling phase does the following:

1. Analyzes all statements included in the source program.
2. Expands macrocode instructions to machine-language code.
3. Uses pseudocodes to bring each specified subroutine into the program at the desired point.
4. Develops a symbol table and assigns absolute addresses to symbolic addresses and data-names, starting with the origin point specified by the programmer.
5. Performs diagnostic routines to check for common mistakes by programmers. The mistakes may be incorrect use of standard mnemonics; erroneous definition of symbols through failure to define, multiple definition, or failure to adhere to rules for an initial alpha character in a symbolic address (to avoid confusion with absolute addresses written in all numerics); failure to use special characters or blanks within a label; failure to observe punctuation, special symbols, literals, and spacing rules for writing operands; and exceeding machine capacity.
6. Defines and allocates areas for the program and for other purposes, either as constants or literals.
7. Prepares a sequence of instructions to load the program into the correct storage locations for running the program.
8. Punches the object program in cards or writes it on tape ready to run.

Processor control statements in an operating compiler give the programmer some control over the compiling process. For example, the control operations enable the operator to tell the processor (1) how to identify the job for distinguishing programs or sections of programs in the output listing, (2) where to place the origin of the program or a particular part of the program in storage at object time, (3) where to place literals, address constants, and closed library routines in storage, (4) when to temporarily interrupt the object program loading process in order to execute the part of the program that has been loaded, (5) when to place a suffix character in the right-hand character position of the label field of all labels that are blank in that position in order to differentiate sections of the program and avoid the confusion from use of the same label in different sections, and, (6) when all of the symbolic program entries have been read and the program is ended, cause the processor to produce a transfer instruction to the first instruction to be executed after the object program is loaded.

One of the more important features of a compiler—the bringing together of subroutines to form a program—can be illustrated by means of open subroutines that are fitted directly—compiled— into the operational sequence of the main program at each point where they are needed. The relationship between instructions written expressly for the main routine and the subroutines merely included in the main program is shown as follows (each line may represent a few or even dozens of instructions):

	——————— }	*Subroutine to load remainder of*
	——————— }	*program*
Program prepared {	———————	
expressly for the {	———————	
application {	———————	
	——————— }	*Subroutine to perform a desired*
	———————	*operation—perhaps read in file*
	———————	*records, unpack, and place in*
	——————— }	*suitable storage locations*
Program prepared {	———————	
expressly for the {	———————	
application {	———————	
	——————— }	*Subroutine to read instructions—*
	———————	*edit for accuracy of data, rear-*
	———————	*range for efficient processing, and*
	— — — — }	*so forth*
	— — — —	
	———————	

(Continued)

The open subroutine scheme is straightforward because each subroutine is included where it is wanted in the main program. Entry to and exit from the subroutine is simple because the whole program—both the handwritten parts and the subroutines—can be located in consecutive storage locations. Each subroutine must be written with symbolic or relative addresses so that it will operate satisfactorily wherever placed in the main program. However, the open subroutine has a drawback in that it must be repeated each time it is used in the main program; therefore, it occupies more storage after read-in, both on tape and in the processor. The compiled object program is available whenever desired to process files and transactions or other kinds of data.

Although assemblers, compilers, and interpreters have much in common, they also have some important differences. For assembly and compiler programs, two passes through the processor are required, although both passes can be handled by the machine one after the other. One pass assembles or compiles the source program into an object program; the second executes the source program for processing data. The object program thus produced is available for reuse. An interpreter routine is executed with the relevant data in only one pass—*load and go*. However, it does not produce an object program that can be reused, and the source program must be reinterpreted each time it is executed.

An assembler offers a programmer little leverage because the mnemonic instructions with symbolic addresses are in a near-machine language, and are converted on a one-for-one basis into machine order code with absolute addresses. There is more flexibility in the interpreter approach to programming, for, when the calling routines in the source program call in closed subroutines from the library, they in effect expand a few instructions into many machine instructions. In other words, interpreters simply draw upon the closed subroutine library and immediately execute the instructions. This approach is more compact than the compiler approach which uses pseudocodes to bring in subroutines and builds the whole program out of open subroutines repeated throughout the program. However, compilers are appreciably more powerful than basic assemblers because, in addition to handling mnemonic instructions and symbolic addresses, they also make use of macrocodes and subroutines, define and allocate storage areas, and prepare load routines for the object program.

It should be pointed out that the distinctions between assemblers, interpreters, and compilers are not rigid and that all may have some features common to each other.

COMPILER-LEVEL LANGUAGES

Typically, a manufacturer supplies a compiler-level language for each machine that he offers. With such a language, the programmer is able to use mnemonic codes and symbolic addresses for the parts of a program that he wishes to write at the detailed level, plus macrocodes for more powerful instructions, and subroutines for the parts of a program that have been developed. Two compiler languages, COBOL and FORTRAN, are discussed here.

COBOL

In Chapters 8 and 9, many of the features of COBOL-61 were treated in the simplified version of COBOL-1. The mechanics of compiling a source program written in COBOL to produce an object program ready to execute were described from the programmer's viewpoint in the latter part of Chapter 8. An additional point, which should be made explicit, is that COBOL uses the data descriptions written at the beginning of the program to set up a *dictionary* of data names for checking the programmer's use of them throughout a program. This is similar to the symbol table which ensures that symbolic addresses make correct references to labels. The concept of the dictionary for assisting the programmer in checking the accuracy of use of data names within instructions is a valuable aid in programming.

As a problem-oriented language, COBOL carries the techniques described earlier in this chapter a step further by making much of the programmer's work independent of the processors on which his program will be compiled and executed. The data and procedure divisions are largely independent of the source and object processors used. By means of the environment division, the programmer specifies the processor to be used at each stage, as illustrated in the problem example in the latter part of Chapter 8. At the risk of oversimplification, it may be said that, merely by changing the description of processors in the environment division, it is possible to compile and execute COBOL programs on a different processor. Thus users of various types of equipment made by one manufacturer, and even various types by different manufacturers, may write a program once and use it on any equipment for which the manufacturer furnishes a COBOL compiler. With this versatility, not only is it possible to use one program on a variety of machines; COBOL can even be used to test the relative merits of different machines for the same application. However, proof that this versatility is oversimplified lies in the fact that each machine has certain strengths and weaknesses in logic, data organization, and other features. A program written for a particular machine is likely to be superior to a program written for just any machine because it may be able to exploit its strengths and avoid its weaknesses.

In addition to problem orientation and machine independence, COBOL contains several other features of interest. Less-experienced programmers are able to write programs in a shorter time in COBOL than in other compiler or machine languages, since many of the contingencies that cause a new programmer trouble are handled automatically. Debugging takes less time, documentation is easier, production runs are obtained in a shorter-elapsed time, and program modification is easier. The power of COBOL as a programming language is shown by the fact that each instruction in a COBOL source program can be expanded in the compiling phase into about five machine-language instructions in the object program. This five-to-one leverage means that the programmer's work—detailed flow-charting, coding, testing, debugging, and documenting —in producing a tested program ready for production use is cut by 80 per cent.

FORTRAN

FORTRAN, for *For*mula *Tran*slating System, is a problem-oriented language developed by IBM primarily for engineering and scientific computations. The language itself is designed to resemble the language of mathematics in order to facilitate program preparation for mathematical problems; however, it can also be used for business applications. A person knowing mathematics can write his program in FORTRAN using the symbols he is accustomed to; he does not have to spend time learning the programming features of a particular processor. Many equipment manufacturers have prepared FORTRAN compiler programs; these compile FORTRAN source programs into machine-language object programs that can be run on their machines. The object program can be executed immediately after it is compiled or it can be written on tape or punched into cards for future use. ALGOL, an algorithmic language, was devised as an international mathematics language in 1958 (and revised in 1960) as a reference, publication, and hardware representation language. Although ALGOL has features similar to FORTRAN, and, in fact, is more powerful, it is not used as widely for computational purposes.

FORTRAN source programs are built from four kinds of statements:

1. Arithmetic statements that specify a numerical computation
2. Control statements that govern the flow of the program
3. Input and output statements
4. Specification statements necessary for allocating storage

Since FORTRAN consists of statements rather than machine-language instructions, the programmer must be familiar with the conventions of the language and observe them in writing a program. Some of the features of FORTRAN can be shown by a simple example in which the cost of material required to make a cylinder of a certain diameter and length is calculated.

The formula for the cost of the material is

$$C \times H \times 3.1416 \times \left(\frac{D}{2}\right)^2,$$

where C is the cost per unit of material, H is the height of the cylinder, 3.1416 is the constant π, and D is the diameter. A programmer can calculate the cost of material for one cylinder merely by writing the statement

$$COST = C * H * 3.1416 * (D/2.0) ** 2.$$

The ** means that the following number, 2, is treated as an exponent in order to square $(D/2)$. The *'s mean multiply C by H by 3.1416 by $(D/2)^2$. The operations are performed in the correct sequence and follow the usual rules for squaring, multiplying, dividing, and, if required, adding and subtracting, as indicated by the use of parentheses and sequences in which written. Using the formula as written, the FORTRAN compiling routine will generate a program of machine instructions to perform the following operations:

1. Divide D by 2 to get D/2
2. Square D/2 to get $(D/2)^2$
3. Multiply $(D/2)^2$ by 3.1416
4. Multiply $(D/2)^2 \times 3.1416$ by H
5. Multiply $(D/2)^2 \times 3.1416 \times H$ by C

The cost department of the factory may want, for example, a list showing the cost of material to make cylinders 3 inches in diameter and 4.1, 4.2, 4.3, . . . , 5 inches in height. The programmer could write the FORTRAN program given below to calculate cost, and print the first line on a list for the basic height of 4.1 inches. In each subsequent "trial" for a total of 10, the height would be increased by 0.1 to 4.2, 4.3, . . . , 5 inches.

Line	Statement
10	D = 3.0
20	H = 4.1
30	C = 1.73
40	DO 80 N = 1, 10, 1
50	COST = C*H*3.1416*(D/2.0)**2
60	PRINT 70, N, H, COST
70	FORMAT (1X, I2, 5X, F3.1, 5X, 1H$, F6.2)
80	H = H+0.1

The symbols and operations can be explained as follows. The equal sign in FORTRAN has a special meaning: set the data-name on the left to the value on the right. Line 10 sets the data-name D, for diameter, to 3 inches; line 20 sets H to the height of 4.1 inches for the first trial; line 30 sets C to the unit cost of material of $1.73 per cubic inch.

Line 40 says to perform the following statements—50 through 80 inclusive, 10 times—varying N from 1 to 10 by 1 each time. The COST calculation in line 50 was explained above. The PRINT operation in line 60 says to print the values of N, H, and COST according to the format specified in line 70. The format, line 70, specifies the following: (a) 1X means that the line starts with one blank and that this blank produces single-spacing carriage control; (b) I2 represents a two-digit integer for N—b1, b2, . . . , 10; (c) 5X means five blank spaces; (d) F3.1 means a fixed decimal-point number (as opposed to an integer or a floating-point number) consisting of three characters—two digits and a decimal point one position from the right corresponding to a format of 9.9 in COBOL; (e) 5X signifies five blank spaces; (f) 1H$ means one Hollerith character from the punched-card character set and, in particular, the dollar sign $, which is comparable to an alphanumeric literal in COBOL; and (g) F6.2 means a fixed decimal-point number of six characters—five digits and a decimal point two positions from the right corresponding to a format of 999.99 in COBOL. Line 80 increases the height used in the previous trial by 0.1—from 4.1 in the first trial to 4.2 in the second, etc. It sets the new value of H to the current value of H plus 0.1, and is equivalent to the COBOL statement ADD 0.1 to H.

The programmer works in a simple, set format, and the formula translation routines work by generating programs from the skeleton subroutines and parameters given in the programmer's instructions. For example, to generate the part of the program needed to find the cost of the cylinder, the compiling routine would use the equal sign as an indication that something called COST in symbolic language should be stored in some location for further use. To calculate COST, the compiler has to divide D by 2, square D/2, multiply by 3.1416, etc. The values of N, H, and COST are printed, H is increased, and the cycle is performed a total of ten times. The routines for performing these simple things are made up from skeleton subroutines that have been previously prepared.

Figure 12-1 shows part of the output that results from running the FORTRAN program given above. The first page simply lists the program cards. The number above the program listing is a job number that identifies the programmer. The next two statements print a title line for the output. Statements 10 to 80 are identical to the program as written. The last statement, END followed by a series of zeros and ones, is generated by the FORTRAN compiler to guide the processor in the execution phase.

The second page of output shows the results produced when the program is executed. The word EXECUTION is supplied by the compiler to signal the start of the results. The final page is produced entirely by the compiler and is, as indicated, an accounting summary. It gives the time (rounded to the nearest ten seconds) required to compile and run the program.

FORTRAN has the usual advantages of a problem-oriented language. It permits a programmer to use mathematics, a language that he is familiar with and that is suited to the problem, thus allowing him to concentrate on problem solution instead of trying to memorize the machine code or language. Some important differences between FORTRAN and COBOL are worth noting. COBOL is normally in English words and phrases (although FORTRAN-like equations can be used), and data-names and pictures can be as long as thirty characters. Arithmetic is normally done in fixed-point notation, and a dictionary is used by the compiler to set up descriptions before use and check them during use. FORTRAN, on the other hand, is in mathematical notation, and names are limited to six characters. Arithmetic is normally done in floating-point notation, and a dictionary is not used for controlling the use of data names.

```
 B

 C      232901

 D          PRINT 5
        5   FORMAT(21H NO.      DIA.        COST /)
 E      10  D = 3.0
        20  H = 4.1
        30  C = 1.73
 F      40  DO 80 N = 1,10,1
        50  COST = C*H*3.1416*(D/2.0)**2
        60  PRINT 70, N,H,COST
        70  FORMAT (1X ,I2,5X,F3.1,5X,1H$,F6.2)
        80  H = H + 0.1
            CALL EXIT
            END(1,0,0,0,0,0,1,0,0,0,0,0,0,0,0)
```

```
              EXECUTION
      NO.     DIA.      COST
       1      4.1      $ 50.14
       2      4.2      $ 51.36
       3      4.3      $ 52.58
       4      4.4      $ 53.81
       5      4.5      $ 55.03
       6      4.6      $ 56.25
       7      4.7      $ 57.47
       8      4.8      $ 58.70
       9      4.9      $ 59.92
      10      5.0      $ 61.14
```

```
 B

 C      ACCOUNTING SUMMARY

 D
        *    JOB      2329,GREGY,RCS834,02,10,10,0
 E
             PROGRAM              TIME
 F           FORTRN                      30SEC
             EXECUTION                   10SEC

             TOTAL                       40SEC

        65 LINES OUTPUT THIS JOB.
```

FIGURE 12-1. *Output from a FORTRAN program.*

Generators

Generators are general routines that accept a set of conditions specified by the programmer and that cause the processor to prepare a routine tailored for a specific application. A programmer can modify a general routine to perform a particular task—for example, file-sequence checking or report writing—by incorporating certain facts about the task in the routine. There are two stages involved in using a generator, and the basic ideas behind them are as follows. First, the generator for the *type* of task and facts about the *particular* task are processed to give an object program in machine language. Second, the object program and the data are processed to give the desired result—for example, a certain report in the desired media, whether printed, on cards or tape, or in some combination. Three examples of generators are discussed briefly here: file-sequence checking, sort-merge, and report writing.

File-Sequence Checking. The problem in checking the sequence of a file is to specify enough facts about the media, record structure, and key to enable the processor to start with a generalized skeleton of file-sequence checking and generate a suitable sequence-checking routine. For example, the following parameters or facts would be needed to generate a routine for checking the sequence of records in a file:

1. Input media used—cards or tape
2. Code used in file—alphabetic, numeric, or alphanumeric
3. Record format and length
4. Number of records per block and their repeat pattern, if on tape
5. Length of items to be sequence-checked—two or more words, one full word, or a part of one word
6. Position in the record—first, second, last, or other word—of the items to be sequence-checked
7. End-of-file tag
8. The output desired

A generating routine can, by using a skeleton sequence-checking routine and these parameters, compile a sequence-checking program for the specific application.

Sort-Merge. Equipment manufacturers furnish skeleton programs for sorting records into sequence which a user can tailor to his particular requirements. A sort generator may differ from the programming techniques described earlier in that it has to be used separately from the main program. In this sense, it is a service or utility program, which performs a useful function in processing data but is not within the main operating stream.

A generalized sort program can modify itself according to information supplied by the user and can be further modified within the program to produce a specific sorting program. An adequate sort program should be able to do most or all of the following:

1. Sort blocked or unblocked, fixed-length records
2. Sort either numeric or alphanumeric records into ascending or descending order
3. Use control data from a number of fields with little restriction on total length
4. Provide checkpoint and restart procedures
5. Handle additions and perform deletions by class or control data
6. Permit deletion of characters from selected parts of the records
7. Allow program modification
8. Provide for input and output on various media

The programmer must supply various facts concerning the file and its records in order to generate a particular object program from a generalized skeleton. These facts include the following: (1) input media as cards, tape, or disks, (2) ascending or descending sequence, (3) maximum number of control fields, (4) types of additions to and deletions from the file at object time, (5) accuracy control features wanted—record count, hash total, or sequence check, (6) equipment configuration and features available for compiling the program, and (7) exits desired at various phases in the program to permit program modification.

Additional factors required for controlling execution of the object program to sort a file of records into sequence include (1) details about the equipment configuration to be used for executing the program to sort records, (2) collating sequence for the object program, (3) record format and length, (4) number, location, and length of control fields, (5) blocking factor for input and output, (6) expected file size, (7) checking features to use, (8) addition of records, (9) deletion of characters, (10) restart points, and (11) linkages to starting addresses of user's programs associated with particular phases. In order to generate an object program and to execute the object program with a file of records to sort them into sequence, a programmer must supply formidable lists of facts. The number of facts that must be supplied indicates that the preparation of sort programs is both difficult and time-consuming. Obviously, efficient sort programs would be far more difficult to construct if generalized routines were not available.

Report Generators. Report generators are useful in several ways. Their use relieves programmers of the burden of preparing particular report-writing routines and speeds the production of tailored reports to meet specific requests.

A reasonably elaborate report-program generator for a medium scale processor, for example, permits the user to specify the following features for a desired report:

1. Define the position of each item appearing in the report, including recurring information consisting of headings and editing symbols
2. Describe record type and distinguish record codes and control fields of the file serving as the source of the report
3. List the data fields necessary for processing the report and specify how the fields will be manipulated and what calculations should be performed—addition, multiplication, division, and comparisons
4. Specify format and conditions for output of each line on the report —print, punch, or tape—and control over paper or card handling; also, for each line, list all the constants, data fields, and edit controlwords, plus the conditions for including a field within a line

This brief description of file-sequence checking, sort-merge, and report generators should give some idea of their general nature and use.

OPERATING SYSTEMS

The concepts and techniques described thus far aid the programmer in preparing programs. Equipment operation is still an important task and can contribute to, or detract from, efficient system operations. Regardless of their skill and experience, it is impossible for people to cope with all the situations that can arise in machine operation or anticipate all the conditions necessary to get the most efficient use of equipment.

Many aspects of processor operations are common to all programs. It is possible to handle these as part of each program, but it is more efficient to prepare programs to handle machine operations. From the programmer's viewpoint, such operating systems serve as an extension of the machine itself; they are extra capabilities of the machine much like those built into the equipment, but more flexible because they are merely machine programs.

There are many complete operations that must be carried out in every installation, and these operations are independent of the common functions appearing in many different procedures. These operations include:

1. Controlling the compilation and execution of programs
2. Controlling input and output operations
3. Converting data from one medium to another and organizing data in storage
4. Testing programs to debug them
5. Simulating the operation of one processor on another

Several examples of operating systems—executive routines, input-output control systems, test routines, and simulators—are discussed in this section.

Executive Routines

Executive routines are, in a sense, at a higher level than the programming techniques discussed above because they set up, monitor, and control the operation of other programs. The objective of executive programs is to simplify the machine operator's work so that the machine can run more efficiently. The functions of executive routines range from the assignment of specific locations in storage to enabling a processor to execute several different programs concurrently. The following material describes sample executive routines for simple execution of one program, concurrent execution of several programs, and serial translation and execution of several programs.

A basic executive routine controls the execution of one program by initializing storage—placing zeros or blanks in work areas and setting up counters—and loading the program into storage.

After the program starts, the input-output control portion of the executive routine, as described later, handles the details of reading and writing records, swapping tape units as required, blocking and unblocking records, and checking labels. If the processor has data channels and trapping features, the executive routine supervises the transfer of control after each input or output operation. Certain kinds of errors encountered during processing—for example, the program exceeding storage capacity—transfer control to the executive, which takes correction action or halts execution.

A more advanced executive routine controls the concurrent operation of several programs—*multi-programming*—and increases processor utilization. For example, while one program is using a data channel to write data on tape, a second program may use the arithmetic unit for computation, and a third program can rearrange some data in storage. If several programs will run concurrently in less time than separately, then multi-programming has a potential pay-off even though they sometimes interfere with each other.

A multi-programming executive routine performs complex functions. It is easiest to explain the concepts by assuming that the processor is supposed to execute three programs, named A, B, and C; the concepts apply to any number of programs. First the three programs A, B, and C are placed in non-conflicting storage locations and assigned input-output units. After operations start, the executive routine examines in turn the next instruction to be performed for each program. If the units needed to execute the first instruction in program A are available, it is performed. If execution is not possible because the unit is in use, the executive examines the first instruction in program B to determine whether the units needed are available for use. In order for program B to use a common unit such as an index register, storage area, or accumulator, the executive routine must store any contents relevant to program A. The executive restores the contents for program A to their original places when the next instruction from A is executed. Instructions from each program are executed in turn until a program is completed and a new program can be read in for execution. Some processors provide extra hardware to simplify multi-programming; but, in any case, the executive routines are highly complex.

An elaborate executive routine is required for a data-processing system with a number of remote input-output units. In the case of an airlines reservation system, for example, the executive routine must handle incoming messages for the processor, control the processing of each input, and send outgoing messages back to the communication network. Each incoming message is examined and a file search initiated for the appropriate file record. Since file search is relatively slow, the message can be put aside until the file record involved is obtained. When the record is found, the executive then retrieves the input message and starts processing. To send outgoing messages to the communication network, a particular channel must be requested and other processing continued until the channel is available and connected so that it is ready for use.

A third major type of executive routine handles a series of programs sequentially without manual assistance. This type of executive routine is especially useful in scientific data-processing installations that run many small programs. A sequential control executive routine enables the user to program in either machine language or source language and subroutines. If a source language program is used, the executive employs a translator program and combines the result with any subroutines already in machine language. If translation was satisfactory, the executive loads the machine language program into storage and uses it to process the data. This operating concept is called *compile and run* because the source program and data are read in and the desired results are produced. A complete program also is produced for subsequent use.

More elaborate executives accept programs in several source languages—for example COBOL or ALGOL, the international scientific language, an assembly language, and machine language to operate in the following fashion. If a program uses a source language, the executive gets the appropriate translator, loads it into storage, and initiates translation into an assembly-level language. If translation is satisfactory, the executive gets the assembly routine, loads it, and assembles the output of the translator into machine language. The executive can then load the machine-language program and start processing data. Executives of the compile-and-run type also have partial options by which the programmer can insert appropriate control cards or characters which translate the program without executing it. Or, he can program in a mnemonic-symbolic or machine-oriented language and have the executive take the steps necessary to run it.

Although compile-and-run type executive routines are used mostly for mathematical applications, they have some good features for business applications. Managers, accountants, and business analysts have numerous problems requiring extensive file searches and laborious manual processing. A large business data processor with a simple source-programming language, remote input-output units, and a good executive routine can provide the manager with a powerful in-office capability for immediate solution of problems.

Figure 12-2 summarizes the role of an operating system for a large processor. If the next job is to compile and run an ALGOL program, the process might proceed as follows. The basic monitor directs the loader to load the ALGOL translator into high-speed storage. The ALGOL translator then controls translation of the ALGOL program into machine language. At the conclusion, control is returned to the basic monitor which directs the loader to load the newly prepared machine-language program into high-speed storage. The machine-language program then executes its instructions with the help of execution control and input-output control. When execution is finished, control returns to the basic monitor to get the next job. In short, any incoming job is examined by the basic monitor and the appropriate control routines are set into action. This operating system is more elaborate than most current ones, but it indicates the existing trend toward comprehensive control.

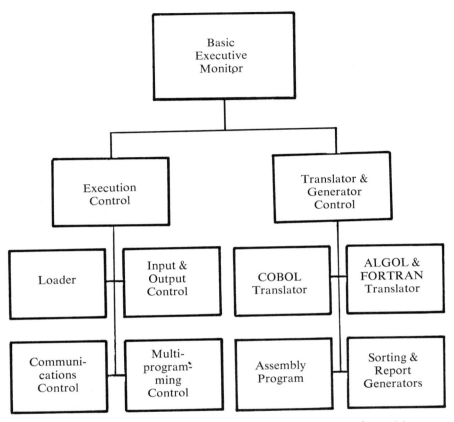

FIGURE 12-2. *Operating system for a large processor (schematic).*

Input-Output Control System

The input-output control system developed for a medium scale processor illustrates how an operating control system aids the programmer by eliminating the need for detailed programming to control these operations. This system consists of standardized routines for performing all card, printer, and disk input-output operations, and supplements the compiler-level language using macro instructions and mnemonic instructions with symbolic addresses available for this processor. When writing a source program, the programmer describes the requirements of a specific input-output job and writes an input-output control macro instruction at the point in the program where the operation is to occur. During the assembly phase, the processor inserts the appropriate machine-language instructions in the object program and provides error-correction and label-handling routines.

The programmer describes in general terms all the files to be processed and the machine configuration for running the object program. He specifies where the input-output subroutines, when generated, are to be located in core storage, the input-output devices to be used, special features affecting input-output operations, disk record organization and operation features, and the capabilities of the equipment in performing overlapped operations for card reading and punching, disk seeking, and printing.

The programmer must define each individual file in appropriate detail for the factors involved in order to indicate whether it is on cards or disks and whether it is to be printed. Each file must be defined by type of file—read, punch, disk, or print—type of processing—random, consecutive, or control-sequential—and method by which spacing and overflow are handled in printed output. The description and definition entries are punched in cards and placed ahead of the source program cards when the program is assembled.

Input-output macro instructions are entered in the user's source program to link the control-system library routines that read, write, block, unblock, and check records. These library routines operate without further programming by the programmer. The macro instructions available to the programmer are: GET, PUT, OPEN, CLOSE, SEEK, SCAN, and STACK.

After the programmer determines the type of records to be handled and plans the input, output, and work areas for a job, he writes only one instruction each time the program needs to read, punch, write, or print a record. The files are opened by an OPEN macro and records are handled by the GET and PUT macros. Special conditions concerning disks are handled by SEEK and SCAN, and card-stacking is handled by the STACK instruction.

The input-output control system is able to transfer records in units of a sector of 100 characters, track sector of 2000 characters, or track record of about 3000 characters, and it has some capability for handling records in two modes. The input-output control system can process records in various sequences, or in random order by using control data in the record to calculate the records disk address, which corresponds to the address assigned to that record when the disk file was set up. Only if the disk address is known or can be determined is it possible to random-process records organized in consecutive or control-sequential order. Consecutive processing is used when consecutive records on disk start with a beginning disk address for the file and continue in order across sectors or tracks to the end of the file. Control-sequential processing applies only to input records arranged in sequential order by control data, such as inventory stock numbers, and stored successively on disks wherever possible. If a record is not stored in successive order—for example, because it was added after the file was originally set up— it may be obtained for processing by providing a linkage between the point where the record would ordinarily be stored and the actual location used.

The versatility of the input-output control system is demonstrated by the types of records it handles, which includes fixed-length unblocked records for card reading or punching and for printer output. Disk files may be fixed-length unblocked, fixed-length blocked, or variable-length blocked, but not variable-length unblocked. The range of record length, by proper definition, is 5 to 2985 characters for unblocked records, and 5 to 999 characters for blocked records. Unblocked record-transfers to disk are one record at a time, whereas blocked records are two or more records at a time.

The programmer is responsible for allotting and defining an input or output area in core storage for each file handled. Individual records are processed in the input-output areas or moved to work areas for processing, depending upon the complexity of the program and type of records handled.

The input-output control system automatically checks whether certain errors have occurred, and either follows up with corrective action or calls on the operator for assistance. Error conditions and corrective actions are as follows: (1) Disk access inoperable; the program halts and indicates the number of the inoperable device. (2) Wrong-length record; if the error is not corrected after three attempts to reread or rewrite, the program halts to allow the operator to restart or to check for program error. (3) Unequal address compare; if the error is not corrected following three attempts to reread or rewrite, the program halts to allow the operator to change the address from the console, if he has been instructed to do so. (4) Parity error; if the error is not corrected after three attempts to reread or rewrite, the program halts and the operator can, on a read operation, scan for incorrect characters and correct, if possible, before restarting. Similar error checks are supplied for card reading and punching, disk writing, and for printing. For example, upon detecting a card-punch error, the input-output control system will attempt to punch the card correctly nine more times, but if it is not finally corrected the program will halt and allow the operator to act.

Utility Routines

Utility routines are completely self-contained programs and support the production work of a data-processing center. They are flexible generalized programs, and the programmer need only specify certain facts about his particular problem in order to use them. Typical utility routines for processors with disk storage are clear disk-storage, disk-to-card, card-to-disk, copy disk, print disk, and disk record-load.

To use a disk utility program, a programmer merely prepares control cards that specify the following for each of the utility programs:

1. Disk storage-area limits—upper and lower—to be operated on
2. Whether operations are in the move mode or the load mode
3. Identification numbers of the disk drives to be used
4. Option to be used for an error-halt condition
5. Track format to be used in each area

The *clear disk-storage* utility program can clear any specified area of disk storage and fill it with any desired valid character. Ordinarily, an area is filled with blanks before a file is loaded into disk storage, but some other character may be used to indicate which locations were unused when later a track or record is read from the disk.

The *disk-to-card* program punches into cards a copy of the contents of specified disk areas to guard against the loss of records through erroneous processing. After correction of the cause of any error, the cards can be used to reload the disk and the deficient processing operations repeated. The number of cards punched by the disk-to-card program depends on the mode and format used to write the track. Each card contains the track address, card sequence, number of data characters in the card, sector address, and up to 70 characters of desired data from the disk, including the sector address.

The *card-to-disk* program simply reloads into disk storage the data punched into cards by the disk-to-card program. The data on cards can be loaded into any disk pack using the addresses as punched and in the same relative locations from which they were punched.

The *copy-disk* utility program writes the contents of one disk pack onto a second disk pack. The copy-disk operation is comparable to the disk-to-card operation, but it is more useful for duplicating a large number of records to protect against erroneous processing. The particular controls to be specified for copy-disk are the numbers of the disk drives on which the packs being read and written are located, and the number of the disk drives to which the addresses of the pack being written are referenced.

The *print-disk* program produces a copy of an area of disk storage exactly as it is written on the disk. A copy of any number of areas can be printed without any effort by the programmer and is especially useful during program debugging. Printing is 30 lines per page and 100 characters per line; the copy also indicates the mode used to write the sector and the sector address.

The *disk-record-load* program is designed to facilitate loading disks and to modify records. This program loads addresses, single records, parts of records, or entire tracks into disk storage. It is also used to read the specified track or sector into core storage, insert data from cards into desired locations, and load the record into disk. The record-load program is useful for setting up a sample file of test records in order to test programs, and for correcting or changing existing files. Cards to be read in for loading disks can contain up to 60 columns of the data to be inserted, and up to 20 columns of control information.

The utility programs discussed here are indicative of the kinds of utility programs available for one kind of processor; other utility programs are also available for it, and, of course, many kinds of utility programs are available for different processors. The important point is that utility programs are simple, handy tools readily available for performing basic, repetitive functions in a data-processing installation. Since they are completely self-contained and can perform highly specialized tasks, no programming is required; the user merely supplies certain control information in order to use them.

Test Routine

Test routines are used to aid the programmer in debugging programs. Two examples of test routines discussed here are postmortems and traces. They are special kinds of interpretive routines that translate a macro-instruction program into machine code and immediately perform the indicated operations by means of subroutines. The machine program is not saved, so that the interpretation must be repeated to run the program again.

Post-Mortem Routines.   A post-mortem routine or examination, either automatically or on demand, will cause the processor to print a snapshot of the contents of registers and storage locations. This is done while the routine is stopped in order to help locate mistakes in coding. With this static listing of storage, register, and index contents a programmer can determine why the program has stopped and find the faulty instruction or instructions. For example, suppose the exit steps following a compare instruction were set up wrong and that indexing was erroneous because of mistakes in setting the index register, counting during each loop, or testing for exit from the loop. In order to debug the program, it is valuable to know the contents of the instruction counter, each index register, and several of the indexed instructions—both operation code and effective address—that were executed before the program halted.

Post-mortem routines are also used when debugging programs during the testing stage to find why they do not perform as planned. Most programs of any length contain mistakes that may require a large amount of time to test and debug. Some simplified forms of post-mortem routines give only a *storage snapshot,* which is a complete copy of all storage locations at the time the processor stopped. A snapshot routine may also list the instruction that caused the program to stop, the current contents of arithmetic units and indexes, and, perhaps, several of the most-recently executed jumps, thus indicating the path of program control. A *differential snapshot* lists the contents of storage locations that have changed from their initial value or from their value in a prior snapshot, if several of these changes have been made during program testing. Differential snapshots are more useful to the programmer than storage snapshots because they help him focus on the changes that have occurred since the prior snapshot and ignore those locations remaining unchanged.

Trace Routines.   A trace routine is used to observe how the object program—the program to be run—operates while it is being executed. The instructions in the object program are fed to the control unit one at a time while the trace routine actually controls the program. After each instruction in the program is executed, the executive routine keeps track of the following:

1. Location of the object program instruction
2. The instruction itself
3. Contents of the accumulator, M-Q, and index registers

The object program may be traced through its difficult or new, untested parts only; the simpler parts and those checked out earlier need not be traced. When testing the object program, instructions can be included in it for entering and leaving the trace routine at any point desired. Of course, executing the trace routine may be wasted if the object program runs to the end without stopping. A post-mortem routine may be incorporated into a trace routine to get a snapshot of storage and selected registers, if the program halts. Snapshots and traces can be included in a program which are executed dependent upon switch settings in the program or on the console. After the program is debugged, the switches can be turned off so that it will run without bothering with snapshots or traces.

Simulator Program. Interpretive routines can be used in processor simulation, whereby one processor operates with instructions and coding designed for another processor. A simulator program is essentially a group of subroutines. For each instruction to be executed—for example, ADD A137, CMP B290—the executive program jumps to a subroutine that performs the indicated operation in the real machine's codes. After completing the subroutine for one instruction, the simulator returns to execute the next instruction in the object program.

A simulator is useful when changing from one processor to another; with it, the user can run existing, tested programs until he can rewrite his own programs and test them for the new machine. Programs that are seldom used may be run by means of the simulator for an indefinite period, despite some loss in machine efficiency. Major programs that are constantly used and for which the extra running time of simulation is too costly can be handled by reprogramming.

If a similar processor is not available for emergency use, a simulator may be used for running urgent programs on whatever processor is available that has enough capacity and speed. Simulation can also be used for testing programs when a new processor is to replace one already in use; the existing processor can, by means of a simulator routine, test the new programs. A medium-sized processor may be used economically to test and debug programs for a larger one. Processor simulation can thus eliminate, to a certain extent, the incompatibility of two processors.

In general, a processor operates best with programs written in its code. A large processor interpreting a program written for a medium processor will act essentially as a medium machine. A medium processor, on the other hand, may not be able to efficiently simulate a large machine. Limited storage or complete lack of certain facilities, such as tape units, index registers, or ability to handle alphabetic characters, limits the simulation ability of medium processors.

SOFTWARE SUPPORT

An electronic processor with machine coding alone is an inefficient tool for processing data because of the intricacies of programming and using it and the expense to each user of repeating operations already performed by others but which are better handled by the processor itself. A *software package* contains programming aids offered by manufacturers to users, and may rival the hardware itself in importance. A complete software package includes the following programming techniques and aids to users:

1. Basic machine code and absolute addressing.
2. Assembly routines for converting mnemonic codes and symbolic addresses on a one-for-one basis to machine code.
3. Macro instructions, which have the appearance of instructions, but which give a programmer leverage, since one instruction written in a program becomes many instructions upon execution.
4. Subroutine libraries, which, by means of interpreters or compilers, permit the incorporation of tested subroutines into new programs.
5. Generator routines, which are skeleton routines that the programmer can select and tailor to fit a particular task—for example, file-sequence checking, sort-merge, and reports—by specifying the conditions involved.
6. Service programs or operating systems, which consist of executive routines; input-output control systems; utility routines—card-to-tape, clear-storage, and others; and test programs—snapshot and trace.
7. Compilers that offer the programmer the opportunity to write source programs in a combination of macro instructions, pseudo-codes to bring in subroutines, and mnemonic instructions and symbolic addresses that are translated into an object program before execution. More elaborate compilers such as COBOL and FORTRAN are in problem-oriented languages for both instruction codes and addressing rather than machine-oriented languages.
8. Program packages complete and ready to operate have been prepared by manufacturers for many industries: demand-deposit accounting, material and stores for utilities, brokerage accounting, and retail stores.
9. Each manufacturer maintains one or more associations of users of its equipment to foster the development of programs and the exchange of new ideas.

During the 'fifties, the development of software packages for a processor ordinarily followed the delivery of first-, second-, and third-generation equipment. By the early 'sixties, advanced programming techniques had assumed such importance, both from the users' and manufacturers' viewpoints, that elaborate software packages were likely to be announced along with the equipment itself. Early announcement and availability of advanced programming techniques cuts a user's costs and increases the efficiency of his programming effort. In a sense, software packages are comparable to another generation of equipment, since they make the equipment seem far different from its real design and make it much easier for the user, by his programming efforts, to gain full benefits from the equipment.

SUMMARY

Programming techniques have changed greatly in the fifteen years since data processors were invented. Initially, the programmer worked at the basic language of the machine; now, a variety of sophisticated languages are available to suit a programmer's abilities and problem needs. Underlying these developments is the concept that a programmer can write a *source* program which the processor, under control of another program, can convert into an *object* program for processing data. Furthermore, many programs are available that demand little of the programmer, and a variety of programs can be obtained to make the machine operator's work easier.

Instruction orders and addresses may be written in *mnemonic codes* and *symbolic addresses* to ease the task of learning the machine order code and to make it easier to assign absolute addresses to operands. Both symbolic addressing and relative addressing are valuable techniques because programs using them can be relocated anywhere desired in storage. *Macrocodes* are a higher-level language than machine language, and one instruction written by the programmer does the work ordinarily requiring many instructions. *Pseudocodes* are program entries that superficially resemble coding and are written in a program in order to bring in subroutines to produce an object program.

A *symbolic assembler* converts each mnemonic-symbolic instruction in a source program to a machine order code—an absolute address instruction in the object program ready to run in a processor.

The *interpretive* approach to the use of subroutines—a set of instructions is used to instruct the processor to carry out a sub-unit of a routine—calls a subroutine into play, supplies the information needed for operations, and immediately executes the subroutine. That is, each closed subroutine is called from the library and executed where needed in the program.

Compilers are processor programs for converting a source program consisting of macrocodes and pseudocodes into an object program that processes data and that can be run later on the machine. Compilation, which is an important tool for the programmer, performs the following functions: it analyzes all statements in the source program, expands macrocodes to machine-language code, uses pseudocodes to bring specified subroutines into the program as open subroutines at the desired point in the program, develops a symbol table (which is more elaborate in some compilers and is called a *dictionary*) and assigns absolute addresses to symbolic addresses, defines and allocates areas for the program, prepares a sequence of instructions to load the program, and places the object program on cards or tape ready to run.

COBOL and FORTRAN are two widely used compilers for business and scientific purposes, respectively. One is written in English and one is written in mathematics, thus fulfilling the two types of problems and preferences of programmers.

Generators are general routines that accept a set of conditions specified by the programmer and cause the processor to prepare a routine tailored for specific applications. Examples are generators for file-sequence checking, sort-merge, and report preparation. Since these operations are performed at all installations, their use can save much programming work.

Operating systems are programs that increase machine operating efficiency by controlling the compilation and execution of programs, supervising input and output operations, converting data from one medium to another, testing programs to debug them, and simulating the operation of one processor on another. *Executive* routines set up, monitor, and control the operation of other programs individually, concurrently, or serially. *Input-output* control systems may, for example, have standardized routines for performing all card, printer, and disk input and output operations to supplement the languages available for programming a particular processor. The programmer describes the requirements of a specific input-output job and writes an input-output control macro, so that the processor will insert the appropriate machine-language instructions in the object program during assembly and provide error-correction and label-handling routines.

Utility routines are completely self-contained routines which support the production work of a data-processing installation. Typical utility routines for a processor with disk storage are disk clear, copy, print, and load and conversion from disk to card and card to disk.

Test routines are useful for *tracing* the execution of a program or for determining the status of a program after it halts—a *post-mortem*.

Simulator programs are used to permit the execution on one machine of a program written for a different machine. The processor used interprets each instruction in the program and executes the interpreted instructions to handle the data.

Software support—all the programming aids supplied by the manufacturer and those developed by others—are an important adjunct to a processor and increase efficiency by reducing users' programming and operating costs.

13
File Processing and Sorting

The preceding chapters dealt with the fundamental building blocks of business data processing—machine-processable data, data organization, processing equipment, systems analysis and design, and programming. This chapter combines these building blocks to illustrate three major facets of business data processing: editing, file processing, and sorting. Editing and file processing are basic to nearly all business data processing; sorting is essential for processing files not maintained in addressable bulk storage.

Editing is done at two stages of data processing: first, during input to ensure that the data are accurate and in suitable form for the processor to handle, and second, during output to prepare understandable and useful reports for people.

Business record file *maintenance* introduces new records into a file and deletes old records from a file. File *processing* changes the content of individual records in a file to reflect transactions involving each record. Although file maintenance and processing frequently are handled together in one file run, treating them separately ensures more careful control over the opening and closing of records in the file. Bank officers, for example, try to guard against an employee's improperly opening or closing depositors' accounts in order to reduce the risk of internal embezzlement. For inventory control, on the other hand, the risk of loss is small from each account incorrectly opened; for example, a transaction for a nonexistent stock number can lead to opening a new account and posting it with that transaction. While this mistake doesn't really facilitate fraud, it does mean that another account—the correct stock record—is not posted and therefore is incorrect. Ways of guarding against these problems will be discussed later.

Sorting is the arrangement of items into sequence on a *key*—one or more selected data elements in each record—that consists of alphabetic or numeric characters. Customarily, files consist of a

479

homogeneous class of records that are sequentially ordered. This organization means that transactions must be separated by class, each class sorted into sequence on the same key—say, stock number—used to organize the file, and all transactions affecting a record must be ordered for logically correct processing, as described in Chapter 7. But in many cases, the data-system requirements and the equipment available for use are such that nonsequential processing is preferable to sequential. When random-access processing is used, transactions need only be classified by type for handling in a logically correct order—for example, receipts ahead of issues —without regard for key sequence.

EDITING

Input editing is done during the initial stages of data handling or read-in. Input editing makes the transaction data conform to the format and standards of quality of data already in files in order to facilitate processing. Output editing is done during the write-out operation or at a later stage to select and arrange the desired information in usable form. Editing is approached here primarily from the viewpoint of its *operational aspects*. From the user's viewpoint, the meaning of data is more important than its form and the operations performed, but the question of *meaning* depends strongly upon the particular circumstances.

Input Editing

Input editing ensures, or at least increases the probability, that data being processed are what they are supposed to be. For example, input editing, in broadest terms, might be used to determine whether an inventory file about to be updated is the current version of that file and not some prior and obsolete copy of it or some entirely different file.

File Labels. One way to check whether the desired file is being used is to identify the tape or card files by written labels that people can read. In addition, a file label that identifies or describes the contents of a file can be included as the first record in a file. Then, before using a file, the processor program reads the file label and checks it against the file wanted for processing, as specified by the label in the program being run.

Although this kind of input editing sounds complex, the reader may understand this by an analogy with his check book. File-label checking corresponds to making sure that you have your *check book* (the file) to write a check (the program), because it must be written in the check book and not on a desk pad, blackboard, or in some other check book. The file label on the check book is implicit in its appearance, for a check book seldom has "check book" printed on it. The "file label" in your check-writing "program" is your remembrance of how a check book looks. This sounds trivial, but imagine the problem if you could not perceive general shapes by visual examination or touch, and all labels were omitted. Electronic processors don't see or feel; they must be instructed by means of the program to call for the necessary file *and* have a way of identifying that the wanted file is available for processing. Programmed checking of file labels is more effective than visual inspection of written labels by machine operators because processors follow programs more consistently than people do.

Input-Editing Operations. Input editing deals primarily with the transactions that cause changes in files and only secondarily with the files themselves. If good control is maintained over all inputs, then the files are bound to be satisfactory. Input-data editing includes several kinds of tests and operations:

1. Field content: input editing determines whether alphabetic and numeric characters are where they are supposed to be and not elsewhere.
2. Accuracy of numeric data *per se*: check-digit, check-sum, and "hash-totals" rules are tested against totals summed at a prior stage for checking purposes to determine whether data meet them.
3. Completeness of data: the presence of all data elements in each transaction record and all records required for the particular type of transaction is ascertained by examining each record, counting records, and testing for gaps in the numerical sequence of records originated and transmitted through the communications network.
4. Code compatibility: editing determines whether input-data code— say, punched-card alphanumeric—differs from processor code, in which case a conversion is made to seven-bit code during read-in.
5. Rearrange data element sequence: data elements in an input record are put into suitable sequence for efficient file processing.
6. Expand or compress data: characters are introduced or deleted to make data element and record length of input data correspond to lengths in files for efficient processing.
7. Remove non-numeric data: money amount symbols—decimal points, commas, and dollar signs—are removed from input data that will be used in arithmetic operations.
8. Examine internal consistency: several data elements within one

record or a data element within the record and an external constant are examined for the existence of a specified relationship.

9. Check for correspondence of data with files: proper names, descriptors, and numeric amounts are compared to see whether they correspond with file content.

Editing and Files. Most of these input-editing operations are handled by programmed subroutines or features built into the machine. In either case, the processor—or, perhaps, a satellite processor—examines the data and performs operations on individual data elements, each transaction record, or on all transaction records. The first eight types of editing—field content, accuracy, completeness, code conversion, rearrangement, expansion or compression of data, non-numeric extraction, and internal consistency—can be performed by a processor without reference to the master files that the transactions will later update. Most of these editing operations can be performed during the first pass of data—perhaps input conversion—through the main processor or satellite because files are not needed.

To determine whether an input record corresponds to the content of its related record in the master files—say, employee payrate action and employee master-record, the transaction must, of course, be compared with the master-file record. Proper names, numbers, descriptors, and even amounts in the input data can be compared with file content to determine whether they correspond.

Conversion of data code often is handled automatically by the machine during data read-in, especially in processors using a seven-bit code for each alphanumeric character. For processors using pure binary for numbers, the conversion from, say, decimal on cards to binary inside the processor may require a programmed computation. Newer machines handle these conversions automatically and the programmer need not worry about them.

Card Format and Editing

A brief description of card input illustrates some of the features of editing listed above. Compatibility of the processor and peripheral card equipment can be achieved either by editing devices associated with the peripheral units or by editing techniques programmed for the processor. In the case of punched-card equipment, limited editing may be done after reading the card and before transferring the data to storage in the processor.

Data Rearrangement.   Data from several fields on a card—columns designated for particular purposes—can be combined into one processor word for a "word" machine. On the other hand, data from card fields containing fewer than the number of characters specified for a word in processor storage can be filled out with zeros or blanks. Of course, variable-field processors can deal directly with fields of any length in the input data, since there is no need to fit characters into words. It is also possible to shift, transpose, or suppress digits within a field and to rearrange fields with input-edit devices. Blanks, zeros, and plus or minus signs are supplied where wanted in a word by the editing unit during input. Any vacant positions not wanted in a numeric word must be filled with zeros (not blanks) during read-in so that the word can be manipulated arithmetically. The card reader may check for field content—alphabetic or numeric characters only where specified—and for format and completeness in a rudimentary way by means of double-punch and blank-column detection.

Other editing operations are programmed for the processor to perform. Since each type of transaction has a specified format, elaborate editing programs are possible on the input data *per se* and, especially, in conjunction with the file records affected by the transaction.

The edit operations for expanding or compressing and rearranging input data to correspond to file records are much simpler in a programming system designed specifically for business data processing. Both the input data and master files are organized as files, records, and data elements. By appropriately defining the data elements in records in both the input and the files as either elementary items or group items, the processor automatically handles the expansion-compression and rearrangement phases of editing. Many of the other phases of editing, however, must be handled by tailor-made programming.

Some processors have a *scatter read* feature for rearranging the individual data elements of each transaction anywhere desired in processor storage. In this way the 80 characters or less of data that are read from each card can be formed into processor words or fields and stored (under simple program control) in the locations that are most convenient for subsequent processing. Without scatter read, the characters read from each card probably would be stored in sequential locations and rearranged in subsequent operations. This pattern is true unless record descriptions organize the characters as words, fields, or data elements (depending upon the design of the machine and the programming system used), and place them wherever wanted in storage.

As discussed in preceding chapters, most processors cannot perform arithmetic operations on data that contain such non-numeric characters as decimal points or dollar signs. If input data does contain these symbols, then an edit routine is required to extract them. In most instances, these symbols are omitted when numeric data are first converted to machine media and the need for subsequent editing thereby is eliminated.

Editing for internal consistency is a powerful means of checking input. Often several data elements within a record bear a known relationship to each other. For example, the start time of a production order must be earlier than the finish time. Other data elements within a record can be compared to a known constant. The issue date on an inventory transaction must not be later than the day of processing and should not be older than, say, one week. An issue dated in the future is clearly a mistake; however, other kinds of comparison may give *unreasonable* but not necessarily wrong answers. An order from a retail customer for 100 suits needs further investigation. He might want 100, but more likely he wants one or ten.

Sequence Checking.   The arrangement of instructions on a card may leave some spare columns that can be used to hold identifying data or remarks. For example, if there are six remaining columns after punching as many instructions as possible in a card, they might be used to identify a program deck, such as LOAD 1 and LOAD 2 for the load-routine cards and SEQCHK for each card in a sequence-check routine. Furthermore, two columns might be reserved (if available) for sequence-numbering the cards (00 through 99) to help keep them in sequence for input. The total of these sequence numbers can be punched into the transfer card to allow a check on peripheral equipment during read-in to assure that all cards are loaded. The processor can, by a small loop in the load routine, also check card sequence within the program or data. A simple check scheme for serially numbered cards might be the comparison of the card number with the contents of a counter, and accepting the card if the two numbers correspond. A 1 should be added to the counter, of course, before comparing the counter contents and next card number. Slightly more elaborate schemes are required if the interval between card numbers is not uniform. Similar schemes can be used for identifying and sequence-numbering input data cards to guard against loss of cards or mixups within and between decks.

Devices. A plugboard wired for input of a particular card format is kept for reuse to avoid the trouble of rewiring the board each time. Clever editing saves card-reading time and processor time for packing or unpacking characters that need to be rearranged for efficient processing. Similar plugboard devices are used for editing data for card-punching units.

Magnetic-tape-handling units lack editing facilities, and using a large processor to perform editing may be expensive. Instead, a satellite processor is often used to edit and rearrange data. In some cases, peripheral equipment, such as card-to-tape converters and off-line printers operating from magnetic tape, do limited editing operations. Processor programs are also used for further editing and rearranging input data during read-in and for editing results during output processing.

Edit Limitations. Some input, such as certain instruction words for a program kept on cards, are difficult to edit for accuracy. The first word—the word-count and storage-location word—on a program load card may have a format different from other instructions and be numeric with a *minus* sign. Two cards to load the routine and the transfer card (to initiate program execution at the desired starting instruction) can start with an instruction word and a *plus* sign to indicate the different use made of the cards. Since the first word on most cards may be used in any one of several ways, this word cannot be edit-checked during read-in. If a plus is erroneously marked a minus on a program card, the program will not run correctly when execution is attempted. In fact, an erroneous sign may prevent loading the whole program and cause a premature attempt to execute the program.

Output Editing

Output editing is actually done after file processing, which is discussed later in this chapter; however, it is desirable to cover output editing at this point, for it has many similarities to input editing, and it bears on file layout and processing. The quantity and quality of information issued by a data-processing system depend upon the caliber of both the input- and output-editing schemes.

User Requirements. Output editing is required because people need their information in a different form than is most efficient for processing. People are accustomed to short documents and reports containing only a few items and to longer reports of orderly rows and columns of names and numbers on sheets of paper with appropriate headings. Common types of reports are statements, statistical summaries, checks, payroll, and cost distributions—lists or summaries about any facet of a business.

The most important questions about report preparation are, "What information should this report contain?" and "How should it be arranged?" The answers depend on several factors. Content of a report depends on *transaction·events*—what and how many transactions are being reported. The intended *audience*—who will read and use the report—determines format, and, to some extent, content. And the *management operating plan*—how the organization responds to reports about what has occurred—influences the content, arrangement, emphasis, and distribution of reports. The exact content and format of any report depends on bargaining between report users and people who operate the data-processing system.

In more concrete terms, and viewed at the operational level of data processing, the desired content of reports needs to be selected from records in a file and arranged for printing as separate words in a readable format in reports. Specifically, this includes the following: editing individual words for spacing; inserting punctuation, special symbols for dollars or units of weight, and abbreviations; and suppressing leading zeros or other symbols in order to improve readability. Also, spacing (or breaks) by minor and major classes must be planned for, headings supplied, and totals and subtotals computed for printing.

In short, output editing bridges the gap between, on the one hand, the most efficient data layouts for processor storage and manipulation and, on the other, the presentation of lengthy reports or merely selected facts to people. Processors have limited primary-storage space; therefore, to economize storage, the format arrangements and redundancies that make data more readable for people are usually eliminated from the input data during read-in. These special format arrangements and redundancies are then restored during output editing so that people can readily use the results without being distracted by the make-up of reports.

If the processor output is used by equipment instead of people, then the output, of course, is edited for machine usage. Examples of machines using processor output are automatic devices for machine or process control in the plant, communication networks to disseminate results, or the processor itself during the next processing cycle.

Output Format. Output editing concentrates on selecting data elements from files, rearranging them—perhaps by *scatter write,* the opposite of scatter read—expanding data elements into separate visual words for readability, and developing attractive page layout. Processors perform several operations, and some in parallel, when handling files to prepare reports:

1. Select desired items or groups of items from specified records (ignore others) in a file and organize them into readable words.
2. Assign desired words to one report output on tape or cards or to several report outputs—say, payroll and earnings report—if wanted in each report.
3. Sort the items for each report into sequence by name, number, quantity involved, or other elements of data, as desired.
4. Develop "breaks" in the data on major and minor classifications and calculate subtotals and totals for each category.
5. Introduce report titles, page headings, page numbers, and special symbols; delete repetitive descriptions and unwanted leading zeros; plan horizontal and vertical spacing and alignment; and select a suitable amount of printing per page.
6. Count the number of records and calculate the totals for all items going into each report and proved against the items selected from files for report preparation.

Some of the critical problems concerning input data—field content, data accuracy, completeness of data, and correspondence of data with files—are most efficiently handled during input editing. During output editing, it is generally assumed that these problems were handled correctly earlier, because little or nothing can be done efficiently about them at this stage. This is true except for the discovery of mistakes that cast doubt on input editing and lead to further investigation. But relationships among items in files can be determined by testing their validity in terms of *standards,* past *actual* results, or even *reasonableness* according to an intuitive feel of the situation. If, for example, purchase orders for a particular item have been issued for quantities ranging from 100 to 350 during the past two years, an order for either 1 or 1000 units deserves investigation. The unusual quantity may arise from a special order or a change in the production schedule, but it is probably an error. Such testing augments input editing by concentrating on the meaning of the output. The *meaning* of the output depends on the logic of processing—

whether the program was designed to do what was actually wanted —and on an understanding of the nature of the input data and file content at any point in time and during any stage of processing. These are vastly broader problems, and more difficult to deal with at the procedural level than input editing, for which many techniques are available.

Report Programming.   Programming all of the editing required for report preparation can be extremely time consuming, if done at the level of machine language. Report generators represent an advanced form of programming and are often more efficient than tailor-made report-writing programs. These generators provide a simplified means of preparing statistics—totals, averages, and standard deviations—and setting up format—titles, spacing, and special symbols. Assuming the availability of a report generator prepared by the equipment manufacturer or other programming specialist, the user must first learn how to work with it, which may be nearly as onerous as writing a program afresh. After he comprehends the generator and still feels that it fulfills his requirements, he specifies certain facts about the data arrangement in the records to be used and the content and layout of reports. The processor, first, *generates* the report-writing program and, second, *executes* the report-writing program to process the files and prepare the desired reports.

FILE MAINTENANCE AND PROCESSING

Business data processing involves huge files of records on employees, material in stock, customers, production scheduling, and other items. These files are *maintained* or updated to reflect nonarithmetical changes in records and *processed* to change the contents of individual records by means of arithmetical operations.

File Maintenance

File maintenance is the modification of a file to incorporate additions, deletions, transfers, and substitutions. Emphasis is placed on the whole record rather than the data elements. The following types of changes in an inventory stock file illustrate the transactions involved in file maintenance.

1. Addition of new stock items to the approved list
2. Deletion of discontinued items
3. Transfers from one section of the file to another because items are reclassified or switched between warehouses

4. Substitution of new identification data—part number, part name, item cost—for old.

If the master file is stored on tape in catalogue-number sequence, the changes are sorted into the same sequence in order to maintain the file. If the file is kept in random-access storage, preliminary sorting of file changes is not required. However, for both file-processing techniques, transactions affecting each record must be handled in a logical sequence.

Inputs and Outputs.   In addition to the processor program, the inputs for file maintenance are the master file, new changes, and pending changes left over from the prior maintenance cycle. The outputs are an updated master file, change list, pending changes, and mismatches. The *updated master file* will reflect additions, deletions and transfers of stock items, and substitution of new facts for stock items that are otherwise unchanged. A *change list* is useful for keeping track of the kinds of changes made in the master file and for tracing them, if necessary.

Pending changes is a type of output peculiar to maintaining files that are kept in sequence. In one file run, an item can be transferred forward by removing it from its original location and inserting it in the file at a later point. The reverse is not possible because the desired insertion point is passed before reaching the item to be moved. To move the record for an item to an earlier point in the master file, the record for the item is taken out of the file during one cycle and inserted at an earlier point in the next cycle. The fact that records to be moved upstream are extracted from the master file and kept in a pending-change file between two cycles may require that the different types of transactions be handled in a certain order. Otherwise, futile attempts will be made to process the item while it is temporarily out of the master file.

Accuracy Control.   *Mismatches* arise in file maintenance whenever the key for an item is incorrect. An attempt to delete, transfer, or substitute an item in the file will end up on an error tape or console print-out, if the input-item key does not match the key of a file item. On the other hand, an incorrect key that happens to match the key of another item will update the wrong record. In one amusing example, a mail-order house reported extremely high sales of fur coats because keypunch operators introducing input data tended to transpose the stock number for another item and punch the number for fur coats. Daydreaming and wishful thinking outfoxed the processing system, and an inventory count and reconciliation was required to correct the records.

A new record can be introduced into a file even though it has an erroneous key. A record with a key 23451 that is erroneously punched as 12345 and used during a file maintenance run will be introduced at the wrong place. The next transaction processed against item 23451 will be rejected as a mismatch (because the earlier item was introduced as 12345) and written out on an error tape for examination.

The accuracy of file-maintenance operations can be controlled, to some extent, by keeping track of the number of records in the file. The initial number, plus introductions, minus deletions equals the final number of records. Transfers within the file change the number of records in a category, but not in total. Obviously, control over modifications within individual records requires more thorough techniques.

Housekeeping Runs.   The file-maintenance requirements of an application affect the initial selection of equipment, modes of storage, arrangement of master-file data, conversion and housekeeping programs, and amount of processor time devoted to nonproduction runs. Systems analysts tend to concentrate on getting tangible output from production programs without giving careful consideration to housekeeping runs—that is, to the sorting, merging, extracting, editing, and updating programs that must be written and run regularly in order to make a production run possible. A single production run can grow into a half-dozen preparatory programs and a like number of one-time file conversion and editing programs.

File Processing

File processing updates a file to incorporate changes involving arithmetical operations. Examples of inventory transactions handled by file processing are:

1. Purchase and use commitments
2. Receipts
3. Issues
4. Financial accounting.

These transactions require arithmetical operations to update the quantity or value of a stock item available or on hand. The transactions are sorted into the same sequence as the master file and processed, by means of suitable programs, against the master file. A program can process many kinds of transactions in the same run if each type is properly identified and handled in a logical sequence.

The essence of processing files kept on tapes—which has been touched on in several earlier chapters—is basically simple. First, a suitable file-processing program is read into the processor. Second, the program directs the read-in of one or more transactions and master-file records (depending upon the length of the records and quantity of processor storage available) to compare them for identity on stock-number or other key until a match is found. Third, each master-file record without a transaction match (inactive file record) is copied onto the new master file. And each transaction lacking a corresponding master-file record—incorrect sequence, or invalid stock number—is written out on a mismatch tape. Fourth, when a match on stock number is found, the program directs the processor to handle all transactions affecting that record to update the master file. Fifth, the updated record is written out on the new master-file tape, and the cycle is repeated starting at the second step.

For files kept in random-access storage, file processing is simpler because transactions need not be sorted into stock-number sequence (although each type has to be handled in a logical sequence) and each updated file-record merely takes the place of the old record in storage; the file is not rewritten. Mismatches are written out for analysis and correction.

Transactions and Subroutines. The transaction identifier is used in the following way to calculate instruction addresses and execute the required subroutine. Assume, for simplicity, that a subroutine of 100 program steps is required to process each of the four types of transactions that occur for the stock file: purchase, receipt, issue, and financial accounting. These subroutines are in processor storage starting at locations 100, 200, 300, and 400, respectively. The main program first takes the transaction type—1, 2, 3, or 4, for the four classes of transactions—from the input record for each transaction. Next, the program multiplies the transaction type number—1, 2, 3, or 4—by 100 to obtain a number indicating the starting point of the subroutine for that kind of transaction. The calculated result—100, 200, 300, or 400—is then inserted into a program jump instruction that can then be executed. When executed, this instruction step makes processor control go to the correct starting point to execute the subroutine. The last step in each of the four subroutines—storage locations 199, 299, 399, and 499—contains a jump to return program control to the main program and handle other transactions in a similar way or continue with other parts of the program.

An important feature of the addressing scheme outlined above is the creation of an address by calculation in order to complete an instruction. Several important aspects of this feature should be noted. The address of the branch instruction is omitted when the instruction is written—that is, it is a *dummy* instruction. Three program steps are used to fill in the address of the dummy instruction. First, the transaction type number is obtained. Second, this number is multiplied by 100. And, third, the product—100, 200, 300, or 400—is incorporated in the dummy instruction by copying or moving it to the blank part of the instruction without changing the instruction code. In the next cycle, a new address is merely written over the address that was copied into the dummy-instruction address. This cycle can be repeated indefinitely to operate correctly on any and every example of the four types of transactions. This is a simple example of the ability of a processor to modify an instruction to fit conditions encountered in the data.

Other schemes, which vary in nature depending on the processor's features, are available for using the desired subroutine in the program. Machines with *indirect addressing* can do this more simply, as follows. The starting points 100, 200, 300, and 400 of the subroutines for the four kinds of transactions are placed in the corresponding storage locations—1, 2, 3, and 4, respectively. Upon reading in each transaction, the transaction class number is used to form the address of an instruction which will obtain from location 1, 2, 3, or 4, as directed, the address of the starting point—100, 200, 300, or 400—of the required subroutine. Thus, in two steps, one address, which corresponds to the type of transaction, is used to find the address of the subroutine starting point. This indirect-addressing scheme of using storage at one address to find another address is carried through several stages by some processors. Corresponding to clues in a "treasure hunt," two (or more) steps are required to reach the goal.

Although this example of how a transaction code may be used to direct the program to a selected subroutine is highly simplified, it should convey the idea of how a program develops, or at least completes, some of its own instructions. The reader may see how transfers to subroutines that have different numbers of instructions can be set up without wasting storage space by padding them out to the same length. It may also be visualized how less orderly-looking schemes for coding transactions can be coped with.

Trial Runs for Processing.   On the surface, file processing seems to be a simple, straightforward process in which all that needs to be done is to process the transactions and carry out the related physical actions—fill orders, pay workmen, or whatever. However, many factors make processing complicated; one factor, which bears on the sequence used for processing, is the fact that it is possible to substitute one stock item for another. More important, a trial run with calculations and perhaps tentative update of the file may be required where reciprocal effects are involved. After deciding what action to take, the file can be updated.

Assume that when stock item A is ordered by customers, if it is not available, then B is the first substitute, and D the second. Substitution of an alternate color or a higher-priced item for the one ordered may be made. A wag once said that mail-order houses try to maximize substitution by sending the alternate or wrong item to each and every customer even though they could fill every order as placed. Ignoring the possible intention of that remark, it is nevertheless possible that every order could be filled "correctly," according to some definition, yet every customer get a substitute. Similar patterns of choice may exist for machine-assignment in a factory and for selection of transportation routes.

A matrix can be developed to show how one item can be substituted for another:

Item Wanted	Substitution Choice					
	A	B	C	D	E	F
A		1		2		
B	1				2	
C	No	substitutes				
D		1				
E			1			2
F	2			1		

The matrix means that, if A is wanted but is not available, B is the first choice and D is the second choice as a substitute. When processing requests for issues, the decision rules might be to (1) try to fill all orders with the items requested, (2) then fill any unfilled orders with first substitutes, if possible, and (3) fill any remaining orders with second substitutes, if possible.

In the simple case, supply equals or exceeds demand, and every order can be filled with the item wanted. The situation is more complex if supply of some items falls short of demand. Two or more attempts may be made to fill orders—initially, with the item wanted; next, with the first substitute; and, finally, with the second substitute. If the demand for A exceeds the supply, the remaining demand is filled with B and D, but only after the primary demands for those items are filled, and so on.

Another rule for filling orders might be to fill all the orders for A—use A and substitutes B and D, if necessary, before going to B, etc. Obviously, the outcome of this scheme depends on whether the order-filling procedure starts with orders for item A and works through to F, or vice versa. More intricate rules might be developed to keep the frequency of substitution at a minimum or to maximize the quantity ordered that is filled by the item wanted or its first substitute.

Two important points are involved in applying substitution rules to maximize the number of orders filled by first-choice items, if the supply of some items is short: (1) the allocation requires a trial run involving *all* orders, and (2) some rules are needed to decide how to allocate items in short supply. The allocation rules, once formulated, can then be applied as part of the data-processing routine to update files and initiate shipping action.

Controls. File maintenance and file processing have enough in common so that they might be handled in the same processor run. Joint treatment may cause some difficulties because control over each kind of operation becomes more difficult. For example, a bank found that checking-account transactions, which were processed in the same run as file changes, sometimes resulted in opening new accounts because of mistakes in account numbers. File-maintenance procedures, it will be recalled, handle insertion of new accounts, and an erroneous transaction account number may either open up a new account or post the transaction to another depositor's account. Erroneously opening a new account causes some difficulty, but posting to the wrong account is at least twice as bad, for it affects two depositors and both may be annoyed by the mistake. One remedy is to handle file maintenance and processing in two separate runs so that tighter control can be kept over the opening and closing of accounts.

The fact that file processing leaves unchanged the number of records in a file facilitates control over a file to guard against erroneous gain or loss of a record. Money amounts can be controlled by keeping control totals—today's balance equals yesterday's balance plus additions and minus deductions—for proving the total of individual account balances. Quantities can be controlled on a unit basis by adding all items to get a control total, even though dissimilar items are involved.

File Handling

Maintaining and processing files kept on magnetic tape usually require reading and rewriting the whole file during each processing cycle. There are several ways to cut down the work of reading and recopying the whole file at each cycle just to update the small fraction of active records.

Fractional Updating. One way is to update a fraction—one-fifth or one-twentieth—of the master file each day so that the whole file is updated once in a week or a month. The whole file is never really current but, on the other hand, it is almost current, for it averages only two days old, if one-fifth is updated each day. On any given day, one-fifth is current or zero days old, and the other fractions are one, two, three, and four business-days old, respectively. Many billing operations—charge accounts, utility bills, insurance premiums—operate in this fashion.

A second way to keep files current without rewriting the master tape completely is to retain the master tape intact and accumulate the changes on a change tape. This approach can save much time for a processor lacking the feature of concurrent read-process-write. Modifications to the master file are accumulated on the change tape until it becomes unwieldy. Finally, the change tape is processed against the master file to update it, the change tape is discarded, and the cycle started afresh. At any time, both the master tape and the change tape must be considered together to find the current status of a record. Although writing time is reduced, the entire master file must be read during each cycle.

The use of addressable bulk-storage devices—mainly disk or drum—is a third approach to the problem of reducing the time used to read and rewrite whole files to change a few records. These devices read a master record only if a transaction is present and provide for writing the revised record in the space occupied by the original and leaving the other records unchanged. Precautions are necessary, of course, to keep the new record within the space occupied by the old and to ensure that data are available for reconstruction in case of mishap. Maintaining files on disk or drum storage offers several advantages, therefore, for large files with low activity.

Retention Period. After setting up, maintaining, and processing a file the question arises, "How long should the file and transactions be kept before they are discarded?" A commonly-used plan is to keep three "generations" of files. For example, Monday's output is retained until Wednesday's output is successfully used as input on Thursday. Then Monday's files can be discarded, leaving the files for Tuesday and Wednesday for back-up in case Thursday's output is defective. Wednesday's file alone may be sufficient back-up for Thursday in most cases. Certain files—those for the end of each month, for example—may be retained longer to prepare reports and answer unexpected questions. The ability to reconstruct all records from a specified date to the present may be wanted as protection against mishap. If so, copies of the master file for that date and all interim transactions must be kept.

The general rule for deciding when to discard output files, and even raw data, is easy to state: discard the file when the cost of keeping it exceeds the probable value of having the data on hand. However, application of the rule is difficult because it is not possible to forecast accurately when and what demands will be made on the files that are saved and when a discarded file will be wanted.

Magnetic-tape files pose problems similar to those of retaining paper records, but some problems are accentuated. The tendency to save data and processed results is stronger for magnetic tape than for other media because of the high density of data and the possibilities of economical reprocessing. Furthermore, the possibility of selectively rewriting tape files to eliminate or consolidate some of the detail, while keeping the more consequential facts, is a plus factor in retaining tape files. Selective condensation may be done one or more times before the files are discarded and the tape reused. Economic analysis would predict that a higher fraction of data in magnetic-tape files will be saved than is the case for paper and card records. This is true even though tape is reusable. As the cost of an item decreases, the quantity used is likely to increase. For example, the Bureau of the Census reports that many *thousands* of magnetic tapes of data are being stored for statisticians and others who may want to process them at some future date to answer questions that are not yet formulated. Of course, if all future questions likely to be asked about data in the files could be formulated now, the questions could be answered and the files discarded.

SORTING

The obvious, immediate objective of sorting data is to arrange records according to rules. The basic reason for sorting data, which is inefficient *per se,* is to make subsequent processing more efficient considering the equipment available and the data-information system requirements. Records are classified by category, sorted into file sequence, and logically ordered by type before processing. Sorting into sequence by numeric or alphabetic key is of primary interest here.

Off-line data-flow plans that use serial storage require sorting transactions by class, sequence, and type to facilitate processing. Most data-processing equipment can more efficiently handle one class of transactions—as viewed from the standpoint of programs and files—than several classes of transactions. Furthermore, an orderly sequence is often easier to deal with than a jumbled sequence.

Random-access equipment operating on-line works more efficiently with one class, or a small assortment of classes, of data than with a wide variety. Arrangement in some orderly fashion may be easier to handle than a disordered mass. The classification and sorting of data into sequence will continue to precede processing until equipment with much larger, low-cost storage capacity is used in business.

An inventory record might contain these data elements along with dozens of others:

Stock Number	Stock Name	Size	Quantity
35079	Truck tire	650-16	12,327

Inventory records are commonly sorted by stock number or name. If the records are to be sorted by stock number, then the key is five digits—35079. Sometimes inventory records are sorted on the basis of stock name, location, size, quantity on hand, or even the number of days overdue for outstanding orders. The point is that any data element in a record can be used as a key. A file sorted into sequence on one key may require rearrangement for further processing. Rearrangement on another key can be avoided if processing that would seem to require resorting can be done by other processing schemes, such as searching, extracting, tallying, or summarizing.

Records are generally sorted into sequences on their keys so that they form either an ascending or a descending string. Each key in an ascending string is larger than the preceding key: 1, 2, 5, 12, 27, 28. Each key in a descending string is smaller: 50, 13, 5, 2, 1.

Alphabetic sorting treats "A" as the smallest (or earliest) letter and "Z" as the largest letter in the alphabet. The assignment of codes to numerals and letters during machine design determines the sorting sequence, which makes up a collation table for the particular processor being used.

Three methods of sorting are discussed here: digital, comparison of pairs, and merge. People, tabulating equipment, and electronic processors can do digital sorting, but comparison- and merge-sorting is restricted, for practical purposes, to electronic processors.

Digital Sorting

Digital sorting starts by sorting records on the right-hand digit in the key and finishes with the left-hand digit; it might be called "minor-major" sorting. The output for sorting on digital keys is ten classes. Each class contains items with the same right-hand digit, but with different left-hand digits. For two-digit keys, the result of the first pass of digital sorting is ten classes: 00, 10, 20, . . ., 90, 01-91, 02-92 and so on through 09-99. The classes can be abbreviated as X0, X1, X2 through X9, with X any digit or digits.

The ten classes from the first pass of digital sorting can be combined in ascending sequence and sorted on the second digit from the right. When the ten output classes are "stacked," the items are then in sequence from 00 to 99 on the two right-hand digits. The process can be repeated until all digits in longer keys are handled and the items are in sequence on all digits 0 . . . 0 to 9 . . . 9. A schematic diagram of digital sorting is shown in Figure 13-1.

A simple example shows how to sort records with a three-digit key (for each additional digit, it is necessary merely to repeat the third step below) into ascending sequence. This procedure can be done either by hand or by machine, depending on whether the data media are paper, cards, or tape, as follows:

1. Sort on the right-hand or units digit.
2. Stack or combine in ascending sequence on the units digit—X0, X1, X2, . . ., X9—and sort on the second digit from the right, or tens, digit.
3. Stack in ascending sequence on the tens digit—0X, 1X, 2X— and sort on the third from right, or hundreds, digit.
4. Stack in ascending sequence on the hundreds digit and the sequence is 000 to 999.

Alphabetical Sorting

Ten output pockets are useful for sorting digital keys one digit at a time, if a simple decimal code is used. An eleventh pocket takes rejects—cards not punched in that position. Two more pockets are included to accept cards punched in the "11" and "12" positions (above the 0 to 9 positions) to sort alphabetical keys using a combination of zone and numeric punch. In short, most card sorters have twelve pockets for alphanumerical sorting, which takes two passes to handle the combination of zone punches—10, 11 and 12 —and the numeric 1 through 9 punches in each column.

Any number of output pockets, from two upward, can be used for sorting, but a small number requires more passes to get the items into sequence. Sorters have been built with dozens of pockets for checks and even hundreds of output pockets for ordinary letter mail, because the availability of more output pockets permits sorting with fewer passes of the items through the sorter.

Physical handling of each separate item is an important feature of manual and mechanical sorting. A slip of paper, a card, or an ordinary envelope used for letter mail contains both the key and record. When sorted on its key, the record itself is also sorted. On the other hand, some records cannot be separated for sorting. High-density storage makes records so small that physical separation for sorting is not feasible, and such records are usually recopied during sorting.

Electronic Sorting

Sorting records in electronic data-processing systems using magnetic-tape storage involves recopying data from one tape to another. The essential feature is the comparison of two or more items to find which one should be recopied first to build a sequence. Since records on long magnetic tape cannot be sorted by physical rearrangement in the same way that paper or punched cards are sorted, they are transferred into processor storage for sorting and rewriting on tape. Many schemes exist for sorting records with electronic equipment: comparison of pairs, merge sorting, and digital sorting. Each is discussed briefly here.

Comparison with Exchange. There are several ways to sort records by comparing their whole keys at one time and exchanging them in storage at each step. By one plan, the keys of the first two items are compared to select the record with the smaller key. The smaller key from the first comparison is then compared with the key of the third record. Whichever record-key is smaller is saved for the next comparison, and the other record is placed in the storage location of the second. Comparison of the keys of two records

First pass: Sort cards from Input-1 stack on "units" digit.

Input-1	338
	250
	960
	506
	287
	819
	621
	208
	082
	585
	451
	688
	895
	263
	557
	630
	789
	124
	017
	392

First Pass—Output

| 250 | 621 | 082 | | | 585 | | 287 | 338 | 819 |
| 960 | 451 | 392 | 263 | 124 | 895 | 506 | 557 | 208 | 789 |
630							017	688	
0	1	2	3	4	5	6	7	8	9

Pockets

Second pass: Stack cards from first pass in ascending sequence on "units" digit to get Input-2 stack.

Sort cards from Input-2 stack on "tens" digit.

Input-2	819
	789
	338
	208
	688
	287
	557
	017
	506
	585
	895
	124
	263
	082
	392
	621
	451
	250
	960
	630

Second Pass—Output

								789	
								688	
					557			287	
208	819	124	338		451	263		585	895
506	017	621	630		250	960		082	392
0	1	2	3	4	5	6	7	8	9

Pockets

FIGURE 13-1. *Digital sorting.*

Third pass: Stack cards from second pass in ascending sequence on "tens" digit to get Input-3 stack.

Sort Input-3 stack on "hundreds" digit.

		Input-3	895
			392
			789
			688
			287
			585
			082
			263
			960
			557
			451
			250
			338
			630
			124
			621
			819
			017
			208
			506

Third Pass—Output

		287							
		263			585	688			
082		250	392		557	630		895	
017	124	208	338	451	506	621	789	819	960
0	1	2	3	4	5	6	7	8	9

Pockets

Stack in ascending sequence on "hundreds" digit to get Stack-4. The items are now in order.

FIGURE 13-1. *Digital sorting (cont'd).*

at a time with exchange at each stage continues until the record with the smallest key is the one saved at the end of the cycle. This record is either placed at the end of the space originally occupied by the file or removed from the set and placed in a separate block in storage. Completing the compare-and-exchange loop for all records in the file merely puts the record with the smallest key at the end of the file. The loop is repeated from the beginning to get the next record in sequence. As the ordered sequence gets longer, the number of records remaining to be sorted in the next loop gets smaller.

The scheme for sorting by comparison of pairs obviously involves many comparisons. To sort 100 records into sequence involves 99 comparisons in the first cycle, 98 comparisons in the second cycle after one record is selected, and so forth. Only one comparison is needed in the last cycle when two records remain. If provision is made for immediate recognition of the end of the sorting operation—it is reached when no record moves toward the small end of the sequence—the number of cycles performed can be reduced.

Sorting by comparison may be used with automatic equipment when all items are kept in internal storage throughout the process. The location of items can be exchanged after each comparison, if desired, so that only the original storage occupied by the items is used during sorting. If the item selected after each pass is put into another section of storage, additional space is required, although programming is simpler.

Sorting by comparison of pairs is limited to the number of items in internal storage at one time. If desired, the sorted items can be read out, storage reloaded, and the sorting process repeated. The result is to sort into sequence the block of items that just fills the working space available in internal storage. Separate blocks of items are not related so that the whole set is not in sequence. A plan is needed to merge individual sequences together into one over-all sequence.

Merge Sorting. Business records usually involve so many items that internal storage capacity is exceeded, and the sequences developed in storage must be merged into longer sequences. Furthermore, it is highly desirable that any sequences in the original data should be exploited. The merge-sorting scheme takes advantage of whatever sequence exists in the data when the operation starts. A set of data already in sequence is handled only once, and the sorting operation merely checks the sequence. Data in the worst possible sequence—completely inverted order—are passed through the processor many times to merge into sequence. Most situations actually lie in between these extremes, for there is usually some order in the data. If two or more sequences exist in the data, each sequence should, of course, be saved and then merged into an over-all sequence.

The basic feature of merge sorting is that it produces a single sequence of items from two or more sequences that are already arranged by the same rules. Viewed in simplest terms, the number of sequences is reduced in each merge-sorting pass corresponding to the number of input tapes used—for example, reduced to one-half for two input tapes—until all the data are arranged in one sequence.

The merge-sorting scheme is frequently used for sorting data stored on magnetic tape. The mechanics of merge sorting are the reading of data from two or more input tapes, arranging the data in sequence on the desired key, and writing the data on output tapes. Longer sequences, which are not limited by processor storage capacity, are developed in each pass through the processor until all items are in one sequence. Merge sorting is easier to follow in detail if only two input and two output tapes are used, and one item at a time is read from and written on a tape as soon as its place in the sequence is determined. The processor follows an instruction program to compare the keys of items received from each input tape with the key of the item just written on the output tape. Actually, longer strings are developed internally and written as a block on tape.

The procedure for merge sorting can be stated simply: build the longest string possible at each stage on an output tape. This requires comparing the preceding item written on that tape and the two items that are available which may be added to the sequence. As each item is written on an output tape, another item is read from the input tape that was the source of the item just written. If it is not possible to continue building the string on one output tape—because both items available are too small—switch to the other output tape and start a new string. In short, a three-way comparison is made each time between two items in storage and the item just added to the sequence.

Merge sorting into ascending sequence is illustrated in Figure 13-2. For simplicity, only the key is shown for each item, but the remainder of the record is assumed to follow the key at every stage. This is not to say that handling the rest of the item is trivial, because considerable detail is involved merely in keeping a record associated with its key. Data movement involved in making internal comparisons can be minimized by forming *key-location* records that consist solely of the key and storage location of each record. The key-location records are sorted into sequence on the key alone, and the location part is then used to get the record with the corresponding key and write it on tape.

Four-Tape Merge. Merge sorting with four tapes—two input tapes, A and B containing items to be sorted, and two output tapes, C and D—can be illustrated for the following initial conditions:

Tape A: 5, 2, 18, 7, 15, 27
Tape B: 20, 8, 9, 3, 21, 13
Tape C: blank
Tape D: blank

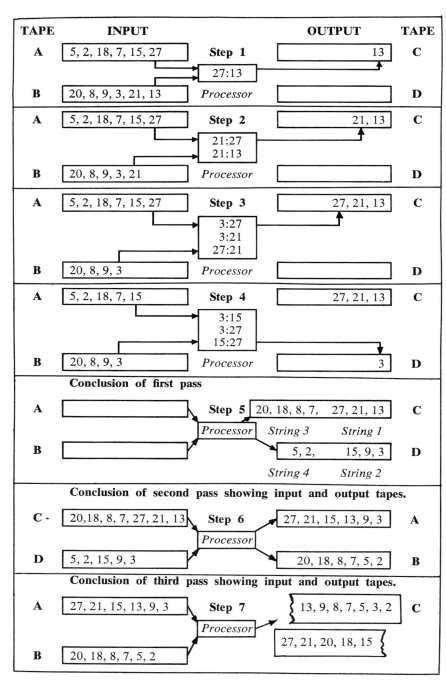

FIGURE 13-2. *Four-tape merge-sort.*

504

The steps involved in the four-tape merge sorting shown in Figure 13-2 can be described as follows:

1. Read in the first key, 27 and 13, from tapes A and B. Compare 13:27 and write the smaller, 13, on tape C. (See Step 1.)
2. Read in the next key, 21, from tape B and compare with 27 already in storage to find the smaller. If the smaller, 21, is larger than the key, 13, just written on tape C, then write 21 on tape C. (See Step 2.)
3. Read in the next key, 3, from tape B and compare with 27 to select the smaller of the two. If the smaller key, 3, is larger than the key, 21, just written on tape C, then write 3 on tape C. Since 3 is smaller than 21, do not write it, but compare 27 with 21, and write 27 on tape C since 27 is larger than 21. (See Step 3.)
4. Read in the next key, 15, from tape A and compare with 3 to select the smaller. Since 3 and 15 are both smaller than the last number written on C, neither can be used to build that sequence. The smaller, 3, is transferred to tape D to start a new string. (See Step 4.)

The procedure described in Steps 2 and 3 is repeated to build the longest possible sequence on tape D. When the available keys will not increase the sequence, a new sequence is started on the other tape. The first pass is completed when all the items on tapes A and B are transferred to tapes C and D. The first pass gives two strings on each output tape. (See Step 5.)

The output tapes for one pass are input tapes for the next pass. The second pass (tapes C and D are now input) yields one string on each tape. (See Step 6.) The third pass, with tapes A and B as input, arranges the items in one sequence. (See Step 7.)

Alternate output is used to get the same number of strings (plus or minus one) on each tape, but it is not necessary to build each sequence on the alternate tape. For a huge number of items, strings can be written on one tape until it is filled. The other tape is then filled. About the same number of sequences is built on each tape, if there are enough items to fill two or more tapes.

A decision table for the logic of four-tape merge sorting is shown in Table 13-1. The three conditions of the problem—input-key-1 is smaller than input-key-2, input-key-1 will build the sequence on the output tape, and input-key-2 will build the sequence on the output tape—are listed at the top of the stub. Here, "input-key-1" means the key of the record read from input tape 1. The actions —write the appropriate input record to build the sequence on the active output tape, read a new input record to replace the one writ-

DECISION TABLE	Table Name	**MERGE-SORT**		Page *1* of *1*
Form	Chart No. **DT-1**	Prepared by **WILL HARRISS**		Date **OCT 10**

Stub	Body															
	Rule Number															
Conditions	1	2	3	4	5	6	7	8	9	10	11	12	13	14	15
INPUT-KEY-1 < INPUT-KEY-2	Y	Y	Y	N	N	N									
INPUT-KEY-1 > PRIOR-OUTPUT-KEY	Y	N	N	N	–	Y									
INPUT-KEY-2 > PRIOR-OUTPUT-KEY	–	Y	N	N	Y	N									
Actions															
SWITCH OUTPUT TAPE		×	×												
WRITE INPUT-1 ON OUTPUT TAPE	×	×			×										
READ NEXT-RECORD ON INPUT-TAPE-1	×	×			×										
WRITE INPUT-2 ON OUTPUT TAPE		×		×	×										
READ NEXT-RECORD ON INPUT-TAPE 2		×		×	×										
GO TO MERGE-SORT TABLE	×	×	×	×	×	×									

TABLE 13-1. *Decision table for four-tape merge-sort.*

ten out, and switch to the inactive output tape when neither input will fit into the sequence on the active output tape—are listed at the bottom of the stub. After each set of actions is completed, the action path returns to the beginning of the table to process the new set of inputs. In actual practice, the complete sorting process would need some tests and actions for the end-of-file conditions on one or both inputs, but such parts are omitted here for simplicity.

In Rule 1, INPUT-KEY-1, the smaller key, is larger than the prior key on the output tape; so INPUT-1 is written and a new record brought in to replace it. Since, in Rule 2, the input with the smaller key will not build the sequence on the output tape, the input with the larger key, which will fit, is written. Rules 3 and 4 cover the case in which neither input record belongs on the current output tape, so the processor switches to the other output tape and writes the input with the smaller key. Rules 5 and 6 are similar to Rules 1 and 2 except that INPUT-2 has the smaller key.

This simple table clearly specifies what actions to take for each set of conditions. It is unnecessary to trace the action path through a series of branches which would be true if flow charts were used. After all the conditions are identified for a particular set of inputs, the correct set of actions follows directly. This particular table is complete in that all possible rules are stated. Since there are three binary conditions, a complete table contains eight rules ($2^3 = 8$). Although the table shown appears to contain only six rules, each rule with a blank for one condition counts for two rules—one rule with a "yes" and one with a "no" for that condition—so the effective total is eight. For analyzing processes of this type, decision tables are likely to be clearer and more consistent than other means.

Three Tapes on First Pass. The merge-sorting example given above assumes that the items are originally stored on two tapes. If the items are on one tape, they are separated or dispersed in the first pass. Two items are read in and comparisons are made to build strings as before. The output of the first dispersion pass starting with one tape corresponds to the result obtained in the illustration involving two tapes. After the first pass, similar procedures are followed for subsequent merge passes.

The merge-sorting procedure described here uses only one item from each tape. A three-way comparison is made between these two items and the item just added to the sequence on one tape. In a processor with fast internal speeds in relation to input-output speeds merge sorting is faster, if more items can be compared at one time because longer strings can be built at each stage. The ultimate, for a machine with fast internal-operating speed and large storage, might be to put all items in storage, sort them into one sequence, and write them in one pass.

Available storage may be filled with the items to be sorted, and later refilled as items are written out in sequence. In this way, the length of each string, counting both key and record, can be about twice as big as the available storage on the first pass. Developing longer strings on the first pass reduces the number of passes required, but increases the number of comparisons. The number of items handled simultaneously depends on available storage, record length, number of tape units, input-output speeds, and programming complexities. Input-output speeds become crucial when data are read in and out through many passes.

More Inputs, Fewer Passes.   Using more than two input tapes permits building sequences faster and reduces the number of passes required for the case where only two inputs are available. With n input tapes (and n is two or more), each pass builds longer strings so that the number of sequences on all the tapes is divided by n. Sorting is complete, of course, when only one string remains. The exact number of passes required depends on the arrangement of data before the sorting operation starts.

The easiest sorting problem occurs when checking the sequence of data from cards sorted into sequences and converted to tape for further processing. The first processor operation may check the sequence of data on tape because of the risk that some cards were out of sequence before conversion. Each tape starts through the merge-sorting procedure and if the input is in sequence, only one output string is obtained, and the sequence is checked. If the input is out of sequence because cards were not correctly sorted before conversion, two or more output strings are obtained from the first pass. Additional passes are then required to build one sequence.

Digital Sorting.   Records on magnetic tape can also be sorted by the digital scheme—as described above for punched-card equipment. One plan is to use a single input tape and ten output tapes corresponding to the ten outputs of a punched-card sorter. On the first pass, items with the right-hand digit 0 are put on one tape, with 1 on another tape, and so forth. Outputs are consolidated in order from 0 to 9 and resorted on the next digit. When ten outputs are combined, the sequence is XXX00 to XXX99 where X represents any digit from 0 through 9. After three more passes, items with five-digit keys are in sequence from 00000 to 99999. One pass is required for each digit in the key regardless of the number of items, when one input and ten output tapes are used. If the key is short and the number of items large, digital sorting may be fastest.

Other Techniques

One approach to the problem of electronic sorting is to arrange items in sequence at an earlier stage—*pre-sorting*. Although this approach does not really solve the sorting problem, the idea of pre-sorting has some merit. Input data might be kept in order as they originate or be sorted before they are put on magnetic tape. Sequence checking might still be desirable, but it can be handled as part of the input-editing routine.

On-line and in-line data-flow plans also eliminate the need for internal sorting during processing since the original sequence of transactions is adhered to.

Items on magnetic tape might be converted to punched cards, sorted by conventional methods, and reconverted to tape for further processing. This scheme involves the cost and time of two conversions. It also increases the possibility of mistakes during sorting, for punched-card sorting is less accurate than processor sorting. Experience shows that one or more cards may be lost or a stack dropped or misplaced in some fashion when numerous cards are involved. Some people say it is impossible, or at least nearly so, to sort a huge number of cards into perfect sequence because too many things can go wrong in the process.

Some data-processing systems avoid sorting by using random-access storage. Data in the master file are quickly available by means of one of several plans. The key for an item may indicate where the record is located in storage. A *table look-up* or *index* may be used to find where a record is stored in order to obtain it. Another plan for placing items in storage and later finding them is to use the *item number* itself as a locator. Some calculations may be performed on the number; for example, squaring the identification number to get a random-like number and selecting the center digits. This approach will convert, say, twenty-digit identification numbers into four-digit numbers and facilitate compact storage.

System Selection

A system designer may want to minimize either the time or the cost of sorting. An efficient system depends on the equipment available, the sorting scheme employed, and the application involved. Important factors about the application are the number of items, length of record, and number of keys—since the items may have to be sorted several times on different keys. Also important are the sequence of the original data, the manner in which data are processed before and after sorting, the speed with which results are wanted, and other functions—editing or checking—that can be combined with sorting.

Sorting data on punched cards is slower, but may be less expensive, than on magnetic tape. Processor sorting is more nearly automatic than punched-card sorting. Less manual effort is involved, which reduces the risk of mistakes. Punched-card sorting may be preferable if data are already on cards and need be sorted only once.

Sorting data one time merely to count one type of item or resorting to accumulate another item is not necessary when a processor is used. Several items can be counted and accumulations made in one pass by the processor with the data arranged in any sequence.

After the data are analyzed, merge-sorting plans can be programmed to take advantage of any sequence already in the data, and partially-ordered data can be sorted with fewer passes than completely unarranged data. A study might show that a set of items wanted in ascending order is already in descending order. Inverting the sequence would be faster than sorting to rearrange, if it is possible to read the input tape while it is moving backwards and write the items out in the desired sequence on another tape, or more simply, merely to process the tape by read-reverse.

Digital sorting, on the other hand, ignores any order in the data and treats every set of items in the same way—any sequence that does exist is destroyed on the first pass. Digital sorting takes the same number of passes whether items are in the desired, inverse, or random order.

The number of merge-sorting passes depends on the number of items and their initial sequence, regardless of the length of the key. Digital sorting, on the other hand, depends on the length of the key, so that lengthy keys increase the number of digital-sorting passes.

An efficient balance is needed between the number of tape units, their arrangement for input and output, programming costs, and processor operating time. Having more input units reduces the number of merge-sorting passes but increases the number of processor comparisons and other operations on each pass. Each pass takes more machine time, but fewer passes are required. Generator routines can analyze the records and "generate" a sorting routine tailored to the application.

SUMMARY

This chapter discusses three major facets of business data processing: editing, file processing, and sorting. Editing during input operations increases the probability that the data are accurate and in suitable form for the processor. Input editing concentrates on getting input transactions into a suitable condition for processing.

Thereafter, the input, having been carefully edited during its first processing, ranks as part of the file; and tape-label checking alone is considered adequate for files, unless mistakes are discovered.

Input editing deals with the following facets: field content, accuracy of numeric data, completeness of data, code conversion, item sequence, data field-length, non-numeric symbols in numbers, internal consistency, and the correspondence of new data to data already in files. The first eight types of editing can be done in a pre-processing stage without reference to files, although specifications about the data format and the checking schemes are needed. Checking for correspondence between transaction data and files— say, customer's name and address are identical—requires, of course, availability of the master file.

Elaborate techniques are available for manipulating data on cards to do certain kinds of editing during conversion operations or during read-in to a processor. More often, satellite processors serve as general-purpose converters and editors for data before reaching the main processor. The main processor still performs any editing requiring availability of the master file.

Output editing focuses on the preparation of reports with content and format suited to the users' needs. This involves selecting desired data elements from files and making them readable for people, assigning data elements to appropriate reports, sorting items into sequence, developing major and minor classifications, calculating subtotals and totals, introducing titles and headings, deleting repetitious and distractive elements, and proving the number of items and their values against prior totals. Values in the output can be tested in terms of standards, actuals, or even reasonableness on an intuitive basis. Report generators, which the processor follows in compiling a report-writing program for later execution, facilitate report preparation.

File maintenance is the modification of a file to incorporate additions, deletions, and transfers. Examples are additions to an approved stock list, deletion of discontinued items, transfers between warehouses, and substitution of new facts for old. Inputs for file maintenance are a master file, new changes, pending changes and, of course, a processor program. Outputs are an updated master file, change lists, pending changes, and mismatches. The number of records within a file can be controlled, since the prior number of records, plus records introduced, minus records deleted, equals the current number of records.

File processing is the modification of a file to incorporate changes involving arithmetical operations. A processor program controls operations to read in transactions and master-file records, compare them for stock-number identity, update active stock records and write out a new master file consisting of both active and inactive records. File updating for random-access storage is easier than for tape records because transactions need not be sorted into sequence; and each updated record merely occupies its same space. A variety of transactions can be processed against a file in one run because the transaction-type identifier directs the processor to go to the correct subroutine in the program. Calculation, indirect addressing, and other schemes are used to select the desired part of the program. File maintenance and file processing are often done together.

Preliminary processing is useful, or even vital, in some situations to determine what action to take. For example, a trial pass of all orders against stock files may be needed to develop decision rules about how to fill customers' orders. Then it is possible to process the orders against the file to update it and prepare shipping documents.

The maintenance and processing of magnetic-tape files usually involves recopying the whole file each time some records are changed, but some processing schemes accumulate changes for a few cycles and then rewrite the whole file. Interesting problems arise concerning how long to keep files to enable reconstruction of files lost through erroneous processing at the next cycle and to make analyses for unexpected questions at any time in the future.

Classification of a transaction in terms of the program or file needed for processing—as payroll, stock transactions or the collection and payment of money—is often done before sorting. *Sorting* consists of arranging items into sequence on their keys—fields of characters used to identify or locate an item. Any data element in a record—part number, size, or location—may be used as a key. Records may be sorted on one individual key or on two or more keys—one major and one minor. Commonly-used sorting schemes are block, digital, comparison, and merge sorting. Punched-card equipment uses a digital plan and also *block* to break up large quantities of cards into manageable quantities. Processors generally use the comparison and merge-sorting schemes.

A processor merge-sorts by reading items held in external storage, comparing them in internal storage, and writing them out in longer strings. The process is repeated in succeeding passes until one continuous string is developed. The number of passes required is related to the number of items sorted, regardless of the length of the key. Merge-sorting often uses two or more tapes for input and two or more tapes for output. Satellite processors are useful for sorting if the main processor is heavily loaded and the volume of special types of work is high. High-speed sorting of records in disk storage is possible by using multiple-access arms according to the "cylinder" concept, in which the read-write heads handle all records in all the tracks in one reading position before moving to a new position.

The selection of equipment and sorting scheme depends partly on whether the objective is to minimize the cost of sorting or the time required. Important factors in system selection are the number of items, length of key, length of record, sequence of original data, processing required before and after sorting, available time, and whether other editing or processing functions can be combined with sorting. Sorting with electronic processors is faster and more accurate than punched-card sorting, but it may be more expensive unless the equipment, sorting scheme, and application are closely attuned.

PART V
PRINCIPLES OF
PROCESSING SYSTEMS

14
Accuracy, Control, and Auditing

The quality of data and information can be described and measured in terms of accuracy, timeliness, predictability, relevance for decision-making, and the consequences of use. These features determine the usefulness of information for management purposes and are important for the design and operation of a data-processing system. Certain steps are necessary in developing a data-processing system to assure that the results produced will have the desired qualities. This chapter deals with accuracy, control, and auditing for a data system. The following chapter deals with timeliness, predictability, and relevance of output for decision-making.

ACCURACY

Accuracy is defined here as the long-run ratio of correct answers to total answers that comprise information—in short, its reliability. For example, information that reports the real situation as condition A ten times when in fact it is condition A nine times and condition B once has an accuracy of 0.9. The degree of accuracy required for information to be useful may vary from being extremely high to being only a rough approximation of the facts. A person often expects his bank to keep his account to the exact penny—banks, furthermore, encourage an aura of infallibility—although he may have trouble keeping track of the simple fact of whether his balance is overdrawn. The bank is expected to know exactly which one of many conditions—x dollars and y cents—his bank account has; whereas he may operate on a binary basis—account *overdrawn* or *not overdrawn*. The difficulties of maintaining a high degree of accuracy grow with the number of possible conditions that are to be reported, and more care is needed at all stages from data origination through reporting to achieve that desired degree.

Accuracy is, in simple terms, the condition of being accurate. Accuracy may mean the precision or amount of detail in a datum. The number ten may mean exactly 10 if integers are intended, or any number between 9.50 and 10.49 if decimal fractions are permitted. Details may be dropped by expressing items in large units— tons instead of pounds—or by dropping digits in order to round to the nearest dollar or nearest thousand dollars. *Precision* exactly defines limits beyond which an item cannot fall. *Accuracy,* on the other hand, defines limits beyond which an item probably will not fall—the degree of dependability in a datum, or, statistically speaking, the standard deviation of a datum. Although a person's bank statement and checkbook stubs are probably kept with the same degree of detail and precision—to the nearest penny—there is usually a lower degree of accuracy in the latter. An organization usually knows the total amount of accounts receivable more accurately than it knows the value of inventory. The costs of determining inventory value may force the organization to stop short of the absolute in pursuing accuracy. The retail inventory scheme, for example, uses the ratio of cost to selling price for merchandise bought to convert inventory on hand at selling price back to a calculated cost. The use of ratios indicates that the loss of accuracy in finding the cost of inventory is probably more than balanced by the reduction in expense from not keeping detailed costs. Taking physical inventories periodically reflects the economies of counting what is on hand rather than keeping detailed records. If records are kept, errors creep in and inventories are taken to reconcile the records with reality or to displace the records and start afresh.

Results may differ from true values because of human mistakes, errors in the calculation plan, or malfunctions in equipment. Inaccuracies can arise at any stage from data origination to report preparation. People can misunderstand or misread original data and make mistakes in operating typewriters and keypunches to prepare data for input. Instruction routines may have errors in logic that make some or even all results erroneous. Even when most cases are being handled correctly, others that are not anticipated may give erroneous results. Equipment malfunction can be either repetitive or intermittent and either easy or difficult to detect.

The Need for Accuracy

Accurate reports for operating and management purposes are needed because of the degrading effect of inaccurate reports on operating results. Accurate reports serve as the foundation for sound decision-making, whereas inaccurate reports may, and frequently do, lead to faulty decisions. The need for accuracy depends on the user and the situation. More accuracy is warranted, if a higher margin of inaccuracy—reporting condition A when in actuality it is condition B, and vice versa—is likely to cause the user to make a different decision. But in some cases, the margin of inaccuracy may have little bearing on the outcome. Assume that a stock item is reordered when the quantity on hand and on order declines to 1000 units. If 2000 units are on hand, the decision is the same—do not reorder—whether 1001 (apart from anticipation orders) or 1,000,-000 units are reported available. In such a case, a large margin of inaccuracy between actual and reported availability—ranging from minus 50 per cent to plus hundreds—does not affect the reorder decision. On the other hand, when the true quantity is 1010, an inaccuracy of even 1 per cent leads to an incorrect decision since a reported quantity of 1000 triggers a reorder.

Figure 14-1 suggests the relationship between the accuracy of

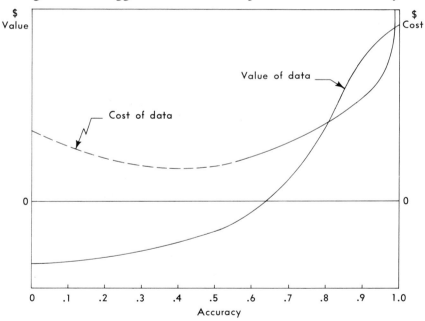

FIGURE 14-1. *Value, cost, and accuracy of results.*

information and its value for management. Value is small or negative when accuracy is low. That is, if prior reports have been correct, inaccurate information may be more likely to lead to profit-losing decisions than would a complete lack of information. The value of information increases rapidly as the degree of accuracy increases, for the more nearly accurate information is, the more it facilitates correct decisions. But the value of information probably levels off as near-perfect information is achieved because decision-making is not sensitive to slight improvements in the range of near-perfect accuracy.

How Much Accuracy

The optimal degree of data-system accuracy depends on both the costs of obtaining and the value of having that accuracy. In general, for any data-processing system, costs increase with higher degrees of accuracy, although low degrees of accuracy lead to higher costs because of the resultant chaos and the drastic steps required to cope with the chaos. The nature and causes of inaccuracies are discussed later, but some cost implications of increasing the degree of accuracy can be discussed here.

The best methods for achieving a high degree of accuracy are those that eliminate most errors when they first occur and that later detect and correct the ones remaining. Many practical schemes for handling both types of errors are based on partial or complete duplication of operations to increase the accuracy of results. The accuracy of data origination is commonly verified by repetition. A check-digit associated with each number or a parity-bit associated with each character increases the probability of originating and maintaining data accuracy. Message numbering at each stage helps ensure that any message entering the system goes through the communication network and reaches its logical conclusion. Processor routines are checked for logic and test-checked with simulated or real data to debug them. Duplicate circuitry or programmed checks, or even both, are used to detect malfunctions in equipment. Balancing and proof-schemes are commonly used to ensure accuracy in manual or mechanical accounting systems; more elaborate plans are used with automatic processing systems.

The steps outlined above for improving the accuracy of system output also increase processing costs. Additional precautions are required to increase the accuracy from 0.7 to 0.8 to 0.9, etc. The precautions required—and the costs—are likely to grow rapidly as the degree of accuracy increases from 0.98 to 0.99, 0.999, etc., because a broader range of precautions must be applied more intensively to reduce the incidence of inaccuracy from 2 in 100, to 1 in 100, 1 in 1000, etc. Figure 14-1 *suggests* the relationship between the cost of processing data and the accuracy of results. Costs increase sharply as the accuracy increases from about 0.95 onward. Much of the cost increase arises from the trouble involved in organizing and policing data origination, transcription, communication, and processing. Even though a smooth curve is drawn, certain step functions or breaks are likely to occur. For example, keypunchers may increase their accuracy from 0.95 to 0.99 accuracy merely by being more careful. To increase to 0.999 may require verification or an entirely new approach to input preparation. For example, some companies type lists of data and, after sight checking, run the lists through a character reader to convert them to machine-processable form. Occasional requirements for extreme accuracy have led to the preparation of *five* independent sets of input data and use of the processor to compare them and indicate discrepancies for correction. Clearly, costs increase rapidly when trying to eliminate the last mistake in 10,000 or 100,000 characters.

For most of the lower range of accuracy, the value of output is probably below the cost of processing the data and producing the output. Excess of cost over value means that the results are not worth the costs of producing them. Above an accuracy of 0.8 or so, the value of output probably goes above the processing costs and rapidly exceeds it. The most desirable degree of accuracy is reached when the value exceeds cost by the greatest difference. The optimum accuracy is probably close to, but slightly below, 1.0 for most business situations, and costs are likely to increase very sharply as output accuracy is pushed much beyond 0.995. It will be recalled that these value and cost relationships for accuracy of output are generalized and do not apply to particular cases.

INACCURACIES AND REMEDIES

Errors, mistakes, and malfunctions are different factors in giving incorrect results. An error is the difference between the accurate quantity and its calculated value that arises because of the numerical methods used. A mistake is a human blunder that occurs in program preparation, coding, data transcription, and processor operations. A malfunction is a failure in equipment operation.

Errors

Rounding errors, such as when the average unit cost of a stock item is treated as $467.37 instead of $467.375, are caused by the finite lengths of processor operating elements or the logic of the processing scheme. The error from rounding is relatively more important for short numbers, say of one or two digits, than for long numbers, say of six or eight digits. The most commonly-used rounding scheme—add 5 to the right of the last digit to be retained, make any carry, and drop unwanted digits—may introduce a large error. For example, workers in a factory may report job time to the nearest half hour. Reported times of 0.5, 1.5, and 2.5 hours are rounded to 1, 2, and 3 hours by the usual rounding rule. Either more sophisticated rules are required for rounding or it should be postponed by retaining more digits throughout the operations than are wanted in the final answer.

Addition of two numbers may yield a total that exceeds the capacity of a word in storage. One remedy is to test for occurrence of overflow after performing the addition and, if it occurs, shift both numbers one position to the right before repeating the operation. If overflow is detected, the net effect of correction is to discard the right-hand digit. Alternatively, the partial result before overflow occurred may be useful; it can be saved and calculations started afresh.

Sometimes it is necessary to use double-precision arithmetic to obtain more digits in the answer than seems possible with fixed-length storage locations and arithmetic registers. Operands longer than a processor word are split into two parts, placed in adjoining storage locations, and treated as semi-independent operands. The results of calculations are first stored in separate words and then joined together to yield a precise answer. For example, suppose the numbers 42,864 and 75,793 are to be added in a processor with fixed word-length storage that, for simplicity, is assumed to be three characters. Using double-precision arithmetic, each data word is split into two words for storage: 42,864 becomes 042 and 864; 75,793 becomes 075 and 793. First, the 864 is added to 793 to get 1657. Next, the 657 is stored and the 1, which appears as an overflow digit, is retained. The sum of 042 and 075 is 117 plus the overflow 1, giving 118. An overflow occurring when the left-hand parts are added may be handled by the usual remedy of shifting all operands one position to the right and repeating the operation. The two parts of the sum are then put together to get 118,657. In tabular form, double-precision addition is as follows:

Numbers	Split into two operands		
42,864	042	864	
75,793	075	793	
	117	1657	*Separate sums*
	1 ← ———————		*Add right part over-*
	118	657	*flow to left-hand part*
	118,657		*Join parts to get total*

Double-precision operations can also be used for subtraction, multiplication, and division. The disappearance of significant digits when taking the difference of two numbers that are about the same size—for example, $123,479 - 123,456 = 23$—demands care in order to keep the desired degree of precision in the remainder. It is easy to treat the remainder as zero, when digits are shifted off the right to avoid overflow so that rounding destroys whatever precision the answer had. The sequence of performing arithmetical operations affects the precision of an answer. Multiplication should be done before division, when possible, to retain precision.

The numbers used for arithmetical operations in accounting, inventory, and related applications seldom exceed the length of processor elements or storage. On the other hand, in statistical or operations-research calculations, long numbers frequently arise requiring caution to obtain suitably precise answers. The loss of precision in business processing due to the computational methods used may be important only where numbers are shortened too much in order to pack several items into one processor word.

When deciding how many digits to use for an item, the programmer should first check the degree of precision necessary in the results as specified, preferably, by the output user or, second, by the systems analyst. The effect of a certain error can be determined by tracing through the numerical operations, which may indicate that it is sometimes imperative to increase the precision of both input data and numerical computing methods. In other cases, less precision is tolerable so that fewer digits in the data and some short cuts in processing are permissible.

Mistakes

Mistakes are human foibles that result in incorrect data-processor instructions or manual operations. Mistakes in transcribing input data and instructions into machine-readable form may be detected by verifying key-punching or tape-writing operations. Totals developed in an earlier stage of processing are often useful for checking the accuracy of input data. Mistakes in punching a program may be discovered from printed copies of the card data. The original programmer or another one may study a program and trace through test cases to isolate mistakes, for desk-checking often discloses many programming mistakes. Mistakes that cause the processor to stop before completing the program include the following types:

1. Invalid operation codes
2. Incorrect instruction addresses
3. Arithmetical operations on alphabetic characters
4. Untested overflow

Other types of mistakes may not halt execution but allow the program to continue beyond the instruction containing the mistake. For example, a jump instruction with an incorrect address may transfer program control to a fragment of some previous program left in the machine or to an unexpected part of the present program. Many instructions may be executed before the processor encounters an instruction or data word that halts operations. Mistakes that may yield the wrong answer without halting program execution are:

1. Input data inaccuracies
2. Incorrect (but legal) operation codes or addresses in instructions
3. Misalignment of decimal points in numbers operated on arithmetically
4. Logic mistakes in program because of incorrect solution method

Built-in checks and program tests are necessary to detect mistakes that give wrong answers without halting operations. A typical program test is a special operation to determine whether an intermediate result is within specified limits. For example, weekly gross pay can be computed and then tested whether it is a positive amount but less than $200. Amounts outside the limits of 0 and $200 may point to a mistake in decimal point (for instance, 450 hours instead of 45.0) or in logic. When a check number, such as a total, is available from a prior operation, it is useful to program a zero-balance check to find whether the newly computed total minus the prior total equals zero. If the difference between the check numbers is zero, the program continues; otherwise, a segment of the program can be repeated, the occurrence of the failure to check can be printed on the supervisory console, or processor operations halted, as desired.

Testing a processor program for a business application involves using data for which the solution is either known or can be determined. One fairly common test is to run the program in parallel with an existing system long enough to detect and eliminate discrepancies. In some cases, only part of the data need be processed in parallel, but in others all data should be handled both ways for an extended period. Devising a thorough test for all parts of the program is sometimes a major task, but since program testing also serves as a training and testing ground for personnel, the time spent is probably justified.

Malfunctions

A malfunction is a failure in equipment operation. Some malfunctions are detected automatically by the processor and will either transfer control to a special routine or halt operations. Other malfunctions can be detected only through checks included in the program. Malfunctions are rare in properly-operating equipment, but a high fraction of those that do occur plague input and output operations. The gain or loss of a pulse results in an invalid character code being transmitted. A parity-code scheme, as discussed in Chapter 2, is generally used to detect invalid characters. The machine stops and turns on an indicator light to show the nature of the malfunction. Some processors use the parity-bit scheme with data on cards or tape but drop it in internal storage, since the risk of losing a bit in internal storage is small. Other processors are designed with the opposite approach of using parity-bits internally but not on cards or tape.

Tape-reading malfunctions are often transient, so that a second or third attempt at reading is satisfactory. Some processors provide for automatic rereading of tape, if the first attempt does not pass the parity test. Input cards are read at two stations in the card reader and the data rejected if there is any discrepancy. Editing devices on input-output units may also perform special checks to determine whether a numerical field contains any alphabetic data or if a sign is missing.

Malfunctions occurring during output have more serious implications than during input. Faulty tape or card output may not be discovered until the tape is used in the next processing cycle, which may be an hour, day, or week later. To guard against malfunctions during output operations, another reading station may read the actual content of cards or tape and compare them with the content of storage or the write buffer for identity *echo-checking*. This reading test must be passed for each card punched or tape block written, else operations are halted. Other schemes determine whether the data just written will pass the parity test, or whether the number of holes punched in each column of a card (or the complete card) matches the *hole count* for the data supposed to be punched in the card.

Some processors check parity each time a word is handled inside the machine, whereas others have data checks at key points in a program. Further, at short intervals, say, of five seconds, contents of all storage locations may be tested for parity. If the test fails, the program returns to a prior checkpoint where the contents were stored for use in case of subsequent malfunction. Special checking programs, also called *engineering decks,* are commonly used to check the operation of all instructions and units just after power is turned on when malfunctions are most likely to occur.

Parallel tests built into the equipment for selected operations are outside a programmer's control. Serial tests may be included in the equipment or devised by programmers when writing programs. Selected types of operations can be tested by two kinds of schemes designed into processors:

1. Parallel testing involves simultaneous execution of an instruction along two paths in the equipment followed by an equality test.
2. Serial testing involves one set of circuits used to repeat an operation and perform an equality test. For example, the product of 345×987 minus the product of 987×345 can be tested for zero.

Malfunctions are rare and may occur once in many million or billion operations. Built-in checks are best suited to detecting malfunctions in business data processing. Frequently, the correct results for a business application are not known before processing is completed, although results for limited sample cases may be obtained by other means. Programming business applications may be so intricate that devising an alternate checking program—in effect, preparing two programs—to guard against malfunctions is inefficient. From the programmer's viewpoint, it is desirable to have the manufacturer design checking features into the equipment. Built-in checks increase effective processor speed by performing checking operations while executing a single program.

The alternate scheme of detecting malfunctions by programming —performing the essential features of an operation in two different ways—increases programming work and processor running time. As an example of a programmed check, it is suggested that the accuracy of multiplication be verified by a second multiplication involving slightly different numbers. Assume that the problem is to calculate inventory value for the following quantities and prices, first by a straightforward and then by a "proof-figure" scheme:

Stock number	Quantity	Price	Value
1234	4	2	8
8765	8	7	56
2391	3	19	57
	15		121

A proof-figure scheme for programmed checking of multiplication uses an artificial basis for either the price or quantity, so that different numbers are involved in the multiplication. Correction then eliminates the effect of the artificial base. By introducing an artificial price base of 20, the calculation is as follows:

Stock number	Quantity	Artificial basis	Price		Proof cost	Quantity proof cost
1234	4	20	—	2 =	18	72
8765	8	20	—	7 =	13	104
2391	3	20	—	19 =	1	3
	15					179

The quantity 15 multiplied by the artificial base of 20 gives a product of 300. The original value of 121 plus the proof cost of 179 totals 300, which proves the coincidence of the answer by two different program routes.

More important than the occasional incorrect results from malfunction is the risk that equipment may be nonoperational for several hours or longer during testing and repair. Down-time—representing the inability of equipment to operate—is likely to be high at first because of injury to equipment during shipping and the early breakdown of defective components. After the initial break-in period, most automatic data-processing equipment is extremely reliable. The availability of similar equipment nearby for emergency use on a reciprocal basis furnishes some protection against protracted down-time. Scheduling operations at 80 to 90 per cent of capacity, after allowing for preventive maintenance, permits making up most down-time. Priority applications may be kept on schedule by postponing less urgent jobs and new program check-out.

Errors, mistakes, and malfunctions are usually far less troublesome in automatic systems than in manual systems. Accuracy and reliability are higher in automatic systems because more emphasis is placed on systems design, "special case" treatment is minimized, "rush" handling is reduced, and there is less chance of human error.

Additional Capacity

It is generally thought that a well-designed system should be capable of producing perfectly accurate output—no discrepancy between the results obtained and the true results. Accuracy can be increased by providing enough capacity to handle both the message and the mistakes that arise—erroneous characters, dropped digits, lost messages, and transpositions. If a system with sufficient capacity is efficiently used, it is possible to detect and even to correct mistakes in data origination, transmission, calculation, and output. Increased capacity for accurate data processing can be obtained by using more sophisticated codes, more elaborate equipment, and better channels. In the final analysis, the question of the degree of accuracy warranted is answered by balancing the cost of achieving greater accuracy against the cost of using inaccurate results.

It is useful to explore how the concept of additional capacity can be applied to improve the accuracy of data during the input and communication phases by coping with uncertainties that arise. Examples of additional capacity are check digits, parity-bits, tape reread, echo-checking, check-read after write, proof-figures, and other schemes already described. The basic feature is that enough capacity devoted to processing data at each stage makes it possible to obtain almost any desired degree of accuracy in the output even though inaccuracies persist. To achieve extremely high degrees of accuracy a large fraction of total capacity may be devoted to detecting and correcting errors so that near-perfect accuracy is obtained either by selecting correct messages, or by correcting erroneous messages and discarding the redundant parts. As an example of the fraction of additional capacity, remember that one parity bit for each six-bit character is a 14 per cent redundancy. The capacity must be large enough at each stage to handle both the accurate and inaccurate components of the data. Systems designers have broad freedom in deciding what methods to use to provide additional capacity: more of the usual factors, a different combination of them, or entirely new factors.

Equipment and Labor for Input. Some input plans rely heavily on manual methods for getting data into processable form, while others make important use of equipment. The ratio of equipment to labor and commonly used input methods can be stated briefly as follows:

Ratio of equipment to labor	**Input methods**
Low	Key-punch for cards
	Tape-producing typewriter

Ratio of equipment to labor	**Input methods**
Intermediate	By-product data recorders
	Sensing marks in specified positions
	Tags attached to inventory items
	Cards in tub files
	Production recorders
	Point-of-sale recorders
High	Direct input of prior output in suitable form
	Character-reading devices

A *low ratio* of equipment to labor means that manual operations are important for preparing input. Two stages are used to get data into processable form. First, people write or type documents; second, they read documents and operate keyboards to punch cards or paper or write on magnetic tape.

An *intermediate ratio* of equipment to labor means that more equipment and less labor is used than in systems with a low ratio. The separate stages of preparing paper documents and converting them to a processable medium are telescoped into one operation. A single manual operation yields data in machine-processable form. By-product data recorders yield two outputs: a printed record considered essential for people and data in a form suitable for automatic processing. Mark-sensing schemes give visually readable and mechanically processable data in one manual operation, but emphasis is usually placed on the feature of automatic processability rather than on readability. Verified cards are mass-produced for attachment to items until they are used, when the cards are detached for processing. A tub file is convenient to store mass-produced cards until they are selected for processing. In some cases the cards are attached to items or kept in "pockets" near the items involved. Production recorders and point-of-transaction recorders may combine data from several sources: manual entries on keyboards; reproductions from cards, plates, or tags; and data set up automatically by equipment and transmitted to a central recorder or processor by communication channels.

A *high ratio* of equipment to labor means that the system is essentially automatic. Almost no labor is required to use the output of one stage of processing as input at the next stage. Punched-card, punched-tape, and magnetic-tape output can be used as input at the next stage. The ratio of equipment to labor is also high for character-recognition devices. Such equipment recognizes or reads characters and converts the signal to a form convenient for further processing.

Different ratios of equipment to labor in input systems have implications for the accuracy of input data. Although everyone seems to believe that his data-processing system is based on good input data, careful analysis often shows that input data are far from accurate. The problem of getting accurate input data can be attacked from two directions. One approach is to increase the manual effort; the other to increase the use of equipment and minimize the manual work of input preparation. Both have the common feature of more concentrated effort on the same data. Each approach for reducing the margin of inaccuracy—the difference between actuality and the reported result—deserves brief consideration.

Manual operations used in preparing input data may be repeated to detect errors. One method is to *repeat the manual operations* involved in going from a readable to a processable form. Mechanical comparison of the results of two manual operations discloses discrepancies to be eliminated. Data verified in this fashion are far more accurate than those resulting from manual operations alone. Another way to verify the accuracy of input data is to read the results against the original source. Experience indicates that duplicated manual operations are more effective than visual comparison for disclosing mistakes. Accuracy can be greatly improved, some analysts say, by making the originators of input data responsible for their accuracy; people are more careful about the accuracy of data they originate if they must eliminate mistakes when discovered.

Input data accuracy can be improved by *more intensive use of equipment*. Control totals developed in an early stage are used to guard against mistakes in input operations. Control totals for dollar amounts or quantities are useful as part of the data. Other control totals—"nonsense" or "hash" totals of unit prices or even code numbers—may be developed solely to improve processing accuracy. In such schemes, the total is recomputed at the next stage and compared with the prior total to detect mistakes. A variation of the control total scheme is to include a check-digit calculated according to certain rules for catalogue numbers, or other identifying numbers. A simple rule is to attach a digit to a number so that all digits, including the check-digit, add to a multiple of ten. More elaborate rules are required if digits are likely to be switched. Each alternate digit, starting with the right-hand digit, may be multiplied by two before adding and attaching a tens-multiple check-digit.

Equipment can be used to edit input data to detect simple mistakes, such as a double-punch or no-punch, in each column of a card. Other input media can be edited in a similar fashion. More elaborate input editing can determine the plausibility of data, and new data can be compared with prior data to disclose unusual changes or variations from past patterns.

Communication Schemes.   Some schemes used for achieving a high degree of accuracy in communication deserve some elaboration here. Various methods are used to try to assure that the message received is identical to the one transmitted. The idea of transverse and longitudinal parity-bits or check sums may be extended to include duplicate transmission of part or all of a message. For example, numbers may be repeated after the body of the message, as is done for commercial telegrams. Numbers may be given in numerals and also spelled out, as in bank checks—"270.30" and "two hundred seventy dollars and thirty cents." Each of these schemes attempts to overcome "noise" by including enough redundancy or repetition in the message so that it can be understood even though some of the message is garbled. A check that is written "230.70" and "two hundred seventy dollars and thirty cents" is valid and will be paid according to rules that specify the precedence of letters over numerals in case of discrepancy.

Some communication schemes increase redundancy still further by means of duplicate transmission in opposite directions. Point A transmits to point B which then retransmits to point A, where the messages making the round trip are compared for discrepancies. This is an example of the *transponder* scheme for assuring accurate transmission by means of an immediate response from the receiver. Quick detection of mistakes in transmission, as reflected by discrepancies, increases the effective amount of data transmitted because equipment and line malfunctions are detected as soon as they occur and can be corrected. Accuracy of accepted messages can approach very close to 1.0 even though a substantial fraction of defective messages is sent. Transmission is repeated if the trouble is only temporary. If repeated transmission does not give two messages that check as identical, the equipment or lines need servicing. The transponder scheme, like other plans for trying to get accurate transmission, has certain costs associated with it. Here a return circuit is used as much as the forward circuit, if the transmission speeds are the same in both directions and the response includes the whole message to give a redundancy rate of 100 per cent or more of the messages accepted.

Two general points are worth considering. The first point is that these two schemes, and all others for improving the accuracy of data transmission, increase costs because more capacity—better equipment, lines, etc.—is required to accommodate noise *and* to transmit the message. A second point is that there is never complete assurance that the message received is identical to the message as it originated, there are only varying degrees of probability that the input and output messages are identical. In other words, perfectly accurate transmission is probably impossible to achieve.

Arithmetic and Control Operations.   Some processors have additional capacity to cope with built-in inaccuracies occurring in arithmetic and control operations. A highly reliable processor requires a method, first, for detecting malfunctions that occur and, second, for correcting them in one of various ways:

1. The processor checks each arithmetical operation or transfer in a way likely to catch most malfunctions, then repairs itself and continues operations.
2. The processor automatically detects most malfunctions, then repeats operations if erroneous results are detected, and continues.
3. Automatic malfunction detection circuits cause the processor to stop so that the operator can take appropriate action.
4. Every problem is run at least twice and results are compared. Diagnostic tests run at intervals verify that the processor is operating correctly at that point. Maintenance and problem-result correction are taken upon detecting a malfunction.
5. Complete reliance is placed upon programmed checking to insure correct results since no automatic checking is included. Diagnostic tests, including marginal testing, are used to indicate correct operation of the processor.

The third scheme—automatic malfunction detection circuits—is used in some processors and increases central processor cost about 25 to 30 per cent, although less for the entire system. The fourth scheme is widely used for punched-card equipment and is sometimes advocated for computers. The fifth scheme—complete reliance on programmed checking—depends on the nature of the application. Mathematical applications may be ingeniously checked for less than a 30 per cent increase in programming cost and running

time. Business applications, on the other hand, may require extensive checking that increases programming and operating costs by
two-thirds. Furthermore, some applications are not amenable to
programmed checking so that the merits of programmed and built-in
checking are not directly comparable.

Electronic and Other Systems. Despite the precautions available to increase the accuracy of electronic data-processing systems,
they sometimes appear to have a lower degree of accuracy than
other systems. This seems paradoxical considering that new systems are carefully designed and that electronic equipment is much
more reliable—both logically and arithmetically—than manual or
punched-card systems. Actually, the incidence of errors, mistakes,
and malfunctions in an electronic system is probably lower than in
the prior system. But inaccuracies arise to plague an electronic
data-processing system for various reasons:

1. Discrepancies existing between different files maintained by the
   organization, if not reconciled during file conversion, are disclosed
   for the first time during file consolidation.
2. Many errors discovered and handled quietly and informally by
   people throughout the prior system might have been overlooked
   when designing the new system.
3. A data-processing system integrates control and correction procedures with routine processing and stops the diffusion of errors
   throughout the whole processing stream.
4. Data-processing systems apparently are exposed to a higher risk
   of inaccuracy because of more careful processing logic and the
   use of output for operating control that quickly discloses inaccuracies.
5. The conversion phase from the prior system to the new system is
   fraught with difficulties and risks of error because it is a one-
   time job occurring during a rush period.
6. Insufficient feedback from the operating organization to the data
   processing system may keep it from reflecting corrections and
   changes made informally by operating personnel.

CONTROL

More than just accurate reporting—making reports conform to
reality—is involved in controlling operations. The results of operations must be appraised in terms of the goals that the company is
trying to reach. Determination of some, and perhaps many, facts
about the results of operations are subject to differences arising from
methods of gathering facts and interpreting them. Also, possibilities

of manipulation arise because people, ranging from the president to the office boy, have an interest in both what happens and how it is reported.

Internal control methods reflect the organizational arrangement and data-processing methods in use at any time. Important changes now occurring in data-handling methods warrant a review of internal control objectives and methods to see how data-processing operations fit into the over-all control scheme. *Internal control within a business comprises the plan of organization and coordinate methods and measures to safeguard assets, check the accuracy of accounting and other types of data, promote operational efficiency, and encourage adherence to prescribed managerial policies.* Internal control and auditing encompass far more than merely safeguarding assets. Operating efficiency can be improved through accurate data and reports to facilitate measurement of adherence to prescribed managerial policies. A system of internal control and auditing extends beyond the functions of the accounting and financial departments to include budgetary control, standard costs, reports and analyses, training programs for personnel, and an internal control staff to assure management of the adequacy of procedures and their implementation. Management is responsible for devising, installing, and supervising a system of internal control and auditing that is adequate to promote operational efficiency, encourage adherence to prescribed managerial policies, ensure accurate and reliable operating data, and safeguard assets. In short, all information used to develop operating results of a company should be covered.

Internal Control and Audit Techniques

Accurate reflection of operating results in accounts and reports is fundamental to appraising the organization and analyzing performance. The essence of internal control and auditing is to determine the accuracy of reports and improve their quality as required. The possibility of errors exists at every stage. Errors, at best, result in inaccurate reports and, at worst, may be related to fraud. Internal auditors guard against errors by sampling to analyze operations and determine that records conform to policies in the following ways:

1. Limit origination of transactions, as reflected by signed authorization papers, to people specified in the organization chart.
2. Divide duties among originator, custodian, and recordkeeper to reduce the manipulative ability of any one person to omit or modify the record for a transaction.
3. Analyze transactions for logical conformance to approved pro-

cedures of classification, use of data in files, timing, and for ultimate consequences, to make sure that none of these transactions die en route.

4. Achieve accuracy in basic arithmetic operations, stage-to-stage recopying, and files maintained for operations: inventory, customers, wage rates, suppliers, etc.

5. Investigate periodically to reconcile records with actuality and to eliminate discrepancies.

Documents.   Documents have long been the foundation of business operations and records. They are, of course, fundamental to internal control procedures now in use. Critical documents are controlled at every stage from preparation to disposition. Control is achieved by pre-numbering, assigning forms to responsible people, issuing through approved channels, signing or initialing at each stage to indicate responsibility, duplicating arithmetical operations, dividing duties to eliminate complete control by one person, reconciling at one or more stages, and safeguarding at disposition.

But readable documents have important deficiencies that are often overlooked. Documents prepared in advance are subject to mishandling even though pre-numbered. Signed or initialed documents serve only as *prima facie* evidence. People are not always good at preparing, issuing, reading, or using paper documents. Often they will tend to fill in documents incorrectly, send them through wrong processing paths, or lose or misplace them, do arithmetic inaccurately, and individually perform such a small fraction of total procedures that too many people are involved.

Audit Trail for Documents.   A large fraction of internal and external audit procedures is devoted to determining whether people do, in fact, follow prescribed procedures. Original transaction input is linked to report output via documents, journals, ledgers, and summaries. These make up an audit trail that permits tracing transactions forward to reports. Conversely, reports can be traced back to original transactions. The small discrete steps of manual processing of documents yield a visual trail that auditors can trace to tie output to input. There is the disadvantage that, because of the small steps involved, people are able to manipulate results at any stage so that extra precautions are required to ascertain and control the degree of manipulation.

Electronic Processing Methods

Electronic data-processing methods are different in several important respects from manual methods as far as internal control is concerned.

Procedures and Programs. The operating procedures books, whether current or semi-obsolete, are an important factor in flow charting and in preparing processing routines. Intensive checking and testing under varied conditions eliminate most mistakes that arise during conversion from approved procedures to instruction routine. Furthermore, mistakes in logic and inefficient procedures in existing methods are often uncovered and corrected during programming. Programs for processing data are detailed, explicit instructions for electronic equipment. Processing rules are used at every stage instead of merely being listed in operating guides for people to try to remember and apply when they process data. Equipment follows the processing rules precisely even though the rules may lead to illogical results, unless such an outcome is anticipated and some provision made for dealing with it.

The formidable task of modifying or rewriting operating programs for processors gives some assurance that individuals will not collusively alter programs. The possibility of procedure and program manipulation is further reduced by program documentation, approval procedures, test routines, monitoring schemes in the form of operating schedules and logs, control limits, and message counts.

Reliability. People are apt to make several mistakes in a thousand arithmetical operations, but electronic equipment malfunctions once in many million operations. Nearly error-free results are obtained in a variety of ways: by considering reliability during initial design of equipment, duplicating circuitry to perform operations in parallel and compare the dual results, operating components at a fraction of their rated strength, simulating adverse operating conditions during testing periods, including a parity bit with each character to guard against malfunction, repeating arithmetical operations, and reading after writing to ensure that actual output matches computer results. Built-in checking features add to equipment cost, but they need not affect the user either for preparation or for operating time.

In addition to built-in reliability of equipment, instruction programs are designed with features that further guard against erroneous results. The programs edit input data for content and test for plausibility, check for origination authority, count records and control sequences to guard against loss of transactions either inside or outside the equipment, develop operator routines to monitor human operators, maintain prior results several tape generations until succeeding results prove satisfactory in actual use, and perform arithmetical operations in two ways and compare results for identity.

Programmed checks increase the accuracy of results, although both program preparation and processor operating time are increased.

Processing Span. The span of processing operations—the amount of processing done at one time with instructions and files—differs greatly for manual and electronic systems. Manual systems generate intermediate results—listings, schedules, and working sheets —as processing aids because processing ability is limited and transactions are handled one small stage at a time. Intermediate output at one stage serves as input at the next stage. The intermediate records are an integral part of the trail followed by auditors to trace the relationship between transaction input and record output.

The span of processing operations is much larger for systems relying on electronic equipment rather than people. More processing steps are performed when a transaction is handled. Intermediate results are available at fewer stages, and since the results are produced in the form best suited for input to the next processing stage, they may not be available for people to read. Intermediate results are sometimes printed out in readable form for precautionary purposes, but printed listings can be suppressed when output of one stage is satisfactorily handled as input at the next stage. Reducing the frequency and volume of intermediate results printed in readable form may at first trouble people responsible for internal control. One remedy, although not especially efficient, is to print intermediate results solely for their control purposes. A superior remedy is to adjust procedures to fit the new techniques and take full advantage of them.

Processing Control. The most likely possibility for controlling system accuracy is to modify internal control procedures to exploit the best features of the system and equipment. It is not necessary to examine the data-processing stream in detail to know what is happening; everyone uses sampling techniques. It is possible to find the "pulse" of operations and keep them under control in other ways than by means of detailed audit trails.

Three factors permit sound control without tracing transactions in detail: (1) instruction programs tested for logical and arithmetical accuracy to cover most situations and reject others; (2) equipment operating reliably enough to execute programs and process data to logical conclusions; (3) procedures covering proper usage of programs, files, and data that will monitor variations from plans.

Control can be achieved by analyzing programs, equipment reliability, and adherence to procedures. Controlled input data, correctly processed, must yield accurate output. The path of individual transactions and test cases can be traced to verify that the system is functioning as planned. Processing variability, so troublesome in manual systems because of the personal element and variability in following procedures, is virtually eliminated. Standardized processing has the virtue of producing results that are either valid or so badly mangled that difficulties are detectable fairly readily. Further, equipment does not have the inherent bias, as do some people, of manipulating results in its favor. In this regard equipment is neutral.

Controlling the flow of data through an electronic system corresponds to continuous processing operations in the chemical and petroleum industries. The processor and a program correspond to the network of pipes and related equipment that determine how inputs are handled to get desired outputs. For some purposes, each processing stage is analyzed; for other purposes, an over-all balance of outputs against inputs indicates whether operations are under control and meet standards.

It is sometimes thought that the data-processing center should operate as a service unit receiving data from other units, processing them, and producing necessary reports. The data-processing center does not originate information, but processes data it receives from others. Under such conditions, controls can be established over employees in the center to ensure accurate handling of the data and preclude fraudulent alterations. Procedures initiated in data-originating departments—payroll, production, and sales—are used to control results developed by the data-processing center. Variations discovered during processing operations are returned to originating departments for approval or investigation.

Origination of Data. Increasing the span of processing operations reduces the need for intermediate results in readable form. Original transaction documents are, from a broad viewpoint, merely intermediate between two processing stages and economies can be gained by changing the nature and use of original transaction documents. Readability of documents is only one factor among many that determine the economics of processing. Ability to keep data in the most economically processable form varies greatly for different situations. Internally produced data are more amenable to origination in the desired form than external data. But in a growing number of cases, data transferred between companies are in the form desired by the recipient for most efficient processing.

Old and New Problems

The form and content of internal control and audit procedures will evolve over time as recordkeeping methods change. A few hundred years ago "auditor" meant listener because recordkeepers and examiners could not read and write. Auditors *listened* to recitations of accounts. Written records replaced tally sticks and similar methods because of the increased processing efficiency and the density of storage. Auditors learned to read when recordkeepers learned to write. Similar changes will occur as electronic equipment and invisible records replace manual and punched-card operations and visible records.

Some Problems Disappear.   Some age-old internal control problems will decrease in importance or disappear. Management plans and operating procedures will be hampered less by such difficulties as the inability of operating personnel to comprehend and adjust to new requirements. Procedures will be embodied in flow charts and carefully tested instruction programs for equipment to follow without variation, if they can be followed at all. The occasional, and even frequent, variations from prescribed procedures that occur in manual systems will be minimized. The inaccuracies of manual arithmetical operations will cease to be a problem. Equipment using built-in circuitry and programmed steps for checking operations will eliminate the problem of arithmetical inaccuracies.

Input data can be screened for accuracy and plausibility before they are used. For example, programmed screening census of manufacturers' data on average sales price per unit disclosed such mistakes as stating units in pounds instead of tons and vice versa. High-low limits for average wage rates of, say, $4 and $.90 an hour can disclose erroneous input or calculation of gross pay in payroll applications. Limits of $200 or $50 might be used for screening total pay calculations. Programmed tests can reject incorrect input data for further investigation and correction. More important is the ability to reconstruct incomplete or even inaccurate data so that garbled input can be used rather than discarded. The screening, testing for plausibility, editing and reconstructing of defective input that is now done by people will soon be performed by sophisticated programs developed for data processors.

There is some danger in manual systems that transactions originate correctly only to disappear from the processing stream at a later stage. Document pre-numbering, proof or control totals, and message counts are useful to guard against loss of transactions recorded on discrete documents. Records on magnetic tape are less subject to loss than paper documents but the same control features to guard against loss can be used. New schemes to safeguard against loss of individual transactions are *hash totals* of letters and numbers not ordinarily totalled for operating purposes, proof totals, numbering original input messages and immediate checking for missing messages, sequence checks, and self-checking numbers.

Some operations, such as payroll preparation, are subject to rigorous operating controls. Program controls are more important for less rigorously controlled areas. The auditor wants to be sure that the control structure appears adequate in concept and in performance. Further, he tries to avoid plodding along making routine checks that are either being done or can be done more effectively in the normal flow of machine operations.

Reading and transcription errors are minimized by means of either built-in or programmed checking, or both. Input can be read twice and the signals from the two readings compared. If both agree, data are considered correctly read and are used. A parity bit is generally used with each character to detect malfunctions upon transfers. Corresponding to double reading on input, some form of reading after writing is used in output operations to compare actual with intended output. Operations are repeated to eliminate discrepancies or, upon repeated failure, to halt processing.

Operations monitoring is facilitated because processing procedures are an integral part of processing, not merely manuals on shelves for people to refer to occasionally. Tight control over instruction programs and their use minimizes variations from approved routines. Operating logs are useful to keep track of equipment operations, programs, files, and transactions being handled.

New Problems Arise.   New methods may eliminate many of the problems that existed with previous methods. New problems will arise, some foreseen but others unanticipated, and additional difficulties will occur during the transition period from old to new system. Internal auditors see three new risks arising. First, excessive reliance will be put on machine results as a substitute for judgment. Second, high-speed machines will produce stifling volumes of reports and records at each processing stage to maintain the usual audit trail, though some selectivity may be exercised and the volume of printed output reduced. Third, possible substitution of machine storage for intermediate accounting records will leave apparent gaps in the audit trail. To some extent, the second and third points are in conflict.

New equipment has probably been introduced at a faster rate than old procedures modified to fully exploit such equipment. Several early users of electronic equipment for payroll preparation did not make any radical changes in basic records from their punched-card procedures. In one company, for example, the permanent records of rates and deductions and the current records of clock cards, job tickets, and piece-work production records were originated, checked, and approved in the same form and manner as before. Processing control was achieved by use of significant totals of hours or pieces for all employees.

Partial or complete disappearance of intermediate results of processing in readable form will require other means to appraise the flow of data. New sampling and testing procedures will be used to determine what is happening. Such methods will, at first, seem indirect because they put greater reliance on equipment that follows different paths and in steps of different scope than the manual processing methods used. Familiarity with new processing methods will, in time, compensate for most of the lack of conventional audit trails and will help to develop new ones.

Origination of accurate input data will become critical because of the difficulty and cost of correcting mistakes if they are allowed to diffuse throughout the system. Although people will themselves make mistakes while handling data, they can be ingenious at detecting mistakes made by others and at working around errors in records. Detection and elimination of erroneous input data become more difficult as processing methods become more nearly automatic. The *prima facie* value of documents as evidence will probably decline with wider use of other means of substantiating transactions and tracing them back to originators whenever required. On-line transaction processing poses new control problems. When used in one or a few areas of a business, transactions are homogeneous and, for control purposes, processing operations correspond to batch processing in many respects. Widespread use of on-line processing within a business is likely to make operations so heterogeneous and programming so intricate that it will bear little or no relation to specialized processing of the batch or random-access type already in use. More experience with company-wide use of on-line processing is required before it will be possible to draw conclusions about its control implications.

AUDITING

The remainder of this chapter reviews auditing fundamentals from the viewpoint of the public accountant. It considers the impact of electronic methods on auditing methods and speculates on future developments. *Auditing* may be defined as a critical review by a person of the internal controls and accounting records of a business enterprise in order to express his opinion about the propriety of its financial statements. An auditor attempts to obtain enough information about the operating system and the records to express an informed opinion about the statements that are prepared. But auditing is more intuitive than scientific, despite much work in recent years on "scientific auditing" for selecting samples and drawing conclusions about the population.

Auditing Techniques

Auditing, as an art and profession, began over a hundred years ago or so when recordkeeping consisted primarily of manual methods using paper, and has developed increasingly during the past fifty years along with the advent of special-purpose office equipment. The widespread use of punched cards in recent decades seemed to have little impact on auditing procedures. The immediate question now is how much electronic techniques will affect auditing methods. Auditors have traditionally relied strongly on documents and records as source material to determine the accuracy of reports. Therefore, changes in data-processing methods, and especially those that upset the traditional availability of readable records, will eventually demand new auditing methods. Auditing methods can, for our purposes, be examined in three parts: systems design, system operation, and reliance on external evidence.

Auditors must examine systems design and operation of a system before relying on its outputs. External and internal auditors are likely to cooperate with systems designers to develop a reliable system for protective features to increase output accuracy.

People are certainly indispensable for originating transactions, keeping records, and maintaining custody of assets. However, the weaknesses as well as the strengths of people must be considered when designing a system. Both internal and external auditors continuously reappraise the internal control system to improve its efficiency by strengthening weak controls and reducing excessive controls. The character of the internal control system thus reflects company policies, managerial objectives, and the abilities of the people setting up and maintaining the system.

The control features designed for a data-processing system must be incorporated into the operating system in order for the features to be useful. An examination of the operations determines the implementation of control features, compatibility with operating methods, and the degree of control obtained. Systems can be examined at both the paper-design and actual operating stages. In order to reach an informed opinion about a system, auditors should have information about the following: over-all accuracy of the system's logic, adherence to system rules, responsibility for transactions, authenticity of data, errors of both omission and commission, arithmetical accuracy, and the possibilities of fraud.

Internal and external auditors seldom verify more than a small fraction of individual transactions. Instead, they place strong reliance on the ability of management and systems designers, the character of the data-processing system, and external evidence. They sample and test to determine whether the system operates as planned, or if not, the nature, extent, and consequences of variations. By several methods auditors obtain additional information outside the formal data-processing system. Company management signs certificates about inventory valuation and ownership, contingent liabilities, and other areas of which it has special knowledge. Third parties, such as banks, suppliers, and customers, are asked to confirm balances and, perhaps, specific transactions, to furnish independent evidence for appraising the accuracy of the data system.

Since manual and electronic processing methods have different operating characteristics and warrant individual audit approaches, their unique features deserve discussion.

Audit of Manual Records

There are several features about manual recordkeeping systems that make them easy to audit. Most important is the fact that the present generation of auditors "grew up" on manual systems through study and long experience. Manual systems rely upon paper documents that can be printed, numbered, signed, counted, and traced. Paper records prepared at each stage of processing bridge the gap between original transactions and final results. Since people handle only a small part of the over-all flow of data at one time, they have to communicate with other people working at the next stage. Such intermediate communications include journals, ledgers, trial balances, summaries, and working sheets. The small, discrete processing steps are reflected in paper yielding a visual trail traceable in an unbroken path from start to finish. The large number of people working in the processing stream facilitates detecting and correcting errors made in earlier stages. Put in different terms, there is enough redundancy in a manual system to discover many of the mistakes that occur. For example, a ledger contains essentially a rearrangement of the journal contents and, therefore, little new information. Responsibility for transactions, records, and asset custody can be separated, and even atomized, to achieve checks and balances important to internal control.

On the other hand, some properties of manual systems which facilitate making an audit also add to the problems of auditing. As stated earlier, people are liable to fill in documents incorrectly, send them through wrong processing paths, lose or misplace them, do arithmetic inaccurately, and individually perform such a small fraction of total operations that a lot of time is often spent picking up and laying down loose ends. Furthermore, the many small steps involved permit people to manipulate results, either accidentally or willfully.

Procedures for manual systems may be ambiguous enough to allow excessive latitude to circumvent them. Worse, variations occur during application because procedures are in books on the shelf while clerks must apply rules from memory supplemented only by occasional reference. Misapplications of rules have clear-cut costs in some cases, such as paying more taxes than required by correct interpretation of the law and rules, and using old price lists after changes occur. Mispricing losses can be severe during rising-price periods.

Individual documents are exposed to risk of loss or disappearance from the processing stream. Precautions are required to guard against improper origination, incorrect processing, and even reuse after the documents are supposedly invalidated or destroyed. Such risks necessitate elaborate schemes for pre-numbering, controlling by batches, and invalidating.

In short, manual systems have many features that facilitate their audit and control, but such features are obtainable only by duplication of work at the expense of increased costs and general inefficiency. It is difficult to distinguish between the inherent inefficiencies and those associated with precautions added to achieve a satisfactory level of control; perhaps these two problems are inseparable.

The traditional methods of auditing manual records are to examine the accounting system and its internal control features; trace transactions from origination to ultimate destination (and vice versa) through an audit trail consisting of documents, summaries, journals, ledgers, and reports; and gain additional facts from outsiders and from management personnel and others not directly involved in recordkeeping.

Audit of Electronic Records

Electronic data-processing methods introduce several important environmental changes for the auditor, the most fundamental of which is the substitution of equipment for clerical personnel. The high ratio of capital to labor in an automatic system entails more equipment and pre-planning but with fewer people directly involved in operations than does a corresponding manual system. The use of more equipment for data processing changes operating methods enough to alter the nature of auditing. The ramifications can be discussed in terms of data readability, adherence to programs, availability of intermediate documents, personnel requirements, and reporting practices.

The use of machines imposes certain restrictions on the nature of original input data for efficient processing. The commonly used media of punched cards, punched tape, and magnetic tape are efficient for machine usage but not for people who want readable data. Two comments are appropriate. First, providing readability in a manual system may increase system operating costs and restrict opportunities for improved efficiency. Second, although reference to files in readable form has useful features, frequent reference may occur partly because the files are readable and access seems easy.

Since carefully prepared and tested programs form an integral part of processing and are executed with minimum participation by people, it is possible to distinguish between mistakes in preparing and running programs. The high cost of input-output operations in relation to processing leads to more emphasis on comprehensive processing whenever files and data are handled. The upper limit to comprehensive processing might be a single run for complete processing of data without either using people at any stage or preparing intermediate records for people to read. Increasing the scope of processing runs and eliminating intermediate records, summaries, and analyses will modify or even obliterate the traditional audit trail connecting input and output.

At the present stage of business data systems development, control over large volumes of data is now concentrated in the hands of a few people. This small group of people, who may be new to the company, are likely to have different backgrounds from those traditional for accountants and auditors. The concentration of responsibility and control over data processing in fewer people will change the nature of internal control and auditing plans. Many of the traditional checks and balances, whereby people at one stage have the opportunity to verify the work of others, may disappear. However, this loss is not necessarily deleterious, for it accompanies a decrease in the manual element and, therefore, risk of mistakes by people.

Changes in data-processing systems resulting from the introduction of processors do not alter the basic objectives of auditing but will require development of new techniques. The problems of equipment and system reliability and accuracy take on new dimensions when processors replace some of the tasks now performed by people. Public accountants are vitally interested in the reliability and accuracy of a data-processing system because it is from these factors that they must draw conclusions about the quality of the system's output. The analogy of learning about a process being carried on inside a "black box" is useful. An observer trying to appraise what occurs inside a black box will adjust his attack in keeping with what he knows usually goes on inside similar boxes and within the limits imposed by the cost of examining by sampling, testing, probing, questioning, experimenting, or even opening the box. Some factors of electronic data-processing systems that auditors are interested in are:

1. Equipment reliability and ability to repeat operations or halt if unreliability develops
2. Precautions to safeguard records against the risk of partial or complete loss
3. Logical and computational accuracy of programs and adherence to programs for routine processing operations
4. Treatment of exceptional cases—either by seeing whether they are handled correctly under program control or, if they are rejected and dealt with by people, ascertaining whether manual treatment is adequately controlled
5. Control over input data in order to ensure that complete and accurate data are originated for all transactions and that none are lost in communications or processing

New Audit Procedures

Changes in recordkeeping methods will give rise to new auditing techniques. The features of electronic processing likely to have the greatest impact on auditing in the near future deserve examination.

A processor executes programs without deviation, thus permitting the auditor to concentrate on detecting and preventing willful manipulation. The problem of unintentional and even unconscious variations from prescribed procedures, which plagues most manual systems, is essentially eliminated when a processor is used. But the continual revision of programs following changes in operating conditions and organization objectives causes difficulty in keeping track of when and how the program was revised and which program was actually used to process what data. Some organizations experiencing a high rate of continuous revisions of their programs have been forced to "batch" the modifications and introduce them at, say, monthly intervals.

Opportunities for intentional manipulation in an electronic system arise at three points. The first occurs when programs are designed to give special treatment to certain items—for example, when the cash collected from some customers is treated as sales returns in order to cover an extraction of cash. However, such a design can be detected, since programs must be examined, tested and approved before use. In theory at least, the usual plan is to draw flow charts and then prepare detailed operating programs. Flow charts may be examined carefully, although problem-oriented languages such as COBOL facilitate program examination. But in either case, an opportunity exists to write the program differently from the flow charts. Adequate program testing may disclose how selected transactions have been manipulated. Also, special programs can convert operating programs back to flow charts, which can be examined for the actual programs in use. This facilitates the search for modifications, both planned and manipulated, that have occurred since the flow charts were officially updated. The manipulation of programs during use can be controlled in several ways. Console typewriters keep operating logs showing all program changes that operators introduce. The number of steps in the program actually run can be counted by the processor and proved against the corresponding number in the approved program. Surprise audits of processor operations help determine whether an approved program is actually being used to process data.

The second opportunity for manipulating data occurs during origination, conversion, transmission, and processing; here, spurious data can be introduced or real data modified or discarded. To guard against these machinations, transactions can be numbered when originated, and checked each time they are handled by matching input against output at each stage and by isolating the place where any transaction was lost or modified.

The third occasion for manipulation arises when the data-processing group is not separated from other groups throughout the company. Opportunities for manipulation are reduced when the data-processing group is established as a separate unit. A data control unit may be set up to keep totals and other control figures for comparison with detailed work of the data-processing unit. For example, one company set up a payroll bureau to handle rate and deduction changes and variations from normal pay for weekly accumulation on standard equipment for comparison with processor print-out. The paymaster receives all checks from the processing center before signing in order to compare with the bureau's man-count and other controls. A data-processing center does not originate data but concentrates on processing data received from others. Division of authority reduces the auditor's fears about concentrating in a few people control over too many key data.

Implications for the Future

Audit procedures for electronic data processing will place more reliance upon the system embodied in processor programs and operating instructions. This is inevitable as the manual element declines. Such age-old problems of manual systems as the failure to adhere to processing instructions, arithmetical inaccuracies, and limited-scope processing will shrink or disappear. New problems that will affect audit methods are the broadened scope of processing in which all ramifications of a transaction are handled at one time, consolidation of records and files, automatic instead of manual origination of transactions, communication via wire and microwave channels instead of paper, maintenance of records in machine-sensible instead of visually-readable form, and concentration of responsibility for system design and operation in a small group of people who are often newly employed.

Clearly, auditors and others responsible for the accuracy and control of system output need to keep abreast of new developments in processing equipment and understand how they affect design and operation of efficient data systems. They should be close enough to systems design to understand the program and the internal controls. They should also be able to comprehend the checks included in the system, which ensure accurate master files, plan for intermediate and final results in a form to facilitate auditing, and ascertain that maintenance and operating procedures give reliable and accurate results.

Viewed in the broadest terms, the auditor's *function,* as opposed to his *techniques,* is likely to continue essentially unchanged. He must continue to obtain enough facts to form an opinion about the relationship of reports and the transactions that occurred. New control and audit procedures will be required, however, to meet the challenging task of devising controls for guarding against fraud and carelessness that may be more ingenious than the new system. Protective measures will be designed into operating programs to ensure better control over processing. Elimination of intermediate results and documents in readable form will lead to new sampling and testing procedures to determine what is happening. At first, such methods will seem indirect because they place greater reliance on equipment which follows different paths and in different steps than manual or punched-card processing methods. In time, new audit procedures equal or superior to those in use today will be developed.

It is possible, conceptually at least, to perform an audit of a company with little or no direct reference to its records and data-processing methods. It is necessary to determine only the credibility of the relationship between transactions and reports. The plausibility of input and output for a data system *might* be appraised by simulating some fraction of the processing already done without examining it as such. The idea is that essential features of an operation can be repeated in order to verify the original outcome without precisely duplicating the operation. The timing, sequencing, and degree of intermediate detail produced can be simplified during the second processing of transactions, yet enable the auditor to validate the results of initial processing by comparing the final results of the original, actual run and the simulated test processing.

SUMMARY

One aspect of the quality of data and information is accuracy, which is defined as the long-run ratio of correct answers to total answers. A report of condition A is treated as correct if the situation is actually condition A and not condition B, and vice versa. For some purposes there may be only two conditions—an employee arrives on time or is late. But in other situations, there may be much finer gradations of interest—what a person's bank balance is to the nearest $100, $10, $1, etc. In each case, the number of possible conditions increases and also the difficulty of determining which condition actually exists. The question of precision arises when the number of possible conditions is quite large, reflecting a desire to have an answer stated to a very small margin of error. In most data-processing work, precision is taken for granted; the real problem is to achieve a satisfactory degree of accuracy.

The degree of accuracy needed for satisfactory decision-making depends on the inputs required for the decision-making rules used. Decisions based on limits are not affected by inaccuracies if the reported value is on the same side of the limit, either above or below, as the actual. However, the degree of accuracy in reports becomes critical as the actual approaches the trigger point. In such cases, a higher degree of accuracy is more valuable because it removes the ambiguity from the reported value. The question "how much accuracy?" is answered by determining the cost of achieving successively higher degrees of accuracy and comparing such cost change with the corresponding change in the value of accuracy. The optimum degree of accuracy is reached when the net benefit—value in excess of cost—from an increase in the degree of accuracy starts to decline.

Higher accuracy is achieved by providing enough capacity to handle the accurate segment and also cope with inaccuracies that persist. Examples of extra capacity in a system to increase accuracy are (1) check digits and verification for originating data, (2) message numbering, (3) proof- and hash-totals, and (4) duplicate processor circuitry or programmed checks to monitor processing operations.

Errors, mistakes, and malfunctions have different origins and remedies. Errors arise from the use of deficient numerical methods. Mistakes are human failures occurring in program preparation, coding, data transcription, and processor operations. Malfunctions are failures in equipment operation. Electronic data-processing systems have an inherent capability of higher accuracy than manual and punched-card systems. However, elaborate processing systems often appear to be less accurate during the conversion phase and perhaps afterwards. Severe problems arise from consolidating fragmentary files that may be incomplete or in conflict, from insufficient programming for errors previously handled informally by people, and from the inexperience of operating personnel about how to work with the new system.

Internal control is the plan of organization and coordinate methods and measures of a business to safeguard assets, check accuracy and reliability of accounting data, promote operational efficiency, and encourage adherence to managerial policies. Internal auditors enforce adherence to policies by restricting the origination of transactions to authorized personnel; dividing duties among originator, custodian, and recordkeeper; analyzing transactions for logical conformance to approved policies and procedures; achieving accuracy at all stages of processing; and investigating differences between reports and actuality to eliminate discrepancies. Systems based on the use of documents have audit trails which can be traced in the forward direction to learn the effect of transactions on reports. Audit trails can also be traced in the opposite direction to learn the source of transactions composing reports. The size of processing steps is much larger with electronic processing and many traces of the audit trail disappear. New approaches to control and auditing are required which will exploit the new equipment yet not burden the data-processing system.

From the viewpoint of control and audit, automatic data-processing methods pose new problems. First, journals and ledgers, and, perhaps, documents, are in machine-sensible form; readability is achieved by printing desired facts. Second, a detailed, continuous audit trail probably does not exist in a well-developed electronic system because of the broad scope of processing when a transaction and its related file are brought together. Third, processors slavishly follow programs, are almost infallibly accurate, and are highly reliable, so that auditors can eliminate errors and mistakes by concentrating on program logic, rather than tracing the program details and proving logical and arithmetical accuracy. Fourth, edit programs can check input data for consistency and adherence to prescribed standards so that control over processing becomes an integral part of processing *per se*. Fifth, processors are impersonal and do not have a selfish interest in the outcome of processing, although the programmers and operators may have biases.

Some problems of control and audit decrease or disappear with the use of processors while other new problems arise. The variability of people in following procedures and their difficulty in sometimes adjusting to new processing procedures is replaced by almost complete certainty about program execution and control over revising and using new programs. Arithmetical accuracy is greatly improved. Control over data from origination through all stages of handling to final disposition gives more assurance that processing is correct and that no data are lost at any stage. Breaks in the audit trail resulting from the increased scope of each stage of processing and the use of machine-sensible data raise the challenge of new and different means of relating data input to report output. Auditors will need to know more about processing procedures and their application than before, since it will be difficult, if not impossible, to trace the audit trail.

An early step in improving control and auditing techniques is the incorporation of control methods into processing programs. In time, auditors are likely to make active use of equipment for selecting samples, testing the logic of processing programs, tracing the effect of translations from beginning to end, and comparing the contents of records with evidence obtained externally. In order for processors to be effective in controlling and auditing data-processing activities, improved automatic programming techniques must be devised to cut the cost of audit-programming and there must be more initiative on the part of auditors for fully exploiting the latest technical developments.

15
The Value and Cost
of Information

Various groups in an organization have different interests in the data-information system, the costs of operating it, and what it produces for the benefit of the organization as a whole and each group in particular. Of interest here are management, operations, and data-processing groups.

The management-planning, policy-making group is interested solely in making policies and decisions concerning the future. Group members want to know what relationship is likely to exist between the results of yesterday's activities and tomorrow's developments. Forecasts about future events are the basis for making decisions affecting only the future, for, obviously, decisions never affect the past. Outputs from the organization's data-processing system indicating, in general terms, what happened yesterday and today are an important input for management. Another input is a projection of what is likely to happen to the organization in both the short- and long-run resulting from its activities. A third input is a forecast of what is most likely to happen outside the organization which will have an important effect on it: competition, new products, prosperity, war, etc.

Generally, operating departments of an organization make decisions only from day to day or for the near future in controlling their operations, solving problems, and keeping score on individual people, departments, and divisions. For operating-control purposes, a substantial amount of detail about individual transactions is required. Thus, operating personnel are more interested than management in outputs from the organization's data-processing system concerning yesterday's and today's activities—what happened and how it compares to objectives—and are less interested in projections and external developments. Operating departments are the primary source of input—data about events as they occur—to the data-processing system, and, therefore, act as both input suppliers and output users.

The group or department responsible for gathering data, processing files, and preparing outputs has some aspects of both management and operating groups. In serving management, it deals with the future to the extent that it attempts to project the results of the recent past. In serving operating departments, its range is less ambitious, covering only the recent past and near future in its day-to-day activities and score-keeping. Compared to the job of management and operating groups, who must state their requirements entirely in advance, the task of data-processing groups is relatively simple: they have only to produce the specified outputs and discard the inputs and files when they are no longer useful. However, difficulties arise if outputs are not completely pre-specified but more reports are called for by later developments. It may be necessary to keep large quantities of data on file for analysis and summary in new kinds of reports.

There are other facets of the data-processing department's relationships with management and operating departments. Management is responsible for either specifying the outputs it wants from the data-processing system or of describing the rules for decision-making carefully enough so that the data-processing group can design the system to provide the necessary outputs. Lacking either of these, data-processing design work is partially done in a vacuum. Operating departments, since they are responsible for furnishing the data-processing group with raw data about events as they occur, spend much effort as a by-product of their primary operating activities in originating data for processing. Data-processing groups have their own interests, of course, in addition to responsibilities to management operating groups. At present, data-processing groups are interested in developing and implementing ambitious systems using large, complex equipment and high-speed communications networks. Important system changes are accepted upon the introduction of a new system, but, thereafter, personnel operating the system appear to desire nothing more than a high degree of stability for several years to consolidate their gains, though they seldom get it. Data-processing groups usually avow an interest in economy, but this objective often seems to be overwhelmed by the urge to have the latest and largest equipment that looks useful.

These brief introductory comments have attempted to bring into perspective the relationships between the interests of management, operations, and data-processing groups. This chapter deals with two of the most fundamental areas in the design and operation of a system: (1) outputs, files, and inputs; (2) the values of having the outputs in contrast to the costs of gathering and processing the inputs and of keeping files to furnish such outputs.

INFORMATION, FILES, AND DATA

It is useful to go over again the distinction between information and data in order to show their relationship to business files. In oversimplified terms, information is the output from files, and data are the input to files, which contain data that are still considered useful. Often the words information and data are used interchangeably, but attaching different meanings to them may help clarify three questions that puzzle all systems designers: "What outputs should be produced from files?" "What data inputs should go into files?" "What content should be retained in files?"

Information

For present purposes the meaning of the word *information* can be considered at three different levels. Considered at the *syntactic* level, data consists of collections of symbols or characters arranged in some orderly way to serve as the vehicle for information. Information is the meaning derived from data and represents the *semantic* level—the relationship between a symbol and the actual object or condition that is symbolized. The impact of the objects or conditions on the receiver represents the *pragmatic* level of information.

At the pragmatic level, which is the one of primary interest from the information user's viewpoint, the impact depends on, first, how much the user knows of the picture presented or, according to his knowledge of the situation, has already guessed, and, second, how correctly he can utilize the picture presented in view of both his abilities and the surrounding circumstances. The value of information at the pragmatic level depends on the quality, quantity, and timeliness of the reports received and the ability of the receiver to act on the basis of the knowledge received. Discussion and some examples will clarify these ideas.

A purchasing agent bought three carloads of plywood at a "bargain," even though his company used little in manufacturing. After a long period, one member of the purchasing department sold it below market. The shipment was recorded as a routine issue, since the data system provided for recording only one kind of transaction to reduce stock on hand. The quantity on hand fell to zero and immediately triggered another purchase to rebuild the inventory.

The distress-price sale was not meaningfully recorded and reported—a semantics error occurred—and had the same effect on inventory-control activities as a routine issuance of stock for manufacturing purposes or for an ordinary sale. Misunderstanding (or lack of information) about the exact nature of the sale led to incorrect action by the purchasing department and a return to the original overstocked condition. Since the data system failed to distinguish between the causes of several kinds of issues and to show why the balance on hand had fallen below the reorder point, the semantics error had an incorrect pragmatic effect.

Another example shows how the attempt to ensure complete reporting may cause duplication and an adverse effect on maintenance efficiency and service life.

> Each member of a plane flight crew is, according to one organization's rules, supposed to report every malfunction that comes to his attention during a flight or at debriefing. Maintenance crews accumulate all the malfunction reports, make repairs or replacements as required, and sign off all the reports even though they may be duplicative. These reports are the basis for analyzing failure experience of parts and for calculating standard hours to measure the efficiency of repair crews.

In the attempt to ensure that all malfunctions are reported by having each crew member report each one he encounters, some duplication arises. An error occurs in information at the syntactic level because multiple reports are made for one malfunction. The report by each crew member is semantically correct. But the combined reports are incorrect syntactically because the data processing system doesn't screen inputs to eliminate duplicates and, therefore, allows the contents of the file to violate the rules ordinarily used for maintaining files: each event that occurs should be reflected once and only once. Mechanics usually make the repair or replacement just once, of course, and sign off the other copies. Mechanics and supervisors may want these duplicates counted to improve their performance rating, which is measured as standard hours for jobs reported done divided by actual hours required to do the jobs. But projects aimed at improving parts repair may focus on certain parts simply because they are reported by several crew members who see a different facet of the same malfunction. This example of multiple reporting of the same problem may seem unique, but actually it is quite common. A "bandwagon" effect seems to prevail in every organization, for people are likely to repeat reports of bad, and even good, news as soon as they learn it. A difficult part of the receiver's task is to separate the information from the "noise." Syntactic mistakes that are the converse of duplicate origination of data are the failure to originate data about events and the loss of messages somewhere in the communication network after they are originated.

The quality of information is influenced by the degree of detail obtained about each event that occurs. Some details are lost when gathering facts about events because it is economically impossible to capture all facts. The question is how much detail can be discarded and a useful quality representation of events still maintained. Pragmatic mistakes—wrong decisions based on the right picture—can occur at the point where information is used. A pragmatic mistake can arise because the decision rule is incorrect. The rule, for example, might be to decrease production as the stock is depleted. Then, too, the correct rule could be incorrectly applied. Correction of pragmatic mistakes may be made through a second look or a review, and even by calculating or simulating the results of a proposed decision before implementing it.

It is easy to produce an excessive *quantity* of information. Care must be taken to keep information tailored to a user's needs and restricted to his ability to use it. Business data-information systems should attempt to produce information that is useful and relevant to decision-making and that is related to a manager's scope for making decisions. There are usually more decisions to be made than a manager can handle and he does not have complete freedom of decision. The point is that information must be related to areas where the manager has elbow room to take action.

> Responsibility accounting summarizes the expenses incurred under the jurisdiction of each manager and reports the details to him. Because he alone is considered responsible for and able to control these details, they are not reported to other managers or even to his superior. But—and this is an interesting aspect of responsibility accounting—a manager's salary is listed on the expense report of his superior since the superior is the one person able to control the manager's salary—increase, decrease, or terminate it.

A manager needs information about a problem while his decisions can still affect its solution. *Timeliness* covers this aspect of information, and control that occurs quickly enough to influence the operations involved is called real-time control. Information that pertains to a *point* in time is called status or condition information—for example, number of seats available to sell on flight 123 from New York to Washington scheduled for June 30. Information that covers a *period* of time is called operating or dynamic information—for instance, the number of passenger miles flown during the week or month ending June 30. The timeliness necessary for status and operating information depends upon the use made of it. For merely learning what did happen during the period ending June 30, a report by July 15 might be suitable for some purposes; for others, reports on July 1 or even June 30 may be necessary. Planning operations and achieving real-time control requires the following: forecasts of what *will* happen; a system that has the capability of gathering and processing data to report results on a timely basis; decision rules for the action to be taken for each condition that may occur; and a controller—a person, automatic device, or computer— to make and implement decisions. After-the-fact reports are suitable in some cases, but other cases require before-the-fact forecasts and therefore require more timely information.

> Commercial banks often treat a day as a unit of time when deciding whether an account is overdrawn. That is, a check paid in the morning may cause a negative balance but a deposit later the same day resulting in a positive balance is considered to erase the overdraft. For some purposes the bank merely needs to know at the close of the banking day whether an account is overdrawn. Possible action on N.S.F. (non-sufficient funds) checks received through the clearing house from other banks must await a possible deposit before returning them to the sending bank. But a decision by a teller to pay a check across the counter may warrant an up-to-the-minute balance of the account involved since a bank has more difficulty recovering on checks paid in cash than on those received through the bank clearing process.

The point of the check-payment example is that immediate information can be valuable for certain purposes, but that for other situations a much longer period of time—say, a banking day—is the shortest period for which the bank can take action. The minimum interval of time for taking action has an important parallel in the capacity of management to take action. In any organization, capacity for taking action may be limited by other factors than the information received about situations that need attention.

A management decision-making capacity may be built up to handle somewhat more than the average load of situations deserving action. Above-average loads cause backlogs; below-average loads enable managers to whittle away the backlog or to survey new areas. There are, of course, several other ways to adjust to the load variation. One is to increase the capacity of management through more people or people with more skill. Another is to report all problem areas but have managers attend to only the most fruitful situations. A third way is to adjust the definition of a situation deserving management attention so that managers will be just fully loaded all the time. This raises a new concept for reports: the amount of management skill and time required to deal with situations needs to be related to the pay-off obtainable from such decisions.

> An electric utility company developed the following scheme for adjusting data-system outputs to the capacity of users. Collectors of delinquent bills need current information about a customer's balance when demanding payment or threatening to discontinue service. Delinquent bill notices are printed for collectors during file-update runs. To be sure that notices can be used while current, the company restricts the number produced to the projected daily capacity of collectors minus the number of notices left over from the previous day.

While the adjustment of bill collectors' notices to their daily capacity is a reasonably simple situation, it is a step in the direction of adjusting information output to the capacity for using it at the next stage of operations. There are two ways to restrict output in this case. The first is to apply the usual rules for creating notices for bill collectors to use, but stop printing notices at the desired number. The second is to modify the delinquent bill collection rules by tightening or loosening them, so that, while processing the whole file, only the number of notices that can be handled will be produced.

Files

In business data processing, a file is a collection of data considered useful in the future and arranged for convenient reference. Files are the system memory, and, as such, are the connecting link between outputs in the form of reports and inputs in the form of data about events as they occur. Under idealized conditions, files would just exactly fulfill requirements for reports that are pre-specified in content, degree of detail, period covered, and other features. If all the requirements for information are pre-specified, file contents can be fully utilized and then downgraded or perhaps discarded since they are no longer useful. But this closely linked and orderly relationship between outputs and file content seldom exists. People throughout the organization raise either new questions or variations of old questions, since their innate curiosity and external events require reference to files for answers. Furthermore, as internal events unfold, situations are revealed that warrant additional processing and the distribution of more information.

In order to meet a high fraction of future *ad hoc* requests for information, most files are designed to contain many more facts than are immediately wanted. It is necessary to design the files to contain all the facts that are certain to be wanted and also fill a high fraction of the other demands. The importance of unplanned demands might be measured in terms of both their frequency of occurrence and the benefits likely to be derived from filling such requests. Files should contain all the obligatory data required by law, regulations, and rules. Another large fraction of file content is determined by operating problems, organizational practices, and managerial requirements. A third category, which might be called *optional data,* is included in files, if the prospective value of having the data available when wanted appears to outweigh the cost of retaining such data in files when they may be used only occasionally.

In order to be useful, the contents of files must be organized in some meaningful way. A few of the many factors affecting the development, maintenance, and use of files are considered here. The *degree of detail,* which is determined by the definition of events for which data are gathered and by the number of data elements in the record for an event, may result in a small number of short records in the file or a huge number of very long records. The reason long records are numerous and short records are few is because of a self-generative effect: if more detail is wanted about an event, it is useful, if not mandatory, to organize these details into a larger number of discrete records. An example will clarify this point.

The controller of an automobile parts manufacturing company says that, for inventory valuation purposes, he doesn't care whether all fenders are lumped together. But he is well aware that the inventory-control and production departments must identify them as left-right, front-back for assembly purposes. For still other purposes—for example, parts replacement—it may be necessary to keep track of auto make, model, year, and perhaps serial number to ensure compatibility.

The increase in degree of detail in the identification of fenders causes not only an increase in the degree of detail in each record but also a growth in the number of records themselves. The ultimate result is so much detail about each stock item that a separate record must be kept for that item, which is commonly true for individual fixed-asset records. Also, as will be shown later in the discussion of data input, the amount of data required both to set up the file and to keep it current will increase along with the detail in the file record.

The *classification scheme* used for organizing data affects files in several ways. Classifications may be made fine or coarse by using many categories or few. One file may be organized by having one data element in a record serve as a key. More elaborate files may be organized by repeating the records one or more times in other files that are arranged differently and using other elements as keys Permissible *response time* for filling a request for information has an important effect on file content, detail, and classification. If quick responses are demanded for interrogations, then file content must be in essentially the form needed to fill the request. That is, there is little time available for processing files to produce information to fill the request and there is probably no time whatever to plan how to process files to develop answers to questions. Therefore, it appears that most, if not all, quick-response reporting from files is likely to be based on essentially raw data or on the results of first-order processing—accumulating, summarizing, updating. Second-order processing—analyzing and correlating to find relationships or to project and extrapolate into the future—is probably ruled out for quick-response reporting.

> Airline reservation systems are elaborate on-line, real-time systems with huge processor capabilities and vast communication networks. But they are designed to answer simple questions: "Is space available on a desired flight and date?" "How late is the plane from X likely to be?"

But even elaborate on-line systems have difficulty dealing with unusual questions that interest many people. For example, airline sales vice-presidents want to know, "What type of passengers are our steady customers, what are their characteristics, and what influences them most?" Often as a result of penetrating questions, more data are gathered and additional processing performed over an extended period of time.

How long should the system *retain contents* of files and how should these contents be discarded? The general rule is simple: retain file contents, measured at the level of data elements, as long as their prospective value from future use exceeds the cost of retaining them. But it is usually possible to discard file contents on a selective basis. The routine steps of calculating new balances by updating files and summarizing individual transactions are based on the principle that increased value can be derived from incorporating new events with old to develop an over-all history. The data about individual events are discarded in the practical sense of not being readily available or of even being destroyed. An example of how file contents can be selectively discarded is shown by a summary of repair and replacements parts issues:

> Records for parts issued are retained for one month and show the following detail: part number, name, quantity issued, date of issue, person issued to, serial number, etc. Issues are summarized by part number into weekly and monthly totals. Quarterly totals are retained for seven quarters and then completely discarded. At any time, the following file contents about parts issued are available: seven quarters, one or two months in the current quarter, one to three weeks in the current month, and individual issues for one month.

By way of summarizing the discussion of content of files in an organization, it is useful to look at two examples which illustrate the range from huge active files to almost none whatever.

A manufacturer leasing data-processing equipment must keep a record containing several dozen data elements for every piece of equipment in order to cover financial and technical matters. These data elements include unit name, model number, serial number, date of manufacture, engineering configuration, plant modifications, field modifications, lessee name and address, date installed, rental rate, one-time charges, expiration of lease, etc.

At the other extreme for file content, a cemetery keeps a bound ledger book which is indexed with a letter for each page, and simply lists the name and date of each person interred. Since there is no turnover of "accounts," the problem of discarding records does not arise and the simple ledger is kept indefinitely.

A third example, in which file content is neither large nor small in detail, is the practice of immediately summarizing details about events in order to discard the detail.

A mail-order house fills as much of a customer's order as possible, updates the summary record of the customer—money terms and, for statistical purposes, amount of order—and returns all papers (both those received from the customer and those prepared internally) to the customer without making any file copies. The customer can return them if he questions the order; otherwise, he may discard them.

The mail-order house approach to file maintenance is ingenious, for it solves in one stroke several problems about detailed records in files—what contents to put into files, how long to retain the contents, and when and how to discard them.

Data

Data can be defined as any facts that are a matter of direct observation. As used in business data processing, data means collections of symbols or characters arranged in some orderly way to make up facts and figures. Numbers and words are examples of data at the *syntactic* level of a data-information system—the patterns of messages formed from words in a particular language. Numbers and words are organized in various ways to serve as a vehicle for information. Examples of organization of numbers and words are documents that represent transactions, files that accumulate the transactions affecting each record in that file, and reports that contain summaries of records in one or more files. Each level or organization of numbers and words—document, record, and report—has a specified structure, contains certain kinds of data, and reflects an increasing degree of summarization with reports being the most highly condensed.

Data-processing systems are designed to handle data that describe various situations and to produce information. Viewed in this sense, data are essentially the input or raw materials for a system designed to process data and to produce some desired output. In order to be useful in subsequent stages of processing, data must have certain attributes of *quality, quantity,* and *timeliness.*

The quality of data is important to all subsequent processing operations. As described in Chapter 14, it is possible to cope with inaccuracies in data and still produce accurate outputs, but it is more efficient to try to prevent inaccuracies or remove most of them shortly after they originate. Many verification procedures aim at detecting syntactical mistakes, such as incorrect numerals or letters. A processing system may include procedures to detect some semantic mistakes by performing limit-tests on the data, comparing reports with files to determine logical plausibility of the data, or matching inputs from two sources to check their plausibility.

A worker's report that he put in 99 hours for one week exceeds ordinary limit tests of the number of hours that workers usually spend on the job.

A report by an automobile mechanic that he fixed a broken windshield by painting it is incorrect according to the file showing authorized action for each job, to say nothing of the violation of common sense.

Similarly, if an airline mechanic reports that he made external repairs on a plane, whereas the crew reported it was in flight at the time, there is a logical inconsistency according to the data received from two sources.

The mere act of gathering data about factory, sales, or administrative activities will affect them in several ways. First, operating personnel are required to know and to adhere to the prescribed procedures for gathering data; both of these requirements detract from their primary activity. Secondly, people have an interest in the content of reports reflecting their performance and therefore may adjust some of the data that they originate—for example, overstate production or understate costs. Gaps and duplications sometimes appear in data that have been originated manually because people may fail to originate any data or may repeat some already started through the communication channels. These deficiencies in the manual origination of data are two important reasons for the trend toward introducing data-origin devices that can accept pre-prepared inputs. These devices, which range from sales registers to factory recorders, restrict manually-created data to the variables that cannot be prepared in advance. Thus, data are originated directly for input to processing instead of being merely collected as already available or created without any direct control by or connection with the data-processing system.

The *quantity* of data that are originated or that are collected in a data-information system is also governed by file content. Enough data elements must be collected to fill the requirements of files both during their initial creation and their subsequent maintenance. If there are any extra data not specified by the record design, they are discarded or the record expanded. Record design *per se* has an interesting effect on the quantity of data that must be gathered to keep files current. A record containing many data elements requires the collection of more input data just to keep the records current, even though physical operations remain unchanged.

Consider the case of a company that wanted to know the current manufacturing status of every item in production in each of its four plants. The manufacturing plant is in Connecticut, the assembly plant is in Puerto Rico, and the two finishing plants are in Puerto Rico and New York.

> At one time the company kept track of a production order only through the manufacturing-assembly stage and through the finishing stage, when the job was split up into several finishing orders. In other words, only two processing stages—make and finish—were kept in the records for reporting production status, and data were originated at only four points—start of manufacture, end of assembly, start of finishing, and end of finishing.

Actually, 19 departments were involved for the typical product: 6 in manufacturing, 5 in assembly, and 8 in finishing. In addition, each lot of goods was shipped twice, so that, at any point in time, there were a total of 21 places where a given production order might be located.

> The new reporting scheme, designed to keep better track of production orders by reporting them by individual operation, required describing each transfer between operating departments and each shipment between plants. Thus, data about the movement of jobs between departments had to be originated at 22 points—start of manufacture, 19 departments, and 2 shipping points.

As a result of reporting production-order status by department instead of by plant, the number of points for originating data increased from 4 to 22. The portion of the file record reflecting the status of each production order was also about five times as long as before.

The problem of *timeliness* of data poses fewer conceptual problems than does the problem of timeliness of reports. Data about events must be obtained as the events occur. It is impossible to obtain prime quality data afterwards, although, within narrow limits, it may be possible to reconstruct essentially what happened. A retail shoe store, for example, usually records each sale as it is made. However, sales also may be calculated by using inventories in conjunction with stock receipts: beginning balance plus shoes received minus ending balance equals calculated sales. But calculated sales may be erroneous because of returns, shoplifts, clerk's losses, and mistakes in inventory accounting. In practice, both schemes for originating data are used: each transaction is recorded as it occurs and inventories occasionally are taken in order to detect and reconcile any discrepancies that occurred in originating data.

The time limits for processing files and issuing reports fixes the time limits for transmitting input data to files. Short time limits require high-speed communication links and, perhaps, automatic devices at all stages from data origination to report preparation. Report time limits also fix the amount of processing possible and the capacity of equipment required to handle such processing.

MANAGEMENT INFORMATION SYSTEM

The data-processing unit is an element of a much larger system—namely, the management information system, which furnishes management and operating personnel with the facts necessary and useful for making decisions and conducting operations. The main purpose of a data-processing unit is to provide information, not merely to marshal facts.

Sources of Information

Managers have several sources in addition to data-processing systems for obtaining information; they examine operations, talk with people to learn about trouble brewing, and observe conditions. To learn how many "widgets" are in stock, a manager may read an available report, wait for a new report, interrogate the data-processing unit's stock-record file, question the head widget-keeper, or simply make a guess on the basis of the prior report and what he knows or thinks has happened since. If he arrives at the right number of widgets in stock, within a margin of error suitable for the problem under consideration, an additional report will be of little value to him. A complete study of management information should consider all methods of originating and communicating data; here only formal systems will be discussed.

Selection of Information from Facts

An important aspect of systems design is the selection from all the facts available of just the information useful for making decisions. This is an age-old problem and is common to all systems. One solution is to appraise each situation individually and decide what information is needed to deal with it. However, there are several reasons why such after-the-fact decisions are not efficient. First, management must spend a great deal of time merely in stating what it wants, even though the requests shortly become highly repetitious. Second, the delay between requesting information and obtaining it is probably too long because of the number of steps in processing and reporting. Third—and this point is crucial even if the other two are not—data are not available to fill management's needs unless they were specified before the event occurred.

For these reasons, managers, operating people, and data-information systems designers must develop rules and procedures that will make a data-processing system responsive to the user's needs. Such a system requires planning in advance the kind of information probably wanted for operations and decision-making, the files necessary to support these outputs, and the input data required to set up and maintain the files. An important point is that this approach to system design is *output-oriented,* since it concentrates first on the outputs wanted and then on the files and input data required to produce these outputs. The opposite approach is *input-oriented,* since the system is designed to gather all available data, store them in a more or less organized fashion, and then try to fill requests for information as they arise. The output and input orientations are oversimplified, but in practice it is possible to find close approximations of both.

After the decision-making rules have been formulated, the first step in making a decision is to obtain information that is pertinent to the rules. If the decision-making rules can be pre-specified, the information needed is determined in advance and its preparation and selection facilitated. The automatic selection of relevant and consequential information permits management to concentrate on decision-making without having to worry about the mechanics of gathering data and preparing reports.

A straightforward way to prepare reports is to develop a list of required items that should be included in each report and a time schedule for its issuance. Each specified item is included in a report without regard to its information content. The procedure simply is to collect data, process them, and produce reports. Managers may then study the reports to find significant facts for decision-making, as suggested by the block diagram in Figure 15-1.

Exception Principle. The exception principle is a first step beyond merely processing the data to supply management with information. Selection of informative data can be accomplished by equipment for reporting desired information to management.

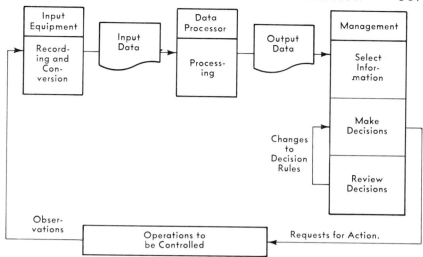

FIGURE 15-1. *Data processing to produce reports.*

One method is to have readers scan complete reports to find significant differences. Complete reports can show actual results, planned or expected results, and differences. The differences may be in the same units—dollars, hours, or tons—as the individual items. Percentage variations from expected results can be shown and readers can scan reports to find significant differences for making decisions and taking action. Such complete reports are widely used because their preparation is simple: every reported item is shown in a fixed format regardless of the amount of the item or its variation from actual, budgeted, or standard values. This format makes it easy to compare an item over a period of time, since it is at the same place on succeeding reports. But management's selection task may be difficult because significant items get buried in a mass of data.

A second approach to the exception-principle scheme is to report only those items that vary significantly from planned results. The processing system examines each variation to find whether it is worth managerial attention—it is likely to lead to some action because of the decision-making rules that are used. If it is worth attention, the item is reported; if not, it is omitted. Data must, of course, be collected and processed in order to be available for possible inclusion in reports. But only those items that have significant variations are included in managerial reports. Figure 15-2 is a block diagram of the scheme for processing data and preparing

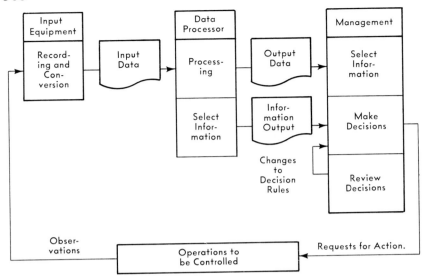

FIGURE 15-2. *Data processing to produce information.*

reports by the exception principle. It shows that selected output goes to management. Complete reports are available for back-up reference and for further analysis to select other items when necessary. Management still makes all decisions.

The formulation of operating targets or budgets must precede establishment and use of the exception-principle system. A normal range above or below the projected result is established for each item in a report, so that, if actual results are within the range, it is suitable to follow a single plan of action. The idea of a single plan of action is quite simple. An item falling inside the normal range is omitted from reports because no new action is required. An item falling outside the normal range can be reported in detail—name of item, target or budgeted amount, actual amount, and difference. The manager responsible for its control can apply the prescribed action rules. The normal range selected for each item to be reported is, of course, critical to the action rule and success of the plan. The normal range should be set wide enough to cover all results that do not require new action, so that such items will not be reported to managers. The width of the normal range is limited by the fact that a plan of action for a particular item will give good results. If the range is too wide, an action plan that is suitable when the actual result is near the top of the range is unsuitable when the actual result is near the bottom of the range. The process is assumed to be in control if actual results fall anywhere within the normal range;

the process is considered out of control and new action is required when the actual results fall outside this range.

Management may be able to set the planned or projected values for some items, but not for others. For example, the planned amount of direct labor is controllable within narrow limits, but the amount of sales generally is not.

The normal range may be based on:

1. Actual amount in the past month, quarter, or year
2. Average, either fixed or moving, of amounts in several past periods
3. Forecast of future results, if the future is expected to be much different from the past.

The amount of variation from the expected value depends more on operations and is less subject to management control. The permissible amount or degree of variation from the expected amount might be measured in one of several ways: the absolute difference in the original units, the percentage difference, or the amount of difference in relation to the typical difference occurring in the past. The normal range and difference must, of course, be adjusted to the particular level of operations being considered.

Part X is manufactured for stock, and inventory is reviewed weekly. The action rules are as follows: take no action if 21,000 to 30,000 of these parts are in stock; start manufacturing if less than 21,000 are in stock; and stop manufacturing for inventory if more than 30,000.

Each of these values—less than 21,000, 21,000 to 30,000, and more than 30,000—implies a single plan of action. The range of 21,000 to 30,000 is suitable as the normal for reporting by the exception principle. It is "best" in the sense that it excludes part X from weekly reports for management when no action is wanted. Part X is reported only when its balance is outside of normal—less than 21,000 or more than 30,000. The person responsible for inventory control takes appropriate action when informed by the data-processing system that the quantity is below 21,000 or above 30,000.

Unless precautions are taken, some waste motion, and even mistakes, may occur in reporting and making decisions with this plan. A second weekly report is made if inventory stays below 21,000. Since a production order was supposed to be issued after the first report, duplication of the production order must be avoided. To guard against repeating a decision already made, the inventory might be defined as "available supply"—the quantity on hand and on order—so that part X would be reported only when the available supply is below 21,000. Each definition should, of course, reflect an actual situation.

Exception-principle reporting decreases the volume of reports furnished to management. The use of a normal range for screening items that are out of control is not limited to the final stages of report preparation; it can also be applied at earlier stages of data processing. Reductions in report volume can save printing and distribution time. Managers are saved time, since they are dealing with shorter reports which pinpoint the needs for action, and since they can analyze the items reported only rarely to see if they should be dropped. The level of management receiving a report may not be able to take appropriate action; a certain manager may be too high or too low in an organization to rectify a situation, or it may be outside his area of responsibility. Still, the problem of reporting only relevant information to a manager is probably as easy to deal with in this scheme as in any other. Managers postpone action on some items outside normal range because action on other items will have more effect on the over-all results—the most fruitful areas deserve most attention.

Internal-Decision Plan. *Internal decision* means that the data-processing system is programmed to take appropriate action. An internal-decision plan does more than merely report situations outside an established normal range. The action may include issuing instructions to a clerk or to a manager, or it may involve preparing documents—purchase or production orders—for distribution. Even physical action—starting, changing, or shutting off a production line—can be taken, if both the data-processing and factory operations are automatic and are linked together.

Figure 15-3 is a block diagram of an internal-decision plan. The block labeled "data processor" now includes three functions: processing data, selecting information, and making decisions. The processor handles tasks that are covered by rules, while a manager sets up and reviews objectives, policies, and decision rules. Management deals with situations that are not handled by the processor, but its main task is to review decisions made automatically. Management gets data and information concerning only those items not covered by decision rules.

The formulation of decision rules for various conditions is fundamental to an internal-decision plan. These problems are similar

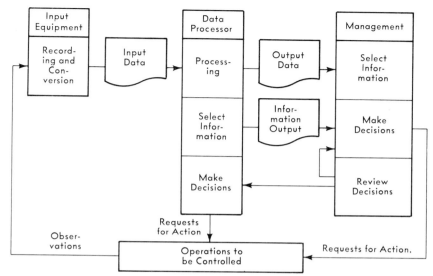

FIGURE 15-3. *Data processing and decision-making.*

to those involved in setting normal ranges, but they are more complex. Management decisions based on available data may follow explicit rules that can be programmed for the data processor to apply. Many operations may be better controlled with internal-decision systems, for automatic equipment is more efficient than people at applying specified rules in order to make decisions.

Variable-Processing Plan. A variable-processing plan examines selected items at key points when it first handles the data. Any key points that do not fall within the normal range of expected values are examined in more detail by processing the supporting data on a second run. This process is repeated until the original data, if necessary, are examined in detail. Limited processing may show that some areas are inside the normal range of control. Data for such areas need not be processed further. Attention can then be concentrated on areas where results are outside the normal range.

Consider a report of total and detailed operating costs covering several manufacturing plants. On the first pass, only data on total cost for each plant are computed. If the total cost for a plant is outside the normal range, the costs for each department's major operation, or other area of interest, can be computed. If any of these costs is out of range, a detailed analysis is made and printed out.

Processing can be extended to any desired degree of detail, although highly detailed information is seldom useful for managerial purposes. By concentrating on areas that need attention, management can examine them more thoroughly than would be warranted with standardized reports on all plants.

Manual-Intervention Plan.   One plan for automatic systems is to have programs provide for every situation, both common and rare, that may arise. Such an ambitious scheme may be expensive because of high programming costs, large internal storage for extra programs, and delays in getting the system into operation. A second plan is to have the processor handle high-volume transactions. When a rare case arises, the processor notifies the operator and either puts the case aside or waits for instructions. Manual intervention, either later or immediately, enables the processor to cope with the unusual situation.

All automatic systems, it should be remembered, require manual assistance for data preparation, problem analysis, and programming, but they attempt to minimize manual intervention during processor operations. The chief point is that, while manual effort is always applied in advance of processing, in the manual intervention scheme, some manual effort is also applied during processing to handle situations not covered in the program for the processor to handle alone.

Adaptive System.   An adaptive system keeps track of demands placed on it and makes changes to cope with them. To do this, it must recognize features of the environment and adjust to new situations. For example, an adaptive data-processing system might keep track of demands for information and organize files so that the most frequently-demanded information would be most readily available.

A bank found that employees asked most of their questions about payroll shortly after checks were distributed. Ninety-five per cent of the questions were asked within one day and ninety-nine per cent within one week. To meet such brief demands for information, the details of calculation were kept readily available for supervisors for one week and then placed in inactive storage.

To take a more elaborate example, the system might be designed as follows to adjust to the broader problem of how much use is made of published information and how many demands arise for new information.

Keep track of the use made of published reports by asking for users' requests to stay on distribution list, by omitting reports occasionally and watching for complaints, and by observing whether decisions indicated as being necessary by reports are actually made. Also examine requests for information to determine whether they are covered by existing reports, can be filled by modifications, or actually require new reports. In order to efficiently handle requirements for new information, it is necessary to modify techniques of preparing reports, reorganize the structure and maintenance of files, and gather new kinds of data for processing.

All viable systems have some degree of self-adaptation. The important question for data-processing systems is whether they are designed with enough self-adaptation so that they can adjust to changing requirements on their own initiative rather than being forced to adjust. A system designed to make internally-generated adjustments is likely to be responsive to requirements placed on it and less likely to require a complete overhaul from time to time.

VALUE OF INFORMATION

Information, files, and data for management and operating purposes were defined above and schemes were suggested for increasing the information content of reports. The value of information and the cost of obtaining and processing data to produce information deserve study, for final design of a system is usually governed by economic considerations. The concept of the value of information is basic to a study of data processing and information production. *Value* is usually defined as that property of a thing which makes it esteemed, desirable, or useful, or the degree to which this property is possessed. Theories of the value of information fall into three categories: intangibles, cost outlay, and managerial use. The first two are only mentioned here; the third is discussed in detail.

Intangibles

When systems are being discussed, the comment is often heard that a proposed system is "worthwhile because it will provide *better* information for operations and for management decisions." But "better" is seldom defined in measurable terms. Improvements are merely treated as plus factors, or intangibles, and no value is assigned. Although intangibles are often used to reinforce a decision to adopt a new system, if they are treated as unvalued factors, the result may be a wrong decision. A change not warranted when the value of intangibles is omitted might be warranted if their value is counted. This point is considered later under the managerial use of information.

Cost Outlay

Many systems analysts, and business managers too, adhere to the theory that the value of information is equal to the *cost outlay* for obtaining it. When considering changes for an existing system, analysts may insist that the same information, or even more, should be acquired without any increase in cost. They are, in effect, accustomed to the existing outlay for processing data and are satisfied with the results obtained. An extremely simple change, such as a large decrease in processing costs, poses an interesting test of the cost-outlay theory of value. One choice is to save the reduction in cost and spend less than before for processing. Another choice is to spend as much as before and obtain better quality, larger quantity, or more timely information. But the cost-outlay theory of value cannot answer the simple question of whether to save the cost reduction or spend the savings to produce more information.

Managerial Use

A more useful concept is that the value of information should be studied in terms of its effect on an organization's operating performance or the revenue obtained. Assume that all factors influencing operating performance can be held constant. If some report or portion of a report is dropped or changed, the resulting decrease in performance would be an indicator of the value of information supplied by that report. If no decrease occurred, the report might be considered valueless.

Actually, the effect of a single report on an over-all result is difficult to measure. Within a large organization many departments may not sell their products in the market but merely transfer them to other departments at arbitrary values. Changes in revenue associated with any particular report are difficult to estimate. Nevertheless, it is worth examining the value of information in four of its aspects: quality, quantity, timeliness, and relevance to management's ability to take action.

Quality. The quality of information, it will be recalled, is judged by the degree of correspondence between the report about a situation and the actual situation. Information of high quality is valuable for several reasons, two of which are that it reduces the range of uncertainty about what action to take and that it makes management more willing to take prompt and vigorous action. If a report about a given situation lacks the minimum degree of accuracy, a user is likely either to demand another report or to simply wait for it and take no action in the interim. At the other extreme, there is a limit to the degree of accuracy useful for decision-making purposes because management rules are usually broad enough that they are not sensitive to a minor drop in quality. Operating personnel, however, may need higher-quality reports, since they deal with a higher level of detail. Higher quality is warranted whenever lower quality is likely to cause the user to make a less desirable decision.

The inventory replenishment rule applied to item X is to reorder when the quantity on hand falls to 1000 units. If 2000 units are actually on hand, the decision to reorder is the same whether 1001 or 1,000,000 are reported to be on hand.

In such a case, the decision is not affected by the degraded quality of the information, even though the reported quantity of units on hand ranges from minus 50 per cent to plus hundreds above the actual quantity. On the other hand, if the actual quantity were 1010, an inaccuracy of even 1 per cent could lead to an incorrect decision. Nevertheless, when carried to the extreme, the apparent quality of information may be increased beyond the point where it aids decision-making; such superfluous increases may be ignored or discarded.

One organization set up inventory control records with six-digit fields for the size and weight of each item. Size was supposed to be stated to the nearest .01 cubic foot and weight to the nearest 0.1 pounds. The organization found that it was not practicable to measure the size of an item more closely than about 10 per cent. Commercial grade scales would not weigh heavy items more accurately than about one pound in 500.

The specified quality of data for size and weight—0.01 cubic foot and 0.1 pound—could not be achieved in practice and was therefore fictitious. For the purposes intended—warehousing and shipping—less accurate volumes and weights were adequate.

Quantity.   The quantity of information available to management depends on the predictability of events and the degree of detail worth having about each event. Information value is related to the difficulty of predicting what is going to happen next and the potential action that can be taken to improve the situation. If it is possible to predict events with certainty, there is no need to have an elaborate data-processing system. Predictable events are similar to the cowboy movies in which the good guys always beat the bad guys: there is no need to watch the movie to know the outcome nor any need, some would say, to make the movie at all. Similar comments apply to processing data and preparing reports when the outcome is fairly certain. A simple example illustrates the idea of a high degree of predictability and the consequent reduced usefulness of pertinent reports:

> Commercial banks use essentially identical procedures to update all depositors' accounts despite the fact that a large fraction of depositors rarely have an overdraft and, if so, readily pay it. Different processing and reporting schemes might well be used for classes of depositors based on past and probable future experience with them. For most depositors, it probably is not worthwhile, from a management and operating viewpoint, to update their accounts every day.

Unpredictability—as reflected in the number of possible alternatives and variations—has an important bearing on the value of information and the design and implementation of business data systems. A system to handle the number of hours worked on individual jobs is more elaborate than a system to keep track of the number of people on the payroll, for variations in the number of hours worked is much greater than in the number of people employed. A job-order production shop demands a more complex data-processing system than a factory operating an assembly line. And highly standardized factory operations are adequately served by relatively simple data-processing systems. Careful observation of the alternatives and variations that may arise helps determine how much detail is useful for an information control system.

Timeliness. Information may be timely in the sense of being available at a suitable time or being well-timed. Timeliness, or the age of information, has three components: interval, delay, and reporting period. *Interval* is the period of time—minutes, days, months, etc.—between the preparation of successive reports or answers to inquiries. *Delay* is the length of time between the cut-off point—the time when no more transactions are accepted for inclusion in the particular report—and the distribution of reports to users. The delay covers the time required to process data and to prepare and distribute reports or to answer questions. *Reporting period* is the length of time that an operating report covers and may be longer or shorter than the interval between the preparation of reports. That is, the time periods covered by successive reports may be continuous, overlapping, or have skips.

At intervals of one month, a filling station owner prepares an income-expense report for a reporting period of one month.

Each month a data-processing service bureau prepares its operating report of revenues and expenses for the current month and the year to date.

A Christmas tree retailer prepares, each December 26, a cash receipts and payments report for the period December 1 to December 24.

For moving or running totals or averages—for example, shipments during the most recent thirteen periods of four weeks each—the reporting period consists of a series of four-week periods extending over 52 weeks, but the reports are prepared at four-week intervals. In short, the reporting periods may be entirely different from the interval used.

Managers often think they must have immediate or up-to-the-minute information in order to operate effectively. *Immediately* literally means pertaining to the present time or moment. The interval, delay, and reporting period would have to be extremely short or even zero in order to get immediate information. The practical results of immediate information would be immediate issuance of a continuous stream of reports covering only a short reporting period. Since a flood of reports without any time coverage is hard for the reader to assimilate and use, "up-to-the-minute information" more often means reports issued with a short delay but with the interval long enough to keep the number of reports manageable and the reporting period long enough to make their contents meaningful.

For *status or point-of-time information,* the minimum age of the newest information ever available is equal to the processing delay involved. The *delay* is the number of units of time—seconds, hours, days, etc.—that it takes to prepare and distribute reports to users. If it takes ten units of time to produce a report of inventory as of December 31, then it is first available ten units of time later. That is to say, the information is ten units of time old when it becomes available. If reported as of the end of each month, the next time new information will become available is January 31 plus ten units of time. Therefore, the age of information pertaining to a point in time ranges from a *minimum* of the delay involved in preparing the report to a *maximum* of the interval plus the reporting delay. For on-line, real-time systems, it is possible to make inquiries whenever desired to find the most recent status and to keep the maximum age near the minimum. But attempting to keep the maximum age extremely close to the minimum may keep the system fully loaded with in-quiries and replies.

If information is used as soon as it becomes available, the proc-essing delay is the primary determinant of age. The time that a man-ager spends reading reports to make decisions counts as part of the processing delay for operational purposes. Reports may come so thick and fast that the receiver cannot make full use of one before he receives other reports, or even the next issue of the same report. He must then decide whether to plow through all the reports and try to get on a current basis or to skip some and start afresh. There-fore, the timing of reports must, of course, be matched with the user's ability to use them.

> The North Country sourdough's approach to reading newspapers is interesting in this regard. The sourdough may get all the news-papers for a whole year at one time and spend the next year reading them at the rate of one a day. The news of the world unfolds for him day by day just as it does for everyone else, except that it is a year or so late.

The sourdough could, of course, discard all but the most recent issue or, preferably, order only the most recent copy of the paper. The businessman can seldom afford the luxury of steadily progress-ing through a huge backlog of reports. He must skip to the current situation and return to prior reports only to obtain background for later situations and to get answers for long-range questions.

Operating information about events occurring throughout a period of time—widgets manufactured, hours worked—covers the period of time during which the events happened. Therefore, the age of operating information depends on the length of the operating period, since some of the events happened early in the period, some near the middle, and some near the end. Information about opera-tions throughout a period of time has an inherent age of one-half a period merely because the events involved are spread throughout the reporting period. The processing delay involved in producing re-ports must be added to this inherent time lag of one-half a period to give the minimum age of information before it is available for use. As was pointed out earlier, the reporting period can be the same as or different from the interval between reports.

The maximum age of operating information is reached one report preparation interval later just before new information becomes available. The age of operating information is one-half a reporting period more than the corresponding age of status information because operating information has an inherent age of one-half a reporting period, no matter how long or short the period is. That is, the age of operating information is more dependent on the length of the reporting period and the interval than is the case for status information; delay is less important as a determinant of age.

General rules for the optimum length of the interval, delay, and reporting periods are easy to state, although they may be difficult to apply in practice. The optimum length interval is determined by two factors: (1) the amount of variation away from the projected operating result that is likely to occur during the interval used, which corresponds to the sampling period; and (2) the cost of sampling, processing, and reporting. Highly variable processes deserve short-interval reporting, even though costs of data processing increase, so that variations from plans can be detected before they grow excessive. Short-interval reporting does, however, have a drawback in that it increases the number of reports that must be prepared and used or merely scanned and discarded. During a year, the use of monthly intervals will result in 12 reports, weekly intervals in 52, and hourly intervals in 2000 or more.

The optimum length delay is determined, on the one hand, by the amount of variation away from the situation existing at the time of cut-off that is likely to occur before reports are ready for use. On the other hand, the optimum length delay depends on the cost of a higher capacity processing-reporting system to furnish outputs with an extremely short delay. A shorter delay in reporting is beneficial because a quick fix on a situation is more useful than one obtained after a long lag in which important variations may have occurred. Short-delay reporting has the advantage of enabling management to take action earlier. The value gained from earlier action is equal to the amount of improvement in operations for the time saved by the shortened delay. For most business-management situations, decision-making and delays in reporting are measured in days, and any consequential improvement requires reducing the delay by a half day, a day, or more. But many operating-control situations need reporting delays measured in hours, minutes, or seconds. In such cases, a small reduction in delay, measured in hours, minutes, or seconds, can sometimes yield large relative improvements in the degree of control over operations.

There is no clear-cut relationship between the length of the reporting period and the value of results. Extremely short reporting periods may permit unusual or superficial events to outweigh the real developments. Conversely, long reporting periods submerge unusual events in longer-term totals or averages. Some intermediate-length reporting period permits optimum sampling to obtain information that represents what is actually happening in the particular situation.

Two examples show the relationship between interval, delay, and reporting period and help draw the discussion together.

Each department manager in a store may demand reports by 10 o'clock each day showing inventory for the previous day, daily sales for the past week, weekly sales for a month, and cumulative sales for the season to date. Details are wanted for item, style, size, color, manufacturer, etc. Reports at daily intervals and one business hour of delay emphasize yesterday's activities but also cover a longer period to put each day in perspective—each report has four reporting periods: day, week, month, and season to date.

Fire alarm messages are so simple that merely pulling the handle of an alarm box transmits the message, and the firemen roar out of the station whether the call is real or false. A fire call gets a standard response with short delay and with little regard for the interval since the last call, although, if alarms occur too frequently, the whole system will be overtaxed and they cannot be answered except with an increased delay or the aid of additional equipment.

Relevance and Consequences. In order to be useful, information must be relevant to a manager's problems—or, more carefully stated, to areas needing improvement. A manager is able to make either better or more decisions when he does not have to spend his time sorting relevant facts from irrelevant ones. If available information is not related to the decision to be made, it has little if any value. The problem of information relevance is intimately related to the managerial organization pattern. The quantities and location of truck tires in inventory may be valuable information to a motor pool commander but useless to a tank company commander.

Another measure of the value of information is the consequence of having it. One useful yardstick is the benefit obtained from the information over a period of time. An inventory-control procedure that saves a penny per part is valuable if millions of parts are involved.

In some cases, a manager cannot act on information because the decision required is made at a different level of management. Or past decisions may limit his present ability to act because "sunk costs" carry over to the future. In such cases, the consequences of more information are trivial.

The possible range of consequences should be considered. If operations are already 85 per cent efficient, perfect information can increase efficiency by only 15 per cent. Information is more valuable in areas that are greatly in need of improvement. However, despite this fact, some areas of business data processing that are easy to understand and change are favorite targets for improvement. Since these areas have had so much attention already, it is unlikely that further attempts at improvement will have much pay-off. There is greater potential gain in attending to areas that were neglected in the past when satisfactory processing methods were not available. The fact that the consequences are a final link in determining the value of information must be kept in mind. The effect of a manager's knowing or not knowing some piece of information and the action that follows such knowledge are important determinants of its value.

COST OF DATA AND INFORMATION

Cost is the price paid for obtaining and processing data to produce reports. This section discusses methods of cost assignment for processing data and producing information and the factors affecting such costs.

Cost Measurement Schemes

There are two widely used methods for assigning cost to data: average cost and marginal cost. Long used for factory cost accounting, these methods are equally applicable to the costs of processing.

Average Cost. Some costs can be identified with a particular project or job for obtaining and processing data. These costs correspond to factory production costs of direct material and direct labor. Other costs of processing data cannot be easily identified with a particular project but must be distributed over all the work done. Such costs correspond to indirect factory costs—equipment depreciation, supervision, space, supplies—and are distributed by overhead rates that supplement the direct costs.

Data-processing costs for large operations may be identified readily with such major areas as purchasing, inventory control, production control, and payroll. But a detailed costing by jobs within each major area may be difficult to obtain because data-processing operations in these areas are interrelated. One set of data may be used for several different purposes, and data from different sources may be combined for one purpose. If costs vary with the amount of work done, job cost accounting can give useful answers for guiding management. Direct costs may be closely related to the volume of work; indirect costs may be essentially fixed and change little or not at all with changes in production volume. The average cost scheme is often used to distribute costs so that the total costs are completely distributed among all the users. The arithmetical niceties of the average cost scheme appear to give it stature beyond its actual merits for decision-making. Highly automatic operations, whether in a factory or office, have a high fraction of fixed costs that vary little with changes in the volume of data handled. In such cases, job cost accounting loses much of its meaning, and another method for assigning costs is more useful.

Marginal Cost. Marginal cost, popularly called "out-of-pocket cost," is the amount that costs change as volume changes. Despite large changes in the volume of data handled or reports produced, the operating costs of an automatic data-processing system are essentially constant and marginal cost is small. Marginal costing charges a job with only the additional costs incurred because of that job. For example, a report might be prepared at a small marginal cost by starting with data already collected for other purposes and be completed within the basic operating schedule for both equipment and people. The marginal cost concept is often used when considering the installation of a data-processing system. People talk of starting equipment on important "bread-and-butter" applications to absorb the total cost of the system. They start other applications that benefit by not having to absorb any costs. No charge is made against additional applications because the marginal cost is zero.

The use of either the average cost or the marginal cost scheme has certain consequences when changes occur in the volume of data handled. For an automatic system with large fixed costs, the average cost per unit is high when volume is low and such costs may further discourage use of the equipment. The opposite is also true. Average costing may lead to either too little or too much work.

Actually, it is probably wise to encourage use of an idle system and discourage use of an overloaded system. Marginal costing is sensitive to the system load. If equipment is idle, marginal cost is small and encourages use. If equipment is fully loaded, marginal cost is high and discourages use. Marginal cost is the full increase in costs for equipment, personnel, and supplies, and is high for the first application and the application that requires more equipment or that causes second-shift operation. To overcome this feature of marginal costs, basic system costs may be lumped together and not allocated to individual jobs. Actually, decisions either to tolerate idle capacity of equipment or to use it to full capacity are often made implicitly on the basis of marginal costs.

Factors Determining Cost

The costs of operating a data-information system depend on many factors, the most important of which are discussed here: quality, quantity, timeliness, and capacity. Some other factors are touched on briefly: flexibility, communications, processing schemes, and rate of transition.

Quality. The nature of the quality of data and information were covered earlier in this chapter when discussing the value of information and also in Chapter 14 where the cost aspects of accuracy were emphasized. The point was made that costs increase rapidly as the degree of accuracy of information is pushed toward the limit of perfection. The degree of quality maintained in a system is related to the costs of achieving any particular degree and the benefits obtainable from having it. An organization usually keeps track of the total amount of accounts receivable with more accuracy than it does the value of inventory. Costs involved in determining inventory value, or even the identification of items and the number of units on hand, may force the organization to stop appreciably short of the ultimate degree of accuracy. The retail inventory scheme, for example, uses the ratio of cost to selling price for merchandise purchased in order to convert the inventory, valued at selling price, back to cost. The use of ratios is an indication that the loss of accuracy in finding the cost of inventory might be more than balanced by the expense reduction from not keeping detailed records.

Results may differ from true values because of people's mistakes, errors in the calculation plan, or malfunctions in equipment. Inaccuracies can arise at any stage from data origination to report preparation. People may misunderstand or misread original data, or make mistakes in operating typewriters and keypunches when preparing data for input. Instruction routines may have errors in logic that make all results erroneous. Even when most cases are handled correctly, others are unanticipated and may give erroneous results. Equipment malfunctions on either a repetitive or intermittent basis.

Many schemes based on partial or complete duplication of operations are used to increase the accuracy of results, and data origination is commonly verified by repetition. A parity-bit associated with each character helps guard against the accidental gain or loss of a bit that would change a character. Instruction routines are checked for logic and test-checked with simulated or real data to debug them. Duplicate circuitry, programmed checks, or even both, are used to detect malfunctions in automatic processors. Double-entry, balancing, and proof schemes are commonly used to ensure accuracy in manual or mechanical accounting systems; more elaborate plans are used with automatic processing systems.

These plans for increasing accuracy (decreasing the difference between results and the true value) also increase the cost of processing data. Additional precautions are required to increase the margin of accuracy from 0.99 to 0.999, 0.9999, and so forth. The precautions required grow rapidly as the margin of accuracy approaches 1.0. The important point here is that increasing the accuracy of results—measured in terms of either their precision or their reliability—adds to the cost of originating and processing data. Much of the cost increase arises from the trouble involved in organizing and policing data origination and transcription methods.

Quantity. The quantity of reports, files, and data handled has an important effect on the costs of systems operations. For example, an increase in the number of transactions of a particular type may cause a strictly proportional increase in the costs of originating raw data. Some costs may remain essentially constant, provided there is any idle capacity. An increased volume of data may be transmittable over leased lines at almost no cost.

Important economies may be available in other ways, such as by processing a larger volume of transactions by means of the same programs so that only small additional programming and set-up costs are involved. Cost increases that are less than proportional to volume increases are obtainable in most systems using large amounts of equipment. The fixed costs of the system buy a large basic capability; increased capacity is obtained at a small outlay merely by more intensive use of equipment.

Some costs, on the other hand, probably increase more rapidly than larger volume alone would indicate. More intensive and more elaborate controls are required to achieve a certain degree of quality when the number of transactions increases. More care is required to ensure that data are originated for all transactions, that none are lost in the communication network, and that the right programs and files are used in processing transactions. The quantity of data in each record in the files, as reflected in the number of data elements, appears to have more than a proportional effect on processing costs. A larger number of data elements in the record design requires the preparation of a more elaborate program to process the file and to prepare the myriad analyses that are possible from the larger quantity and variety of data. Also, a larger quantity of input data is required to set up the initial record and to keep it current thereafter. The mere fact that a record has more data elements in it means there is a higher incidence of change: a wider variety of input data must be obtained, and obtained more frequently, in order to keep an elaborate record current and correct. Also, a more elaborate record offers better potential for analysis and is likely to be retained longer and analyzed more carefully than a short record. Consider the implications of just one aspect of a utility record—the amount of electricity consumed and the quantity of detail kept in the record for each customer.

Consumption for the most recent month.

Consumption for the most recent month and the minimum and maximum amounts for any month in the current calendar year.

Consumption for the most recent month and for each of the twelve preceding months.

The effort involved in establishing the file is appreciably greater for the second and third cases. In fact, when first adopting the latter record design, it is impossible, at any reasonable cost, to set up the record, since a year's history is not available. Only the new meter reading is necessary each month to calculate consumption for the most recent month, but appreciably more processing is involved in keeping track of the minimum and maximum consumptions for the year to date or consumption by months for the preceding year. This progression in the work involved in file updating arises solely because of record design and content, for only one input each month is actually needed to update the record. From this simple case involving only one part of a record it is possible to gain some idea of how a large and intricate record is likely to increase data-gathering and processing costs.

Timeliness.   Three classes of operations are worth considering here. Some operations involved in processing data are carried on throughout a reporting interval without regard for the length of the interval. Data origination and some processing operations may be continuous. Other operations, such as file maintenance and processing, may be variable, but they must be done at least once before reports are prepared.

The use of short *report preparation intervals* involves additional processing cycles during any time period. For example, a high fraction of the total cost of processing magnetic-tape files is incurred merely by passing tape through the processor. The tape read-write time may be essentially the same for low or high activity of the records. In such tape-limited processing—file updating can be done during the time required to read and write the files—costs are more closely related to the number of file-processing cycles than to the number of transactions handled. The cost of summarizing files and preparing reports is related to the number of reports prepared, and some costs of processing—updating files and preparing reports—may double if the reporting interval is cut in half. The ultimate, as the interval between reports approaches zero, is for costs to become infinite.

Going in the other direction, as the report preparation interval becomes longer, the costs of processing data are also likely to increase. Extremely long intervals require holding more data in active storage until reports are prepared and a new period starts. The preparation of reports serves the useful but little noticed purpose of permitting a purge of active files and adoption of a new starting point. The cost implications of extremely short intervals have practical importance for systems utilizing magnetic-tape files.

> Systems analysts in one company reported that, over a long period, weekly processing of a policy holder's file was about four times as expensive as monthly processing. Similarly, a manufacturing company reported that daily inventory processing would cost about four times as much as weekly processing.

To the extent that tape file processing is limited by internal operating speeds, processing at shorter intervals may be obtained at little cost, since processor running time is not increased in proportion to the frequency of updating. This discussion of the effect of changing the length of the processing interval presumes that the processing technique remains constant. Another method of file storage would, of course, have a different set of cost curves, although probably with similar characteristics. It appears that the cost of random-access file processing on addressable bulk-storage disks or drums would be at a minimum for some report preparation interval, but would increase if the interval was either shorter or longer. But costs would increase less rapidly for processing disk or drum files than for tape files at short intervals because random-access files get at the next active record in less time. On the other hand, a long interval for file updating and reporting would, it seems, greatly increase processing costs because of the large number of disks or drums required to hold the larger volume of files. Protracted intervals mean that data must be carried forward for a long time before reports are prepared and files can be purged. A curve with a minimum point in the center and higher points on either side is said to be "U" shaped. The objective in systems design is to avoid ending up in either of the high cost areas.

Report preparation may cost less for random-access equipment than for magnetic-tape files because the data transfer rate from some types of disks and drums is faster than for sequential data on magnetic tapes. This is especially true for limited volumes of data to be selected from a large file. In short, data-origination costs may be the same for systems using either magnetic-tape or random-access storage; short-interval processing may be less for a random-access system; and report preparation may be less for a random-access system, especially for small volumes of reports and short intervals.

For any particular system using certain methods—manual, electromechanical, or electronic—there is some optimum *processing delay* that gives the lowest operating costs. System and equipment capacity are used at a high fraction of capacity throughout the interval and neither an overload nor idleness occurs. Shortening the processing delay, for a particular type of system and equipment, increases costs. Shorter delays increase costs because additional capacity is required, scheduling is more difficult, and average usage is likely to be lower. As the delay is decreased toward zero, costs skyrocket because no system, even a "blue-sky" one, is capable of producing results with zero delay. Moving in the other direction, longer delays are also likely to increase processing costs. The system may bog down because it must store and deal with a great quantity of data before processing can be completed and the files purged or downgraded to inactive storage.

These general comments on the cost of processing and length of delay are not restricted to any particular system and type of equipment, but apply to all. Changes in a system or its equipment merely alter the cost-delay relationship but do not destroy it. It appears that a "U"-shaped cost curve is generally true for the costs of processing delay for any processing scheme.

Capacity. The capacity of a system must be large enough to handle peak loads. For a steady work load, the use of either faster equipment or more equipment can reduce delay. But work loads are uneven; some trade-off must be made between increased system capacity and longer processing delays. The fixed costs of a system for equipment, space, basic personnel, and programming are likely to be determined chiefly by the maximum capacity of the system. Operating costs for supplies, second-shift rental, and others, are more sensitive to total volume. When the peak load is far larger than the average processing load, either more capacity must be provided to handle the peak, or the elapsed time required for processing will grow. Such added capacity may then be idle until the next peak load occurs.

Staggering or overlapping intervals so that peak loads occur at different times may smooth out loads on the system. Cycled work loads can increase the use of processing facilities, but this approach does not directly attack the basic problem of short delays and the high cost of adequate capacity for peak-load processing. Eventually, a "one-hoss shay" effect occurs because a number of different-length intervals end at the same time to cause a huge work load. In effect, the staggered scheduling system falls apart, and a new schedule has to be adopted to ease the work load. As the acceptable delay is permitted to increase, the maximum capacity required drops off from the peak-load quantity, and levels off just above the average load. Obviously, a system must have enough capacity to handle present applications, and additional capacity may have to be obtained in advance because available equipment comes in only a few sizes. The choice among central processors is restricted to a small number of sizes, although much more freedom exists to add relatively small units of peripheral equipment later when needed.

Other Factors. Several other factors affect the cost of a data-processing system. Some that are merely touched on here are flexibility, communication methods, processing scheme, and rate of transition.

Flexibility costs money. A system limited to one or a few specific applications that do not change has a minimum cost. At the other extreme, a system may be flexible enough to deal with any application. In such a case, more capacity, systems analysis, and programming capability are required to handle applications. *Communications methods* used may range from regular or air mail to wire and radio transmission. Each, of course, has different cost functions that vary with the channel capacity and volume of data transmitted. *Processing schemes* may be standardized or selective. The exception principle, internal decision, adaptive, and variable processing plans described earlier in this chapter are examples of selective processing schemes. Analysis and programming costs for a selective processing scheme are higher than for standardized processing. After a selective processing scheme is set up, however, its operating costs may be low because attention is focused on situations where it is needed.

The *rate of transition* from the old system to the new also affects costs. Rapid changes from one system to another result in confusion and lost motion. Some people, in fact, hold that important changes in a system cannot be made efficiently more frequently than once every three to five years by a large organization.

RELATIONSHIP BETWEEN VALUE AND COST

From an economic viewpoint, information is a factor in production similar to manpower, equipment, and material. Obtaining better information—measured in terms of quality, quantity, and timeliness—may permit larger savings in other factors.

Railroads have recently introduced automatic systems for reporting train location and, by using sidings for passing, are able to get most of the benefits of double tracks yet save the investment and maintenance costs. If high-speed communication and control systems had been available a hundred years ago, probably few double-track roads would have been built.

Many companies buy credit reports to get more information about a prospect's rating in order to balance the risk of loss against the profit from accepting an order. The organization supplying credit reports deals solely in gathering data and interpreting them into credit ratings for sale to any purchaser. The report buyer weighs the costs of information against the increased profits from accepting orders from customers whose credit can be appraised.

The general rule for deciding how much data and information to obtain corresponds to the rules applicable to the other factors of production. Continue to use more of a factor until the cost of the next unit is just equal to the benefits obtained from using it. While applying this rule to data-information systems is difficult, it is probably no more so than applying it to other production factors.

PROBLEMS IN DEVELOPING GENERAL PRINCIPLES

The foregoing discussion of value and cost of information has been lengthy because few general principles or rules exist to serve as guides for designing data-processing systems. Truly general rules could, if they existed, be stated very briefly. The causes of this lack of general principles deserve some comment.

The first reason for a lack of general principles is that operating data-information systems are *difficult to describe* in simple terms. This is true whether the system uses manual, punched card, or electronic methods. Analysis is expensive and time-consuming. Systems do not remain in a "steady state" but continue to change even during analysis. In fact, the rate of change may outrun the analysts who must keep abreast of the old system while designing a new one. Any attempt merely to analyze a system will change it and, where people are involved, change it appreciably. Simply asking a responsive person, "What do you do?" or "Why do you do it?" is likely to lead to some change.

Second, the operating *environment* and the *problems* to be handled differ from one case to the next. Reports, files, and data inputs are different, even though equipment and operations are similar; and such differences limit the value of comparing operations in different environments. Comparison of a proposed system with one that does not change or with an extrapolation of the present system may be valuable for drawing valid conclusions about the effect of new proposals. Laboratory models or controlled experiments are sometimes useful for showing the effect of certain changes. But it is difficult to use a business *per se* as a laboratory for testing new ideas about data processing because of the unsettling effect of experimentation and the risk that untested initial operations may fail and discredit the whole system effort. Hard-headed managers insist upon having solutions that work when first installed.

A third reason for the lack of any general rules is that the use of electronic equipment and advanced *techniques* is still relatively new. Experience now available covers only a small number of years and a limited number of complete cycles from initial installation to introduction of still newer equipment or discard of the system and return to the old. Imagine the problem of an insurance actuary asked to predict average life expectancy from life histories of many children and a few adults, but no deceased persons. The massive introduction of electronic equipment by many organizations in a few years has foreclosed many of the benefits from learning from the experience and mistakes of others. More knowledge would have been generally available from a slower rate of introduction. Important changes in both equipment and the systems built around the equipment occur frequently, and they will continue to occur indefinitely.

Fourth, data-processing systems are *complex*. Many alternate configurations of equipment are available to solve a particular problem. The system built around the equipment in order to handle the origination of data and distribution of results reaches throughout all parts of a business organization. The combination of equipment configurations and highly complex management information systems produces a set of possible data-processing systems that are too numerous to evaluate properly.

These four factors—difficulties of description, lack of laboratory conditions, newness of electronic equipment, and complexity of equipment and systems—impede the development of exact rules for systems design and operation. A formula would be useful for determining system and equipment needs and ways of using them. Lacking a formula, one approach to solving the problem—an approach useful in any field—is to search for some of the basic ideas involved for an understanding of the concepts or general principles. This approach is especially important in such a new and developing field as automatic data processing. General principles must be developed before useful, specific rules can be devised. A search for general principles reveals new facets of a subject, puts various features into perspective, and discloses new relationships.

SUMMARY

At the *syntactic* level, data are collections of symbols or characters arranged in some orderly way—for example, documents, files, or reports—to serve as the vehicle for information. Information is the meaning derived from data and represents the *semantic* level—the relationship between a symbol and the actual object or condition that is symbolized. The impact of the objects or conditions on the receiver and the action that he can take represent the *pragmatic* level of information.

Complete, detailed reports may show the variations between actual and forecasted results; this is a first step toward reporting by the exception principle, which can be extended to omit items that do not have significant variations. Using a normal range is one way to set limits for reporting exceptional values. Items within the normal range can be handled by one decision rule, whereas items falling outside require different action. Normal ranges for screening items that are not controlled can be used at many stages of report preparation.

Expected values may be based on the actual or average amount experienced in the past or upon a forecast of future results. Variations from budgeted or projected values can be measured in the same units as the data or in relative terms—percentages, or variations. The exception-principle scheme is designed to improve the content of *action* reports by increasing their impact on the receiver. Items reported infrequently can be dropped from action reports; complete reports can be prepared for *reference* purposes.

A processing plan for making internal decisions applies management decision rules during the main stream of data processing. Managers can still review the results of applying the rules before using the results from processing, and analyze in detail any situations out of control. A manual intervention plan provides for equipment to follow rules where suitable, but situations not covered by rules are turned over to people in order to combine the best abilities of man and machine. More elaborate and sophisticated systems that can better adapt to their environment are in the offing.

The *value* of information is often treated as an intangible not amenable to analysis. Another approach is to treat the value of information as being just equal to the cost of processing. A better approach to studying the value of information is to examine its managerial implications. The crucial question is, "What does the information contribute to managerial decisions and over-all operations?" Factors that affect the value of information are quality, quantity, timeliness, and relevance. The timeliness of information depends on the length of the interval, the reporting period, and the processing delay. The minimum, average, and maximum ages of information suitable for each situation must be considered during systems design.

Information needs to be relevant to the problems that the receiver of a report can handle. The consequences arising from knowing something depend on how much change in operations that knowledge will lead to in actual practice. Operations that are predictable require little or no information for effective control, whereas dynamic operations require elaborate control.

The concepts of *cost*—both average and marginal—are pertinent to the volume of data handled and to decisions for changing procedures. Factors that have an important bearing on the cost of processing data are quality, quantity, timeliness, and relevance. Short intervals and frequent reports go together; they are two sides of the same coin. The costs of reporting probably double each time the interval is cut in half. On the other hand, the value of reports first increases and then may actually decrease as intervals are made shorter. In extremely short intervals, unusual events may outweigh and mask the underlying events. The delay—the length of time before a report about a single event or a series of events is available —can be shortened to get up-to-date reports. Costs may increase rapidly, if large facilities are used to meet peak demands for quick processing because such facilities are underutilized most of the time. The increase in the value of results learned sooner—whether an hour, minutes, or seconds earlier—depends on the circumstances of the situation.

Some of the basic ideas in this chapter are summarized in Figure 15-4. The *process* column shows the operation of an information system starting from input data and extending to the action flowing from decisions. The *considerations* show the factors important at each stage of processing. The nature of input data is fundamental to the design and operation of the whole system. All four factors are considered for selection of input data. The data-processing system has some measure of control over kind, quality, quantity, and timeliness, at least at the syntactic level. The makeup of reports is determined in terms of their information content. A decision maker gets certain quantities of reports with some specified degree of kind, quality, quantity, timeliness, and format. The primary considerations for a report user are the meaning and impact of reports— their semantic aspect. Following these, he must consider the practical consequences of his action.

The *cost and value* emphasize the point that costs are incurred at every stage of processing while benefits result only from managerial action utilizing system output. The *raison d'être* of an information system is to improve the operation of the organization. Even good decisions are valueless unless they lead to action.

For several reasons, few general principles or rules exist for guidance in designing data-processing systems: analysis is expensive and time-consuming, systems are essentially unique to an environment, insufficient experience with new equipment is available to permit long-run conclusions, and data-processing and information-production systems are complex because they pervade an entire organization.

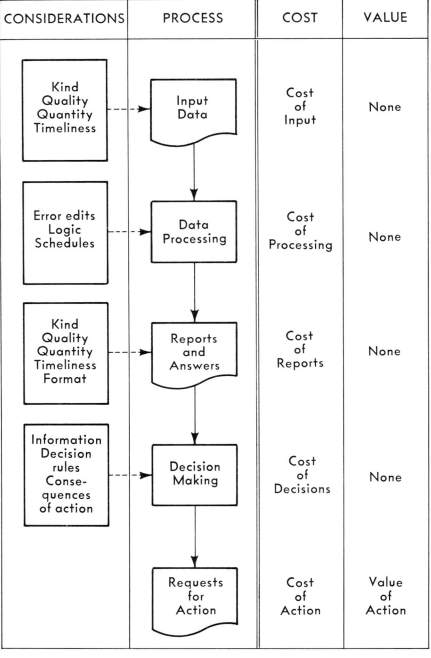

FIGURE 15-4. *Value and cost in a data-processing system.*

PART VI
EQUIPMENT ACQUISITION
AND UTILIZATION

16
Feasibility and Applications Studies

Earlier discussion has made it clear that setting up an effective data-processing system is a complex and lengthy job. A detailed and carefully organized plan for examining and weighing facts and opinions is necessary. Many policy and operating decisions must be made involving long-run commitments and therefore large amounts of money, for the costs of such commitments are likely to exceed the direct, immediate outlays for equipment.

In the feasibility study, the data-processing requirements of an organization and the equipment that will be available are analyzed to determine whether new equipment and a related data-processing system will be more efficient than the system in use. Application studies are more detailed and careful extensions of the feasibility study and should be conducted within the framework of the general planning and scope of that study. The feasibility and applications studies are the first two steps in a long chain of events leading to the introduction and operation of a new system. The steps in making any important change in a system may be listed in the following order:

1. Feasibility study: preliminary process of determining the over-all suitability of applying or not applying data processors to specific operations
2. Applications study: detailed process of designing a system or set of procedures for using data processors for selected functions or operations and establishing the specifications for equipment suitable to the needs
3. Equipment acquisition proposal: recommendation for management action supported by feasibility and applications studies and other facts

4. Procurement: arrangements necessary to buy or rent equipment and supporting facilities
5. Preparation for installation: training, programming, testing, debugging, site preparation, organization adjustments, and communications arrangements
6. Parallel operations and conversion: a period during which the old and new systems are operated concurrently until the new one is proved adequate

FEASIBILITY STUDY

The interrelationships of the many systems that make up the data-information structure of an organization must be examined. An integrated approach requires the most thorough effort by the systems analysts and management conducting the study. In fact, the terms "automatic" and "integrated" are sometimes used interchangeably in describing data-processing systems. A sound feasibility study must consider all of the organization's systems; it cannot be performed on a piecemeal basis.

After starting with a period of orientation and then pursuing over-all and detailed investigation, the feasibility study group will reach one of two conclusions. One conclusion is that the present system seems better than any new system studied, in which case the study group has two choices. First, it may examine additional systems in case any were overlooked originally or any new developments occurred during the study period. Second, if all available systems were studied with care and none found superior to the existing system, it may discontinue the feasibility study pending new developments that merit consideration. The other conclusion is that one or more new systems appear to be better than the present system, in which case the feasibility study group may proceed to the applications study, described later in the chapter.

The feasibility study is important to the success of a prospective system, for initial decisions affect all future actions. A negative decision is all-important because it may be the only one made for a long while. A premature conclusion that a proposed system will be highly profitable may cause important factors to be overlooked later. The feasibility study is an extremely important step and a time-consuming, complicated process that should be taken seriously. If other improvements can be made, there may be no need for an automatic system. The feasibility of installing automatic systems should be determined only after considering all the practicable improvements in procedures and systems that can be made without installing elaborate equipment. Two valuable by-products of such a study are the discipline it requires of analysts and the opportunities it opens up for systems improvement.

Orientation

Since it is not clear at the start how extensive the change should be or how much to spend on a new system, early phases should attempt to reduce the degree of uncertainty. The initial task is to understand the unsolved problems and learn how to deal with them, rather than to make system changes or buy equipment.

Obtaining Support. The first step in planning a feasibility study is to enlist management support and establish good employee relations. The support of top management can be obtained by suitable presentations, orientations, and briefings. Such support is vital because of the long period of time spent following a feasibility study in gathering facts and doing detailed systems analysis. Support of all personnel who will be affected is also required to bring about the organizational and procedural adjustments necessary to improve the system. The point should be made crystal clear that top management wants effective results from the study.

The initiation of feasibility studies may alarm the staff and working force because of the possibility of machines replacing people. Employees should be completely informed in order to obtain their full cooperation. If resulting personnel adjustments are to be absorbed by attrition or minimized by reassignment, in preference to any reduction in force, the announcement of this policy will be reassuring. Some employees will be retrained and reassigned within the organization to higher-paying jobs; others may be shifted sideways and, possibly, downward.

Preliminary Study Group. The first step in a feasibility study is to determine study objectives, then assign people to the project. An accountant from the controller's department, a systems or industrial engineer, and an operating department head might work together. There should be one person working full time who is responsible for keeping the study going; others may serve full time or part time. A group representing diverse interests can establish close liaison throughout the organization, recognize and understand the problems, and compensate for the biases of individual members.

At least one member of the group should be familiar with operations and with the major problems that each section faces. If possible, there should be a member with several years of experience at the location being studied. One member should be familiar with data-processing equipment and modern business control procedures. Such knowledge can be acquired through books and articles dealing with equipment and its application to situations similar to those being studied. Firsthand discussion with more experienced users is invaluable for learning the good and bad features of equipment under operating conditions. Members should attend classes, conferences, and seminars dealing with data-processing equipment, programming, methods, and machine operations. At this stage, group members need to understand only the abilities and limitations of data-processing equipment and methods, although at least one member should have detailed knowledge about the data-information requirements of each area of the organization.

Preliminary Investigation.   The study group should complete the preliminary investigation in a feasibility study within a few months and should try to determine the following:

1. Requirements throughout the organization for data processing and information in the present and in the near future
2. Available equipment and methods
3. Estimated costs in personnel, time, and money to complete the feasibility study
4. Estimates of costs and benefits for a complete study and installation; if possible, estimates should be supported by the experience of other organizations

The study group should keep management informed by oral and written reports. Although ordinarily management is unfamiliar with the technical aspects of data-processing systems, it should be able to decide from the feasibility study preliminary report whether to continue the project with costs and benefits as estimated. If management is unwilling to continue, the feasibility study should be terminated or shelved awaiting further developments. However, the expense of further study seldom is by itself sufficient cause for shelving a project. The loss from over-extending a study is likely to be small compared with the potential gains from important system improvements. If the study is continued but leads to the decision that change is not feasible, only the cost of the study, at most, is lost. On the other hand, large potential benefits may be lost from prematurely stopping the study.

Over-all Investigation

Over-all investigation requires setting objectives, defining problems, organizing the feasibility study, and obtaining competent personnel. A proper balance is needed between experience with operations under study, knowledge of new kinds of equipment to be used, and experience of others in tackling similar problems.

Selection of Objectives. If management concludes from the preliminary study that an extended feasibility study should be made, the preliminary report can help define the objectives. The careful selection of objectives is important, although it may be desirable to modify them or even completely change them as the study progresses. Since the selected objectives influence the nature of the end product, the advantages and disadvantages of each possible objective must be determined. Examining the probable results of each objective determines whether they are desirable. For example, over-emphasis on up-to-the-minute information may result in a high-cost system. Unless current information is extremely useful for operations or for management, it should not be a primary objective for the systems study.

The study group should use objectives as real, working guides for the detailed feasibility study. Since the main objective is to increase company profits, any and all operations that affect the cost of processing data and the value obtained from information are relevant for study. This wide scope creates a problem: a broad approach is desirable for developing the best system, but it may introduce complexities beyond the time and money budgeted for the feasibility study group. One simple way to identify areas for further analysis is to list important users, processors, and suppliers of data in the organization. For each organizational unit, it is useful to consider the following items:

1. Reports and documents produced by or for the unit
2. Files maintained by the unit for reference purposes
3. Processing done by or for the unit
4. Data collected within or obtained by the unit
5. Volume, cost, and time requirements for the above items
6. Requirements imposed by external conditions that are easy or difficult to change
7. Internal changes desirable for each unit, such as more, newer, or cheaper information

Another approach to selecting areas for study is to start with the obvious targets for improvements, such as high-volume operations or repetitive operations with high clerical costs. These operations may by themselves justify the use of new equipment and a new system.

Definition of Problem.   The object and scope of the feasibility study should be defined in a written charter. A careful outline is important because the study cuts across organization lines and requires authority for suggesting possible changes in procedures, forms, reports, or organization. A written charter helps ensure the study's progress against intervention by management and supervisory personnel and reduces the possibility of branching onto tangents. A time-schedule of goals and priorities helps bring the study to a satisfactory conclusion and provides benchmarks for reviewing the progress achieved. In any event, management should firmly fix responsibility for the study and assign adequate authority, staff, and resources to meet time schedules.

Organization of Study.   In organizing the study, management must decide on the composition and education of the working group, and whether to use consultants.

The *working group* may include, because of their study experience, members of the preliminary study group. Since the full-time effort of those directing the study is usually required, it is preferable to select individuals who will remain with the organization and can be assigned to later applications studies.

The chairman of the group should be well informed on the functions and operations of the entire organization and personally able to plan and carry out major projects. The following qualifications are desirable:

1. Ability to communicate persuasively
2. Ability to reason
3. Ability to work with groups representing diverse functions and processes
4. Experience in the operating areas of the business

Working members of the group should be supervisors or executives of the organization, management engineers or analysts, and people experienced in various functional fields throughout the organization.

The *education* of the working group should cover methods of conducting a feasibility study, data-systems design and operation, and enough of the fundamentals of electronic data processing so that members can understand the capabilities and limitations of electronic equipment. The group should study the technical literature of the field and keep informed on new and possible future developments in methods and machines. Some members should learn about programming techniques in order to be able to appraise them. Certain members may benefit by attending professional society meetings, or by taking courses given by universities, service schools, and manufacturers. Several manufacturers offer programming courses in which the abilities, complexities, and limitations of equipment are taught. The minimum *scope* of training for the working group should cover the capabilities, limitations, and characteristics of electronic processors, punched-card equipment, communication devices, and conventional office machines. By obtaining a broad perspective, the group can appraise equipment and avoid a bias toward one particular kind.

Industry frequently employs specialized *consulting firms* to make feasibility studies and do systems analysis. Although consultants are likely to have greater objectivity and experience, which enables them to avoid mistakes they have previously encountered, one disadvantage is that they must be trained in the client's operations. Also, if their services are terminated after the equipment is installed, they take with them much of the knowledge required for successful and continuing operation of the system. Generally, an organization's own personnel, with appropriate assistance from consultants or specialists, are capable of doing the feasibility study and systems analysis.

Detailed Study Area

The feasibility study team first develops the over-all picture of an organization's data-processing requirements. Next, it selects areas likely to derive the largest benefits from using new procedures and equipment. It should study these areas in detail to determine whether they merit using advanced data-processing methods. The ideal approach is to study the largest possible area at one time in order to gain good perspective. Many functions operate jointly and receive data from or send data to other functions. Studying them together permits considering their common as well as their individual problems. This is the *systems* approach, which examines the whole operation rather than its parts. But because analysis of large areas raises many problems that must be dealt with simultaneously, there is the risk that resultant increases in cost and confusion may outweigh some of the benefits of the systems approach. If prompt results are wanted or if personnel and funds are limited, a study of more limited scope is probably suitable.

Some factors to consider when choosing an area of data processing for detailed study are the history of the operation, experience with similar applications, expected benefits, costs, personnel, resources, flexibility, and relationships of various areas.

History of an Operation.   The history of a particular operation, both locally and elsewhere, often helps to determine whether it should be considered for detailed study. Two important facets are the previous efforts to improve similar operations and the prior systems work for the area in question. Data-processing operations fall into three classes for this purpose: operations already successfully handled with advanced techniques elsewhere, untried operations, and automatic techniques tried but not yet successfully used.

An operation deserves detailed study if other companies have *successfully converted* a similar operation to advanced methods and equipment. The experience of others is valuable for pointing out fruitful areas, typical costs, and efficient system design. Risks are reduced when new techniques are applied to areas where successful applications already exist.

Untried areas, despite the uncertainty, should be studied in detail if potential benefits seem large. Proven areas are preferable, of course, to untried areas when the possible benefits are roughly equal, since unexplored areas offer little or no experience for guidance. However, the lack of experience of others may encourage finding an excellent method rather than accepting a mediocre one already available. Electronic processing methods are new enough that many fruitful applications are still untried; some worthwhile applications are untried because they exist in only a few organizations. Untried areas probably involve higher conversion costs than areas with a successful history of conversion and application. The risks of complete or partial failure are higher in new areas, but new applications must be tried to realize full benefit.

Operations initiated by others but *not yet successfully implemented* should be examined afresh. Proper analysis and a scientific approach will determine specific areas for improvement regardless of past history or degree of mechanization through punched-card equipment or other methods. The issue is not what other people have failed to do in the past, but what positive steps can be taken in a particular case to develop improved systems.

Usually an area under study will have been subjected to some *prior systems work*. Some areas may have progressed through several cycles of improvement, as from manual methods to book-keeping machines to punched-card equipment. In other areas, however, limited analysis and change may have left them dormant over long periods of time. Before thoroughly analyzing and mecha-nizing an area, two important points should be considered. First, for an operation previously analyzed or mechanized, the cost and time required to convert it to a new technique are less than for a similar operation not analyzed or mechanized. Second, the cost savings or additional benefits are smaller, however, than for a simi-lar operation presently being handled by less efficient methods. In other words, although areas incompletely analyzed or handled by inefficient methods have higher conversion costs, their prospective benefits are greater.

Expected Benefits.   The *present costs* of data-processing opera-tions can indicate whether it is economically feasible to use new equipment. Such costs are either *replaceable*—they can be saved by the introduction of new methods—or *nonreplaceable*—they continue despite the adoption of new methods. Some kinds of data-processing work will continue unchanged even with new methods, and the cost of these cannot be completely avoided; for example, the work of preparing input data and handling exceptions may re-main unchanged or even increase. If a new system is introduced which is not expected to gain any important new benefits, the area chosen should have replaceable costs at least equal to the costs of the proposed equipment and related system. An area with small replace-able costs is a dubious prospect for conversion if no additional bene-fits are expected or desired.

Areas with limited replaceable costs which may derive additional benefits by *improving results* should be considered for conversion. In addition to accuracy, speed, and flexibility, automatic equipment will produce the following benefits: quicker reporting of results by decreasing the processing time; more frequent reporting, permitting real-time control of rapidly changing operations; solving mathe-matical and logical problems involving sequences of calculations too elaborate for punched-card or manual solution; and gaining the ability to handle increased workloads at small additional costs.

Office *personnel* can benefit from automatic systems that reduce routine tasks. Although several months may be required for training, the routine of an office job may thereafter lead to discontent and a large turnover of personnel. Thus, employment and training costs are high and operations are inefficient. Since electronic systems do not become bored or have personal prejudices, they can take over routine tasks, leaving people to do more interesting and productive work.

Automatic data processing can also reduce *space* requirements. Sometimes management may want larger quantities of more useful information, but there will be no room for more clerks, desks, and files. More space may be obtained and existing methods continued or an automatic system may replace enough filing cabinets and desks to continue operations within the available space.

Another benefit obtainable from an automatic system is the training and *practical experience* it will give personnel. If an organization plans eventually to use automatic methods on a large scale, an early venture may be partly justifiable for the experience it provides. A well-trained group, which takes a long time to develop, is invaluable in view of the general scarcity of experienced people.

Relationship of Operations.   The operating areas throughout an organization may be either independent or interdependent. Inventory control, for example, is essentially independent of personnel records, but it is closely related to production control. Operating relationships have an important bearing on the plans for data processing, for both must have the same scope and boundaries to achieve efficient operation. An example will show the nature of the *system-wide* approach.

Assume a plan is being considered in which punched-paper tape is to be used by one part of a business to communicate with other parts of the business. An intensive study of the first area's operations might show the plan to be worthwhile, but such a study is too narrow in scope. Data and reports are sent to and from many other parts of the organization so that punched-paper tape equipment is needed in many places. The entire organization should be studied, not just one segment of it. The basic problem is intra-company communications between the first department and all others that deal with it.

Interdependent operations should be analyzed by *functional areas* rather than organizational areas. More can be gained by analyzing an important functional area, such as inventory control, than by concentrating on organizational areas, such as cost accounting or production control. All related areas must be considered, even though later excluded, when a function is chosen for study. The inventory function, for example, includes inventory control and the stock-room operations, but it is closely related to purchasing, production, shipping, receiving, cataloguing, and cost accounting. All these organization areas, which make interrelated decisions on inventory, may use similar forms and common or duplicative reference files.

If, on the other hand, the *minimum-area* approach is used—the study is kept within modest limits—it is mandatory to pick an area that is independent of other areas or isolated from them. One plan for selecting a problem area for study is to find the smallest one justifying the proposed system. A single functional area should be considered first, but if it does not justify the proposed system, several functions may be considered, or the size of the proposed system may be reduced until the areas and the proposed system are in balance.

The U.S. Army Finance Center, for example, after carefully studying many areas that might benefit by automatic data processing, decided to limit the initial application to the processing of soldiers' deposits—a savings bank operation. Accordingly, a medium-scale processor was rented which would provide training and experience that could be used later when large-scale equipment was acquired covering a broader range of activities.

A large industrial company found that, by processing the payroll at one plant on a processor working ten hours a week, the money saved covered the total cost of renting, installing, and operating the processor. By concentrating all systems work in one area, the company was able to start operations months sooner than if it had used a broad approach, and other areas were converted after the payroll analysis was completed. Since the company had more than a year's experience in processor operation when it finished the major systems study work, it quickly discovered its early mistakes during actual operations and was able to avoid them later. A smaller systems study group was able to handle one area at a time.

The minimum-area approach has merit if management desires to start new operations with a minimum delay, if personnel are not available for a large study, or if no reasonable basis exists for enlarging the study area. An objection to the minimum-area approach is that the equipment obtained may be too small for future use. As further application studies are made, it may be necessary to obtain additional units or replace the original units with larger-scale equipment. However, the cost of switching from small to big equipment may be reduced by renting instead of purchasing initial equipment, although important costs are likely to be involved later in reprogramming, conversion, and installation, following a step-up from small or medium to large equipment.

One serious problem in developing a system around small equipment is that individually developed procedures may be difficult to integrate later. Generally, individual applications are converted to advanced processing equipment with minimum changes in system structure—the general scheme as opposed to exact mechanics. If additional areas are actually interrelated, as is typical, it is difficult to change one area without making changes in others, and an area-by-area approach discourages viewing the system as a whole. Two functions producing almost identical reports under the prior system will probably continue to duplicate each other's efforts under the new system. Systems analysts aware of this problem can reduce its incidence and severity, but it will persist.

The area chosen for a feasibility study should not be considered fixed. The study of problems in one area almost always leads into other areas, and large potential benefits may be discovered for an area not originally studied. On the other hand, the area first selected may turn out to be too large to handle effectively. If important new factors are discovered, the study team should consider redefining the selected area.

A decision table for selecting a course of action for certain conditions uncovered during a feasibility study is shown in Table 16-1. Preparation of this particular table assumes that the preliminary study is finished and the company is selecting a plan for further action. The conditions in the upper part of the table represent the facts uncovered during the preliminary study—for example, the amount of potential savings or the availability of trained analysts. The possible courses of actions range from discontinuing the study to enlarging the effort to a system-wide study.

Each rule represents a set of actions corresponding to a particular set of conditions determined by the preliminary study, just as it did for the decision table described in Chapter 7. For example, rule 1 states that if the preliminary study shows top management support is unavailable and savings are small, then the study should be discontinued. In this context, decision tables are useful for describing a complex management decision process rather than a data processing application *per se*.

DECISION TABLE Form	Table Name **FEASIBILITY STUDY GUIDE**		Page *I* of *I*
	Chart No. **FSG-I**	Prepared by **WILL HARRISS**	Date **JULY 20**

Stub	Body														
	Rule Number														
Conditions	1	2	3	4	5	6	7	8	9	10	11	12	13	14	15
TOP MANAGEMENT SUPPORT IS AVAILABLE	N	N	N	N	Y	Y	Y	Y	Y	Y	Y	Y			
POTENTIAL SAVINGS ARE LARGE	N	Y	Y	Y	Y	Y	Y	Y	–	–	–	N			
TRAINED ANALYSTS ARE AVAILABLE	–	N	Y	Y	N	N	N	N	–	Y	Y	N			
TIME FOR STUDY IS SHORT	–	–	–	–	–	Y	N	Y	N	Y	Y	N	–		
CONSULTANTS ARE ACCEPTABLE	–	–	–	–	Y	–	N	–	–	–	–	–			
AREAS ARE CLOSELY RELATED	–	–	Y	N	N	Y	N	N	Y	N	–	–			
Actions															
DISCONTINUE STUDY	X	X	X				X		X			X			
TRAIN ANALYSTS							X		X						
HIRE CONSULTANTS					X										
USE MINIMUM-AREA APPROACH					X	X					X				
USE SYSTEM-WIDE APPROACH							X				X				

TABLE 16-1. *Decision table for selecting a course of action in a feasibility study.*

Resources. The development and implementation of an automatic data-processing system require the following resources:

1. Manpower to
   (a) Study system and equipment feasibility and application
   (b) Conduct systems analysis and design
   (c) Program and code instruction routines
   (d) Operate and maintain equipment
   (e) Prepare input data
   (f) Use output reports

2. Money for
   (a) Personnel
   (b) Equipment acquisition and maintenance
   (c) Installation of equipment
   (d) Conversion from the old to new system
3. Space for
   (a) People
   (b) Equipment
   (c) Supplies
   (d) Files
4. Time to
   (a) Conduct studies
   (b) Obtain and install equipment
   (c) Get the new system functioning properly

The scope of problem areas selected for study should be consistent with available resources. Studying a problem requiring vast equipment is worthwhile only if resources are available for such equipment, for management may restrict funds allotted regardless of how profitable a system is likely to be. Demands for and limits on the organization's resources, whatever the reasons, must be considered in setting the scope of feasibility studies.

Conduct of Feasibility Study

Actual execution of a feasibility study requires careful planning, thorough analysis, and constant supervision to tie together the many related facets. A common error is to underestimate the time and personnel needed for a substantive study. A study of possible conversion to electronic processing should be more thorough than most management studies because it covers a broader area, requires more systems improvements, and presages larger expenditures. The feasibility study is important because it establishes the direction and intensity of systems study for a long period of time. Feasibility studies should seldom be considered too extensive, for even a simple study of one area will take several months to complete.

Procedures proved effective for one actual feasibility study are outlined here. Such procedures are intended as a guide only and, of course, require adaptation to a particular situation.

Framework of Operations.   The initial step is to determine the framework of operations for the operating activities. Legal limitations, policy directives, and managerial restrictions have an important bearing on the framework, and should be examined to determine the organization's goals. The examination also promotes early recognition of important problems, encourages considering the system in the light of its limitations, and provides criteria for checking the area studied.

The second step is to define the *organizational area* being studied for the proposed data-processing system and chart it in detail. A simple code scheme can be constructed after the organization and its components are defined. Major elements to identify are company or service, division, branch, department, unit, and sub-unit. The preliminary analysis of the organization will require correction later. A chart may be prepared showing the grade or rank of all personnel in order to keep new operations within the estimated personnel costs of the currently authorized manpower.

Procedures for Analysis.   The next step is to make a detailed analysis of the specific system in two phases: orientation and fact-finding. In the *orientation* phase, analysts obtain complete information about the existing operation from both internal and external sources. Questions to ask at this point are: What does the system do? How does this fit into the operations of the over-all organization? How well does it fulfill its intended mission? What integral links exist between this and other operations? The purpose is to fit this operation as a link into the productive or administrative chain and see exactly where it fits in relation to the whole chain. With these questions answered, the next phase can be started.

The second phase entails *collecting and cataloguing facts* about internal functioning of the system. Fact-finding can start by having the supervisor of each major organizational element describe the data-processing or paper-work activities occurring in his bailiwick. The supervisor should collect all the working documents, including local forms, used in his activity. Systems-analysis techniques discussed in Chapter 6 are appropriate here.

In the next step, analysts study the areas to be converted. A step-by-step analysis of operations will, to an imaginative analyst, suggest alternatives. The possibility of eliminating basic and intermediate records should be considered, for an electronic processor requires fewer intermediate records than a manual or mechanical system. Such records have a doubtful future value and should be examined critically. Analysis may show that data no longer needed are still being compiled or, conversely, that vital facts are not available. Useful aids for analysis are flow charts, data on workloads, time schedules, and manuals or memoranda of procedures. The objective is to get a "blow-by-blow" description of what happens. Careful analysis is likely to reveal startling facts and may produce real benefits no matter what the final decision is on a new system.

A summary should show the work related to each record and provide a validity check of the total manpower for each organizational element. Total man-hours per year should correspond with the total manpower available. If not, the difference indicates omission of some data-processing activities or inclusion of some extraneous activities. Analysts should, of course, investigate and reconcile any significant discrepancies.

Supervisors should review the summary of facts prepared for each source document and for each end-product. Workload data in man-hours per year for each source document and each end-product can be converted to an annual cost at the average hourly direct rate and also at the total cost per worker. Work-sampling techniques may be used when appropriate for the conditions under study.

Next, *cost summaries* for major organization units should be prepared. All source documents and end-products should be listed and the total costs, based on earlier estimates, for organizational sub-elements shown. The cost summary form reveals the total annual *personnel cost* for present operating methods and is the basis for determining whether mechanization can be economical. The costs should be examined to see whether they can cover the costs of various size data processors. If the operation does not justify a full-time processor, part-time use of service-bureau equipment might be considered.

The study group decides on the least-cost equipment suitable for the data-processing system requirements. Equipment, as such, is not selected at this stage; the objective is to determine comparative costs for analytic purposes. Estimated costs should cover site preparation, air conditioning, parallel operations, conversion, and supplies. Accumulated cost data are analyzed to find the economic soundness of introducing the proposed methods and equipment.

Concluding the Feasibility Study.   The feasibility study group develops a tentative design, including costs and benefits, for one or more proposed new systems. The group should prepare the following summary for each area selected and for each system considered:

1. Cost by functional area for operating the present system
2. Cost of the proposed system
   (a) Nonreplaceable costs that carry over from the present system
   (b) Additional costs for the new system

3. Cost differential for the present and the proposed system
4. Additional benefits, if any, expected from the proposed system
5. Resources for the proposed system: capital expenditures, time, space, and personnel
6. Adjustment problems: personnel relocation, equipment disposition, and others
7. Future plans for additional work, new procedures, and operations analysis

In evaluating a proposed system, its costs and benefits should be compared with those of the present system; the present system is used as a *yardstick*—either as is or with improvements. Some analysts believe the proposed system should be compared with the present system as such. Others argue that both the existing system and any possible improved version, because it may be improved by minor changes at small cost, should be used as yardsticks for a wholly-new system. Using the present system with prospective short-run improvements—whether minor or major—as a yardstick is more likely to result in the most efficient system. The time and cost required to study every possible system restricts detailed analysis to the one or two with the most promise. But the haunting question always persists whether any particular system was studied thoroughly enough to disclose its merits before it was dropped.

A new system may be justified by the *additional benefits* that can be obtained from it. A report should list the benefits, explain their desirability, and show the costs that will be increased or decreased. Continuing costs can be omitted since they should not affect the decision. Management may decide whether the benefits justify the costs by an intuitive approach—a sort of educated guessing. However, it may be possible to evaluate the extra benefits in dollars. The factors discussed in Chapters 14 and 15 that help determine the value of information are accuracy, timeliness, predictability, relevance, and consequences. Even a rough estimate of the value of information is preferable to labeling it an "intangible benefit" and not estimating the amount involved. More careful study is required if the intangible benefits seem large and the determination of value is complex.

Reporting to Management.   The feasibility study group should report to management on its activities, findings, and recommendations. These reports should be prepared intelligently and carefully, since they are the foundation for building a future data-processing system. The following list of points can serve as a useful guide:

1. Concise statement of conclusions and recommendations
   (a) Cost differences between the present and the proposed systems
   (b) Major resource requirements of the proposed systems
   (c) Extra benefits of the proposed systems
   (d) Major recommendations of the study group
2. Detailed statement of conclusions and recommendations
   (a) Breakdown of cost figures
   (b) Explanation of extra benefits
   (c) Detailed reasoning supporting the group's recommendations
   (d) Plans for initiating an applications study
   (e) Rough estimate of time scale for developing and implementing the proposed system
3. Supporting material for the study
   (a) Group's preliminary report to management
   (b) Outline of how the study was conducted
   (c) Brief description of available equipment considered useful
   (d) Copy of the over-all findings of the investigation
   (e) Discussion of why the areas for the proposed system were chosen

Sufficient detail should be included in the report to permit a decision whether to authorize an applications study. In addition, plans should be included for initiating an applications study that will develop a new system to achieve the estimated savings and that will lead to the equipment selection.

All estimates and forecasts have some degree of *uncertainty*. In the early stages, no one knows for sure how much the proposed equipment and a new system will cost to install and operate or how satisfactorily it will function. The problems which a system has been designed to handle may turn out to be trivial or the size and scope of an application may be inaccurately estimated. Feasibility study reports should make the degree of uncertainty as explicit as possible for the reader because the conclusions reached frequently hinge on many conditions. The conclusions are valid, *if* the system works as planned, *if* the equipment meets specifications, *if* people work as expected, *if* the costs do not exceed estimates, and *if* no material mistake was made in fact-finding or estimating.

Planning a data-processing system affects the long-term future of an organization and requires *looking ahead*. The transition from an existing to a proposed system is time-consuming and, for a large application, likely to be several years. After the system is in operation, another year or two may be required before it works as efficiently as planned. The data-processing requirements that deserve primary consideration are not today's problems. More important are the problems that will exist two or more years from now. Present requirements may serve as the only available guides, if estimates about future requirements, which may be much different from today's problems, are hazy.

APPLICATIONS STUDIES

Applications studies are careful, detailed extensions of the feasibility studies and should build on them. An *applications study* is defined here as the redesign of a system or set of procedures for the use of electronic data processors and the establishment of specifications for selecting equipment suitable for the system requirements.

Scope and Content of Study

The task of the applications study group is to determine the precise form of the new system by ruling out many of the alternatives considered in a feasibility study. The applications study group makes decisions on many important factors: methods and procedures to change, files to set up or eliminate, equipment to obtain or discard, and organizational changes to make in the area of data processing. After carefully designing the system, the applications study group should review it to see whether it should be studied further or shelved awaiting new developments. An important part of the applications study is a review of the whole economics of the proposal. Because the feasibility study group was not in a position to determine the precise form of the new system, new estimates of cost and value may be greatly different.

After the new system is outlined, the applications group can develop flow charts and data sheets showing workloads for the operations covered. Complete flow charts of processes and techniques are useful for preparing programs and instruction routines and for estimating processing time and costs. A separate task is to appraise the value of information to be obtained from the new system. A proposal is then prepared for top management recommending either to introduce a new system and its required equipment or to maintain the status quo. If management approves, system specifications are developed in order to prepare bid invitations with functional specifications to send to manufacturers. Following the manufacturers' replies, it is possible to evaluate and select the most promising one.

Content. The applications study should use techniques leading to optimum systems design. An initial task in an applications study is to relate source documents to the end-products by means of flow charts or lists showing data flows as described in Chapter 6. Emphasis should be placed on the importance of detailed fact-finding about everything that is done, the way in which it is done, the frequency required, man-hours needed, and the complexity of processing. Detailed analysis uncovers existing areas of duplication and overlap of source documents, data, records, and reports. It also discloses whether it is necessary to verify the data obtained and gather more data. The components of an applications study are fact-finding, preliminary evaluation, basic system design, and development of systems specifications. The applications study, if approved, leads to the preparation and submission of proposals to equipment manufacturers, followed by the evaluation and selection of equipment, which are covered in Chapter 17. Here each component of an applications study is discussed briefly.

Fact-finding must be more intensive and extensive than it was during the feasibility study, but facts available from the feasibility study should be used. The initial task of fact-finding is to ensure that all source documents are collected and related to the end-products and organizational elements. Functional specialists are interviewed to obtain facts about system operations and gain the benefit of their experience. Flow charts or lists are prepared to furnish a detailed description of the present system. Strong emphasis should be placed on gathering detailed facts about what, where, and how data are processed, the uses made of them, frequency required, and the complexity of processing. Careful development of the current organizational and personnel charts is equally important.

Preliminary evaluation is an over-all examination of the facts and flow-process charts. This analytical evaluation establishes the basis for eliminating duplication, combining details, rearranging sequences, validating records, and summarizing requirements. Any unnecessary processes can be eliminated; however, the addition of new processes and essential records or new reports wanted should be considered.

Basic Design.   Basic systems design is the first stage in *synthesizing* the new system as opposed to *analyzing* the existing one. Three goals of design are to achieve multiple use of common source data, organize files for appropriately timed reference, and develop procedural instructions to minimize the repetitive use and manipulation of data. The new system can be constructed in the form of source document designs and flow charts or decision tables, as described in Chapter 7. Organization requirements, including the need for supervisors and clerks, must be restated for the new procedures.

Equipment manufacturers and others can help in systems design, but the user is ultimately responsible for system success. The need for equipment is dictated by over-all systems requirements. Coordinated functioning of all the subsystems is required to ensure proper handling of source documents and records and to make these fill the needs of auditors as well as the requirements of management. The objective at this stage is to design a system in general terms that can make use of any capable equipment without becoming "locked" into equipment of one class or brand. Classes and types of equipment are considered at this stage of the study, but selection of particular models is postponed until later.

Development of Specifications. Development of systems specifications provides a basis for relating and evaluating the potentialities of various equipment. Such criteria are used to solicit manufacturers' proposals, to evaluate their equipment proposals, and to select equipment. For these purposes, the following minimal specifications about a system should be ascertained:

1. Input—a description of all planned inputs
    (a) Method for originating data and the media used
    (b) Format, message length, and use of numeric or alphanumeric
    (c) Daily volume, including weekly, monthly, and annual peaks for data origination
    (d) Hourly rate of data input to equipment
2. Maintenance of files—description of records to be maintained
    (a) Record types, length, and volume
    (b) Methods of file organization and processing
    (c) Rate of file activity
    (d) Numeric and alphanumeric requirements
    (e) Interrogation and reporting requirements
3. Data handling
    (a) Types of transactions to be handled and quantity of each
    (b) Quality of transactions data, checking required, and correction problems
    (c) Kinds of processing required
4. Output—a description of output needs
    (a) Kind of output and its distribution: printed copy, punched card, magnetic tape, or paper tape
    (b) Daily volume by type of output

(c) Format requirements planned in advance or *ad hoc*
(d) Time after cut-off for producing each kind of output report
5. Special requirements—timing and compatibility
  (a) Time cycle to handle each transaction: process a requisition or answer an inquiry
  (b) Required date for delivery and installation of equipment
  (c) Equipment maintenance arrangements
  (d) Compatibility with other equipment
  (e) Expansibility to accommodate an additional workload
6. Additional information
  (a) Equipment cost, including make, model, number, and quantity
  (b) Cost of site preparation and equipment installation
  (c) Space requirements
  (d) Cost of maintenance and parts
  (e) Cost of operation
  (f) Cost of training personnel
  (g) Manufacturer's assistance in programming through software and manpower
  (h) Cost of converting existing operations to proposed system

The applications study does not deal with specific methods of operation and processing because various types of equipment require different procedural steps to accomplish the same results. The study places emphasis on specific data-processing jobs, and should proceed only upon the evidence that a complete systems analysis was performed. It is desirable to summarize the scope of and problems encountered in the present data-processing system; for example, the inability to obtain information for internal operation and management, time limits for reporting, workloads, and maximum cost. The scope of the proposed data-processing system covers the data currently available and all projects to be mechanized, cost of the system, and benefits to be expected from it. A work-load summary by specific projects includes the type and number of documents, line entries, input messages, and reports to be prepared. The workload and tables of machine operating speed are used to calculate the required complement of machines.

Conduct of Applications Study

A comprehensive applications study covers the schedules for preparing and completing the study, the organization and personnel requirements, and the basic structure of a new system. Each of these points is discussed in some detail in order to show the relationship among them.

Study Schedule.   Substantial manpower and money are required over a long period of time to make an applications study. Each phase of the applications study should be given definite starting and ending dates. Otherwise, there is a tendency for each phase to drag because people believe that another week or two will permit tying up more loose ends or exploring other interesting possibilities. Of course, schedule revisions can be made if more time is required for satisfactory completion of each phase; important opportunities should be explored and problems solved. On the other hand, the impact on the schedule from including new areas in the study must be considered. Schedule extensions and addition of new areas should be reviewed formally rather than pass unnoticed. Schedules should cover the expected time required for each of the following:

1. Organize, select, and train an applications study group
2. Flow-chart or flow-list the basic structure for processing data
3. Tabulate the workload on data sheets
4. Prepare systems specifications
5. Evaluate prospective system structures, apart from the equipment involved, and select the most promising one
6. Complete the flow charts or decision tables for processes and techniques, perform some coding, calculate processing time, and estimate the costs and values of the expected results
7. Prepare a proposal for submission to top management

It is useful to have both an over-all schedule plus a detailed schedule for each member of the applications study team.

Organization and Personnel.   Participants in the feasibility study can be the nucleus of the applications study group. Additional people are needed to handle the increased work involved and to represent the departments affected by the new system. The applications study group should include the study supervisor, systems analysts, project analysts, programmers, operating department representatives, and clerks and technicians.

The *study supervisor* should be able to work with the organization's executives and group members and have enough knowledge of data processing to lead the study group and appraise its work. He must be a capable administrator, since he is responsible for:

1. Keeping the study on schedule and within budget
2. Making initial contact with operating and staff groups involved in the study
3. Providing training and facilities for the study group

4. Contacting equipment manufacturers
5. Participating in policy determinations that affect data processing
6. Informing management and other people of developments that will affect them

Opinion is divided about the most desirable qualifications for the study supervisor. Some say he should have a thorough knowledge of the organization and its data-information problems. Others stress a need for thorough knowledge of and experience with the data-processing equipment likely to be used. In some cases, the problems related to the unit's operations and data processing are more complex and more difficult to understand than the equipment involved—at least from the user's viewpoint. In these instances, the supervisor should have extensive experience with the organization and its requirements. In other cases, the data-information problems are simple and problems associated with the use of equipment are relatively complex, so that knowledge and experience with equipment is more useful. Supervisors with detailed knowledge of equipment may be recruited from the manufacturer or from other organizations. Study supervisors experienced with both systems and equipment are scarce, but the number is growing.

Systems analysts are the applications study technical experts and should have experience with data-processing equipment and management methods. Systems analysts are chosen for their technical knowledge of accounting, economics, mathematics, production, or systems design. They should be aware of new developments, capable of original thinking, and open-minded enough to consider any reasonable idea. They should be able to understand problems and limitations of operating areas without being directly involved in such operations. Although the study supervisor is in charge, systems analysts are primarily responsible for developing approaches to design, determining feasibility of various plans, and designing the over-all system. Thus, they should be encouraged to consider unusual opportunities and completely different ways of doing jobs.

One or more systems analysts are required, depending on the scope of the applications study, and their duties include the following:

1. Developing a general plan or design for the system
2. Assigning tasks to project analysts
3. Reviewing the work of project analysts, determining additional requirements, and furnishing advice and guidance to them
4. Evaluating all study group reports for accuracy and completeness

Project analysts do the groundwork for applications studies. Since they work in specific areas on assigned jobs, they do not need as much skill and background as systems analysts. The success of project analysts depends on their analytic ability, personal initiative, and ability to work harmoniously with operating people. A project analyst determines the following facts for areas that a systems analyst assigns to him:

1. Documents and information wanted
2. Data available: kinds, quantities, format, and media
3. Processing required to convert the data into desired results
4. Conditions limiting the freedom to make changes that might be proposed

A project analyst uses data sheets to accumulate facts and flow charts or lists to organize his findings. He may also investigate various equipment available, prepare cost data, or assist the systems analyst in developing the over-all system.

A *programmer* plans a computation or process from the first formulation of a question to the final delivery of results, including the integration of operations into the existing system. Programming consists of planning and coding, which includes file processing, specification of printing formats, and other functions necessary to make the system operational. A programmer's work may be as broad as that of a systems analyst, in which case it covers all or a segment of a whole application from the initial formulation to the finished program ready to run on equipment. A beginning programmer's assignment may be limited to coding. If so, he starts with flow charts or decision tables prepared by analysts and lists processor operations in a problem-oriented language, such as COBOL, FORTRAN, or ALGOL or a machine-oriented language. Since analysis and flow-charting represent about three fourths of the total task of program preparation, it is rare to have anyone work for long solely as a coder.

Some organizations use aptitude testing, along with interviews and supervisors' ratings, to select personnel for systems analysis and programming work. Selection methods attempt to locate people with the right combinations of basic abilities, imagination, logical reasoning power, perception of details, and persistence. Different abilities and aptitudes are required for each level of personnel ranging from supervisor to clerk. Some test users claim a high correlation between test scores and long-run success in analysis and programming. Equipment manufacturers have devised tests for screening capable prospects, although some tests concentrate on the subject matter of programming and may prove unfair to capable people with no programming experience. Some organizations have devised their own tests which may consist of many kinds of questions or perhaps only a single question requiring analytic ability. Two examples of single-question tests, which are actually age-old puzzles, are:

1. At 1:17 P.M. a camper started paddling his canoe upstream at 4 miles an hour against a current of 1.5 miles an hour. At 2:05 P.M. he saw a bottle floating downstream, but continued upstream. Later, overcome by curiosity, he turned around and paddled downstream to catch up with the bottle just as it reached camp. How far did he go from camp before he started after the bottle?

2. Given only a set of balance scales (two pans with no weights), determine which *one* of twelve apparently identical balls is heavier than the others by using the scales as few times as possible. Repeat the operation if you do *not* know whether the odd ball is heavy or light. (The minimum number of weighings in each case is three.)

Longer tests covering general ability to read numbers and solve simple problems in algebra, logic, spatial perception, probability, and other fields are often given to prospective analysts and programmers. An example of a multi-part aptitude test like those used in business, is shown in Figure 16-1. The example shown here is merely a "for instance" and has not been validated.

Part I

Read the following problem carefully. List your answers to the questions in clear, readable form.

A man lives in a small Alaskan town at the point marked "X." Every street in the town is shown on the map on page 622. A friend from Ohio is coming to visit the Alaskan and may arrive on highway U.S. 31 (point A), U.S. 42 (point B), or Jones Road (point C). The Alaskan wishes to telegraph instructions to his friend. At the telegraph company he finds that he will be charged one dollar for each single instruction, such as (1) "turn right on Yukon Drive," or (2) "turn left at the end of the street."

Question 1. Write a complete set of instructions that will (a) cover the three different arrival points, and (b) minimize the cost of the telegram. Be very specific, for the friend will do exactly as he is told. Each instruction should be numbered and must contain only one command, as explained in the problem.

FIGURE 16-1. *Suggested aptitude test for analysts and programmers.*

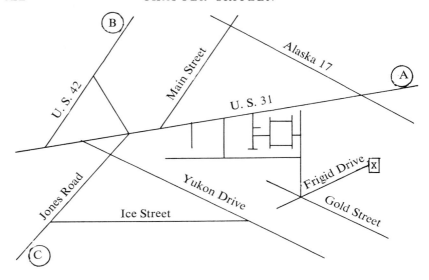

Question 2. At each intersection, the friend must make a decision to take one of the possible alternative routes. For example, at the intersection of Yukon Drive and Jones Road, he has three choices: (1) turn right, (2) turn left, (3) go straight.

(a) If it takes the friend five minutes to make a decision, what route should he follow from point C to minimize the thinking time required, and what is this minimum time?

(b) If it takes him two minutes to consider each alternative and no time to make a decision, what are the answers to part (a) above?

Part II

1. Draw a continuous line consisting of four straight segments so as to pass once and only once through all nine dots.

       · · ·

       · · ·

       · · ·

2. What number leaves a remainder of 1 when divided by 2, 3, 4, 5, or 6 and no remainder when divided by 7?

3. A doctor advised a patient that he had no cause to worry about his operation because the doctor's last nine patients had died from a similar operation and medical statistics indicated that one person in ten survived such an operation. What were the patient's chances of recovery?

FIGURE 16-1. *Suggested aptitude test for analysts and programmers (cont'd).*

4. A grocer attempts to weigh out identical amounts of sugar to two customers, but his scales do not have equal-length arms. The first time he puts the weight in one pan and the sugar in the other; the second time he reverses the procedure. Does he gain or lose? How much?

5. If I were to give 7 cents to each of the beggars at my door, I would have 24 cents left. I lack 32 cents of being able to give them 9 cents apiece. How many beggars are there, and how much money have I?

6. Find the least number of standard weights needed to weigh every whole number of pounds from 1 to 40 by placing weights in only one pan of an ordinary balance scale.

FIGURE 16-1. *Suggested aptitude test for analysts and programmers (cont'd).*

Selecting an *operating representative* from each data-processing area for cooperating in the applications study is useful. An operating representative should be alert and observant with a good general picture of activities in his area. Several years of solid, well-rounded experience in the area that he represents is desirable, provided he is imaginative enough to devise improvements and willing to accept changes proposed by others. Each operating representative can furnish project analysts with facts on information requirements, data available, procedures, and problems. Additional facts can be collected under his supervision. Since he is familiar with the problems and people involved, the operating department representative can work more effectively than the project analyst alone.

Clerks and technicians assist systems analysts. Analysts may make rough drafts of flow charts, data sheets, and other forms, but others can handle the time-consuming work of preparing final copy.

The applications study group will function best if it represents a balance between analysts and operating people. Management may insist that each group member have both qualifications, but such a requirement may limit progress and decrease the effectiveness of systems analysis.

Basic Structure for a New System. The applications study team may start by focusing attention on the kinds of information wanted, the times when required, and the data available or obtainable. The analyst also considers the structure of files and the processing procedures needed to convert input data to desired output. These factors are important in the structure of the data-processing system. One method for developing a new data-processing system is simply to introduce equipment for the first time or to replace the present equipment with more advanced equipment. The second is to redesign the whole system to develop new plans for processing data, keeping files, and preparing reports. The two approaches for developing a new system—mechanization and redesign, which were discussed at length in Chapter 6—deserve brief consideration here.

The basic structure can be developed by making flow charts or lists of the existing system, if the objective of the applications is primarily to introduce either new equipment or more equipment— the *mechanization* approach. The currently used techniques that will continue unchanged can be shown on the flow charts with appropriate technical symbols. Areas that will be changed in the process of mechanization, such as files and processing methods, are first represented by general symbols and later shown in detail after decisions are made. Data sheets can be prepared for all inputs, files, and outputs in the old system, since their content presumably will be changed little by more mechanization. New media, if known, can be listed on the data sheets. Volumes and time schedules for the present system should be recorded if they will be useful in developing the new system. Under the increased-mechanization approach, data sheets and flow charts for the present system plus facts on minor changes to be made are sufficient to start designing the new system.

If, on the other hand, the study team's goal is to *redesign* the system's basic structure, the value of flow charting is reduced. It is necessary to carefully examine the merits of a detailed analysis of the existing system before flow-charting it. The structure of some parts of the system may change little or none. Detailed analysis of the static parts of the present system by means of data sheets and flow charts has some value. But detailed flow charts and data sheets for the present system are less valuable if the system will be changed appreciably. The existing system should be studied primarily to get the specifications that will carry over to the new system; beyond that, the group should concentrate on developing the desired system.

Most systems studies fall between the two extremes of mere mechanization and complete redesign. There are several reasons for a middle path. First, it is difficult to introduce radically new equipment without making important changes in the system. Second, complete overhaul of a system may seem too expensive because of the analysis required and the disruption during transition. Third, complete redesign is risky because the new system, while it may provide a few big improvements, might not be as successful in all respects as the system it replaces, and small deficiencies *seem* to outweigh large improvements.

It is often said that mechanization and structural redesign are more efficient when accomplished in one step than in two. The argument goes that, since the structure of the system must be redesigned eventually for the best use of new equipment, redesign may as well be done when equipment is first introduced. This viewpoint is more acceptable when analysts are familiar with equipment and can concentrate their attention on systems redesign at the same time equipment is being installed.

Available *input data* may limit the basic structure of a proposed system. Any combination, form and size of files, type of processing, and set of outputs is theoretically possible if the necessary input is available. But the cost of devising and operating the system is a practical limiting factor. Some facts that are desired and others that are critical may not be available at any reasonable cost. The job of converting actions and operations into processable data is largely a manual operation. People read numerals and letters on paper and operate key-stroke devices to convert them to processable form. Data origination is costly, time-consuming, and subject to mistakes. Newly introduced automatic recording and direct-input devices reduce the costs and increase the accuracy of input data, and input problems at subsequent stages can be avoided by keeping data in processable form throughout.

A system that is otherwise well designed may be unsatisfactory because the necessary input, if available at all, is inaccurate or too costly. The analyst should specify exactly what quality of input data are required for a proposed system. Efficient system design requires use of all input data entering the system, minimum duplication of data, and elimination of high-cost manual handling after the first stage.

Every manager has certain requirements for *information*. Much information is most efficiently obtained from the data-processing system. Some other types of information arise outside the formal system: supervisors supply their secretaries with the contents of letters and engineers communicate with machinists via blueprints. If information available from the existing system requires improvement, the analyst should examine, in cooperation with output users, each separate activity in the study area. They try to find the decisions made or functions performed by the activity, the information useful to the activity, and the required features of information, such as accuracy, timeliness, predictability, and relevance. The analyst may have firsthand knowledge about decision-making and information requirements. He can get additional facts from organization charts, job descriptions, and work procedures, and check them with operating representatives and managers. New requirements for data and information can be obtained either by improving the present set or by starting afresh with an examination of managerial decisions and functions. A complete re-examination gives the analyst freer rein, since he does not use the existing scheme as a point of departure, but this entirely fresh approach tends to take more time and money, and there is some risk that he may merely "reinvent the wheel."

The analyst makes far-reaching decisions about data *files* while designing a system. Size, composition, and arrangement affect the usefulness of files for different processing operations. Various files may be kept separate or consolidated into one compact file by eliminating duplications. Efficient processing, it should be pointed out, requires ingenious schemes to ensure that the entire consolidated file will not have to be processed merely to handle individual transactions. Completely consolidated files have other disadvantages. Congestion can arise during file search because many requests are made on the file at one time. Record arrangement may be awkward because each use involves scanning unwanted data to find desired items. Consolidated files can sometimes be used efficiently in selected areas of data processing, such as inventory, personnel, payroll, and customer accounting. The concept of a *completely consolidated file* for a whole organization does not appear practical at the present stage of technical development because of equipment speeds, programming complexities, and operating costs.

Records of different lengths raise problems similar to those of consolidated files. The record for an inventory item stocked in a hundred warehouses contains more elements of data than the record for an item stocked in a dozen warehouses. Accordingly, equal-length records in files waste file space, whereas different-length records take more ingenious file design and processing. One plan for solving this problem is to classify the items in the records by the frequency of their *occurrence*. The most frequently occurring items make up records in one file while infrequently used items are kept separate as trailer records. Both must be handled, of course, for complete processing. Another plan for classifying records within a file is by the frequency of *processing*. The most frequently processed items can be kept in records in one file, with the infrequently processed items in records in a separate file. The optimum number, size, and composition of files represents a balance between the costs of establishing, updating, and maintaining the file and the costs of using the file to obtain desired information.

One point should be crystal clear. Some orderly arrangement of files is required for their efficient use. An inventory file may be arranged by part number, supplier, user department, end-use, or in other ways. Various uses may require different arrangements of records, which may be obtained by sorting records as required for each purpose, maintaining separate files for each arrangement, and maintaining cross-reference lists. Each file should be examined during both the systems analysis and design phases to determine the best arrangement for the proposed applications.

Facts about input, files, and output are obtained in order to analyze the system *workload*. The source and destination of documents can be traced to identify data and output by summarizing the workload for each functional area studied. The summary shows the work attributed to each record and can be used to check the total manpower in each organizational element. The input-load facts for each source document are their daily volume, including cyclical peaks and hourly rates. Useful details are the media used, their format, message length, and alphanumeric-code requirements. Facts needed about files are the volume, record length, form, codes, serial or random-access storage, degree of duplication, rate of change, processing frequency, and complexity of processing. Output-load facts cover the daily volume of each type of output, format, permissible processing delay, requirements for unscheduled interrogation, and kind of output wanted—tape, paper, or card media.

SUMMARY

A detailed and carefully organized plan is necessary for gathering and weighing both facts and opinions for feasibility and applications studies. The feasibility study and applications study are steps leading to an important change in a system.

The feasibility study analyzes data-processing requirements and equipment to determine whether new equipment and a proposed system for data processing appear to be more efficient than the equipment and system in use. The study is important, for it affects all subsequent action. The initial step in a feasibility study is to assign several competent people to a preliminary study group. Some study group members should know the data-information environment of the company or the part of it involved. Some members should know the characteristics of equipment that may be used and the experience of other companies in using it. Top management support should be enlisted by suitable presentations and briefings, and employees should be reassured that personnel dislocations will be minimized.

A preliminary feasibility study should be completed in a few months and should determine the data-information requirements, available equipment and methods, costs of completing the feasibility study, and the estimated costs and benefits of carrying out applications studies and installing the proposed system. If the outcome of a preliminary study is favorable, the study group should continue with a full-scale study.

The objectives—reduced costs, improved information, maximum profit—should be spelled out in order to focus effort on them when obtaining facts for making the decision against the desired standards. Broad or narrow areas may be selected for study. Important users, processors, and suppliers of data should be listed to find areas for further analysis. Obvious targets for improvement are areas with high-volume and repetitive operations with large clerical or manpower costs and areas where better information permits improvements in business operations.

A written charter should define the object and scope of the feasibility study to ensure constancy of direction and to serve as the basis for reviewing progress. After developing the over-all picture of data-information requirements, the most fruitful areas should be studied more carefully. Factors to consider when selecting an area are the history of the operation, known experiences with similar applications, expected benefits, costs, personnel, relationship of areas, resources, and flexibility. Expected benefits are reduced costs, improved information, and the ability to handle large volumes without further increases in facilities. The relationship between operations in an organization determines whether one or more small areas should be tackled or a broad-gauge attack made on all related problems. The costs, benefits, resources, conversion problems, and future plans for one or more systems should be developed for each area studied.

Concluding a feasibility study requires a formal report to management to gain acceptance of recommendations. A concise statement of conclusions and recommendations is usually backed up by a detailed statement and supporting material. The range of uncertainty involved in estimates should be specified so that conclusions can be tempered by the range of estimates used.

Applications studies are a vital step in bringing a proposed data-processing system to reality. The applications study group designs a system or set of procedures and establishes specifications for the equipment required. In cooperation with others, the group decides on methods and procedures to change, files to set up or eliminate, equipment to obtain or discard, and related organizational changes.

This group takes the general proposals developed in the feasibility study, reviews their economic aspects, and develops specific proposals.

Applications studies aim at creating optimum systems design. Systems design involves developing inputs, constructing flow charts or decision tables, integrating operations, determining personnel needs, and exploring equipment potentials. Designing an efficient system requires providing for multiple use of common source data, minimum repetitive use of data elements, and maximum use of automatic facilities. Specifications are developed for input, files, data handling, output, and special requirements.

Conducting an efficient applications study involves advance planning for time schedules, organization and personnel, systems analysis, systems design, new equipment evaluation, and correlation of system and equipment. An applications study schedule should be rigid enough to ensure that work progresses, but flexible enough to permit intensive coverage of selected areas and exploration of new areas.

Required personnel include the project supervisor, systems and project analysts, programmers, representatives of operating departments, and clerks and technicians. Some are recruited from the feasibility study group and others are chosen by aptitude tests, interviews, and superviors' ratings. A balance of knowledge about both equipment details and system environment is desirable in the applications study group.

In system redesign, an entirely new processing structure may have to be invented, as well as new equipment obtained. On the other hand, it may be limited to mechanization—introducing new equipment with minimum changes in procedures. The cautious approach is to introduce some new equipment and limit initial changes in the existing system, thereby postponing important system changes until later. The rate and extent of change affect the applications study scope and content. The controlling factors in system design are the outputs required, inputs available, and files to link them. The workload is determined by tracing inputs through files to outputs; facts are organized on flow charts, decision tables, and data sheets. The most important problem of feasibility and applications studies is to avoid merely solving "yesterday's" problems that are still causing trouble. A long-term viewpoint is vital to recognize and cope with requirements that are not yet clearly discernible.

17

Equipment Selection, Systems Implementation, and Operation

This chapter describes the steps that follow the feasibility and applications studies; these steps lead to positive recommendations on developing an electronic data-processing system. The phases of systems development covered here are equipment selection, systems implementation for equipment and operating procedures, and operations.

EQUIPMENT SELECTION

In order to make a rational choice of equipment, facts must be collected about equipment and its suitability for proposed applications. These facts can be obtained from manufacturers' publications, contract schedules, and solicited proposals; from personnel with knowledge or experience; and from other users of equipment. In analyzing competing equipment, it is important to use an identical specification base and desirable to examine all manufacturers' equipment suitable for the application.

Bid Invitation

Bids or proposals should be solicited from manufacturers after discussing application requirements and proposed equipment with them. Their proposals are necessary to reduce discussions and negotiations to concrete terms. The applications study group can request manufacturers' bids after the basic structure of the data-processing system is outlined and the needs for equipment are clarified.

One plan for getting bid invitations is to send copies of all flow charts and data sheets to manufacturers and request submission of bids for equipment necessary to handle the applications. To gain a clearer understanding of the problems, manufacturers may send representatives to talk with the applications study group. A manufacturer working without contact with the study group can, at best, develop only an approximate idea of the equipment needed.

An organization should send bid invitations to all equipment manufacturers who can most likely fulfill the requirements. A new manufacturer may devise new equipment for a system superior to that devised by the applications study team. Newcomers to a field often develop more novel equipment and advanced systems than do established manufacturers, who tend toward conservatism because of their vast engineering and administrative know-how. On the other hand, there is more risk that radically different equipment and advanced systems may not work as planned. Both new and established manufacturers occasionally fail in this regard so that prototype equipment put out for field testing often goes "back to the drawing boards." A well-planned description in the bid invitation is useful for it tells the manufacturer what requirements he must meet, reduces the number of questions a manufacturer needs to ask, and provides a fair basis for comparing different equipment.

The bid request should differentiate between what is desired and what is demanded. *Desires* are stated as the basis for discussion, whereas *demands* are the basis for equipment selection. The equipment storage and processing capacity required should be stated. The adequacy of controls and accuracy of equipment, whether provided by built-in or programmed checking, and adaptability to long-range plans are important. Points to be included in the bid invitation are discussed in detail here from the viewpoint of the manufacturer's proposal.

Manufacturer's Proposal

A manufacturer's bid should cover all details about the equipment proposed to meet the bid request. These features are described here and later summarized in a check list.

Operating Requirements. The manufacturer should clearly describe operating methods and machine running times. Each type of equipment may require varying methods for efficient performance of the same job because of differences in data representation for the processor and external storage, input-output speeds, and concurrent operations.

The ability to achieve input-output, processing, and interrogation cycles determines the time needed to handle required jobs. It is then possible to calculate the number of hours of use in relation to potential hours and possibilities for expansion. Whether access to storage is random or serial may be an important factor in determining processing times and the ability to meet short deadlines. Another important feature is the permissible delay in report preparation after either a scheduled or an unscheduled cut-off time. Quick reporting may involve storing current records, updating records as each transaction is processed, and answering inquiries or printing reports at high speed whenever wanted.

The manufacturer and study team together agree how much flow charting, programming, detailed coding, and estimating of machine running time to do. Manufacturers tend to restrict their attention to general-level charts and do little detailed flow charting and coding except under pressure or with considerable help from the prospect.

Equipment.   A point that must be decided early by the manufacturer and the user is the desired degree of automation for the system. An automatic system with a high ratio of capital to labor is essential for some applications. The manufacturer should specify in detail—make, model, number, and quantity—the equipment to meet the applications requirements. Often, several models and makes of one type of equipment are available, so that, for example, the term "magnetic-tape unit" is not explicit enough; tape units of a particular manufacturer can have greatly different read-write speeds, densities, and rewind times. The input-output media and other operating supplies involved should be stated.

The manufacturer should give a definite date for equipment delivery and installation along with any additional time required to check out the equipment and get it in operation. Penalties may be agreed upon for failure to meet schedules that cause the user loss through delay. The time between an order for and the delivery of equipment often runs from six to eighteen months and check-out may take from several weeks to a few months. It should be pointed out that manufacturers do a good job of meeting delivery schedules for equipment already in production, although different combinations of equipment that include some new units, may cause delays in development and manufacture. But users often have trouble in meeting installation and systems design schedules for utilizing equipment after it is released by manufacturers.

Sizes, weights, and recommended floor space for all equipment must be specified so the user can prepare housing for the equipment.

Arrangements must be made for bringing in necessary electric power and for wiring units together by under-floor, false-floor, or overhead conduits. A central location, in relation to data origination and use, is desirable. The user needs guidance on the amount of space he should provide for the following:

1. Data-processing equipment: input, processor, output, and supporting units
2. Related equipment: air conditioners, water coolers, and motor-generator sets, if required
3. Personnel: supervisors, analysts, programmers, coders, operators, and technicians
4. File vaults and supply storage
5. Maintenance parts, testing equipment, and testing operations
6. Visitors gallery

Most electronic equipment requires air conditioning to control temperature, dust, and humidity conditions. Production-control processors operating under unusual conditions, such as high temperature, corrosive vapor or gas, vibration, dust, or fluctuating power supply, may require additional special precautions.

Manufacturer's Assistance.   A manufacturer, in his proposal, generally offers assistance in setting up a new system by furnishing trained analysts and programmers for extended periods. Engineers are usually available for consultation on installation and operation. Equipment manufacturers also offer training courses for programmers and operators. The extent, condition, and location of all assistance should be specified.

A manufacturer usually furnishes processor time for testing programs before delivery of equipment. Forty hours or so is helpful for debugging programs and speeding up efficient use of equipment when it is ready to run. The amount of time available and location of equipment should be specified in the bid. The "software" package of programming aids, as described in Chapter 12, facilitates programming and reduces the user's cost. Manual programming, unless it uses the best compiler techniques, can be extremely expensive and should be minimized.

Equipment rental usually includes manpower, parts, and supplies for maintenance on the prime shift and perhaps the second and third shifts or for some specified number of hours per month, but the number of engineers and hours of work should be spelled out to avoid questions. Maintenance contracts for purchased equipment should specify the parts and supplies included, number and skills of personnel, and hours reserved for scheduled testing. Scheduled test time should not, hopefully, interfere with regular working hours for the operating staff. A maintenance-service contract should specify renewal terms to guard against unusual increases in rates after the initial contract expires.

Contract and Design Changes. A proposed rental contract should cover the cost for different levels of usage, length of rental period, maintenance service, and renewal or cancellation terms, as described in Chapter 5. Some agreements may also be made covering the conditions for obtaining an improved model. Terms should be stated for payment of purchase price, discounts, and guarantees on replacement of parts. Crediting a fraction of the rental payments for one or two years toward purchase is often provided, if the option is exercised during a stated period. Some manufacturers require an initial deposit to cover the right to exercise the option.

Occasionally, a unit will not work satisfactorily after it is installed and the manufacturer must redesign it or replace it with another unit or by a later model. A manufacturer's bid should cover prospective design changes for installed units that are frequently improved. Another point to cover is the arrangement for exchanging present equipment for a new model. The trade-in price and preference to owners of present equipment may be specified. Alternatively, used equipment may be sold on the second-hand market at prevailing prices.

Initially, large units of equipment are seldom used at full capacity. Time is required to develop applications that make full use of additional input-output, storage, processing, and special-purpose devices and thus reach a balance with the central processor's capacity. The manufacturer should specify the possibilities of expanding and integrating his equipment with other types.

Check List. Points to be covered in a manufacturer's bid, as discussed above, can be summarized in a check list as shown in Table 17-1 below.

1. Degree and extent of automation in the system
2. Equipment composition
    (a) Description: make, model, number, and quantity of each unit
    (b) Form of data handled: numeric or alphanumeric, and fixed word or variable or selected field

TABLE 17-1. *Check list for manufacturer's bid.*

    (c) Storage capacity and method: random or serial access

    (d) Adequacy of controls, method of checking, and average length of time between malfunctions

    (e) Operating instructions for each major unit

    (f) Operating supplies needed

3. Operating requirements

    (a) Acceptance of input documents and data

    (b) Time required for each type of equipment to handle each major job and the total time available

    (c) Delay after cut-off before reports are available

    (d) Flow charts of jobs showing recommended techniques

    (e) Examples of detailed coding for applications

4. Delivery of equipment

    (a) Delivery date

    (b) Length of time to check equipment and get it into operating condition

    (c) Penalties for late delivery or complete failure to deliver equipment that is contracted for

5. Installation requirements, including both recommended and extreme conditions for manufacturer's guarantee

    (a) Size, weight, floor space, and height for each unit, including auxiliary equipment

    (b) Electric power—public utility or special equipment—and wiring requirements

    (c) Air conditioning: humidity, temperature, dust, and special protection

    (d) Space for files, supplies, maintenance parts, test operations, personnel, and visitors

6. Manufacturer's assistance

    (a) Availability of engineers or technicians for analysis, programming, and installation

    (b) Training courses for customer's programmers and operators

    (c) Availability of manufacturer's or a customer's equipment for use in program debugging

    (d) The manufacturer's software package for programming and assistance available by participating in the equipment users' associations

7. Rental or purchase or combined agreements

    (a) Rental rate, term of contract, renewal, and cancellation clauses

    (b) Number of hours for operating in one, two, or three shifts or on a monthly basis and rate adjustment for excessive down time

    (c) Terms of payment, discount, and financing arrangement

    (d) Guarantees on equipment operation, availability of magnetic

TABLE 17-1. *Check list for manufacturer's bid (cont'd).*

tape and special supplies, cost of maintenance parts and supplies

(e) Terms of any purchase option: initial deposit required, fraction of rental payments credited toward purchase, and option expiration date

8. Maintenance contracts
    (a) Maintenance contract cost, service personnel, scheduled maintenance period, availability of a similar machine during extended down time, and renewal conditions
    (b) Term and rate of initial contract and renewal period
    (c) Provision for replacing parts, testing equipment, and maintenance

9. Design changes
    (a) Replacement of unsatisfactory units
    (b) Arrangements for securing improvements or new models, including trade-in value

10. Expansion and integration
    (a) Additional units that can be added: input, output, storage, processing, and interrogation
    (b) Other equipment that will accept media directly from this equipment
    (c) Equipment available for media conversion

TABLE 17-1. *Check list for manufacturer's bid* (cont'd).

Equipment Evaluation

After manufacturers' bids are received, the applications group makes a final evaluation of the proposed data-processing equipment and system. In this regard, those evaluating equipment should remember that manufacturers and users have different interests. Manufacturers sell equipment to make profits; users buy equipment to get information from data. Neither is primarily interested in the equipment; it is only a means to other goals. A manufacturer can readily specify the technical capabilities of his equipment. The user is primarily responsible for determining whether certain equipment will meet his particular application requirements. This is true even though the manufacturer assists in analyzing applications requirements. An exception arises when a manufacturer guarantees satisfactory performance for an application instead of merely delivering equipment and leaving the customer to efficiently apply it. Evaluation and selection of equipment require emphasis on operating time and costs, but full analysis is required for the following factors:

1. Compliance with terms of bid request
   (a) Equipment composition
   (b) Operating requirements
   (c) Delivery of equipment
   (d) Installation requirements
   (e) Manufacturer's assistance
   (f) Rental-purchase agreement
   (g) Maintenance service and contracts
   (h) Design changes
   (i) Expansion and integration
2. Capabilities of machine to meet requirements
   (a) Acceptance of input documents and data
   (b) Sufficiency of storage and processing capacity
   (c) Production of output in required form
   (d) Adequacy of controls and accuracy
   (e) Reliability of equipment
   (f) Adaptability to long-range plans
3. Time taken to do the job
   (a) Hours of use in relation to potential hours
   (b) Capability to achieve desired processing and interrogation cycles
   (c) Potential for expansion and emergency needs
4. Advantages of use
   (a) Timeliness of information production
   (b) Production of information desired but not available
   (c) Economic evaluation
   (d) Other tangible or intangible benefits to be gained

The points listed above should be considered to determine whether the manufacturer's proposal and bid are meaningful. The fundamental question is: "Is the manufacturer's proposal in sufficient detail to show he understands the problems and is in a position to submit appropriate equipment recommendations?" This question can be answered by evaluating the equipment proposal against the criteria established during the applications study and stated in the bid invitation. The dollar bid price is only one factor among many.

Selection of the best equipment may proceed along two paths. If one set of equipment is outstanding, it is merely identified. If none is wholly satisfactory, lower-ranking equipment is rejected until only one set remains. The applications study group screens out any bid covering equipment that does not meet the bid request or that falls down on critical points. If only one bid passes initial screening, the group's job may be limited to re-examining it. Re-examination is required to make certain that the equipment offered will operate satisfactorily in the proposed system. If several bids pass the initial screening, the study group must select the best equipment and related system.

Selection may be difficult because the equipment offered is not wholly suited or is even unsuited for handling the proposed applications. Any manufacturer's equipment will usually have both strong and weak points for a particular application. The decision to select certain equipment may represent a rough judgment about the relative merits of various features which are not easily summarized into a single score for comparison.

Equipment Acquisition

Before equipment is acquired, proposals are prepared and submitted to management. If the acquisition proposal is approved, procurement and preparation for installation follow.

Proposals. The applications study should be summarized and the system and equipment proposals submitted to management. Each proposal should contain, as a minimum, the following information:

1. Identification of the organizational element sponsoring the proposal and the location where the equipment will be installed
2. Description of the application scope and objectives to be achieved
3. A sufficiently detailed description of present methods to identify its deficiencies
4. Description of the proposed system in enough detail to indicate how it will overcome deficiencies of the present system
5. Reference to investigation of other methods of processing data and the reasons for rejecting them
6. Pertinent workloads, costs, and other facts relating to both the present and the proposed systems essential for evaluating the proposal
7. Summary of the makes of equipment evaluated and the method used to select the proposed equipment; name of manufacturer, specific components, and cost of equipment selected; justification for selection in terms of equipment capabilities in relation to processing time requirements; and justification for purchase or rental of proposed equipment
8. Personnel requirements: number, capabilities, and sources
9. Funding implications with a statement concerning the availability of funds
10. Estimated cost of site preparation and proposed installation schedule

Responsible levels of management should review proposals to make sure that the justification for action is adequately documented and to make recommendations and comments on the action.

Preparation for Installation.   Upon deciding to introduce the new system, the user should complete all plans and arrangements for installing and using the equipment when ready. Factors to consider in planning equipment installation are:

1. Space, power, air conditioning, furnishings, and building construction
2. Organizational changes for the systems operating group
3. Recruiting, orienting, training, and retraining personnel
4. Procedures for flow-charting, programming, and testing
5. Conversion procedures, parallel operations, discarding the old system
6. Rental, and maintenance arrangements
7. Obtaining supplies
8. Communications arrangements

During the period before equipment delivery, systems plans should be completed. All initial applications requiring conversion should be programmed and tested on equipment furnished by the manufacturer. Workable and efficient operating instructions should be prepared for all personnel working with the system. Instruction routines, based on analyses and flow charts should, of course, be programmed for equipment operation. All remaining personnel required for the automatic data-processing system should be trained and plans adopted for softening the impact of the system on personnel throughout the organization.

SYSTEMS IMPLEMENTATION

The group responsible for implementation gets the new equipment and related systems in operation. This group, which may include some or all members of the applications study group, first sets a schedule for converting from the old to the new system. Ideas and detailed plans developed in the applications study must be put into actual practice: obtain equipment, install it, and start work. The implementation group also deals with physical features, such as space, power, air conditioning, structural clearances, and floor loading. A major task of the implementation group is to orient and train people to work with the new system to achieve a smooth transition from old to new.

Problems of installation occur both before and after equipment delivery. The numerous problems considered during the feasibility and applications studies appear in an entirely new perspective at implementation time. Problems of scheduling, organization, personnel, programming, and physical requirements must be solved in order to fully implement a system.

Scheduling

Schedules are useful to put installation work in the proper time perspective and ensure that all important points are covered.

Lead Time. A long period of time—the lead time—usually exists between contracting with a manufacturer and the delivery of electronic equipment. For developmental equipment, a long lead time arises because the manufacturer may take longer to design, construct, and test than he planned. Thereafter, customer demand may create a backlog and a long delivery time persists. A long period between order and delivery, with some provision for adjusting the delivery date, is advantageous for the user's flexibility. The scheduled delivery date for equipment is a target for completing all preliminary work. Some customers find that they have insufficient analysis, programming, and debugging time when they try to make their schedule fit the manufacturer's lead time. There is some merit in a different plan whereby equipment delivery is scheduled after the end of programming and testing is in sight, unless the lead time then is likely to be too long. As systems analysts and programmers gain skill and experience, it may be possible to squeeze systems work into a period shorter than the manufacturer's lead time. The lead-time problem is much simpler when new equipment replaces similar equipment and especially so if only minor changes are made in the operating system and processor programs. Regardless of the scheduling plan used, it is highly desirable to time-phase equipment delivery so that it can be used when installed.

Installation work should be scheduled realistically and in detail. Despite the uncertainty of requirements at this stage, explicit scheduling is valuable. Schedules may be prepared on charts with time marked along the bottom line and a horizontal bar showing the starting and finishing date for each phase of each application area. Such charts help point out peaks in workloads and aid in sequencing work in the proper order. Clear indications of work peaks and lulls are obtained if units of work are indicated on the vertical scale.

Sequence of Work.   Data-processing activities for each application and the steps in installation should be listed, taking into consideration records design, data analysis, and the clean-up and organization of data. The term *data discipline* covers the work involved in making incomplete or erroneous data sufficiently complete and accurate for efficient processing. The man-hours required to accomplish all the tasks involved are estimated and totaled to arrive at the man-month requirements for each application. The work during the system development and conversion period can be divided into four parts:

1. Systems analysis and design: methods improvement, data-discipline, records design, determination of input and output requirements, and development of functional flow charts of operations
2. Preliminary programming and conversion: development of detailed flow charts, writing of detailed operating programs, testing and revising programs, developing procedures for converting present data to automatic equipment codes and media, scheduling operations, and final testing and shakedown of equipment
3. Extended research of discrepancies: careful screening of all procedures to ensure they are adequate to meet requirements for efficiently handling applications; further refinement is made of system methods and data collection and processing, including pre- and post-processing operations
4. Operation of both systems in parallel: the time required for the conversion phase depends on the complexity and diversity of programs and data processing for each application, and the skill and thoroughness of systems design

Schedules are invaluable for acquainting management with the magnitude of problems envisaged and ensuring that important points are covered. But flexibility is needed and schedules should be revised as events require.

Scheduling Techniques.   Various techniques exist for preparing schedules. A good scheduling technique should provide the scheduled start and end time for the whole project and the relationships between tasks or jobs—job X must be finished before jobs Y and Z can be started. The scheduling technique should also help the user to evaluate the impact of changes—for example, a delay in starting or ending a job—on the schedule.

On Gantt charts, a bar with length proportional to time, which runs horizontally, is used to represent the planned time for each job.

Jobs that must be performed sequentially are represented by bars placed end to end; whereas a job that can be performed in parallel is shown by a bar under another one. In this way, a graphical display is obtained showing the time to finish an entire project, the scheduled stop and start time for each job, and some of the relationships between jobs—perform in parallel or sequentially. Gantt charts are useful when the number of jobs being studied is only a hundred or so.

When a huge number of jobs are involved, Gantt charts are difficult to construct and use. Furthermore, they usually fail to show an explicit relationship between jobs and the allowable range of time—for example, how early a job can be started or how late it can be finished without interfering with the completion date for the whole job.

On the other hand, network flow scheduling techniques, of which PERT (Program Evaluation and Review Technique) and CPM (Critical Path Method) are the best known, describe both the explicit relationships between jobs and the range—earliest and latest—of starting and finishing times for jobs. The availability of data-processor programs for preparing network flow schedules permits the analysis of large and complicated activities.

A sample network flow schedule for a job of interest throughout this chapter—the design and implementation of a new data-processing system—is shown in Figure 17-1. Each horizontal line represents a job and the connections between horizontal lines represent the relationships between jobs. All jobs terminating in a circle must be complete before any of the jobs originating from that circle can start. For example, general design and the hiring and training jobs to the left of circle 3 must be completed before the four tasks to the right—special design study, subsystem A and B detail, and the preliminary evaluation—can be started. Each line is drawn long enough to indicate the relationships and does not indicate the time for a task. The estimated time in calendar months required to perform each task is shown beneath its title.

The heavy line shows the longest path through the network, which is *critical* for completing this job—successful implementation of a data-processing system. A critical path between any two points is found simply by searching for the path with the longest elapsed time between the two points. Any paths superseded by longer paths between the same two points—for example, subsystem B detail at 6.0 months is longer than special design study 4.0 and subsystem C detail at 1.5 months—are discarded until only one continuous path remains from the starting to the finishing points.

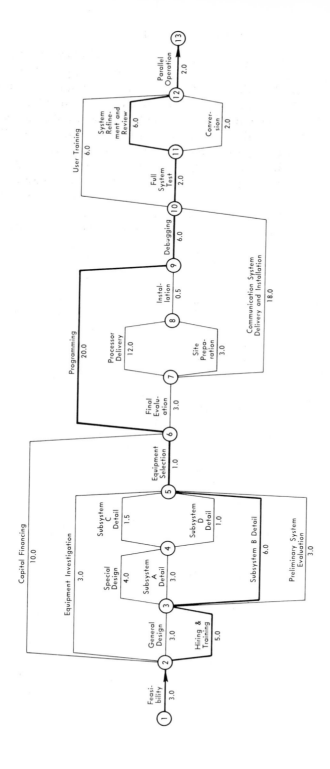

FIG. 17-1. *Network flow chart for scheduling data-system implementation.*

The tasks along this path will determine the total elapsed time to design and implement the system. Any delays in starting or finishing tasks on the critical path will delay the final completion date. Consequently, tasks on the critical path need careful management and control. Some delays in tasks outside the critical path are permissible within the over-all schedule; but others may cause a switch from the original critical path to a new one that includes the delayed task. For example, if financial approval exceeds twelve months, it becomes the critical path between points 2 and 6. The amount of time a job can slip without affecting the schedule is called *slack time*.

The network flow can be reduced to calendar dates by selecting a desired starting or finishing date for the entire project and moving along the critical path assigning dates. For the critical path, the list below shows the schedule point number, time, and date.

Point number	Schedule Year	Schedule Month	Description Finish	Description Start	Months for next activity	Total elapsed months
1	1	Jan		Feasibility study	3.0	—
2	1	April	Feasibility study	Hiring and training	5.0	3.0
3	1	Sept	Hiring and training	Subsystem B detail	6.0	8.0
5	2	March	Subsystem B detail	Equipment selection	1.0	14.0
6	2	April	Equipment selection	Programming	20.0	15.0
9	3	Dec	Programming	Debugging	6.0	35.0
10	4	June	Debugging	Full system test	2.0	41.0
11	4	Aug	Full system test	System refinement	6.0	43.0
12	5	Feb	System refinement	Parallel operation	2.0	49.0
13	5	April	Parallel operation	Regular operation	—	51.0

Critical Path Description

Although this example has a small number of activities, sketching out a flow network simplifies the description of relationships among jobs and the assignment of schedule completion dates. For large and intricate scheduling problems, an organized approach is imperative.

Organization

The form of an organization reflects its functions. The functions, operating personnel, and equipment are important factors in determining an efficient organizational structure for data processing. The reason for making organizational changes can be seen from a look at the procedures used before and after installing an automatic system in an organization.

Before. Data processing at one stock control point required paper work to process demands from customers; extracts from the warehouse; shipping orders from the headquarters office; receipts from vendors and other warehouses; returns from customers; and adjustments to stock balances, due-in, due-out, and reserved stocks. This processing required multiple clerical operations involving logical decisions and arithmetical computations. Operations at the stock control point required exhaustive data processing, sorting, calculating, summarizing, transmitting, storing, and recording in huge files to maintain detailed records by item stock number. Depot activities of receipt, storage, issue, and maintenance were accomplished through the use of detailed records of inventory and financial accounting. This required maintaining reference files and performing many computations. Control information was duplicated because of manual operations and mechanical limitations. Files showing quantities required duplication to handle transactions affecting property and financial records.

Manual operations inhibited the rapid production of timely information for logical decisions and computations. Limited transaction records required both processing and controlling blocks of data from one process to the next. Costs were greater than they would be for an integrated system not hampered by limited-scope processing and intensive block control. Decision-making associated with manual operations was not completely formulated and gave rise to multiple errors. Verification of all transactions was required to minimize the consequences of errors.

After. The system planned for this stock control point proposed on-line data flow to provide necessary reports of timely information and permit management to make decisions based on current events rather than on history. The new system uses a medium-scale machine offering random access to data in bulk storage. Automatic transaction editing is used before posting. Logistical data for stock and financial inventory accounting are processed on-line so that the need for block controls, duplicative files, and repetitive operations is reduced. The simplified processing offered important possibilities for a streamlined organization. Larger and more intricate organization structures usually accompany bigger systems applications.

Personnel Considerations

Placing an order for automatic data-processing equipment is the signal for establishing a working organization for the personnel involved. The principles of sound organization apply here as well as elsewhere, and it is vital that a qualified individual be given overall responsibility at the outset. Some centralization of automatic processing is required to get maximum benefits, which suggests that the people involved should report to a higher level of management than the units they serve. Typically operating primarily as a service group, the data-processing unit requires enough line support to ensure cooperation and uniformity for efficient operations.

The introduction of new systems and equipment is received well by most people in an organization, but changes will cause some dislocations and hardships. The impact of new systems on personnel tends to be moderate, for the job categories affected usually are in clerical areas that have a moderate to high turnover of personnel. Fortuitously, the planning period preceding equipment installation may give enough time for some reduction in the work force through normal turnover. Furthermore, the present tendency to increase the volume of data-processing work often requires additional employees in supporting activities. More new jobs may be created than were eliminated, although these jobs are likely to be different and thus frequently require reassignment with training or entirely new people.

Publication of Facts. New systems are adopted for their expected benefits. The decision to introduce a new system is made after extensive analysis to find what impact the new equipment and system will have on the organization's interests. By the same token, the employee is anxious to learn what impact the new system is likely to have on his interests. But an important difference exists: management can independently obtain facts and make decisions, whereas employees are dependent on management for most facts and decisions. Frank and open discussions by management can reduce rumors that otherwise may give a distorted view of the situation.

A well-planned information policy throughout the organization has advantages after a commitment is made to obtain equipment. Introduction of a new system and equipment indicates progressive management and confidence in the future. If this belief is tactfully presented, it can generate pride and satisfaction in the organization, but the program should not be oversold or potential difficulties minimized. Dislocated individuals or groups are best served by giving them specific advance notice so that they can formulate individual plans. The important point is the realization by management that all employees need complete and accurate facts.

Personnel Required.   The most striking change in personnel requirements is the increase in the number of upper-level jobs and decrease in lower-level jobs. Several factors cause this shift upwards. The new system and equipment is more intricate than the old and requires more capability of supervisors, analysts, and operators. Complex problems are likely to increase during the period of analysis, installation, and conversion and demand more skill for satisfactory solution. Newly created job positions at the upper level need, of course, to be approved by management. An interesting problem arises in getting new, upper-level job descriptions approved. There is a widespread tendency to think of the importance of upper-level positions in a manual data-processing system as being related to the number of clerks requiring supervision. A dilemma arises because a larger fraction of high-level job classifications is needed for efficient system operation even though fewer people are involved. People managing and operating a system involving fewer clerks than before have a critical influence on system efficiency. But after the transition period, when operations are expected to return to normal, the need for top-level skills and management attention declines. Such a reduction in management's attention follows in part, at least, from a slower work pace after the difficult period of installation and conversion.

The skill of a console operator, for example, partially determines the efficiency of work otherwise involving several hundred clerks. Processing time can easily increase 20 per cent or more merely because one operator is not as quick, accurate, or well versed as others; however, executive routines take over much of the work of the console operator. Similar observations are true for other posts—supervisors, analysts, and programmers. Qualified personnel are critical for system efficiency. When equipment is used for clerical work, new ideas about personnel classifications are required to replace the idea that the mere number of clerical personnel supervised determines classifications.

Personnel Selection.   One of the first jobs of a data-processing manager is to staff his organization. Members of the applications study group are obvious candidates, since their recent experience is valuable for detailed planning and operations. But the change from a temporary study to a permanent assignment involves a risk at this stage. The feasibility and applications study groups were temporary, having been formed from people with a variety of backgrounds. Some people who willingly served on a temporary basis in the feasibility and applications groups may want to return to their basic career fields. Other people doing feasibility or applications study work may not be suited either by training or temperament for a career in systems analysis and data processing. A person may not fulfill a continuing assignment because he is either underqualified or overqualified. Then too, a person who finds preparatory studies interesting because of their variety may not do well when work becomes routine.

The manager should explain to interested people who are qualified for key positions that the installation and operating requirements are different from those faced by the study group. These people will be concerned about their prospects for advancement and security. Top management must assure them that the data-processing organization has a long-run future. Setting up preliminary job classifications and descriptions helps orient potential employees to long-range opportunities; these job descriptions should be carefully prepared to serve for a reasonably long period because revisions are troublesome and disruptive.

Employees within the existing data-processing group are another source of personnel. Their knowledge of operating procedures is a valuable background to the specialized skills that can be acquired in operating assignments. The transfer of people from the old to the new data-processing group also reduces the problem of personnel dislocation. In general, it is desirable to seek people from within the organization rather than from outside, since the people already available are probably equally capable and are acclimated to the organization. The effect on employee morale must be considered, for people resent managerial indifference to their plight as much or more than they do the equipment that appears to be the immediate cause. Employees within the organization are selected by means of posting job announcements to get expressions of interest, interviews, supervisors' ratings and recommendations, general ability tests, and analyst-programmer tests. Analyst-programmer tests are designed to test the candidate's ability to think clearly and reach conclusions for problems similar to those he will encounter as an analyst. Such tests are considered useful even though a person is not familiar with the equipment and tools for systems analysis.

People with specialized skills for programming are apt to be in short supply. Any people trained during the systems analysis and applications projects should be used, if possible. Despite all the arguments for obtaining staff within the organization, there is merit in having a balance of viewpoints and experience. People already skilled in using specific equipment are a desirable complement to people with company experience and systems know-how. They can speed up successful system implementation.

Training.   Adequate training is desirable whatever the source of personnel. An equipment manufacturer's training courses and on-the-job training give a practical working knowledge of equipment. Courses in programming and processor operations are offered regularly at customer-service locations by most manufacturers and, in addition, many provide resident instruction for specified periods. Large companies and government agencies often conduct their own courses in programming and operating principles at both elementary and advanced levels. Key personnel should be *educated* as well as trained. University courses and association meetings are valuable for learning more than basic programming and operating principles; they also furnish background knowledge and permit the exchange of ideas about new equipment and application development.

The classroom, it should be remembered, is not a substitute for experience on the job. Analysis and programming work should be started as soon as some people are trained to develop essential experience toward getting the work done. Formal training is most valuable when supplemented with on-the-job training, for in this way, advanced techniques can be absorbed and used as soon as the programmer is ready. A tentative schedule for training and programming used by one organization in conjunction with medium-scale equipment installation included training sessions for programmers, management, and operators. The training periods were interspersed with periods spent designing the proposed system, flow-charting and programming, and correcting programs. Training and programming were, in this case, done at the organization's location. In addition to the training periods, programs were scheduled for testing on equipment at the manufacturer's plant on several different occasions. Program test periods served several purposes. They determined whether the programs would handle test data and offered concrete operating experience with equipment. Looked at from another viewpoint, program testing also furnishes an opportunity to re-examine the quality of programmer education and training.

In the concurrent approach to work scheduling, the first phase of another application is started when beginning the second phase of the initial application. Eventually a different phase of each application will be in progress and each will be handled at the same time. The workload in any one phase is thus kept nearly constant and the organization is able to learn lessons from the early applications and apply them to the corresponding phase of succeeding applications. The work-scheduling plan affects the number of people to train, the timing of their training, the duration of their assignment to a particular kind of work, and even the "learning curve" and efficiency of their performance.

Treatment of Dislocated Personnel.   Careful planning and close cooperation are essential to minimize the personal hardship of displaced workers. Management is interested in reducing such hardship, not only to help dislocated personnel, but also to strengthen the morale of other employees and to retain good public relations. Subsequent lay-offs might be avoided by reduced hiring before the new system is installed, although this approach poses difficulties during the implementation phase. Assuming that the present staff is working at full capacity, the question arises as to how reductions can be accomplished before the new system is operating smoothly. Staff reductions over a long period of time are desirable to avoid abrupt cutbacks, but, unfortunately, no simple answer exists for this and many other personnel problems, although planning and scheduling can help.

In the later stages of systems implementation extensive overtime can help spread a limited work force. Temporary employment, borrowing other personnel, and use of service bureau assistance can help. The reaction of employees to such measures is determined in part by whether management has a coordinated plan for conversion. Management's responsibility does not end with reduced hiring and temporary employment, for many transfers may be required because of changes in job structure. Management should handle transfers efficiently and with consideration for employee interests, although some problems will arise in areas that management does not control directly.

Some companies find that each level of employees poses different problems. Turnover and reduced hiring may cover clerks and machine operators. Middle-level supervisors may be young enough in skill, ability, and outlook to retain for assignment in data processing or in other areas. Handling upper-level supervisors presents a more difficult problem in view of the limited opportunities for transfer at their level; furthermore, if the number of clerical jobs shrinks, the need for supervisors decreases.

Programming

Workable and efficient processor routines must be prepared before the new system is installed and operating. Application flow charts and analysis may justify acquiring the equipment, but, in order to be useful, plans must be reduced to specific instructions for the equipment and people.

Instruction Routines. The work involved in preparing detailed instruction routines for electronic equipment has been discussed in several other chapters on systems analysis, design, and programming. The tasks of analyzing a proposed application and preparing instruction routines blend into each other. Together they may cost as much as the purchase price of the equipment involved: analysis is thought to run about three-fourths of this, and preparation of instruction routines makes up the remainder. Furthermore, programming costs do not stop with the first successful application, but in most cases seem likely to continue indefinitely at high levels. Changing applications deserve program revision and new applications require new programs. Even reasonably satisfactory programs are rewritten to cut processor time, to improve their logic, and to produce better reports.

Debugging. Some mistakes are acceptable in many areas of data processing. Manual systems produce several mistakes or errors per thousand operations. But such systems continue to operate reasonably well for two reasons: first, some clerks specialize in locating and correcting mistakes and errors of others. Second, people can tolerate a modest number of some kinds of mistakes and errors and still function fairly efficiently. The number of gaps in files and deficient procedures usually uncovered during the conversion phase indicates manual systems have more faults than is generally realized.

Data-processing instruction routines, when first prepared, are almost certain to contain human blunders and erroneous logic. Equipment does not overlook a typographical mistake, but either stops operations or follows such a mistake to what may be absurd conclusions. Elaborate procedures, such as "desk-checking" and debugging, are useful for screening out many mistakes in program preparation. Programmers, perhaps even beginners, desk-check programs by studying draft versions to try to correct mistakes and errors in logic. In machine debugging, a program is run with fabricated or real test data and perhaps live data to find most of the remaining mistakes, although some may remain undiscovered through many cycles.

Locating program mistakes is essentially a refined process of trial and error. Several programming aids simplify the chore of error detection. The processor can be stopped at predetermined checkpoints to give snapshots of the contents of the accumulator, particular registers, and storage locations, as described in Chapter 12. Another approach is the program post-mortem, which may be made if the routine will not function, as is usually true on the first few attempts. Debugging can take a lot of time, especially in the early stages of processing, before the programmers develop skill in writing routines. Accordingly, they should write routines and substantially debug them before the equipment is installed. Debugging time is usually furnished by the equipment manufacturer, although additional time is often needed and may be obtained at a service center or at another user's installation.

Physical Requirements

Management is likely to be more familiar with the problems related to the physical installation of large units of production equipment in factories than to implementation of office systems *per se*. The new feature, from the viewpoint of the people directly responsible for data-processing operations, is the surprising complexity of installing large equipment, since they are accustomed to dealing with relatively small units of office machines and punched-card equipment. A hundred and one points, many individually small and simple, can snowball into an immense task. Complete planning and scheduling are essential to avoid last-minute complications and increased expense.

General Planning. The data-processing manager may not be directly responsible for the physical aspects of equipment installation, but he must be sure that adequate and complete plans are formulated to achieve serviceable operation on schedule. Factors to consider are space, location, and layout. Space is necessary for the major components and supporting equipment as well. Space for maintenance work, parts storage, and test equipment is also needed; and a reception and visitors' area is useful to avoid interference with production operations. Room should be allowed for possible short-range and long-range expansion; the cost of additional space initially may be small compared to the expense of alterations or future expansion.

Space and facilities comparable in quantity and quality to those provided for other office and supervisory employees are desirable. Some of this may be located near the processor; but the nonoperating research, analysis, and design personnel may be located elsewhere away from the hurly-burly of the immediate problems of machine operations. The location of space for equipment and personnel depends on many factors. Cost is important and is a suitable criterion, if all costs—intangible as well as tangible—are counted. The impact of a remote location on communications between the data-processing center and other parts of the organization is just as important as the cost of installing an air-conditioning system. Other factors in selecting a suitable location and layout are:

1. Adequate floor strength to support the weights involved
2. Head room sufficient for largest components
3. Isolation from machinery or other factors creating an unfavorable environment
4. Electricity, water, and other utilities
5. Location of entrances and exits adequate for equipment and suitable for convenience of personnel and flow of traffic
6. Adequate operating and maintenance space around each component
7. "Showroom" window for use by casual visitors

The layout of space should be determined early to fix the location of power lines, lighting, and air conditioning. The manufacturer's representatives and the user's building engineers are best able to convert equipment specifications into space layouts and facilities plans.

Detailed Planning. Routine operating groups can handle engineering and detailed planning of the area to be used or constructed for data-processing equipment in the same way as other plant modifications. A building or plant engineer can supervise the preparatory work, the awarding of contracts, and actual installation. Specific facts about power requirements and air-conditioning loads are obtainable from the equipment manufacturer. An alternative approach, probably best suited to special design equipment, is to contract with the manufacturer for a completed installation. In this case, a manufacturer's representative functions much like a building or plant engineer during the construction and installation phase.

OPERATION

Systems implementation has two phases. The first is to move the equipment into place, set it up electrically and mechanically, and test it for meeting specifications. The second phase is to start conversion of operations from the old system to the new. A shakedown period is required to ensure that the new system will function as planned or to revise it to achieve the desired level of operations.

Acceptance Testing

Manufacturer's field-service engineers should completely install and test all equipment before turning it over to the user. The manufacturer has diagnostic routines specifically designed for testing various features. These routines test major features and parts, although it is nearly impossible to make thorough tests at the detailed component level. One testing method is to use previously verified data to run a proven program for an extended period. A complex program with real data for testing both the equipment and the data-processing system should use all system components at some point. Verification of the program on other equipment, if available, is useful but not necessary. Periods of forty to eighty hours of operation with no more than one or two hours of unscheduled down time is considered an excellent indicator of reliability and should reveal weak components. The manager of data processing is responsible for accepting the equipment after it is functioning reliably.

Off-line equipment is similarly tested, but a word of caution is in order for planning tests. High-speed printers, for example, consume not merely reams but miles of paper during several days of continuous testing. Continuous operations testing becomes practicable only after the system is installed and printers are in routine use.

Newly developed equipment may deserve more thorough testing than established equipment. The engineering design of new equipment requires checking along with the construction—both electrical and mechanical—of the product itself. Also useful are specially designed programs for "marginal checking" of each feature by operating it over a range of conditions simulating unfavorable operating conditions to test its performance. Arrangements for developing programs to meet the user's test specifications may be made with the manufacturer or with consultants.

Conversion

The pressure to attain maximum use increases quickly after the equipment is accepted. This pressure will critically test the adequacy of all prior planning; hence, an established plan is imperative for guiding an orderly conversion. It is also useful for evaluating the progress of conversion. Data-processing procedures themselves are merely a means toward the end of obtaining specific information at certain times and places. A careful check of actual system operations will show how well this end is met. It is useful to operate the new system on a test basis for a period so that mistakes and errors can be detected without contaminating real data and disrupting actual operations. One approach is to provide a period of parallel operation with the existing system. The new system can handle a sample of transactions parallel with the old for comparison of results; the old system continues to handle all transactions and is the primary source of information.

When system reliability is proved by small-scale parallel operations, processing can be shifted to the new system. The old system may be operated a short time longer to verify the accuracy of results and to serve as a safeguard against system failure during conversion. Some users of automatic equipment find that the output from a logically correct and debugged program is extremely accurate, so that not much parallel operation is required to verify the accuracy of new system results. Parallel operations are likely to disclose mistakes in the results obtained by the old system rather than the new, and reconciliation of such differences is fruitless. Furthermore, parallel operations are a heavy drain on manpower during the critical stages of conversion. After proving reliability of the new system for both accuracy and ability to handle proposed applications, the old system is discontinued.

Publicity about new developments is highly desirable. All people concerned or interested should be advised of the conversion plan and time schedule. Furthermore, every person whose duties will be changed by the conversion should be informed what his new responsibilities are and when they start.

Operating Procedures

Successful operations require attention to many points: communications, time schedules, operating procedures, and retention of records.

Communication channels are set up to get data when available and to deliver reports when wanted. Efficient channels depend on the form of data, volume, distance, time requirements, and available facilities. Physical delivery of paper or cards may serve in some cases; in others, data on punched cards is sent by wire circuits. Magnetic tape is physically delivered or, in some cases, is sent by low- or high-speed wire or extremely high-capacity microwave circuits.

Output reports are often merely printed copy for direct delivery, but the content of some reports may be sent over wire circuits and printed by the user. Communication channels—wire circuits, messenger, or mail—need have capacity for only slightly more than the average message loads, if short "waiting lines" are permissible. For minimum delay, capacity must be large enough to handle peak loads. Some compromise is usually accepted between the huge capacity required to handle any peak load and the small delay associated with near-average capacity.

All processing operations must be scheduled, but flexibility is obtained by *scheduling* at less than full capacity to avoid the chaos resulting from schedules going awry. Slack capacity makes it possible to get operations back on schedule. Each stage—data origination, conversion, processing, and output—must be scheduled for smooth operations. Work needs to be done on time and must be done in the right sequence. Assignment of deadlines for processing puts the information wanted within fixed, short time limits ahead of information that is wanted merely when convenient to produce. Short-cycle processing gets a high priority to ensure prompt handling and avoid having to combine several cycles to get back to schedule, if a cycle is lost. Applications having longer cycles—week, month, and quarter—are phased in with daily operations and with each other to try to get a reasonably level workload.

Testing of new programs poses interesting scheduling problems. Production processing tends to push aside new program debugging because it does not seem immediately productive. However, unless an organization continues to prepare and test new programs, it soon has neither up-to-date programs nor new applications. Some organizations give high priority to debugging new programs during the day shift when analysts and programmers are available. Equipment testing can certainly be done outside regularly scheduled hours for the whole processing group. Some users find that maintenance causes the least inconvenience if engineers start work about an hour before operating personnel. Maintenance engineers should, desirably, be quickly available to find and correct equipment malfunctions that occur during scheduled operations.

As processing loads grow, the question arises whether to run equipment more hours per day or to obtain additional equipment. Multi-shift operation costs less per unit of time because equipment rental rates are lower and many costs increase less than proportional to the number of hours operated. On the other hand, employees may dislike working a second shift because it violates traditional "office hours." A similar scheduling problem arises for nation-wide or world-wide operations when office hours at several places are out of phase merely because of time zone differences. The use of wire or other high-speed circuits to cover the operating hours observed at all locations extends central operations beyond one shift.

Many policy decisions are required to achieve uniform and efficient *operating procedures*. Systems analysis and programming must incorporate such procedures during the development phases and not merely tack them on at the end. Some routines for people and machines are required to check the accuracy of console operators and tape handlers. Others are needed to guard against mixing programs, inputs, and files, which may cause loss of data and machine time. Console operating logs are included in programs to give instructions to the operator, keep tabs on what he does, and provide for reconstructing files when severe difficulties occur. Programs should include restart and rerun procedures for those occasions when the processor malfunctions.

Separation of duties among the people responsible for originating and processing data and maintaining custody over property—supplies, inventory, equipment, or money—meets the internal check and control standards of sound management. Auditors are also interested in a division of duties to safeguard property and records.

Operating procedures are needed to deal with intermittent questions about the results of processing. Questions may arise that need more current answers than those produced in the last regular processing cycle. If the equipment is able to handle random questions, answers can be obtained by interrogating the system. If equipment does not have random interrogation ability, an answer may be obtained during the next regular processing cycle. A random interrogation capability gives more current answers, but at the expense of more equipment and perhaps more elaborate programming.

Questions about the long-term history of any record—customer, employee, inventory item, etc.—may be answered by reference to occasional, complete print-outs of files. Each individual print-out may be noncumulative to cover only the period following the prior print-out, and the files themselves may be purged after printing. An index or chain-link scheme may be used to trace the record of a particular item from one print-out to the preceding one. In this way, it is possible to get the whole story by tracing a record as far back as is desired and fairly quickly assembling the individual print-outs. Unanticipated questions pose far more difficult problems; they may require developing new programs and procedures to get answers from files. Some questions may be unanswerable because the necessary facts were not obtained or were obtained and then discarded.

Standard operating policies should control the *retention of records*. The basic question about retention is "How, where, and how long should original data, interim results of processing, and files be kept?" Strictly for operating safety, many organizations keep magnetic-tape files for several processing cycles until it is clear that the most recent version is satisfactory for further processing. Current transactions are processed against the previous day's file and, if the output seems satisfactory, preceding tapes are released. In short, keeping files for several cycles guards against having to go back too far to reconstruct files in case of difficulty during any particular run.

Input data may be kept for a longer period so that they can be further processed to answer unexpected questions and to meet legal and other requirements for historical facts. Data on tape are useful for economical processing and the original paper or punched-card data used in producing the tape may be retained for record and audit purposes. The prior processing programs and related instructions for operators and tape handlers also must be retained in order to utilize old files after new programs are introduced.

In the matter of destroying records, magnetic-tape files are most efficient, since they can be selectively erased and condensed. Daily receipts and issues of widgets, for instance, may be useful facts to keep for a month. After a month, when daily activity is of less interest, transactions may be summarized by weeks or for the month. With this feature of partial destruction through condensation, data items can be gradually eliminated from each record in keeping with the future value of the record. It differs in some respects from the all-or-nothing plan of retaining or destroying paper and card records.

Alternative Facilities

An organization may become extremely dependent on a well-designed data-processing system, since the system records supply much of the information needed to operate, evaluate, and control the organization.

Emergency Plans.   Any system may fail either partially or completely. Failure may be temporary when caused by power interruption or equipment malfunction that involves lengthy diagnosis and correction; the failure may be near-permanent when caused by fire, explosion, or a similar catastrophe. Complete alternate processing plans for emergency operations should provide for all reasonable possibilities. A plan might be started by making the following lists:

1. List in order of criticalness all data-processing jobs and indicate those that can be handled without the automatic system
2. List the location of similar automatic data-processing equipment
3. List duplicate files to be maintained and suitable locations for them

The ranking or priority of jobs varies widely. Some may be needed daily; others can be suspended for a time without seriously hindering operations. Few jobs are absolutely necessary because much information of this type can be handled outside the formal system by telephone, memo, or personal contact. A larger number of jobs, such as payroll, accounting, and stock control, rank as highly desirable; some of these might be done manually in an emergency, despite reduced efficiency. Most other data-processing jobs are important enough that their suspension for a long time would be harmful. Optional jobs are probably least important; these are jobs to be done if conditions are suitable, such as longer-range applications to improve the performance of the organization.

If equipment failure is expected to continue for a long time, quick availability of other equipment is desirable. The user may have identical equipment at another location that can handle part of the load, or equipment may be available in a nearby service bureau. When planning the load on one set of equipment, the possibility of performing high-priority jobs from other installations should be considered.

Duplicate Files. A disaster that destroys equipment may also destroy all files at that location, or they can be lost or destroyed from lesser causes. Duplicate files at separate locations are desirable for preserving instruction programs and basic records but it is necessary to keep them correct and current. Duplicate files can be produced on magnetic tape or punched cards corresponding to the original files. As such, they are fairly easy to reproduce, transport, and store. Duplicate instruction programs and files can be stored at an installation with similar equipment. If current or nearly current duplicate programs and files are already at the alternate facility, an emergency system can be activated quickly.

Reference information—lists of items in inventory, part numbers, uses, and suppliers—can be efficiently contained in duplicate record files, since they are updated only occasionally. Maintenance of duplicate record files containing operating data is troublesome because such data continuously change. If conditions change slowly, occasional updating may yield duplicate record files sufficiently current for most purposes. If changes are rapid, current duplicate records can be maintained only by frequent updating, which may be costly. The cost of preparing and storing duplicate record files and the frequency of updating them should be related to the probable value of their occasional use.

Reviewing New Operations

Successful conversion of the first major application inaugurates a new period of challenge. Following the conversion to a new system, there still remain intricate problems to be solved before management can reap full benefits. New programs and procedures generally require *modification,* for preparation of the complete program for an application is usually so complex it is almost impossible to do it efficiently the first time. Furthermore, the magnitude of systems analysis and programming is usually underestimated. Lengthy programs written to get operations started can be improved by systematic review during operations. Operating programs can also be improved by continually reviewing the basic functions of the procedure. The question "What information is required, when, and by whom?" deserves to be asked and answered again and again. As people throughout the organization learn equipment and system capabilities, they will think of ideas for extending and modifying information output. The data-processing group may evaluate proposals and implement the changes and improvements considered worthwhile. The cost of making such changes must be weighed against the probable benefits, just as it was in the initial installation. But the fact that programming experience and skills have improved and automatic equipment is available with excess capacity weighs heavily in favor of any application that shows reasonable promise.

Studies for developing *additional applications* should be exploited and the changeover from manual or semi-automatic to automatic processing should be accomplished in much the same way as for initial applications. Each application profits from the same follow-up approach discussed above. At this point, it is worthwhile to recall the course of development that resulted in the new operating system. First, a feasibility study was made of key areas that would appear to benefit by automatic processing. This was done on the basis of preliminary estimates and, perhaps, with some working knowledge of advanced equipment. Second, an applications study elaborated the key areas and formulated the general plan for data flow through the processing system to reach the desired objectives. Third, the flow charts were reduced to detailed programs and operating instructions and the applications were installed. Vast experience, both in programming and operating techniques, was accumulated after the early days of the feasibility study. Experience available at any stage should be used to re-evaluate the foundations of the data-information system by determining:

1. Where is a greater degree of integration suitable for data, files, and processing?
2. What data-information requirements should be added or eliminated?
3. What new areas can be incorporated in the automatic system?

These questions and others should be raised periodically on a systematic basis to gain maximum benefit from experience. The system should reflect changes in information requirements, and all the data economically processable should be handled. Most users emphasize electronic equipment for mass-volume data processing. Such emphasis is suitable because routine data processing is the staple diet for business data processors. In general, routine problems that need frequent solution—for instance, keeping up with and controlling the number of widgets in stock—are the primary and immediate justification for equipment. Some striking benefits can be derived from using electronic computers for *special studies*. Specialists conduct organized approaches that are more efficient than haphazard approaches and occasional studies to satisfy management's immediate need for specific information. A systematic approach is valuable for the following reasons:

1. Operations-research techniques improve quantitative analysis for business operations
2. Machine-processable data obtained as a by-product of routine processing are useful for further studies and eliminate the need for costly collection and manual handling of data
3. High fixed costs of installed and operating processors permit intensive analysis at small additional costs

Electronic data-processing equipment is a remarkably powerful and versatile tool. It is worth remembering that, as with any tool, efficient use requires much skill, imagination, and hard work. The result may be a level of control and efficiency not otherwise obtainable in a large, complex organization.

SUMMARY

Equipment selection begins by obtaining the facts about equipment and applications. The specifications on data input, processing, files, and output are collected. Special requirements and installation and operation features are also ascertained.

Bid invitations reduce discussions and negotiations to concrete terms. A well-planned bid invitation describes what is wanted, answers questions about applications, and provides a fair basis for comparing equipment. Manufacturers' proposals should be detailed and explicit enough to show they understand applications requirements and can deal with them. Proposals should cover the degree of automation planned, equipment needed, operating requirements, the manufacturers' assistance, rental and purchase terms, maintenance, design changes, and expansibility for handling a growing workload. Equipment evaluation determines whether terms of the bid request are met, capability of equipment to handle applications, and equipment operating time. Bid price is only one factor among many to consider in selecting equipment.

Although the user must rely on the equipment manufacturer for facts about equipment, he is ultimately responsible for determining the acceptability and advantages of using equipment and a newly designed system. The margin of error in estimates is critical to the final success of the project; the user should estimate and appraise their implications for the proposed system.

Equipment acquisition hinges on preparing and submitting a proposal showing an adequate and thorough study justifying acquisition of the selected equipment and system. The proposal can be supported by all investigatory work starting from the initial feasibility study. If proposal review leads to approval, normal procurement procedure is followed. Advance planning for delivery and physical installation assures prompt and efficient use. Applications must be programmed and tested, and personnel obtained and trained in order to start operations when equipment is installed and checked.

The installation group is responsible for installing new equipment and implementing the related system. This responsibility involves making ideas and plans operational, installing equipment, training people, converting operations to new procedures, discontinuing old procedures and equipment, and transferring personnel. Before delivery of equipment, it is necessary to plan for the installation schedule, operating organization, analytical and programming work, and site requirements.

Development and conversion may be divided into four broad phases: (1) systems analysis and design, (2) flow-charting, programming and preparing operating instructions, and testing, (3) dual operations of both the new and the old systems during final testing, and (4) elimination of deficiencies to get smooth, efficient operations. Data-processing organizational structures are revised to reflect changes in operating methods, manpower involved, and concentration of responsibility. Personnel considerations require informing all people involved, selecting and training required personnel, and dealing with dislocated personnel. Competent, enthusiastic personnel are just as important as new equipment to the success of a system.

Systems programming in the broad sense—systems analysis and preparation of instruction routines and procedures for people to follow—is likely to cost as much as the purchase price of equipment itself and take many man-years for an important application. The use of advanced programming techniques and cooperative work by users and manufacturers can reduce the programming costs for each user.

Alternative facilities are valuable safeguards against long down time or complete disability. Plans should be made to give vital jobs priority, plan use of other equipment, and store duplicate record files and programs for safety and convenience.

Continuing review and improvement should follow successful installation. Here, as elsewhere, hindsight is better than foresight for seeing how something should have been done. Additional applications make full use of the skilled manpower and equipment capacities. Operations research studies offer techniques for improving data processing and getting more valuable information for management.

Appendixes

Appendix I

QUESTIONS AND PROBLEMS

1. **a.** Why are data processed? **b.** What is the most important reason? **c.** What operations are included in the processing of data?

2. **a.** What is the distinction between *data* and *information*? **b.** How can this distinction be used in designing and operating a system?

3. **a.** Why is it so difficult to solve the problem of deciding precisely what data to gather and store for use in the future? **b.** What is a rational approach toward answering the question, "How much data should we obtain now and save on the chance that we will need it someday"?

4. **a.** Describe briefly some reporting system with which you are familiar and then answer the following questions. **b.** How satisfactory is the structure of reports judged by the definition of "information" given in the chapter? **c.** Suggest improvements in the report structure. **d.** How much back-up data are retained and how long are they retained primarily for the purpose of dealing with unexpected requests for information? **e.** How frequent and important are such requests? **f.** In view of the frequency and nature of such requests and the penalty that results from not being able to fill them, would it be better to reduce the quantity of back-up data and shorten the retention period?

5. **a.** What data-processing capabilities does a trained clerk have? **b.** What arithmetical and logical operations can a clerk perform? **c.** How would you reply to the supervisor who demands that clerks originate perfect data—either they should be trained thoroughly and work hard enough to reach perfection, or more checking must be done to make the data perfect?

6. **a.** What determines the form and method for originating data? **b.** Why not originate data in the precise form and media wanted for input to the processing unit?

7. **a.** Why verify data? **b.** What are the different kinds of verification and how are they performed? **c.** Does verification assure perfection? If not, why bother to do it? **d.** Would it be feasible to do all the steps in verification when data are first originated so that no problems— errors, incomplete data, etc.—will arise in later stages of processing?

8. What equipment and support are necessary for an electronic data-processing system?

9. a. What steps should be taken to evaluate a data-processing system? **b.** What changes in the way business operations are organized and carried out are likely to accompany the introduction of electronic data-processing systems?

10. One proposal for report preparation is to use the same format every time so that the location of an item will not change in each edition of a particular report. A second proposal is to include in a report only those items that have a suitably high information content and omit all other items. Answer and explain the following questions. **a.** Are fixed format reports compatible with high information content? **b.** Which scheme for preparing reports is more efficient? **c.** Which type of report is more efficient for the user? **d.** Which scheme uses the least quantity of paper to print?

11. a. Since sorting anything—invoices, checks, or vouchers—into sequence seems such a chore for people or equipment, why not merely avoid doing it when processing data? **b.** What changes would be required in the equipment and techniques used for processing?

12. a. Since advanced data-processing systems are likely to accelerate the growth of scientific decision-making and take over routine decisions, the question arises, "What kinds of education and training should be given to a prospective manager?" **b.** Where and how will a junior manager get any practical experience in order to grow into a bigger job by first making small decisions, if the system makes all small decisions but leaves important decisions to senior managers?

13. Random-access files are often claimed to be superior to magnetic-tape files, which are sequential. **a.** What do the terms "random access" and "sequential" mean in this context? **b.** Since random-access files cost more to operate than sequential files, how would you go about selecting the type most suited for an application? **c.** Does it seem compatible to use both kinds of files within one data-processing system? Explain.

14. a. What are the differences between historical reports, forecast reports, and action documents? **b.** Name an example of each drawn from the area of production for a company that you are familiar with and describe their content and use. **c.** Similarly, from the area of marketing for a company.

15. a. Explain why it is necessary to distinguish between these two facets of time for reports: (1) the frequency of report preparation, and (2) the length of time available after the close of a period (or when a request is made for information) before reports have to be submitted. **b.** What is the practical effect of trying to get immediate or up-to-the-minute reports on everything that is happening throughout an organization? **c.** Why do unexpected and even unscheduled requests for information pose a difficult problem for a data-processing system? **d.** Why should one turn the question, "Look, we have these kinds of facts on file, what useful reports can we get out of them?" over to statisticians or researchers to try to answer rather than attempt to develop a solution to the question and immediately incorporate it into the data-processing system?

16. An electronic data-processing system reads in its instruction program in just the same form as the data to be processed, whereas a clerk reads (or already knows) operating instructions expressed in words and handles documents containing words and numbers. **a.** How do the processor and the clerk keep the instructions and data separate so that they correctly use each? **b.** What happens if they switch the instructions and data before they use them? **c.** How does a clerk modify the instructions as he works through the data and finally reaches the end? **d.** How does a clerk know which set of instructions to use on the next stack of documents that he receives? **e.** What does a clerk do if a document does not fall within any of the categories that he knows how to handle? **f.** What does an electronic processor do in the unique-document situation?

17. a. Under what circumstances is the division of a company's records into files useful for efficient processing? **b.** When does a segregation by files reduce processing efficiency? **c.** Describe the organization and maintenance of completely integrated files for a company.

18. Until the beginning of the twentieth century, letter presses were commonly used to make copies of handwritten or typed letters. A copy was made in a bound book by wetting the copy paper and pressing it against the letter in a way similar to the operation of a hectograph spirit duplicator. What changes in making copies of business documents have followed the invention and widespread use of typewriters and carbon paper?

19. Typewriters were designed in the eighteenth century to type raised characters for the blind to read by touch. What differences would you expect to find in data collection, storage, and output if people could read faster by touch than by sight?

20. Describe the important differences between on-line and off-line systems in terms of feedback, response time, and the role that people play in system operation.

21. a. How does process plant control differ from airline handling of space, reservation, and ticketing for customers? **b.** What additional features would be required in order for an airline system to be as fully automatic as a process plant control system?

22. Describe the importance of each of the following for data-processing system design and operation: **a.** number of points where data originate; **b.** distance between points where data originate and the central processor; **c.** time limits for processing data to produce an answer; **d.** amount of loss that will occur if control information is delayed or erroneous; **e.** the different kinds of transactions that must be treated together and the times when they originate in order to develop a useful answer.

CHAPTER 2

1. It is possible to punch a hole in any of twelve positions in each column of a punched card. **a.** How many different symbols can be represented by one punch in a column? **b.** How many different symbols can combinations of not more than two punches in a column represent?

2. Packing density is the number of bits or characters in a unit of media. **a.** Compare the packing densities in characters per linear inch for paper tape, magnetic tape, and a track on a magnetic drum. **b.** What is the ratio of the packing density of punched cards to magnetic tape in characters per square inch?

3. Observe the arrangement of alphanumeric characters on a telephone dial. **a.** How many three-letter exchange names can be formed using any combination of letters? **b.** How many three-digit exchange names can be formed? **c.** What increase in the number of possible exchanges is gained by changing from alphabetical to numeric exchange names? **d.** Repeat (a), (b), and (c) for two-letter and two-digit exchange codes. **e.** If numeric exchange names are used, is there any need to keep the letters on the dial? **f.** Will elimination of letters from the telephone dial occur as quickly as the initial introduction of automatic dialing on a local basis? Explain.

4. **a.** Explain the purpose and use of parity-bits. **b.** How does a simple-parity-bit scheme operate to detect malfunctions? **c.** How does an elaborate scheme operate to detect and correct malfunctions? **d.** Explain how parity-bits might be used on ordinary punched cards.

5. **a.** What is the relationship of characters, data elements, records, and files for organizing data? **b.** What is the purpose of dividing an item of data into two or more parts (for example, the data element "city-state" can be redefined as "city" and "state")? **c.** Give five other examples of redefinition of one data element into two or more sub-elements that are useful in processing data.

6. **a.** Is English the "natural" language of an electronic data-processing system? **b.** How might a processor be modified to read and print the 32 characters of the Russian alphabet? **c.** How would the processor sort the Russian characters into sequence?

7. a. Sort the following characters into ascending sequence by using the code collating sequence illustrated in the chapter: P, K, End Data,), #, O, A, $, and *. **b.** Why should numeric data be right-justified and alphabetical data left-justified before sorting? **c.** What scheme would you suggest for a processor to keep the decimal point straight in performing addition operations? Remember that decimal points are not ordinarily shown in punched cards used for data read-in, and even if they were, a processor cannot add numbers containing nonnumeric characters.

8. What sequence of accounts—numeric, alphabetical, or random—will result from the sorting operations performed on customers' accounts in each of the following cases? **a.** Use account number as the key when account numbers are merely assigned sequentially to accounts when they are opened. **b.** Use account name and number (name is major, number is minor) as a combined key for the account number scheme described in (a). **c.** Use account number as the key when account numbers are assigned from a table designed to keep names in alphabetical sequence. The scheme works 99.6 per cent of the time, but 0.4 per cent of the time a pre-assigned number block becomes filled with names, which requires the assignment of numbers from a reserved block at the end of the whole series. **d.** Use account name and number as a combined key for the account numbering scheme described in (c).

9. a. How are items separated on tape and in processor storage when the processor is designed to handle variable-length items? **b.** What kind of addressability of storage is required for a processor designed to handle fixed-length fields? **c.** Variable-length fields? **d.** Selectable length fields?

10. The address element of a customer's record on magnetic tape using the code scheme illustrated in the chapter is given below:

**Channel
number**

7	0 0 0 0 1 0 1 1 1 1 1 0 1 1 0 1 1 1 1 1 1 0 1 0 0 1 0 1 0
6	1 0 1 0 0 0 1 1 1 1 1 1 1 1 0 1 1 1 0 1 1 1 0 1 1 1 1 0 0 0 1
5	1 1 1 1 1 0 1 0 0 1 1 0 1 1 0 0 0 1 0 0 0 0 1 0 1 0 1 0 0 1 1 1
4	1 0 1 1 1 0 0 1 1 0 0 1 0 0 0 0 0 0 1 0 1 1 0 0 1 1 0 1 0 0 1 1
3	1 1 0 0 0 0 1 1 1 0 1 1 0 0 1 0 0 1 1 0 1 1 1 0 0 1 0 0 0 1 0 1
2	1 1 0 1 0 0 1 0 0 1 1 1 0 1 1 0 0 0 0 0 0 0 1 0 0 1 0 1 0 0 1 0
1	0 0 1 0 0 0 0 0 1 1 0 0 1 1 1 0 0 1 0 0 1 0 0 0 0 0 1 0 0 1 1 1

There are, for purposes of illustration here, five single-bit errors in recording the address data element.

a. Detect as many errors as you can by means of the column or vertical parity rule (row parity is not used here).
b. Correct as many errors as you can by applying the parity rule.
c. How many more errors could be corrected by means of the row parity rule (in addition to column-parity) if it were used?
d. Correct as many errors as you can by decoding the message (determine each character from the code illustrated in the chapter) and applying what you know about the composition of addresses.
e. What conclusions would you draw about the accuracy of the system—equipment and people—if you were told that this element of a record was the customer's name?

11. The following numbers have a decimal base:

2	64	.5	64.25
4	260	.25	324.75
9	4096	.375	4356.33
17	32768	.4375	36864.9375

a. Convert each number from the decimal to the binary base. (In most cases, one may do the conversion by inspection. Start from the brief description in the chapter and build from your own solutions; e.g., $4356 = 260 + 4096$.)
b. Convert the binary numbers from part (a) to octal. (Octal uses the digits $0, 1, \ldots 7$ to represent binary digits taken three at a time on either side of the binary point: $1_{octal} = 001_{binary}$, $3_o = 011_b$, $7_o = 111_b$, etc.)
c. Convert the numbers from the decimal base to binary-coded decimal. (Each decimal digit, $0, 1, \ldots 9$ is converted to bcd (8421): $3_{decimal} = 0011_{bcd}$, $9_d = 1001_{bcd}$, etc.)

12. What changes will probably occur in data representation, input-output, and processing methods, if data processors and physical operations—selected machines, individual processes, or even a whole factory—are more closely linked as another step toward the "automatic factory"?

13. a. Given the following description about manpower data for a manufacturing organization, show how they can be organized from lowest to highest level as data elements, records, and files by using the outline form given below. Show the level numbers similar to those in ordinary outlines, and indicate the *class* (numeric, alphabetic or alphanumeric) and the *size* (average number or range of characters) of each item. For each item that may be repeated, merely describe it once and indicate how many times it may occur. Each possible occurrence must be counted to determine size. Indicate the class and size for only the lowest level description of each item—which may be a data element, sub-element, etc.—so that there is no duplication of description in the outline.

b. Calculate the estimated size of each file that is required and the total file content. Make any reasonable assumptions required about the number of characters in each element and the number of times that each repetitive element occurs—for example, ten children, etc.

   I. Name of file.
      A. Name of record.
         1. Name of data element with class, and size (if lowest level).
            a. Name of sub-data element with class, and size (if lowest level).
               (1) Name of sub-sub element with class and size.
               (a) Etc.

The ABC organization has 2600 employees on the active payroll, 1800 work in the main plant located in state A, 500 in plant 2 located in state B, 100 in sales throughout the United States, and 200 in general administration in state A. In addition, there are 150 retired employees still on the employee newsletter mailing list (pensions are handled through a trust); two-thirds reside in state A and the others in state C. For each active employee, the data on file, although not arranged in any particular order, covers name, address (in the usual detail), social security number, sex, birth date and place; marital status, name of spouse (usual format), sex, birth date and place; name, birth date and sex of each child; number of dependents claimed for tax purposes; participation in medical and hospital plans, family coverage, and amount of deduction each month; savings bond deduction amount for specified weeks in each month, and denomination to purchase when enough is deducted; deduction for specified organizations, amount, and pay periods for deduction (repeated for ten possible deductions); name and address of bank to mail check to, if so requested; department employee assigned to and date assigned; rate of pay and date of change to that rate (repeated for all work assignments and rates for the past ten years or five work assignment changes or rate changes whichever is longer).

Each record for a retired employee consists of his current address and the presently useful part of his active payroll record (which you are to select for purposes of this question) at date of retirement. It also lists his annual total earnings for each of the last five years.

14. a. Why is the binary scheme favored in the design of electronic computing equipment? **b.** Is the decimal number system the only reasonable one for people to use?

15. A base 26 number system contains the symbols A, B, C, . . . , Z where A is the zero symbol, B the one symbol, and Z the highest order symbol. Represent each of the following decimal numbers in the base 26 system: **a.** 5; **b.** 27; and **c.** 676.

16. a. How many bits are needed to represent a decimal digit? **b.** How many characters can eight bits represent?

17. a. In designing payroll cards that must be sorted into alphabetic order, what are the advantages of using a *selected-length* data element as compared to a *variable-length* field for names? **b.** Are there any disadvantages?

18. Various kinds of paper records have features well suited to storing variable, selectable, and fixed-length items. Classify each kind of paper in terms of its item storage characteristics:
a. Accountant's ruled working paper;
b. Blank 8½ inches × 11 inches paper;
c. Ruled square grid paper;
d. Roll paper of the type used in tabulating machines;
e. Printed card records for inventory;
f. Ruled accounting ledger sheets;
g. Printed bill forms.

19. A utility that bills customers on a bi-monthly cycle basis (assume a twenty business-day month) wants to identify each day's group of accounts with the shortest possible code.
a. How many characters are required if the code is either numeric, alphabetic, alphanumeric, or any alphanumeric and special symbol that can be represented by six bits?
b. How many characters are required for cycle identification if the utility switches to (1) a monthly cycle, (2) a tri-monthly cycle?

20. Five-channel punched-paper tape directly represents 32 characters ($2^5 = 32$). Mode shifts are used to represent a wider variety of characters at the expense of using one character to shift from one mode to another. Further, some characters (blank, carriage return, line feed, and space) may be provided in each mode similar to the typewriter arrangement of space, period, and comma in both upper and lower cases. The general rule for the number of characters that can be represented in two or more modes by n channels, with M modes shifts, where C characters are common to all modes is $(2^n - M - C)M + C$.
a. Determine the number of characters representable by five-channel tape when used in 1, 2, 3, 4, 5, 6, and 27 modes.
b. Repeat for six-channel tape with 1, 2, 3, 4, 5, 6, and 59 modes.
c. Which is a simpler approach to representing more characters: (1) more channels, or (2) more modes? Why?
d. What would a typewriter that is limited to 40 keys look like if it operated in 1, 2, 5, 10 and 20 modes?

e. How many characters could be represented in each mode?

f. At what point does the number of modes become so high that only one key is used for characters and all others are used for mode shifts?

21. Standard cards can be punched in binary fashion with one word of 36 bits in columns 1 to 36, and another word in columns 37 to 72 in each row across the card. Nine rows (0 through 8) are used for data and row 9 is used for a parity-bit for each column.

    a. What is the largest binary number that can be represented by 36 bits? What is the octal equivalent? Decimal equivalent?

    b. What is the largest decimal number that can be represented in binary-coded alphanumeric form in each word?

    c. How many letters can be represented in binary-coded alphanumeric form in each word?

22. The Travelers National Bank issues its travelers' checks in blocks of 100, numbered xxxx00 to xxxx99 for each amount ($10, $20, $50, $100), to agent banks on consignment and collects for them after they are sold by the agent banks. The Travelers National Bank wants to keep track of the following facts for each check: (1) issued to agent bank on consignment; (2) sold by agent bank; (3) collected proceeds from agent bank; (4) paid check after use by purchaser; and (5) stop-payment order received from purchaser because check reported lost or stolen. Each block of checks requires 40 characters of constant data.

    a. How can each check be represented by one column in a card and how many cards are required to control a block of checks?

    b. The Travelers National Bank's systems department is proposing that one row across four columns be used to store data for one check. Devise a scheme to implement the proposal and show that 40 columns will control 100 checks by using ten rows for ten checks. What savings in punched cards can be achieved by this scheme?

    c. How much more compression of data could be obtained if punched-card equipment worked with three kinds of punches (▬ , ▌ , and ●) instead of just one?

CHAPTER 3

1. **a.** What are the major components of data-processing systems? **b.** What is the flow-path of data among them? **c.** How much freedom does the user have to choose the equipment that he wants at each stage? What is available and how compatible is it with equipment used at other stages?

2. Draw a block diagram showing the relationship between the follow-

ing elements of a data processor: **a.** input; **b.** internal storage; **c.** arithmetic function; **d.** control function; **e.** output.

3. a. What are the control functions in a processor? **b.** How are instructions given to a processor? **c.** Which method is most flexible and why? **d.** If an externally-stored program is difficult to change, why is an internally-stored program not equally difficult?

4. Instructions and data are said to have the same appearance in storage and either can be stored anywhere in an internally-stored program processor. **a.** How can you·distinguish between instructions and data to avoid confusion? **b.** What is the meaning of the sentence, "It is useful to modify instructions but it is not meaningful to execute data"? **c.** How can the address part of an instruction be modified? The operation part? **d.** Why is it useful to modify either part of an instruction? **e.** Give an example of address modification and show how it can be used in programming and processing.

5. a. For the instruction "SUBTRACT 200, 300," what is the meaning of the explanation, "Subtract the contents of location 200 from the contents of location 300"? **b.** Is the result 100; if not, what is it exactly? **c.** Where is the result located? **d.** Develop an example to show the operation.

6. a. What is an *operand*? **b.** How is an operand related to storage locations and the instruction command in one-address instructions? Three-address instructions?

7. a. Explain what function is performed by the following: (1) accumulator; (2) M-Q register; (3) instruction counter; (4) instruction register? **b.** How are the accumulator and M-Q registers used in performing addition and multiplication instructions? **c.** Would it be possible to use both the accumulator and M-Q registers together to perform double-precision addition—addition of operands twice as long as the usual word in storage—by having each register handle one half of an operand?

8. a. What are the steps in an operating cycle to execute one instruction? **b.** Can the console be used efficiently to monitor the execution of one instruction? **c.** What is the function of the console in debugging on the machine, and preparing traces and post-mortems?

9. a. What are the similarities and differences between arithmetical and logical operations? **b.** Give three examples of logical operations and show how they can be used.

10. a. How is it possible to make decisions within a program since it is essentially sequential—instruction-after-instruction—but decision-making may result in skipping forward or backwards ("jump" or "go to") various parts of the program because of conditions that are encountered in a program? **b.** Draw a simple flow chart to illustrate decision-making for joint conditions. For example, accept customer's order *if* no bill exceeding 10 per cent of credit rating is overdue *and* the value of this shipment will not cause his new balance to exceed credit limit. **c.** Draw a simple flow chart to cover the order-credit case described in (b), if the rule is to grant credit to a customer who meets one of the two conditions. **d.** Ambiguity is raised by the condition, "No bill exceeding 10 per cent of the credit rating is overdue." How should you cope with it? (Flow chart symbols are illustrated in Chapter 6.)

11. Explain why it is necessary to eliminate the symbols "$", "," and "." from an item of data before read-in to a processor, if used for: **a.** arithmetic operations; **b.** decision-making operations; **c.** merely forming part of the output record?

12. **a.** What are *concurrent* operations? **b.** How are they achieved? **c.** What is the practical effect of concurrent operations for processor operations? **d.** What is the importance of trapping from the programmer's viewpoint? **e.** From the program execution viewpoint?

13. Describe and appraise the efficiency of the various schemes used to represent stored data.

14. Define: **a.** stated storage capacity; **b.** effective storage capacity; **c.** access time; **d.** volatility; **e.** word time; **f.** transfer rate.

15. **a.** What scheme is used to address an element of data in storage organized as fixed-word? **b.** As character-addressable storage? **c.** Under what conditions are absolute addresses useful? **d.** How can symbolic or name-addresses be used in programming since a processor works with numerical addresses only when executing instructions? **e.** What are *data-names* and *procedure-names* and how are they used in addressing data in a program?

16. What is the nature and importance of each of the following for evaluating storage-unit characteristics: **a.** data representation; **b.** addressing scheme; **c.** operating mode; **d.** capacity; **e.** access time?

17. **a.** For a magnetic drum, how are packing, access, and capacity affected by revolver loops? **b.** Why is it possible for magnetic cores and thin films to operate a hundred or more times as fast as magnetic drums? **c.** Why are combinations of storage used for a processor instead of only one type of storage throughout?

18. **a.** What are the chief differences between high-speed and bulk storage? **b.** Under what conditions is each useful for processing data? **c.** What is the relationship of bulk drum to high-speed drum storage and to disk in terms of access speed, capacity, and function within a system?

19. a. What storage requirements do disks fill for file processing? **b.** For on-line processing and interrogations that require quick answers to routine questions? **c.** How is access time to records on disk storage reduced by the cylinder concept of data storage when each diskface has one or more read-write heads? **d.** How might disks be used in conjunction with tapes for efficient sorting of large volumes of data by means of the cylinder concept?

20. a. What is the purpose and the effect on data density, read-write speeds, and organization of data in blocks of the inter-block gap on magnetic tape? **b.** Explain how the following contribute to tape operating efficiency: read-write speed, density, transfer rate, read backwards, rewind speed, tape swaps, search.

21. Explain how the following factors affect the selection of storage equipment: **a.** type of processing; **b.** size of file; **c.** time limit for processing and interrogation rate; **d.** cycle up-dating; **e.** retention period and selective condensation and discard.

22. Internal storage capacity has increased over the years while access times have decreased. **a.** What is the effect of this dual change on practical capabilities of processors? **b.** One might speculate that a suitable design objective is to keep the product of storage capacity and access time roughly constant. Would keeping this product constant mean that effective storage capacity of processors for handling data will remain almost constant? Explain.

23. a. If a 4 inch diameter magnetic drum rotates at a speed of 5000 revolutions a minute, what are the maximum and average latency times in milliseconds on a standard band with one read-write head? **b.** What are the latency times if the drum is 8 inches in diameter? **c.** What are the latency times for data on a revolver loop if the read and write heads are one eighth of a drum circumference apart?

24. A programmer facetiously said that his company produced one pint of oil during one word time. The drum involved stored 1000 words on 20 tracks and revolved at 12,500 revolutions a minute. How much oil did his company produce per month?

25. a. What is the cost, at $.05 each, for magnetic cores alone to make a storage of 1024 words if each word has a sign and 12 alphanumeric characters each with parity-bit? **b.** What is the cost of a 16,384-word storage if each word has a sign, 36 data bits, and a parity-bit? **c.** What is the most economical configuration for each storage unit, considering the cost of read-write circuitry?

26. When using magnetic tapes for data storage, it is customary, although not universal, to remove inactive tapes and replace with active tapes. **a.** Could a similar replacement plan be used for magnetic drums, disks, cores, and cards? **b.** How would you appraise the merits of such a replacement scheme?

27. Tape transport units customarily are assigned by pairs for handling multi-reel files so that a "tape swap" can be made from one tape to the other without interrupting processing.
a. How much processing time is saved by arranging for tape swaps?
b. What is the effect on the number of tape transports required and their utilization?
c. Could equipment utilization be improved by having one (or perhaps more) tape transports assigned as "roving spares" to swap with any tape transport on a first-come, first-served basis?
d. Would a combination of one assigned spare transport for each major tape file and a roving spare for all minor tape files increase equipment utilization without making programming unnecessarily complex?

28. The following estimates are available about the number of tape files and input-output time:

	Number of Tapes	Input-Output Time
Master file	10	8 min. each
Trailer file (contains overflow of each record from master file)	4	20
Transactions	2.7	30
Error tape (from prior processing cycle)	.2	80
Program	.1	

a. How many tapes are required for the current processing cycle and two complete prior cycles of the file for back-up purposes?
b. What arrangement of tapes on tape transports will give fastest processing if tape-change time (rewind a tape, dismount, and mount a new tape) is 2.5 minutes and 10 tape transports are available?
c. What arrangement of tapes on tape transports will give fastest processing if tape-changing time is the same as (b), but 15 tape transports are available?
d. Draw a line chart (with time shown horizontally) to show the use of each tape transport (running, change, and idle time), if 12 are available.
e. What is the ideal number of tape transports if they rent for $600 a month, computer time costs $300 an hour, and three jobs similar to this one are being run every business day?

CHAPTER 4

1. **a.** What are the steps in the chain of activities leading up to data input to a processor? **b.** What is the distinction between *symbols* and *data* in this context? **c.** Why is an *event* the basis for starting the data input operation?

2. **a.** Describe an example of data origination that you are familiar with to illustrate the steps in the activities leading to data input to a processor. **b.** Show how the performance of each of these steps can be improved. **c.** How much combining of these steps is feasible if important changes in system design are permitted?

3. **a.** What are the advantages of originating data in a form suitable for processing as a by-product of another operation? **b.** What is the net effect on system efficiency? **c.** What are the audit control features of remote by-product preparation of data when the machine operator is excluded from the tape room (the input keyboard is wire-connected to a tape punch in a central room) and therefore never sees the by-product output?

4. **a.** What is meant by *prior* or *advance preparation* of data?
   b. Under what conditions is prior preparation of data input useful?
   c. What is the feasibility of prior preparation when your organization has sole control over the data media at all stages (for example, time cards and inventory tags), and when your organization shares control with others (for example, checks and public utility bills)?
   d. What spoilage rate and reconstruction costs are permissible, yet can still make prior preparation worthwhile?

5. **a.** What are the advantages of on-line data input? **b.** What problems does on-line input pose in trying to keep processors operating at capacity?

6. **a.** Since equipment is available, or can be developed, for converting data from one medium to almost any other, or a satellite processor can be used, why should a system designer worry about data incompatibility? **b.** What are the merits of direct data conversion—as from punched cards to processor—instead of an indirect scheme —punched cards or tape to magnetic tape and then to processor?

7. **a.** Obtain copies of bank checks printed for MICR (magnetic-ink character recognition) and study them to determine what characters are specially printed on a check when first issued by the bank and after it is paid by the bank. **b.** Are the characters readable in both cases? **c.** What are the chief features of the MICR scheme? **d.** How much advance preparation of checks is possible with this approach to bank automation? **e.** What features would an optical character-

reading system need to have in order to compete with the magnetic-ink system? **f.** What combination of circumstances, as you view the situation, caused bank automation to become a reality only in the 1960's in view of the fact that punched cards were widely used starting about 1920 or 1930?

8. **a.** What features are required in a data-collection system to make it suitable for use in a job shop factory? **b.** What are the merits of installing and using a factory data-collection system? **c.** How many other features would have to be built into a data-collection system in order for it to be able to communicate operating instructions about the next job to the machine operator? (Consider the central processor's capabilities to store data about men, machines, and jobs in order to calculate what to schedule next.) **d.** How closely does a factory data-collection system approach the automatic factory? **e.** What else would be required to warrant the name "automatic factory?"

9. **a.** What is the relationship between a satellite processor and the main processor? **b.** What are the merits of a satellite processor for input-output conversion instead of a number of specialized media converters to handle conversions between the processor, cards, magnetic tapes, and printers?

10. **a.** Assuming typical densities and inter-record gaps, how much tape is required during the initial card-to-tape conversion to record the content of 30,000 cards punched in all columns, if the card-to-tape converter writes the data from each card as a separate record? **b.** If the satellite processor used for conversion has 10,000 characters of storage for data and program and it forms long data blocks before writing on tape? **c.** If blocked records are superior to unblocked records, why not combine all records into one super-block? **d.** What determines the practical upper limit to block length?

11. Explain the implications for processing speeds of each of the following features of magnetic tapes: **a.** long or short interblock gaps; **b.** unblocked and blocked records; **c.** vertical parity-bit for each character; **d.** horizontal-parity check word for each record or block; **e.** concurrent "read-process-write" or "overlapped" operations; **f.** high-speed rewind; **g.** read-reverse; **h.** back-space in order to read a prior record (but no read-reverse feature); **i.** back-space and reread a faulty record as many as five times before halting operations.

12. People are sometimes considered too slow and unreliable to operate on-line keyboards for data input. **a.** How does multiplexing cope with the speed and accuracy problems? **b.** What functions do special devices—agents' desk sets, bank tellers' machines, and others—per-

form to facilitate manual inquiry and output? **c.** What is the purpose of providing remote interrogation of, and data input to, a processor file via a communication network?

13. **a.** What part does the document or report format—headings, lines, number of characters, sub-totals, and blank spaces—play in determining the speed of editing, output, and printing? **b.** What is the effect on report format and printing speeds of adopting a perfectly uniform format so that the same item will appear in just the same position on every report to facilitate the reader's finding the item that he wants to study? **c.** How would you choose between the constant report format described in (b) and a variable format that emphasizes off-standard performance and omits items that are on-standard? (Consider the user's problems of reading voluminous reports or searching through shorter reports that may not contain the desired items.)

14. Explain how the following factors are balanced out in trying to design an efficient communication scheme: **a.** volume of data to be transmitted; **b.** number of origin and destination points; **c.** time limits within which data must be transmitted; **d.** degree of reliability required; **e.** media containing the data at origin point and media wanted at destination; **f.** capacity of the communication channel; **g.** the need for on-line processing and immediate reply of current information to interrogators.

15. **a.** What are the merits of using characters that are readable by both people and machines? **b.** Give examples of character readers for data input. **c.** What are the advantages of character recognition devices to prepare machine-usable data media? **d.** How are character-readable data verified?

16. **a.** What types of mechanical printers are used in data-processing systems? **b.** How do they differ in operation from each other?

17. **a.** What does *multiplexed* input mean? **b.** What are the merits of multiplexed input for utilization of both the processor and the input units?

18. Assume that a processor is capable of supplying output at the rate of 100,000 characters a second. The choices offered are to operate output units (cards, paper tape, and magnetic tape) either directly connected or through buffers. If the output units are directly connected, the processor must supply characters when they are wanted by the output unit. If a buffer is used, the processor merely loads the buffer and then continues other operations while buffer content is transferred to the output unit.
a. What fraction of the processor output capability can be absorbed

by a card punch, a paper-tape punch, or a magnetic-tape unit, if a buffer is not used and the processor is able to deal with only that unit?

b. What fraction of the processor's time will be absorbed in output if a suitable buffer is available for each output unit (80 characters for cards, 1 character for tape, and 1000 characters for magnetic tape) that can be filled at processor speeds (and emptied at output unit speeds), but 10 character cycles of the processor are required for the processor to test each buffer for readiness to load in the latter part of each output cycle?

19. The printed copy output requirements of one organization are 30,000,000 characters a day, on average. **a.** What printing capacity is required if the output load throughout the week is level and printing deadlines merely require that output be available by the end of the day following processing? **b.** What printing capacity is required if the peak day load in a week is three times the average and the tight time schedules require completion of printing two hours after processing (which takes three hours) is complete? Assume that final data start becoming available for printing halfway through the processing cycle. **c.** If the conditions in either case (a) or (b) seem too loose or too tight, what changes would you recommend?

20. The following facts are given concerning a tape file that contains 12 million characters of data: tape density 400 characters per inch, tape write speed 150 inches per second, rewind speed 300 inches per second, block length not exceeding 511 words of six characters each (a block can contain any integral number of records not exceeding 511 words), start-stop time each 10 milliseconds, one inch inter-block gap. Compute the tape-writing time, tape-rewind time, and length of tape for each of the following cases:

a. records 80 characters long are to be written on tape, in blocked fashion for use in the next processing cycle;

b. records 80 characters long are to be written on tape as individual card records (content of each card separated by a gap) ready for punching;

c. records 20 characters long are to be written on tape as individual card records ready for punching.

21. Paychecks and stubs are printed on card stock 3¼ inches by 7½ inches with a maximum of 50 and 100 characters, respectively. A border of ¼ inch on each edge of the check and stub cannot be used for printing, and ¼ inch must be allowed between successive cards to compensate for the difference between card size and the spacing interval for feeding card stock through the printer. A high-speed printer prints 10 characters per inch along a line, and six lines per inch at the rate of 1000 lines per minute. Skips of one to eight lines are made at the print rate, but skips of eight or more lines are made at the high-speed skip rate of 25,000 lines a minute.

a. Determine the layout of data for fastest printing of check and stub.

b. Compute the printing time for 1000 checks and stubs.

c. How much faster is side-by-side printing of check and stub instead of serial alternate printing (check, stub, check, stub, etc.)?

CHAPTER 5

1. a. Describe the ranges of internal storage capacities and operating speeds for the small and large processors listed in the tables in the chapter. **b.** Explain the usefulness of these two factors as general indicators of data-processing capability.

2. Explain the meaning of the following terms: **a.** capacity in decimal digits; **b.** word content in alphanumeric characters and binary bits; **c.** three-address addition time for operands with five decimal digits; **d.** indirect addressing; **e.** character addressing; **f.** floating-point arithmetic; **g.** number of addresses for an instruction.

3. a. What factors determine the theoretical transfer rate for magnetic tape? **b.** What are the implications of long tapes on effective processing speed and processing capability? **c.** How are block size, inter-block gap, and the read-reverse feature related to effective tape capacity?

4. a. In converting data from cards to tape, how many card records can be written on a typical tape as individual records? **b.** How much more data can be written on a typical tape if, say, one half of the processor storage is available for assembling data before writing on tape? **c.** What are the characteristics required for efficient use of tape by both a main processor and its satellite?

5. A maxim in data-processing circles is that "processing capability increases faster than systems rental." **a.** How can this maxim be evaluated to determine its validity? **b.** If the maxim is true, what action should a company about to order some data-processing equipment take? **c.** What action should it take if it has recently received some new equipment?

6. Some manufacturers offer users the choice of a small or medium processor, others offer a satellite and large processor, and a few offer a complete range from very small to very large processors. **a.** What are the advantages and disadvantages from the user's viewpoint? **b.** How can a user wisely choose from the array of equipment to best fill his short- and long-term requirements?

7. Explain the difference between computing for engineering-scientific purposes and data processing for business in terms of their requirements for electronic equipment.

8. a. Compare the features of *ideal* and *available* processing equipment. **b.** What steps may be taken to compensate for the lack of ideal features in equipment actually used by a company?

9. a. What does the phrase *system balance* mean and what is its relationship to applications? **b.** How can a lack of system balance be corrected short of purchasing new equipment?

10. a. What does the phrase *tape-limited operation* mean? **b.** What does *processor-limited operation* mean? **c.** What changes might cause an operation that is tape limited to become processor limited, and vice versa?

11. If a user is offered the opportunity of choosing one feature of processing equipment to be improved 100 per cent at no cost to him, which feature should he choose?

12. The following choices may be available when a parity-bit error occurs when reading tape: reread one or more times under program control, reread automatically one or more times under control of equipment, read the faulty record onto a reject tape, or halt all operations. What is the order of desirability of each of these features for achieving the highest validity in data that are processed and for processing the largest volume of data?

13. It is sometimes said that, "If a processor has more than four index registers, it should have a hundred." **a.** How can the usefulness of having a hundred index registers in a processor be appraised? **b.** How can the optimum number of index registers be selected?

14. What factors determine the most efficient amount of addressable bulk storage in relation to the amount of internal storage in a processor?

15. a. What factors make the track-to-track access time for magnetic disks shorter than the disk-to-disk access time? **b.** What is a typical transfer rate for data after the desired disk track is located? **c.** What is the relationship between the storage capacity of a set of disks, a magnetic tape, and a random access magnetic card unit? **d.** How does the comb concept for disk reading and writing affect data transfer rates for small quantities of data? For large quantities?

16. a. What is the maximum number of tape units that can be connected to a typical processor? **b.** What factors determine the optimum number of tape units to use? **c.** What is the minimum number of tape units that are useful for a file-processing run? **d.** Minimum number for a merge-sort run?

17. **a.** Rank five processors by basic storage cycle time as described in the chapter. **b.** How much difference is there between the rank and the addition speed or the multiplication speed alone for each processor? **c.** How suitable as an index of speed is the following scheme: total the time required for each processor to perform the operations common to all processors under consideration including an addition, a subtraction, a multiplication, and a comparison?

18. Describe the potential effect on the data content of magnetic tape from making each of the following changes: **a.** eliminating the frame and row parity-bits; **b.** doubling the length of tape; **c.** eliminating the inter-block gap; **d.** making the tape four times as wide.

19. Assess the merits of each of the following *schemes* for effectively cutting rewinding time, which is typically from one to five minutes: **a.** Assign tape units in pairs and swap to a new tape while the filled tape is rewinding. **b.** Dismount tapes without rewinding and use a special device to rewind them. **c.** Dismount wound tapes and do not rewind them, but mount the reel backwards the next time it is used so that it can be reused without bothering to rewind it. **d.** Process the reel by reading it backwards in the next cycle, if the processor has a read-backwards feature.

20. Explain the merits of the following features for facilitating processor operations: **a.** program interrupt; **b.** simultaneous read-process-write; **c.** simultaneous tape search; **d.** real-time input; **e.** off-line printing.

21. One processor records variable-length records on tape at a density of 100 characters per inch with an inter-record gap of .75 of an inch. **a.** Draw a chart with the length of the record along the horizontal and the effective data density (as a percentage of specified density) along the vertical to show the percentage of tape occupied by records of different lengths: 25, 50, 75, 100, 200, . . . , to 800 characters. **b.** Draw another line for a specified density of 400 characters an inch and .75 of an inch inter-record gap. **c.** Repeat for 400 characters an inch but assume an inter-record gap of .25 of an inch. **d.** What length of record is necessary in each case to get an effective density of 25, 50, and 75 per cent of the potential density? **e.** What improvement in tape use can be gained by blocking several short records into a longer block? **f.** What is the relationship between tape use and processor read-write time for file processing?

22. A manufacturer is considering offering a new model processor. His choices are either to offer the same processing capacity as before

at a reduced price, or to offer more processing capacity at the same price. Furthermore, the new machine can be designed to handle programs prepared for the earlier model. If the new model is lower priced and programs are compatible, users of the prior equipment may insist that the equipment already in use be reduced in rent or that it be replaced by the new equipment.

a. What strategy should the manufacturer adopt for introducing new features and pricing new equipment?

b. How can he guard against users turning in relatively new equipment and demanding newer models?

23. The formula for the multiplication operation time in one processor is, in milliseconds:

$$.017[N_r(N_d + 4) + 2],$$

where

$N_r =$ the number of digits in the multiplier
$N_d =$ the number of digits in the multiplicand

a. Use this formula to calculate the multiplication time for each of the following: (1) 1234×4567; (2) 4567×8989; (3) 12×9876543.

b. Make a table with N_r along the horizontal and N_d along the vertical and fill in the multiplication times for N_r and N_d from 1 through 10. Connect the points that have the same value.

c. Explain how to arrange the multiplication operation to minimize the time required.

24. a. What benefits can a prospective user of equipment gain from the manufacturer's software package? **b.** When does a user need to know the specifications of the software package in order to make full use of it? **c.** How are the manufacturer's costs of producing a software package and the users' benefits from using it shared between them?

25. Describe each of the following plans for evaluating equipment and describe the merits of each plan in terms of the costs involved and the benefits obtained by both the prospective user of equipment and the manufacturer.

a. Prepare and run a program for an actual application with real, live data.

b. Prepare and run a program for a test problem with simulated data.

c. Plan the program for an application and calculate how long it will take to run the program.

d. Calculate a profile of equipment capability by considering every feature of both hardware and software for which specifications can be obtained.

e. Simply calculate an index by totaling the time required to perform nine additions and one multiplication, using data already in storage and placing the results in storage, plus the time required to read and write 100 records on tape.

26. a. What features of the traditional rent-or-buy decision for production equipment need to be changed in order to apply it to data-processing equipment? **b.** Explain the importance of each of the following for a rent-or-buy decision: (1) length of time the equipment under consideration has been available; (2) option deposit; (3) credit of rental payments toward purchase price; (4) maintenance contract rates on various pieces of equipment; (5) number of hours equipment is operated per day; (6) adequacy of equipment for future loads; (7) technical and economic obsolescence of the equipment involved.

CHAPTER 6

1. a. What are the steps in systems analysis? **b.** Why is it any more important or difficult to determine the outputs that users want than it is to do the other steps?

2. Explain the meaning of each of the following terms related to systems analysis: **a.** event; **b.** event chain; **c.** station; **d.** data collection sheet; **e.** editing; **f.** station characteristics; **g.** network load analysis; **h.** document activity analysis.

3. a. What are the objectives of systems analysis? **b.** How do they differ from the objectives of any other kind of analysis? **c.** What factors determine how much analysis is worthwhile for a company that has just completed installation of a radically new and improved system? **d.** How much analysis is suitable for a company that has not made any important changes in its system in twelve years?

4. a. What work is involved in the systems analysis and approaches to design phases of developing a new system? **b.** Since the selection of a design approach may be important for guiding systems-design work, why not choose a design approach first in order to minimize the analysis work that is done for no useful purpose? Explain. **c.** If the design approach is selected in advance with no possibility of change, can the new system be designed immediately without analyzing the existing system? Explain.

5. Some observers say that initial estimates of new system benefits are usually too high and costs too low. **a.** What is the meaning of this statement and under what circumstances is it likely to be true? **b.** If you were responsible for appraising and selecting proposals to develop new systems, how would you apply this observation in accepting or rejecting individual proposals? **c.** How does the statement,

"Note that the criterion for continuing or stopping analysis and design work is not how much has been spent to date, but how much will be spent to completion," correspond with what you know about decisions to continue or stop systems work?

6. Systems analysts were told that the frequency of processing was "as required" for certain kinds of documents. Document activity analysis and file analysis indicated a disproportionate fraction of as-required processing. Further investigation disclosed that people meant documents were not processed if there were no documents either because of a delay in receipt or because no transactions had occurred, and that a daily or weekly schedule was ordinarily followed.

a. How is it possible to describe processing schedules when replies of this type are obtained?

b. What would be the effect on system design if this unusual definition of "as required" was not discovered?

c. What is the practical effect of the two no-processing situations upon the workload for the following day or week?

d. Should delayed processing be adopted so that a small backlog of transactions of each type awaiting processing can be built to help keep the processing load steady by filling the gaps in receipt of transactions? Explain.

e. If a small backlog is used to keep the processor workload steady, what is the effect on timeliness of reports?

7. a. What is a *flow list*? **b.** How is it related to events, documents, files, outputs and stations? **c.** Why is a flow list superior to a flow chart when one picture is often said to equal ten thousand words? **d.** Can flow charts be developed from flow lists? Flow lists from charts? Explain. **e.** How are gaps or breaks in the event chain discovered from flow lists? From flow charts?

8. a. What are the important features of automated analysis of a system? **b.** How does automated analysis differ from traditional systems and procedures analysis? **c.** Why go to all the bother of interviewing people and obtaining copies of forms when it is possible to analyze a system automatically?

9. Two definitions of file redundancy are that it exists (1) if two or more files make common use of the same document(s), and (2) if they are based solely on an identical set of documents.

a. What is the nature of forms-to-file redundancy?

b. Reconcile these two definitions.

c. Is it possible for two files based solely on an identical set of documents not to be redundant from the user's viewpoint? Explain.

d. Why, and under what conditions, does file redundancy have merit for operating purposes?

e. Would it be possible and feasible to eliminate file redundancy by having only one file that contains all transaction data in original raw form for analysis and presentation when information is wanted? Explain the merits and demerits of this scheme.

10. **a.** Why is it important to consider selecting an approach to systems design before starting the actual design work? **b.** What are the essential features of each of the four approaches to design discussed in the chapter? **c.** What are the consequences for the system designer of a broad degree of freedom when selecting an optimum approach to design? **d.** What is the optimum approach if freedom is small or nil?

11. Describe in moderate detail the analysis and design-approach selection work for a system that you have first hand experience or some familiarity with. Answer with explanations the following questions:
a. Was the analysis group set up with a sufficiently high-level and explicit charter and enough manpower and money to cover the work it was supposed to do?
b. Did the analysis group adequately examine all fruitful areas? Over-examine any?
c. Did the approach to system design most likely to be selected have any bearing on the initial analysis phase? On subsequent phases?
d. Were the facts obtained by analysis efficiently organized in flow charts, tables, or other forms for use in selecting a design approach and later designing the system?
e. How much analysis work was wasted because improvements were not possible in a particular area or a prior decision had been made to proceed along a certain path?
f. What steps should and could have been taken to make the analysis and design selection work more efficient?

12. Explain the effect on systems analysis and design of the following changes: **a.** Important improvement in communication techniques or data-processing equipment. **b.** Increase in complexity of the business by acquisition of new factories, introduction of new products, and expansion into new markets. **c.** Increased competition from improved services on products and lower prices of competitors. **d.** Reduction in the data-processing budget because management believes the company cannot afford the usual outlay.

13. Some organizations are vertically integrated to cover all operations from the production of raw material to the final stage of selling to consumers.
a. How different are the data requirements of vertically and horizontally integrated organizations?
b. What opportunities exist for making data processing more effi-

cient in a vertically integrated organization than in a horizontally integrated one?

c. Are there any operating areas within an organization that are completely unrelated to the main stream of operations? If so, explain how data processing for them can be handled most efficiently.

14. a. What is the difference between static and dynamic business operations? **b.** In what ways do the data and information requirements of a dynamic organization differ from the requirements of a static organization? **c.** How are these differences in data and information requirements reflected in efficient systems design?

15. The controller of one corporation said, "We will continue to use decentralized management throughout our widely scattered organization no matter what changes we make in our data-processing system."

a. Under what conditions is such a strong adherence to decentralized management warranted?

b. What changes would warrant complete re-examination of the controller's announced position?

16. Managerial control plans are said to range from being carefully specified in advance to being developed as problems arise. **a.** Why do most actual control plans fall somewhere between these two extremes? **b.** What are the data-processing requirements for these two extreme plans of managerial control? **c.** Under what conditions would it be efficient to specify completely detailed control plans in advance for every conceivable problem that is likely to arise? **d.** How does the management control plan being used influence data-processing system design?

17. Why should a systems analyst consider, first, the data and information requirements and, second, the organizational structure when designing a data-processing system?

18. a. How is it possible for a small organization to have bigger data-processing problems than a large organization? **b.** Since data and information systems are relatively simple for large organizations, does it follow that these organizations are likely to have a much faster growth rate than small organizations?

19. a. Explain how the geographical location of data processing is influenced by the cost of communication, in view of the fact that the volume of data usually exceeds the volume of information. **b.** What geographical location scheme would be used if the volume of output from data processing were several times as large as the input?

20. In recent years there has been a strong tendency for communication companies to increase their rates by charging more for services, requiring longer-term commitments by users, and restricting the freedom of users to add and drop circuits at will. How should a company modify its extensive communication network if these cost increases are occurring?

21. a. How would you reconcile the economies of uniform processing with the desire to have complete freedom at the local level? **b.** What degree of freedom to meet local information requirements is compatible with the need to consolidate reports for an organization as a whole?

22. a. What is the relationship between capacity and flexibility for a data-processing system? **b.** If the .statement, "larger systems have lower unit processing costs than smaller systems," is true, should an organization have one completely consolidated data-processing system? Explain. **c.** Why is centralized processing more critical for dynamic operations than for static operations?

23. What are the implications of centralized data processing for each of the following areas: **a.** document preparation; **b.** operating information; **c.** freedom of local managers from interference by central management; **d.** system flexibility.

24. What are the merits of using a joint communication network to handle both data-processing and administrative messages? Try to reconcile this joint use of a communication network with this often-expressed opinion: "The communication network is merely an extension of the data processor that permits it to operate effectively throughout the organization."

25. A large company is considering adopting one of the following organization plans for its data-processing activities: **a.** application—payroll, inventory control, sales, engineering, operations research; **b.** functions—engineering, production, finance, marketing, management, accounting, special analysis; **c.** data flow—data collection, transmission, processing, distribution; **d.** systems—analysis, planning and development, systems design, programming, systems installation, communications, computer operations; **e.** geographical areas—eastern, midwestern, and western U. S. What useful guidance can you give toward selecting the best organization plan since there are strong proponents throughout the company for the use of each plan?

26. A company that has the manufacturing plants of its five major household appliance divisions located in adjoining buildings is planning to introduce one or more processors to forecast demand, schedule and control production, control inventory, analyze sales, etc. The company has not decided whether to establish one data-processing department in each of the five divisions or to establish one center to serve all divisions.
a. What factors would bear on the use of five data-processing departments or one data-processing center?

b. If the idea of a data-processing center is approved, should it be set up within a manufacturing division or set up as a separate service center? Explain.

27. The Blackout Electric Power Company has a very large staff, at an excessive cost, for manually preparing monthly bills for customers and processing collections against customer accounts. **a.** Describe reasonable alternative systems within the following framework: (1) develop an improved manual system, (2) subcontract the billing operation to an outside firm, (3) develop an automated system. **b.** Describe some typical costs and benefits that are probably associated with each of the above.

28. The Moneyland Savings Bank is experiencing trouble with its manual recordkeeping system partly because the clerical force is large and turnover is high. Inexperienced girls too frequently post transactions to the wrong accounts. A customer who wants to deposit or withdraw money must sometimes wait in line 15 to 20 minutes and then spend another several minutes at the window while the bookkeepers find and process his account.
a. Develop several reasonable alternative systems for Moneyland.
b. Appraise the costs and benefits associated with one of the alternatives.
c. The Bank management wants to construct a simulator to test operation of a proposed system. Describe (1) the kinds of input data required, (2) the process that will occur in the simulator, and (3) the output statistics that should be collected.

29. Use the information about the mail-order company described in the Systems Evaluation section of this chapter to prepare an "explicit" report. Make whatever compatible assumptions are required to explain the following: (1) the foundations of the study, (2) the source of data used in the study, (3) techniques used, (4) results obtained, (5) limitations of the results, and (6) recommendations.

CHAPTER 7

1. a. What bearing do input and output requirements have on systems design? **b.** Do output requirements or the available inputs deserve more emphasis in systems design? Explain. **c.** If a system can be described precisely in terms of its inputs and outputs, why is any consideration given to the processing operations between input and output?

2. a. What is the relationship between reporting requirements and file design?
b. Explain *timeliness* of reports and show how it affects file design.

c. What factors should be considered in designing an efficient file structure?

3. a. How are unexpected requests for information planned for in designing files? **b.** Develop an example to illustrate the definition of "efficiency of file design" described in the chapter. **c.** Develop and illustrate a better measure of efficiency, if possible.

4. a. Evaluate the following statement: "Concentration on data inputs, when designing a system, is incorrect because it is based on the assumption that if enough data enter a system, the desired results are *pushed* out. Instead, concentration on outputs is correct because their careful definition will cause the necessary data to be *pulled* into the system." **b.** If not satisfactory, develop a superior statement of the design relationship between inputs and outputs.

5. a. Why should long-run systems objectives be spelled out when starting design work? **b.** What are the sources of information about systems objectives? **c.** Who establishes systems objectives?

6. a. What is a *run diagram*? **b.** What is the function of run diagrams? **c.** What level of detail does a run diagram have? **d.** Draw a run diagram for an application you are familiar with.

7. a. What is the purpose of *structure flow charts*? **b.** What is the relationship between run diagrams and structure flow charts? **c.** How can a structure flow chart be drawn without taking equipment into account and still be useful in systems-design work?

8. Explain how each of the following is shown on flow charts: **a.** main flow of data; **b.** identification of blocks, documents and files; **c.** quantity of items handled at each stage; **d.** repetitive loops; **e.** branching; **f.** merging; **g.** connectors; **h.** reuse of a file in a following run.

9. a. Study the run diagram and flow charts in the chapter and describe the ambiguous situations, mistakes, or duplications in them. **b.** Redraw any flow charts that you can clarify, correct, simplify or improve. State your assumptions in making any changes.

10. A manager of a programming and analysis staff says that one of his most difficult problems is to get people to document their work so that program maintenance work can be done easily several months later by the same programmer or by another one, in case the original programmer is not available. What suggestions can you offer to solve this almost-universal problem?

11. a. Why does the number of flow charts required at each successive level of detail increase so much? **b.** Can this number be reduced efficiently? **c.** How big (or small) a gap should exist between the most detailed flow chart and the program to be prepared from the flow chart?

12. From studying the flow charts, what rules can you devise that would serve as a guide for finding bugs in similar flow charts? For example, following a test, there must be two branches (or perhaps three, to cover the less-than, greater-than, and equal-to cases).

13. Prepare a run diagram and suitably detailed flow charts for the following stock-control application: The management of a machine parts manufacturing company wants a daily listing of every stock item and a separate listing of each item falling below its reorder point. The stock file from the previous cycle is available and transactions are classified by items completed, items shipped, returns from customers, returns to the factory, and reworked parts received from the factory.

14. Assume the same conditions as in Question 13, but suppose that management realizes it is able to deal with only a limited number of reorder items each day. Two possibilities exist: (1) a complete list of reorder items may be printed, permitting management to use the portion it can and carry over the remainder of the list for the next day; (2) a list of reorder items may be printed that is only as long as management can deal with each day, and printing of the list is started at that point during the next processing cycle.
a. How should these two schemes be shown on run diagrams?
b. On flow charts?
c. What are the merits of these two schemes for simplicity and efficiency of both data processing and management operations?

15. Expert programmers of scientific and engineering problems discount the value of detailed and elaborate run diagrams and flow charts. Equally expert programmers of business applications say that good run diagrams and flow charts are invaluable. How would you reconcile these viewpoints?

16. A series of tests are performed on 1000 items to identify those that fall into certain categories. The initial test yields 800 items (usually) in category A and 200 in category B, which might be abbreviated initially as $1000 \rightarrow A800, B200$, and thereafter abbreviated as $A800 \rightarrow C750, D50; B200 \rightarrow E190, F10; C750 \rightarrow G715, H35; D50 \rightarrow I45, J5; E190 \rightarrow K100, L90; F10 \rightarrow M6, N4; G715 \rightarrow O650, P65; M6 \rightarrow Q5, R1$.
a. Draw a flow chart to show the sequence of parallel testing suggested by the nature of the data and the number of items identified by each binary (yes-no) test.
b. Calculate the number of tests required for ultimate identification of every item. (H, I, J, and seven other categories are ultimate.)

17. Assume that the conditions are the same as for Question 16 except that the ten ultimate cases can be classified directly by a serial pattern of testing. **a.** Draw a flow chart to show the testing sequence to classify ultimate cases in alphabetical sequence (H, I, J . . .) and calculate the number of tests required. **b.** Draw a flow chart to show the testing sequence when the most frequently occurring item is classified first, the next most frequent item is classified second, etc., and calculate the number of tests required. **c.** What conclusions can you draw about the sequence for performing tests?

18. An electric utility issues bi-monthly bills to residential customers. Follow-up action for uncollected bills is taken on the basis of the uncollected balance, number of days overdue, the customer's credit rating, and whether the customer has a deposit. The conditions for issuing a reminder and a warning notice can be summarized as follows:

Uncollected Balance	Days Overdue	Customer Credit Rating	Customer Deposit	Action
$25 or more	30	2	None	Reminder
$75	60	1	Yes	Reminder
$22	30	3	None	Warning
$20	60	2	None	Warning
$50	90	1	Yes	Warning

a. Draw a flow chart showing the steps involved in determining whether to issue a reminder, issue a warning, or take no action.
b. What changes can you suggest in the rules followed by the utility to simplify processing without upsetting their business practices?

19. **a.** Why is continual review of forms and reports important for the efficient operation of a data-processing system? **b.** What recommendations can you suggest for reconciling the conflict that is likely to arise between the desire to standardize the preparation of reports and the need to keep the information content high in order to make reports useful for management?

20. *Compatibility* may be defined as "the ability to exist together in harmony." **a.** What kinds of incompatibility exist in data-processing systems? **b.** Why is it possible to reconcile some kinds of incompatibilities but not others? **c.** Describe the nature of a perfectly compatible system, then evaluate the argument that "compatibility can be achieved for any system because it is possible to convert data from any media to any other media, so that there is no need to worry about compatibility during the design phase."

21. **a.** What possibilities exist for organizing data-processing operations within a company that operates at a single location? **b.** How would you decide which plan to select?

22. Test the flow chart in Figure 7-7 for inventory-file reading and balance updating by tracing through its application to several different

situations. Determine the number of times that each path is followed and balance these against the number of master records and transactions. (One way to do this is to simulate the processing operations and tally on the chart each path as it is used.) Master-file contents to use in each of these cases are limited to stock record numbers: 1, 2, 3, 5, and 8.

Case **a.** Stock transactions for stock record number and type: 2 issue, 5 receipt, 5 issue, and 8 purchase order (in that sequence).

Case **b.** Transactions: 2 issue, 5 receipt, 5 issue, 3 receipt, and 8 purchase order.

Case **c.** Transactions: 2 issue, 5 issue, 5 receipt, 5 purchase order, and 7 receipt.

Case **d.** What other master record and transaction situations should be tested through this flow chart to determine its validity?

Case **e.** Redraw the flow chart to eliminate any bugs that you can find.

23. Explain the meaning of each of the following terms related to decision tables: **a.** condition; **b.** action; **c.** rule; **d.** limited entry; **e.** extended entry; **f.** Else-rule.

24. **a.** How can the sequence numbers assigned to rules be used to simplify the writing of rules and the order of execution? **b.** In what sequence are actions performed? **c.** How do rules relate conditions and actions?

25. This question pertains to the decision tables illustrated in the chapter: **a.** What effect would switching ">" and "<" in Rules 2 and 8 have on the solution logic? **b.** What effect would omission of Rule 5 have on the solution logic? **c.** Omission of Rule 9? **d.** If an Else-rule should be included in this table, what conditions and actions would be appropriate for it?

26. Calculate the number of rules needed to handle all the possible combinations of C conditions in a decision table, each of which may have entries of "Y" or "N": **a.** $C = 2$; **b.** $C = 4$; **c.** $C = 7$; **d.** $C = 10$. Repeat if three entries "Y," "N," and "–" are permissible for **e.** $C = 2$; **f.** $C = 5$; **g.** $C = 10$.

27. Revise the decision table illustrated in the chapter to write two output master-file records, one for the updated active-inventory-item records and a second for the inactive-inventory-item records.

28. Revise the decision table illustrated in the chapter to handle insertion of new catalogue items, transaction type 6, in the master-file record.

29. A fire completely destroyed building 10 and its contents. Building 11 was damaged with complete loss of contents from aisle 25 upwards and 60 per cent smoke and water damage to the remaining contents. The insurance company wants a detailed listing based on the inventory master-record form in the chapter: stock number, name, quan-

tity on hand, unit cost, fraction of loss, and dollar amount of loss for each stock item suffering a loss of 100 dollars or more. For items with smaller losses, the insurance company requests that merely the number of items and dollar amount of loss occuring in each building be accumulated. Prepare a decision table to make the fire-loss listings, as specified.

CHAPTER 8

1. a. What are the essential steps involved in programming? **b.** How do they differ from the steps in merely preparing instructions telling an experienced person how to do the job?

2. For the program on how to reach a friend's home given in the chapter, many points are implicit.
a. Rewrite the program with a *completely explicit* data description and procedures description. ("Completely explicit" means that all details are handled for the level of detail that is selected as suitable, not that every conceivable detail or contingency is covered.)
b. What details and contingencies are likely to cause your program to fail to work and when will they be discovered?
c. Show how these weaknesses can be handled: higher degree of detail, cover more contingencies, pre-test the program yourself, ask your friend to pre-test it, or let him try it and call for help in case of trouble.

3. Explain what the following terms used for programming mean: **a.** subset of English language; **b.** macro-level; **c.** translation; **d.** sequence; **e.** execution; **f.** interpret; **g.** compile.

4. a. What is a problem-oriented language and how does it differ from a machine-oriented language? **b.** How is a problem-oriented language useful since there are many different kinds of problems and many different kinds of machines?

5. Explain the meaning of each of the following terms used with COBOL: **a.** data division; **b.** procedure division; **c.** data-name; **d.** procedure-name; **e.** compiling run; **f.** execution run.

6. The level numbers assigned to a stock record are the same as in the chapter, except as follows:

02	WAREHOUSE-LOCATION
04	BUILD-NO
05	AISLE-NO
06	BIN-NO
03	UNIT-COST
04	STOCK-VALUE

a. What effect do these differences have on the organization of data?
b. What changes occur in the single-element, group-element arrange-

ment? **c.** What element(s) will be obtained by an instruction that refers to (1) BUILD-NO; (2) UNIT-COST; (3) WAREHOUSE-LOCATION; (4) BIN-NUMBER; (5) UNIT-VALUE?

7. a. If a programmer can select and use any data-names and procedure-names he wants, what prevents confusion within each group and between the two groups? **b.** What are the rules for writing pictures of data? **c.** Why must data used for calculations have numeric pictures?

8. Prepare a data description for customer-account records containing the following elements (in no particular order) on a COBOL-1 programming form and making necessary assumptions that are compatible: (1) customer name; (2) address for billing purposes; (3) address for shipping purposes (if different); (4) salesman; (5) sales territory; (6) sales to customer for "season history" (each season in current and preceding year); (7) date and amount of first order for season history; (8) returns in units and dollar amount for season history; (9) two most recent credit ratings by Dun & Bradstreet and by the company's own credit department; (10) account-balance high and low amount for season history; (11) dollar-days (dollar amounts X days overdue) for invoices now overdue 30 days and 90 days; (12) current balance of account; and (13) open-to-buy balance—that is, credit authorization minus current balance of account minus orders on hand to be filled.

9. Show the general form and illustrate the operation by means of simple numerical examples using appropriate data-names for each of the following instructions: **a.** ADD GIVING; **b.** ADD TO; **c.** SUBTRACT FROM GIVING; **d.** DIVIDE INTO GIVING; **e.** MULTIPLY.

10. a. How is decimal-point alignment handled in input data and inside the processor? **b.** How are the decimal points handled in the three numbers involved in the multiplication operation? **c.** What steps are used to assure that the desired number of digits are retained in a result without losing any significant digits?

11. a. How are decision-making choices written in a program? **b.** Show how the three conditional expressions—greater than, equal to, and less than—can be used in the format of the IF—THEN instruction, which has only two outlets. **c.** What is the relationship between conditional expressions, truth or falsity of expressions, and statements in an IF—THEN instruction? **d.** Why and how are imperative statements included in IF—THEN instructions?

12. For the example discussed in the chapter, develop a program—flow chart, data description, and a procedures description—to determine the following:

a. Number of stock records in the inventory file.
b. Total number of all units on hand for all inventory items ignoring the differences in unit of measure.
c. Total value of all stock items.
d. Number of stock items with unit-cost below $10.00 and above $100.00.
e. Calculate a "hash total" of all stock-record numbers in the inventory file. Show how the total can be updated during file-maintenance runs (when catalogue changes are made) to prove against a new hash total calculated before the next processing cycle to guard against incorrect entry or elimination of a file record.

13. a. For the stock-record file described in the chapter, design an output record to show the number of line items on hand, total number of inventory units on hand, and average dollar value on hand per stock item. **b.** Prepare a program to produce this output record.

14. a. Redesign the stock-record file described in the chapter to contain reorder point and reorder quantity. **b.** Design an output message format (assuming new order can be placed at prior unit cost shown in record) to show the following:

ITEM ORDERED _____ QUANTITY _____ EST-COST _____

c. Write a program to prepare this output message for each stock item below the reorder point. **d.** Describe how to modify the program to restrict the placing of orders to the first X items that should be ordered. **e.** Describe how to modify the program to restrict placing orders for those items resulting in the largest dollar-cost orders, yet remain within a financial limit set by the controller.

15. a. Design a simple customer-account record. **b.** Write a program to check whether the file is in order (assume the file is prepared in an appropriate medium and sorted into sequence). Write out a message FILE IN ORDER or count the number of records out of order (in relation to the immediately preceding record) and prepare the following record:

_____ RECORDS OUT OF ORDER.

16. a. Starting with the stock-record description in the chapter, develop appropriate data descriptions for receipts and issues transactions. **b.** Assuming that the two types of transactions are available as two files, each in sequence, draw a flow chart for updating the stock record, if not more than one receipt and one issue have occurred for each stock item. **c.** Prepare a program to update the stock record.

17. a. Design a master record for employees to contain name, number, department, starting date, rate, and 200 other alphanumeric characters. **b.** Design a "new hires" transaction record with appropriate data elements. **c.** Draw a flow chart to merge hires records into master-record file. (Assume any sequence wanted for each file.) **d.** Write a COBOL program to merge hires into the master file.

18. This question makes use of the employee master record required for the preceding question. **a.** Design an employee termination record with appropriate data elements. **b.** Draw a flow chart to eliminate terminated employee records from master-record file and write them in a termination-record file. (Assume any sequence wanted for each file. Provide for erroneous employee numbers in termination records.) **c.** Write a COBOL program to eliminate terminated employee records from master file.

19. a. Draw a flow chart to handle new hires and employee terminations described in the preceding two questions to update the employee master file in one pass. **b.** Write a COBOL program to update the master file.

20. a. How are files organized into three levels for COBOL purposes? **b.** Describe a record you are familiar with that contains at least twenty data elements and show two ways that these elements can be organized for file processing. **c.** How are single and group elements related to a record for file organization purposes?

21. Explain any inconsistency between correct COBOL-1 and the data description and contents for each of the following:

	Data-Name	**Picture**	**Contents**
a.	COST	9(6)V99	$000360.34
b.	NET-COST	9(3) . 99	137.56
c.	NAME	9(10)	GEORGE UTE
d.	GROSS COST	9(3)V99	312734
e.	XYZ993	X(4)	1331
f.	COST-E	$X(3).99	$127.44

22. Point out the errors in the following data description:

Level No.	Data-Name	Picture
DATE-DIVISION.		
FC	TEST-FILE DATA RECORD IS TESTING-RECORD.	
02	TEST-RECORD	PICTURE X(15)
40	TEST-DATA.	PICTARE 9(10).
60	TEST-DATA	PICTURE 5(9).

23. The following program is supposed to read in a stock-record, compute inventory value, and write an inventory record containing the stock value:

Proce-dure Name	Procedure	
Level No.	**Data-Name**	**Picture**

```
DATA-DIVISION
FD        INVENTORY-FILE  DATA-RECORD  IS  STANDARD.
01        INVENTORY-RECORD
02        STOCK-NUMBER.                    PICTURE-9(10).
03        QUAN-ON-HAND                     PICTURE X(3)V99.
04        UNIT COST                        PICTURE 9(6)V99.
05        VALUE                            PICTURE 9.
FD        INVENTORY-VALUE-FILE  DATA-RECORD IS VALUE-RECORD.
01        VALUE-RECORD.
02        VALUE-RECORD-CONTENTS            PICTURE X(50).
PROCEDURES-DIVISION
          READ INVENTORY-RECORD AT END
          MULTIPLY QUANTITY-ON-HAND BY UNIT-COST.
          MOVE STOCK-NUMBER TO STOCK-NUMBER-O.
          WRITE INVENTORY-VALUE-RECORD.
          GO TO START.
```

a. Explain why the program will not run correctly.

b. Rewrite the program, without changing the description of IN-VENTORY-VALUE-FILE, so that it will work.

24. At one point in a program, the contents of three names are as follows: NAME-1, 05; NAME-2, 07; and NAME-3, 04. Describe the contents of the three names, after executing each of the following individual procedures:

a. MOVE NAME-1 TO NAME-2.

b. ADD NAME-1 to NAME-2.

c. IF NAME-1 IS GREATER THAN NAME-2 THEN ADD NAME-1 TO NAME-2 OTHERWISE SUBTRACT NAME-1 FROM NAME-2.

d. SUBTRACT NAME-1 FROM NAME-2 GIVING NAME-3.

25. The *data-name* COST has a PICTURE 9(5)V99 and contents of 0034037. Show the result of the statement MOVE COST TO COST-EDIT if the picture for COST-EDIT is each of the following: **a.** 9(5)V99; **b.** X(10); **c.** 9(10); **d.** 9(5).99; **e.** $(5).99; **f.** $Z(4).99; **g.** 99ZZZ.99; **h.** $99,999.99; **i.** $ZZ,Z9.99; **j.** 99.9.

26. a. Why is STOCK-FILE a legal name, if FILE is a reserved word? **b.** Is SUBTRACT-FILE a legal name? **c.** Why is it possible to use more than one FILLER data element in a program?

27. a. What are the three functions of the Environment Division? **b.** Why are separate descriptions provided for the source computer and object computer, instead of merely having one description for the computer to do the job? **c.** When the plans are to write a program for one computer and run it on another computer, what items in the environment division must be changed?

28. Because of a change in equipment availability, the illustrative program at the end of the chapter is to be compiled and run on a WORDCOM-1000 with 15,000 words of storage. Aside from storage size, all WORDCOM-1000's have the same features. The only input-output units available for the WORDCOM-1000 are four magnetic tape units identified as TAPE-1, TAPE-2, TAPE-3, and TAPE-4. Rewrite the environment division of the sample program to compile and execute it on the WORDCOM-1000.

29. Modify the illustrative program in the chapter to do the following: **a.** Compute and print the stock value and print all the input data for each record. **b.** Assume that the last two digits of each stock number are check digits—they are simply the sum of the first eight digits. Make appropriate changes in the Environment, Data, and Procedures Divisions to do the following: Test each stock number to determine whether it is valid. If valid, proceed as shown in the illustrative program; otherwise, punch the complete record into a card. The punch is called the 1402-P.

CHAPTER 9

1. a. Why are COBOL names and verbs used in the flow charts given in the chapter? **b.** Describe three uses of flow charts in COBOL programming.

2. a. What are *literals*? **b.** What are the two main types of literals? **c.** What restrictions apply to the writing of literals? **d.** Why are literals used in programs? **e.** How can a program be written without using literals?

3. Give several examples of and explain how literals are used in **a.** the Procedures Division; **b.** the Data Division.

4. a. What is a *figurative constant*? **b.** How do figurative constants differ from other literals?

5. Six literal statements—data-name and picture—are given below. **a.** State whether each literal is figurative, numeric, or alphanumeric. **b.** Is each statement legal? Explain.

(1) MOVE ZEROS TO 93107.	PICTURE 9(5).
(2) MOVE ZEROS TO A9307.	PICTURE 9(5).
(3) MOVE 00103 TO COUNT.	PICTURE 9(6).
(4) ADD "107" TO COUNT.	PICTURE 9(6).
(5) MOVE SPACES TO COUNT.	PICTURE 9(6).
(6) MOVE "WRONG" TO RIGHT.	PICTURE X(10).

6. a. Why does COBOL have ACCEPT and DISPLAY statements in addition to READ and WRITE statements? **b.** Can programs be written without using ACCEPT and DISPLAY statements? **c.** Is the DISPLAY instruction useful for writing out individual data-elements from a record storage area used by an input or output file?

7. a. Describe two uses for working storage. **b.** Why is it more useful to set initial values for items in working storage than to set initial values of items in the File Section? **c.** If STATUS is part of a group-work-area, can it also be defined as an independent-work-area?

8. a. What unique restriction applies to an item defined in the Constant Section that is not applicable to an item in the Working Storage or the File Section? **b.** If TAX-RATE is defined as a constant, are the following statements legal? Explain.

```
MULTIPLY TAX-RATE BY INCOME GIVING TAX.
DIVIDE BUDGET BY ASSESSED-VALUE GIVING TAX-RATE.
DISPLAY TAX-RATE.
ACCEPT TAX-RATE.
```

9. a. Why are condition names used in a program? **b.** If MALE is the condition name corresponding to a value of 1 for SEX, write the conditional phrase that MALE is equivalent to.

10. a. What is the nature and use of a *mask* for describing data? **b.** Why are different masks used? **c.** How does the use of a redefinition clause change the content of the storage area involved?

11. a. Where several different record-names appear in the same file, how does the programmer arrange to read in the one he wants? **b.** What data are obtained if the program uses a data-name associated with record-1 when record-2 is actually in the storage area?

12. a. Why are subroutines used in a program? **b.** Can one subroutine call on another subroutine? **c.** Why are GO TO statements necessary instead of merely writing all instructions in one continuous sequence? **d.** Explain why the following program could run indefinitely without producing any results.

Main Program

```
START.
    ADD A TO B GIVING G.
    GO TO NET.
NEXT.
    ADD G TO F.
    GO TO PRINT-OUT.
NET.
    ADD F TO H.
    GO TO NET.
PRINT-OUT.
    WRITE OUTPUT-RECORD.
    STOP RUN.
```

13. The value of TRANSACTION-TYPE is 06 for RECEIPT, 13 for ISSUE, and 21 for ORDER. **a.** Can the selective GO TO be used to select the proper process routine? Explain. **b.** Can condition-names be defined and used in IF statements to select the proper routine? Explain.

14. A selective GO TO verb is followed by four data-names. Describe what will happen if the value of the data-name in the DEPENDING ON phrase has each one of the following values: **a.** 2; **b.** 5; **c.** −3; **d.** 2.5.

15. a. What two major tasks does a PERFORM statement control? **b.** What function does a PERFORM statement accomplish that is difficult to obtain with one or more GO TO statements? **c.** Why is this unique feature of a PERFORM statement useful?

16. a. What is the *range* of a PERFORM statement? **b.** How much variation is possible in the range of PERFORM statements that can be executed. **c.** Can the range of a PERFORM include the entire Procedure Division, one sentence, or one phrase (part of a sentence)?

17. a. If a particular paragraph consists of three sentences, how can the program be set up so that a PERFORM will include only the first two sentences? **b.** If a PERFORM should include two adjacent paragraphs called FIRST-ITEM and LAST-ITEM, how should the PERFORM statement be written? **c.** If the paragraphs to be performed are not adjacent, how should the PERFORM statement be written?

18. a. What feature does the PERFORM...UNTIL instruction have in addition to the features in the PERFORM? **b.** Name three situations where the PERFORM...UNTIL is useful.

19. How should a programmer write the instructions to execute exactly ten times a section of a program called FILE-CHECK SECTION?

20. a. What is a *table*? **b.** What are the similarities and differences of a table and a *file*?

21. a. What is meant by the *dimension* of a table? **b.** How is a particular item in a table identified?

22. The examples of tables in the text have only one dimension. **a.** Describe the nature of a two-dimension table and give an example. **b.** Develop a scheme for subscripting for a two-dimensional table. **c.** Design a PERFORM VARYING statement capable of working with any desired item in a two-dimensional table.

23. a. How can tables be defined without using an OCCURS clause? **b.** What advantages does an OCCURS clause offer over the longhand method of defining a table?

24. a. What is the function of *subscripting*? **b.** How are subscripts written in COBOL-1? **c.** Does the description defining a table include subscripts? **d.** Is a subscript always necessary for referencing an item in a table? Explain.

25. SALES is an item in a table. Explain whether each of the following entries is legal in the same program: **a.** SALES (3); **b.** SALES (2.5); **c.** SALES (STATION); **d.** SALES (COUNTER-1); **e.** SALES.

26. a. How are a counter and a PERFORM...UNTIL statement used to process the items in a table? **b.** What two functions does the counter serve? **c.** What features does a PERFORM...VARYING statement have that a counter and a PERFORM...UNTIL statement do not?

27. a. What are the advantages of assigning two tape units to multi-reel tape files? **b.** Explain why a programmer might assign only one reel to a file that always consists of multiple reels? **c.** Why is it desirable to describe a file as multi-reel even though it often has only one reel? **d.** How are specific physical tape units assigned to files?

28. a. What is *blocking*? **b.** Why are records blocked? **c.** Why are punched cards and printed records not blocked? **d.** How does the programmer deal with blocking in COBOL?

29. a. What is the content of each label record on magnetic tape? **b.** Are label records mandatory for tapes? **c.** What functions are served by tape-label records? **d.** What instructions must the programmer write in the Procedures Division in order to write and check labels?

30. This question pertains to the inventory updating program in the chapter. Each time an item is issued the remaining balance should be checked to find whether it is below the reorder point. If it is, an order is placed to increase the balance to the stock level. Modify the data description for the master record and the program procedures to reflect this change.

31. The inventory-update program in the chapter is designed to produce an audit record with a set of totals for each batch of transactions. Modify the data divisions and program procedures to accumulate and print a grand total of the number of transactions read in, and the number of issues, orders, and receipts processed.

32. The inventory-updating program in the chapter stops when it encounters a sequence error. Revise the program, including the Environment, Data, and Procedures Divisions, to write the erroneous record on a special file and continue with processing for each of the following conditions:
a. The master file is in correct sequence so that only the transaction file may be out of sequence.

b. Either file may be out of sequence. (Hint: File-sequence checking and corrections require that at least two records be available in storage for comparison purposes.)

33. The Ultrapower Oil Company has 6427 service stations. Each submits a monthly report each 30 days showing daily dollar volume of gasoline sales. Write the data descriptions and procedures to compute total sales for each station for the month and total sales by day for the company.

34. Heigh-Pryce's Department Store has charge accounts for several thousand customers. Each sales slip—containing customer account number, date of sale, amount of the sale, and department—is sent to the data-processing center. Each month the sales slips and any collections received are processed against the master file (assume any format consistent with the problem requirements) to prepare bills. Provide data description and proper procedures for the following:

a. Prepare a billing record for each customer containing the customer's name, address, and account number; the date and amount of each sale or collection; and the balance due. Place a letter S between the date and amount for each sale and a C in the same location for each collection. If the balance due is negative (collection exceeded a balance), place the word CREDIT after the balance due.

b. Indicate the modifications required (without repeating the program) to suppress preparation of a bill if the balance due is zero.

c. Put the account number in a "reminder file" if the amount due is positive and no collection has been received in the preceding 60 days.

CHAPTER 10

1. a. What is the instruction format for WORDCOM? **b.** What is each character used for in an input-output instruction? **c.** In an indexing instruction? **d.** In an arithmetic instruction?

2. Explain the operation of the following instructions from the programmer's viewpoint: **a.** RECyxxx; **b.** WTtyxxx; **c.** CAAyxxx; **d.** ADDyxxx; **e.** JMPyxxx; **f.** RWt.

3. The following instructions are supposed to make WORDCOM read in 120 words of data from tape and 20 words from cards and then duplicate them in the same media so that two copies are available:

RT3 160	PNC 180
REC 170	RW3
REC 180	WT3 160
PNC 170	WT3 220

a. What will this program procedure actually do?
b. Point out the mistakes in the intended routine.
c. Write the routine correctly.

4. **a.** How are index registers used to control the number of times that cycles are performed? **b.** What causes a program to leave the cycle after it is executed the desired number of times? **c.** Which instructions can a programmer use to alter, and in what way, the contents of an index register in WORDCOM?

5. **a.** What is an effective address? **b.** How is an effective address formed? **c.** Why and how are instructions written with effective addresses? **d.** What does effective addressing do to the instruction and to the index register involved?

6. A routine using an index has five elements: set up or *initialize* index, *compare* index to a criterion, *increase* the index count, *perform* the operations specified in the main program, and *go to* the location specified for repeat or exit from the loop.
a. In what sequence are these elements used in the illustrations involving cycle counting in the chapter?
b. A program is supposed to add ten numbers that are available on ten cards—one number per card. Write two different logical versions of a program with different sequences for the indexing and operating elements after setting the index, such as (1) increase, count, operate, test, and jump; and (2) operate, test, jump, and count.
c. If a loop in the main program is occasionally supposed to be performed zero times (that is, not at all), what sequence of elements and what criterion should be used to guard against performing the main program one time before testing the index content?

7. **a.** List the conditions necessary for the use of each kind of comparison instruction described in the chapter. **b.** State the instructions that must follow each kind of comparison instruction in order to handle each condition.

8. **a.** What are the three types of jump instructions? **b.** Give an example of each. **c.** What provision is required in a program to make the jump operate?

9. Answer the following questions about the multiplication operation for WORDCOM: **a.** What set-up operation is required? **b.** Where is the multiplier placed initially and how is it used during multiplication? **c.** How long is the product and where is it located? **d.** How is the product stored?

10. **a.** Where is the assumed decimal point located in the product after a multiplication operation? **b.** Develop a general rule for the location of decimal points for the multiplication operation.

11. **a.** Write a program to read and punch ten cards. **b.** Draw a flow chart for the program to read and punch 2000 cards. **c.** Write the program for (b).

12. **a.** Write a program to read two blocks of data on tape that contain records of ten words each and punch cards containing one record each. **b.** Draw a flow chart for the program to read 10,000 blocks of data from tape and punch a ten-word record in each card. **c.** Write the program for (b).

13. Suppose the problem is to find the total value of 200 stock items on cards with the stock value punched in word 6. **a.** Write a program to summarize the stock value and punch in word 2 of a new card. **b.** What will the program do, if there are only 199 instead of 200 cards? **c.** If there are 201 cards instead of 200?

14. For a deck of cards containing stock number, quantity, and unit cost in words 1, 2, and 3, respectively, the problem is to calculate the value on hand for each item and punch a new deck containing the original three words plus stock value in word 4. Also, punch a summary card with the *number* of stock-record cards processed in word 3 and the *total value* of stock on hand in word 4.
a. Draw a flow chart for the program.
b. Write the program. State any compatible and consistent assumptions you need to solve the problem.

15. Repeat the prior question but restrict the calculation, card punching, and summarizing to items having a value on hand exceeding $100 each. **a.** Draw a flow chart for the program. **b.** Write the program with provision for the possibility of overflow.

16. Write a program to unpack each of the following items stored together in one word:

        JR 3, 782, S
                     └ Storage location in warehouse
              └ Quantity in stock
        └ Item description

17. The following three versions of a program procedure are supposed to total the quantity of units in stock where the item record contains five words with the quantity in the third word. There are 110 inventory items stored in locations 200 and following. Location 099 contains zero, location 100 contains 550, location 101 contains 110, location 102 contains 445, and the main program continues in location 125.

Location	Version 1	Version 2	Version 3
060	SISA099	SISA100	SISC102
061	CAAA200	CAAB204	INCC005
062	ADDA205	ADDB209	CISC099
063	INCA005	CISB099	JMPC125
064	CISA099	INCB004	CAAC203
065	JMP 060	JMP 062	ADDC208
066	JMP 061	JMP 065	

a. Trace through one cycle of each version of the program.

b. Describe the plan in each version for dealing with each item in turn.

c. Revise the nearest correct version of the program so that it is correct.

d. Draw a flow chart and write a program following a different plan to meet the problem requirements.

18. This question deals with the program example in the chapter to read tape records, calculate stock value, summarize stock value, write tape records, and punch a summary card.

a. Why is provision made for accumulator overflow and what will cause it to occur in this program?

b. What are the operating consequences of overflow?

c. If overflow occurred three times before the end of program was reached, how many subtotal or total cards would the program punch?

d. Write a program just to summarize these total cards to find total value. (Hint: Shift each total right one place, summarize and adjust for the shift. Or split each total into two parts, summarize the two parts and put them back together—double-precision addition.)

19. This question deals with the card sequence-check example in the chapter.

a. How many cards will the program handle if all are in sequence?

b. What is the effect on the number of cards read and converted to tape if one card in fifty is out of sequence and one card in a hundred is a duplicate?

c. Revise the program to use an index register to count the number of duplicate cards.

d. Can WORDCOM unload the content of the index register used in (c) so that the number of out-of-sequence cards is available for use? If not, define a new instruction for the designers to build into WORDCOM II to unload an index register.

e. Revise the program to use a storage location for keeping count of the number of duplicate cards. (Hint: Assign a storage location

to keep count, and initially load it with zeros. Then include the
following steps in each cycle involving a duplicate card: Clear accumulator and add the prior count, add 1, and store current count
back in the same location.)

20. This question deals with the load-program example in the chapter.
a. What is the merit of using the contents of location 030 to set
index register A?
b. What are the risks involved, since location 030 has an active
instruction?
c. Can this load program be run a second time (for another program) without another read-in? Explain.
d. What will happen, if the transfer instruction in the main program
being run is punched "—" instead of "+"?
e. Rewrite the load program to cure any real risk pointed out in
(b) above and also relocate the whole load-program in the high end
of storage—locations 999 and immediately below.

21. Write a program to read in four blocks of data from tape and write
out as follows: **a.** four blocks on tape; **b.** two blocks on magnetic
tape, consisting of words 0 through 29 from each input block after
discarding words 30 through 59. **c.** Repeat (b) but save words 30
through 59 after discarding words 0 through 29 from each input
block. **d.** Repeat (c) but use punched-card output instead of tape.

22. **a.** Why must a programmer know how many digits are involved in
each number when multiplying them? **b.** Suggest a method of multiplication that eliminates the problem of keeping track of the size of
numbers.

23. The problem is to find the total value of inventory for 200 items
stored in locations 100 to 299 as five groups of 40 items each. **a.**
Program the addition as specified, using index registers, to place
subtotals in locations 500 through 504 and the total in 505. **b.** Prepare a trace of program operations showing the contents of index
registers and the effective addresses of locations used during the
set-up and cycles 1, 39, 40, 41, 199, and 200.

24. Answer the following for the multiplication operation described in
the chapter: **a.** What set-up operation is required? **b.** Where is the
multiplier placed initially and how is it used during multiplication?
c. How long is the product and where is it located? **d.** If the product
contains six significant digits that are in both the accumulator and
M-Q registers, how can the product be stored? **e.** Repeat (d) but
with the product containing eight significant digits.

25. Assume the following values are in storage:

Storage Location	Value
500	12.3
501	200
502	10.01

Write a program to compute x to the nearest one-hundredth (.01) and store the result in location 500.

$$x = 200 + \frac{(10.01 \times 12.3)}{200}$$

26. Locations 201 to 252 contain the rainfall at Boston, in hundredths of an inch, recorded in each week of 1963. Put in location 10 the least rainfall occurring in any period of four consecutive weeks.

27. Location 2 contains two three-letter English words. Put them into the left-hand halves of locations 3 and 4 in alphabetical order.

28. Location 5 contains a money amount in pennies. Put in locations 10 to 19 inclusive the number of bills or coins of each of the various denominations from 1 cent to $50.00 required to make up this amount.

29. Read twenty cards, each containing an amount of money in dollars and cents (four columns for dollars and two for cents), and punch one card carrying the total.

30. Assuming any convenient punched-card layout, read a card containing the following: **a.** two consecutive electricity meter readings of six digits each, in kwh (remember that the meter may have overflowed from 999999 to 000000); **b.** amount of previous bill in dollars and cents (three digits for dollars and two digits for cents); **c.** method of charging (1 or 2: see below); **d.** whether previous bill has been collected (1 = uncollected, 2 = collected); **e.** name and address (59 characters allowed).

Punch a card containing items (c) and (e) as in the input card, the value 1 or 2 for item (d), the later meter reading transferred to the position of the earlier one, and the amount of the new bill computed as follows:

Method 1: Fixed charge of $15 plus 0.9 cents for each kwh over 1000.

Method 2: Fixed charge of $3 plus 1.3 cents per kwh.

In either case round to nearest penny and add the previous bill if uncollected.

31. Explain the meaning of the following terms for WORDCOM II: **a.** partial word logic, **b.** compact addressing, **c.** two-address instructions, **d.** binary operations.

32. a. What is gained by the way in which WORDCOM II uses the bits in an instruction over the way that WORDCOM I uses them? **b.** Suggest, if possible, additional changes in WORDCOM II for better exploitation of the bits.

33. a. How can three 6-bit characters contain addresses to more than 999 storage locations and also to some index registers? **b.** What is the maximum number of storage locations that can be addressed by the bits in three 6-bit characters if they must also be used to address 31 index registers? **c.** Same as (b) except include 63 index registers. **d.** Develop a general rule for the number of storage locations and index registers that can be addressed by the bits in three 6-bit characters.

34. a. Which version of WORDCOM II described in the chapter is most efficient for business data-processing operations? **b.** Describe how to determine the value of the preferred version of WORDCOM II over a standard WORDCOM I.

CHAPTER 11

1. Explain the relationship between the following features of FIELD-COM-S and WORDCOM: **a.** storage capacity; **b.** organization of storage; **c.** length of a word and length of a field; **d.** number of addresses per instruction.

2. a. What is the minimum amount of storage used for an instruction in WORDCOM? **b.** Minimum in FIELDCOM-S? **c.** Which method of storage gives a higher density for instructions in high-speed storage? **d.** Higher density on tape?

3. a. Why must a programmer worry with fieldmarks for FIELD-COM-S? **b.** How does a fieldmark indicate the end of an instruction, since the controlling fieldmark is in the next instruction? **c.** How does a fieldmark terminate the processing of an operand?

4. a. How does a programmer put fieldmarks in the exact storage positions he wants? **b.** What is the effect on the character of fieldmarking a position containing a character? **c.** What is the effect of storing a character in a position containing a fieldmark? **d.** Why is it necessary to clear FIELDCOM-S storage before starting a program, since it wasn't necessary to clear WORDCOM storage?

5. Compare the following factors for WORDCOM, FIELDCOM-S, and FIELDCOM-V: **a.** freedom to use any amount of storage desired for a data element and for a record; **b.** ease of expanding or contracting the length of a record as requirements change; **c.** density of data storage on tape; **d.** density of data in high-speed storage considering the use of an eighth bit (one above the six for alphanumeric and seventh for parity) for fieldmark, a special character for field separator, and a fixed-length word.

6. **a.** What is the effect on FIELDCOM-S instruction format of having the machine designer assign positions in storage for reading and punching cards? **b.** How can a programmer use these areas for, say, arithmetic operations involved in card-updating operations? **c.** How can he use them for working-storage areas during magnetic-tape file updating?

7. Storage contains fieldmarks at positions 1001 and 1201. Explain the result of each of these instructions: **a.** CP 1010 1210; **b.** CP 1010 1205; **c.** CP 1005 1210; **d.** RC 1080 1280; **e.** PC 1280 1080.

8. **a.** Write a program to read and duplicate-punch three cards. **b.** Write a program to read three punched cards and duplicate-punch them, but change their sequence from 1, 2, 3, to 3, 2, 1 in the card-punch hopper.

9. Give the meaning of the following terms for FIELDCOM-S: **a.** add-to-storage logic; **b.** fieldmark; **c.** field mistake; **d.** switch; **e.** chaining; **f.** instruction counter; **g.** "c" modifier.

10. Explain the result of executing the following instructions: **a.** R3 4567; **b.** PT; **c.** CM 1234 4321; **d.** FM 2345; **e.** ZR 2345; **f.** CP 4567 8901; **g.** AD222 3333; **h.** HL HALT; **i.** NP WRITE; **j.** AA 0321 STRT; **k.** JS READ U.

11. Explain what determines the amount of data handled in each of the following operations: **a.** card read; **b.** print; **c.** tape write; **d.** add; **e.** copy; **f.** copy edit; **g.** disk read.

12. **a.** What is the sequence for handling characters in an instruction? **b.** Sequence of character-handling in an operand? **c.** What is the setting of the address registers for the A and B addresses after executing an instruction? **d.** How is this feature of address registers used in "chaining" instructions? **e.** What are the merits of chaining instructions?

13. **a.** Write a program to clear storage and set fieldmarks for reading and printing two cards with the following changes in sequence of the data from the cards.

Card Columns	Print Positions
1–5	101–105
6–20	16–30
21–30	6–15
31–70	31–70
71–75	Discard
76–80	1–5

b. Reprogram the read and print operations for two cards using only the one fieldmark obtained from the clear storage instruction; that is, do not use any fieldmark instructions, as such.

c. Rewrite (b) to use "chaining" so that only two B addresses are used in the copy instructions.

14. These questions pertain to the first program given in the chapter to read cards and write them on tape. **a.** Is adequate or excessive storage cleared initially? **b.** What does the instruction BM 1000 do? **c.** Could the series of CP 0080 1080, etc., instructions in ascending sequence be written in descending sequence? **d.** What does the JS READ U instruction do? **e.** How many cards will this program handle? **f.** What terminates the read-write cycle? **g.** Would this program operate satisfactorily if merely restarted for another deck of cards? **h.** How many instructions are written in this program solely for set-up and housekeeping? **i.** How many instructions are written for card-to-tape conversion? **j.** Calculate the total number of instructions that will be executed to convert 3000 cards to tape.

15. These questions pertain to the card-to-tape conversion program given in the chapter to convert and count all the cards put in the hopper. **a.** Why is the CS 1001 1480 the ninth instead of simply the third instruction in the program? **b.** What function does the JS PRTB C instruction perform, and how many times is it executed if the program is used for 3000 cards? **c.** 3004 cards? **d.** What does the AD ONE ACNT instruction perform and how many times is it executed for 3000 cards; 2997 cards? **e.** What does the JS CLRS U instruction do in each cycle? **f.** Is the instruction address WNDP (wind up) required; does it interfere with program execution? **g.** Does the sign of DIFFERENCE correctly represent a shortage or excess number of cards? **h.** What is the difference between the two instructions AL ONE +1 and AA* 1 ONE, and why have both?

16. a. Draw the flow chart that seems to have been used for the card-to-tape conversion program given in the chapter to count all the cards in the hopper. **b.** Test the accuracy of your flow chart and trace the program in the chapter for a total of one, two, five, six, and seven cards. **c.** Are these tests satisfactory for 2999, 3000, and 3001 cards? **d.** What will happen if only the control card indicating 3000 cards is put in the read hopper without any data cards? **e.** What will happen if the control card is omitted? **f.** How many cycles will the program execute if no cards—control or data—are placed in the reader when program execution is started?

17. Revise the program for card-to-tape conversion given in the chapter to count all the cards put in the hopper to include two and four blanks (instead of one and two) in the message punched in a card as follows: CONTROLbCOUNTbbXXXXbbbbACTUAL. . . .

18. Revise the program for card-to-tape conversion given in the chapter to count all the cards put in the hopper. In addition to punching the count control card, also accumulate a four-digit field in each input card and punch a total control card with the message:

CONTROLbTOTALbbXXXXXXXbbACTUALbTOTALbYYYYYYYbb
DIFFERENCEbb±ZZZZZZZ.

19. These questions pertain to the card-to-tape conversion program in the chapter as modified to handle exactly 3000 cards. **a.** What will happen if there are 2999 cards? **b.** 3000 cards? **c.** 3001 cards? **d.** When is the CM 0118 ACNT instruction executed? **e.** What causes the JS PRTB E instruction to execute and how many times is it executed?

20. Combine the program for card-to-tape conversion designed to handle and count all cards and the modification supposed to handle a stipulated number of cards, as given in the chapter. In developing the combined program (without rewriting the whole program), modify it to give an internal auditor the option of using either scheme for any particular conversion simply by indicating in a specified column or columns in a header card which plan he wants.

21. Revise the actual-count scheme for card-to-tape conversion given in the chapter to use only one tape-write instruction, if feasible. It should be possible to eliminate the effect of the JS CLRS U instruction by changing it to a NP CLRS U instruction after reading the last card. The program could then execute the first write instruction and skip the NP CLRS U instruction (previously the JS CLRS U) to continue with program wind-up.

22. For the flow chart and program of the utility-bill calculation in the chapter, letter each block in the flow chart A, B, C, . . ., and associate the block letter with instructions in the program. Reconcile (or correct) any blocks not properly programmed—steps, sequence, degree of detail, etc.—and any instructions not covered by a flow-chart block.

23. a. Trace through the utility-bill calculation plan in the chapter for handling the following customer-number records to show what happens in each case:

Card	Tape
1	1
3	2
8	3
6	4
9	6
10	8
	9
	12

b. Use these same transactions and master file numbers to show what will happen if they are used for the inventory-file update described in the chapter on systems design.

24. Modify the utility-bill calculation scheme given in the chapter to handle a five-digit rate field, instead of four, and a meter reading of six digits instead of five. Show new record formats, storage assignment, and instructions, with an indication of any instructions displaced. Do not rewrite the whole program.

25. In addition to containing the most recent meter-reading quantity in characters 11 through 15, the example of utility customer record in the chapter contains actual consumption for each of the preceding eleven months stored in fields of five characters each starting with character 101. Total consumption for the twelve preceding months is in positions 156 through 161 and the average is in 162 through 166.
a. Draw a flow chart to compare current consumption with past consumption to determine whether it is within "limits" calculated by one of the following plans: (1) average for twelve months plus or minus 40 per cent; (2) range of highest and lowest individual monthly consumption in twelve prior months plus 15 per cent and minus 10 per cent, respectively. If current consumption is outside of "limits" for the plan used, provide for punching a card for an account investigator containing appropriate details from the available data.
b. Revise the program given in the chapter to include the limit scheme that you flow-charted in (a).
c. Describe a scheme for keeping track of and updating the "limits" for the scheme used for (b) so that it need not be recalculated afresh each month. Two fields can be included in the record for containing the high and low monthly consumptions for the past year, if desired, to facilitate the limit test.

26. These questions relate to the preceding question for utility-bill calculation. **a.** Would it be satisfactory to store consumption for each preceding month as a four-digit number for purposes of past history and limit calculations? **b.** Describe programming to discard one digit from most recent consumption when storing in the "history" section of the record. **c.** What bias creeps into the consumption history, if the discarded digit is either simply dropped or the number is rounded? **d.** Modify the bill-calculation program to update the monthly consumption history and discard the oldest month, after the current month consumption is calculated. Minimize the number of instructions.

27. Assume that after a period of years, the 24 rate classes used for the utility-bill calculation in the chapter has grown to a total of 146 including only 13 of the original 24. The range of rate-class numbers is then from 3 to 206 because of rates dropped. The rate table now has dual entries consisting of each rate-class number and its corresponding rate in pennies. You may assume that the rate-class numbers are three digits stored in addresses 5903 and following. The rates themselves are stored in addresses 6404 and following.
a. Prepare a flow chart showing how to do a table look-up to find the desired rate for bill calculation.
b. Modify the program in the chapter to include the new table for determining the rate.

CHAPTER 12

1. Explain the meaning of each of the following terms: **a.** mnemonic code; **b.** absolute address; **c.** symbolic address; **d.** label; **e.** macrocode.

2. a. What is the nature of mnemonic codes and machine codes? **b.** Why is it desirable to have order codes other than machine codes for a processor?

3. a. Why are symbolic addresses preferable to absolute addresses? **b.** What are the disadvantages of absolute addresses? **c.** If processors are designed to operate with absolute addresses only, how can programs that are written with symbolic addresses be used efficiently on a processor? **d.** What is the scheme for converting symbolic addresses to absolute addresses?

4. Explain what is meant by each of the following terms: **a.** automatic programming; **b.** machine-oriented language; **c.** problem-oriented language; **d.** assembly routine; **e.** compiler routine.

5. a. What is the difference between an *assembler* and a *compiler* in terms of the levels of programming languages involved? **b.** What are their differences from the programmer's viewpoint in terms of how much work he must do in writing a program, how much is done for him during the assembly or compiling phases, and their leverage factors?

6. a. What benefits does a programmer gain from using a subroutine in a program? **b.** How can a subroutine be useful if it must either be included in the program at each point where it is wanted or program control must be transferred to a subroutine each time it is needed in the program? **c.** What are the merits of open subroutines and closed subroutines from the viewpoint of high-speed storage required to hold the program and the time lost through calling in some subroutines from bulk storage to overlay the program because of its total length?

7. a. What is the relationship between a *label* and a *symbolic address*? **b.** What are the consequences of using a symbolic address for an operand without a corresponding label for an instruction or number? **c.** What are the consequences of using a label without a corresponding symbolic address? **d.** How do undefined- and multiply-defined labels occur and what are their implications?

8. a. What is the relationship among a generator, utility routine, and a manually written program? **b.** How does a programmer file in the skeleton of a generator to prepare a generator routine? **c.** What kinds of facts must be supplied to make generator, utility, and manually written programs ready to operate?

9. a. Why and under what conditions is it useful to have both post-mortem and trace routines available for use? **b.** How does a differential snapshot operate in relation to a trace and how are their outputs used? **c.** If limited to either a snapshot or a trace, which should be selected as more useful?

10. a. Why does the problem of programming for minimum access time arise with the use of drum and disk storage, although it does not usually arise with magnetic core storage? **b.** A manufacturer promising 0.5 microsecond access time storage when the fastest magnetic cores available had a 2 microsecond access time hit upon the plan of dividing core storage into four banks and sequentially pulsing each one 0.5 microseconds later. (1) Is such a magnetic core storage random access? (2) Do optimum programming problems arise with this core storage comparable to those usually associated with drum and disk? Explain.

11. The use of subroutines is sometimes criticized because they are only 85 per cent as efficient as hand-written programs, they require much study in order for the user to understand them, and they require additional computer storage. The advantages of subroutines are reductions in program writing time and debugging time. How would you compare these and other advantages and disadvantages to decide whether it is more efficient to prepare and use subroutines or to write programs for each specific application?

12. a. What is the relationship between a post-mortem and a trace routine? **b.** A trace routine appreciably increases processor running time. Since this additional time is wasted if the program works correctly, explain the conditions under which a trace can be used advantageously.

13. a. What is the purpose of generator routines? **b.** Why are so many parameters required to generate a routine to check the sequence of records in a file?

14. a. Why are two entirely different compiler-level languages such as COBOL and FORTRAN or ALGOL offered to computer users? **b.** How would you appraise the value of a compiler level language?

15. At one time entirely different electronic computers were offered to business and engineering-scientific users, although this may have reflected the organization of marketing departments of some manufacturers as much as anything else. More recently, the same equipment has been offered to both types of users. There is some speculation that languages such as COBOL and ALGOL will also converge and end up as one compiler language.
a. What requirements would a composite problem-oriented language need?
b. What are the apparent prospects for development of one composite language?
c. How many more and what kinds of facts would you consider necessary to make an informed judgment on this matter?
d. What are the implications of a common language instead of separate languages from the user's viewpoint?

16. It is sometimes said that high programming costs reflect the fact that automatic processing equipment is not well-suited to business application requirements and that equipment manufacturers are not meeting their obligations.
a. How would you appraise the merits of this statement?
b. What remedies would you propose in order to reduce the user's programming costs?

17. a. How can a set index and jump instruction (an instruction that sets an index register with the contents of the instruction counter and jumps to a specified location) be used to enter a subroutine? **b.** To return to the main program? **c.** Can a set index and jump instruction be used repeatedly in a program? **d.** How can the return point in the main program be selected dependent upon conditions encountered in the subroutine?

18. a. Would it be possible to write a program, using symbolic and relative addresses, so that the programmer need make no commitment whatever about where it should be placed in storage? **b.** If not, what is the minimum that he must specify?

19. A star or asterisk is sometimes used to indicate the location of the "present" instruction in a program when using the relative addressing scheme. Thus * + 3 means three storage locations after the present location. There is a traditional story that a fisherman once suggested that the good fishing spot be marked by an X on the side of the boat; he was farsighted enough to see that even if he did not always use the same boat, he would probably get a boat that someone else had marked with equal care.
a. What is the relationship between the two relative addressing schemes in programming and fishing?
b. What keeps the * in relative addressing in programming from being as fluid as the X on the boat?

20. a. What is a simulator program? **b.** How does a simulator program bridge the gap between installed equipment and equipment about to be installed? **c.** What are the implications of using a simulator program in order to continue running old programs on new equipment without bothering to rewrite them? **d.** How useful are simulator programs for gaining back-up capacity on different types of equipment when identical equipment is not available for use in case of breakdown?

21. Describe the implications of compiler-level languages for each of the following: **a.** program documentation; **b.** debugging; **c.** program modification; **d.** leverage.

22. a. What are the functions performed by an input-output control system? **b.** What is the relationship between an input-output control system and the main program? **c.** What level of instructions—machine, mnemonic, or macro—is used in the input-output control system described in the chapter?

23. a. What kinds of facts must a programmer supply to a report generator? **b.** What kinds of facts to a sort generator? **c.** What are the implications of the large number of facts required and the complexity of writing a program if a generator routine was not available? **d.** Why are so few facts adequate for a utility routine in contrast to the number required for a generator?

24. In order to debug a program written in an assembly- or compiler-level language, a programmer needs to know both the programming language and the machine language. Is it possible to reconcile the need for a programmer to be bilingual with the advantages claimed for advanced languages? Explain.

25. Internal storage contains 200 account balances with debits as plus numbers and credits as minus numbers. The identifying account number for each is stored in one location and its balance in the next location in pairs 001 through 399.

One hundred and fifty transactions (consisting of one or more transactions per account) are read into the processor in account-number order, each consisting of identification number and amount with debits as plus and credits as minus. These transactions are stored in locations 700 through 999.

Location 401 contains the number 400, which is the total number of accounts times 2, and location 699 contains the number 300, which is the total number of transactions times 2. Index register A might be used to keep the file count and index register B the transaction count.

a. Draw a flow diagram of the steps involved in locating an active record, updating the account balance, and moving to the next transaction.

b. Prepare a decision table to show the logic of the solution developed in (a).

c. Write a program to update the account balances, using the order code for WORDCOM and labels as follows:

FILE	First file record address
TRANS	First transaction address
FCOUNT	Number of records times 2
TCOUNT	Number of transactions times 2
MATCH	Start of processing routine for matches
ERROR	Start of error processing routine

d. Assign absolute addresses to the labels to show that the program locations written in symbolic addresses (c) can be converted to absolute addresses for execution.

e. If a program is used to assemble the symbolic address program into the minimum storage space, what absolute address will be assigned to the symbolic addresses?

26. This question pertains to question 14 for WORDCOM in Chapter 10. **a.** Answer the question, but use labels and symbolic addresses instead of absolute addresses in writing the program in part (b) of that question. **b.** Prepare a table of absolute addresses for labels with program origin at location 150.

27. This question pertains to the load-program example for WORDCOM in Chapter 10. **a.** Rewrite the load program with symbolic addresses so that it can be located anywhere desired in storage, but use the minimum number of labels as addresses for instructions. **b.** Place the origin of the program at storage location 500 (assuming an instruction "ORIGIN" that can be used to assign an address to a label—for example, Begin, ORIGIN, 500), and prepare an address table to show the absolute addresses for the labels used. **c.** Rewrite the load program with *relative addresses* and show where the instructions referred to in the program will be located if the origin is placed at storage location 990.

28. This question pertains to the utility-bill calculation program example in Chapter 11. **a.** Prepare a symbol table to show the assignment of absolute addresses to labels starting at location 0400. Remember that FIELDCOM is a character machine and that only the minimum number of characters need be used for each instruction. **b.** "Assemble" the program by rewriting it with absolute addresses for labels. Indicate any symbolic addresses that are not defined and any labels that are either not used or that have duplicate definitions.

CHAPTER 13

1. a. Explain why data are edited during both input and output operations and what the chief differences are in the edit operations? **b.** What is the nature, purpose, and use of file labels?

2. a. What kinds of input editing can be done without reference to the master file? **b.** What assurance does such editing give that input data are correct? **c.** How does further editing by use of the file improve accuracy of input data?

3. a. What do the terms *proof totals* and *hash totals* mean? **b.** Develop an example of proof totals and hash totals. **c.** Under what conditions is each type of total suitable? **d.** How is each type of total obtained most efficiently under operating conditions?

4. a. What are the special problems involved in editing input data on cards and how are they handled? **b.** What are "explicit data" on cards and why is it not possible to edit them? **c.** How is it possible to ensure that cards are in sequence during read-in, when they are subject to mishandling during sorting and feeding? **d.** How is it possible to ensure that the card sequence is correct if the processor's card-reader accepts only 74 columns of data?

5. a. What are the objectives of output editing? **b.** What operations are performed during output editing? **c.** How is *scatter write* used during output editing?

6. a. Evaluate the statement, "During output editing, it is generally assumed that these problems were handled correctly earlier, because little or nothing can be done efficiently about them at this stage." **b.** If this statement is true, would it be suitable to omit either input or output editing? Explain. **c.** What is the relationship between report generators and editing operations?

7. a. What is the difference between *file maintenance* and *file processing*? **b.** What are the arguments for combining or for separating file maintenance and processing? **c.** Why and how do pending changes arise in file maintenance? **d.** How does the quantity of available processor storage affect efficient file maintenance and processing methods?

8. Explain the meaning of the following items related to file maintenance: **a.** master file; **b.** change list; **c.** pending changes; **d.** mismatches; **e.** number of records in files; **f.** housekeeping runs; **g.** logical sequence of transactions; **h.** transfers between sections of the file; **i.** insertion point.

9. a. What is *trial processing*? **b.** Why is it necessary and under what conditions is it useful? **c.** Describe an example of data processing with which you are familiar that does use or could advantageously use trial processing.

10. Explain the meaning of the following items related to file processing: **a.** key; **b.** orderly sequence of transactions; **c.** match; **d.** random-access storage; **e.** subroutines; **f.** dummy instruction; **g.** indirect addressing; **h.** retention period; **i.** fractional updating.

11. a. Why and under what conditions is it necessary to rewrite files during updating operations? **b.** What is the smallest fraction of a file that can be updated during each file pass and still give efficient file processing?

12. The following file-maintenance plan is proposed for file updating: Accumulate all transactions that occur over a period of time and organize them in a suitable fashion for use with master files to permit determination of current results whenever wanted.
a. How should the files and transactions be arranged and stored for this scheme to make any sense?
b. What storage media are implied?
c. Over how long a period of time is it feasible to accumulate transactions before updating the master file?
d. What processing and calculating operations are required to answer each file interrogation?
e. How would you appraise such a scheme, if file activity is low and inquiries are few; if activity is high and inquiries are numerous?

13. a. Why are data sorted? **b.** How does sorting facilitate the subsequent stages of data processing? **c.** How can data be processed efficiently if they are not sorted? **d.** Some people object to the term *sort*, since no item is eliminated (unlike sorting bad apples from good) but prefer the term *marshall,* or *sequence.* Evaluate the argument.

14. a. Explain the steps involved in digital sorting on a five-digit key. **b.** Why is digital sorting called *minor-major*? **c.** What are the similarities and differences between digital and alphabetical sorting of data on cards? **d.** What is the relationship between the number of output pockets, the base for the number scheme (or alphanumeric scheme) used, and the number of passes required to sort a large number of items? Develop a general rule or use several examples to show the relationship.

15. You are told that a series of items is sorted into ascending sequence when you receive them. **a.** How can you check their sequence most efficiently? **b.** How much work is involved, if you conclude they are not in sequence and try to sort them into ascending sequence by the digital scheme and by the merge scheme? **c.** What sorting schemes exploit any existing sequence in the data? **d.** What scheme is most efficient for sorting into descending sequence a series of items that is in ascending sequence?

16. Define and distinguish between the following schemes for sorting data: **a.** digital; **b.** comparison with exchange; **c.** merge.
Suppose you are given records with the following keys:

>13, 39, 35, 43, 11, 28, 04, 26, 32, 30, 37, 98
>38, 60, 07, 43, 19, 11, 75, 31, 36, 82, 95, 46.

Show how records with these keys would be sorted by each of the following schemes: **d.** digital; **e.** comparison with exchanges; **f.** merge; **g.** Describe the effect on each of these sorting schemes, if some additional records with alphanumeric keys are included: 8G, AF, ML, B4.

17. a. What is the relationship between digitally sorting data on cards and on tape? **b.** How is it possible to sort digitally if there are fewer than ten output pockets or tapes for each digit position?

18. A manufacturing company codes each master-file record to indicate its origin—for example, customer or stock number—and its destinations—for example, list of delinquent customers or of stock items depleted. In order to prepare reports, each record is repeated once on tape for each report in which the item will be included. One way to arrange the items for report preparation is to block-sort the items for each report and fine-sort each subset into report sequence. Another method is to devise a combined report and item code so that all items can be sorted directly into one over-all report and item sequence.
a. What are the advantages of sorting a large set of items into one

over-all sequence instead of block-sorting first and then fine-sorting into individual sequences?

b. Devise a combined report and item-code classification useful for the second method of arranging items for report preparation.

c. What are the implications of each method for report editing and printing operations?

19. Explain the effect on merge-sorting operations of the following: **a.** Using larger internal storage to develop longer sequences on the first pass. **b.** Using three tapes instead of four on the first pass. **c.** Using four input and four output tape units on each pass. **d.** Using six input and two output tape units on each pass (with swaps on the output units for filled tapes).

20. **a.** Why might block sorting be called major-minor and digital sorting minor-major? **b.** What are the differences in the operations involved in the two sorting schemes?

21. **a.** What is the general rule for the number of tape passes required for merge sorting randomly arranged items? **b.** How many more passes are required to sort items that are in the reverse sequence than to sort items that are in random sequence when first received? **c.** How is the calculated number of passes rounded to find the actual number of passes required? **d.** What is the effect of the number of tape inputs on the number of merge passes required to sort data?

22. **a.** What are the consequences for file processing of having incorrect keys in (1) input transactions and (2) the main file? **b.** How can each type of mistake be detected and corrected?

23. **a.** Why is it either desirable or necessary to process different kinds of transactions (for example, receipts, shipments, orders, returns, cancellations) in a specified sequence? **b.** What sequence of transaction types would you suggest for processing inventory transactions?

24. Any change in account numbers or classifications reduces or eliminates the comparability of results obtained before and after the change date. Examples are the introduction of account numbers for a bank's depositors, new catalogue numbers and classes for a company's products, and a redefinition of a trade area for collecting census data.

a. Under what conditions is a proposed change in account numbers or classifications warranted in view of the loss of comparability?

b. What preparations should be made to facilitate such a change?

c. What additional processing is required to obtain comparability of the results obtained before and after such a change?

25. How should a file be organized for efficient processing, if any item within a record may need to be used as the sorting key?

26. Prepare charts to show the time required to sort randomly arranged items into sequence with a punched-card sorter and with a large scale automatic processor that can handle each pass within the time required to pass tapes. Assume that data are already on cards or tapes as desired. Facts about automatic equipment are given in Chapter 5. Card sorters are available to sort 400, 1000, or 2000 cards per minute on one column.
a. Cover the range of 1000 to 100,000 records of 80 characters each with a key of eight characters.
b. Cover the range of 10,000 to 500,000 records of 200 characters each with a key of 20 characters.

CHAPTER 14

1. a. How is *accuracy* defined in the chapter? **b.** What are the practical consequences of many items being slightly inaccurate or a few items being grossly inaccurate? **c.** Why is it possible for different parties to operate satisfactorily with entirely different levels of accuracy—for example, the recordkeeping practices of banks and depositors?

2. a. What are the chief causes of inaccuracy in business data processing? **b.** How can the level of accuracy be increased most economically to .995? To .999? To 1.0? **c.** What is the optimum degree of accuracy for business data?

3. a. What are the differences in the nature of errors, mistakes, and malfunctions? **b.** How do systems designers and internal auditors determine the importance of each of these causes of inaccuracy and cope with them?

4. a. Explain the meaning of the statement that "Accuracy can be increased by providing enough capacity to handle both the message and the mistakes that arise—erroneous characters, dropped digits, lost messages, and transpositions." **b.** If this statement is true, why worry about the mistakes that occur, since they can be handled?

5. Determine how much extra capacity is required to handle each of the following schemes for increasing accuracy: **a.** parity bit for each six-bit characters; **b.** 1 parity character for each 25 characters; **c.** retransmission of faulty messages occurring at the rate of 3 in 100; **d.** return transmission of all messages—full transponder scheme.

6. a. What kinds of inaccuracies plague electronic systems? **b.** Are these inaccuracies actually more important for electronic than other systems and, if so, why?

7. What is management's responsibility for devising, installing, and supervising a system of internal control and audit in view of the schemes available for detecting and correcting processor malfunctions? In short, why not leave the whole problem to equipment designers and maintenance engineers?

8. a. What is an *audit trail*? **b.** What changes in auditing methods will accompany the use of automatic equipment? **c.** Can you visualize auditing procedures for systems that do not use any hard copy? **d.** What is the relationship of an audit trail to manual, punched-card, and automatic data-processing methods?

9. a. What old problems disappear with the introduction of new data-processing methods? **b.** What new problems arise? **c.** What steps are available to cope with the new problems?

10. a. What is the relationship between the interests of internal auditors, external auditors, and systems designers in controlling system operations? **b.** How are their differences, if any, reconciled to achieve their objectives and still give efficient operations?

11. a. What is the purpose of a data control group or bureau? **b.** How should it operate to achieve adequate control without hindering productive processing operations? **c.** How would you determine the optimum degree of control to use, since the costs of achieving perfect control are inordinate?

12. a. What is the distinction between an auditor's *functions* and his *techniques*? **b.** How much can auditors modify their techniques yet satisfactorily fulfill their function? **c.** If audit techniques are modifiable, why are auditors concerned about the internal control system and recordkeeping practices that an organization uses?

13. a. How much freedom does a systems analyst have to separate the actual work of originating data from the originator's responsibility for collecting accurate and timely data? **b.** What are the advantages of making the data originators take full responsibility for the quality of data?

14. A newspaper controller suspects that the list of subscribers includes names for which no collection has been made. **a.** How might names incorrectly enter the list? **b.** How would you try to find the nature and extent of the mistakes? **c.** What procedures should be used to correct the present situation? **d.** To prevent its recurrence?

15. a. What is the relationship between the cost of data collection and the ratio of equipment to labor used in data origination? **b.** How can the accuracy of input data be improved by changing the ratio of capital to labor used in originating data? **c.** How would you determine what degree of accuracy in input data is most efficient for over-all processing? **d.** What is the relationship between the degree of accuracy and the cost of obtaining that degree of accuracy?

16. Indicate which of the three kinds of inaccuracies—errors, mistakes, and malfunctions—can be minimized by the following: **a.** verification of data collection; **b.** using more digits in calculations than are required in the final answer; **c.** desk-checking; **d.** using care to perform operations in the correct sequence; **e.** routine test and maintenance of equipment; **f.** built-in program checks; **g.** double-precision arithmetic operations; **h.** testing the program on live data; **i.** designing duplicate circuitry into the processor; **j.** duplicating operations within the processor by programming; **k.** using hash totals and proof figures.

17. The usual rule for rounding a number is to add 5 in the extreme left position to be discarded, make any carry, and discard the unwanted digits. An upward bias may result because all numbers ending in 5, 50, 500 in the positions to be discarded are rounded to the next higher number. A more careful rule for rounding numbers ending in 50...0 is to make the right hand retained position an even-valued digit—odd-valued digits are increased by the add-five rule, but even-valued digits are left unchanged.

a. Determine the amount of bias that can arise by applying the usual rule for rounding when only a few digits are rounded off and when many digits are rounded off.

b. Devise a program routine to apply a more careful rule—the one described above or some other—for rounding.

18. Show how the proof-figure scheme described in the chapter can be used to increase the probability of accurate results in computing inventory value for the following items:

Item	Quantity	Unit Price
1	2368	$ 4.67
2	5192	10.11
3	37	59.88
4	244	1.23

19. Classify the following as errors, mistakes, or malfunctions, and propose remedies: **a.** Confusion of the withholding tax and federal insurance contribution rules, so that withholding tax is not deducted for gross pay exceeding $4800. **b.** Processor multiplication of gross pay times tax rate gives incorrect amount of withholding tax. **c.** Federal insurance contributions rates for the prior period used after the rates were increased. **d.** New cards prepared to replace those failing the verification test, but not verified before being used as inputs.

20. a. What are the implications of trying to maintain the audit trail when designing for electronic processing? **b.** What are the audit-trail implications of exploiting the largest possible span of processing between stages where readable copy is produced? **c.** Discuss the changes that might be expected to occur in both business data processing and auditing techniques if paper were to cost one hundred or even ten times as much as it now does.

21. **a.** What are the merits of verifying data by reading the original copy against the machine-prepared copy? **b.** What are the merits of having page copy, as well as machine-readable media, when operating manual keyboard devices? (You can get the feel of *not* having readable copy by starting to type an original and carbon copy but leaving the ribbon in the "off" position so that the original copy is blank. Try it to test your skill and ability to work in the "dark." Remember, no peeking at the carbon, because in an actual situation that does not produce readable copy, you cannot read a page until it goes through one or more stages of processing.) **c.** What factors would you consider in appraising a proposal to send unverified documents (shipping notices, bills, etc.) to customers and rely on them to report mistakes?

22. **a.** What are the merits of using characters that are readable by both people and machines? **b.** Give examples of character readers for data input. **c.** What are the advantages of character-recognition devices to prepare machine-usable data media? **d.** How are character-readable data verified?

23. Appraise these three proposals for printing out files to answer questions in terms of printing requirements, ease of finding answers to questions, and economy: **a.** print complete file at short intervals; **b.** print complete file at long intervals and supplement the file with a list of transactions (arranged in some organized sequence) following the prior printout; **c.** rely upon transaction lists only (with a "prior-transaction reference" scheme to locate the previous entry) and never print the file.

24. Banks are interested in preventing customers from utilizing *float*, which is defined as balances arising from items deposited that will not be collected for a certain number of days. Items in float may be considered collected either a specified number of days after deposit or when notice of collection is received from the drawee bank. What processing procedures are required to restrict depositors' use of float, when trying to manage it by each of the two schemes?

25. Many precautionary controls are exercised by one company over data sent to the data-processing department. These include message numbering, control totals, hash totals, limit checks, and editing of numeric and alphabetic fields. Despite these precautions, some mistakes are not discovered until file-processing runs are started. The question is whether the data-processing department should take the

responsibility for correcting input data or whether they should ask the originators of the data to make corrections.

a. How would you determine which scheme for making corrections is preferable?

b. Would you recommend a different scheme for making corrections if the data originating locations are several hundred miles from the data-processing center instead of being in the same building?

26. Some magnetic-tape units are designed with a reading head beside the writing head to check-read the data just after they are written on tape. **a.** Why worry about the quality of data written on tape if parity-bits are used? **b.** About how many characters are there between the write and read heads if they are three quarters of an inch apart? **c.** How should the intervening characters (between the writing and reading heads) be treated in processor storage so that they are available for checking against the data being read from tape? **d.** What are the merits of a read-check to determine that each character merely passes the parity test without comparing it against the corresponding character in storage?

27. The following facts are available for three cases of data preparation, verification, and correction:

	Case 1	Case 2	Case 3
Ratio of numeric to total characters	.5	.7	.9
Mistake rate in original preparation of data, per thousand characters	4	2	2
Cost to verify, per thousand characters	$ .20	$ .15	$ .10
Fraction of mistakes found	.95	.9	.9
Cost to correct a located mistake	$ .05	$ .05	$ .05
Probability of making satisfactory correction	.7	.8	.9
Penalty for incorrect character going to next stage of processing			
Alphabetic character	$1	$1	$1
Numeric character	$2	$2	$2

For 100,000 characters of data for each case, calculate the following:

a. The quality of the alphabetic and numeric data after each stage in the verification-correction process.

b. The cost of the operation, including the penalty for mistakes remaining in the final data.

c. Whether more than one verification and correction operation appears worthwhile, if the ratios and costs given above apply to mistakes still in the data when the next verification is started.

d. Whether more verification and correction processes are warranted if the penalties are $3 and $10 for incorrect alphabetic and numeric characters, respectively, because of interruptions in later stages of processing, confusion in factory operations, and customer ill-will.

28. The First National Bank of Ipswich handles the introduction of new accounts and deletion of closed or transferred checking accounts in the same cycle as deposits are entered and checks are paid. There are 40,000 checking accounts and average daily activities are 6000 deposits, 70,000 checks paid, 105 new accounts opened, and 90 accounts closed. Customers are identified by initial of last name and four digits with initial spacing of four digits to insert other names in the sequence—for example: John Doe—D3275; Johnny Doe—D3280.

The error rate in manually key-punching account numbers is about 2 per cent, but only account openings and closings are verified before processing. After key-punching, dollar amounts are summarized and proved against a batch total, calculated in the preceding operation, to discover and correct mistakes.

File maintenance and processing are handled together so that transactions involving one account number may be posted to another customer's account or a new fictitious account may be opened.

A list of remedies proposed to reduce the incidence of mistakes is as follows:

1. Scan account names and numbers after posting and merging with other checks and deposit slips.

2. Control the number of accounts handled in daily cycle: number of accounts at start plus accounts opened minus accounts closed equals number of accounts at end.

3. Control the money balances of accounts in daily cycle: beginning balance plus deposits minus checks paid equals ending balance.

4. Immediately investigate any overdrafts to find mistakes from posting to the wrong account.

5. Attach a simplified check digit, either 0 or 1, to each number to make the individual digits add to an even amount. For example, D3275 would be given a check digit of 1 to become D32751, so that $3 + 2 + 7 + 5 + 1$ is an even sum, but F6965 would be F65690. A mistake such as F69660 would be detectable because the sum of $6 + 9 + 6 + 6 + 0$ is an odd total.

6. Verify keypunching of account number and money amounts and drop the summary and proof on money total, as described above.

a. Which of the proposed schemes might be effective?

b. Which schemes are likely to give a high degree of accuracy?

c. Which scheme has lowest costs?

d. Which scheme is most efficient per unit of effort spent to reduce mistakes? (Make any assumptions required that are consistent with the facts given.)

29. A company has achieved the near-ultimate with its advanced data-processing system, for it uses no paper at all. Each employee authorized to originate transactions has access to a desk equipped with an input keyboard and an output view-screen. He can enter any transaction or interrogate the central storage to obtain an answer to any proper question in an average of 30 seconds. The view-screen capacity is 10 lines of 120 characters each. A code book describes the file structure and how to formulate each of 437 specific questions, each with numerous variables, that the reply program can handle.

a. How would you go about developing an audit program to work with this on-line paperless system?

b. What effect would this system have on typical audit procedures and the time required to make an audit?

c. If the interrogation scheme is not satisfactory for audit fact-finding, what remedies would you propose?

d. What are the implications of these input-output desks for control over input, accuracy of records, and control over information the company considers confidential?

CHAPTER 15

1. a. How are *data* and *information* defined in the chapter? **b.** Why are two different definitions used here when dictionaries use quite similar definitions? **c.** Why are relevance and freedom of action considered in defining information? **d.** If the definitions of the two words, data and information, do not satisfy you, develop new meanings for them.

2. The words *data* and *information* are sometimes considered to be synonymous with *condition* and *operating* results. **a.** Should a distinction be drawn? **b.** If so, what distinction?

3. a. If all facts are necessarily past history, why do managers and operations researchers rail at accountants for reporting what has actually happened? **b.** If accountants stopped dealing with past financial events, would another group develop to fulfill the same function? Explain. **c.** If facts about the past are not wanted, how might the data-processing system be redesigned to cut costs?

4. a. What sources of information are available to a manager in an organization? **b.** How do managers get information outside the formal data-processing system? **c.** Does the acquisition of information outside the formal channels imply that the formal system should be expanded or scrapped? Explain. **d.** How would the managerial function change, if only formal information channels were available to a manager?

5. a. Describe the nature and operation of a data system that supplies full reports to managers who must select information to make decisions. **b.** What is the *exception principle* applied to report preparation? **c.** What are the implications of the differences between full reporting and exception reporting?

6. a. How is the idea of a normal range related to exception reporting? **b.** What methods can be used for setting normal ranges? **c.** Why is it important not to set the normal range too wide? Too narrow? **d.** What are the advantages and disadvantages of the exception-reporting plan?

7. a. What is the distinction between *internal decisions* and *information selection*? **b.** Why is it easier for a data-processing system to select and report information than it is for it to make internal decisions?

8. a. What is the difference between *quality* and *quantity*? **b.** How is quality measured? **c.** Describe how a system may produce precise but inaccurate results?

9. a. What aspects of information deserve study in formulating a theory of value? **b.** Discuss the relationship between three of these aspects and the value of information. **c.** Under what conditions (considering each aspect) is the value of information the highest?

10. a. How is the age of information defined? **b.** Why is the age of status and of operating information defined differently? Explain.

11. If i indicates interval, d delay, and r reporting interval, develop formulas to calculate the minimum, maximum, and average age of status and operating information.

12. a. Under what conditions is a data-processing system optimized in terms of accuracy, interval, and delay? **b.** Why not simply push each factor to its limit—perfect accuracy, shortest interval, and least delay—when designing an advanced data-processing system?

13. a. How does the degree of predictability of report contents affect the value of reports? **b.** What factors determine the relevance of information for management's use? **c.** Why is it important to examine the consequences of having (or not having) information when designing or altering a data-processing system?

14. a. What causes the quality of system output to fall? **b.** What is the relationship between the cost of processing and the quality of output as quality increases toward perfection?

15. a. What is the relationship of the length of the processing interval and the cost of processing? **b.** Why do processing costs increase rapidly as the interval approaches zero, whereas they increase slowly if the interval is greatly extended? **c.** Could an indefinitely long interval be used to minimize processing costs? Explain.

16. What is the effect of the degree of automation, the type of processing scheme, and the rate of transition on the costs of data processing?

17. In doing some analysis to formulate cost and value models, it is learned that a manager needs to make only yes-no decisions. **a.** Why does the manager want information? **b.** Will he always make the wrong decision when he lacks information on the current state of the real world? **c.** What are the best and worst limits for his situation? **d.** Does a manager ever have zero information? **e.** What is the best policy for the manager to follow in obtaining information?

18. The benefits obtainable by forecasting or reporting timely events— elections, security prices, weather, fast- or slow-moving stock items— may place a high premium on getting results quickly. **a.** What is the nature of the reporting period, interval, and delay in each of the examples cited? **b.** What factors determine the value of timely results obtained from data processing in each example? **c.** Why are merchandise flash reports and Dow Jones and Associated Press wire reports for security price indexes considered invaluable?

19. a. Show what will happen over a period of one year to the time-phasing of transactions for a company that plans to bill customers, pay bills, and so forth, on a 28-day month when all others use a calendar month. **b.** What will happen to depositors' balances at a bank if the delay in clearing checks is suddenly cut from several days to one day? **c.** What are the implications of April 15 instead of March 15 as a tax return filing date if a pay-as-you-go plan is used that withholds too much (or too little) tax?

20. A census bureau is instructed to take a decennial population census. It is also planning other censuses: biennial for manufactures, triennial for agriculture, quadrennial for service industries, and quinquennial for government, religious, political, and educational institutions. Since the bureau wants to process all data on the same equipment, it is interested in the minimum required capacity if a staggered schedule is used.
a. Determine the worst case, as reflected by uneven work loads and equipment capacity required over the indefinite future if census taking is poorly timed.
b. Determine the best case—level work load and minimum-capacity equipment—if the initial starting date for each census is carefully selected but cannot be postponed longer than its specified interval.
c. Repeat (b) if the work involved in processing each census is proportional to its interval.

d. How much can the work load in (c) be leveled, if the permissible processing delay can be extended to the year after taking the census plus one fourth of its interval, but not to exceed a total of two years?

21. a. Why are models for determining the cost and value of information not frequently used? **b.** Why are general principles for system value and cost so slow in developing? **c.** Is it possible to build valid rules for system design without a theoretical foundation of information value and system costs?

22. Some insurance companies may start the preparation of premium notices six weeks before the due date and mail them one month before the due date because of processing time and legal requirements. During this six-week period, the following kinds of changes occur and have certain costs for correction:

Kind of change and example	Frequency per 1000 policies per year	Cost to prepare each correction	Estimated loss associated with each uncorrected mistake
Trivial—change of address	250	$ 1.40	$ .20
Consequential—premium change	140	3.80	5.00
Critical—lapse or death	50	12.00	50.00

Five per cent of the notices that should be changed slip through unchanged or incorrectly changed.

a. How would you describe the six-week and one-month periods involved here in terms of interval, delay, and reporting period?
b. What costs can be saved and what benefits obtained by reducing the six-week period to one month?
c. Is there enough at stake to warrant asking state insurance authorities to reduce the premium notice period from one month to, say, ten days?

23. Managers in one large organization requiring huge amounts of data say that they are not able to get sufficient precision but they must rely on daily, weekly, or monthly results instead of hourly data. Untangle the concepts that they have mixed.

CHAPTER 16

1. a. What logical conclusions can be expected from a feasibility study?
b. Why is the cost incurred from prematurely making a feasibility study likely to be less than the potential loss from postponing it too

long? **c.** What by-product benefits can be expected from making a feasibility study?

2. **a.** Why is it necessary to obtain the support of top management before making a feasibility study? **b.** How can top management support be obtained most readily?

3. **a.** What factors are used to identify areas deserving a detailed feasibility study? **b.** What factors are involved in deciding whether to enlarge or limit the number and scope of the areas selected for detailed study? **c.** Why is it imperative to define carefully the object and scope of a feasibility study?

4. **a.** What attributes are necessary for members of the working group assigned to the feasibility study? **b.** How broadly and thoroughly should the working group be trained?

5. Explain which is preferable when planning for a detailed feasibility study: **a.** to accept a consultant's offer to furnish either senior analysts at full rates or junior analysts at half rates; **b.** to take an equipment manufacturer's offer to make the study at no cost; **c.** perform the study with inexperienced employees.

6. When selecting areas of data processing for feasibility study, explain how much consideration should be given to each of the following factors: **a.** length of time since important improvements were last made; **b.** degree of automation already achieved in the application; **c.** potential improvement by using newest equipment and developing the most advanced systems; **d.** experience of other organizations in the same area using the equipment that is being considered.

7. **a.** Why must replaceable and nonreplaceable costs be treated differently when analyzing proposed changes to a data processing system? **b.** What are some of the costs that might easily be misclassified as replaceable costs?

8. **a.** What direct benefits are likely to be obtained from introducing advanced data-processing methods? **b.** What indirect improvements are obtainable from an advanced data system and why are they so difficult to evaluate?

9. An old saw about committee inaction is that "individually we can do nothing and collectively nothing can be done." How can this difficulty be avoided when selecting the limited-area or system-wide approach to systems analysis?

10. **a.** What is the minimum area within a data-processing system that is worth studying? **b.** What are the advantages and objections to the minimum-area approach to systems analysis?

11. **a.** What resources are required for an automatic data-processing system? **b.** What is the relationship between available resources and scope of the area selected for study?

12. **a.** What points should be covered in addition to those included in the outline for the feasibility study report given in the chapter? **b.** How are uncertainties about present and future plans of the organization handled in preparing a feasibility study report?

13. **a.** What steps are involved in designing a data-processing system? **b.** What principles of systems analysis are involved? **c.** Why are the steps in systems design and the principles of analysis entirely different?

14. **a.** Why is an applications study focused on specific data-processing jobs? **b.** Is it possible to make an applications study in general terms or for a hypothetical situation without regard to actual applications? Explain. **c.** What are the practical merits of a hypothetical applications study?

15. **a.** What schedules are useful for conducting an applications study? **b.** How should the uncertainty arising from the possibility of including new areas in the applications study be treated in making initial schedules?

16. **a.** What is a desirable composition of personnel for the applications study group? **b.** Sketch the qualifications—capabilities, experience, and background—of each kind of personnel that should be included in the study group.

17. **a.** Solve, unless you have already done so, the two individual questions that are suggested for use in selecting analysts and programmers. **b.** Solve the hypothetical multi-part aptitude test given in Figure 16-1. **c.** Identify the areas covered by these two tests and try to appraise them for their usefulness in selecting analysts and programmers.

18. **a.** What steps would you suggest in order to validate the illustrative questions and tests given in the chapter? **b.** What information would you want about a person, besides scores on either individual questions or tests, in order to select potential analysts and programmers?

19. **a.** How is a satisfactory balance of capabilities, backgrounds, and experience obtained among members of the applications study group? **b.** Why are operating representatives included in the applications study group?

20. **a.** What is covered by the phrase, "basic structure for a new system"? **b.** For developing a new system, what are the merits, and demerits, of mechanization and of redesign? **c.** Why do so many people

advocate complete redesign of a system, but restrict their efforts to mechanization of procedures already in use when they design systems?

21. Are the *input* and *output* of a data-processing system synonymous with *data* and *information* as developed in an earlier chapter? Explain.

22. a. What factors must be considered in designing an efficient file structure? **b.** Explain how the following situations can be handled when designing files: (1) duplication because varying data elements for one item are in several different files; (2) different length records because some fields are not needed for some items; (3) different length records because some fields are repeated many times for some items.

23. a. What facts should be obtained about workloads during an applications study? **b.** How are these facts used in designing a system? **c.** What is the relationship between the facts about workloads obtained in an applications study and corresponding facts obtained in the feasibility study?

24. A firm of data-processing consultants says that there are three reasons why new systems are unprofitable: no reduction in costs, no increase in revenues, and no improvement in the company's market position. Another situation is said to arise, however, in which automatic data processing must be applied regardless of profit in order to fulfill the data-handling requirements of the company because personnel are unavailable or the work load is so great that no reasonable number of people can do a day's work in a day's time. **a.** Are there actually four arguments here, instead of only two since reductions in cost and increases in revenue should, it seems, cover all specific situations?
b. Is the situation involving high volume and high labor costs merely an example of high costs and low revenue that need correction? Explain.

25. Alpine Airlines has 537 ticket offices throughout the United States and each maintains an inventory of unsold seats for the flights originating there. A customer wanting a return flight or a flight originating in another city is asked to wait for a confirmation to be obtained from the office at point of departure. Alpine promises to advise the customer of the confirmation, but often "forgets." If the customer calls after two or three days Alpine advises whether the desired space was available and it generally is because Alpine's flights are seldom full. Top management is unhappy with this situation and demands that the vice president of passenger traffic improve this defect of the reservation system within six months. A WORDCOM salesman told the vice president of the superb on-line system that can be built around a WORDCOM processor to connect every office directly to a master reservation file at headquarters for instantaneous control over reservations. In off-peak hours, the WORDCOM could handle payroll, flight scheduling, and stewardess selection.

a. What path of action should the vice president follow for the next few months?

b. If the vice president should consider an automated system, what would be the various facts about airline operations to collect as the basis for systems design?

c. How should the vice president or his feasibility study team examine the WORDCOM proposal?

d. Design the formats for transmitting reservation inquiries to the central office, sending replies to the agent, and for keeping records in the master file.

e. What costs and savings are relevant to the problem and proposed solution?

f. Devise a time-schedule bar chart for the feasibility and applications studies. Identify the important check points and show the alternative results of various decisions.

g. What features should the input-output devices located in each ticket office have? Evaluate the merit of having different devices in various size offices.

h. What specifications and features should be available in the central processor located at headquarters?

26. The City Electric Company wants to automate the billing procedure for its customers. Describe the relevant costs, savings, and volumes associated with each of the following proposals:

a. Print bills with special characters in order to read them with an optical reader after they are received with collections from customers.

b. Bill bi-monthly instead of each month.

c. Send a reminder to each customer who is overdue 30 days or more.

d. Use the same processing system to process the company's payroll.

e. Issue all bills on the 25th of each month computed from meter readings on the 20th instead of issuing one twentieth of the bills each business day.

CHAPTER 17

1. a. What are the steps involved in selecting data-processing equipment? **b.** What should a user put in a bid invitation and how widely should he distribute it? **c.** Why should both new and long-established manufacturers of equipment be given bid invitations?

2. a. How can an equipment supplier separate a user's *desires* for certain features in equipment from his *demands*? **b.** What are the implications of each for short- and long-run equipment design and development?

3. a. What should an equipment manufacturer cover in his proposals to supply equipment in response to a user's requests? **b.** Why should a manufacturer restate systems loads and processing procedures in his proposal when he obtained the facts from the user who is responsible for satisfactory operation of his system? **c.** What interest does a user have in a firm or a flexible delivery date for equipment that he orders?

4. a. What are the installation requirements for a large-scale data processor? **b.** How much do these requirements change if a fully transistorized processor is obtained instead of a vacuum tube processor? **c.** If a vacuum tube processor is already installed and operating, how much can be gained by replacing it with a transistorized processor?

5. Explain what consideration the user should give to each one of the following points in the manufacturer's proposal: **a.** rent or purchase option; **b.** maintenance service; **c.** education and training of user's staff; **d.** equipment-design changes before and after installation; **e.** specific units, models, and capacities of equipment proposed; **f.** programming software package—compilers, executive routines, service routines, etc; **g.** machine time for testing programs before and after delivery of equipment.

6. a. What factors must be considered in evaluating equipment? **b.** How can various excess capabilities and deficiencies of different equipment be weighed in order to select the equipment best suited to application requirements? **c.** Where does the ultimate responsibility for equipment acquisition rest within an organization?

7. a. What steps are involved in preparing for equipment installation? **b.** Since equipment manufacturers have far more experience in delivering equipment than users have in installing it, how is it possible to synchronize the work of both parties for prompt, efficient installation?

8. a. What is the relationship between the form and function of an organization? **b.** How does the introduction of automatic data processing affect the structure of the organization responsible for data processing?

9. a. How much difference is there in the work involved in the three phases of studying, installing, and operating a data-processing system? **b.** What skills, education, training, and experience are required for personnel working in each phase?

10. **a.** Plan a program for training key personnel and working personnel. **b.** Who has the primary responsibility for educating and training personnel to make the study, install, and operate a data-processing system?

11. **a.** When a new data-processing system is introduced, why does the total amount of manpower required increase before it can be reduced? **b.** How are the problems of dislocated personnel handled most effectively? **c.** Why are upper-level personnel sometimes said to pose a bigger relocation problem than lower-level personnel?

12. Some companies promise employees that no one will lose in any way—reduction in rate of pay or loss of job—upon introduction of advanced data-processing equipment. **a.** How can such a policy be rationalized if one of the objectives is to reduce clerical costs? **b.** If smaller manpower requirements are met by reduced hiring rates, what are the future employment implications for white-collar workers?

13. **a.** Why does debugging receive so little attention in manual data-processing? **b.** How are errors in logic corrected most efficiently for manual systems? **c.** For automatic systems?

14. **a.** What does a user gain by joining a voluntary association of users of similar equipment? **b.** How is it possible for a user to contribute experiences to a cooperative association without revealing trade secrets? **c.** What would you recommend to an organization that claims to have unique applications and therefore believes it should not join any cooperative association, for it could neither contribute to nor benefit from membership?

15. False flooring, costing $5 to $10 a square foot, is recommended by many equipment manufacturers as the best way to provide space for connecting cables and power lines. A prospective user is offered two choices: one processor usually set up with 3000 square feet of false flooring or a competitive processor of equal or higher capacity needing only 600 square feet of space and no false floor.
a. What consideration should a user give to this possible saving when selecting equipment?
b. Should the manufacturer, user, or both jointly benefit from the savings in space and flooring costs? Explain.

16. How should the reduction in air conditioning costs, which are estimated to be $60,000 for a large vacuum tube processor and $20,000 for a comparable transistorized processor be shared between the manufacturer and the user?

17. One equipment manufacturer's estimate for handling four major applications is 12 hours of central processor time a day, whereas two other manufacturers estimate 7 and 9 hours a day for their equip-

ment to handle the same applications. The first manufacturer's sales representative proposes unofficially to count only the first shift time of 8 hours a day and ignore any additional time in order to retain the posted price for one-shift operation yet be competitive on this job. Explain what reaction you would have to such pricing practices if you worked for the following:

a. the customer;

b. the first manufacturer;

c. one of the other manufacturers;

d. some other user not offered similar price concessions;

e. the General Services Administration, which obtains equipment for the Federal Government and insists that a manufacturer adhere to his posted price and not offer discounts to anyone.

18. a. What problems are involved in the conversion from one set of equipment to another? **b.** How can the optimum amount of parallel operation of the old and the new system be determined?

19. a. How is it possible to balance the cost of long-term retention of files against the benefits obtainable from having the data available in the future? **b.** What differences in operating procedures arise for reconstructing files when (1) the immediately preceding "generation" of files is still available, and (2) the most recent file available is two generations old?

20. Explain how you would make a careful appraisal of the following argument: "All the talk about the value of getting faster, better, more complete data and making intensive studies to improve operating practices and managerial policies is mere rationalization for the fact that the originally promised cost reductions for routine data-processing have not been achieved."

21. a. What kinds of personnel problems accompany the introduction of new systems and equipment? **b.** What are the advantages and disadvantages of freely distributing information about the organizational changes—both levels and numbers involved—that will occur?

22. a. Why is feasibility and applications study work considered short-term in contrast to career work in systems analysis and operation of a data-processing system? **b.** Where within a company can personnel be obtained for installation and operations work? **c.** How can management eliminate apprehension about advancement and security among the members of the installation and operations group?

23. a. Why is parallel operation of the manual and mechanized systems commonly used during the conversion period? **b.** How long should parallel operations be continued? **c.** What are the merits of reconciling every difference discovered between the old and new system until the two operate in perfect harmony?

24. a. What is the purpose of scheduling processor operations? **b.** What difficulties tend to disrupt schedules? **c.** How is it possible to get back on a schedule after an important deviation?

25. Describe the kinds of operating procedures that should be established at an efficient data-processing installation.

26. The General Supplies Company has decided to implement a large and complex data-processing system for handling receipts, issues, and orders at four different locations.
a. What are the important factors in evaluating random access and batch processing equipment for this application?
b. How can the company decide whether to rent or buy equipment?
c. What are the merits of using a medium size processor for two shifts per day, two medium size processors for one shift, or one large processor for less than one shift?

27. For the General Supplies Company project perform the following:
a. Describe briefly the contents of each phase and prepare a detailed time schedule covering the following: bid invitation, equipment evaluation, equipment acquisition, programming, debugging, installation at one site, parallel operation, installation at the remaining three sites, and other relevant phases. **b.** Prepare test and check-out procedures for the system.

28. The General Manufacturing Company is planning the design and installation of a large, new data processing system. Each equipment manufacturer promises delivery eighteen months after a firm order is placed, and, moreover, points out that equipment delivery date cannot cause any problem since the programming work is estimated to take twenty-four months consisting of ten months for subsystem A, ten months for subsystem B, and four months for subsystem C. A consultant will undertake to program subsystem A starting at the time an equipment-selection decision is made. While this programming work is going on, General will spend six months training its own programmers. After subsystem A is finished, General's programmers will program subsystems B and C in serial fashion—one after the other. After the equipment arrives, the program debugging will take an estimated one month before the system goes into full operation.

The company plans to start this development project with a two month orientation program for all personnel followed by a six month preliminary design study and a parallel effort covering eight months to hire and train analysts. After training and preliminary design, the detail design can start and will take six months for subsystem C and one month for A and B together. As soon as A and B are designed, three months of equipment evaluation will start. At the end of the evaluation period, equipment will be selected and programming work can start. However, subsystem A must be pro-grammed before a firm order for equipment will be placed. Further-more, at the beginning of the orientation period, the company wants to embark on a twelve-month market-analysis study so that it can have the results available before the equipment-evaluation period. The president reported to stockholders that the new system will be operating in three years.

a. Construct a network-flow schedule for the planned development work and show the critical path.

b. Determine how long the development will take.

c. What elements implied by this schedule are missing or unrealistic?

d. Show how the development effort might be modified to stay within the time limit promised by the president.

Appendix II

GLOSSARY

This glossary is intended for people without special training who are interested in business data processing. Therefore, it attempts to define only the terms most often used in data processing and to provide a useful meaning for these terms. It does *not* ordinarily include instructions, for which the order codes for individual machines should be consulted, nor does it generally deal with technical words related to equipment design.

To reduce the over-all length of the glossary, cross-referencing has been minimized by listing most multiple-word entries under their first word. In some cases it is necessary to look under the more important word to find a desired entry.

Access Time—Time required to read or write a character, word, or field in a particular location. Frequently used to mean average access time for all locations in a particular storage unit.

Accumulator—A register in the arithmetic unit in which operands are placed and in which arithmetical results are formed; also used for logical-arithmetic operations and for intermediate storage.

Accuracy—The degree of correspondence between data, files, and outputs and the true results obtainable by extremely careful data gathering and processing. Accuracy is measured in terms of either the number of items that are different or the amount of difference between the calculated and true result.

Action—The processing steps to take when the related conditions are satisfied.

Address—A label consisting of numeric or alphanumeric characters which identifies a storage location, register, or device containing data.

> **Absolute Address**—Actual location in storage of a particular unit of data; an address expressed as a number that the control unit can interpret directly.

> **Address Modifier**—A plus (or minus) number added to (or subtracted from) the address of an operand to get a shifted-address for a character-addressable machine; the result is to shift the operand to left or right respectively.

> **Assigned Address**—During the compiling phase, the absolute address that is associated with an address label written in a source program.

Effective Address—The address obtained by combining the contents of a specified index register with the address in an instruction.

Relative Address—A label used to identify a word in a routine or subroutine with respect to its position preceding or following other instructions in that routine or subroutine. A relative address is translated into an absolute address during an assembly or compiler run by introducing a specific starting address for the subroutine within the main routine.

Symbolic Address—A label assigned to a selected word in a routine for the convenience of the programmer. The label is independent of the location of a word within a routine; it identifies the field of data to be operated on or the operation to be used rather than its storage location. Before the program is executed, the symbolic address is converted to an absolute address.

Addressing—Method of identifying operands in storage.

Field Addressing—The right-hand character position of an operand is used as its address in selected-length field storage; the left-hand character position is used for instructions.

Indirect Addressing—The address in an instruction referring to a location that contains the *address* of the operand instead of the operand itself; may be carried through two or more stages.

Add-to-Storage Logic—Processor logic designed to add any operand in storage to any other; an accumulator, as such, is not available.

Align—Placing operands within words so that operations can be performed correctly—for example, shifting numbers to put the units values (and others) in corresponding positions before adding.

Alphabet—Sets of letter symbols—for example, A through Z—used to form words. More broadly, any set of symbols used to represent data.

Alphanumeric—A coding system capable of representing alphabetic characters, numerals, and other symbols.

Applications Study—Design of a system and related procedures plus development of equipment specifications to perform a certain data-processing job.

Areas in Storage—Characters, fields, or words in processor storage assigned for the following purposes in a program: editing, printing, punching, read-in, constants, working, and write-out.

Arithmetic and Logic Unit—The part of a processor that performs the arithmetical operations of adding, multiplying, etc., and the logical operations of comparing one number or name with another.

Arithmetic Operation—Addition, subtraction, multiplication, and division.

Assemble—*See* "Assembly Routine" under "Routine."

Asynchronous (Processor)—That portion of processor operations in which performance of the next command is started by a signal that the previous command has been completed. Synchronous processors, on the other hand, have a fixed time cycle for the execution of operations.

Audit Trail—The path left by a transaction when it is processed; consists of the original document, entry in a transaction list, posting to a file record, and inclusion in a report. Auditors use the audit trail of a transaction for determining the validity of records.

Auditing—Examination of source data, methods of processing, and contents of reports to draw conclusions about the validity of the system and credibility of reports; auditors use many sources of information and various techniques for verification.

Automatic Data-Processing System—A system that makes maximum use of an electronic data processor and related equipment for processing data.

Automatic Programming—A way of writing programs based on a problem-oriented language and a translator routine for translating this language to machine language.

Automatic Transaction Recorder—Systems for recording several of the facts about a transaction with minimum manual input. For example, in a job shop the recorder will pick up the worker and job identification from plates or cards and the start-stop times from a built-in clock, so that only the quantity completed is punched into the keyboard or set up in dials for recording.

Batch Processing—Collection of data over a period of time for sorting and processing as a group during a particular machine run.

Binary-Coded Alphanumeric—A scheme for representing all alphabetic characters, digits, and special symbols in binary notation. The use of six bits for each character is common since $2^6 = 64$, which is generally adequate for the alphabet involved.

Binary-Coded Decimal—A system for representing *each* decimal digit by a code written in binary notation. Among the several systems are the 8-4-2-1 and the Excess-3 schemes.

Binary Number—A number with the base 2 having the following positional values: 64, 32, 16, 8, 4, 2, 1, ½, ¼, ⅛, etc.

Bit—A binary digit; hence, a unit of data in binary notation; abbreviated from *bi*nary digi*t*.

Block—A group of words, fields, or data elements transferred as a unit for input and output purposes.

Blocked—The arrangement of records in blocks for input and output. Generally two or more data records are placed in a block on tape, depending on the length of records and blocks. *Blocking* is the combining of two or more data records into one block for writing on tape. *Deblocking* is the separation of blocked records preparatory to processing. *Unblocked* data records are recorded as individual blocks on tape.

Blocking Factor—The number of data records that can be contained in a given block on tape.

Blockmark—A mark placed in storage to indicate the end of a block of data to be written on tape for a processor that handles variable-length blocks on tape.

Bootstrap—The use of prior steps to advance operations at the next stage; for example, a few instructions entered through the console can cause a processor to start reading a load routine which then takes over to read the remainder of the load routine and the whole program.

Branch—*See* "Jump."

Breakpoint—A point in a program at which a processor may be made to stop automatically for a check on the progress of the routine. A *conditional* breakpoint permits the programmer to control operations by means of a switch setting and to continue the program as coded, if desired conditions are satisfied.

Buffer—A device for compensating for differences in speed between two devices to permit them to operate together.

Bulk Storage—Large-volume storage used to supplement the high-speed storage; may be addressable, as with disks and drums, or nonaddressable, as with magnetic tapes. Also called "secondary" and "external storage."

Business Application—A closely related set of activities that are treated as a unit—for example, each of the following: customer accounting, inventory control, or order entry and sales may be treated as a unit for conversion to automatic data processing and operation.

Business Data Processing—Processing of data for *actual* transactions—purchases, sales, collections—involving file processing, calculations, and reporting; also includes processing *planned* transactions for budgeting and operating control purposes. Characterized by large volumes of input and output with limited amounts of computation during processing.

Capacity, System—The power of a system to store data in files, accept transactions, process files, and furnish results.

Card Punch—A device for punching data in cards. Examples are simple hand punches, keyboard print-punches, paper-tape-to-card converter punches, and high-speed punches for magnetic-tape-to-card conversion, or for direct output from the processor.

Carry—(1) Digit to be added to the next higher column when the sum of digits in one column equals or exceeds the number base. (2) Process of forwarding the carry digit.

Chaining—(1) For some processors, instructions in sequence that have sequential addresses (the address register contains the address of the next operand wanted after the preceding instruction is executed) can be "chained" together and the operand address(es) omitted. (2) Printed listings of transactions each of which contains a reference to the preceding transaction for the record involved; may also have an index to the most recent transaction for every record in the file.

Changes, Pending—Transactions not successfully processed against the file because of mistakes in data, program errors, records not yet established or already deleted from file, account "frozen," or record was moved within the file and, therefore, was not available in the expected sequence.

Channel—A path along which data, particularly a series of digits or characters, may flow or be stored either in a particular set of equipment or a communication network. In storage that is serial by character and parallel by bit (for example, a magnetic tape or drum in some coded decimal processors), a channel comprises several parallel tracks.

Character—(1) One of a set of elementary symbols, such as those corresponding to the keys on a typewriter. The symbols may include decimal digits 0 through 9, the letters A through Z, punctuation marks, operation symbols, and any other single symbol that a processor can read, store, or write. (2) A binary representation of such a symbol. A correct representation of a character in any media is a *valid* character, whereas a combination of bits or punches not representing an accepted character is called *illegal*. For example, in punched-card code, the 0 and 2 punch represent S, a legal character, but the 2 and 3 punch are invalid because they do not represent a character.

Character Reader—A device for scanning and identifying characters on documents that can also be read by people. *Magnetic-ink* readers work with specially-shaped characters printed in metallic ink that is magnetized before reading. *Optical* readers use ordinary-shaped characters printed in ordinary inks.

Check—A means of verifying the accuracy of data transmitted, manipulated, or stored by a unit or device in a processor.

Check Digit—A check scheme that attaches one or more extra digits to a word according to certain rules so that, if any digit changes, the mistake can be detected.

Code Check—Determination that the character representation is in the "legal" set of characters for the machine being used and that fields have valid characters—that is, numerics are not in alphabetic fields, and vice versa.

Mathematical Check—A check making use of mathematical identities or other properties—for example, checking multiplication by verifying that $A \cdot B = B \cdot A$.

Summation Check—A redundant check in which groups of digits are summed, usually without regard for overflow, and that sum checked against a previously computed sum to verify accuracy.

COBOL—*C*ommon *B*usiness *O*riented *L*anguage; an English-like programming language designed primarily for business-type applications and implemented for use with many different data processors.

COBOL Word—A word given pre-assigned meaning in the COBOL language, including both optional and key words that must be used in their prescribed context; also called "reserved words." The list of COBOL-61 reserved words is supplemented by a manufacturer's list for each machine with a COBOL compiler.

Code (noun)—A system of rules for using a set of symbols to represent data or operations.

Instruction Code—The symbols, names, and descriptions for all the operations that a processor executes.

Machine Code—The code that the processor hardware was built to interpret and execute.

Macrocode—An instruction written by a programmer in a source program to specify a routine to be extracted from the library and to give the processor program information required to tailor the routine to fit into the object program.

Mnemonic Code—An instruction code using abbreviations, instead of numeric codes, to permit easy recognition. For example, "subtract" is represented by "SUB" instead of the number "12." Mnemonic code must be converted to machine code before a program is executed.

Multi-Mode Code—The character represented by a pattern of bits, holes, etc., depends on whether the device is in the "letters" or "figures" mode. Corresponds roughly to the upper and lower case characters on a typewriter obtained by use of the shift key.

Numeric Code—A code in which the symbols used are all numerals. Four- and six-bit codes for electronic equipment; five-, six-, seven-, and eight-channel code for punched-paper-tape; and Hollerith code for punched cards.

Pseudocode—An arbitrary code, independent of the hardware of a computer and designed for convenience in programming, which must be translated into computer code in order to direct the computer.

Two-for-One; Three-for-Two—The combined use of the four bits of each numeric character to represent alphabetic characters with six bits each.

Two-for-Three—The combined use of twelve bits of two alphanumeric characters to represent three numeric characters.

Code for Computer (verb)—To express a program in a code that a specific computer was built or programmed to interpret and execute, or in a code that can be translated into machine code.

Collate—To produce a single sequence of items, ordered according to some rule, from two or more similarly ordered sequences. The final sequence need not contain all of the data available in the original sets. If, for example, two sets of items are being matched, items that do not match may be discarded.

Collating Sequence—The sequence of special symbols, letters, and numerals to which the binary values, ranging from 000000 to 111111, are assigned by the equipment designer. The collation table value for each character determines the results of making comparisons—smaller, equal, or larger—and the sequence when sorting.

Common Language—A single code used by several different devices—for example, typewriters, calculators, and transmitters—manufactured by different companies.

Communication Channel—Messenger, voice, mail, telegraph, telephone, and microwave available for transmitting business data over short or long distances.

Telegraph Channel—A low-capacity communication channel with a maximum data-transmission rate of ten characters per second.

Telephone Channel—A medium-capacity communication channel with a maximum capacity of 300 characters per second.

Telpak or Microwave Channel—A high-capacity communication channel with data-transmission rates up to 100,000 characters per second.

Compare—To examine two *numeric* data items to find if one is equal to, smaller, or larger than the other. To examine two *alphabetic* data items to find if one is the same, earlier, or later than the other in the collating sequence.

Compiler—*See* "Compiler" Routine under "Routine."

Computer—Any device capable of accepting data, applying prescribed processes to them, and supplying the results of these processes. The word "computer" usually refers to an internally-stored-program data processor; the term "processor" is preferable for business applications.

> **Digital Computer**—A computer capable of accepting and operating on only the representations of numerals or letters coded numerically. More broadly, a digital computer handles numerals, letters, or symbols represented as discrete items of data, as opposed to measurements.

> **Stored-Program Computer**—A digital computer capable of performing sequences of internally stored instructions, as opposed to calculators on which the sequence is impressed manually. Such computers also usually possess the ability to operate upon the instructions themselves, and to alter the sequence of instructions in accordance with results already calculated.

Condition—(1) An expression that, taken as a whole, may be true or false. A *simple* condition has only one element—for example, "if account balance exceeds credit limit, reject customer's order." A *compound* condition has two or more elements—for example, "if account balance exceeds credit limit but account is current and the new order will not cause balance to exceed twice the credit limit, then accept order." (2) The result of a test—for example, greater than, negative, overflow. (3) A value that an item may have.

Condition-Name—A name assigned by the programmer to denote one of a number of values that an item of data can assume.

Configuration, Machine—The pattern of equipment making up a system: size of storage, number of tape units and input-output channels, printer speed, etc.

Console—Equipment that provides for manual intervention and for monitoring processor operations.

Constant—A value used without alteration throughout a program.

Control Counter—A counter built into the control unit of a processor and used for sequencing instructions to be executed. It normally contains the address of the next instruction to be performed, but its contents can be changed by means of conditional or unconditional jump instructions.

Control Field—The field used to edit data before output for printing. For example, $$$Z,ZZ9.99 will result in the insertion of a "$", a "," and a "." as well as the suppression of leading zeros in the number 0000345678 to give an edited field such as $3,456.78.

Control, Internal—The procedures used within an organization to achieve accuracy at each stage of processing to ensure adherence to policies and to make reports conform to reality.

Control, Operating—The system used to obtain information about events as they occur, process them against files containing the results of previous events, draw conclusions about developments, make decisions, and implement the decisions. *Closed-loop* control relies upon equipment and excludes people. *Open-loop* control uses people in some stage of the control process—most frequently for appraisal and decision-making. *Real-time* control (also called "on-line" control) is comprehensive enough and operates quickly enough to permit control of a process while it is going on.

Control Sequence—Normal order of selection of instructions for execution. In some processors, one of the addresses in each instruction specifies the control sequence. In most processors, the sequence is consecutive except when a jump is made.

Control Unit—The portion of the hardware of an automatic digital processor that directs the sequence of operations, interprets coded instructions, and initiates proper commands to the circuits to execute instructions.

Converter—A device for transferring data from one storage medium to another—for example, from punched cards to magnetic tape.

Cost—The outlay for data, equipment or operations. Relevant cost concepts are average, fixed, marginal, and replaceable.

Criterion—(1) A value used for judging, as in determining whether a condition is true or false. (2) A rule or test for making a decision.

Cycle (verb)—To repeat a set of operations a prescribed number of times including, when required, supplying necessary address changes by arithmetical operations, by an index register, or in other ways.

Cylinder—For disk units with multiple read-write heads, all of the data tracks under the read-write heads can be accessed without mechanical movement of the heads. If each disk surface has one read-write head, the tracks under them can be thought of as a *cylinder* consisting of one track from each disk.

Data—Figures, words, or charts that refer to or describe some situation.

Data Description—An entry in the data division of a COBOL program describing the characteristics of a data item in terms of level, name, length, and alphanumeric content.

Data Division—A division of a COBOL program describing the characteristics of data: files, records, and data elements.

Data Element—A group of characters that specify an *item* at or near the basic level. An *elementary* item—for example, "month,"—contains no subordinate item. A *group* item—for example, "date," which consists of day, month, and year—contains items that may be used separately and therefore treated as elementary items.

Data Item—A unit of data that can be identified by a name or combination of names and subscripts.

Working-Storage Section—Describes areas of storage where intermediate results and other items are stored temporarily during program execution; consists of a series of record description entries each of which describes an item in a work area.

Data Density—The number of characters that can be stored per unit of length, area, or volume. Specifically, for magnetic tape, the number of bits in one row per inch of tape where one bit in each row across the tape makes up a frame representing one character.

Data Origination—The steps used for obtaining data at the points where events occur. The operations may be manual or mechanical and the data may be obtained in a form that requires conversion or that are directly usable for further processing.

Data Processing—Rearrangement and refinement of data into a form suitable for further use; often involves file processing to update files for transactions that occur.

Debug—To test a program by running it with test, simulated, or live data on a processor to find whether it works properly, and, if mistakes are revealed either in the final answer or at various stages of processing, to discover the source and make corrections.

Decentralized Data Processing—Processing data at many (or perhaps only one) locations for an organization that is decentralized managerially, geographically, or both.

Decimal—Pertaining to the number 10. A number system whose base is the quantity 10; a system of notation utilizing ten symbols, 0, 1, . . . , 9.

Decimal Number—A number with the base 10 having positional values of 1000, 100, 10, 1, $\frac{1}{10}$, $\frac{1}{100}$, $\frac{1}{1000}$, etc.

Decimal Point—The separating mark "." between the positional values of 1 and $\frac{1}{10}$. The *actual* decimal may appear in data and is usually wanted in output for "display" purposes. If the actual decimal point is retained in data, it occupies an actual space in storage and precludes arithmetical operations.

Decision—(1) In management, a conclusion arrived at after consideration. (2) In programming, a choice between alternatives depending on prior conditions and use of specified parts of the program.

Decision Plan—The system used for making managerial decisions; consists of rules prepared in advance or developed *ad hoc* and applied by men, machines, or some combination. Systems include the exception principle, internal decision, variable processing, manual intervention, and adaptive plans.

Decision Table—Organized tabular representation of relationships between variables, sets of conditions and the related sequences of action that make up rules.

Delay—The length of time after either the occurrence of an event for individual event reporting or the close of a reporting period for summary reporting before reports are made available. Delay covers the time needed to process data and to prepare and distribute reports.

Design Approach—The view that the designer takes of the restraints on the design process; his freedom may range from nearly none to almost carte blanche to design whatever seems most useful for the organization.

Data System Redesign—Stresses redesign of files, inputs, data flows; outputs and management procedures are viewed as fixed. New equipment is introduced when warranted.

Information System Redesign—Stresses complete freedom to redesign both management decision rules and the entire data system.

Mechanization—Stresses the introduction of new equipment processing procedures with the current inputs, files, outputs, and data flows.

Simplification—Stresses better forms, elimination of useless data, more efficient flows of data, consolidated files, and improvements in existing techniques.

DETAB-X—Decision Tables, Experimental; a programming language that combines decision tables with COBOL.

Disk—A circular metal plate with magnetic material on both sides, continuously rotated for reading or writing by means of one or more read-write heads mounted on movable or fixed arms; disks may be permanently mounted on a shaft or, as a package, they may be removable and others placed on the shaft.

Display—Visible representation of data on a console, in a printed report, or by other means.

Display, Direct—Television-like tubes that display various alphanumeric or graphic results from a processor for viewing or photographing for the record. More simply, a desk set on which selected facts—for example, availability of a seat for a desired airflight—may be viewed.

Division (noun)—The parts in which a COBOL program is organized. *Identification* division provides information to identify the source and object programs. *Environment* division specifies the equipment to use for translating and running a program. *Data* division contains entries to define the nature of the data to be processed. *Procedure* division consists of the processor program to be run with data.

Documents, Readable—Papers containing data about transactions, or, loosely, any report written, typed, printed, or imprinted that people can read (often called "hard copy"); also includes printed or interpreted cards and punched-paper tape.

Down-Time—The period of time that a processor is malfunctioning because of equipment failure.

Dummy—An artificial address, instruction, or other unit of data inserted solely to fulfill prescribed conditions (such as word length or block length) without affecting operations. A dummy instruction may be converted to an instruction and executed in a later cycle.

Dump—To record the contents of internal storage at a given instant of time, usually to help detect program mistakes or errors, or to remove a program and data from the processor to permit running another program.

Edit—(1) To arrange or rearrange information for the output unit of the processor to print. Editing may involve deletion of unwanted data, selection of pertinent data, and application of standard processes, such as zero-suppression. (2) To examine raw data to check or improve their accuracy and relevance before keypunching. (3) To examine data during the input operation or at other stages of processing for completeness and correctness.

Electronic Data-Processing System—A machine system capable of receiving, storing, operating on, and recording data without the intermediate use of tabulating cards. The system is also able to store internally at least some instructions for data-processing operations, and to locate and control access to data stored internally.

Else-Rule—A catch-all rule in decision tables to handle the conditions not covered by explicit rules; written by leaving all conditions blank ("irrelevant"). Action taken may be to halt processing, note the condition, or to correct the situation and continue processing.

End-of-File—Special symbols and a trailer label indicate end of a file. Several short files can be recorded on one tape, whereas a long file may extend over several reels—a multi-reel file. Automatic procedures are used to finish processing when the end of a record file on tape is reached.

End-of-Tape—A reflective spot or other indicator is placed near the physical end of the tape to signal the end. Automatic procedures are used to handle tapes when the physical end of an input or output tape is reached.

Entry—A notation written in a stub of a row or in a cell of a decision table. Any row must be in the form of either a limited entry or an extended entry.

Extended Entry—A notation other than a limited entry with part of the condition or action written in the cells—for example, less than, greater than, or equal to an amount; excellent, good, poor, none, any.

Limited Entry—A notation restricted, to yes, no, X, and blank in a cell in a decision table. Conditions and actions are restricted to the stubs of the rows.

Environment Division—The division of a COBOL program in which the programmer lists the features of the equipment needed to run a program: input-output devices, storage size, etc.

Error—The difference between an accurate quantity and its calculated approximation. *Errors* occur in numerical methods; *mistakes* are human blunders that occur in programs, coding, data transcription, and operating; *malfunctions* occur in equipment operations.

Error Tape—A tape used for writing out errors in order to correct them by analysis after printing or further machine processing.

Quiet Error—Errors occurring in manual-mechanical systems that are corrected by people familiar with the situation before the errors spread throughout the system. In automatic systems, this type of error is likely to spread throughout the records before it is discovered and corrected.

Size Error—The size error condition arises in COBOL whenever the number of positions to the left of the assumed decimal point in a computed result exceeds the corresponding positions in the *data-name* supposed to hold the result.

Event—Any action that gives rise to data that affects the contents of the files of a business—for example, purchase, shipment, or sale.

Event Chain—A trace of the series of actions—preparing documents, processing data, and updating files—that results from one initial event.

Exception-Principle System—An information system that reports on situations only when actual results are outside a "normal range"; results within normal range are not reported.

Excess-3 Code—A binary-coded decimal system that represents each decimal digit as the corresponding binary number plus three. For example, the decimal digits 0, 1, 8, 9 are represented as 0011, 0100,

1011, 1100, respectively. The 9's complement of the decimal digit corresponds (also in Excess-3 code) to the 1's complement of the four binary digits.

Exit—A possible outcome from comparing items of numeric data—equal to, smaller than, larger than, or zero, negative, positive—or from comparing alphabetic data items: same, earlier, or later. An outcome from checking the truth of a condition statement: yes or no. Each outcome may be used to send program control to a different, appropriate subroutine.

Externally-Stored Program—Instruction routines set up in wiring boards or plugboards for manual insertion into a small-scale processor.

Extract—(1) To obtain certain specified digits from a machine word. (2) To replace contents of specific columns of another machine word, depending on the instruction. (3) To remove from a set of items of data all those items that meet some arbitrary condition.

Factory Data Collection—Devices placed throughout a factory for workers to report production by inserting plates or cards representing themselves and their jobs and by keying in the quantity completed. The data are transmitted to a central compiler that records them and picks up the start-stop times from an internal clock.

Feasibility Study—Preliminary process of determining the over-all suitability of applying data processors to specific operations; involves both technical and economic considerations.

Field—A set of one or more characters treated as a unit of data. Used for the organization of data on punched cards where enough columns are assigned to each item to handle the longest case likely to occur. Similarly applied to character-addressable processors, although often called "variable word."

  Field Name—A symbolic name the programmer gives a field of data; an absolute address is assigned during program assembly.

  Field Shifting—The adjustment of the address of a field to left or right to shorten or to realign the item of data.

  Selected-Length Field—A fixed number of characters selected for each data element; requires filling out shorter data items with zeros or blanks to reach the fixed number. Corresponds to the field assigned to an item during the design of a punched-card layout.

  Variable-Length Field—The number of characters used for each item of data is just the number needed for it; there is no need to fill the item of data out to a certain length. Item separators indicate the end of each item. Punched-paper tape uses blanks for separators between items in ordinary communication, but an explicit symbol (not a blank) must be used as an item separator for data on tape read into a processor.

Fieldcom—*Field Com*puter, a hypothetical processor used to illustrate the features of and programming for a processor with character-addressable storage that handles data as fields.

Fieldmark—An indication of the left-hand character for an item of data in FIELDCOM. Commonly called "wordmark," even though data are organized as fields.

File—One or more records concerning people, things, or places that are closely related and handled together for processing.

> **Change File**—A list of the transactions effectively processed against a master file. May also include selected parts or all of each changed record from the master file.

> **File Label**—A record placed before (and after) the records on tape to indicate their nature, when written, when to use, and how long to retain the file.

> **Master File**—A file of records containing a cumulative history or the results of accumulation; updated in each file-processing cycle, and carried forward to the next cycle.

> **Transaction File**—The transactions occurring over a period of time and accumulated as a batch ready for processing against the master files that are affected.

File Analysis—A study of file characteristics to locate file redundancies or similarities and to list documents affecting a file and data elements contained in a file.

File Maintenance—Modification of a file to incorporate changes that do *not* involve arithmetical operations—for example, insertions, deletions, transfers, and corrections.

File Processing—Modification of a file to incorporate changes that involve arithmetical operations—for example, receipts, issues, returns, and losses of stock items.

Filemark—A mark placed after the last record in a file and its trailer label on tape to indicate end of the file. May be followed by another file. The last file on a reel is followed by trailer label, filemark, and reelmark.

Fixed-Point Arithmetic—A method of calculation in which operations take place in an invariant manner, without regard for location of the decimal or binary point. This is illustrated by desk calculators or slide rules, with which the operator must keep track of the decimal point, and by many automatic computers, with which the programmer is responsible for the location of the decimal point.

Floating-Point Arithmetic—A method of calculation which automatically accounts for the location of the decimal or binary point. This is usually accomplished by handling the number as a signed mantissa times the radix raised to an integral exponent. For example, the decimal number $+88.3$ might be written as $+.883 \times 10^2$; the binary number $+.0011$ as $+.11 \times 2^{-2}$.

Flow Chart—A systems-analysis tool consisting of a graphical representation of a procedure.

Structure Flow Charts—General flow charts showing types, times, and quantities of input, processing, files, and output but *not* indicating how jobs are performed.

Technique Flow Charts—Specific flow charts showing data and information requirements *and* the methods proposed for filling them.

Format—The arrangement of output for printing: page numbering, headings, vertical and horizontal spacing, minor, major, and page totals, etc.

FORTRAN—*For*mula *Trans*lating system; consists of a language and translator designed for programming problems expressed in a mathematical-type language.

Frame—The group of bits across magnetic tape, usually seven, consisting of one from each row that make up a character; also, five, six, seven, or eight punches across punched-paper tape.

Hardware—The electric, electronic, and mechanical equipment used for processing data; consists of cabinets, racks, tubes, transistors, wires, and motors.

Hash Total—Sums of data items not ordinarily added, such as the stock numbers of units shipped, which are used to control the accuracy of the data at each stage of processing.

High-Low Limits—Maximum and minimum values used for checking the plausibility of data or results. If the limits are exceeded, corrective action may be taken or the item rejected for investigation.

Identification Division—The part of a COBOL program in which the programmer gives information to identify the source and object programs.

Implementation—The steps involved in installing and starting successful operation of a system and related equipment. These steps include feasibility study, applications study, equipment selection, systems analysis and design, physical installation, operation, and review.

Index Register—A register to which an integer, usually one, is added (or subtracted) upon the execution of certain machine instructions. The contents of a register are used with other instructions to get effective instruction addresses during execution and for counting the performance of cycles. The register may be reset to zero or to any desired number.

Indirect Addressing—The operand in an instruction is the address of a storage location containing the *address* of the desired operand; may be carried two or more stages.

Information—Knowledge that was not previously known to its receiver. Information can be derived from data only if the data are accurate, timely, unexpected, and relevant to the subject under consideration.

Information Flow Analysis—A technique for organizing and analyzing the facts obtained about the flow of documents throughout an organization; can be performed manually or on a processor. One mechanized version is called AUTOSATE.

Initialize—Preparatory steps required *before* executing a repetitive cycle in order to get it started correctly; performed initially and not repeated within the program unless the cycle is started afresh.

Input—The process of introducing data into the internal storage of the processor.

Input-Output Control System—Library routines that a programmer can select and tailor to the application by means of macro instructions and certain facts supplied in the source program for handling input and output for cards, tape, disk, drum, and printer. Involves a description of machine configuration and definition of files.

Instruction—A set of characters that defines an operation together with one or more addresses to cause the processor to operate accordingly on the indicated operands. *Single, double,* and *triple* address instructions have one, two, and three operand addresses, respectively.

Instruction Routine—The set of instructions prepared to direct the processor to process data—for example, update master inventory files—or to perform some calculations.

Integrated Data Processing—A business data system designed as a whole so that data are initially recorded at the point of origin in a form suitable for subsequent processing without manual recopying.

Internally-Stored Program—A program prepared by programmers and converted to a suitable input media—cards, paper tape, magnetic tape —for reading into the processor and storing for execution when data are read in. Instructions in the program itself can be manipulated in much the same way as data and the whole program can be replaced by merely reading in another program.

Interrogation—An inquiry, usually of a simple nature—for example, "How many widgets are on hand?"—for which a quick reply is expected; requires the use of random-access equipment.

Interrupt—The ability of one device to stop the operation of another to indicate readiness to supply or receive data; for example tape units can interrupt the processor when ready to read or write.

Jump—To transfer control by executing an instruction that specifies the location of the next instruction to be executed by the program. Also called "branch" or "transfer." An *unconditional* jump is made to occur whenever the jump instruction is encountered in the program. A *conditional* jump transfers control only if some specified logical condition is satisfied; if the condition is not satisfied, the next instruction is taken in normal sequence.

Justify—To shift alphanumeric items to put their left (or numeric items to put their right) characters in the corresponding positions.

Key—A field used for identification of a record; a selected element in each record used for sorting records into a desired sequence.

Keyboard—The whole arrangement of the keys on a card punch, teletype, or other data origination or communication device, consisting of special symbols, numerals, and letters.

Key-Punch (noun)—A typewriter-like machine for recording data on punched cards by punching a code into them, and, often, printing the same data on the cards.

Label—In symbolic programming, a name consisting of several alphanumerics (perhaps required to start with an alpha) to serve as an address while writing a source program; absolute addresses are assigned during assembly or compilation.

Labels—(1) A written or printed sticker on a tape reel or container identifying contents of tape. (2) A record on tape describing file content.

> **Header Label**—Label recorded on tape preceding the first record in the file to identify the file—file name, date written, and reel number.

> **Trailer Label**—Label recorded on tape following last record in a file—number of records on tape and whether file is continued on another tape.

Language—Expressions used to define the operations of a processor.

> **Machine-Oriented Language**—A language intelligible to a processor with little or no translation—for example, the programs written in WORDCOM and FIELDCOM order codes. Mnemonic order codes need to be translated into the machine's numeric order code on a one-for-one basis and the symbolic addresses need to be converted into absolute addresses.

> **Problem-Oriented Language**—A language designed for solving a particular class of problems—for example COBOL for business and

FORTRAN for mathematics. Requires elaborate translation or compiling—each program instruction becomes several machine instructions—before the program can be run on a processor.

Level—In COBOL, the status of one data item relative to another, indicates whether one item includes subsequent ones or whether, as reflected in the numbering scheme which must follow certain rules, data items are independent of each other.

Leverage—The number of instructions compiled in the object program for each instruction written in the source program. From the programmer's viewpoint, leverage is an indication of the power of a programming language and its processor.

Library—An organized collection—for example, tape-file library or subroutine library.

List—A single series of similar items—for example, the names of states and their current census. A one-dimensional array.

Literal—One or more characters used to represent the value "literally" expressed.

Logical Operation—(1) An operation in which a decision affecting the future sequence of instructions is automatically made by the processor. The decision is based upon comparisons between all or some of the characters in an arithmetic register and their counterparts in any other register on a less-than, equal-to, or greater-than basis, or between certain characters in arithmetic registers and built-in standards. (2) Operations on a word on a character-by-character basis without regard for other characters as in "logical and" and "logical or" operations.

Machine-Independent Solution—A procedure or program organized in terms of the logical nature of the problem rather than in terms of any data-processing machine used in solving it.

Machine-Processable Form—Data on a media suitable for machines to accept; commonly magnetic tape, punched cards, or punched tape.

Machine-Readable Characters—Printed, typed, or written symbols on documents which both people and character-reading machines can read.

Macro-Instruction—A mnemonic instruction that a programmer writes in a source program to call for a library routine that performs desired functions—for example, open, close, or seek. The programmer specifies conditions in the operand part of the macro to tailor the library routine to the program requirements.

Magnetic-Core Storage—A storage device consisting of magnetically permeable binary cells arrayed in a two-dimensional matrix; a large storage unit contains many such matrices. Each core is wire-connected and may be polarized in either of two directions to store one binary digit. The direction of polarization can be sensed by wires running through the core.

Magnetic-Disk Storage—A storage device consisting of magnetically coated disks accessible to a read-write arm operating similar to records in an automatic record player. An arm is moved mechanically to the desired disk (unless there is an arm for each disk) and then to the desired track on that disk. The arm reads or writes data sequentially as the disk rotates.

Magnetic-Drum Storage—A device that stores data on tracks around a rotating cylindrical drum surfaced with a magnetic coating. A magnetic read-write head is usually associated with each track so that the desired track can be selected by electric switching. Data from a given track are read or written sequentially as the drum continually rotates.

Magnetic-Ink Character Recognition—A system using specially-shaped characters printed in magnetizable ink for machine reading; originally developed for commercial check processing.

Magnetic-Tape Storage—A storage device consisting of plastic tape or metal coated with magnetic material. A read-write head is associated with each row of bits on tape so that a frame can be read or written at one time as the tape moves past the head.

Malfunction—Incorrect function occurring in equipment.

Management Information System—A data-processing system designed to supply management and supervisory personnel with information consisting of data that are accurate, timely, and new.

Mask—To replace characters in the accumulator with characters from a specified storage location that corresponds to the "ones" positions in the mask, which is in a specified storage location or register.

Master Record—The official updated record for use in the next file-processing run. The master record is usually on magnetic tape or cards, but a card copy of it may be used as a visual file for reference purposes.

Match—Comparison of keys (of records) that are identical—for example, transaction record and master-file record; also called a "hit" or "strike."

Matrix—(1) A rectangular array of numbers, subject to mathematical operations, such as addition, multiplication, and inversion, according to specified rules. Any table is a matrix. (2) An array of circuit elements, such as diodes, wires, magnetic cores, and relays, arranged and designed to perform a specified function—for example, conversion from one number system to another.

Media—Magnetic tape, punched cards, and punched tape used to hold data and used primarily for input and output.

Merge—To produce a single sequence of items, ordered according to a certain rule, from two or more sequences previously ordered according to the same rule, without changing the items in size, structure, or total number. Merging is a special kind of collating.

Microsecond—A millionth of a second; "µs."

Microwave—Extremely short electromagnetic waves used in high-capacity communications networks. Usually subdivided into many channels of various capacities to transmit voice or data messages at high rates.

Millisecond—A thousandth of a second; one thousand microseconds; "ms."

Mistake—Blunders by people causing inaccurate results.

Mnemonic—Memory-aiding instruction names—for example, PRT and SUB for "print" and "subtract," respectively, instead of the numeric code used by the machine. Mnemonics codes are converted to machine code during program assembly.

Mode—The style of operation; for example, paper-tape punches have both letters and figures modes to increase the number of possible characters from 32 (five channels on tape offers a maximum of 2^5 or 32 characters) to 52 after allowing for control characters common to both modes and for shifting characters. Typewriters, for example, have the upper and lower case modes of operation.

Modular—Standardization of processor components to permit combining them in various ways.

Modulate—Conversion of one form of signal to another suitable for transmission over communication circuits. For example, a modulator converts the bits representing a frame of data on punched-paper tape or magnetic tape from the parallel mode to the serial mode for transmission.

M-Q Register—A register used in conjunction with the accumulator for performing arithmetical operations. For example, in multiplication, the M-Q is first loaded with the multiplier. After multiplication, the M-Q contains the low-order digits of the product; the high-order digits are in the accumulator and the multiplicand remains in its storage location.

Multiplex—A technique for transferring data from several storage devices operating at relatively low transfer rates to one storage device operating at a high transfer rate in such a manner that the high-speed device is not obliged to wait for the low-speed units. The high-speed device is time-shared by offering service to each low-speed device in turn.

Multiply Field—A field in a character machine used to hold the results of the multiplication operation. A multiply field, which can be located anywhere in storage, must be as long as the multiplier and multiplicand fields plus one character. Initially, the multiplier is copied into the left end of the field and the product occupies the right end after multiplicaton is completed.

Names—In COBOL, a combination of one to thirty alphanumeric characters containing at least one alpha (although procedure-names may be all numeric) and no blanks, not starting or ending with a hyphen. Names are used for *conditions, data, procedures,* and *special* purposes.

Nanosecond—A billionth of a second; a thousandth of a microsecond.

Nesting—The relationship between the statements contained in two perform statements. The statements included in the second (or "inner") perform statement must be wholly included within or excluded from the first (or "outer") perform statement; they must not *partially* overlap.

Network Load Analysis—In systems analysis, a listing of the flow of messages between stations to develop station characteristics by volumes of documents, frequency of processing, and special time requirements.

Noise—Errors introduced into data in a system, especially in communication channels.

No Operation—A "dummy" operation inserted in a program which, depending upon conditions encountered in the program, can be replaced by a specific instruction formed by the program itself. Also sometimes used at intervals throughout a program written with absolute addresses to provide space to write additional instructions with minimum rewriting of other instructions. A "no operation" instruction *per se* is skipped and not executed.

Normal Range—A range of values with specified limits set up so that, if results of a particular plan of action fall within the range, the results are considered satisfactory. This concept is used in "exception-principle systems" for reporting only results not within the normal range.

Number Base—The base of a number system; that is, a quantity that defines a system of representing numbers by positional notation; the number of digit symbols required by a number system. Examples:

System	Number Base
Decimal	10
Octal	8
Quinary	5
Binary	2

Numeric—Composed of numerals; a number consisting of numerals; the value of a number (as opposed to the characters representing it).

Object Computer—A computer used to execute an object program in machine language (after being compiled from the problem-oriented language in which it was originally written) and process data; may be the same or a different machine from the source computer.

Object Program—A program in machine language resulting from the translation of a source program by a source computer. For example, a source program written in COBOL and compiled into machine language results in an *object* program ready to run on an object computer.

Object Time—Occurring when an object program is to be executed; for example, index registers are initialized with desired values, and constants used in the program are introduced.

Occurs—In COBOL, describes a sequence of data items of the same format—for example, the items appearing in a list or table. Subscripting is used to refer to a particular item in a procedure statement.

Octal—Pertaining to the number 8; a number system whose base is the quantity 8. The symbols used are 0, 1, . . ., 7. The octal and binary number systems bear a convenient relationship to one another because each is an integral power of 2.

Off-Line Equipment—Equipment *not* connected directly to the central processor but working through an intermediary device. For example, a processor can write output on an on-line magnetic tape that is *later* used as input to an off-line printer for printing reports.

On-Line Equipment—Equipment connected directly to the central processor to furnish or receive data—for example, card readers, high-speed printers, inquiry stations, and direct-display devices.

Operand—Any one of the quantities entering into or arising from an operation. An operand may be an indication of the location of the next instruction or a result from computation.

Operating System—That part of a software package designed to simplify housekeeping programming. May include an input-output control system, sort-merge generators, data-conversion routines, and test routines.

Operation—(1) A defined action. (2) The action specified by a single processor instruction or pseudo-instruction. (3) An arithmetical, logical, or transferral unit of a problem, usually executed under the direction of a subroutine.

Order Code—The complete set of instructions that a processor can execute; also called "instruction repertoire."

Output—Process of transferring data from internal storage of a processor to some other storage device. A specific output area may be used for organizing data prior to the output operation.

Overflow—In an arithmetical operation, the generation of a quantity that is too large for the capacity of the register or location that is to receive the result.

Overlap, Processing—Processor operations performed at the same time by using different parts of the circuitry—for example, read-process-write or any two of these.

Pack—To combine two or more different items of data into one machine word. For example, the three fields of employee pay number, weekly pay rate, and number of tax exemptions might be stored together in one word. To *unpack* is to separate the individual items for processing by means of shifting or partial-word logic.

Parallel—The internal handling of data in groups, all elements of a group being handled simultaneously.

Parallel Operation (of a System)—The period of time when the old and new system are operated together in order to prove both the logic of the programs and the capability of people and equipment to function properly.

Parameter—A quantity in a mathematical calculation which may be assigned any arbitrary value.

Parity Bit—A bit associated with other data bits to get some specified relation, such as an odd or even total number of bits for each character. A parity bit is usually associated with the frame for each six-bit character on tape; also, parity bits may be placed at frequent intervals to associate them with the seven rows of bits (six for data and one for parity) along the tape.

Parity Check—A summation check in which the binary digits in a character or word in storage or a character, word, or row on tape, are added (modulo 2) and the sum checked against a single, previously specified digit; for example, a check which tests whether the number of ones is odd or even.

Perform—In COBOL, a verb for departing temporarily from the normal sequence of the program to execute some other procedure a specified number of times and return to the normal sequence.

Photographic Storage—(1) Miniature facsimile copies of readable documents or of direct output of the processor. (2) Photographic copies of data shown on direct-display tubes. (3) High-density storage of data in binary form on photographic disks for quick reference purposes.

Pictorial—The layout of headings, columns, totals, blank spaces, etc., used in planning a report for printing.

Picture—In COBOL, a symbolic description of each data element according to certain rules concerning numerals, alphanumerics, location of decimal points, and length.

Printer, High-Speed—High-speed printing that makes use of rotating print wheels or a chain with raised type faces and fast-acting hammers to press the paper against the desired character at the instant it is in the correct position.

Process-Time—The time for translating a source program into an object program through the action of a processor program and a computer.

Processing Plan—The interaction of man and machine to process data, produce information and control operations of the organization. Examples are *manual intervention* by people to handle situations not planned for, advance planning for *automatic* handling of all situations, *variable* treatment of differing situations depending on circumstances, and *adaptive systems* to adjust to new and unexpected situations as they arise.

Processor—(1) Any device capable of accepting data, applying prescribed processes to them, and supplying the results of these processes. Usually internally-stored program, but may be externally-stored or built-in. (2) An internally-stored-program electronic computer and peripheral equipment used for business data processing. (3) A program used in compiling a source program to produce an object program ready to execute with data.

Program (noun)—A plan for the automatic solution of a problem. A complete program includes plans for the transcription of data, coding for the processor, and plans for the absorption of the results into the system. The list of coded instructions is called a "routine."

Programming—The process of creating a program; includes applications analysis, design of a solution, coding for testing to produce an operating program, and development of other procedures to make the system function.

Punched Card—A card of standard size and shape in which data are stored in the form of punched holes. The hole locations are arranged in 80 or 90 columns with a given pattern of holes in a column representing one alphanumeric character. The data content is read by mechanical, electrical, or photoelectrical sensing of the hole positions.

Punched Tape—Tape, usually paper, in which data are stored in the form of punched holes arrayed in a frame across the tape.

Qualification—In COBOL, the technique of making a name unique by adding IN or OF and another name, according to certain rules.

Random Access—Access to storage under conditions in which each set of data records is directly addressable. Access to data at random—in any desired sequence. More commonly used to mean bulk storage with access within several milliseconds to several microseconds for data at any location.

Read—(1) To copy, usually from one form of storage to another, particularly from external or secondary storage to internal storage. (2) To sense the meaning of arrangements of hardware or visually readable patterns.

Read-Process-Write—To read in one block of data, while simultaneously processing the preceding block and writing out the results of the previously processed block. Some processors concurrently perform any two of the three operations; others are restricted to concurrent read-write.

Read-Write Head—A small electromagnet used for reading, recording, or erasing polarized spots on a magnetic surface.

Real-Time Operation—Processing data in synchronism with a physical process rapidly enough so that results of data processing are useful to the physical operation. Sometimes called "on-line, real-time control."

Record (noun)—A set of data elements closely related in the sense that they pertain to the same person, place, or thing.

Record Description—In COBOL, a record is described in terms of the data elements it contains. For each element in a record, a picture is used to specify its level, name, and format.

Record Name—In COBOL, the name given to a record within a file and assigned the level number 01. Data names for elements within a record have lower-level numbers 02, 03, etc.

Redefine—In COBOL, to reuse the same storage area for different data items during program execution by means of appropriate descriptions in the data division.

Report—Data-processing system output that has high information content; more broadly, any planned and organized output from a system.

Report Interval—The length of time between the preparation of two issues of a corresponding report. For example, monthly operating reports have a report interval of one month and daily sales reports an interval of one day. The interval may be variable in length when events, rather than the passage of time, trigger the preparation of reports—for example, when stock on hand falls below the review quantity or when a manager requests the preparation of a report whenever he thinks it useful.

Reporting Period—The length of time covered in a report. For example, in year-to-date reports issued each month, the reporting period is 1, 2, 3, . . ., 12 months, while the interval between the issuance of two successive reports remains constant at one month.

Rerun Point—One of a set of planned-for points in a program, used so that, if an error is detected between two such points, the problem may be rerun merely by going back to the last rerun point. Rerun points are often three to five minutes apart, so that little time is required for a rerun. All information pertinent to a rerun is kept in standby storage during the time from one rerun point to the next.

Rounding—Dropping certain less significant digits of a quantity and applying some adjustment to the more significant digits retained. A common round-off rule is to add 5 in the left-most position to be dropped, make the carry (if any), and discard unwanted digits. Thus, π, 3.14159265 . . ., rounded to three decimals is 3.142.

Routine—A set of coded instructions arranged in proper sequence to direct the processor to perform a desired operation or series of operations. *See also* "Subroutine."

Assembly Routine—A routine that, before the desired processing starts, converts a source program in mnemonic instructions and symbolic addresses into a machine-language object program. Since the conversion is on a one-for-one basis, assembly-level languages facilitate programming but give the programmer no leverage.

Compiler Routine—A routine that, before the desired computation is started, translates a source program expressed in a problem-oriented language into an object program in machine code. In accomplishing the translation, the compiler may be required to:

Allocate—To assign storage locations to the main routines and subroutines, thereby fixing the absolute values of any symbolic addresses.

Assemble—To integrate the subroutines (supplied, selected, or generated) into the main routine—that is, to adapt, incorporate, orient.

Generate—To produce a needed subroutine from parameters and skeletal coding; called a "generator routine."

Diagnostic Routine—A specific routine designed to locate either a malfunction in the processor or a mistake in coding.

Executive Routine—A routine designed to process and control other routines.

Generalized Routine—A routine expressed in computer coding designed to solve a class of problems that can be specialized to a specific problem when appropriate values are supplied.

Generator Routine—A generalized skeleton routine that accepts specifications about a particular situation and causes the processor to prepare a specific routine for further use. For example, in a report generator, specifications must be supplied about printer spacing, input file, record format, calculations desired, and format of each output line.

Interpretive Routine—An executive routine which, during the course of data-handling operations, translates a stored pseudo-code program into a machine code and immediately performs the indicated operations by means of subroutines.

Post-Mortem Routine—A routine that either automatically or on demand prints data concerning contents of registers and storage locations after the routine stops in order to assist in locating a mistake in coding.

Rerun Routine—A routine designed for use in the wake of a processor malfunction or coding or operating mistake to reconstitute a routine from the last previous rerun point.

Service Routine—A routine designed to assist in actual operation of a computer. Includes tape comparison, block location, certain post-mortems, and correction routines.

Simulator Routine—An interpretive routine to enable one processor to interpret and execute instructions and coding designed for another processor.

Trace Routine—A routine used to observe how the object program operates while it is being executed.

Translator Routine—*See* "Compiler Routine" under "Routine."

Utility Routine—Subroutines for handling machine operations necessary to data processing but not contributing directly to the output—for example, labeling tapes, loading and organizing disks, clearing storage, printing, copying, and converting from one data media to another.

Run—The act of processing, under the control of one or more programs, a batch of transactions—for example the inventory receipts, issues, etc., for the week—against all the files that are affected to produce desired outputs consisting of updated files and reports.

Run Diagram—A generalized graphic representation of the files, transactions, and data that are handled together under program control to produce an updated file, list of changes, and errors.

Run, Trial—A preliminary run of transactions against files, but without producing any outputs, for the purposes of finding errors and omissions in the data and determining the correct effect for interrelated events—for example, substitution of merchandise to fill priority customers' orders, or payroll calculations involving group bonus plans where the composition of the groups changes frequently. An actual run is made to update the records using knowledge gained from the trial run.

Runs, Housekeeping—The sorting, merging, editing, and operating runs required for file maintenance; the nonproduction runs. In a limited sense, the set-up and clean-up parts of a program as opposed to production processing.

Satellite Processor—A small processor designed primarily for card-to-tape conversion, printing of tape contents, and other selected, high-volume operations. Used to support a large processor to increase its productivity.

Scatter Read-Write—A *scatter-read* operation performed under program control reads a block of data from tape and breaks it up into processable elements that can be placed where wanted in storage. A *scatter-write* operation picks up the dispersed data elements in storage and writes them on tape as a block.

Sentence—In COBOL, a sequence of one or more statements specifying one or more operations, according to certain rules, and terminated by a period.

Sequence—In sorting, the ordering of items on an element—for example, records on a selected key—according to some rules that utilize the processor's collation table.

Alphanumeric—A sequence developed for records containing alphanumeric characters. The exact sequence depends on the binary value assigned to each alphabetic and numeric character—whether alphabetic precedes numeric or vice versa—by the machine designer.

Numeric—A sequence developed for records with keys containing numerals only; usually ascending but may also be descending.

Random—A sequence that is not arranged by ascending or descending keys but which actually may be arranged in an organized fashion. For example, each record may be placed in bulk storage in a location determined by some calculations performed on its key to develop an address; the calculations are repeated in order to get the address and locate the item.

Serial Number Control—The control of messages by assigning a number from a master list when it first originates and, perhaps, adding a suffix number from a local list for each point the message passes through to its destination.

Shift—To move the characters of a unit of data to the right or left by means of a shifting register. Used to unpack words to isolate data items and to multiply or divide a quantity by a power of the number base.

Simulation—An experimental analysis of an operating system by means of mathematical or physical models that operate in a time-sequential manner similar to the system itself.

Snapshot—A listing of the contents of storage locations, registers, and indexes at a given instant in time either at intervals during the execution of a program or when it stops running; may be complete or differential to list the contents of only those locations that have changed since the prior snapshot. Useful in program debugging.

Software Package—The programming aids supplied by the manufacturer to facilitate the user's efficient operation of equipment. Includes assemblers, compilers, generators, subroutine libraries, operating systems, and industry application programs.

Sorting—The arranging of records so that they are in ascending or descending sequence for some data element used as a key.

> **Comparison-of-Pairs Sorting**—To compare the keys of two records and put the record with the smaller-valued key ahead of the other to get the two items into ascending sequence; or to put the smaller behind to get a descending sequence.

> **Digital Sorting**—A procedure for first sorting the records on the least significant (right-hand) digit in their keys and re-sorting on each higher-order digit until the records are sorted on the most significant digit in their keys. A commonly used punched-card technique.

> **Internal Sorting**—The sorting of items contained in internal storage to develop strings preparatory to merge sorting. All items contained in storage can be sorted into sequence and written out as one string. Or blocks of items in sequence can be written out and replaced by other input items to build longer strings. Uses the comparison of pairs or a similar scheme.

> **Merge Sorting**—To produce a single sequence of records, ordered according to some rule, from two or more previously ordered (or perhaps unordered) sequences, without changing the items in size, structure, or total number. Although more than one pass may be required for complete sorting, during each pass items are selected on the basis of their entire key to build the sequence.

> **Minor-Major Sorting**—Arranging records in sequence on their keys starting with the right-hand digit only on the first pass and continuing to the left with all records used in each pass. Commonly used for punched-card sorting.

Source Computer—A computer used to compile a source program as written by a programmer in a problem-oriented language into a machine-language program for running on an object computer. The compilation is done under control of a processor program designed especially for the computer and the two languages involved.

Source Program—The program as written by a programmer—for example, COBOL—before being translated or compiled by a source computer and a translator into an object program in machine language.

Storage—A device capable of receiving data, retaining them for an indefinite period of time, and supplying them upon command.

Addressable Bulk Storage—Storage with the primary function of augmenting capacity of internal storage for handling data and instructions. Data from addressable bulk storage must be transferred to internal storage in order to use them in operations.

Buffer Storage—(1) Secondary storage used exclusively for assembly and transfer of data between internal and external storage. (2) Storage used to facilitate transfer of data between any two storage devices whose input and output speeds are not synchronized.

High-Speed Storage—The quickest access internal storage of a processor; this is composed of magnetic cores in most processors, although some use special cores or thin-film elements for limited amounts of ultra-high speed.

Internal Storage—Storage that is directly accessible to the arithmetic and control units of a computer. It is used for storage of instructions and for data currently being operated upon.

Storage Capacity—Number of units of data that can be stored in a device at one time; variously expressed in terms of bits, characters, or words, depending upon the method of organization.

Storage Density—The number of characters stored per unit length or area of storage medium—for example, number of characters per inch of magnetic tape.

Storage Location—A storage position holding one machine word and usually having a specific address; the character position used to address a data field in a character-addressable machine.

Stored Program—A program for instructing a processor how to manipulate data. Generally taken to mean internally-stored program in which data and instructions are placed interchangeably in storage. Also covers (1) special-purpose equipment with instructions designed into the circuitry and (2) externally-stored programs set up in wiring boards or plug boards for physical insertion into the machine.

Structure (of a System)—Refers to the *nature* of the chain of command, the origin and type of data collected, the form and destination of results, and the procedures used to control operations.

Subroutine—A set of instructions in machine code to direct the processor to carry out a well-defined mathematical or logical operation; a part of a routine. A calling sequence of a few instructions and factors are used to initialize a subroutine, transfer control to it, and provide for return to the main program after the subroutine execution is complete. Simpler schemes are available in compiler-level languages to go to a subroutine and return to the main program or merely to perform the subroutine and continue the main program. A subroutine is often written with symbolic relative addresses even though the routine to which it belongs is not.

> **Closed Subroutine**—A subroutine stored outside the routine which refers to it. Such a subroutine is entered by a jump, and provision is made to return to the proper point in the main routine at the end of the subroutine.

> **Library Subroutine**—A standard and proven subroutine which is kept "on file" for use at any time.

> **Open Subroutine**—A subroutine inserted directly into the program; it must be recopied at each point where it is needed in a routine.

Subscript—An integer used to specify a particular item in a list or table, according to COBOL rules, and consisting of a numeric literal or data-name.

Suspense File—The file of transactions or records that are awaiting some anticipated event. For example, rejected transactions are retained in a suspense file for control purposes until corrections are returned for another attempt at processing.

Switch—A device within the processor that stores an indication of various conditions encountered during processing—for example, greater than, less than, or equal to following a comparison operation. The switch contents can be tested by a conditional jump instruction to execute appropriate routines in the program.

System—Any regular or special method or plan of procedure. In a broader context, a system consists of an organization, people, hardware, and procedures that operate together to perform a set of tasks.

Systems Analysis—An orderly study of the detailed procedure for collecting, organizing, and evaluating information about an organization with the objective of improving control over its operations.

Systems Design—Formulation and description of the nature and content of inputs, files, and outputs in order to show how they are connected by processing procedures and for the purpose of developing a new or improved system.

Table—A dual series of similar items—for example, the names of states, their current census and one or more prior censuses. A two dimensional array.

Tag Reader—A device for reading punched or notched tags, plates, and cards pre-punched and attached to physical objects or given to employees and others for identification; also may be used for accepting keyboard input. Examples are garment tag readers used in department stores which also read customers' charge plates and sales clerks' identification cards.

Tape Unit—A device for reading data from magnetic tape and writing new data (after erasing prior data) on tape. Some tape units read in either direction, although they write in only the forward direction. The device also rewinds tape ready for removal and replacement by another reel.

Technique (of a Data-Processing System)—Refers to the *method* used to collect data inputs, to process them, and to convert processed data into reports or other usable form.

Teledata—A device for introducing parity bits and transmitting over telegraph circuits data already punched in five-, six-, or eight-channel paper tape. The receiving unit at a distant point checks parity for code accuracy, and reperforates valid data into paper tape.

Teletypewriter—Basically an electric typewriter that can be operated manually or by reading and reperforating paper tape; it is connected to a leased or dial-switched telegraph grade circuit for transmitting text and also data messages in readable form.

Telpak—Broad-band communication channels for transmitting data from magnetic tape to magnetic tape or directly between computers at rates up to 60,000 characters a second.

Testing—Examination to determine the real character of a thing in a particular aspect. *Acceptance* testing for equipment determines capacity and reliability. *Program* testing determines whether programs do what they are supposed to when used with test, simulated, or live data.

Thin Film—An ultra high-speed storage device consisting of a molecular deposit of material on a suitable plate.

Total—The sum of numeric items. A *batch* total is the sum of all the items handled as a unit for processing, such as a bundle of checks or other documents. A *control* or *proof* total is a sum developed at one stage of processing that must be matched at a later stage of processing. A *hash* or *nonsense* total is a sum of numeric items not ordinarily added, such as catalogue numbers for items on a customer's order, to help control accuracy during processing.

Track—A sequence of binary cells arranged so that data may be read or written from one cell at a time in serial fashion. For example, a track on a magnetic drum is a path one-bit wide around the circumference of the drum; the bits in several tracks make up a character.

Transaction—Event that affects the status of a business—for example, purchase, sale, issue, and collection. Also called "event."

Transceiver—Card-reading, modulating, and punching equipment for card-to-card transmission of data over telephone or telegraph grade circuits.

Transition, Rate of—The period of time during which system changes are made or new equipment introduced. The rate is affected by the degree of change, size of the organization, length of time since the last change, and whether the organization has reached a reasonably steady state following the preceding systems change.

Truncate—To cut off by discarding part of a number without rounding. Usually applied to the low-order (right-hand) digits but may occur for high-order digits under some conditions.

Unconditional—Without any conditions; for example, an unconditional statement is executed whenever it is encountered during a program.

Values, Initial—The information represented by a data item, arithmetic expression, or conditional expression before manipulation in the object program.

Variable—In COBOL, a named data item in storage that assumes different values during execution of the object program.

Verb—In COBOL, an instruction word that specifies one or more operations to be performed by a data processor.

Verify—(1) To check, usually with an automatic machine, one typing or recording of data against another in order to minimize the number of human errors or mistakes in the data transcription. (2) In preparing data for a processor, to make certain that data prepared are correct.

Word—A set of characters occupying one storage location; it is treated by the processor circuits as a unit and transported as such. Ordinarily, the control unit treats a word as an instruction whereas the arithmetic unit treats a word as a quantity.

    Fixed-Length Word—The number of characters to be handled as a unit as determined by the equipment designer and built into the circuitry.

Key Word—In COBOL, words that must be included in statements (unless they are in an optional phrase) and correctly spelled to avoid an error in the program.

Optional Word—In COBOL, words that may be used solely to improve readability, but, if used, must be correctly spelled.

Selectable-Length Word—The number of characters assigned by the programmer to each item of data; must be long enough to handle the longest instance of each item that will occur. Spaces not used for a particular item are filled out with zeros if numeric and blanks if alphanumeric.

Partial-Word Logic—The ability of a processor to select specified bits or characters from a word for processing and ignore others.

Variable-Length Word—The number of characters used for an item of data is exactly equal to its length, whether short or long; item separators are used to indicate the end of each item.

WORDCOM—*Word Com*puter, a hypothetical processor used to illustrate the features of and programming for a processor with storage organized into words.

Write—To cause the contents of one or more storage locations to become the contents of other locations after erasing the contents of the location to receive the data; for example, to write a block of data on magnetic tape after erasing the previous contents at the block written.

Zero Suppression—Elimination of nonsignificant zeros to the left of the integral part of a quantity as part of the editing routine before printing.

Zone—(1) In processors, two bits used in conjunction with four numeric bits to represent alphanumeric characters. The zone bits may be used separately to represent signs, to identify index registers, and for other purposes. (2) For punched cards, the 11 and 12 punches used with numeric punches 0 through 9 to represent alphabetic and special symbols. Zone punches may be used independently to indicate signs and for special control purposes.

Appendix III

GUIDE TO THE LITERATURE

The books and magazines listed here represent a brief guide to literature of interest in the field of business data processing. It is divided into two sections: books and periodicals. The periodicals are devoted to computers and data processing; in addition, professional and trade journals are available to anyone interested in particular fields. Manufacturers should be consulted for descriptive bulletins about equipment and for literature about "software" packages available.

BOOKS

Baumes, Carl G:, *Administration of Electronic Data Processing, Business Policy Study,* No. 98. New York: National Industrial Conference Board, 1961; 136 pages.
Based on a survey of 124 companies, this report covers the planning, the feasibility study, and the systems study. It also deals with the study of electronic equipment, organizing the data-processing operation, defining jobs and selecting personnel, evaluating performance and progress, and gaining employee cooperation.

Canning, Richard G., *Electronic Data Processing for Business and Industry.* New York: John Wiley & Sons, Inc., 1956; 332 pages.
This book, a classic in its field, discusses electronic data processing as a management tool; it covers the patterns of data processing, equipment characteristics, programming, systems study, initial design, and detailed design.

Chapin, Ned, *Programming Computers for Business Applications.* New York: McGraw-Hill Book Company, Inc., 1961; 279 pages.
Directed at programming for business data processing, this book discusses how to prepare programs for two different situations: where the problem is carefully defined in advance, and where the problem must be developed by the programmer. A chapter each is devoted to special problems of programming such as saving storage, improving accuracy, and increasing speed. Subroutines and library programs are also discussed.

COBOL—1961: Revised Specifications for a Common Business Oriented Language. Washington, D.C.: U. S. Government Printing Office, 1961; 175 pages.
This manual gives the official specifications for COBOL-1961. It

covers the general structure of COBOL, details of format and notation, and available features, including both optional and required ones. Equipment manufacturers use these specifications to prepare a COBOL language for their machines.

Computer Applications—1960: Proceedings of the 1960 Computer Applications Symposium. Armour Research Foundation, New York: The Macmillan Company, 1961; 193 pages.

A symposium dealing with both business-management and engineering-scientific applications of computers. The business and management applications cover a wide range of topics: subscription fulfillment, library usage, economic research, brokerage accounting, and mail-order house operations.

Conway, B., J. Gibbons and D. E. Watts, *Business Experience with Electronic Computers.* New York: Controllers Institute Research Foundation, Inc., 1959; 191 pages.

This report surveys the experience of a number of companies in introducing electronic data processing. The topics covered are the decision to introduce the system, company education and the programming group, development of the applications and conversion from prior methods, operating electronic equipment, and relations with manufacturers. Also included is a discussion of some unresolved matters and some thoughts on the next five years.

Data Processing Today: A Progress Report. New York: American Management Association, 1960; 143 pages.

Conference proceedings dealing with management and data processing, advances in data-processing technology, computer applications, and an intensive study of information processing at one company.

Electronics in Action: The Current Practicality of Electronic Data Processing. New York: American Management Association, Inc., 1957; 156 pages.

A report of an early AMA Conference containing thirteen papers dealing with feasibility studies, electronics at work, and new frontiers.

Gallagher, James D., *Management Information Systems and the Computer.* New York: American Management Association, Inc., 1961; 191 pages.

This book undertakes to put the management information system into perspective by showing how to organize a system for management planning and control and develop the relationship between systems work and the management information system. It contains case studies of the American Airlines SABRE system and the experience of Sylvania Electric Products, Inc. with business data processing.

Gatto, O. T., *Autosate: An Automated Data Systems Analysis Technique* (Memorandum RM-3118-PR). Santa Monica, California: The RAND Corporation, 1962; 50 pages.

Describes an organized, automated technique that provides information on data system flows and characteristics in a more usable form and more economically than usual manual methods.

Haskins and Sells, *Introduction to Data Processing*. New York: Haskins and Sells, 1957; 107 pages.

This book discusses the principal methods and devices used in data processing and relates them to the basic operations they perform: classifying, sorting, calculating, summarizing, recording, and communicating. Chapters are devoted to punched-card equipment and to electronic data-processing equipment.

Hattery, Lowell H., *Executive Control and Data Processing*. Washington, D. C.: Anderson Kramer Associates, 1959; 92 pages.

A short guide to the executive in meeting the challenge of using new data-processing tools for more effective control. Heavy emphasis is placed on reporting systems, data for management systems, and human resources.

Kaufman, Felix, *Electronic Data Processing and Auditing*. New York: The Ronald Press Company, 1961; 180 pages.

This book focuses on the problem of control in electronic data processing and shows how data flow through an organization by means of two examples: (1) payroll and sales functions, and (2) accounts receivable, purchases, and disbursements. The book will be of interest to auditors and others concerned with controlling the accuracy of data processing, since it covers redundancy and the reliability of data and the effects of data processing systems on internal control and audit-trail conditions. It also raises some of the control problems associated with the use of data processors.

Ledley, Robert Steven, *Programming and Utilizing Digital Computers*. New York: McGraw-Hill Book Company, Inc., 1962; 568 pages.

A digital computer programming text; it covers machine languages, automatic programming languages (ALGOL and COBOL), and data-processing techniques (numerical analysis; Boolean algebra; and searching, sorting, ordering, and codifying).

Malcolm, Donald G., and Alan J. Rowe, *Management Control Systems*. New York: John Wiley & Sons, Inc., 1960; 375 pages.

The proceedings of a symposium that dealt with the concepts of management control, the impacts of computers on the design of management controls, research in systems design, new approaches to future possibilities in management control, and information systems. It contains some examples of automated management controls.

McCracken, Daniel D., Harold Weiss and Tsai-Hwa Lee, *Programming Business Computers*. New York: John Wiley & Sons, Inc., 1959; 510 pages.
In 21 chapters, this book covers the structure of files, flow-charting, data-processing equipment, programming (arithmetic operations, address computation, loops and index registers, subroutines, and input-output devices) and verification of program accuracy. Also covers machine-aided coding, sorting, operating techniques, steps in planning and programming computer applications, and auditing.

McNerney, John Peter, *Installing and Using an Automatic Data Processing System: a Case Study for Management*. Boston: Division of Research, Graduate School of Business Administration, Harvard University, 1961; 314 pages.
A case study of a manufacturing company converting from punched-card equipment to the installation of a small computer for sales control and inventory control. The areas covered are background and systems evaluation, investigation and results, and evaluation of equipment.

Nett, Roger and Stanley A. Hetzler, *An Introduction to Electronic Data Processing*. Glencoe, Illinois: Free Press of Glencoe, Inc., 1959; 287 pages.
An introductory book covering the history of computation, the operating principles and language of computers, computer applications, and personnel organization and training for system operation.

Optner, Stanford L., *Systems Analysis for Business Management*. Englewood Cliffs, New Jersey: Prentice-Hall, Inc., 1960; 276 pages.
This book deals with systems analysis focused on business data-processing systems. Part I covers the systems concept in business, fundamentals of systems design, postulating data-processing systems, preparing for the systems study, and evaluation and cost estimation for data systems. Part II contains ten case studies covering a wide range of business problems.

Proceedings, 1962 Joint Computer Conference, American Federation of Information Processing Societies—AFIPS. Palo Alto, California: The National Press, 1962; 392 pages.
Proceedings of one conference in a continuing series covering a wide range of topics of interest to systems designers and users; some coverage of business and other applications.

Saxon, James A., and William S. Plette, *Programming the IBM 1401*. Englewood Cliffs, New Jersey: Prentice-Hall, Inc., 1962; 208 pages.
A self-instructional book covering programming for the IBM 1401 in 42 lessons.

Schmidt, Richard N. and William E. Meyers, *Electronic Business Data Processing.* New York: Holt, Rinehart and Winston, Inc., 1963; 482 pages.

Presents the principles of data processing from the operating management viewpoint to cover: planning, processing, control, and organization with some attention to COBOL. Covers in some detail programming for the UNIVAC I and IBM 1401.

Sprague, Richard E., *Electronic Business Systems: Management Use of On-Line—Real-Time Computers.* New York: The Ronald Press Company, 1962; 168 pages.

As the preface states, this book undertakes to show that "by 1970, all electronic data-processing systems will be of the on-line—real-time variety." The book covers the effect of pressures upon system requirements, developments in data processing and communications, and current potential developments in on-line real-time systems. Chapters deal with the impact of data systems on industrial manufacturing and the organization structure.

Wallace, Edward L., *Management Influence on the Design of Data Processing Systems: a Case Study.* Boston: Division of Research, Graduate School of Business Administration, Harvard University, 1961; 259 pages.

An intensive case study of a shoe manufacturing company's products, management organization, and methods of planning; some discussion of its previous mechanization of data processing. The proposed system for automatic data processing is covered and comments are made about the company study group's proposal for new system development with an alternative proposal for information handling.

PERIODICALS

Business Automation. OA Business Publications, Inc., Room 1716, 100 East 42nd Street, New York 17, New York.

This monthly magazine contains articles of general interest in business data processing. The topics range from self-checking numbers to background material on successful new firms.

Business Automation News Report. OA Business Publications, Inc., Room 1716, 100 East 42nd Street, New York 17, New York.

This nontechnical publication is a weekly newsletter. It covers data processing applications, announcements of new equipment, financial status of manufacturers, contract announcements, meetings, and similar items.

Communications of the ACM. Association for Computing Machinery, Mt. Royal & Guilford Avenues, Baltimore 2, Maryland.

Published monthly by a professional society, the Association for

Computing Machinery (ACM), this magazine informs subscribers on such topics as standards, techniques, and applications in the areas of scientific and business data processing. Most of the articles are of a specialized and technical nature. An ACM member also receives *Computing Reviews* (a comprehensive, bi-monthly abstract of literature in the field) and the *Journal of the Association for Computing Machinery* (a quarterly journal that describes new research).

Computers and Automation. Berkeley Enterprises, Inc., 815 Washington Street, Newtonville 60, Massachusetts.
This monthly magazine has articles on the construction, applications and implications of data processors. One of the regular features is a computer census giving for each computer the number of installations, unfilled orders, average monthly rental, and date first installed.

Computer Characteristics Quarterly. Charles W. Adams Associates, 142 The Great Road, Bedford, Massachusetts.
Salient features of all general-purpose stored-program electronic data processors that are actively used in the United States are described in this quarterly report. It covers typical price, internal speed, storage capacity, input-output equipment and special features for each system. New equipment or changes are added as they appear.

Data Processing. Iliffe Production Publications Ltd., Dorset House, Stamford Street, London, S.E. 1, England.
This British journal has articles on data-processing equipment—both American and European—punched-card equipment, applications, and new ideas or techniques. A complete subject index is provided yearly.

Data Processing Digest. Data Processing Digest, Inc., 1140 South Robertson Boulevard, Los Angeles 35, California.
A monthly abstract service, this digest reviews most of the articles and books relevant to business data processing. Articles of interest in such related fields as management science are also covered. In addition to abstracts, each issue may contain a brief article on a topic of special interest. The contents of the *Computer Characteristics Quarterly* are also reprinted here. A comprehensive index to past abstracts classified by subject is available as the *Data Processing Digest Fact Finder.*

Data Processing for Management. American Data Processing, Inc., 22nd Floor Book Tower, Detroit 26, Michigan.
This monthly publication covers a variety of business data processing topics in a nontechnical fashion. Regular features include sections on equipment, forms, books, and coming events.

Datamation. F. D. Thompson Publications, Inc., 141 East 44th Street, New York 17, New York.

A basic source of current information in the data processing field, this monthly magazine discusses controversial topics as they arise. Sections are included each month covering meetings and new literature and products.

EDP Weekly. Industry Reports, Inc., 1327 F Street, N.W., Washington 4, D. C.

This bulletin contains nontechnical news reports on subjects of general interest in data processing—equipment, applications, contracts, meetings, and people.

Journal of Machine Accounting. Journal of Machine Accounting, 1750 West Central Road, Mt. Prospect, Illinois.

Published under the auspices of the Data Processing Management Association (DPMA), this journal covers data-processing equipment and applications related to accounting and financial management. Activities of the DPMA are also covered.

Office Automation. OA Business Publications, Inc., 288 Park Avenue West, Elmhurst, Illinois.

This handbook contains extensive and detailed specifications by manufacturer and model of data-processing equipment—punched-card devices, electronic data processors, transmission facilities, and peripheral equipment of all types. A monthly updating service provides information on changes and newly-announced equipment. Other volumes are available from this publisher on selected applications of data-processing equipment.

Systems Management. Data Processing Publishing Corporation, 200 Madison Avenue, New York 16, New York.

Articles in this magazine are oriented toward the recording, retrieval and reproduction of data, although articles on other aspects of data processing also appear in each issue. Regular sections are included for such areas as microfilm topics and reproduction techniques.

ACKNOWLEDGMENT FOR COBOL

The COBOL-1 chapters of this publication are based on the COBOL System developed in 1959 by a committee composed of government users and computer manufacturers. The organizations participating in the original development were:

Air Materiel Command, United States Air Force
Bureau of Standards, United States Department of Commerce
Burroughs Corporation

David Taylor Model Basin, Bureau of Ships, United States Navy
Electronic Data Processing Division, Minneapolis-Honeywell
    Regulator Company
International Business Machines Corporation
Radio Corporation of America
Sylvania Electric Products, Inc.
UNIVAC Division of Sperry Rand Corporation

In addition to the organizations listed above, the following other organizations participated in the work of the Maintenance Group:

Allstate Insurance Company
The Bendix Corporation, Computer Division
Control Data Corporation
E. I. du Pont de Nemours and Company
General Electric Company
General Motors Corporation
Lockheed Aircraft Corporation
The National Cash Register Company
Philco Corporation
Standard Oil Company (New Jersey)
United States Steel Corporation

This COBOL-61 manual is the result of contributions made by all of the above-mentioned organizations. No warranty, expressed or implied, is made by any contributor or by the committee as to the accuracy and functioning of the programming system and language. Moreover, no responsibility is assumed by any contributor, or by the committee, in connection therewith.

It is reasonable to expect that many improvements and additions will be made to COBOL. Every effort will be made to insure that improvements and corrections will be made in an orderly fashion, with due recognition of existing users' investments in programming. However, this protection can be positively assured only by individual implementors.

Procedures have been established for the maintenance of COBOL. Inquiries concerning the procedures and the methods for proposing changes should be directed to the Executive Committee of the Conference on Data Systems Languages.

The authors and copyright holders of the copyrighted material used herein: FLOW-MATIC (Trade-mark of Sperry Rand Corporation) *Programming for the UNIVAC® I and II, Data Automation Systems* © 1958, 1959, Sperry Rand Corporation; *IBM Commercial Translator,* Form No. F28-8013, copyrighted 1959 by IBM, have specifically authorized the use of this material, in whole or in part, in the COBOL-61 specifications. Such authorization extends to the reproduction and use of COBOL specifications in programming manuals or similar publications.

Any organization interested in reproducing the COBOL report and initial specifications in whole or in part, using ideas taken from this report or utilizing this report as the basis for an instruction manual or any other purpose is free to do so. However, all such organizations are requested to reproduce this section as part of the introduction to the document. Those using a short passage, as in a book review, are requested to mention "COBOL" in acknowledgment of the source but need not quote the entire section.

ACKNOWLEDGMENTS OF ILLUSTRATIONS

We are indebted to the following organizations for supplying material for the figures and tables indicated:

Ampex Corporation, Figure 4-6.
Burroughs Corporation, Figure 4-1, entries in Tables 5-10 to 5-18.
Collins Radio Company, entries in Table 5-19.
Commercial Controls Corporation, Figure 4-1.
Control Data Corporation, entries in Tables 5-10 to 5-18.
Dashew Business Machines, Incorporated, entries in Table 5-19.
Digitronics Corporation, entries in Table 5-19.
Frieden, Incorporated, entries in Table 5-19.
General Electric Company, Figures 4-4, 5-2, entries in Tables 5-10 to 5-18.
Honeywell Electronic Data Processing, a Division of Minneapolis-Honeywell Corporation, Figure 5-3, entries in Tables 5-10 to 5-18.
International Business Machines Corporation, Figures 2-1, 2-2, 2-4, 3-3, 4-2, 4-6, 5-1, entries in Tables 5-10 to 5-19.
Monroe Calculating Machine Company, Figure 4-1.
National Cash Register Company, Figure 4-1, entries in Tables 5-10 to 5-18.
Pacific Telephone and Telegraph Company, Figures 2-3, 5-4, entries in Table 5-19.
Philco Corporation, a Subsidiary of Ford Motor Company, Figure 5-3, entries in Tables 5-10 to 5-18.
Radio Corporation of America, Figures 2-5, 4-3, 4-6, 5-2, entries in Tables 5-10 to 5-19.
RAND Corporation, Figures 6-1, 6-2, 6-3, 6-4, 6-5.
Soroban Engineering Company, entries in Table 5-19.
Standard Register Company, entries in Table 5-19.
Stromberg, a Division of General Time Corporation, entries in Table 5-19.

Systematics, a Division of General Instrument Corporation, entries in Table 5-19.

Tally Register Corporation, entries in Table 5-19.

Teleregister Corporation, Figure 4-7, entries in Table 5-19.

Univac, a Division of Sperry Rand Corporation, Figures 2-1, 2-2, 3-4, 5-1, entries in Tables 5-10 to 5-19.

Western Union Telegraph Company, entries in Table 5-19.

LIST OF ILLUSTRATIONS

FIGURES

TABLES

Index

Note: This index covers the material in Chapters 1–17 of this book. The Glossary and other appendixes should also be consulted as necessary.

WORDCOM ORDER CODE

RECyxxx	Read a card.
PNCyxxx	Punch a card.
RTty xxx	Read tape.
WTtyxxx	Write tape.
RWt___	Rewind a tape.
SISy xxx	Set index y.
INCynnn	Increase index y.
CISy xxx	Compare index y.
CMPyxxx	Compare accumulator and location xxx.
JIN yxxx	Jump, if accumulator negative.
JOV xxx	Jump, on overflow condition.
CAAyxxx	Clear accumulator and add.
STAy xxx	Store accumulator.
CAMyxxx	Clear and add into M-Q.
STMyxxx	Store M-Q.
ADDyxxx	Add.
SUByxxx	Subtract.
MLTyxxx	Multiply.
DIVyxxx	Divide.
HLT xxx	Unconditional halt.
SHL nn	Shift left.
SHR nn	Shift right.
EXOyxxx	Extract characters.
JMPyxxx	Unconditional jump.